P9-CDV-806

ALSO BY GARY J. BASS

Stay the Hand of Vengeance: The Politics of War Crimes Tribunals

Freedom's Battle

FREEDOM'S BATTLE

THE ORIGINS OF HUMANITARIAN INTERVENTION

GARY J. BASS

Alfred A. Knopf · New York · 2008

THIS IS A BORZOI BOOK
PUBLISHED BY ALFRED A. KNOPF

www.aaknopf.com

Portions of this work were originally published in *The New Republic*.

Library of Congress Cataloging-in-Publication Data

Bass, Gary Jonathan, 1969–
Freedom's battle : the origins of humanitarian intervention / by Gary J. Bass. — 1st ed.
p. cm.
ISBN 978-0-307-26648-4
1. Humanitarian intervention—History.
2. Humanitarian intervention—Case studies. I. Title.
JZ6369. B37 2008
341.5'84—dc22 2007052252

Manufactured in the United States of America
First Edition

For M. B.

For Freedom's battle once begun,
Bequeath'd by bleeding sire to son,
Though baffled oft is ever won.

—Byron

Posted by a Solidarity activist, in the Lenin Shipyards, Gdansk, Poland, 1980

CONTENTS

PART ONE: INTRODUCTION 1

Chapter 1: Humanitarianism or Imperialism? 11

Chapter 2: Media and Solidarity 25

Chapter 3: The Diplomacy of Humanitarian Intervention 39

PART TWO: GREEKS 45

Chapter 4: The Greek Revolution 51

Chapter 5: The Scio Massacre 67

Chapter 6: The London Greek Committee 76

Chapter 7: Americans and Greeks 88

Chapter 8: Lord Byron's War 100

Chapter 9: Canning 111

Chapter 10: The Holy Alliance 117

Chapter 11: A Rumor of Slaughter 123

Chapter 12: Navarino 137

PART THREE: SYRIANS 153

Chapter 13: Napoléon the Little 159

Chapter 14: The Massacres 163

Chapter 15: Public Opinion 182

Chapter 16: Occupying Syria 190

Chapter 17: Mission Creep 213

PART FOUR: BULGARIANS 233

Chapter 18: The Eastern Question 239

Chapter 19: Pan-Slavism 242

Chapter 20: Bosnia and Serbia 248

Chapter 21: Bulgarian Horrors 256

Chapter 22: Gladstone vs. Disraeli 266

Chapter 23: The Russo-Turkish War 297

Chapter 24: The Midlothian Campaign 305

PART FIVE: CONCLUSION 313

Chapter 25: Armenians 315

Chapter 26: The Uses of History 341

Chapter 27: The International Politics of Humanitarian Intervention 352

Chapter 28: The Domestic Politics of Humanitarian Intervention 367

Chapter 29: A New Imperialism? 376

Notes 383

Acknowledgments 483

Index 487

PART ONE

INTRODUCTION

The president of the United States, in his State of the Union speech, gave a grave warning to the American people. He noted that overseas "there are occasional crimes committed on so vast a scale and of such peculiar horror" that the United States had a duty to step in. "In extreme cases action may be justifiable and proper." In a few cases, depending on "the degree of the atrocity and upon our power to remedy it," the president argued, "we could interfere by force of arms . . . to put a stop to intolerable conditions." This was an explicit call for using U.S. troops to save foreigners. It was not from Bill Clinton or Jimmy Carter—the two presidents who claimed to make human rights a centerpiece of their foreign policy. The president was Theodore Roosevelt; the year was 1904; his example was Cuba, where Roosevelt had famously put his own neck on the line against Spanish atrocities.[1]

This was familiar rhetoric. Roosevelt's audience would not have been scandalized or confused by his words on this formal occasion. The president of the United States gave a ringing message about what we today would call humanitarian intervention, in ways that would be stunning almost a century later, and nobody thought too much of it.

Something has been lost since then. The tradition of humanitarian intervention once ran deep in world politics, long before Rwanda and Kosovo came to the world's fitful attention. Over a century ago, it was a known principle that troops should sometimes be sent to prevent the slaughter of innocent foreigners. That principle has recently reemerged with fresh strength in the aftermath of the Cold War, but it is anything but new.

Human rights policies are usually thought of today as being largely an innovation of the Carter presidency, making another appearance in the Clinton administration—or, at most, going back to Woodrow Wilson. Before that, on this account, international politics were run by hard-nosed diplomats, unsentimental about foreign lives and liberties but dedicated to maintaining the balance of power. The fate of the world was worked out at lordly conferences in Vienna, Paris, and Berlin, behind closed doors thick enough to shut out the hubbub of mass opinion. This common belief that humanitarianism has no real historical standing has been used powerfully to oppose U.S. and European missions abroad.

But in fact, the century *before* Wilson's presidency was anything but an age of unbroken realpolitik. Especially in Victorian Britain, this was a period rich in what we today would recognize clearly as human rights rhetoric, all the way up to the highest levels. This was the time of the anti-slavery campaign in Britain, and then of the mass uproar against vicious Belgian colonial rule in the Congo. It was the era of philhellenism in Britain and pan-Slavism in Russia, of liberal sympathy for the national minorities crushed by the Ottoman and Austrian and Russian empires, of intrusive and sovereignty-defying treaties to safeguard minority rights, of French solicitude for Syria's Christians, and of wild popular convulsions in British politics on behalf of the Bulgarians. The most magical names—from Byron to Dostoevsky—entered the lists on behalf of foreign suffering.[2]

These emotional pleas were a regular feature of international politics throughout much of the nineteenth century, resulting in several important military missions. The basic ideas go all the way back to Thucydides, who, horrified at bloody ancient civil wars, hoped for the endurance of "the general laws of humanity which are there to give a hope of salvation to all who are in distress." As early as 1625, in his classic *De Jure Belli et Pacis,* Hugo Grotius argued,

> If the Injustice be visible, as if a *Busiris,* a *Phalaris,* or a *Thracian Diomedes* exercise such Tyrannies over Subjects, as no good Man living can approve of, the Right of human Society shall not be therefore excluded. Thus *Constantine* made War against *Maxentius* and *Licinius;* and other *Roman* Emperors against the *Persians,* or threatned them with it at least, unless they left off persecuting Christians on the account of their Religion only.

Humanitarian intervention was once a relatively familiar European practice, and was understood as such—not just by the intervening countries, but even sometimes by the government whose sovereignty was being violated in the name of humanity.[3]

All of the major themes of today's heated debates about humanitarian intervention—about undermining sovereignty or supporting universal human rights, about altruistic or veiled imperialistic motivations, about the terrible dangers of taking sides in civil wars and ethnic conflicts, about the role of public opinion and the press in shaping democratic foreign policy, about multilateral and unilateral uses of force, about the moral responsibility of political leaders—were voiced loud and clear throughout the nineteenth century. In their elegant cursive, in dispatches ornamentally sealed with red wax and delivered in safe boxes, the diplomats of a century and three-quarters ago were negotiating many of the same questions that Bill Clinton faced in Bosnia and Rwanda and that George W. Bush faced in Congo and Darfur. They knew things then that we have forgotten now.

Human Rights in History

Why do we let evil happen? Why do we sometimes rally to stop it? And, when we do act, how can we act more effectively? These are the core questions of this book. Good-hearted people all too often stand by in the face of enormous bloodshed overseas. As the British scholar Arnold Toynbee fumed, Mussolini could only get away with conquering Abyssinia because of "a negative, weak-willed, cowardly egotism" in Britain and France. The experience of past centuries must show a way to do at least a little better.[4]

So this book has three overarching themes. First, humanitarian interventions are not just a newfangled experiment from the 1990s. Humanitarian intervention has a deep history, which is worth understanding both for its own sake and for the light it casts on current debates. Today's human rights advocates are neither faddish nor even particularly modern; they are the ideological and organizational descendants of the nineteenth century's activists against cruelty in remote places like Greece and Bulgaria.

This activism was not just a matter of imperialism. Unlike the recent advocates of a new kind of American human rights imperialism, I want to keep a bright line between empire and humanity. This book is, in part, a history of activists who campaigned against massacre abroad, while also frowning on the imperialism of their own country. There was a genuine humanitarianism at work in the making of some foreign policy in the nineteenth century, which was not the same thing as that era's imperialism. Of course, I do not mean to suggest that the whole of the nineteenth century was humanitarian—only that there were some important episodes even in a horribly imperialistic age, including several of the biggest foreign policy crises of the day. Rediscovering this long history levels the playing field in present-day debates between human rights advocates and more conservative realists, rather than leaving realists dominant as the exponents of traditional statecraft. Even in the heyday of imperialism and realpolitik, the politics of human rights made a big impact on foreign policy.

Nor was this only a matter of pan-Christian solidarity: of European Christians rescuing fellow Christians overseas. Christianity was certainly part of the story, but not the whole of it. Some of the most important activists hoped to save humanity, not just Christianity. Although much of the diplomatic attention focused on the Ottoman Empire, liberal Europeans also intervened in Naples, and argued for confronting Russia and Austria. Looking at the activists and listening in on the domestic debates about intervention, it was often the most Christian-identified actors who opposed intervention, while the more secular liberals supported it. Most strikingly, the Church of England opposed humanitarian intervention to rescue Greeks, Bosnians, and Bulgarians. Christian identity was a motive for some of the activists, but most Britons supporting the Greeks were drawn more by their pagan past than their Orthodox present. The British voiced substantial sympathy not just for suffering Christians, but also for Ottomans, Druzes, and enslaved Africans. The agitation over the Bulgarians in the 1870s paved the way to the modern human rights movement, with William Ewart Gladstone resoundingly speaking out on behalf of the human rights of Zulus and Afghans.[5]

Second, this book looks at the way freedom at home can help promote freedom abroad. As domestic liberalism grew up in Britain, the United States, and, to some extent, France, the governments there found their foreign policy being pushed by their own homegrown freedoms: above all the power of a newly unshackled free press that could report on foreign atrocities; and then a free society that could react with horror at those atrocities, and politicians inside and outside the government jockeying for political power by trying to capture that public passion. The governments had to sit up and take notice when their so-called atrocitarians demanded heroic rescues of suffering populations, even when the mission would be in some obscure part of the world that served no strategic purpose—or undermined the government's realpolitik policy.

The new mass media played a particularly crucial role in pressuring a free government toward humanitarian intervention. These governments could not silence their own press, nor prevent them from reporting embarrassing news from inconvenient places. Skyrocketing newspaper circulations, better kinds of technology like the telegraph, increasing journalistic professionalism: all of this sometimes made it impossible for politicians to get away with quietly pursuing a foreign policy based on realpolitik. Once the press broke a gruesome story, the officials of a liberal state could find themselves under crushing pressure to respond. The exact placement of the reporters made a big difference. In short: humanitarian intervention is not new, and neither is the so-called CNN effect.

Before the rise of an effective and credible free press, the dark news of an atrocity overseas would reach the halls of power through ambassadors, consuls, or spies; if the government wanted, the information could be largely hidden from the public. But when the news came from the press, or from activist groups, then it went straight to the public. No matter how awkward it might be for their diplomacy, politicians in a free state could do little to stop their own newspapers from reporting hideous news—or to stop newspaper readers from reacting with shock and horror at what they read.

Sometimes senior government officials will genuinely care about suffering foreigners, as Madeleine Albright did for Bosnians and Kosovars, and George H. W. Bush reportedly did for Somalis. But successful politicians are often pretty cold fishes, and are more likely to take the risk of war if they are under pressure at home. So well-organized pressure groups, like today's human rights groups or the London Greek Committee in the 1820s, can have a powerful impact on a government's thinking.[6]

Life was a little easier for despots. In unfree countries, like tsarist Russia, the government can censor the press, or control it so that it only reports stories that are convenient to the government's foreign policy. The state can feed its public the requisite propaganda to encourage only those foreign solidarities that help advance the state's imperialist or expansionist goals. And if the public gets too agitated, the state can try to use its repressive machinery to kill, jail, or cow the activists. None of those options is available to a political leader in a free country.

In other words, humanitarian intervention emerged as a fundamentally liberal enterprise, wrapped up with the progress of liberal ideals and institutions. Ideologically, it grew out of the radical ideas of freedom and the rights of man, a driving force in world politics since the French Revolution in 1789; institutionally, it grew up along with the rise of the mass media, public opinion, and responsive government. Even a little bit of liberalism, as seen in the nineteenth century's major constitutional states like Britain, can lead to surprisingly big effects in foreign policy.[7]

Finally, there is something to be learned from the way that diplomats in the nineteenth century managed the practice of humanitarian intervention. After all, even limited humanitarian interventions—like any use of military force—carry enormous risks. They can be foils for imperialist conquest and occupation, draw big states into rivalry, or spark devastating wider wars between great powers.

Even if a president or prime minister has credible information about atrocities, and there is strong public sympathy for those victims, there must still be a cold realpolitik calculation about the costs of intervening. If the foreign murderers are relatively weak, it may be tempting to confront them. But if a humanitarian intervention would lead to a broader international crisis, or plunge the country—or the world—into a massive war, then most cabinets will decide that it is just not worth it. After all, governments are opportunistic in their humanitarianism, as they are with any military venture; believing in human rights does not make one suicidal.

Still, the diplomats of the nineteenth century developed some important ways to reduce the international dangers from a humanitarian intervention. They engaged in complex exercises in self-restraint to prove that their intentions were limited only to unselfish humanitarianism, rather than conquest or imperialism. These governments voluntarily limited the size and duration of their military missions; relied on specific treaties to delineate what could be called spheres of humanitarian interest; and engaged in successful multilateral practices of consultation that are as striking as anything ever dreamed of at the League of Nations or the United Nations.

The rest of this part of this book will be spent establishing and fleshing out these main arguments. First, there will be a challenge to the influential notion that "humanitarian" interventions are really just veiled imperialism. This will be followed by taking on the related argument that the nineteenth century's "humanitarian" interventions were actually pan-

Christian missions, arguing instead that a broader humanitarianism was actually at work. Next comes a turn to domestic politics, looking at how the mass media shapes this sense of the fellow humanity of foreigners, and how domestic politics plays out in free and authoritarian states. Finally, there will be a look at the diplomacy of humanitarian intervention.

CHAPTER ONE

Humanitarianism or Imperialism?

"Powers Will Be Powers"

Mass murderers have a well-worn argument to defend themselves against outside intervention: that sending troops would be an act of imperialism, not of altruism. Sudan's dictatorial president, Omar al-Bashir, once bluntly rejected United Nations peacekeepers in Darfur: "We will not accept colonial forces coming into the country." He could have been echoing Aleksandr Lukashenko, the Belarusian despot, who told the UN General Assembly: "If there are no pretexts for intervention, imaginary ones are created. To this end a very convenient banner was chosen—democracy and human rights." Even Vladimir Putin, facing international criticism for smothering Russian democracy, retorted that this reminded him of how a century ago "colonial powers . . . cited arguments such as playing a civilizing role, the particular role of the white man, the need to civilize 'primitive peoples.' "[1]

Bashir and Lukashenko may be pretty quickly written off as self-serving. But there is a serious intellectual tradition here. The most influential thinkers about international politics, at least in Britain and the United States since the shattering experience of World War II, are also the most gloomy. These realists see international politics as an amoral and savage struggle for survival and conquest. Sovereign states in the brawl of international anarchy must rely on their own strength to ensure their security. This leaves scant room for moral action. In his Nuremberg cell, Hermann Göring declared, "When it is the question of *the interests of the nation!?*—Phooey! Then morality stops! That is what England has done for centuries; America has done it; and Russia is still doing it!"[2]

Henry Kissinger, as U.S. secretary of state, sent word to the Khmer Rouge: "Tell the Cambodians that we will be friends with them. They are murderous thugs, but we won't let that stand in our way." Today's realists—even at their worst, nothing at all like Göring—are usually conservatives, best represented in the moderate internationalist wing of the Republican Party. In his first major campaign speech on foreign policy, candidate George W. Bush—presumably influenced by Condoleezza Rice, a self-described realist—promised "realism, in the service of American ideals." That was hardly how his crusading administration turned out, but Bush originally forswore humanitarian intervention: "We should not send our troops to stop ethnic cleansing and genocide in nations outside our strategic interest." Today, as Iraq suffers through a horrific civil war, realists like James Baker and Brent Scowcroft are understandably dominating the public debate, demanding that idealists confront the brute realities of international relations. Many liberals have been forced to admit the potency of realist thinking. John Kerry, the Democratic presidential candidate in 2004, said that he found insights from going "backward to Disraeli and Metternich and forward to Henry Kissinger."[3]

According to realists, states will go to war for conquest or for their own security—which could mean self-defense, or some kind of balance of power, or perhaps fighting for the sake of their allies. One should not expect much more than that. As A. J. P. Taylor, a British realist historian so allergic to moral judgments that he once defended Hitler as a normal German statesman, put it, "As a private citizen, I think that all this striving after greatness and domination is idiotic; and I should like my country not to take part in it. As a historian, I recognize that Powers will be Powers."[4]

So for realists, humanitarian intervention—if there is such a thing—is a novel and alarming notion. This realist view that humanitarian intervention is new has become utterly conventional.[5]

Disapproving of the U.S. lifesaving mission in Somalia, Henry Kissinger, the most famous of the American realists—and probably the most respected voice in U.S. foreign policy circles—wrote: " 'Humanitarian intervention' asserts that moral and humane concerns are so much a part of American life that not only treasure but lives must be risked to vindicate them. . . . No other nation has ever put forward such a set of propositions." After the Kosovo war, Kissinger reprimanded Tony Blair, Britain's prime minister, for the "abrupt abandonment of the concept of national sovereignty" and "the advent of a new style of foreign policy driven by domestic politics and the invocation of universal moralistic slogans." He direly warned:

> Those who sneer at history obviously do not recall that the legal doctrine of national sovereignty and the principle of noninterference—enshrined, by the way, in the U.N. Charter—emerged at the end of the devastating Thirty Years War, to inhibit a repetition of the depredations of the 17th century, during which perhaps 40 percent of the population of Central Europe perished in the name of competing versions of universal truth.[6]

In the same vein, Charles Krauthammer, a conservative columnist, wrote that Kosovo "probably qualifies as the first purely humanitarian war." The argument that humanitarian intervention is a brand-new phenomenon has also been made by influential foreign policy thinkers on both sides of the Atlantic like Stephen Glover, Richard Haass, and Michael Mandelbaum. It has also got traction on the other side of the Pacific: Tang Jiaxuan, as China's foreign minister, called NATO's Kosovo air strikes an "ominous precedent in international relations." Leslie Gelb, who has some sympathy for human rights interventions, wrote, "The notion that states could invade the sovereign territory of other states to stop massive bloodshed (call it genocide or ethnic cleansing or whatever) was inconceivable until the 1990s. . . . But in the space of a few years, this pillar of international politics was badly shaken."[7]

This radical new development is, to many realists, an unambiguously bad one. George Kennan, the realist wise man who came up with the Cold War strategy of containment, argued only for interventions to stop practices "seriously injurious to our interest, rather than just our sensibilities." Thus Kennan was appalled at televised images of U.S. marines going into Somalia, dismissing public sympathy as "an emotional reaction, not a thoughtful or deliberate one."[8]

Realists—especially ones of the Christian theologian Reinhold Niebuhr's stripe—are by no means amoral. Rather, theirs is a morality of prudence and restraint, where the paramount goal is the avoidance of war. The point of a balance of power is a profound moral goal: it keeps the peace. Henry Kissinger's heroes are Metternich and Castlereagh, the statesmen of the Vienna settlement of 1815, who, horrified by the Napoleonic Wars, set up the Concert of Europe to prevent future wars—a success, although at the cost of crushing small nationalities and liberals in the name of long decades of great power peace. So realists rightly worry that hotheaded liberals will choose humanitarian intervention as a first resort rather than a last one, and that the perfectionist calls of justice will drown out the nonperfectionist calls of peace.[9]

At best, some realists think that humanitarian intervention might be a kind of luxury item: a frivolity indulged in by a particularly strong country enjoying a rare moment of international dominance—until it gets its inevitable comeuppance from some new challenger and turns back to the serious business of forging a balance of power. As the neoconservative analyst Robert Kagan noted, the collapse of Soviet power freed the United States to intervene wherever it wanted. But realists see this as immature at best, and an arrogant invitation to nemesis at worst. "We proudly and readily allow our young sons and daughters in uniform to participate in humanitarian enterprises far from home," Colin Powell, chairman of the Joint Chiefs of Staff during the Somalia mission, later wrote. "But when the fighting starts, as it did in Somalia, and American lives are at risk, our people rightly demand to know what vital interest that sacrifice serves."[10]

More often, realists worry that any injection of morality into warfare will lead to unlimited crusades. Realists have long worried about a dangerously immature utopian impulse in democratic foreign policy. They particularly distrust feckless public opinion. This echoes old fears (not just those of realists) about mass politics. Alexander Hamilton wrote in *The Federalist Papers,* "The cries of the nation and the importunities of their representatives have, upon various occasions, dragged their monarchs into war, or continued them in it, contrary to their inclinations, and sometimes contrary to the real interests of the state." Alexis de Tocqueville, in *Democracy in America,* criticized democracies for a "propensity . . . to obey impulse rather than prudence, and to abandon a mature design for the gratification of a momentary passion." Thus Kissinger applauded Metternich and Castlereagh for "their indifference to popular pressures."[11]

When the U.S. Senate considered breaking relations with the Austrian Empire to protest Austria's crackdown on Hungarian nationalists in 1848, one senator sarcastically called for also condemning Russia for its suppression of Poland, France for Algeria, and Britain for India and Ireland. Henry Clay asked, "Where . . . are we to stop? Why should we not interfere in behalf of suffering Ireland? Why not interfere in behalf of suffering humanity wherever we may find it?"[12]

More profoundly, realists doubt that states' motives are really humanitarian. The British realist scholar E. H. Carr saw no moral absolutes, only ideological justifications. In perhaps the most sinister version of this argument, Wilhelm Grewe, a leading German international law expert writing under Nazism in 1944, argued that the stronger a state got, "the more its ideas and concepts prevailed, the more it conferred general and absolute validity on expressions of its national expansionist ideology."[13]

Even if one doesn't go that far, ugly motives are all too commonly masked with pretty rhetoric. As Leo Tolstoy angrily wrote, "Men march from west to east, killing their fellow-creatures, and this event is accompanied by phrases about the glory of France, the baseness of England, and so on. . . . Is there any sort of combined action which could not find justification in political unity, or in patriotism, or in the balance of power, or in civilisation?" Max Weber cautioned against the "undignified self-righteousness" of victorious men who claim they won a war because of their moral rectitude. The worst imperialists often claim they are acting from the finest motives, as realists like Hans Morgenthau, Kenneth Waltz, and Niebuhr have eloquently noted. Even the liberal political theorist Michael Walzer warns, "Ever since Roman times, empires have expanded by intervening in civil wars, replacing 'anarchy' with law and order, overthrowing supposedly noxious regimes." The conquest of weaker nations, Morgenthau argued, is always explained away as the advance of humanitarianism, whether the conquerors are British, Japanese, Arab, French, or Russian.[14]

Today's most influential realists stick to this belief. Kissinger and Mandelbaum put the phrase "humanitarian intervention" in quotation marks. Similarly, John Bolton, a neoconservative who served as George W. Bush's UN-hating UN ambassador, said that "this so-called right of humanitarian intervention . . . is just a gleam in one beholder's eye but looks like flat-out aggression to somebody else." In other words, the starkest realist view of humanitarian intervention is, to paraphrase the postmodernist scholar Stanley Fish: there's no such thing as humanitarian intervention, and it's a good thing, too. That is, these interventions are not really humanitarian, but, windy diplomatic rhetoric notwithstanding, are actually animated by the brutal motives that realists think dominate international politics.[15]

Strangely, it is at this point where realism—generally thought of as a conservative or reactionary creed—aligns with radical leftism. Like realists, leftists see darker imperial motives behind foreign policy: either for economic profit (according to Karl Marx, Vladimir Lenin, and J. A. Hobson) or for racism (according to Edward Said), or a blend of both (Noam Chomsky). Marxism and realism thus came to the same conclusion.[16]

Jean-Paul Sartre, in his furious preface to Frantz Fanon's *The Wretched of the Earth,* wrote of "the strip tease of our humanism. There you can see it, quite naked, and it's not a pretty sight. It was nothing but an ideology of lies, a perfect justification for pillage; its honeyed words, its affectation of sensibility were only alibis for our aggressions." In *Orientalism,* Said wrote, "Colonial rule was justified in advance by Orientalism, rather than after the fact. . . . The Oriental is irrational, depraved (fallen), childlike, 'different'; thus the European is rational, virtuous, mature, 'normal.' " During the Kosovo war, Said complained against "the famous idea of humanitarian intervention which so many Western liberals have dragged out as an excuse for the bombing war." He added, "In comparison with what Clinton has done to Iraq alone, Milošević, for all his brutality, is a rank amateur in viciousness. What makes Clinton's crimes worse is the sanctimony and fraudulent concern in which he cloaks himself and, worse, which seem to fool the neo-liberals who now run the Natopolitan world."[17]

In short, many of the main anxieties of realism are shared as much by leftists as by Kissingerian realists. It is a little strange to see deconstructionists like Jacques Derrida and leftist Heideggerians like Jean Baudrillard agree with conservative realists in their skepticism about state claims to be acting morally. As Baudrillard said after the overthrow of the Taliban in Afghanistan, "Human rights have already been subsumed by the process of globalization and function as an alibi. They belong to the juridical and moral superstructure—in sum, they are *advertising.*" Governments have warmed to the theme, too. Criticizing NATO's war in Kosovo, Chinese foreign minister Tang denounced the concept of humanitarian intervention as "new 'gun-boat diplomacy' " and a prelude to "the rampage of hegemonism." Either way, humanitarian rhetoric about suffering Bosnians, Zimbabweans, or Darfuris must be dismissed out of hand as so much imperial cant.[18]

So, in sum, realists tend to view humanitarian intervention as new and either foolish, fake, or irrelevant.

Beyond Realism

There is much to be said for realism as a starting point. Realists are right to focus on raw power rather than just intentions. Like Machiavelli, realists argue that "all the armed prophets conquered and the unarmed ones were ruined," and, like Weber, that "for the politician the . . . proposition holds, 'thou *shalt* resist evil by force,' or else you are responsible for the evil winning out."[19]

The realists correctly remind us that humanitarian intervention is most likely to occur against militarily weak states. In hard cases, it takes power to impose human rights. As this book will show, in the nineteenth century Russian and Austrian oppression, while often prompting elite and even mass outcries in more liberal countries, did not provoke military steps, whereas oppression by weaker powers like the Ottoman Empire and Naples did. Today, China can get away with far worse in Tibet, or Russia in Chechnya, than a weaker state could. It was NATO power that made possible the humanitarian deployments in Somalia, Bosnia, and Kosovo.[20]

Realists are also right to point out the frequent hypocrisy of the national security establishment. Immanuel Kant worried that kings could go callously to war and "blithely leave its justification (which decency requires), to his diplomatic corps, who are always prepared for such exercises." In the era of imperialism, one should be wary of any British hearts that bled over the fate of the insurrectionist Greeks and Bulgarians while remaining inured to the imperial brutalities inflicted on insurrectionist Sikhs and Bengalis by the British themselves. Thus John Stuart Mill shabbily defended British and French imperialism as a tutelary "benefit" for Indians and Algerians: "Barbarians have no rights as a nation, except a right to such treatment as may, at the earliest possible period, fit them for becoming one." It is right to be deeply suspicious of any government that claims its wars are for the good of humanity.[21]

But there are problems with the realist viewpoint—not least that it could be self-fulfilling. Politicians are not always cynics or hypocrites, or at least not always totally so. Sometimes governments will do well by doing good. The fact that a military intervention in some way serves some government's realpolitik interest does not mean that there is no idealism involved in the decision to send troops. Even a realist like George Kennan admits that the American public was genuinely shocked at Spanish cruelty in Cuba. Even if, as Niebuhr argues, hypocritical rhetoric is meant "for the deception of their own deluded nationals . . . [and] to heal a moral breach in the inner life of statesmen," could not activists use these pinpricks of conscience as the thin edge of a wedge, building a more truly moral kind of statecraft?[22]

Sometimes, states are genuinely driven by morality. The prime example is the campaign against the slave trade, and then slavery itself—properly seen as the root of all modern human rights activism. Britain drove hard to stop the African slave trade—even to the point of using military force. As the political scientists Chaim Kaufmann and Robert Pape demonstrate, this principled commitment cost Britain the lives of some five thousand troops in various antislavery missions, soured its relations with the United States and France, and badly damaged the British economy by undermining its own sugar industry. Still, British leaders backed the policy with remarkable vigor. "I need hardly remind you of the slave trade," Liverpool, the prime minister, wrote to his foreign secretary, Castlereagh, immediately upon hearing of the capitulation of Paris at the end of the Napoleonic Wars in 1815. Napoléon had reintroduced slavery in the French Empire in 1802, but now King Louis XVIII, restored to his throne by force of British arms, was in no position to resist the British antislavery position; Castlereagh could soon proudly report to Liverpool "the final Act of His Most Christian Majesty, declaring the Slave Trade for ever abolished throughout the Dominions of France." Although much of the French public resented this imposition by a victorious enemy, Britain continued to complain of French violations of the treaty.[23]

In 1817, Britain insisted on a treaty that called for the abolition of Spain's slave trade by 1820. To the horror of Cuban plantation owners, and in violation of Spanish sovereignty, Britain sent abolitionist officials to look out for the slaves—and even made a dramatic show of military force, dispatching a ship to Havana, with black British soldiers aboard to take freed Africans to British colonies. In 1821, Britain signed a treaty with Madagascar to put an end to the slave trade there, on pain of execution for slavers. Prime Minister Palmerston unsubtly named a fierce British abolitionist as Britain's consul in Cuba. In 1845, Parliament gave the British navy the authority to seize Brazilian slave ships. When British diplomatic pressure failed to convince the slave-trading sultan of Zanzibar to see the error of his ways, Britain in 1873 got the job done with an ultimatum that threatened a full naval blockade. British officials also hassled their counterparts in the Ottoman Empire, Iran, and Texas. By 1862, John Stuart Mill could cheer "the great victory of slavery abolition."[24]

Britain's efforts were matched with echoes from abroad: the coming of emancipation in France and Denmark in 1848, in Russia in 1861, and in the United States in 1863. (In the United States, the Civil War was in large part about ending slavery—and thus is properly seen as, to some substantial degree, a humanitarian war.) These and other efforts, as the historian David Brion Davis argues, were not just a fig leaf over British imperialism, but part of a genuine British commitment to antislavery. Davis even writes—in words that have an eerily familiar ring to debates about Darfur—"Britain's fixation on the slave trade often worked against British interests, damaging or straining relations with Muslim leaders in an era of Islamic insurgency and nationalistic discontent." This was not faked humanitarianism.[25]

As the slave trade example shows, humanitarian interventions are not just a luxury item. They are not, more precisely, the self-indulgence of a hegemonic country with no major security concerns—namely, the United States in the dreamy interlude between the end of the Cold War and before September 11, 2001. Of course, there is no doubt that the collapse of the Soviet Union was a vital precursor to a (fitful) new U.S. and European interest in humanitarian interventions in the 1990s. But that is not all there is to say. Even when states are not totally secure, not in a position of complete hegemony, they have often been tempted by humanitarian military adventures. In the nineteenth century, Britain launched humanitarian missions, even though statesmen in London knew full well that their own state was far from completely secure, and that such missions could have dangerous strategic consequences on the Continent.

In short, realism cannot explain away the humanitarian interventions of the nineteenth century. Britain repeatedly went against its own realpolitik interests, including the core security concern of checking Russian expansionism, in the name of humanity. There really is such a thing as humanitarianism; it is not just veiled imperialism; governments can sometimes be made to send troops not because of self-interest but because of a genuine sense of humanity.

Saving Fellow Humans or Saving Fellow Christians?

When Hitler came to devour the Sudetenland, and then Czechoslovakia, Neville Chamberlain shrugged it off as just a "quarrel in a faraway country between people of whom we know nothing." It is a notorious phrase but not a careless one. After all, Chamberlain, while himself genuinely knowing precious little about Czechoslovakia, was a shrewd politician who had not become prime minister without some real skill in aiming his words at British public opinion. He must have thought that these words would sell Britons on appeasement: that the remoteness and obscurity of the Czechs would make it morally and politically acceptable to sacrifice them to Germany. This was the language of moral unconcern, a deliberate attempt to make the fate of the Czechs a matter of indifference to the British.[26]

Whose lives matter to us? If someone was being murdered right next to you, you would react, even if you did not know the person. But that simple moral imperative somehow seems to fade with increasing distance.

David Hume wrote, "The breaking of a mirror gives us more concern when at home, than the burning of a house, when abroad, and some hundred leagues distant."[27]

Our moral universes radiate outward from ourselves. Our own personal miseries are our foremost concern, even when relatively trivial. "If he were to lose his little finger to-morrow, he would not sleep to-night," Adam Smith mordantly wrote. "But, provided he never saw them, he will snore with the most profound security over the ruin of a hundred millions of his brethren, and the destruction of that immense multitude seems plainly an object less interesting to him, than this paltry misfortune of his own." Virginia Woolf, in *Mrs. Dalloway*, has her elegantly aloof title character think, "And people would say, 'Clarissa Dalloway is spoilt.' She cared much more for her roses than for the Armenians. Hunted out of existence, maimed, frozen, the victims of cruelty and injustice (she had heard Richard say so over and over again)—no, she could feel nothing for the Albanians, or was it the Armenians? but she loved her roses."[28]

We all love our roses. And most of us love them a little guiltily, insofar as we recognize the narrowness of this emotional horizon. This guilt, or discomfort, is a mark of moral progress. At least Clarissa Dalloway feels bad that she doesn't feel bad. So we are also capable of broadening our moral horizons. The next obvious step for our moral sensibilities is concern for our immediate families and friends. These ties come easily, without any particular abstractions of thought. Beyond that, we carry loyalties to our town, our region, our coreligionists, our class, our nation, our country. As Aristotle wrote, "Men also pity their equals and contemporaries, by character, by habit, by esteem and by birth; for in all these cases it seems more likely that it [suffering] could also happen to them." Hume agreed: "There is no such passion in human minds, as the love of mankind, merely as such, independent of personal qualities, of services, or of relation to ourself."[29]

Some solidarities go very big and far: pan-Slavism, pan-Arabism, irredentist national movements. Leo Tolstoy saw himself as part of a larger Christian community, which superseded loyalties to states: "There . . . cannot be any reason for dissension between Christian nations." In an influential recent book, the political scientist Martha Finnemore pointed to the power of pan-Christian loyalties. Aleksandr Herzen went one better: "After Christianity [came] the belief in civilisation, in humanity."[30]

These more expansive moral ties often mimic direct personal relationships. Thus nationalists often, however implausibly, refer to the other distant members of the nation as family: our brothers, our cousins.

In Shakespeare's *Henry V*, the king rallies his soldiers at Agincourt by telling them that they are a "band of brothers."[31]

Realists draw the line at the border. They extol only the community of citizens within a country and ignore foreigners. George Orwell, trying to understand why Germans were bombing him in World War II, argued, "One cannot see the modern world as it is unless one recognises the overwhelming strength of patriotism, national loyalty." Realists are patriotic—loyal to the state—and nothing but patriotic. As E. H. Carr put it, "Most men's sense of common interest and obligation is keener in respect of family and friends than in respect of others of their fellow-countrymen, and keener in respect of their fellow-countrymen than of other people."[32]

Narrow patriotism, for realists, trumps broad humanitarianism. It was in that vein that a young George Canning, who would later become Britain's foreign secretary and prime minister, mocked the purported universalism born of the French Revolution:

> *No narrow bigot he; —his reason'd view*
> *Thy interests, England, ranks with thine, Peru!*
> *France at our doors, he sees no danger nigh,*
> *But heaves for Turkey's woes th' impartial sigh;*
> *A steady patriot of the world alone,*
> *The friend of every country—but his own.*

These advocates of patriotism can lean pretty hard on the unfamiliarity of foreigners. Patriotism, after all, is what underpinned Chamberlain's argument against British interest in the Czechs. "The ordinary Englishman carries in his mind a generalised picture of the behaviour, daily life, thoughts and interests of other Englishmen, whereas he has no such picture at all of the Greek or the Lithuanian," wrote Carr. "Moreover, the vividness of his picture of 'foreigners' will commonly vary in relation to geographical, racial and linguistic proximity, so that the ordinary Englishman will be likely to feel that he has something, however slight, in common with the German or the Australian and nothing at all in common with the Chinese or the Turk."[33]

Governments, at least, have long seen the world that way. Patriotism drives states more often than a broader humanitarianism. In 1850, Palmerston sent a British squadron to Greece after anti-Semitic rioters burned the house of Don Pacifico, a British Jew living in Athens; during the Boxer

Rebellion in 1900, the United States and many European countries dispatched troops to safeguard their citizens (and imperialistic claims) in China; in 1965, Lyndon Johnson publicly justified sending the marines to the Dominican Republic by the need to evacuate U.S. citizens; in 1975, the White House argued that it was entitled to use force to free the *Mayaguez,* an U.S. merchant ship seized by Cambodia; in 1976, Israel reached as far as Entebbe, in Uganda, to rescue Israelis and Jews taken hostage by Palestinian hijackers; and in 1980, distinctly less effectively, the Carter administration launched a botched raid to try to free U.S. embassy personnel held hostage in Iran.[34]

This sort of patriotism, deployed against larger and distant obligations, is likely to increase as things in Iraq go from awful to worse. In the current Scowcroftian moment, when the Bush administration's disastrous adventure in Iraq threatens to discredit any future projects of nation-building and democratization, Americans are likely to emphasize looking out for fellow Americans, and the rest of the world be damned. But the contemporary revival of the patriotic-realist tradition will run up against an obstacle—against one of the primary moral accomplishments of our time: the idea, and the statecraft, of human rights.

The radical premise of human rights is that human lives are human lives, near or far. As Immanuel Kant argued, "Because a . . . community widely prevails among the Earth's peoples, a transgression of rights in *one* place in the world is felt *everywhere.*" Edmund Burke, denouncing British corruption in India, declared, "The laws of morality are the same every where." To a pure liberal, if people are dying in a quarrel in a faraway country between people of whom we know nothing, all that matters is that people are dying.[35]

For the ideological heirs of the Enlightenment, all men are created equal, and our moral sensibilities should recognize that. Adam Smith notes, "We are but one of the multitude, in no respect better than any other in it; . . . when we prefer ourselves so shamefully and so blindly to others, we become the proper objects of resentment, abhorrence, and execration." Victor Hugo compared "the two ideas of country and humanity,—country, the idea which enlarges the heart; humanity the idea which enlarges the horizon." More recently, John Rawls argued that we should make society's rules as if we did not know which family or ethnic group we belong to. For liberals, there is something obnoxious about nationalist discrimination. When patriots or nationalists arbitrarily value one group of people over another, they are, to some liberals, little better than racists.[36]

Thus one of the harshest indictments against bystanders to genocide is that they are lulled by their own bigotry. Would Americans have stood by if the Rwandans were white, or if the Bosnians were overwhelmingly Christian? David Wyman, the leading historian of the United States' reaction to the Holocaust, cannot escape the conclusion that the country's passivity was driven by American anti-Semitism. As the poet Czesław Miłosz wrote, of Bosnia, "The lives of the well-fed are worth more than the lives of the starving." Nelson Mandela said that Africans and Asians had to envy the willingness of the world to save Kosovo.[37]

These kinds of biases are a particular concern for the press, which is supposed to be making judgments about news, not race. As Carr wrote, "An American newspaper correspondent in Europe is said to have laid down the rule that an accident was worth reporting if it involved the death of one American, five Englishmen, or ten Europeans." In 1970, the publisher of the *New York Times,* Arthur Ochs Sulzberger, asked his editors, "Why is it that when the National Guard kills four white students we put it on page 1, and when the National Guard kills six black people we put it on page 32?" When an explosion of army munitions in Lagos killed over a thousand fleeing Nigerians, it was not front-page news in the *Chicago Tribune,* which instead ran pieces on Illinois prescription drug coverage and corruption charges against a Chicago businessman. How can one justify this kind of partiality? At home, it is intolerable; abroad, it may be equally intolerable, but it is commonplace.[38]

Against that kind of discrimination, Percy Bysshe Shelley wrote in 1821 that "we are all Greeks." He was using the same leveling kind of moral language as John Kennedy's "I am a Berliner," or the American civil rights movement slogan "I am a man," or *Le Monde*'s headline after September 11 that "We are all Americans." That is the essence of human rights: the suffering of the distant is put on the same level as that of ourselves.[39]

The crucial point is that, in liberal states—today and in the nineteenth century—the ambit of solidarity is potentially unlimited. Everyone's lives count. Pan-Arabism and pan-Slavism are limited to lands where Arabs and Slavs live; the same is true for even the biggest world religions and nationalisms. And in despotic countries, the apparatus of state power demands fealty to the state, not to other communities; dictators are jealous rulers. But liberal political leaders, while jealous, too, confront a unique problem in trying to keep their populations loyal to themselves alone. Their state ideology has no natural end point. It encompasses the entire human race.

Thus, it is possible to see liberal states pursuing a foreign policy in the interests of humanity. John Stuart Mill scorned

> the eternal repetition of this shabby *refrain,*— . . . "We ought not to interfere where no English interest is concerned." England is thus exhibited as a country whose most distinguished men are not ashamed to profess, as politicians, a rule of action which no one, not utterly base, could endure to be accused of as the maxim by which he guides his private life,—not to move a finger for others unless he sees his private advantage in it.

Instead, Mill cheered at British foreign policy conducted, so he thought,

> rather in the service of others than of itself,—to mediate in the quarrels which break out between foreign States, to arrest obstinate civil wars, to reconcile belligerents, to intercede for mild treatment of the vanquished, or, finally, to procure the abandonment of some national crime and scandal to humanity, such as the slave-trade.

Here was the interventionist language of "crimes against humanity," almost a century before Nuremberg.[40]

CHAPTER TWO

Media and Solidarity

THE "CNN EFFECT" BEFORE CNN

What can close the roughly 650 miles between Neville Chamberlain's London and Prague? The mass media is a crucial part of the political expression of this humanitarianism. Adam Smith's famous example of the man who values his little finger above the ruin of millions of distant people comes with a crucial proviso: he will be able to snore through the slaughter of millions of innocents, "provided he never saw them." But the distance created by space and unfamiliarity can be erased by new media technology.[1]

This is why mass media plays such a major role in the politics of humanitarian intervention. Roméo Dallaire, the Canadian general who led the ill-starred UN mission in Rwanda, reckoned, "A reporter with a line to the West was worth a battalion on the ground." As Michael Ignatieff argues, televised images of Ethiopian famine in 1984 created "a new kind of electronic internationalism"—the kind of image-driven outcry that is now called the CNN effect (after the Cable News Network). Even realists, who disapprove of this, admit its importance. Thus, after the Tiananmen Square massacre, a chagrined George H. W. Bush wrote to Deng Xiaoping: "The wonder of TV brought the details of the events in Tiananmen Square into the homes of people not just in 'Western' countries but world-wide." George Kennan was flummoxed by the images from Mogadishu on his television screen in Princeton, unhappily concluding that the American reaction to remote suffering was caused by television. So did Kissinger during the Kosovo war.[2]

One of the main arguments of this book is that mass media is the crucial first step toward a humanitarian intervention. This builds on the well-established understanding that the media plays a crucial role in forging national identity—the social engineering that creates new group identity, and forges links between groups of people who previously thought of themselves as distinct. Nations are groups of people who think they share a common identity, but these identities shift. People from Savoy and Nice think of themselves as fellow Frenchmen, but they didn't always, and they have so much that divides them that it's remarkable how much they consider themselves united. Similarly for Massachusetts and Alabama, or Sardinia and Tuscany. Conversely, Serbs and Croats, who used to be Yugoslavs, have so much in common that it's remarkable how much they consider themselves divided. As Benedict Anderson notes, there is something artificial about a sense of a common nationhood among distant people who have never met each other. No American can personally know all the other Americans, but Americans do not doubt that that their fellow citizens are out there somewhere. They form, in Anderson's striking phrase, an "imagined community."[3]

The key point is that these imagined communities rest on the mass media. What links these distant disconnected persons, Anderson argues, is, at least at first, print capitalism. By the year 1500, there had been at least twenty million books printed. With the coming of the printing press and the book, languages became standardized, so that individuals far away could understand what the others were saying. And they could also understand that there were other peoples who did not share that common language, and who were therefore different. Although elites and intellectuals would usually be the vanguard of nationalism, the spread of print allowed them to pump nationalist sentiment out to the masses.[4]

This technological shift made the modern nation possible. Anderson says it grew out of the combination of print technology with capitalism. Long-distance transportation is important, too, but the nationalism literature gives pride of place to the mass media. For instance, in colonial America, which by the end of the eighteenth century had more presses than Britain did, printing helped create a new sense of distinct non-British identity. Victor Hugo saw the greatness of the nineteenth century in "the mariner's compass, the voltaic pile, the printing-press, the journal, the locomotive, the electric telegraph." After the French Revolution, Edmund Burke worried that the seeds of revolution

> are sown almost every where, chiefly by newspaper circulations, infinitely more efficacious and extensive than ever they were. . . . There are thirty of them in Paris alone. . . . [T]hey are like a battery in which the stroke of any one ball produces no great effect, but the

> amount of continual repetition is decisive. Let us only suffer any person to tell us his story, morning and evening, but for one twelvemonth, and he will become our master.

These new solidarities among distant Americans or distant Frenchmen were created largely by the mass media.[5]

Imagined Humanity

If new identities can form within borders, they can surely form outside of borders, too. The same kinds of processes that generated national identity could create some kind of solidarity with foreigners, as well. This solidarity might not be as strong as that within a country, but it could nevertheless come to play an important role in international politics.

After all, national communities may create deeply felt solidarity among their members, but they do not rest on any genuine prehistoric primordial ties. Ethnic, linguistic, geographic, religious, or tribal attachments need not be political, and indeed they often are not. It is nationalism that turns them into political commitments. So there is no reason why beliefs should stop at borders. If British national identity was a belief strong enough to agglomerate the English, the Welsh, and the Scots, why should it stop sharply at Britain's borders? There are innumerable examples of ethnic groups whose sympathies extend across their international borders. Just as a start, the anthropologist Clifford Geertz lists pan-Arabism, pan-Africanism, and greater Somali identity, as well as worrying about the potential for India and China to reach out to foreign ethnic Indians and ethnic Chinese, plus Malays in Thailand, and—particularly important since September 11—ethnic Pashtun on both sides of the Pakistan-Afghanistan border.[6]

The humanitarian interventions of the nineteenth century can be seen as, at the least, the froth of that era's cresting wave of nationalism. This was a century of great xenophobia, but there were other more hopeful currents, too. In other words, the same forces of modernity that forged a sense of common British political identity between impoverished Welsh villagers and London aristocrats, or between French citizens in metropolitan Paris and slowly integrating Lorraine, could also create a weaker but still politically important sense of solidarity with foreigners facing massacre. Just as the growth of national consciousness relies on knowing about the lives of other members of the national community living far away, the growth of humanitarian concern for foreigners relies on knowing about the lives of foreigners. So the causes of humanitarian intervention lie with the latter stages of the parallel marches of political liberalization and of mass media technology. In the nineteenth century, this meant telegraphs and newspapers and books, and today blossoms to include radio, wires, computers, television, and satellites, all of which can make the distances between peoples shrink. The phenomenon is bleakly satirized in Danis Tanović's film *No Man's Land,* where a Bosnian soldier sitting in his trench with a newspaper says, "What a mess in Rwanda." Technology does not make us all one, but it has the potential to collapse the distances between us, and help create an imagined community that, at the margin, includes all of us—an imagined humanity.[7]

Domestic Politics and Humanitarian Intervention

The nineteenth-century Russian anarchist thinker Mikhail Bakunin once wrote, "When an Englishman or an American says 'I am an Englishman,' 'I am an American', they are saying 'I am a free man'; when a German says 'I am a German' he is saying ' . . . my Emperor is stronger than all the other Emperors, and the German soldier who is strangling me will strangle you all.' " The important point from this rather chilling assertion is that the particular kind of government makes a big difference in the making of foreign policy—particularly a foreign policy promoting human rights.[8]

Domestic politics is the crucible of foreign policy. Domestic structures and institutions can make the difference between war and peace. Kant prophesied that properly made constitutions would bring perpetual peace. As Samantha Power put it, "It is in the realm of domestic politics that the battle to stop genocide is lost."[9] In liberal states, there are three distinctive institutions—a free press, free civil society, and governments that respond to public opinion—that can create pressure on the government to defend human rights abroad.

In free states, where citizens enjoy civil rights and representative government, press and societal freedom tend to go along with a government that listens to the will of its own society. A free press can outrage a free polity, pushing the government to respond. As Victor Hugo wrote, "Where there is no liberty of the press, there is no vote." In a powerful example, Jean Drèze and Amartya Sen argue that it was India's democracy that prevented the huge famines that had scourged the country before independence, since the relatively free Indian press and opposition could shame the government into action.[10]

This is not to say that publics will always demand humanitarianism, nor that governments will always accede. The fact that liberal ideology mandates sympathies for all suffering humanity hardly means that state policy will follow. The free press can miss or botch the story; the elites and mass public can fail to react to the stories; and the government can decide it would rather face the repercussions at home than take a misstep in its foreign policy. As Gladstone wrote, "Indignation is froth, except as it leads to action." But liberal states are torn between national and international considerations, between self-protection and solidarity—and in that clash lies much of the basic political drama of this book.[11]

The politics of humanitarian intervention look very different in an illiberal state. Despots are less likely to indulge ideological doctrines of solidarity with the rest of humanity. Some postcolonial dictatorships have polities with broader concerns, like the well-being of fellow Arabs or fellow Christians living in other countries, which can sometimes receive the ideological blessing of the state. But there are distinct limits to these solidarities, unlike the potentially universal solidarity of liberal states.

On top of that, illiberal states have a profoundly different relationship with their publics. They do not face a free press or a free civil society. Dictatorial regimes can muzzle their press, shackle their civil society, and jail or kill their political opposition. This gives them a range of what politely could be called policy options that liberal states lack. Credible information about foreign atrocities goes first to the government, not to the public, and the government can coolly decide if it suits its strategic interests to react or not. The regime can mold public opinion. The regime might allow space for civil society to pick up on an issue that serves the government's purposes, but it can also choke off that space when it no longer does. In particular, despotisms can use the state-controlled press top-down to create solidarity with foreigners when that serves the state's own expansionist agenda. In contrast to their example of democratic India, Drèze and Sen argue that China had famines because of the lack of "a political system of adversarial journalism and opposition." Mao, silencing the domestic press and curtailing the handful of foreign correspondents in

China to guesswork, could let millions starve to death without being called to account—much like North Korea today.[12]

"I Am Kept in Ignorance!": Illiberal State, Unfree Press

There is a stark difference between the role of the press under liberal and illiberal governments. For anyone who's ever tried to slog through a state-controlled newspaper, like the stultifying ones in Vietnam, this is not a subtle distinction. In an illiberal country, the press is, at best, at the mercy of government censors, and often is itself a wing of the government.

Napoléon once said to Metternich, despot to despot, "You see me as the master of France; well, I would not undertake to govern it for three months with freedom of the press." From the receiving end of the state's censorship, Victor Hugo wrote,

> What! I know nothing of what has taken place. People have been killed, butchered, fusiladed, assassinated, and I am kept in ignorance! Men have been sequestrated, tortured, expelled, exiled, deported, and I have had hardly a glimpse of the outrage! . . . I am a peasant; I cultivate a bit of land down in one of the provinces; you suppress the newspaper, you stifle revelations, you prevent the truth from reaching me.

On June 4, the Chinese press makes no mention of the Tiananmen Square massacre on its anniversary, leaving Chinese peasants equally as stifled.[13]

Nazi Germany had the highest percentage of radio listeners in the world, at over 70 percent in 1939, thanks in large part to state subsidization of over seven million cheap radios called *Volksempfänger* (People's Receivers). The radios were weak so that, except near the borders, they could only pick up German broadcasts. Josef Goebbels, the propaganda minister, said, "We make no bones about the fact that the radio belongs to us and to no one else." Although Americans read more newspapers per capita than Soviets did, Soviets read more political magazines and journals, and the Soviet press was all united in its state-dictated themes. Soviet citizens only got the official line, meant to inspire Kremlin-friendly views. Today, North Korean radios are literally stuck on the government station, lest anyone hear an opinion not congenial to Kim Jong-il.[14]

On top of that, the press can foment lethal nationalism when it is firmly under the thumb of a government. In liberal Britain or the United States, it was the media that many times moved the government, but in illiberal countries it will often be the other way around. Slobodan Milošević used Serbia's state-dominated media to ratchet up nationalism, in particular by creating pan-Serb solidarity with ethnic Serbs in Croatia and Bosnia. In a kind of mirror-imaging, Franjo Tuđman stoked equal but opposite fears in Croatia. And in Rwanda, Hutu Power hate radio relentlessly drove home the call for genocide against the Tutsi.[15]

The prime example in this book of illiberal manipulation of the press is tsarist Russia, where pan-Slavist attachments were forged with government encouragement and direct help. Even so, many Russian pan-Slavist activists were genuine in their solicitude for their brother Serbs, just as many Arabs are genuinely concerned about the plight of the Palestinians. The pan-Slavists may have been dupes, but they were sincere dupes. Cynicism in the Winter Palace does not imply cynicism in the streets of Moscow and St. Petersburg.[16]

Still, Leo Tolstoy understood well what was really going on. He warned, "Thanks to the development of literature, reading, and the facilities of travel, governments which have their agents everywhere, by means of statutes, sermons, schools, and press, inculcate everywhere upon the people the most barbarous and erroneous ideas." Thus Russians became tools of their government's foreign policy. "We all regard ourselves as free, educated, humane men, or even as Christians," he wrote, "and yet were all in such a position that were Wilhelm tomorrow to take offense against Alexander, or Mr. N. to write a lively article on the Eastern Question, or Prince So-and-so to plunder some Bulgarians or Servians, or some queen or empress to be put out by something or other, all we educated humane Christians must go and kill people of whom we have no knowledge, and toward whom we are as amicably disposed as to the rest of the world."[17]

"A Relentless Inquisition": Free State, Free Press

Things look very different in a liberal country, with a free press. Thomas Jefferson famously wrote, "Were it left to me to decide whether we should have a government without newspapers or newspapers without a government, I should not hesitate a moment to prefer the latter." Under a liberal state, the press is free to publish as it sees fit—prompting free reactions throughout society. As Ralph Waldo Emerson wrote, of the *Times,*

> The English like it for its complete information. . . . Then, they like its independence; they do not know, when they take it up, what their paper is going to say. . . . Its existence honors the people who dare to print all they know, dare to know all the facts, and do not wish to be flattered by hiding the extent of the public disaster.[18]

In London during the Blitz, George Orwell proudly wrote, "After a year of war, newspapers and pamphlets abusing the Government, praising the enemy and clamouring for surrender are being sold on the streets, almost without interference." In the Cold War, American and British government broadcasts tried to break the monopoly on information in Eastern Europe, just as today South Koreans try to sneak normal radios into North Korea. The *New York Times* combatively says every day that it runs "all the news that's fit to print," and if you don't like the paper, you can pick up a copy of the *Wall Street Journal* or the *New York Post; Granma* slavishly bills itself as "the official organ of the Cuban communist party," and if you don't like the paper, you're stuck.[19]

It is this free press that makes possible solidarities with distant victims of massacre. While press freedom is a familiar feature of today's liberal democracies, it was a revolutionary idea.[20]

The free press became an integral part of British parliamentary politics, as part of a growing trend of liberalization that swept away the absolutism of the sixteenth century. In 1695, in a momentous first step, the imprimatur—the government license to print—was quietly allowed to lapse. After the Napoleonic Wars, newspapers trumpeted their role in maintaining British freedom, with support from the courts in libel cases. Emerson thought that free journals were "the driving force" behind British liberalization. The British newspaper, he wrote after an 1847 visit to London, "stands in antagonism with the feudal institutions," fighting "against the secretive tendencies of a monarchy." He rhapsodized:

> There is no corner and no night. A relentless inquisition drags every secret to the day, turns the glare of this solar microscope on every malfaisance, so as to make the public a more terrible spy than any foreigner; and no weakness can be taken advantage of by an enemy, since the whole people are already forewarned. Thus England rids herself of those incrustations which have been the ruin of old states.

The final constraints on the press were heavy taxes on paper and stamps, to help fund the Napoleonic Wars, which were repealed from 1853 to 1861. From the 1850s to the 1880s, the British mass press basked in an unprecedented age of freedom and influence.[21]

The impact of the unshackled press at home in Britain is well known, like its pressure toward abolishing the protectionist Corn Laws. But the impact was just as great in foreign policy. As Emerson wrote, "What would the 'Times' say? is a terror in Paris, in Berlin, in Vienna, in Copenhagen, and in Nepaul." The British government could no longer pick and choose when and how to confront foreign crises. In an earlier era, if there was an inconvenient massacre somewhere, then only British diplomats would know about it, and could sweep it under the rug if that was what realpolitik dictated. But as the press grew robust, there was always the danger that an industrious foreign correspondent would report news directly to the British public, no matter what the cabinet wanted its subjects to know.[22]

This is not to say that the press will always poke into the right corners. As George Orwell wrote, awful things happened in the Spanish Civil War, and "they did not happen any the less because the *Daily Telegraph* has suddenly found out about them when it is five years too late." In 1994, there were twenty-five hundred reporters covering the inauguration of Nelson Mandela and no more than fifteen covering the genocide in Rwanda. Often, dictatorships will make it impossible for reporters to do their job. In Justice Robert Jackson's opening address at Nuremberg, he spoke of Buchenwald and Dachau but not of Auschwitz, because the eastern camps were in Soviet hands and thus not as accessible to British and U.S. officials and reporters. In Algeria and Chechnya, visiting reporters were potential targets, helping ensure that the outside world knows little of the staggering bloodshed there. The Baathist regime in Iraq prevented international television reporters from getting film of Shia refugees in 1991, but not of the Kurds, resulting in public pressure to relieve Kurdish suffering. North Korea imposes strict limits on foreign correspondents, preventing detailed reporting on the country's vast famine. And Robert Mugabe has expelled many foreign correspondents from Zimbabwe. To understand the patterns of humanitarian intervention, the vital first step is knowing where the reporters are.[23]

From Pigeons to CNN

The early newspapers were usually pretty poor. Although ideologically liberalism could encompass all of humanity, in practice liberal moral commitments tend to go only as far as their mass media can go. Without credible information about foreign atrocities, liberal citizens cannot know where to focus their moral concerns—and can return to worrying about more parochial concerns.

It was not so long ago that independent newspapers and telegraph agencies came on the scene. Milton's classic argument against censorship in his *Areopagitica* was published in 1644, but as late as the 1780s, Britain's foreign news still came largely from the *London Gazette,* the official government mouthpiece. British newspapers might agitate on foreign events, like an overhyped threat of a French invasion in 1798, but they could offer their readers no real reporting of their own about what was actually happening in France. It took almost two months for Londoners to get word of Napoléon's death.[24]

Pigeons ruled the news business as late as the middle of the nineteenth century. In 1837, it was relatively bold of the *Times* to set up its own pigeon post between Paris and Boulogne to carry market prices. The Correspondance Garnier, one of France's first news agencies, relied on pigeons to shuttle news from Paris to London and St. Petersburg. Paul Julius Reuter, a young German Jewish émigré newsman (who had discreetly changed his name from Israel Beer Josaphat) also concentrated his attentions on these reliable birds, which were considerably faster than mail trains. In 1850, Reuter bought forty pigeons to carry commercial news. Stock prices, carefully copied onto tissue paper, would be put in a silk bag tucked under a pigeon's wing. Reuter slowly shifted to having his local agents actually write news, including political news. In 1851, Reuter relocated from Aachen to London, attracted by British press freedom. By then, a technological revolution had happened: a telegraph line had been completed between Berlin and Paris, and another between Dover and Calais.[25]

The telegraph carried news at lightning speed, putting railroads and pigeons to shame. So newspapers, for the first time, became full of world news. Reuters, reinvented as a telegraph agency, sent news flashing from Paris to London in minutes, so that its readers could chew it over the next day. By 1848, the *New York Herald* was printing seventy-nine thousand words sent by telegraph. In the U.S. Civil War, the telegraph was a staple of newspaper coverage from the front lines. And in 1866, Reuters opened its first office in Bombay, although there was still no reliable cable link back to London.[26]

Governments also took advantage of the new technology. By 1870 the British Foreign Office had its own permanent lines. Queen Victoria installed a telegraph office in Osborne House, her massive private retreat on the Isle of Wight, which, as the historian Niall Ferguson writes, "perfectly illustrates what happened to the world during Victoria's reign. It shrank—and it did so largely because of British technology." Her prime minister, Benjamin Disraeli, was thunderstruck at how fast he could reach his foreign secretary: "I have just got a telegram from Derby at Fairhill. I communicated with him only an hour ago! I can't get over the feeling of magic when I receive these electronic missives, though I ought to be hardened to them."[27]

The *Times* dominated the landscape. But by 1855, after the repeal of the Advertisement Duty and the Stamp Duty, it had to compete against a variety of less prestigious but much cheaper newspapers aiming at lower brows—most notably the *Daily Telegraph,* as well as provincial newspapers like the *Manchester Guardian* and the *Scotsman.* With the rise of these "penny papers," a fifth the price of the *Times,* the size of the British newspaper-reading public exploded: from a grand total of less than 100,000 a day in 1854, up to 150,000 readers of the *Daily News* alone by 1871. (Those who came to the paper late missed out; it had originally been edited by Charles Dickens, who quit after only three weeks.) There were only 88 newspapers founded in Britain from 1665 to 1800, and another 126 from 1800 to 1830—and then an astonishing 415 more from 1830 to 1855, followed by 492 more from 1855 to 1861. The size of the readership grew with the 1870 Education Act, boosting public literacy from 61 percent in 1850 to fully 97 percent by 1888. The London newspapers spread to the countryside; commuters read them on the trains; newsstands sprang up.[28]

Foreign news blossomed, too. The smaller papers relied heavily on Reuters telegraph copy to fill their pages—just as smaller newspapers today rely on wire copy rather than staffing their own foreign bureaus. Newspapers slowly got serious about foreign coverage. As late as 1848, the *Times* had only a handful of rather relaxed foreign correspondents in Spain, Portugal, India, and the United States, led by a Paris reporter whose job was mostly to lightly edit European newspapers and forward them on to London, along with mail from India that came through Marseille. Slowly giving up its lazy habit of rewriting European newspapers, the *Times* added correspondents in Berlin and Vienna.[29]

The press gradually learned new norms of objectivity, which had to be policed by the editors. In 1850, the *Times* sacked its first eastern Mediterranean correspondent for accepting a cruise from the king of Greece and filing from the royal yacht, and fired its Italy correspondent for letting his son work for the Neapolitan government. (They also dropped the Paris correspondent for another traditional sin of the foreign correspondent: outrageous expenses.) Worse, the editorial line in Printing House Square still sometimes dictated the vigor of foreign reporting. During the 1848 Hungarian revolution against Austrian domination, the *Times* supported the Austrian Empire, scorning the rebels even though it had not managed to get a reporter anywhere near the insurrection. When the *Times* finally decided to send a special reporter, their man was on warm terms with Metternich and anything but intrepid in his coverage. When the paper's regular Vienna correspondent took Austria to task, he was rewarded both with the search of his house by the police and with a note from his boss in London telling him to tone it down.[30]

In time, the hacks got more professional. Before the outbreak of the Crimean War in 1853, the British press had covered wars mostly by getting letters from low-ranking officers at the front. These soldier amateurs tended to be unreliable, and would hardly satisfy the growing public hunger for news. John Delane, the editor of the *Times,* which had a circulation bigger than that of all its rivals combined, felt a special responsibility. So he made the bold innovation of dispatching an actual foreign correspondent, William Howard Russell.[31]

Russell, from Dublin County, had cut his teeth on Irish violence, and became famous for his vivid accounts of the Crimean War—most dramatically the doomed charge of the Light Brigade, which he privately reckoned as folly. The Crimean War was the first war intentionally reported on by civilians for civilians. It was also the first occasion where the mass media played a role that today is painfully familiar in democratic countries: the press initially whipped up the British public to go to war with Russia; then it showed them the horrors of that war, and the epic ineptitude of the ill-prepared and aristocrat-dominated British military, stirring the public to turn against the botched war.[32]

As Lytton Strachey noted in his dyspeptic sketch of Florence Nightingale, one of the first media darlings, the hideous conditions of the British military hospitals in suburban Constantinople were "revealed to the English public in the dispatches of the *Times* correspondent and in a multitude of private letters." (Nightingale had read the early *Times* coverage in London, and was inspired to head out to Constantinople.) The War Office's judgment was now subject to question from any Briton with a newspaper in hand. Delane let Russell hammer away at the War Office and its largely hapless field officers, who tried to impede or outright censor Russell's reporting, which they saw as borderline treason. When the British foreign secretary griped that the *Times* had driven the public to topple his government for the Crimean War, he was sounding a note that would be echoed by Lyndon Johnson.[33]

The press grew so important to leaders that by the Franco-Prussian War, Bismarck himself sent a telegram directly to Reuters complaining that the *Times*'s reporting "rests upon pure invention." But much as Bismarck might have wished otherwise, people were learning to trust the newspapers. The independent British press, led by the *Times* and other papers, as well as Reuters, developed a reputation for honesty and reliability. On the other side of the Atlantic, the first U.S. wire service, the Associated Press, founded in 1848 to use the new telegraph technology much as Reuters had, turned away from partisan editorializing to the now-familiar standard of objective factual reporting. The AP was followed in this by the *New York Times,* which, after Adolph Ochs took over as publisher in 1896, built a reputation for honesty fully as formidable as that of the *Times* in London in its heyday. People believed what they read, even in the more populist penny press.[34]

Reporters were emerging as a distinct professional class, with some professional standards. By the 1880s, newspapers were even employing college graduates, and the profession gained social cachet. William Makepeace Thackeray worked as a Paris correspondent of a short-lived liberal penny paper, the *Constitutional.*[35]

There was one black hole in this surging liberalism: the British Empire. The freedoms that the British reckoned crucial at home were conspicuously absent in gigantic swaths of their imperial domain. In 1823, as press restrictions were faltering in Britain proper, a set of Bengal Regulations kept a firm grip on licensing newspapers in the lands of the British East India Company. Things grew somewhat more open afterward, but there was a harsh crackdown in 1857 after the Bengal mutiny, followed, from the late 1870s on, by a series of acts meant to prevent the rise of an Indian nationalist press. British newspapers and reporters in India all too often shared the prejudices of the imperial center.[36]

There were some Britons who saw the sickening hypocrisy. William Ewart Gladstone, the Liberal statesman, complained, a little too innocently, that India's nascent free press had "discreditably" been "destroyed, and the native press of India has been placed at the mere beck and will of the Viceroy." Gladstone was also angry that Britons had been kept in the dark about their army's cruelties in Afghanistan. The Indian local press tried to report on the massive 1876–79 famine, and managed to stir up liberal criticism back in Britain of the empire's policy. Some British reporters in India aggressively took on the official London line, like James Routledge of the *Times,* who unsparingly covered the Bengal famine. But they often ran into British imperial censorship. The *Times* was allowed to cover the Zulu War of 1879, but British officials in Africa did their best to interfere with the correspondents—including Winston Churchill, in the Sudan for the *Morning Post.*[37]

When it came to their own brutality, British officials understood all too well what press coverage could mean. In its empire, the British government was starkly illiberal. But for the rest of the world, the government mostly let its press run free. The distance between peoples shrunk, allowing moral empathy with people in a faraway country of whom British newspaper readers now knew quite a few things. The limits to the expanding moral universe were the reach of the reporter and the run of the telegraph wire.

CHAPTER THREE

The Diplomacy of Humanitarian Intervention

Scaring the Rest of the World

The foulest invasions have been justified by the invader as serving the noblest ends. In Munich, in 1938, Hitler complained to Chamberlain, "Herr Beneš is using force against my countrymen in the Sudetenland." A German propaganda barrage managed to convince British elites that Nazi Germany was moved by the purported plight of ethnic Germans in Czechoslovakia's Sudetenland. "In reaction against these renewed assaults upon their life and liberty the nationalities have now freed themselves from Prague," Hitler formally proclaimed as German troops marched in. "Czecho-Slovakia has thereupon ceased to exist. Since Sunday wild excesses have taken place in many villages to which again numerous Germans have fallen victims. From hour to hour the appeals for help from victims and persecuted are increasing."[1]

This cynical abuse of humanitarian rhetoric creates a serious problem for the genuine humanitarians. One great danger for a humanitarian intervention is that it will not be seen internationally as humanitarian. John Stuart Mill, with a rosy estimate of British benevolence, complained that Britain's unselfish policies were "a novelty in the world; so much so . . . that many are unable to believe it when they see it." In their own hearts, Americans may know that their motives are pure, that they want nothing but the best for the people of Somalia and Kosovo, and certainly have no territorial ambitions there. But why should the rest of the world believe that? When it comes with troops, humanitarianism looks a lot like imperialism.[2]

After all, the power and will that are required to launch a successful humanitarian intervention must primarily register on other countries as a sign of our own brute ability to make war. British or French troops landing somewhere to protect the innocent look a lot like British or French troops participating in the "scramble for Africa." Milošević portrayed NATO's humanitarian wars in the 1990s as an expression of Western imperial hatred for the Slavs. The most radical foreign policy thinkers—like E. H. Carr and Noam Chomsky—will never believe that U.S. motives are pure, even if they actually are. One's motives, no matter how vociferous one's protestations of goodwill, will always be subject to question; but the crude fact of one's use of force will not.[3]

Boris Yeltsin, Russia's first elected president, was, as Bill Clinton's top Russia aide Strobe Talbott writes, "nearly unhinged on the subject of Kosovo," complaining that "the U.S. was once again acting as though it had the right to impose its will on the world." China felt much the same way—especially after NATO bombed the Chinese embassy in Belgrade, which the Chinese government called "barbaric." Moralizing speeches from the White House will not be enough; humanitarian talk is cheap, and everybody, down to and including Hitler, uses it. As Henry Kissinger warned during the Somalia mission, "We must not seem to be claiming for ourselves a doctrine of universal unilateral intervention, all the less so as we cannot want to encourage some future rogue nation to decide to use the slogan of 'humanitarian intervention' for expansionist designs."[4]

Aggressive behavior by states tends to prompt a counterreaction. If a powerful liberal country goes to war for the sake of protecting human rights, this will probably spook brutal governments who worry that they might be next. By behaving belligerently, even in the name of humanity, the United States could self-defeatingly scare other rival states into forming new alliances to balance against the threat of U.S. power. How can American humanitarian interventionists possibly convince Russia and China that the most powerful country on earth is invading other countries but not really being aggressive?[5]

At worst, this could spark devastating wars. Conservatives in the nineteenth century would point to the Crimean War—the biggest conflict between the end of the Napoleonic Wars and the outbreak of World War I—as a looming example of how rival great power solicitude for Christians in Ottoman territory could lead to ruin (although Russian expansionism was as much to blame). If George H. W. Bush, reflecting American public shock over the Tiananmen Square massacre, had made military threats against nuclear-armed China, the consequences could have been catastrophic.

The problem with realism is it does a better job of identifying this problem than of solving it. Yes, if it were really true that a humanitarian intervention would cause a vastly larger war, or embitter the rest of the world against the intervening state, then the mission probably would not be worth it. But conservatives sometimes give up too easily. Instead, this book will look for ways to manage the practice of humanitarian intervention. The diplomatic challenge is to prove benevolent motivations, with firm and credible commitments not to turn an ostensibly humanitarian mission into imperial aggrandizement. This book will show that, in the nineteenth century, diplomats had some impressively successful ways of doing just that: using a combination of multilateralism, self-restraint, and treaties as tools to reassure other states about the good motivations behind a humanitarian mission. The leaders of that century were remarkably skilled at convincing rival states of their nonthreatening motives—even in a century of rampant imperialism. Just as it is irresponsible for liberals to hold justice so far above peace that they spark major wars, it is unconscionable for realists to hold peace so far above justice that they overlook ways to make it possible to save innocent lives.[6]

The Politics of Humanitarian Intervention

This book is about the nineteenth century, as an imperfect way to better understand our own current predicament. The politics of human rights have a long and tangled history, and the dilemmas faced by today's human rights advocates are often reflections of those faced by like-minded people who have long since turned to dust. Tsarist manipulation of Russian pan-Slavist public sentiments would be totally familiar to Vladimir Putin; Benjamin Disraeli, digging in his heels against public calls for protection of human rights in Bulgaria, sounded fully as exasperated as Richard Nixon and Henry Kissinger struggling to create the United States' alignment with China.

The image of humanitarian intervention as an untested novelty is wrong. There were some more or less humanitarian interventions waged outside of Europe this century: India's war against Pakistani brutality in Bangladesh, and Tanzania's ouster of Idi Amin's junta in Uganda. To this roster, along with Somalia, Bosnia, Kosovo, Sierra Leone, and Ituri Province in Congo, this book means to add the nineteenth-century European experience of humanitarian intervention. As John Stuart Mill wrote, considering bloody civil wars in general and of Greece in particular: "It seems now to be an admitted doctrine" that outside powers "are warranted in demanding that the contest shall cease, and a reconciliation take place on equitable terms of compromise. Intervention of this description has been repeatedly practised during the present generation, with such general approval, that its legitimacy may be considered to have passed into a maxim of what is called international law." Far from being radical innovators in Bosnia after 1995 and in Kosovo, Clinton and Albright were walking in the footsteps of Canning, Gladstone, James Madison, and Theodore Roosevelt, as well as the moral tradition of Lord Byron and Victor Hugo.[7]

This book is not just about a tradition of humanitarian interventionism, but also about a tradition of honorable and principled opposition to such adventurism. Sometimes the politicians who do not want to save oppressed foreigners are callous or willfully ignorant, but not always. Lord Castlereagh and Disraeli were fixated on maintaining the peace of Europe, and were convinced that this would sometimes unfortunately mean the subjugation of smaller peoples. It is no comfort to the victims that they seem to have been quite sincere in this belief, but it does put them in a different category from more current Western leaders who ignored slaughters overseas for rather less lofty reasons. Castlereagh stayed out of the Balkans because he valued peace more than justice, and John Quincy Adams stayed out of the Balkans because a weak United States could only endanger itself; Clinton stayed out of the Balkans until 1995 without any such excuse.

Nor is this book a celebration of interventionism—and still less of imperialism. There are terrifying hazards involved in meddling in other peoples' conflicts. Outsiders are often lethally ignorant of local politics and cultures, as in Vietnam and Iraq; and foreign meddling can exacerbate local tensions. Ostensible humanitarianism can all too easily shade into bigotry, or can be based on ignorant or biased information. It can be manipulated to fit a country's imperialistic or expansionist designs, or it can bring big powers lurching into a major war. The atrocitarians were not always pure of heart, and they were often reckless and blind to the potentially devastating consequences of their activism. But all of these flaws are also why the atrocitarians are worth understanding: a better grasp of previous efforts at taming and routinizing the practice of humanitarian intervention should contribute to a more humble, sober version of the practice in the future.[8]

The pages that follow are mostly about nineteenth-century political brawls: on British, Russian, and U.S. responses to atrocities against Greeks in 1821–27; on French and British responses to atrocities against Syrians in 1860; on British and Russian responses to atrocities against Bulgarians in 1876; and, bringing the story into the twentieth century, U.S. responses to the Armenian genocide of 1915. The book also considers the plight of Poles, Hungarians, Neapolitans, Bosnians, and Serbians. These are not perfect echoes of the more recent U.S. and European democratic debates about humanitarian intervention on behalf of Somalis, Bosnians, Rwandans, Kosovars, Congolese, Liberians, and Darfuris; but they are crucial precursors. They offer a more complete picture of how activists and governments have confronted the challenge of humanitarian intervention. And they show that passivity in the face of the mass death of innocent foreigners is neither inevitable nor traditional.

PART TWO

GREEKS

Lord Byron could see his own death coming. The most famous and most notorious poet in Europe, as unforgiving in his politics as in his stanzas, he had thrown his celebrity behind the most romantic of political causes: protecting the insurgent Greeks from the Ottoman Empire's oppression. By December 1823, at the age of thirty-five, he had followed his political passion to its logical end: a remote Greek island west of the main fighting. There, he gathered up his courage to sail for the worst of it, Mesologgi, a strategic Greek town terrifyingly besieged by Ottoman forces. He knew the risks. Byron spent his final months organizing the war effort, happily blowing his fortunes funding the Greeks, complaining with remarkable political sophistication about Greek infighting, and privately tearing himself apart between his admiration for the Greek fighters and his own darkest fears. He wrote proudly that the Greeks "expect that I should march with them, and—be it even so!" But in a letter to a friend, his terrors surfaced with an eerie listing of poets of all nations who had died in battle: "If any thing in the way of fever, fatigue, famine, or otherwise, should cut short the middle age of a brother warbler,—like Garcilasso de la Vega, Kleist, Korner, Kutoffski (a Russian nightingale . . .), or Thersander, or,—somebody else—but never mind—I pray you to remember me in your 'smiles and wine.'" Two days later, he left for Mesologgi and a miserable death by fever.[1]

Byron was only the most prominent name among the countless Europeans whose hearts went out to the Greeks. These pro-Greeks, known as the philhellenes, helped mightily in the struggle for the liberation from Ottoman rule of a distant corner of the Balkans, which had once been ancient Greece. The news of the Greek struggle reached Britain through its emerging free press, and found an echo in British society. The British philhellenes formed something like one of the first modern human rights groups; they are the distant but unmistakable ancestors of Amnesty International and Human Rights Watch. Led not just by Byron, but also by figures like the philosopher Jeremy Bentham and the economist David Ricardo, the philhellenes had an abiding—if often delusional—cosmopolitan passion for the cause of relieving foreign suffering.

These proto–human rights activists were wildly romantic, eccentrically educated, ill disciplined, and full of bizarre enthusiasms. They were fascinated by a foreign land, onto which they projected their own fantasies of classical virtue and grandeur. For most of them, what was at stake was nothing less than the defense of liberty against despotism, of civilization against barbarism, and of humanity against mass murder. The philhellenes' politics were largely progressive and humanist, or in some cases evangelical, with deep faith either in liberalism or an activist deity. Above all, they acted on their beliefs. Taking full advantage of Britain's domestic liberalism, they raised money, held rousing public meetings, went door-to-door, built party coalitions, managed press coverage, and lobbied the startled British government from within and without. And they did things that today's human rights groups would never dream of, like buying weapons and outfitting troops to help win the Greek war. Some of the most committed or lunatic members—anticipating, by over a century, George Orwell and the International Brigade in the Spanish Civil War—actually took up arms themselves against Ottoman soldiers.[2]

Arrayed against the philhellenes were the mightiest establishment forces in British politics: towering Tory figures like the Duke of Wellington and Lord Castlereagh, as well as the conservative King George IV himself, who all wanted the Ottomans to crush the Greeks. It was a matter of cold realpolitik: the Ottoman Empire was a crucial ally, a vital bulwark against Russian expansion in the Balkans; the Greek insurrection was an inconvenient distraction. So if the philhellenes look curiously familiar to modern eyes, so do their adversaries. Castlereagh and his fellow conservatives are the heroes of today's realists, exalted by Henry Kissinger as the model of wise diplomacy: prudence above risk, enlightened elites above passionate masses, stability above justice. The fight between Castlereagh and the philhellenes carries echoes of much more recent arguments about humanitarian intervention in the Balkans and elsewhere.

The philhellenes played a crucial role in slanting British policy in a decidedly pro-Greek direction, although they were never quite successful in forming a mass base in Britain. At semiregular intervals, the British government renewed its commitment to protecting the Greeks after some fresh, well-publicized Ottoman horror: the execution of Patriarch Grigorios in 1821, the Scio massacre in 1822, the death of Byron in 1824, and a bloody rampage in the Morea (the Peloponnese) in 1825. This litany of slaughter forced Britain out of its ostensible neutrality, and then to the brink of a humanitarian war for the Greeks. Russia, which had imperialistic as well as humanitarian motives, also pushed Britain closer to intervention in the Mediterranean. By 1827, after six years of war and carnage, a British-led squadron, joined by Russian and French ships, would send most of the Ottoman fleet to the bottom of Navarino Bay—a decisive victory that secured Byron's dream of a new Greece.[3]

CHAPTER FOUR

The Greek Revolution

After Bonaparte

The world in the 1820s was haunted, above all, by the memory of the French Revolution. The kings and courts of Europe had been stunned by the overthrow of the French monarchy in 1789, then horrified by the Terror within France and the rise of Napoléon Bonaparte. Soon after, an apocalyptic series of wars raged across Europe, until Napoléon's final defeat at Waterloo in 1815. To radicals in the 1820s, the revolutionary fires were still fresh; to the kings, even the more progressive ones, so was the lingering sense of disbelief and nightmare. King George IV vowed that Britain's government should always be guided by the memory of "the anarchy produced throughout the world by the French Revolution." For the most reactionary empires—Russia, Prussia, and Austria—the need to stamp out revolution was absolute. But even the constitutional government in Britain, for all its slowly growing liberalism, dreaded domestic upheaval. George IV, typically, complained that the "active firebrands of Ireland" were animated "by the same evil spirit, which gave rise to the calamities of the French Revolution."[1]

At the end of the Napoleonic Wars, to maintain peace and prevent another outbreak of revolution, the great powers had created the Concert of Europe. The Concert was a cooperative European attempt to make the world safe for the shaken Romanovs, Habsburgs, Hanovers, Bourbons, and Hohenzollerns. The Concert and the accompanying world order had been hammered out at the Congress of Vienna in 1814 and 1815, hosted and masterminded by Austria's foreign minister, Prince Klemens von Metternich. On top of that, Russia, Prussia, and Austria formed the Holy Alliance—a league of the most reactionary empires.

The emperors of the Holy Alliance believed in intervention, but of a kind that was anything but humanitarian. Intervention meant their massive empires stepping into some small country to crush a liberal revolution and reestablish a wobbly conservative king on his throne. The Ottoman Empire was seen by Britain and other powers as a legitimate government, worthy of that kind of Holy Alliance help. But for many Britons, sympathetic to the more moderate rebels, their government's reluctant alignment with the Holy Alliance was a disgrace—a cynical and cold-hearted partnership with ruthless foreign despotisms, stamping out the flickerings of freedom in small nations. The phrase "rights of man" might be too tainted by the French Revolution to be used widely, but the idea of freedom was powerful. If military or diplomatic force was to be used, many British liberals thought, it should be on the side of the weak, not on the side of tyrannical empires.[2]

"For Foreign Arms and Aid They Fondly Sigh"

Lord Byron first set foot on Greek soil in 1809, and in short order, as one would expect, he fell in love.

The callow young George Gordon, the sixth Lord Byron, still only aspired to be mad, bad, and dangerous to know. He was so handsome—luxurious curls, expressive eyes, strong nose and chin—that people could not resist calling his looks Greek, but this was offset by his lame leg, which had dogged him from birth. So far, his life had mostly disappointed him. While slumbering through Cambridge (and annoying the dons by keeping a pet bear, since Trinity College regulations forbade dogs), Byron put out his first book of poetry, unpromisingly titled *Hours of Idleness,* which some reviewers hated. Years later, he recalled with undiminished bitterness, "A savage review is Hemlock to a sucking author. . . . Instead of bursting a blood-vessel—I drank three bottles of Claret—and began an answer." Unable to find legal means to smash the head of his reviewer, Byron retaliated with a second book, this one peevishly titled *English Bards and Scotch Reviewers.* He was by now heartily sick of English life, and hot for new horizons and bedmates. So, with his long-suffering Cambridge friend John Cam Hobhouse, the otherwise respectable scion of a wealthy Bristol family, Byron set off on a tour of the eastern Mediterranean. He finally found what he was looking for in Greece.[3]

Greece would be Byron's fatal political cause, and the muse for some of his best—and worst—poetry. It was also, Byron being Byron, a playground for prodigious sex tourism. Byron was drawn to the ancient Greek openness about passion. When he first set foot in Greece—not far from Mesologgi—he was struck by the presence of well-armed Ottoman soldiers, a visible sign of oppression. He mourned the ruined Acropolis and thrilled at the plain of Marathon. The literary traveler swam across the Hellespont in an hour and ten minutes, undeterred by some alarmingly big fish, and then duly wrote a poem about it. In 1810, in Athens, he rented an apartment from the widow of a former British consul, and—taking philhellenism to the next level—fell in love with her beautiful daughter, Theresa Macri. For her, he wrote the cringe-inducing "Maid of Athens, Ere We Part," which somehow became one of Byron's most famous works despite seeming to be pitched at the level of his beloved, who was then twelve years old:

Maid of Athens, ere we part,
Give, oh give me back my heart!
Or, since that has left my breast,
Keep it now, and take the rest![4]

When Byron returned to Britain in 1811 from his Greek adventures, complaining merrily to his friends of a hard-earned case of gonorrhea (even the more sedate Hobhouse had managed to get the clap), he had largely finished *Childe Harold's Pilgrimage,* his immortal, self-promoting poetic travelogue. *Childe Harold* is shot through not just with the cloying classicism of a Trinity undergraduate, but overtly political calls for Greek liberation from Turkish oppression. Other Ottoman peoples did not catch Byron's fancy. His *Hebrew Melodies,* written by the waters of Seaham in 1815 and noticeably vaguer in its descriptions of ancient Israel than *Childe Harold*'s descriptions of Greece, might have been the cause of endless trouble if only there had been a Jewish anti-Ottoman revolt afoot. In *Childe Harold,* Byron describes exotic Muslim Albanians but offers no particular sympathy for them.[5]

But Greece was something to fire Byron's imagination, both radical and classical. In *Childe Harold,* he wrote, "Fair Greece! sad relic of departed Worth!/ Immortal, though no more; though fallen, great!" His modern calls for liberation were soaked in ancient Greek glory:

When riseth Lacedemon's Hardihood,
When Thebes Epaminondras rears again,
When Athens' children are with hearts endued,

When Grecian mothers shall give birth to men,
Then may'st thou be restored; but not till then.
A thousand years scarce serve to form a state;
An hour may lay it in the dust: and when
Can Man its shattered splendour renovate,
Recall its virtues back, and vanquish Time and Fate?

Conspicuously absent from *Childe Harold*'s maudlin call to arms is any particular discussion of actual living, breathing Greeks. Byron knew plenty about the real politics there, but could not resist the inspiration of ancient names and the classical tradition. (He wasn't alone; John Stuart Mill could write a forty-four-page review of the eighth volume of a history of ancient Greece without once mentioning modern Greece.) Modern Greeks mostly feature in *Childe Harold* as pale disappointments to their heroic ancestors: "Trembling beneath the scourge of Turkish hand, / From birth till death enslaved—in word, in deed, unmanned." The Greeks fell short of Cambridge standards.[6]

This strange ancient-modern view of Greece was typically British. In the eighteenth and nineteenth centuries, British sympathy for the Greeks was ubiquitous but abstract. Byron, in all his condescension, was a substantial improvement over previous British and Continental visitors on the Grand Tour, for whom Greece was a place for cultured aristocrats to get out of the rain and glimpse the crumbling remnants of the classical world. Byron would grow more realistic and empathetic toward the living Greeks. He would later jeer a naive German philhellene who "wonders a little that the Greeks are not quite the same with those of the time of Themistocles."[7]

When Byron took his first trip there, Greece was not yet a political cause. To most Britons, there was Greece, and there were the Greeks: so much Balkan rabble. They were, admittedly, Christian, but the wrong kind of Christian: Orthodox, and therefore more than halfway to depravity. Many of the early British tourists might have preferred it if the Greeks had been pagans, picturesquely worshipping Zeus instead of Jesus. Protestant missionaries from Britain and the United States brought the Bible to the Greeks, without fretting too much that the Greeks already had it. The withering verdict from many Britons was that the Greeks were barely Greeks at all. An eminent British ethnologist would pedantically identify himself not as a philhellene but as a *prophiloromaios,* meaning someone devoted to the travails of the modern Greeks rather than the ancient ones. Nothing better symbolizes British attitudes toward Greece than Lord Elgin, who blithely stole the great marbles despite what the Greeks themselves might have to say about it. (Byron, at least, hated him for it: "the modern Pict's ignoble boast,/ To rive what Goth, and Turk, and Time hath spared.")[8]

Still, Greece registered infinitely more on well-educated British minds than more obscure Ottoman-ruled lands, even though it was hardly the worst off. Although the Ottoman authorities had been harshly suppressing a Serb revolt since 1804, there was no particular call in Britain to save the Serbs. But Serb epic poems about the battle of Kosovo Polje had none of the cultural familiarity of Homer. In 1690, John Locke had written, in his *Second Treatise on Government,* "Who doubts but the Grecian christians, descendants of the ancient possessors of that country, may justly cast off the Turkish yoke, which they have so long groaned under, whenever they have an opportunity to do it?" Milton sounded the same theme in *Paradise Lost.* In *Childe Harold,* Byron reminded Britons that they were in debt to the Greeks for their very civilization: "Ah! Greece! they love thee least who owe thee most." Greece was a special case.[9]

Byron inspired new waves of British tourists, some of whom literally set off with a copy of *Childe Harold* in hand. Among them were some future philhellene leaders, including military men like Edward Blaquiere and Charles James Napier. And the aura of an ancient-modern Greece proved supremely useful to foreign supporters of the Greeks. Greece had a unique claim to be not just part of the civilized world, but the source of it. Greek nationalists found it irresistible to rally their people with claims that they were the downtrodden heirs of the ancients. It was not always an easy sell. When one foreign scholar deferentially called a local chieftain Achilles, the irritated chief snapped, "Who is this Achilles? Handy with a musket, was he?"[10]

A Problem from Hellas

Childe Harold was a war poem. Byron, trying to spur both the British and the Greeks into action, had written:

For foreign arms and aid they fondly sigh,
Nor solely dare encounter hostile rage,
Or tear their name defiled from Slavery's mournful page.

In March 1821, as Byron and the philhellenes had only dared to dream, Greek nationalists rose up against Ottoman rule.[11]

The first salvo was deeply unimpressive. It came not in Greece proper but in Wallachia and Moldavia (in present-day Romania): two Russian-protected principalities on the Danube under the rule of Greek governors. Worse, it looked suspiciously like a Russian job. The revolt was led by General Alexandros Ipsilantis, a well-connected Russian major general, who was widely assumed to be taking his orders directly from the tsar. Some Russian military chiefs considered a swift intervention. The great poet Aleksandr Pushkin, an ardent Russian imperialist, was beside himself: "Will we occupy Moldavia and Wallachia in the guise of peace-loving mediators; will we cross the Danube as the allies of the Greeks . . .?" Pushkin, with the incisive military judgment of a poet, predicted, "I am firmly convinced that Greece will triumph, and that 25,000,000 [*sic*] Turks will leave the flowering land of Hellas to the rightful heirs of Homer and Themistocles." Not quite: the revolts in Wallachia and Moldavia were swiftly crushed by Ottoman troops.[12]

The uprising spread to the Morea in April 1821. Here it was more popular and durable. Almost from the first, the war was fought with shocking brutality. Although the philhellenes would focus exclusively on Ottoman atrocities, the Greeks were no innocents. In Kalavryta, Ottomans surrendered to the Greeks on the promise of impunity, but were massacred anyway; in countless eastern Greek villages, and in Mesologgi in western Greece, the Muslim population was killed, with whole families exterminated together. In town after town, Greek insurgents slaughtered Turks, killing at least fifteen thousand out of a total of forty thousand in the Morea.[13]

The Ottomans retaliated furiously. They burned Greek Orthodox churches and butchered Greeks in Constantinople and Smyrna. One philhellene estimated that thirty thousand Greeks died in the first three months of the war. On Easter Sunday, the Ottomans committed the first act of repression that would capture wide European attention: they killed numerous Greeks in Constantinople, and hanged the city's Patriarch Grigorios and several bishops. Grigorios, almost eighty years old, had actually excommunicated Ipsilantis, but was nevertheless left to hang from the gate of his church as an example, with a fatwa condemning him pinned to his body. Russia, complaining that the sack of Orthodox churches violated the old Treaty of Kutchuk-Kainardji, withdrew its ambassador from Constantinople.[14]

The British press gave scant coverage to the Greeks' cruelties. There was some pro-Greek bias, and the ravaged towns were so remote that no reporters got close enough to get anything but the sketchiest details of massacres of Turks. Some correspondents were as distant as Warsaw and Vienna. In much the same way, the Ottomans got away with many acts of repression, so long as it was done far from journalistic eyes. They crushed Smyrna, but reporters in Trieste or Vienna had no details. And the British public had almost no idea what had happened in June in Kydonies (Aivali), where Ottoman forces killed hundreds of Greeks and sold scores into slavery.[15]

But in Constantinople, the Ottomans made the mistake of committing atrocities in plain sight of newspaper correspondents and countless letter-writers. Accounts "which make humanity shudder" flooded in, describing how the patriarch's corpse was dumped in the Bosphorus. The hubbub was joined by reports of varying degrees of reliability about massacres of Greeks. As one French report noted, "The only fact which seems to be indisputable is the cruelty practised in the capital and elsewhere towards the Greeks." The image of shocking Ottoman cruelty had been firmly fixed in European minds.[16]

This first publicized Ottoman atrocity set the tone for British understanding of the war. British philhellenes would long remember, as one religious activist put it, "the cruel public execution of the Patriarch of Constantinople, hung like a dog before the gates of his own cathedral." Edward Blaquiere, the former British naval officer turned radical activist, remembered "the massacre of the venerable and virtuous Patriarch Gregory, not to mention thousands of unoffending Greeks at Constantinople and other places" as the moment when Greeks "saw no alternative between resistance and extermination."[17]

Some British philhellenes saw it precisely the same way. There was a small and motley band who joined the Greek insurgency as brothers in arms. Many of them were inspired by Byron, like Frank Abney Hastings, a tempestuous former British naval officer who read Byron and rushed off to the great cause. As early as May, Ottoman authorities were complaining of British aid to the rebels. The sum total of fighting philhellenes, British and otherwise, was probably around five hundred. But some Britons played major strategic roles. Sir Richard Church would become commander in chief of Greek land forces; Lord Cochrane, a renegade former Member of Parliament disgraced in a banking scandal, would make a remarkably innovative commander in chief of a small Greek navy.[18]

Even more important was the political fight in Britain. Byron had laid the seeds for British sympathy for the Greeks. He was joined by his dear friend Percy Bysshe Shelley, who would drown a year later, after a trip to visit Byron in Pisa, with a copy of Aeschylus in his pocket. Shelley's contribution to the war effort was a gorgeous revolutionary poem, "Choruses from Hellas." Choruses they were, but not from Hellas. Shelley, pumped full of the classics but having never been to Greece, mostly imagined the place in austerely classical terms:

A loftier Argo cleaves the main,
Fraught with a later prize;
Another Orpheus sings again,
And loves, and weeps, and dies
A new Ulysses leaves once more
Calypso for his native shore.

. . . .

Another Athens shall arise,
And to remoter time
Bequeath, like sunset to the skies,
The splendour of its prime;
And leave, if nought so bright may live,
All earth can take or Heaven can give.

This is not exactly a precise account of the stink and filth of the actual Balkan revolt, let alone the fiasco in Wallachia. (Ipsilantis referred to Wallachia as the ancient Dacia, which would have mystified most people actually living there.)[19]

And all of Shelley and Byron's best poetry would make no difference unless it could be heard by the British public and the mandarins of foreign policy. Above all, the clamor made by the philhellenes had to penetrate the windows of the Foreign Office on Downing Street and of the St. James's Square house of Viscount Castlereagh, the infamous foreign secretary.

"I Met Murder on the Way/He Had a Mask Like Castlereagh"

Robert Stewart, Lord Castlereagh, was the last man to indulge radical poets. He had none of Byron's brilliance, but worked himself mercilessly.

A graceful man, he had dark sensitive eyes and a big nose, and an innocuous face. He was more comfortable maneuvering behind the scenes than in full view, and was painfully awkward when he had to speak in the House of Commons. (His favorite outfit, incongruously, was a pink hunting coat and riding boots.) He carried himself with English reserve, polite and calm even as inward he was spiraling downward to his eventual suicide by penknife.[20]

Castlereagh was a prime architect of the conservative world order shaped after the Napoleonic Wars. He had been Metternich's main partner at the Congress of Vienna. Castlereagh's secretive and often reactionary foreign policy, cozily aligning Britain with the despotic empires of the Holy Alliance, made him a lightning rod for liberal and radical hatred at home. (Castlereagh, nowhere near as much a friend to the Holy Alliance as Byron thought him, actually strongly disapproved when the Holy Alliance smothered liberal revolts in Spain and Naples.) On top of that, he was notorious for helping to crush an Irish uprising. After a foiled assassination plot, Castlereagh constantly carried pistols, which he called a familiar enough habit from his Irish days. Despite private despair, he affected not to care about the public contempt for him: "Unpopularity is more convenient and gentlemanlike."[21]

Castlereagh had good reason to believe he could afford to ignore public opinion. British foreign policy was shaped largely by king, cabinet, and, far less important, Parliament. British politics was still largely the playground of lords and toffs—the so-called Upper Ten Thousand. The Tory government of Lord Liverpool, the prime minister, basked in the glory of its magnificent victory over Napoléon. Castlereagh only deigned to let Parliament rubber-stamp the treaties he negotiated.[22]

As the Greek insurgency started, most Britons, if they thought at all about the war in the east, were more anti-Russian than anything else. In Parliament, the Whig opposition was too factious to resist the Tory steamroller. There was only one parliamentary faction that was vocal and organized: the so-called Saints, the evangelical Christians led by William Wilberforce, who had brilliantly led the charge for the 1807 abolition of the slave trade, and was still crusading against slavery in the West Indies.[23]

The free press was growing, but it was still a novelty, and a special tax on political publications kept circulations low—no more than twenty thousand each morning in London in 1821. Even so, the press had tremendous influence on the upper reaches of London society, not least the diplomats and parliamentarians. The Tory cabinet tried hard to woo the newspapers. The Tories largely won over the *Courier*, while the *Times*, still in its infancy, kept close to the establishment. The toughest criticism came from the liberal *Morning Chronicle.*[24]

The Greeks were not important to Castlereagh. He knew their classical appeal, but Britain had no territorial aspirations in Greece. Britain had taken the Ionian Islands as a naval base after the Napoleonic Wars, but British diplomats were willing to give them up, and would eventually voluntarily do so. Greece mattered only in the brute logic of the balance of power. Castlereagh saw the Ottoman Empire as "a necessary evil."[25]

The philhellenes were far to the left of the Tory government. They were mostly liberals and Whigs, as well as some evangelicals, and not very used to hands-on politicking. Byron's politics were romantically radical. He announced "my plain, sworn, downright detestation/ Of every despotism in every nation."[26]

Byron despised the Tories. Not even the godlike Duke of Wellington, whose conservative politics were hand in glove with Castlereagh's, was spared. Byron adored Napoléon at a time when most Britons reckoned the French leader as pure evil, and brazenly compared the British victory at Waterloo to "Cannæ's carnage" and called Waterloo "this place of skulls." In *Don Juan,* Byron took direct aim at Wellington:

If you have acted once a generous part,
The World, not the World's masters, will decide,
And I shall be delighted to learn who,
Save you and yours, have gained by Waterloo?[27]

Still, it was Castlereagh who really enraged Byron. The foreign secretary seemed to embody to the philhellenes all the uncaring forces of high policy, the cruelty of the imperial courts, calmly prepared to see Greece meet an Irish fate. The philosopher Jeremy Bentham, an ardent supporter of the Greeks, boasted that no king could "degrade me to a level with the Castlereaghs, the Metternichs." Byron's bitter political poetry seemed designed to drive the seemingly cool but inwardly turbulent foreign secretary toward the penknife. Byron joked about shooting Castlereagh: "I am not now near enough to give him an exchange of shots."[28]

Byron's worst was too much to publish. In the dedication to *Don Juan,* the poet went so far over the top that his publisher and Hobhouse had to censor out a blistering attack on "the intellectual eunuch Castlereagh." In some of the finest—and cruelest—political poetry ever written, Byron fired off exquisitely phrased and metered blasts:

Cold-blooded, smooth-faced, placid miscreant!
Dabbling its sleek young hands in Erin's [Ireland's] gore,
And thus for wider carnage taught to pant,
Transferred to gorge upon a sister shore,
The vulgarest tool that Tyranny could want,
With just enough of talent, and no more,
To lengthen fetters by another fixed,
And offer poison long already mixed.

. . . .

A bungler even in its disgusting trade,
And botching, patching, leaving still behind
Something of which its masters are afraid—
States to be curbed, and thoughts to be confined,
Conspiracy or Congress to be made—
Cobbling at manacles for all mankind—
A tinkering slave-maker, who mends old chains,
With God and Man's abhorrence for its gains.

This could only be published after Byron's death.[29]

While Byron had an undeniable flair for it, he was not the only great philhellene poet to pillory Castlereagh. In 1819, after British troops opened fired on reformers rallying in Manchester, a furious Percy Shelley outdid his friend Byron:

I met Murder on the way—
He had a mask like Castlereagh—
Very smooth he looked, yet grim;
Seven blood-hounds followed him;

All were fat; and well they might
Be in admirable plight,
For one by one, and two by two,
He tossed them human hearts to chew
Which from his wide cloak he drew.[30]

"The Dictates of His Understanding": Castlereagh and the Greeks

Castlereagh's policy on Greece was, above all, about the preservation of peace: "the safety and repose of Europe." The Greek insurgency posed a terrifying threat to that peace—as well as attracting "every ardent adventurer and political fanatic in Europe." Fearing that Russia would use the Greeks as a pretext for expansion, Castlereagh's policy was to avoid giving Russia "any just or even plausible motive for war."[31]

Tsar Aleksandr I was a commanding and handsome leader, proud of routing Napoléon in 1812 on Russian soil. (Oddly, he coined a phrase that is more commonly attributed to Ronald Reagan, calling the foes of the Holy Alliance an "*empire of evil.*") But in his old age, he was running to seed, growing fat, moody, and deaf. Although usually horrified by revolution, the tsar knew that the Greek uprising could both expand Russia's influence into the Balkans and undermine its hated rival, the Ottoman Empire. Russia had in 1774 signed the Treaty of Kutchuk-Kainardji with the Ottomans, which allowed Russia a vague but sweeping right to protect the Orthodox Christians living under Ottoman sovereignty. The soul-searching question for Aleksandr I, in other words, was whether he was more of a reactionary or an imperialist.[32]

At first, Aleksandr I condemned the Greek upstarts. Disgusted with the fiasco in Wallachia and Moldavia, he fired Ipsilantis from the Russian army, and invited the Ottoman government to send some twenty-five thousand soldiers into Wallachia and Moldavia to crush the insurgents. Metternich, the icy Austrian foreign minister who was a mortal foe to all rebellion, was satisfied that he and the tsar were in perfect agreement.[33]

Not so all of Russia. Much of public opinion was strongly pro-Greek, seeing the Greeks as their fellow Orthodox Slavs. So was the tsar's most trusted adviser, Count John Capo d'Istria, a Greek from Corfu who had risen to be Russia's secretary of state. When Patriarch Grigorios was killed, Russian philhellenes pleaded for Russia to send troops. Capo d'Istria, seeing his chance, got the tsar to approve an ultimatum demanding that the Ottomans restore the Greek Orthodox churches and spare those Greeks who were not in revolt. When the Ottomans did not agree within the seven-day time limit, Russia withdrew its ambassador—the last step short of war. Most Russians, Aleksandr I reckoned, thought "a war with Turkey inviting and popular."[34]

As the Greek war smoldered, Castlereagh waged a paper battle against

Capo d'Istria for the tsar's mind. Aleksandr I had once told Castlereagh to write him personally in emergencies; now, for the first time, Castlereagh did. Castlereagh admitted that "humanity shudders at the scenes," and that the "fanatic and semi-barbarous" Ottomans had succumbed to "a blind spirit of internal and exterminating warfare." But despite "the religious sympathy of the great mass of your Majesty's subjects with the Greek population of Turkey," Castlereagh begged him to use all his "commanding authority . . . to reconcile the Russian nation to witness the ministers of a congenial faith so barbarously immolated." Peace had to trump compassion: "It is in vain to hope that we can . . . deliver them from their sufferings, and preserve the system of Europe as it now stands." On top of that, he warned against "the perils and burthens of a military occupation, to be effectuated not amongst a Christian and tractable, but amongst a bigoted, revengeful, and uncivilized population." Finally, Castlereagh, with considerable paranoia, tarred the Greek revolutionaries as "a branch of that organized spirit of insurrection which is systematically propagating itself throughout Europe."[35]

In a second letter, even Castlereagh professed his sympathy for the Greeks: "Ought the Turkish yoke to be for ever rivetted upon the necks of their suffering and Christian subjects . . . ? . . . It is impossible not to feel the appeal; and if a statesman were permitted to regulate his conduct by the counsels of his heart instead of the dictates of his understanding, I really see no limits to the impulse." But, in a ringing statement of his own philosophy of realpolitik, he continued, "But we must always recollect that his is the grave task of providing for the peace and security of those interests immediately committed to his care; that he must not endanger the fate of the present generation in a speculative endeavour to improve the lot of that which is to come." He thus could not "be tempted, nor even called upon in moral duty under loose notions of humanity and amendment, to forget the obligations of existing Treaties, to endanger the frame of long established relations, and to aid the insurrectionary efforts now in progress in Greece."[36]

Castlereagh helped get the Ottoman Empire to accept the terms of Russia's ultimatum, while he urged the tsar to let the Ottoman Empire finish "extinguishing the revolt." The Ottoman government, under British pressure, agreed to withdraw from Wallachia and Moldavia, guarantee religious freedom to the Orthodox Greeks, rebuild sacked churches, and amnesty Greek rebels. But if these humanitarian steps did not satisfy Russia, Wellington feared there might be "revolution from the Atlantic to the Austrian frontiers" and "probably a general war in Europe."[37]

Even Metternich, struggling against Capo d'Istria, was flustered. "These wicked affairs occupy me day and night," Metternich wrote. But, succumbing to Castlereagh and Metternich's pleas, Aleksandr I began to walk back from the brink. Once the terms of Russia's ultimatum were carried out, the crisis seemed to have passed. Defeated, Capo d'Istria took a leave of absence, which turned out to be permanent. (He would later become president of a provisional Greek government, and come to be known as Kapodistrias.) "Not bad," Metternich noted smugly on hearing of Capo d'Istria's fall. The news came on Metternich's birthday, as if a touchingly thoughtful geopolitical gift from the tsar. The Holy Alliance was united and triumphant. Betrayed by Russia, the Greek leadership could only hope to win over Britain.[38]

The Tripolitza Massacre

As the war dragged on, one of the Tories' most damning arguments was moral equivalence—that the Greeks were just as bloodstained as the Ottomans. One anxious British philhellene warned that some believed that "the Greeks themselves are barbarians, & far surpass the Turks in atrocities." He thus wanted to "suggest to the Greeks the necessity of humane treatment of their captives." Blaquiere understood that, to sell the Greek cause, he had to bear witness that they were "an eminently moral and religious people."[39]

In fact, the Greek insurgents continued to show themselves capable of sickening brutality. At Arkadia, Monemvasia, and Navarino, Greek rebels slaughtered the Turks or sold them into slavery. But the scarcity of reliable information from Greece meant that the philhellenes could slant the overall story, airbrushing out many Greek atrocities.[40]

One of the worst demonstrations of Greek brutality was a massacre at Tripolitza (Tripoli) in October 1821. Colonel Thomas Gordon, a British officer from Scotland serving as a military expert for the Greeks, was on the scene for some of the slaughter, and later wrote up a private detailed firsthand report for the British philhellenes. The besieged Turks in the citadel at Tripolitza, starving and sick, tried to surrender to the Greek camp. But although some Turkish civilians were at first not harmed, the capitulation turned chaotic. The Ottomans in the citadel fired on the Greeks. In response, Gordon wrote, the Greeks butchered Turkish civilians who had surrendered: "Neither age nor sex was spared, and the rage of the assailants overleaping all bounds quenched itself in the blood of some thousands of unhappy persons who had previously delivered themselves up and were lodged in the camp." Although some Greek officers tried to hold back the killing tide, and high-ranking Turks and mercenary Albanians were spared, Gordon calculated "at least seven or eight thousand . . . persons that were put to the sword."[41]

To their eternal discredit, many important philhellenes had a flair for excusing Greek atrocities. Lord Thomas Erskine, whom Byron scorned as particularly clueless about Greek realities, invoked the glories of ancient Greece, and unblushingly wrote that even gentle cows could be "goaded by barbarous oppression" into stampeding. Blaquiere complained that reports of Greek "excesses . . . have been mostly wantonly exaggerated." He was sure that "when all the concomitant circumstances which led to the excesses at Tripolizza are made known, they will appear mild, when compared to those committed by the best disciplined and most civilized troops of Europe in many circumstances during the last fifty years." The most Blaquiere would do was "lament, most deeply lament, the excesses"—as if the only problem was one of scale—while still blaming "those centuries of galling and intolerable oppression which the Greek people had to avenge." Later, he would point to Henry V's slaughter at Agincourt, and asked whether "the aggregate excesses in Greece, bear any comparison in point of wantonness and enormity, with those which preceded the partition of Poland, or that occurred during the French revolution, and the wars to which it has given rise in almost every quarter of the globe?" As for why any of that made it morally acceptable to take revenge on thousands of defenseless human beings, Blaquiere was silent.[42]

Gordon left Greece, repulsed; it would take Byron's urgings to get him back there years later. Still, even Gordon, who had seen the bloodshed with his own eyes, partially brushed it off. Given the Ottoman "plan of extermination," the fact of one or two Greek atrocities "can surprise only those who are ignorant of the state of the Country and of the people; of the motives of the war; and of human nature itself." Most of the Greeks, Gordon added, had "to avenge some private injury of the present day, the murder of a father or brother, or the violation of a wife or daughter." The worst killing was done by local Greek peasants, oppressed since infancy. In a kind of apologia that has hardly gone out of style, Gordon asked "what was to be expected from them who had just burst their chains: from a people brutalized by oppression?"[43]

Right after the Tripolitza massacre, Gordon kept largely silent, thus helping the philhellenes swing the press coverage. The pro-Tory *Courier* condemned the slaughter. In rejoinder, the liberal *Morning Chronicle* replied that while the *Courier*'s "false and absurd account of horrible atrocities of the Greeks at Tripoliza" was based on Gordon, Gordon himself remained strongly pro-Greek. So long as Gordon did not speak out against the Greeks, the British press had no reliable proof of what had really happened at Tripolitza. The basic facts remained unknown, so much so that the *Times* could write it off as nothing worse than "Greek *soldiers*" putting "a Turkish garrison to the sword." Without better reporting, and with the philhellenes industriously pushing their cause, the broader European public was kept away from the hard reality of Greek cruelty.[44]

Years later, Gordon would try to make up for this by telling the blunt truth. In a popular history, he forthrightly wrote that "the streets and houses were inundated with blood, and obstructed with heaps of bodies. . . . [T]heir insatiable cruelty knew no bounds, and seemed to inspire them with a superhuman energy for evil." No oppression could justify such vengeance. Although revolutions were "bright and dazzling when contemplated from a distance," up close they had "many dark spots."[45]

CHAPTER FIVE

The Scio Massacre

"Which Makes Humanity Shudder"

Around the time of Castlereagh's moment of triumph over Russia, the Greeks of the island of Scio (Chios) briefly rebelled against Ottoman rule. In swift response, starting in April 1822, a massive Ottoman fleet, led by six ships of the line, descended on Scio and slaughtered the inhabitants. It was the worst atrocity of the war, and the defining moment of the conflict for most Europeans. Scio was a wealthy island in the east of Greece, precariously close to mainland Anatolia, known best to Europeans as Homer's home island. But suddenly Scio became as notorious as Guernica or Srebrenica—no longer just the name of a place, but a synonym for massacre of the worst kind.[1]

The diplomats knew first. Although the British press had no correspondents near enough to Scio to report anything, Viscount Strangford, the pro-Ottoman British ambassador in Constantinople, relying on reports from his consul in Smyrna, Francis Werry, understood that the war had reached a horrible new low. Before the onslaught, Strangford knew that the Ottoman cabinet was violently enraged at the prospect of Scio rebelling. "Scio is completely subdued," Werry reported on May 2. "But nothing hitherto has subdued the exasperated Mussulman's vengeance. . . . The City is ⅔ destroy'd, most of the Villages have shared the same fate." The churches had been destroyed, he said, and the women enslaved or sent to harems.[2]

Thousands of refugees flooded out, many arriving in Smyrna. So the first newspaper to get wind of the gruesome story was a French-owned Smyrna weekly newspaper called *Le Spectateur Oriental,* which the French government occasionally banned. Based on its reporting, and that of his consul, the British ambassador quickly told Castlereagh that Scio was now "a scene of the most appalling desolation." A British warship, HMS *Cambrian,* had actually sailed through the Ottoman and Greek fleets on May 13, but had done nothing to dissuade the Ottoman forces. By May 25, Strangford told Castlereagh that "the ferocity of the Turks [had] been carried to a pitch which makes humanity shudder. The whole of the Island . . . presents one mass of ruin."[3]

The British ambassador asked an Ottoman minister to stop selling innocent people from Scio into slavery, warning that it would anger "the public mind in Europe." The minister replied that Europe had long tolerated slavery. "Why do not the Christian Sovereigns interfere to prevent the Emperor of Russia from sending his subjects into Siberia?" the minister asked. "Because they know very well what answer they would receive! Thus there is one law of humanity for Turkey and another for Russia!"[4]

For all Strangford's shock, he knew that there had been some Greek atrocities, too, although not on the scale of the Ottoman slaughter, and reported that many Ottoman officials were trying to be humane. Still, he was particularly horrified at the public beheading of ten prominent Greek merchants in Constantinople, whom the Ottomans had held hostage to the good conduct of Scio's populace. The British ambassador wrote that "fertile as this place has been in horrors, is beyond all comparison, the one which I have witnessed with the greatest disgust and indignation. I cannot express . . . the pain and concern which it has occasioned to me. I had been in constant private communication with these poor Sciots." In June, *Le Spectateur Oriental* calculated the human toll: thousands enslaved, thousands of refugees, and about twenty-five thousand killed.[5]

Castlereagh in the Storm

Scio threatened to rubbish Castlereagh's hard-won diplomacy. By late June, the British press began reporting detailed news of the massacre—first, as usual, in a letter from Constantinople. The first reported event was the execution of the ten Greek hostages—a remote aftershock of the Scio bloodbath. Some Greeks of Constantinople wrote, "Who can, without shuddering, read of the total ruin, the universal desolation of our famed and once happy isle (Scio) . . . ?"[6]

Castlereagh could. The day after the *Times* ran its first story, the foreign secretary came under ferocious questioning in Parliament, where he could barely be heard. Castlereagh coolly replied,

> A calamity had occurred, which had arisen out of the peculiar acts of barbarity which had been perpetrated on both sides, during the war in the island of Scio. Acts of barbarity . . . had been committed on both sides.—(Hear.) The Greeks had themselves committed certain cruelties, which, though they did not justify, led to the transactions complained of.—(Hear.)

But the press coverage, including reporting and reprinted letters, still mostly from Constantinople, drove home the magnitude of the slaughter. "A cry of horror will resound throughout Europe when the new cruelties in Scio are made known," wrote one. Another added morbid detail about "the total destruction of the island" from Scio eyewitnesses. The *Times* editorialized that the Greeks faced "immediate and total annihilation. . . . We know not that any tragedy on record ever produced in this country a movement of deeper horror than this recital of the atrocities."[7]

In Parliament, Castlereagh and Liverpool were heatedly questioned. One MP asked Castlereagh if "the markets of Smyrna and Constantinople were filled with amiable Greek ladies and children, offered to the caprices of barbarous Mahomedan voluptuaries?" William Wilberforce, the elderly leader of the Christian evangelicals in the House of Commons, led the charge. A dazzling speaker, witty and deeply religious, the tiny Wilberforce had successfully spearheaded the parliamentary fight against the slave trade. In that struggle, Wilberforce had found Castlereagh "a fish of the coldest-blooded kind." Now, to cheers from the House, Wilberforce belligerently demanded military intervention. It was "rather a disgrace" that the great European powers had not already "driven back a nation of barbarians, the ancient and inveterate enemies of Christianity and freedom, into Asia." Wilberforce declared that he always avoided "advocating war . . . unless indeed peace could only be acquired at the price of disgrace and infamy." But he "knew of no case in which the power of a mighty country like England could be more nobly, more generously, or more justifiably exerted than in rescuing the Greeks from bondage and destruction."[8]

Castlereagh fired back, "It was really marvellous to see how the friends of peace, against, perhaps, their own consciences and knowledge, could sometimes advocate the cause, and most unnecessarily, of war." He preferred peace: "Neither the government nor the country were so wild as to be prepared to take up arms with a view to the more effective and impartial administration of justice in the dominions of Turkey." Warning how difficult "a crusade for the restoration of order and tranquillity in Turkey" would be, Castlereagh denied that "all the horrors and atrocities were on one side of this contest, and that there was nothing in it for humanity to deplore, but the cruelty and barbarism of the Turks, and the sufferings and ill-fated benevolence of the Greeks." The Tory benches cheered.[9]

A few days later, in the House of Lords, Earl Grosvenor put the case in more liberal terms. Since Britain had "thought it right to interfere with foreign independent nations in order to prevent the continuance of the slave trade, surely [it] could not object to the employment of similar efforts" to stop "the dreadful atrocities" against the Greeks.

Liverpool replied that this cruelty had "been committed by the Government of Turkey—upon whom? Upon their own subjects, the Greeks. As a matter of right, then, what right . . . had this country to interfere in a matter occurring between a foreign government and the subjects of that government? See the extent to which such a principle, if once admitted, could be carried." The prime minister, bluntly imperialist, warned that Britain might have to put down its own insurrections one day. The slave trade was no precedent, because "there the question was between independent states respecting the inhabitants of Africa—a country over which no European state could have a claim of jurisdiction." Much like his foreign secretary, the prime minister blamed Scio's Greeks for starting it, and insisted that "humanity must deplore" outrages by all sides. He refused to consider going to war.[10]

National sovereignty, moral equivalence, the risk of unending war: the Tories sounded themes that echo all the way down to today.

A British Threat

Although publicly Castlereagh stood his ground, he had decided to reprimand the Ottoman Empire. Complaining rawly of "the painful and disgusting recital of the bloody scenes growing out of the Scio War" and "the most ferocious and hateful barbarism," Castlereagh ordered Strangford to use "the most pointed terms" to express King George IV's "grief." In Parliament, Castlereagh had only said that Britain had no legal responsibility to Greek hostages; but to the Ottoman government, he denounced "the atrocity of their execution," which had "inflicted a sensible wound on the King's mind and filled the British Nation with horror and disgust." Castlereagh told Strangford to drive home to the Ottoman leadership "the fatal consequences of such scenes perpetrated in the midst of their Capital and under the very eye of the Representatives of civilized Nations." He threatened war: any other "such deeds of blood" would "render all pacific arrangements impracticable." Adding teeth to that, he said fresh atrocities would force friendly states to withdraw their ambassadors—a clear step toward war—rather than appear to be "the approving witnesses of Transactions for which no human offences can furnish a pretext, much less a justification."[11]

It took about a month for Castlereagh's fierce letter to get to Constantinople. In the meantime, the Greeks managed to destroy an important Ottoman ship, which drove the Ottomans to ravage the few remaining villages on Scio. Strangford reported famine, pestilence, and the colonization of Scio by Turks to supplant the Greeks.[12]

So when the ambassador got Castlereagh's threatening letter, he took undiplomatic personal satisfaction in delivering it, seeing no need for "treating the feelings of the Turkish Ministers with much delicacy." The Reis Effendi, the Ottoman equivalent of foreign minister, seemed ashamed and taken aback by the British reprimand. But he reminded Strangford of "unremitting Cruelties" by the Greek insurgents, including the Tripolitza massacre, and accused Scio's Greeks of treason. The Ottoman government, Strangford wrote, now understood British outrage. The ambassador was proud that only Britain had "branded the transactions at Scio with the indignant and fearless expression of its abhorrence." Even Castlereagh had shown British outrage.[13]

"Every British Heart Would Have Melted"

Unrelenting press coverage of the Scio massacre solidified British sympathies. "The most civilized, cultivated, and interesting people, the flower of Greece, have been, the greater part, exterminated," wrote the *Times.* The bloodbath shocked Europeans to the core, with the figure of twenty or twenty-five thousand dead in wide circulation. This number was probably exaggerated. But in an era when people had not yet grown inured to death tolls in the millions, Scio was a defining moment—remembered half a century later by the *Times* as "the most appalling chapter in the history of modern Europe."[14]

Blaquiere was sure that when the British public realized what was really happening in Greece, they would demand action: "Had the cries reached our country, of infants torn from their mothers' breasts and flung into the sea, or dashed against the rocks, as at Scio and various other places—of fathers, husbands and brothers, butchered before the eyes of mothers, wives and sisters, who were themselves destined either to share a similar fate, or be dragged into that hopeless slavery in which thousands languish at this moment,—it is needless to say that every British heart would have melted, and every British hand been stretched out to succour or to save a perishing community!" Now, with the reports about Scio, for the first time, the philhellenes had a mass audience in Britain, where the news spread with shock and indignation.[15]

Castlereagh and Liverpool's vigorous performances in Parliament backfired. The *Times* scorned them for all but justifying the Scio massacre. Unaware of Castlereagh's secret threat to the Ottoman government, Blaquiere wrote, "Will posterity believe . . . that while the ambassadors remained quietly at their posts, the lamentable catastrophe rung through Christian and civilized Europe, without exciting much more notice than the loss of an East Indiaman, or a trifling fall in the public funds?"[16]

Each Tory minister's speech inspired a separate widely circulated pamphlet in rebuttal. Lord Erskine's pamphlet was an indignant open letter to Liverpool demanding military action, although undermined by his hyperbolic assertion that "the Negro Slave Trade was nothing in the scale of misery and debasement against the horrors." The other blast came from Thomas S. Hughes, a Tory priest in Cambridge who had written a travelogue on Greece's antiquities and its modern inhabitants, who was so disgusted with Castlereagh's words in Parliament that he dashed off a near-hysterical popular pamphlet. He denounced "the support of what is called, 'the balance power,' . . . or, in other words, . . . the protection of an infidel exterminating government, . . . an alliance with deliberate murderers, barbarians habitually stained with the most abominable vices, and declared enemies of the Christian faith." Hughes held a vicious view of Islam as "hatched and matured in falsehood, hypocrisy, and blood," and unlike more liberal philhellenes, couched his appeal in Christian terms. Rather than "dwelling upon the glories of Salamis and Thermopylæ," he wrote, "the cause I plead is that of suffering Christians—and the name I invoke, is that of Him who died upon the Cross." He challenged antislavery liberals: "You, the advocates of philanthropy in our senate, who have so oft proclaimed the sorrows and vindicated the rights of suffering humanity, who have extended of power to the relief of the captive African, why are ye now silent?" Scio, he wrote, had been turned into "a common slaughter-house. . . . Gracious God! a tenth part of these atrocities in an unenlightened age, would have aroused all the gallant spirits of Christendom to avenge their wrong!"[17]

The shock spread across Europe. In France, Eugène Delacroix—the greatest of the French Romantic artists and an admirer of Byron—would paint his popular oil, *Scenes of the Massacres at Scio,* which created a sensation when it was unveiled and now hangs in the Louvre. It is gigantic, more than twice the size of his *Liberty Leading the People.* The horrifically vivid painting shows chaotic violence everywhere: a dull bloody knife lies on the ground; a Greek boy clutches at his dead mother's breast; a Turk on horseback draws his scimitar as a faceless Greek cowers; a crowd of Turks shoots down Greeks. Delacroix has a symbolic naked classical Greek woman in the ropes of slavery, but also a woman being raped by a Turk still wearing his fez, and an ancient grandmother trembling in despair. Even nature is stunned, with the ground itself cracking and the sky reddening. Not to be outdone, Victor Hugo would imagine finding a sole surviving Greek child in the ruins:

> *The Turks have been here. All is ruin and mourning.*
> *Chio, the island of wines, is nothing but a somber reef.*
> . . . .
> *What do you want? flower, beautiful fruit, or the marvellous bird?*
> *—Friend, said the Greek child, said the child with blue eyes,*
> *I want gunpowder and bullets.*[18]

"So Castlereagh Has Cut His Throat"

If Castlereagh was indeed as demonic as Byron reckoned, he was a sensitive kind of demon. Painfully aware of his cold-blooded image, Castlereagh dared not meet with Metternich for fear of further embarrassment. The foreign secretary, exhausted and isolated by his job, had been privately verging on despair for years. After the long rounds of diplomacy, and the fury over the Scio massacre, he seemed outright suicidal.[19]

In what would turn out to be his final words on Greece, Castlereagh's paramount goal remained preventing a Russian war against the Ottoman Empire. But he also hoped to "soften, as far as possible, the rigour of war between the Turks and Greeks." Although he refused to intervene, he noted that if a Greek government was declared, "it may be difficult for this country . . . to refuse to it the ordinary privileges of a belligerent." He wanted to do so quietly, since legally recognizing the insurgents as legitimate combatants would be a slap to the Ottoman government.[20]

Around the same time, Castlereagh told his personal secretary, "I am quite worn out here"—holding his forehead. "Quite worn out—and this fresh load of responsibility now put upon me is more than I can bear." Meeting with King George IV on August 9, just three weeks after being slammed over Scio in Parliament, Castlereagh worried that the next personal attack would be a charge of homosexuality. After Shelley and Byron's lyrical maulings, small wonder that Castlereagh feared further vitriol. "Everyone hates me and shuns me," the foreign secretary told the king. "When I walk down the street, people take the opposite side to avoid meeting me. I am very unhappy." When the king urged him to fight his "blue devils," Castlereagh burst into tears: "I am mad. I know I am mad. I have known it for some time, but no one has any idea of it." The shocked king, promising to keep this secret, kindly suggested that Castlereagh be bled. Castlereagh, regaining a modicum of composure, melodramatically declared, "Sir! it is necessary to say good-bye to Europe; you and I alone have saved it; no one after me understands the affairs of the Continent."[21]

Wellington, meeting Castlereagh that afternoon, found him exhausted by his responsibilities and terrified about being accused of homosexual acts. Castlereagh, Wellington wrote (in a letter that was supposed to be destroyed), "cried excessively" and was "in a state of mental delusion." Wellington went immediately to try to find Castlereagh's doctor. The king, too, shaken by his meeting, sent a warm and comforting personal note to his shattered foreign secretary, urging him to seek medical help.[22]

Unfortunately, he did. Castlereagh retreated to Cray, his country house in Kent, outside of London, where his doctor drugged and bled him. This induced delirium. Castlereagh asked his wife for his pistol. This was not forthcoming. The next morning, he took an alarming interest in a shave, and she locked away his razors and ordered her maid to check his dressing room for anything sharp. But on August 12, Castlereagh was left alone in his dressing room for a few moments. Britain's foreign secretary enterprisingly found a little penknife in a drawer in his washstand. He slashed his neck, cutting deep into his carotid artery. His doctor entered the room an instant later. Castlereagh, fifty-three years old, spoke his last words: "Bankhead, let me fall upon your arm; 'tis all over." Blood gushed from his neck. He died almost instantly.[23]

Metternich was one of the relatively few people in Europe genuinely upset by Castlereagh's suicide: "What a blow!" But he composed himself with the consolations of realpolitik: "I am, besides, armed against all events; my cause will not be lost until I am felled myself." Meanwhile, in London, mysterious notices began to appear saying that Castlereagh, as a suicide, should not be allowed to be buried in Westminster Abbey—something almost certainly more about public contempt than public piety. An angry crowd jeered in St. James's Square as Castlereagh's corpse lay in state. Even the *Times,* announcing Castlereagh's suicide, added, "We must admire the manifest mediocrity of his genius." Despite the trappings of a full state funeral, a considerable number of spectators actually cheered at the appearance of Castlereagh's coffin in Westminster Abbey, waving their hats joyfully for his welcome demise. Wellington, appalled, tried unsuccessfully to hush the crowd as the coffin was whisked inside.[24]

Some philhellenes disguised their pleasure more than others. After waiting just three days for the corpse to cool, the *Times* editorialized for a more humane policy toward Greece, without Castlereagh's "subserviency to despotic power." Byron was thrilled: "It may at least serve as some consolation to the nations, that their oppressors are not happy, and in some instances judge so justly of their own actions as to anticipate the sentence of mankind." He gleefully drafted a series of acidic verses for the *Examiner* on the theme of slit throats:

> *Oh, Castlereagh! thou art a patriot now!*
> *Cato died for his Country—so dos't thou.—*
> He *perished rather than see Rome enslaved,*
> Thou *cuts't thy throat that Britain may be saved.*
> *Another*
> *So Castlereagh has cut his throat; the worst*
> *Of this is—that his own was not the first,*
> *Another*
> *So* He *has cut his throat at last*—He? Who?
> *The Man who cut his Country's long ago.—*

When it was suggested that this might not be in the best of taste, Byron privately wrote, "His measures do not die with him like a private individual's notions, he is a matter of *history*—and wherever I find a tyrant or a villain—I will mark him." With perhaps a hint of defensiveness, he added, truthfully enough, "I attacked him no more than I had been wont to do." Finally, to his friend Hobhouse, Byron came up with a few lines for the gravesite, inviting perpetual marking:

> *Posterity will ne'er survey*
> *A nobler grave than this:*
> *Here lie the bones of Castlereagh:*
> *Stop, traveller,—[and piss.]*[25]

CHAPTER SIX

The London Greek Committee

"All the Means in Their Power"

In the aftermath of the Scio massacre and Castlereagh's suicide, the British philhellenes tried to cement their new place in mainstream politics. There were also successful philhellene societies in Spain, France, the United States, and Switzerland, but only in Britain were the philhellenes in a position to change the foreign policy of a great power. Although there had been earlier philhellene organizations in both Edinburgh and Cambridge, they were immediately dwarfed by the birth of the London Greek Committee in March 1823. Its fractious membership would come to encompass a daunting selection of radical or reform-minded MPs and a truly breathtaking slice of the British intelligentsia.[1]

The committee was launched by an invitation letter from John Bowring, age thirty-one, a proud disciple of Jeremy Bentham who spoke thirteen languages (including Czech and Serbo-Croatian), and would become the secretary and key activist in the group. Greece was just one of Bowring's liberal causes: he had recently been arrested (along with Blaquiere) by France for carrying letters to revolutionaries in Portugal, and he would later help found the Anti–Corn Law League to fight for free trade. Bowring invited the great and the good to join, announcing that the committee would support the Greeks "by all the means in their power."[2]

By March 8, Bowring could distribute an impressive first list of members. Crowning it was Jeremy Bentham, the great founder of utilitarianism, then at the height of his powers—probably the most renowned philosopher in Britain. With his long white hair, he reminded Bowring of Benjamin Franklin, but with "a profounder wisdom and a more marked benevolence." Bentham believed that the innocent sometimes needed to be defended by force. In one of his ferocious denunciations of the slave trade, he told the president of Haiti that he would like to see Haitian vessels "capturing the slave-trading ships" and then "consigning" the slavers "to the like slavery in your Island." The master of the slave ships should have "an indelible mark upon him" so he would stand out in Haiti as "a man so highly distinguished in barbarity, and in the profit reaped from it. If one of his lips were cut off, he might by this indelible mark, in case of escape or ransom, still impress useful terror, on the minds of all whom he found engaged in the like traffic." He now applied the same fierce passion to the Greek cause.[3]

Bentham was joined by the renowned economist David Ricardo, celebrated for his advocacy of free trade. Among the other original members were Lord John Russell, a future prime minister; John Cam Hobhouse, Byron's close friend and traveling companion from his fateful first trip to Greece back in 1809, now an MP (which made him a fat target for Byron to razz as "My boy Hobbie O"); twenty other MPs, including Joseph Hume and the fiery Sir Francis Burdett; and an eccentric assortment of military and scholarly activists.[4]

Encouraged, Bowring sent out a second round of recruitment letters. By May, the illustrious list had grown to eighty. It had poets like Samuel Rogers; scholars, including, inevitably, classicists; preachers; a dozen more MPs; numerous nobles, like the pamphleteering Lord Erskine; several prominent military officers, among them the adventurous Blaquiere and a doggedly Benthamite colonel named Leicester Stanhope—and, most sensational of all, Byron.[5]

Many of the members of the London Greek Committee could not stand each other, notably the pious evangelicals and the libertine Benthamites. The philhellenes' political base was geographically in Scotland and Ireland; by class, the workers of Manchester and Liverpool and the investors in the City of London; by religion, the nonconformists and evangelicals, as well as the more secular Whigs. They often wanted to slap the Tory government, and to support liberalization in Britain and abroad. Their defense of British workers at home went hand in glove with a defense of the Greeks overseas.[6]

The committee held its first public meeting at the Crown and Anchor Tavern in the Strand (once a favorite haunt of Dr. Samuel Johnson), which had a huge ballroom that was good for raucous and boozy political gatherings. The money began to flow in: a healthy £1,049 at first, with Russell personally subscribing £50, and Hobhouse £25. Ricardo, one of the greatest economists of his century, was quick to contribute a solid £20 to the cause, and was, in faint recognition of his monumental abilities, named an auditor for the group. The money kept coming in, eventually including—to the fury of the Ottoman government—a hefty sum from the mayor of London.[7]

The London Greek Committee constantly referred to ancient Greece. Jeremy Bentham called the Greeks the "first enlightened nation," as opposed to the British, descendants of "naked barbarians, who were never deemed worth taming." One time, in London, when politely introduced to a visiting Greek delegate as "monsieur," Bentham joked, "Monsieur Solon, Monsieur Pericles, Monsieur Epaminondas, Monsieur Philopoemen?"[8]

In the face of that kind of rhetoric, it was clear to those philhellenes who actually went to Greece that the main committee in London was profoundly out of touch. Byron thought that philhellenes who had not set foot in Greece were as naive as Eton schoolboys.[9]

The Greeks won British attention more for their ancient pagan glory than for their contemporary Christianity. The exception was the evangelicals on the committee, for whom the Greeks' Christianity mattered more; but even Hughes, the most influential philhellene cleric, wrote that if he did not speak up for the Greeks, he would be "a traitor to my country, a traitor to humanity." A pamphlet aimed specifically at religious Christians referred repeatedly to a broader human community: "The struggle has been humanized." And for the liberals and Benthamites, the defense of humanity was a recurrent theme. Blaquiere boasted of Britain's "commiseration for the woes of others, no matter what their clime or colour." One activist wrote that they were moved by "the hatred of oppression," not just in Greece but in "the general harvest of grievances in the rest of Europe."[10]

Still, perhaps most important, the London Greek Committee was galvanized by Ottoman atrocities—above all Scio. This was no normal conflict, but "a war of peculiar ferocity." Byron once wished that both Ottomans and Greeks "could be induced to conduct themselves with some regard to the laws of War—or any laws whatsoever." Blaquiere wrote that "the total extermination of the Greek people was now resolved on by the Divan," and that this showed in "the conduct of the soldiery." This was, he wrote, a "war of extermination." One philhellene physician in Greece described "the exterminating system of warfare followed by the Turks," including killing wounded Greek soldiers. The committee warned ominously of what we might today call genocide: "It is clear it can end in nothing but in the independence or the absolute annihilation of the Greek people. . . . Shall the scenes of Scio and Cyprus be renewed, and a whole Christian people be extirpated?"[11]

"Are You the Only Men Who Have Rights?"

The Tory government was the clear enemy for the British philhellenes. A classicist complained that his government, "unfortunately for the honor of England, listened more to the representations of the oppressor than to the cries of the oppressed." An Edinburgh philhellene wrote, "The government of this country under our antijacobins has become an enormous engine for crushing any liberal sentiment, from an inbred consciousness that its existence is bound up with corruption in every shape."[12]

Byron and Bentham, the two most important London Greek Committee members, were hearty critics not just of the Tory government, but of the British Empire. Bentham was not above drafting a reformed legal system for India, as he did for countless other nations, but he was more often stoutly anti-imperial. In a pamphlet sent to the French republic, with the unambiguous title of "Emancipate Your Colonies!," Bentham had written: "You choose your own government, why are not other people to choose theirs? Do you seriously mean to govern the world, and do you call that *liberty*? What is become of the rights of men? Are you the only men who have rights?" He magnificently concluded:

> You will, I say, give up your colonies—because you have no right to govern them, because they had rather not be governed by you, because it is against their interest to be governed by you, because you get nothing by governing them, because you can't keep them, because the expence of trying to keep them would be ruinous, because your constitution would suffer by your keeping them, because your principles forbid your keeping them, and because you would do good to all the world by parting with them.

This was not just a critique of the empires of France and Spain (in his subsequent "Rid Yourselves of Ultramaria"), but of Britain, too. Bentham, who had sympathized with the anticolonialism of the American Revolution, told the French, "By emancipating your own colonies, you may emancipate ours: by setting the example, you may open our eyes and force us to follow it." Byron and Bentham's humanitarianism could not sit comfortably with imperialism.[13]

After joining the London Greek Committee, Bentham quickly

become an indefatigable advocate of a progressive Greek constitution, to the delight of the Greek rebels. Firing off letter after letter to the Greeks, Bentham was particularly eager that Greece not saddle itself with a monarchy, like those ruling the main European courts. Instead, he hoped that Greece would enjoy the "liberty which is the matchless fruit of a Representative Democracy." (When the Greeks received one of his many suggestions for a new constitution, Bentham—named the "father protector of Greece"—shamelessly boasted that "there was an universal burst of exultation, accompanied by tears from many eyes.")[14]

So it was no surprise that many Tories were afraid to have anything to do with the committee. Sir John Gladstone, a Tory philhellene, and father of William Ewart Gladstone, was sympathetic but did not actually join. Nor did the most famous Tory who supported the group, William Wilberforce. One recipient of Bowring's appeal nervously replied that it might be illegal "to support without the authority of Parliament a War in which this Country is not engaged." Another felt it improper for someone "bearing the Kings Commission to take a more active part in the affairs of a people, who are not acknowledged as independent by His Majesty."[15]

This kind of government-inspired reluctance was particularly vexing with respect to the Church of England. Although organizing through the Church might have skewed the committee away from its liberal roots, it would have provided a ready-made network of churches and attentive congregations. One committee activist drafted a special religious pamphlet asking for "the saving of thousands of fellow-Christians from death." But the philhellenes failed miserably with the Church of England. The only strong religious support they got was from the less influential nonconformist denominations and evangelicals.[16]

Blaquiere was disappointed to see the Church of England "resist the performance of a duty" because of Tory partisanship and a fear of being seen to abet revolutions across Europe. George Hadfield, an energetic activist in Manchester, reported that "the Clergy of the Establishment" feared government disapproval and were "afraid of compromising themselves." Even Hughes, the Cambridge preacher known for his Scio pamphlet, dared not formally join the committee because of his "*ticklish* situation as examining Chaplain to the Bishop of London."[17]

The shrewder philhellenes feared alienating Britain's masses of Tories by making Greece a partisan matter between rival Whigs and Tories. When the Tories accused the London Greek Committee of being a "nest of

Whigs," one activist bristled: "We *are* a nest of Whigs, the Lord be praised." But Edmund Henry Barker, a down-on-his-luck Cambridge academic who became a tireless activist for the Greeks, warned Bowring, "Your Committee, consisting as it does of men of the most decided politics, is not . . . calculated to catch the moderate men." Barker suggested that "moderate" activism "will draw within its vortex many Tories, who are well-disposed to the Greeks, but are afraid to act with the Whigs." So one Cambridge political economist was sidelined for being "decidedly too much known as a Whig, & ultra-Whig." Conversely, the philhellenes showered attention on sympathetic Tories. Hughes, the Cambridge cleric, was valued "not merely from his zeal, but because he is a Tory."[18]

They were also cautious about the politics of celebrity. Byron himself was too notoriously radical to be their main public face. As Bowring later wrote, Byron "seemed to live in perpetual vibration between what is divine and demoniacal." Byron's close friend Shelley asked, "Why dost thou curb not thine own sacred rage?" Byron understood that he was the wrong man to rebut an anti-Greek book: "I am *too warm* a controversialist."[19]

Even worse, the philhellenes could be dismissed as useful idiots for the Russians, or as revolutionaries, which carried some of the stigma in post-Napoleonic Britain that communism did in Cold War America. For the former, Tories would have been horrified to learn that a committee representative met with Capo d'Istria, the tsar's sacked hawkish adviser, and discovered that "all his views coincide with theirs." For the latter, Barker bookishly wanted to "vindicate the Greek Revolution from the charge of *rebellion* by adducing the opinions of Grotius & his Commentators."[20]

But the London Greek Committee was undeniably radical. To them, Ottoman sovereignty scarcely mattered, any more than Serbian sovereignty would matter to liberals as Milošević scourged Kosovo in 1999. As Hughes put it, "Gracious heaven! . . . that the epithet legitimate should be attached to tyrannic despotism!" The president of Magdalene College at Oxford wrote that, although he had worried about helping insurgents against a government with which Britain was at peace, he realized that the Ottoman government, "so far from answering the ends of Government, was no other . . . than a system of horrible oppression." He concluded, "As a philanthropist, therefore, I feel myself disposed to assist the cause of suffering humanity in a country distant indeed, yet particularly interesting on many acc[oun]ts.; & as a Xtian, I wish to heal the wounds inflicted by the rage & cruelty of infidels." This was, at the least, a kind of Lockean antecedent to today's UN call for a responsibility to protect vulnerable citizens.[21]

The Man Castlereagh Shot

The most important Tory to win over was the new foreign secretary, George Canning. Far less conservative than Castlereagh, the imposingly bald Canning had confronted Castlereagh in a way that Byron could only dream of: a pistol duel. After a cabinet squabble in 1809, Canning had "cheerfully" accepted Castlereagh's challenge. At six o'clock the next morning Canning went out and, in the mists of Putney Heath, got shot in the thigh by Castlereagh in their second volley. The two ministers were both forced to resign; it took years for Castlereagh to get back into the cabinet.[22]

Aside from shooting at Castlereagh, there were other hints that tempted philhellenes to hope that Canning might be one of their own. Canning had soaked up the Greek classics at Eton and then Christ Church, Oxford, where he briefly gained a reputation as a Whig radical before toning down his politics. Canning, while not seeing Christianity as much of a political guide, had some classical affection for Greece. In his youth, the future foreign secretary had published a thoroughly derivative poem, "The Slavery of Greece," which started with the usual invocations of Plato and Socrates, Marathon and Thermopylae, and ended with a blast at Ottoman oppression: "What! that thy bold, thy freedom-breathing land/ Should crouch beneath a tyrant's stern command!" In private, Canning enjoyed Byron's (much better) poetry. Byron returned the compliment: "Canning is a genius, almost a universal one, an orator, a wit, a poet, a statesman. . . . If ever man saved his country, Canning *can*."[23]

Although Canning had been sickened by the Terror in France, he had also made a few strikingly liberal gestures as foreign secretary. He favored a gradual end to slavery and wanted to allow Catholics to serve in public office. When Mexico, Colombia, and Buenos Aires broke free of Spanish rule, Canning recognized the new republics. He complained that a "spirit of systematic encroachment and ambition" underlay British imperialism in India, and cheered Parliament's "constant laudable exertions . . . to check" or "counteract" imperialism. He detested the Holy Alliance, especially Metternich's complex intrigues. "I confess Prince Metternich's performances sometimes leave me in doubt whether I exactly understand him or not," Canning frostily wrote.[24]

The London Greek Committee hopefully lobbied Canning. They sent an MP to ask his help in repatriating 150 Greek refugees in Switzerland. Canning said that the refugees could come to Britain, but if they went home, "many political Considerations" prevented him from promising that Britain would protect the refugees on their Mediterranean voyage. Another MP on the committee complained that British consuls in Greece were helping the Ottomans, and Canning promised to stop them. More tellingly, he did not prevent the most hot-blooded philhellenes from going off to Greece to fight. And even after the Ottoman Empire lodged a formal complaint about British citizens arming the Greek insurgency, Canning did not stop that either.[25]

"Newspaper Erudition"

The London Greek Committee aimed not just at the highest levels of government, but also at the mass public. For that, the press was vital. As Blaquiere told the committee, "[T]he European public is, as yet, most imperfectly and inadequately informed on the subject." Even though the press had "teemed with the recital of massacres and murders," the public did not know the worst of it: "Would it be possible for the most able pen, or eloquent tongue, to describe the scenes which followed the executions of the capital, at Adrianople, Salonica, Cassandra, Mount Athos, Smyrna, Scala-Novo, Aivali, Rhodes, Cyprus, Candia, and Scio?"[26]

But reliable news from Greece was scarce, and, about a decade before the invention of the telegraph, slow. Shelley, in the preface to "Hellas," apologized "for the display of newspaper erudition to which I have been reduced." It took about a month for a letter to get from Marseille to London. In Genoa, Byron admitted, "*Here*—we can learn nothing but from some of the refugees who appear chiefly interested for *themselves.*" The London activists tried to corroborate details about massacres, like one on Cyprus. Immediately after the formation of the London Greek Committee, Blaquiere was sent off to Greece to root out "correct information." Canning supplied Blaquiere with passports for the mission, and Bowring passed along the committee's military information back to Canning. Still, when Byron finally arrived in Greece in 1823, he would write, "Your newspaper accounts are highly exaggerated for neither Turks nor Greeks have done much this year."[27]

The press could also mold public opinion. As Erskine wrote, "there is *one empire* which they can never hope to subdue—THE EMPIRE OF OPINION, whose throne is THE LIBERTY OF THE PRESS." The London Greek Committee systematically sent letters to the editors of the major publications, from the *Times, Chronicle,* and *Herald* to the *Literary Gazette.* They helped a *Times* reporter cover public meetings. When Blaquiere, "having come piping hot from Greece," gave firsthand stories of the struggle to rapt audiences in Bristol, Manchester, and Liverpool, they were generously covered by the press. The committee set up a "literary Sub Committee" to monitor the press and submit sympathetic articles. Blaquiere gloated that "the daily and periodical press have, with one or two exceptions, uniformly advocated" the Greek cause.[28]

Barker, the Cambridge academic, obsessively monitored the media fight. He bristled at a piece arguing that the committee's fund-raising came "at the expense of the Poor at home"; complained of "the pernicious way" in which the *Inquirer* had covered Greece; urged the committee to rebut an anti-Greek book; and suggested that Blaquiere gather Greek songs for publication in British magazines in order to show off the Greeks' "literary & moral & national character." (One such song makes one wonder what Byron saw in the Greeks: "Hasten on, ye youths, with/ alacrity, retaining the natural/ excellency of your minds, & your friendship/ with the Muses, to the divine Parnassus.")[29]

The committee's paper struggle was limited by the constraints of publishing: the delay and cost of mail, and, most annoyingly, the price of printing. The London Greek Committee crassly exploited the free-mail privileges of its MP members, jamming other letters in with those of an MP, and sending correspondence through MPs. The committee's pamphleteers griped about their expenses. Barker had to cadge off a sympathetic printer around Cambridge. The London Greek Committee even persuaded a printer to join, and then took shameless advantage of his shop.[30]

"Public Spirit Is a Young & Tender Plant"

Outside London, the committee was something that existed in newspapers and pamphlets. The activists had real difficulty in attracting supporters. "We know of the Committee's existence only from the public Papers," wrote Barker, near Cambridge, urging a new round of newspaper advertisements. "Where we make no personal or epistolary application, we have no other means of reaching the public ear."[31]

Cambridge, an academic town, might have been expected to be a hotbed of liberalism, and was the site for a branch committee of the main London organization. But there was not enough support there for a public meeting. "Nothing has given me so mean an opinion of the English University men as their indifference or rather hostility to the Greeks," wrote an activist. Barker begged for more advertisements from London "to shew that your Committee is *still living.*" One Cambridge political economist, finding the public more preoccupied with farming, was cautious: "I find a few willing tho[ugh] lukewarm; & the rest careless at best; some of them perhaps hostile, tho[ugh] not avowedly so. . . . Public spirit is a young & tender plant. I fear nothing can be done."[32]

In Manchester, a traditional left-wing stronghold, the cause seems to have been mostly embraced by the Left, not by moderates. George Hadfield, the leading activist there, had hoped his city would realize that Greece was "the cause of Christianity, Humanity, and Civil Liberty." But, he wrote, "I despair at present of a Committee in Manchester." He asked for "all possible publicity . . . in every Town in the Kingdom—for it cannot be expected that a contest so remote, the nature of which few comparatively are acquainted with, should excite sufficient interest till such explanations, and representations are made as would work upon their feelings." Hadfield requested a mass printing of new pamphlets based on Blaquiere's reports, as "a pathetic appeal to the People of England." Things turned around when the London Greek Committee agreed. Hadfield distributed the pamphlets and lobbied "some of the most respectable Individuals in the Town." He then formed the Manchester Greek Committee, eighteen members strong, which began printing up pamphlets and collecting donations.[33]

The activists were also "almost despairing of success at Ipswich." Suffolk was a split town, whose two MPs were "a staunch Whig" and a "sad Tory." Still, the editor of the *Suffolk Chronicle* and another local worthy started up a committee, which brought the advantage of free advertising. With fifteen members, the Suffolk Greek Committee quickly raised a respectable £200 in subscriptions, including a donation from "A Friend of Rational Liberty."[34]

There were many other towns where the philhellenes never organized, even though they hoped there was latent sympathy for the Greeks to be tapped there. An Edinburgh activist decided not to fund-raise: "I fear we should only expose our poverty and indifference." For all its efforts, the London Greek Committee and its regional offshoots, lacking real mass communications, never managed to become a mass movement.[35]

"Those Sinews of War"

The London Greek Committee was determined not just to rally public opinion, but to defend the Greeks by the force of arms. Unlike Human

Rights Watch or Amnesty International, this was an organization with an active military subcommittee.[36]

Byron, in his letter joining the committee, wrote that what the Greeks most needed was artillery, gunpowder, and artillery officers. As one classicist wrote, "Arms & ammunition appear to me the best resources England can supply to the Morea." Others demanded direct British intervention. Barker wrote, "England had ample means of assisting the Greeks,—by an armed interference." He argued that Britain "could have, two years ago, liberated Greece by strengthening the Greek Flotilla in the Mediterranean with six Ships of the Line & as many Frigates." He wrote that the Tories "would . . . sooner see the massacres of Scio repeated for the 100th time in a ten years' war, than prevent the repetition by proper interference." In one of its first resolutions, the London Greek Committee demanded that "a stop should be put to its [the war's] ravages by enabling the Greeks decidedly & firmly to keep up the land of their fathers."[37]

Thus the committee clashed with Quaker activists who wanted to help refugees from Scio, but refused to have anything to do with the war. Helping the refugees, they thought, was treating a symptom, not the disease. One Edinburgh philhellene, scorning "timorous and religious folks," would have rather given "money to aid the fighting Greeks." In a Yarmouth public advertisement, the committee made no secret of where the money would go: "Greece is POOR in those sinews of war—MONEY and ARMS; but she is RICH in every thing else—in MEN, in SPIRIT, and, above all, in her CAUSE."[38]

Some philhellene military experts made a rallying cry of providing the Greek navy with "*three Frigates,*" since one Greek admiral had said, "If one had but three English frigates, one could easily pass the Dardanelles & light fire works in Constantinople." Colonel Thomas Gordon joined the committee despite witnessing the Tripolitza massacre, and gave Bowring a professional assessment. The insurgents needed forges and artillery officers. They had lots of guns, but "they are cumberous, unwieldy, and totally out of order." Even the use of light artillery was impossible: "At the Siege of Tripolitza we strained every nerve to place in battery 5 pieces of Cannon and 2 mortars." Gordon would have preferred "buying and equipping a body of European troops, and sending them out to Greece," but that was too expensive. Instead, he suggested sending "a brigade of artificiers, clothed, armed, and engaged for one year, with two portable forges, tools, and entrenching tools," and "a brigade of light artillery," plus cattle to drag the artillery. The committee raised the money, and began recruiting artillery officers.[39]

Gordon was sent to command the London Greek Committee's troops. The volunteers, despite wan attempts at vetting them, were a motley crowd: a zealous amateur medic willing to "maintain all the risque of my own *existence,*" an ambitious soldier denied a regular British military commission, and someone recently sprung from prison. In total, seventy-nine British citizens would volunteer for the Greek cause, many of them taking important command posts. One of them would be Byron himself.[40]

CHAPTER SEVEN

Americans and Greeks

"In Search of Monsters to Destroy"

A classically inflected revolution for freedom from imperial rule: the Greek insurgents had an obvious way of pitching their struggle to Americans. The call of liberty had a potent resonance, as did the ancient overtones, in a country dotted with cities named Ithaca and Athens (six of them). Although the Founding Fathers had more often looked to Rome as their classical inspiration, the Greek revolution turned a new generation of Americans to Greece instead.[1]

Ottoman oppression was hardly at the top of American public priorities. A Serb uprising from 1804 onward was either ignored or dismissed as an unruly Balkan peasant revolt. But in May 1821, a few months into the Greek uprising, the Greek leaders in Kalamata sent a message aimed at Americans. First came the appeal to rights: Americans, the Greek leaders pointed out, believed "that all should enjoy those rights, to which all are by nature equally entitled. It is you, who first proclaimed these rights; it is you who have been the first again to recognise them, in rendering the rank of men to the Africans degraded to the level of brutes"—something which, while passable in abolitionist parts of New England, was absurd in the South. Then came the classical appeal: "The fellow-citizens of Penn, of Washington, and of Franklin, will not refuse their aid to the descendants of Phocion, and Thrasybulus, of Aratus, and of Philopoemen." With the execution of the Greek patriarch in Constantinople, U.S. elite opinion swung behind the Greeks.[2]

In response, the first official statement came from John Quincy Adams, the secretary of state to President James Monroe. Monroe was a tall, grizzled Virginia farmer, eager for a military buildup to make Europeans take the United States more seriously. In contrast, Adams was a stout, tough New Englander. The worldly and cerebral son of a president, Adams had been a senator and also served as U.S. ambassador to Britain, Russia, and Holland; he was now maneuvering his way toward the presidency. He knew Europe as well or better than the United States. His looming fear was that European autocracy would crush the United States' independence.[3]

Adams understood that the United States was just "a cock-boat" compared to "the British man-of-war." As a weak republic, the United States both scorned and dreaded the big European empires, especially the Holy Alliance. So the official government line was a self-protective insistence on U.S. sovereignty: a "principle of neutrality to *all* foreign wars."[4]

To dampen sympathy for the Greeks, Adams used a July 4 address to deliver a brilliant and enduring statement of a liberal doctrine of nonintervention. For almost half a century, Adams said, the United States "respected the independence of other nations while asserting and maintaining her own." Adams predicted that "probably for centuries to come," Europe would be torn between "inveterate power, and emerging right." But it was not the United States' place to step in: "Wherever the standard of freedom and Independence has been or shall be unfurled, there will her heart, her benedictions and her prayers be. But she does not go abroad, in search of monsters to destroy. She is the well-wisher to the freedom and independence of all. She is the champion and vindicator only of her own."[5]

Still, Adams admitted that the "prevailing popular feeling" was for the Greeks. Soon after that July 4 speech, the ambassador to France, Albert Gallatin, an aristocratic Swiss-born Pennsylvanian who had served as Treasury secretary, pointedly sent Adams a copy of the Kalamata appeal. Bypassing the White House, an elderly Greek scholar and leader, Adamantios Koraes, mailed another copy to a Harvard professor of Greek, Edward Everett. Around the same time, Russia suggested that the U.S. squadron in the Mediterranean join it in helping the Greeks, but Monroe refused any political ties with Russia.[6]

Everett was launching himself on a meteoric career. While studying in Germany, he met Byron himself. At Harvard, he taught an awestruck young Ralph Waldo Emerson. Everett was a good friend of Daniel Webster, and Thomas Jefferson admired his scholarship. Everett would go on to become governor of Massachusetts, ambassador to Britain, president of Harvard, and secretary of state. His fame was so great that, late in life, he was chosen to deliver the wordy oration preceding Abraham Lincoln at Gettysburg. True to form, at Gettysburg, Everett spoke in the popular Greek-inspired rhetorical style, invoking Pericles' funeral oration and the glorious Athenian dead at Marathon. Lincoln's speech, too, echoed Greek style—a legacy of an American adoration of all things Greek, which dated back to 1821.[7]

As a young activist, Everett, the editor of the prestigious *North American Review,* had the Greek appeal printed there, and distributed around the rest of the country. The plea from Kalamata got a much warmer reception outside of official Washington. Unlike European philhellenes, Americans did not need to tiptoe around the issue of revolution, which they could wholeheartedly endorse in the spirit of 1776. DeWitt Clinton, the governor of New York, signed onto the Albany Greek Committee. Public pressure began to build for an official recognition of Greece. Many philhellenes pushed for government action, and a handful went to Greece to fight. The liberation struggle in Greece helped inspire a new wave of Greek Revival architecture, including the additions that Lincoln built on to his own house.[8]

Americans were, like their liberal compatriots in Britain and France, horrified above all by the Scio massacre in April 1822. Philhellenes in Boston recalled "the catastrophe of Scio" in which "twenty five thousand . . . perished with arms in their hands, or were hanged, impaled, burned, or drowned." William Cullen Bryant, one of the best American poets of that period, wrote:

Weep not for Scio's children slain;
Their blood, by Turkish falchion's shed,
Sends not its cry to Heaven in vain
For vengeance on the murderer's head.

And Daniel Webster, then a congressman from Massachusetts, would accuse Ottoman troops of "an indiscriminate massacre. The city was fired; and in four days the fire and sword of the Turk rendered the beautiful Scio a clotted mass of blood and ashes."[9]

After this, American enthusiasm for the Greeks was growing potent enough that the White House had to join in. Monroe's draft of his annual message to Congress had, as Adams noted, "a strong expression of sympathy" for the Greeks, although it added explicitly that "neither justice nor policy would justify on our part any active interference in their cause." Adams was annoyed to find that a later draft included several paragraphs on the Greeks "with no little invective upon the *horrible* despotism by which they are oppressed."[10]

In his annual message to Congress on December 3, Monroe came out strong: "The mention of Greece fills the mind with the most exalted sentiments and arouses in our bosoms the best feelings of which our nature is susceptible." Since Greece's ancient glories had been suffocated by "a gloomy despotism," the president said, "[i]t was natural . . . that the reappearance of those people in their original character, contending in favor of their liberties, should produce that great excitement and sympathy in their favor which have been so signally displayed throughout the United States." He came close to recognizing Greece: "A strong hope is entertained that these people will recover their independence and resume their equal station among the nations of the earth." But he stopped there, without any specific political or military commitments. Instead, Monroe, wary of getting dragged into Europe's simmering wars, declared: "The United States owe to the world a great example, and by means thereof, to the cause of liberty and humanity a generous support."[11]

"This Holy Cause"

The Greek uprising was still raging as the White House drew up the statement that would become famous as the Monroe Doctrine. The Monroe administration was under great pressure to include in it a recognition of Greek independence. France had helped the United States win its freedom; now the United States should do the same for Greece.

Thomas Jefferson himself backed the Greek cause. In general, even in the face of European tyranny, Jefferson was sure that free government would spread: "The advance of mind which has taken place everywhere cannot retrograde, and the advantages of representative government exhibited in England and America, and recently in other countries, will procure its establishment everywhere in a more or less perfect form; and this will insure the amelioration of the world." He added: "It will cost years of blood, and will be well worth them." As early as 1785, Jefferson hoped to "see the language of Homer and Demosthenes flow with purity, from the lips of a free and ingenious people," although he did not trust any European powers to free Greece. Even so, in 1787, war between Russia and the Ottoman Empire prompted Jefferson, in Paris, to write: "I cannot help looking forward to the re-establishment of the Greeks as a people, and the language of Homer becoming again a living language."[12]

When the Greek revolution came, Jefferson wrote of the world's debt to Homer and Demosthenes (evidently his favorites), and reckoned that he only needed a modern Greek dictionary to read rebel speeches. From Monticello, Jefferson wrote to Koraes, the Greek scholar: "No people sympathise more feelingly than ours with the sufferings of your countrymen, none offer more sincere and ardent prayers to heaven." But Jefferson would not actually intervene: "nothing indeed but the fundamental principle of our government, never to entangle us with the broils of Europe could restrain our generous youth from taking some part in this holy cause." Still, he continued, "Possessing ourselves the combined blessing of liberty and order, we wish the same to other countries, and to none more than yours, which, the first of civilized nations, presented examples of what man should be." Jefferson made a series of suggestions for Greece's constitution, including freedom of religion and the press, and hoped for an elected leader, if the European courts would allow it. If any of his advice proved useful, the drafter of the Declaration of Independence wrote, "I shall fancy it a tribute rendered to the manes of your Homer, your Demosthenes." He concluded: "We offer to heaven the warmest supplications for the restoration of your countrymen to the freedom and science of their ancestors."[13]

Another Founding Father was less cautious. James Madison argued to Monroe that the United States and Britain should "join in some declaratory Act in behalf of the Greeks." Madison also wrote to Jefferson, former president to former president, that he hoped that the White House would join Britain to "make Greece an object of some such favorable attention." This could have meant a Monroe Doctrine that protected not just Latin America, but also Greece.[14]

Other prominent Americans were bolder still. In October 1823, Everett wrote a much-discussed article in his *North American Review.* In what was nominally a review of Koraes's new translation of Aristotle's *Ethics,* Everett extolled the Greeks as a civilized and Christian people resisting "the merciless domination of mahometanism" and the "heart-rending despotism of the Turks." He equated the Greek revolution with the American Revolution: "They have taken the liberty, as we did in 1776, of declaring themselves free." Everett claimed that "a more general opinion never existed in the civilized world, than that the Greeks ought to be aided." So he called on Monroe to send the small U.S. fleet in the Mediterranean to monitor the course of the war. If the navy determined that Greece was in fact free of Ottoman rule, then "let the independence of Greece be acknowledged by the United States, and a minister sent to their government"—presumably Everett.[15]

Gallatin, back from his posting as ambassador to France, repeatedly advocated what would have been the United States' first humanitarian intervention. The provisional Greek government was asking for U.S. recognition and assistance. As Adams noted, Gallatin urged that "we should assist the Greeks with our naval force in the Mediterranean—one frigate, one corvette, and one schooner." It was an odd kind of request, since the United States' Mediterranean navy was smaller than that of the Greeks. Lafayette, the United States' most celebrated foreign friend, urged Henry Clay to back a U.S. military intervention: "Should the Ottoman navy prove impertinent, it might be crushed at once."[16]

Gallatin's plea landed in a cabinet that was, as Jefferson noted, made up of rivals running for president. (Gallatin was aiming to become vice president.) In a cabinet meeting at the White House in August, John C. Calhoun, the fiercely pro-slavery South Carolinian serving as secretary of war, "descanted upon his great enthusiasm for the cause of the Greeks; he was for taking no heed of Turkey whatever." Unlike Adams, Calhoun presumed the United States would have to fight the Holy Alliance sooner or later; and, running for president against Adams, he saw the political usefulness of the Greek cause. Calhoun also suggested sending Everett as a secret agent to the Greeks. The Treasury secretary, William Crawford, another presidential aspirant, backed Calhoun, with one apprehension: "Crawford asked, hesitatingly, whether we were at peace with Turkey."[17]

Adams was not impressed. "Their enthusiasm for the Greeks is all sentiment," he wrote of his cabinet colleagues, "and the standard of this is the prevailing popular feeling." He was sure their bravado was all talk, and scorned "their doubts whether we were at peace with Turkey, their contempt for the Sublime Porte, . . . their enthusiasm for the cause of the Greeks." (As for a secret agent: "Our Agents will never be secret.") Adams told the president, "I thought not quite so lightly of a war with Turkey." Adams did not seize on the more obvious hypocrisy: how could Calhoun enslave blacks and save Greeks? While Britain was pushing the United States to get rid of the slave trade, Calhoun once accused abolitionists of "rendering us [Southern slaveholders] hateful in the eyes of the world—with a view to a general crusade against us and our institutions." The cabinet debated for two hours, without reaching any conclusion.[18]

Adams suggested a clear standard: respecting the sovereignty of independent countries. Since the new Latin American republics had been recognized by the United States, "they themselves, and no other nation, had the *right* to dispose of their condition." But because Adams did not consider Greece similarly independent, his stance ruled out U.S. interference in Ottoman internal affairs. Adams disclaimed "all intention of attempting to propagate them [American principles] by force, and all interference with the political affairs of Europe." In return, he wanted the Europeans to refrain from intervention in South America.[19]

But in a later cabinet meeting, Monroe tilted back toward the Greeks. As the president read his draft declaration aloud, Adams was surprised to find that Monroe had added "a broad acknowledgment of the Greeks as an independent nation, and recommendation to Congress to make an appropriation for sending a Minister to them." (Partisan politics made this embarrassing for Adams: Everett, the likely commissioner to Greece, was a Federalist, so Democratic-Republicans would be irritated by his assignment.) One of the cabinet members warned that if Monroe did not recognize Greece, then the House of Representatives might. Adams warned that Monroe's draft was "a summons to arms—to arms against all Europe, and for objects of policy exclusively European." It would come "like a clap of thunder," and might make France and Russia break off diplomatic relations with the United States.[20]

The next day, Adams went to see Monroe alone, to urge "him to abstain from everything in his message which the Holy Allies could make a pretext for construing into aggression upon them." If the Holy Alliance did try to seize part of Latin America by force, Adams said, "we shall have as much as we can do to prevent them, without going to bid them defiance in the heart of Europe." If Congress recognized Greece, that would still be less provocative than having the White House do so. Adams wanted to stand "against the interference of the European powers by force with South America, but to disclaim all interference on our part with Europe; to make an American cause, and adhere inflexibly to that." Monroe mentioned that he had spoken of Greece in the previous year's speech, and Adams said he would not mind a statement "in general terms and pledging nothing."[21]

Gallatin continued to push the administration. He met with Adams, according to whom Gallatin "proposes, as if he was serious, that we should send two or three frigates to assist them in destroying the Turkish fleet, and a loan or subsidy of two millions of dollars." Adams refused to meet with Monroe anymore on the topic of the Greeks, rather than entertain the prospect of sending "a naval force to fight with the Turks." Later that day, Adams found Gallatin at the White House with Monroe, where they argued it out again: "Mr. Gallatin still builds castles in the air of popularity, and, being under no responsibility for consequences, patronizes the Greek cause for the sake of raising his own reputation. . . . [A]ll the burden and danger of it will not bear upon him, but upon the Administration, and he will be the great champion of Grecian liberty." Adams won the day. After Gallatin left, Monroe read Adams his revised paragraphs on South America and the Greeks. This time, Adams was "highly gratified" to find them "quite unexceptional."[22]

On December 2, the president unveiled the Monroe Doctrine in his annual message to Congress. (Among other things, Monroe called for the suppression of the "odious and criminal" slave trade.) The main presidential message was that the Western Hemisphere was now off-limits to European colonization. Despite Madison's suggestion, Greece was not included in that. But Monroe, in the general terms that Adams could accept, once again expressed hope for Greek victory. The president walked to the verge of de facto recognition of Greek statehood: "There is good cause to believe that their enemy has lost forever all dominion over them; that Greece will become again an independent nation. That she may obtain that rank is the object of our most ardent wishes." But Monroe's paramount goal was defense—protecting U.S. freedom and security from European despotism, not saving Greece. As the president reminded the European courts, "It is only when our rights are invaded or seriously menaced that we resent injuries or make preparations for our defense."[23]

"The Great Political Question of This Age"

After the declaration of the Monroe Doctrine, the public fervor for the Greeks only grew. In late December, John Adams, the former president, seemed to rebuke his own son by telling the New York Greek Committee that his heart "beat in unison" with theirs and those of the Greeks. In Albany, Boston, New York, Philadelphia, and elsewhere, there were meetings held on behalf of the Greeks, hoping to put pressure on Congress. The campuses of Yale, Columbia, and West Point were swept away with enthusiasm. The Maryland state legislature passed a resolution of support. In Cincinnati, the future president William Henry Harrison gave a powerful speech for the Greeks at a benefit concert.[24]

To take one prominent example, the philhellene committee in Boston was led by Everett and Thomas Winthrop, who would soon become lieutenant governor of Massachusetts, and who came from perhaps the toniest political family in the commonwealth. (John Kerry, the Massachusetts senator and 2004 Democratic presidential candidate, is his great-great-

great-grandson.) In a widely circulated pamphlet based on a Boston public meeting, Winthrop and Everett were not above writing of "those Turkish beasts in human form." They were embarrassed that the United States had not helped Greece more, due to "[o]ur distance from the scene of suffering" and "the general want of information. . . . At length, however, the public mind is awakened." Winthrop and Everett noted that Monroe had spoken for the Greeks in front of Congress, and politicians from Maryland to South Carolina had taken up the cause. Finally, the Boston philhellenes invoked the memory of 1776: "We call on the citizens of America to remember the time . . . when our own beloved, prosperous country waited at the door of the court of France and the States of Holland, pleading for a little money and few troops; and not to disregard the call of those, who are struggling against a tyranny infinitely more galling than that, which our fathers thought it beyond the power of man to support."[25]

All of this put pressure on Congress to act where the White House had not. In January 1824, Daniel Webster introduced and put his extraordinary eloquence behind a House resolution to recognize Greece and send an American commissioner. Webster's choice would be his friend Everett. Adams was appalled. "It would destroy all possibility of our doing anything at Constantinople," he wrote privately, "and Everett was already too much committed as a partisan."[26]

Adams had his presidential ambitions on the line. It was widely rumored in Washington and beyond that he had held Monroe back on the Greeks, against public opinion. Worse, there was gossip that Monroe had given Webster the go-ahead, something that Webster himself would later confirm. So a vote for Greece would show Adams's weakness in any presidential election in the House. He risked the wrath of Everett's *North American Review.* He stood to lose popularity in Massachusetts, New York, and elsewhere, while his pro-Greek rivals, Clay and Calhoun, surged. Even the modest-sized faction trying to draft Andrew Jackson as president was largely pro-Greek.[27]

Webster let public support grow for six weeks, including resolutions for recognizing Greece from the legislatures in South Carolina, Kentucky, and Louisiana. Adams fought back as best he could. He hinted—falsely—to the House Foreign Relations Committee that there was a secret effort afoot to help the Greeks. At first the Monroe administration quietly decided not to come out openly against Webster's bill. But Adams evidently pushed the wobbling president back the other way. The secretary of state denounced both "the intermeddling of the Legislature with the duties of the Executive" and Webster's "seizing upon the popular feeling of the moment to perplex and embarrass the Administration."[28]

In the House debate, Webster unleashed one of his rhetorical masterpieces, denouncing the Holy Alliance and the "horrible oppression" by the Ottoman Empire. Webster declared, "The great political question of this age is that between absolute and regulated governments," with Greece as a key example: "If men may not resist . . . the Turkish cimeter, what is there to which humanity must not submit?" Still, Webster, probably only tactically, presented his motion as a modest one: "Are we to go to war? Are we to interfere in the Greek cause, or any other European cause? . . . No, certainly not." Instead, he argued that "the public opinion of the civilized world is rapidly gaining an ascendancy over mere brutal force." Clay followed, saying that Americans must "utter our indignation, at the most brutal and atrocious war that ever stained earth or shocked high heaven." That position was ringingly endorsed by speakers from Massachusetts, Pennsylvania, and Illinois, as well as Sam Houston. Webster was on the verge of triumph. But Adams was saved at the last minute by the bloc led by Crawford, which seemed to want to deny Calhoun a political victory. Some of these congressmen did not want to get involved in European diplomacy; others wanted to guard U.S. interests, not those of foreigners; and some, to Clay's disgust, wanted to protect trade with the Ottoman Empire. A New York congressman said that the United States should set an example, but should avoid "embarking in a military crusade to establish the empire of our principles." Ichabod Bartlett of New Hampshire sounded the enduring theme that Americans would not tolerate casualties: "When . . . the Turkish cimeter is dyed in American blood—where then will be your Greek committees—your Greek dancers?" Webster's bill was tabled.[29]

Adams had won. The government would not help the Greeks. It did not recognize Greece until 1833—long after Greece was, as a matter of fact, independent of Ottoman rule. Any rescue for Greece would have to come from the old world, not the new.[30]

"The Liberties of Mankind"

American society, if not the federal government, continued to agitate for the Greek cause. To help the Providence fund for the Greeks, a Brown professor sermonized about Hippocrates, Plato, and Socrates, as well as the Scio massacre. Rhode Island, he said, was named after the Aegean island Rhodes. His oration was followed by a song:

As, for liberty and right,
WASHINGTON upheld our fight,
So, some Grecian Patriot's might
Shall lead to Victory.[31]

American poets followed Byron's example, like Bryant, who rhapsodized that Greece's sons had

... risen, and drawn the sword, and on the foe
Have dealt the swift and desperate blow,
And the Othman power is cloven, and the stroke
Has touched its chains, and they are broke.

Fitz-Green Halleck's ode to a fallen Greek guerrilla leader was terrifically popular: "thou art Freedom's now, and Fame's;/ One of the few, immortal names."[32]

More important, Americans raised substantial sums for Greece. The New York committee alone garnered $37,000 by July 1824, almost matching the amount raised by the London Greek Committee across all of Britain. Much of this went to military supplies, and the American committees sent muskets, rifles, and small cannons.[33]

Many Americans were inspired by Byron. A small number went to fight alongside the Greeks. The most famous was Samuel Gridley Howe, a young doctor from Boston who would go on to marry Julia Ward Howe, the abolitionist who wrote the lyrics of "The Battle Hymn of the Republic." Howe, who used to recite Byron's poems, graduated from Harvard Medical School and set off for Greece. There he set about "killing Turks, helping Greeks, and taking care of my bacon." He wrote: "Oh, for two thousand American troops, and in three months not a Turk would tread the classic soil of Greece!"[34]

Some state governments supported the cause, too. DeWitt Clinton, the governor of New York, in a message whose foreign policy reach usually extended no farther than border squabbles with New Jersey, told his legislature that the "troubled democrac[y] of Greece" was better than the "hateful tyrannies" bordering it. But U.S. freedom came first. He also expressed relief that "the unhallowed conspiracies of the old world, against the liberties of mankind, can find no means of support and aggression on this side of the Atlantic."[35]

The U.S. government indulged all of this, if not joining in. An American philhellene once called upon Adams to ask for money for the Greeks.

Calhoun and the navy secretary had agreed to donate if the president and Adams would do so, too. Adams refused: "We had objects of distress to relieve at home more than sufficient to absorb all my capacities of contribution." As if on cue, while the philhellene argued with "crusading spirit" against an "inflexible" Adams, a senator from Missouri walked in, requesting donations to build a new Presbyterian church in St. Louis. "I subscribed for that instead of the Greeks," wrote Adams.[36]

CHAPTER EIGHT

Lord Byron's War

Homage to Cefalonia

Conspicuously absent from the London Greek Committee's war councils was Byron, who, having fled Britain in 1816 in fear of accusations of sodomy and of incest with his half sister, was off mooning about in Italy.[1]

While in Ravenna, he had a brief and unsatisfying foray into radical politics, joining up with revolutionary underground cells. He took particular pleasure in the rebels' elaborate sequences of passwords, and bought bayonets and muskets for "our ragamuffins." Byron was naively thrilled at "the very *poetry* of politics. Only think—a free Italy!!!" When Austria joined in cracking down on the radicals, Byron urged an uprising across Italy, and offered to join the fight himself: "It is not one man, nor a million, but the *spirit* of liberty which must be spread." As he noted, "The *Powers* mean to war with the peoples." Small wonder that the secret police opened his mail. Sickened by Austria's "butcher-work," he declared, "No tyrant nor tyranny—nor barbarian Army shall ever make me change my tone—or thoughts or actions—or alter anything but my temper."[2]

The revolutionaries were quickly crushed, to Byron's exasperation. "I can't laugh yet," he wrote to Hobhouse, blaming the weakness of the southern Italians: "Poland and Ireland were Sparta and Sparta*cus* compared to these villains." The panicked rebels used Byron for cover: "My lower apartments are full of their bayonets, fusils, cartridges, and what not. I suppose that they consider me as a depôt, to be sacrificed." When his beloved, the beautiful Countess Teresa Guiccioli, whose father and brother had been leaders of the revolution, tearfully told him that the Italians would now have to return to making operas, he agreed: "*That* and maccaroni are their forte." She was forced to follow her father into exile in

Florence. Byron returned to his "scribbling," as he called his work on his masterpiece *Don Juan*: "Now let us be literary;—a sad falling off, but it is always a consolation. . . . [I]f we cannot contribute to make mankind more free and wise, we may amuse ourselves and those who like it."[3]

The London Greek Committee knew that enlisting the most famous (albeit scandalous) European poet would be a propaganda windfall, linking the Homeric past to the Byronic present. For the less high-minded, Byron had the mass appeal of a rock star. Two years after Byron gave up on the Italian revolutionaries, the committee tried to shake him out of his gloom and get him back into the Greek struggle, which he seemed to have forgotten in Genoa. They begged, flattered, shamed, and cajoled.[4]

There was a chore that needed doing, too. Strapped for cash, the Greek provisional government went searching for a loan from London's banks. Bentham himself was enmeshed in the details of the loan, and deeply worried about the sticky task of finding a suitably shrewd commissioner for it. Blaquiere, headed to the war in Greece, stopped on the way to see Byron—certainly shrewd, although not known for being particularly good with money. Blaquiere begged him to be one of the three commissioners to administer the committee's loan in Greece.[5]

Byron was slowly awakening. After the committee flattered him with a resolution thanking him, Byron snapped out of his haze. He reported, through Hobhouse, that he was eager to help the Greeks. The poet agreed to go to war. "Pray come," Byron wrote to Edward John Trelawny, a self-promoting naval adventurer who modeled himself after Byron's *Corsair,* "for I am at last determined to go to Greece; it was the only place I was ever contented in. . . . [T]hey all say I can be of use in Greece. I do not know how, nor do they; but at all events let us go."[6]

In mid-July 1823, Byron, as the official agent of the London Greek Committee, said his farewells to a sobbing Teresa Guiccioli, and finally sailed for Greece, loaded with cash, weapons, ostentatious uniforms, ammunition, and fourteen stanzas of his *Don Juan,* which he would never finish. He left the literary world behind, hastily replying to a fan letter from Johann Wolfgang von Goethe: "I am returning to Greece, to see if I can be of any little use there: if ever I come back, I will pay a visit to Weimar." Instead of poetry, Byron's head swam with the minutiae of war: "1st. a park of field Artillery—light—and fit for Mountain service—2dly. Gunpowder—3dly. hospital or Medical Stores." Before setting off, he was almost giddy with the prospect of a glorious death: "I should prefer a grey Greek stone over me to Westminster Abbey; but I would doubt if I should have the luck to die so happily."[7]

Aboard the *Hercules,* Byron jotted down a poem in his journal: "The Dead have awakened—shall I sleep?/ The World's at war with tyrants—shall I crouch?" But instead of heading for the main flashpoint—the besieged town of Mesologgi—Byron instead arrived on August 3 at Cefalonia (Kefallonia), an island off to the west of the mainland. As one of the Ionian Islands, Cefalonia was still British territory. Byron could see the Ottoman ships closing in Greece all the way from Mesologgi to Navarino, but did not dare run the blockade. "I believed myself on a fool's errand from the outset," he wrote, but decided to "see whether I *can* be of *any* service in *any* way." He settled down in Cefalonia for four months, enduring one sizable earthquake and waiting for the London Greek Committee to actually set up the loan.[8]

The Greeks were thrilled at the famous arrival. Poignantly, one Greek military leader wrote offering to give Byron a suitable public reception, but died in battle the next day. Hobhouse, who was not on the publicity subcommittee for nothing, sent Byron the dead man's letters to translate and give to British newspapers. Byron did so. He was perfectly aware of his own star power.[9]

The Ottomans had repeatedly asked Canning to stop Byron, but the foreign secretary refused. Canning's government turned a blind eye to Byron's mission. Hobhouse noted, "Lord Byron has been extremely well received by the English civil & military authorities, who . . . seem very well inclined to further the objects of his visit to Greece." Byron encouraged the British governor of Cefalonia, Lieutenant Colonel Charles James Napier, to back the Greeks and secretly talk to the London Greek Committee. "*He* is our man to lead a regular force, or to organize a national one for the Greeks," Byron told Bowring. "Ask the army—ask any one." Napier, although tempted to join the Greek side, would in the end stick to his British military career: invading Sindh in the Indian subcontinent and ruling it with an iron fist, for which he is today honored with a huge statue in Trafalgar Square.[10]

In Greece, a thoroughly practical Byron emerged—sensible, centrist, detail-oriented, every inch the pragmatic man of affairs. Bentham, who had worried about Byron's capriciousness, was now grudgingly impressed and saw his usefulness: "By his connections he is in a way to have political fruits in abundance." Byron was vastly less taken with the Greeks than they were with him. "[T]hey are such d——d liars," he wrote. Unlike dreamy philhellenes in London or Cambridge, Byron faced harsh wartime reality, although a more glorious picture of the struggle would have added considerably to the Byronic legend. "I cannot say much for those [Greeks]

I have seen here," he wrote. Byron was leery of the Greeks' demands for money, and disgusted by their factionalism. As Hobhouse flatly told the London Greek Committee, Byron thought Greek "dissension" was "more formidable to the cause of Greek independence than the Turkish enemy."[11]

Byron's preferred Greek leader was Alexandros Mavrokordatos, who had set himself up as president of the provisional government in western Greece. He was, Byron thought, Greece's only potential George Washington: "the only civilized person . . . amongst the liberators." Mavrokordatos was a cerebral and bespectacled revolutionary of the type to suit Byron and Bentham: Western-leaning, dramatic mustache, smart clothes, seven languages. In exile in Pisa, he had taught Greek to Mary Shelley, and Percy Shelley had dedicated his "Hellas" to him. Bentham, who backed Mavrokordatos for prime minister, hailed him as a particularly enlightened descendant of the Greeks who "in the Garden of Europe for so many ages, kept at bay the Despots of the East, with their ever armed yet still enslaved millions." But Mavrokordatos was increasingly unpopular among Greeks, and Byron became seen as a prize by the various factional leaders. Byron, at the center of the intrigue, found himself trying to prevent a Greek civil war. As Leicester Stanhope, a British colonel fighting in Greece, put it, "All is not sound in Denmark." Byron's own analogy was to Newgate prison.[12]

"The fact is that matters are in great disorder," he direly warned. "No less than three parties—and one conspiracy going on at this moment amongst them—a few steps further and a civil war may ensue.——On all sides they are . . . trying to enlist me as a partizan." Byron resisted it: "I did not come here to join a faction but a nation." He wrote to Mavrokordatos, in one of his many attempts to coax the factious Greek leadership to pull together: "It seems that it falls to a foreigner to guard against all acts that might have some appearance of arousing the parties and feeding discord."[13]

The Greek leaders showed, as Hobhouse paraphrased Byron, "more of the nature of private than public warfare against the Common Enemy." To Byron's dismay, Mavrokordatos was shoved aside. Hobhouse reported that Byron said that "'*money*' is the general demand of the Greeks but that a great jealousy prevails as to the application of it—for instance Lord Byron himself offered to permit a thousand dollars a month for the relief of Messalonghi but, . . . the government itself threw an obstacle in the way of this generosity." Strikingly, Byron wanted the London Greek Committee to "address a formal remonstrance to the Greek Government on the subject of their dissensions."[14]

For all his romanticism, Byron shone a harsh unflattering light on the Greeks. "Of all those who came to help the Greeks, I never knew one, except Lord Byron and Mr. [Thomas] Gordon, that seemed to have justly estimated their character," said Napier. "All came expecting to find the Peloponnesus filled with Plutarch's men, and all returned thinking the inhabitants of Newgate [prison] more moral. Lord Byron judged them fairly; he knew that half-civilized men are full of vices, and that great allowance must be made for emancipated slaves. He, therefore, proceeded, bridle in hand, not thinking them good, but hoping to make them better." As Byron warned the Greek government, "I do not consent, nor will I ever consent to permit the Public or private English citizens ever to be deluded about the true state of things in Greece. The rest depends on you, Gentlemen."[15]

Still, he worried that he might be giving more truth than the more naive members of the London Greek Committee could take. "It is my duty & business to conceal nothing either of my own impressions or of the general belief upon the score of Greeks from the Committee," he wrote. "[B]ut when I add that I do not despair—but think . . . that my exertions should be used in their behalf in the hope that time & freedom will revive for them what tyranny has kept under but perhaps not extinguished—I conceived you will not despond nor believe me desponding because I state things as they really are."[16]

The military situation was worse. Byron was underwhelmed by the committee's own contribution. "We want a military foreign force and military man to lead," he wrote. "Gordon [is] . . . a good soldier and with a thousand men at his back and a little patience might have done much—but alone he can do little—they won't obey a stranger unless he has a force of his men sufficient to make himself respected—so say all the foreign officers who are returning by dozens." When a British captain made the startling suggestion of buying the Greeks a steamboat, Byron gave the plan a crucial endorsement for the committee. Byron mocked the Benthamite educational efforts of the committee: "The mathematical instruments are thrown away—none of the Greeks know a problem from a poker—we must conquer first, and plan afterward. The use of the trumpets may too be doubted, unless Constantinople were Jericho." He also, in a large contribution to the war effort, paid for Mavrokordatos's squadron to help besieged Mesologgi. This resulted in an inconclusive naval battle, which he admitted was "not quite an Ocean-Thermopylæ."[17]

Byron said he was "waiting at Cefalonia only until he can have a positive invitation from the Government to proceed to Tripolitza," on the mainland. Requesting epsom salts (to keep from gaining weight) and his favorite British brand of toothbrush, he seemed to be settling in for a while. In the meantime, the poet made himself prosaically useful to the mainland fighting, centered on besieged Mesologgi. As Hobhouse reported: "Lord Byron has arrived & provisioned forty Suliots & sent them to join in the defense of Missalonghi." He sent medicine and money to the wounded, and "renewed the refugees in the islands." (He also fell in love with one of those refugees, a boy named Lukas Chalandritsanos, who became his page.) Byron signed a contract with the Greek government for £4,000 from the London Greek Committee, which would allow the Greek navy to set sail.[18]

The war news that reached him was pitiable. Blaquiere, presumably trying to guilt the poet into sailing for the coast, had a Greek brief Byron: "The free party of continental Greece, exhausted by the cruel invasion that she has suffered for the past year, and exposed by her location to all the blows of actual war, today finds herself more menaced than ever." Trelawny, whose survival instincts left something to be desired, played to Byron's ego while urging him to go to a congress at Salamis: "Every individual of consequence is to attend." Byron, trying to overcome his own doubts, watching other European philhellenes flee, nevertheless swore to Bowring that he would "stick by the cause while a plank remains which can be honourably clung to—if I quit it—it will be by the Greek's conduct—and not the holy Allies or the holier Mussulmans—but let us hope better things."[19]

Mesologgi

By December, Byron had made up his mind: Mavrokordatos had taken over command in Mesologgi thanks to Byron's £4,000 loan, and Byron would go join him. This was the moment for Byron, no fool, to feel the terror of his own death, and to give his horrifically prescient recitation of fallen warrior poets. But it seemed that his presence could encourage and unify the Greeks. One British philhellene in Mesologgi wrote, "All are looking forward to Lord Byron's arrival, as they would to the coming of a Messiah." Byron, even while doing something genuinely brave, could not help jokily deflating his own fine talk: "I have hopes that the cause will triumph; but, whether it does or no, still 'Honour must be minded as strictly as a milk diet.' I trust to observe both." To his old friend Hobhouse, he wrote, "I may get the Greeks to keep the field—never mind *me*—so that the Cause goes on—if that is well—all is well." Mavrokordatos had told

Byron "that my presence will '*electrify* the troops' so I am going over to 'electrify' the Suliotes." He sailed off with a Suliote Albanian war cry: " 'Derrah! Derrah!' which being interpreted, means 'On—On—On!' "[20]

It was a perilous crossing. Byron's party was nearly shipwrecked, "twice upon the rocks." One of their two ships, ostensibly neutral and under British protection, was intercepted by an Ottoman frigate, with Byron's ship, within pistol range, escaping, in a note of uncharacteristic but heartfelt piety, "by a miracle of all the Saints." To kill his fleas, after five days and nights without washing or changing clothes, the British lord risked a fever by taking a cold ocean swim. On January 5, 1824, in a scarlet military uniform, Byron came ashore at Mesologgi to an ecstatic welcome from a massive crowd of Greeks.[21]

Mesologgi, a swampy fishing village on the Gulf of Patras, was a seriously dangerous place to be. "We are blockaded here by the Turkish Squadron sixteen sail in all," Byron told Bowring. It was dismally swampy: "The Dykes of Holland when broken down are the Desarts of Arabia for dryness in comparison." This meant a horrific danger of disease, as dangerous as the Ottoman siege: "If we are not taken off with the sword—we are like to march off with an ague in this mud-basket—and to conclude with a very bad pun . . . better *mart*ially—than *marsh*-ally." Two philhellenes begged the London Greek Committee to support their families, as "there is some probability of meeting death either in action, or from the effects of a climate not altogether congenial to Northern Europeans."[22]

The Ottomans later freed Byron's compatriots on the other ship, in exchange for which Byron had the Greek government release twenty-eight Ottoman prisoners. He asked the Ottoman forces to treat any Greek prisoners kindly, "[s]ince the horrors of war are sufficient in themselves without adding cold-blooded ruthlessness on either side." These Ottoman prisoners were all that was left of the non-Greek population of Mesologgi—the rest had been killed back in 1821, at the start of the Greek uprising. But, Byron wrote, "When the dictates of humanity are in question, I know no difference between Turks and Greeks." He planned to adopt one of these prisoners, a nine-year-old Turkish girl, whose brothers had been killed by the Greeks.[23]

Of all the ragged crew of British philhellenes sent by the London Greek Committee to dare death at Mesologgi, Colonel Leicester Stanhope was by far the most irritating. He had come to Mesologgi hoping to meet Byron there. But where Byron had turned out to be surprisingly practical, Stanhope was giddily idealistic. The colonel saw the Greeks as a splendid opportunity to put Jeremy Bentham's ideas into practice. But Stanhope stuck to his utilitarian dogma with bulldog consistency even when actually in Greece. Upon arrival, he quickly set about setting up presses, among whose first tasks would be publishing Bentham's works. As Byron sneered, "He came up (as they all do who have not been in the country before) with some high-flown notions of the sixth form at Harrow or Eton."[24]

Others found him equally grating. When Bowring offered to pass along some information from Stanhope to Canning, the foreign secretary recoiled: "No! I do not wish to have anything from that Mr Stanhope." Thomas Gordon, always practical, wrote of Stanhope's "zealous" Benthamite convictions: " 'We want artillerymen, and heavy ordnance,' said the Greeks! the Colonel offered them types and printers. 'The Turks and Egyptians are coming against us with a mighty power!'—'Model your institutions on those of the United States of America.'—'We have neither money, ammunition, nor provisions.'—'Decree the unlimited freedom of the press!' "[25]

This was a man capable of starting a speech to a crowd of Greeks at Nafplio by calling them Athenians, the minor geographical matter of the Saronic Gulf and a chunk of the Peloponnesus notwithstanding: "I call you Athenians because you are the worthy descendants of that ancient, learned, valiant & famed people." Stanhope continued, "I will not tire you by a long dissertation on the advantages that must result from the free exercise of reason on Government," and then launched right into one. What the Greeks needed was some Bentham: "Athenians you are well aware that the end of Govt. is the public welfare or the greatest good of the greatest Many." Stanhope had two radical newspapers created, the *Telegrafo Greco* in Italian (a common tongue in the Ionian Islands) and the *Hellenica Chronica* in Greek, the latter edited by Jean-Jacques Meyer, a Swiss Benthamite. Here was nation-building, circa 1824.[26]

Stanhope's cloying utopianism annoyed Byron beyond endurance. "I am tired of hearing nothing but talk—and Constitutions—and Sunday Schools," he wrote. Byron refused to write for Stanhope's newspaper, hated its humorless style and didactic radicalism, and called its staff "fools" and "mountebanks." When Meyer wrote a provocatively nasty attack on the Austrian monarchy, Byron killed the issue, suggesting that Meyer's "unrestrained freedom of the Press" should be put under "*some* restrictions." As for Meyer, "Of all petty tyrants he is one of the pettiest." This led to a topsy-turvy screaming match with Stanhope: "He charged me with *despotic* principles—and I *him* with Ultra-radicalism."[27]

Byron stayed fixated on military affairs. He and Stanhope proudly informed Mavrokordatos that the London Greek Committee's long-promised military laboratory was complete, ready to produce cannons, bullets, and artillery. Mavrokordatos flattered Byron by naming him "Commander in Chief of Western Greece" and putting him in charge of a raid against an Ottoman fortress at Lepanto (Nafpaktos). Byron wrote, "These fellows do mind me a little." All told, Byron reckoned he spent $30,000 of his own money on the Greeks in Mesologgi, essentially funding his own small army. He shrugged off the expense: "It is better playing at Nations than gaming at Almacks or Newmarket." He was mordantly amused by his motley troops: "Between Suliote Chiefs—German Barons—English Volunteers—and adventurers of all Nations—we are likely to form as goodly an allied army—as ever quarrelled beneath the same banner."[28]

"A Soldier's Grave"

Byron turned thirty-six on January 22, and wrote a celebratory poem that progressed from exuberance toward a grim foreboding:

The Sword, the Banner, and the Field,
Glory and Greece, around me see!
The Spartan, borne upon his shield,
Was not more free.

. . . .

Seek out—less often sought than found—
A soldier's grave, for thee the best;
Then look around, and choose thy ground,
And take thy Rest.

The foreboding was closing in on him. On February 15, Byron suffered "a strong shock of a Convulsive description," which he thought nearly killed him. He was "bled profusely" with leeches at his temples. He did not know "whether it was epilepsy—catalepsy—cachexy—apoplexy—or what other *exy*—or *opsy*." The combination of illness and unrest in his Albanian Suliote ranks made him postpone the Lepanto attack. When they demanded a raise, Byron wrote, "I will have nothing more to do with the Suliotes—they may go to the Turks or—the devil." An earthquake added to the sense of imminent doom.[29]

Byron had one last poem in him, to the Greek beloved of the moment, his page, the boy Lukas Chalandritsanos:

What are to me those honours or renown
Past or to come, a new-born people's cry?
Albeit for such I could despise a crown
Of aught save laurel, or for such could die.
I am a fool of passion, and a frown
Of thine to me is as an adder's eye
To the poor bird whose pinion fluttering down
Wafts unto death the breast it bore so high:
Such is this maddening fascination grown,
So strong thy magic or so weak am I.

Even his love poem had a war background.[30]

Byron's final days were spent on practical matters: he planned to go to a meeting of Mavrokordatos and other factional leaders; he looked forward to an "ensuing campaign"; and he was finally officially named as one of three commissioners who would oversee the London Greek Committee's long-awaited loan. He handled military minutiae. The artillery corps "have mutinied twice on account of bad bread, and really with cause, for it was quite unmasticable." The most celebrated poet in Europe prevented the flogging of a man caught stealing, and stopped a duel between some officers.[31]

To the last, he took the uncomfortable position of not whitewashing Greek affairs for the benefit of the committee. He told Bowring, "I am an enemy to Cant of all kinds." Playing on *Hamlet,* he added, " 'I could mouthe' as well as any of them if I liked it—but I reserved (when I was in the habit of writing) such things for verse—in business—plain prose is best." In happier days back in Italy, while only playing at revolution, he could have found consolation for politics in poetry; in Greece, Byron fixated only on the duty of politics. His final letters, on April 9, were utterly unpoetic: "Have you any further news of the Greek Loan? is it really settled—and how?"[32]

A bit later on the same day, Byron went riding in the rain, and this time caught something serious. Over ten agonizing days, the slow fever progressed. Byron resisted being bled, but finally gave in on April 16: "Here, take my arm, and do whatever you like." He was bled three times more the next day, which caused the debilitated poet to go into fainting fits. "Lord Byron dangerously ill," Stanhope wrote back to London on

April 18. Increasingly incoherent, shouting for his daughter and other relatives, Byron tried to give last instructions to a servant. He seemed to be suffocating, and made a rattling noise in his throat. "I must sleep now," he said, and fell still for twenty-four hours, his throat still rattling. On April 19, during a thunderstorm, Lord Byron died in Mesologgi.[33]

Byron's fame grew even more with his death. The philhellenes were eager to claim him as a relic of their political mission. Meyer, the editor of the *Hellenica Chronica,* claimed, almost certainly falsely, "Lord Noel Byron has died in my arms, strange matter that the man who always spoke against the meaning of my newspaper should die in *my arms.*" Stanhope was more gracious: "The soul of Byron has taken its last flight. England has lost her brightest genius—Greece her noblest friend." But he could not quite help adding, "If Byron had faults he had redeeming virtues too—he sacrificed his comfort, fortune, health & life to the cause of an oppressed nation."[34]

The spectacle of Byron's infinitely romantic death did more to warm public opinion to the Greek cause than almost anything he could have done while alive. His obituaries were a Europe-wide propaganda bonanza for Greece. Pushkin (who had once been drawn to a Greek refugee who claimed, falsely, to have been Byron's lover) wrote, "You mourn Byron, but I am glad of his death as a sublime subject for verse." Aleksandr Herzen later wrote, "If he could have adapted himself to this life he would, instead of dying in Greece . . . , now have been Lord Palmerston or Lord John Russell." Victor Hugo called him "the immortal poet." When Byron's body was laid in state in London, the police were needed to quell near riots. Philhellenism was more entrenched than ever in British consciousness. But for Hobhouse, Byron's old friend, it was not a moment for politics, but only for "an agony of grief."[35]

CHAPTER NINE

Canning

After Byron

Byron's death was an organizational disaster for the London Greek Committee. Byron died as Blaquiere was sailing to Zante with £40,000, the first installment of the loan. Blaquiere wrote, "The death of Lord Byron was the first news I heard from the harbour master when he came alongside!!" He worried that "this most unexpected and Melancholy event of poor Lord Byron's Death" would delay the loan, and rebuked Bowring for not planning ahead.[1]

At Mesologgi, Byron left an immense vacuum. "In consequence of the Death of his Lordship, every thing has been thrown into such confusion," wrote one British philhellene. The remaining philhellenes squabbled about Byron's final orders.[2]

Byron left a void in Greek politics, too. In one funeral oration, a prominent Greek said, "Unlooked-for event! deplorable misfortune! . . . Was ever Greece in greater want of assistance than when the ever-to-be-lamented Lord Byron, at the peril of his life, crossed over to Messolunghi?" Mavrokordatos proclaimed twenty-one days of mourning and a thirty-six-gun salute for each one of the poet's years. But Trelawny noted, "Byron['s] death—is a death blow to Mavrocordato & he already sees it." Without Byron, the Greeks were on the road to civil war. Bentham, worn down by Greek factionalism, wrote, "A guerrilla warfare seems to be all they are fit for." Trelawny, in the midst of the wreckage, was disgusted to his core with the town and the Greeks: "I am at the fountain head of procrastination—the pestilential fumes of these torpid waters seems to have infected every thing—the atmosphere is as dense as a November in London and it is infected by reptiles—every thing is transacted not under the nose but under the mud."[3]

Despite the wave of publicity and support, the philhellenes, though still vocal, lost some of their cohesion and influence. Blaquiere, frustrated by the committee's inefficiency, momentarily declared his "determination to give up greek concerns altogether." Bentham, in a letter to the great Latin American revolutionary Simón Bolívar, accused the Greek envoys sent to him of "ignorance, groundless suspicion, insincerity, faithlessness, incivility, negligence, quarrelsomeness, weakness of judgment, pride, vaingloriousness, frivolity, and in the whole together incapacity for political business." He busied himself giving constitutional advice to Mexico and Guatemala instead.[4]

On the ground, the philhellene fighters found themselves increasingly bound up in intra-Greek disputes, reaching rock bottom when some British philhellenes shot Trelawny in the back (although not fatally). Despite their attempts to keep an eye on where the money went (not least because it was hard to raise funds without being able to show donors the results), the London Greek Committee became mired in questionable accounting. The Greeks only got £300,000 out of the £800,000 total of the loan Byron was to administer. The Whig press singled out David Ricardo for taking a commission for the loan, and for choosing a guileless agent who was overwhelmed by factional politics, in a way that Byron would not have been. Byron, if anything, had been all too suspicious of Greek corruption: he once wrote, "*There is no difference between the JEW and the GREEK.*" The lenders would never receive anything back for their ill-managed investment to what one philhellene called "Homer, Plato, & Co."[5]

The next big effort of the committee was to try to buy the Greeks a better navy. In 1825, they hired Lord Cochrane to build six modern steamships. But Hobhouse proved inadequate without Byron, and Ricardo turned out to be as bad at building a war machine as he was good at economics. Unbeknownst to the rest of the committee, he made a contract with an incompetent firm for four of the steamships. It took two years and a staggering £120,000 before any of the ships left the Thames, and, as Gordon wrote disgustedly, "three rotted in the river." None of the ships was ready before the Allied squadrons at Navarino sank the Ottoman fleet without any Greek help.[6]

The American philhellenes did no better. The Greek authorities decided to buy two frigates from a New York shipmaking company, one of whose partners was the chairman of the New York Greek Committee. The frigates, supposed to cost $250,000 apiece, wound up costing $750,000, far more than the Greeks could possibly pay. The Greeks had to sell one frigate in order to buy the other. This was so embarrassing that the U.S. government quietly agreed to buy one frigate. The other one, the *Hellas,* sailed off for war. From his estate at Montpelier, in Virginia, James Madison winced at the "mortifying topic" of "The Greek equipment at N[ew]. York." As he told Lafayette, "The ample fund for two Frigates at an early day has procured but one which has but recently sailed. The indignation of the public is highly excited; and regular investigation of the lamentable abuse is going on. In the mean time Greece is bleeding in consequence of it, as is every heart that sympathizes with her noble cause."[7]

Neutrality

Byron and Castlereagh were dead, but Canning was still very much alive. He had enormous influence in setting Greek policy, not least because Liverpool, the prime minister, was hopelessly flummoxed by it. Instead, Canning's main conservative antagonist was the Duke of Wellington: master general of the ordnance, the greatest military man in Europe, and Napoléon's nemesis. Wellington saw eye to eye with his late colleague Castlereagh. Byron had called him "Villainton":

I am no flatterer—you've supped full of flattery:
They say you like it too—'t is no great wonder.
He whose whole life has been assault and battery,
At last may get a little tired of thunder;
And swallowing eulogy much more than satire, he
May like being praised for every lucky blunder,
Called "Saviour of the Nations"—not yet saved,—
And "Europe's Liberator"—still enslaved.[8]

Canning saw many of the same realpolitik risks in Greece as Castlereagh had and Wellington did. The foreign secretary urgently wanted to prevent Russia from going to war against the Ottoman Empire, fearing "a new war . . . might presently involve all of Europe." He was wary of rescuing the Greeks: "We had neither the right to interfere, nor the means of effectual interference." Whatever "our sympathies," Britain had to respect Ottoman "national independence," just as Britain would want its sovereignty respected during an uprising. He invoked Britain's own empire: "nor was it for a Christian government which rules, in its distant dependencies, over a population of millions of Mahomedans, to proclaim a war of religion." Still, acknowledging the "public opinion of

England" and Britain's "remonstrances against the atrocities committed at Scio," he warned the Ottoman government that it was "our right, our duty, and our inclination" to urge them "to govern their Christian subjects with a mild and equitable sway."[9]

Canning began tilting toward the Greeks. Officially, he declared Britain to be neutral. This was in itself a slap to the Ottoman government, putting insurgents on the same level as the empire. Then, in March 1823, Canning went a step further: he formally recognized the Greek revolutionaries as belligerents, giving them the protections of the laws and customs of war. Thus British ships now respected the Greeks' naval blockade, rather than treating them as pirates; British merchant vessels were searched by Greek cruisers, who could confiscate enemy property, since Britain was ostensibly neutral.

Britain was the first great power to grant this legitimacy to the insurgency, while Metternich's ultraconservative Austria staunchly refused it. "The character of *belligerency* is not so much a principle as a fact," Canning defensively wrote. If the Greeks were not belligerents, then they were just pirates. He warned of "the monstrous consequences . . . from treating as pirates a population of millions of souls, to whom . . . you would convey the right, and even impose upon them (according to the natural law of self-defence), the obligation of terrible reprisals." In an endorsement of international humanitarian law, he asked, "Can it be necessary to suggest the advantage to humanity of bringing within the regulated limits of civilised war, a contest which was marked on its outset, on both sides, with disgusting barbarities? and of restraining, by those conventional observances and modifications which disarm war of half its miseries, passions inflamed on both sides to so furious a pitch as to aim at nothing short of mutual extermination?"[10]

The London Greek Committee was thrilled. Blaquiere would later write that, under Canning, Britain was transformed "from the ally of despotism to the protectress of freedom and constitutional rights!" In a pamphlet, Barker, the Cambridge activist, wrote that "since the accession of the Right Hone. George Canning to his Majesty's Cabinet, the oppressed Greeks have been treated with Christian kindness—that their blockades have been recognised by the British Squadron in the Mediterranean Sea." British ports traded freely with Greek rebel-controlled ports. When a Greek town fell, Britain allowed some of the fighters to shelter on British-controlled Cefalonia, and then return to the war.[11]

While Canning was receptive to the pleas of the London Greek Committee, he had his limits. In January 1824, Bowring, the committee secretary, had an astonishingly frank meeting, over an hour long, with Canning, who was too gouty to stand up. "The peace of Europe hangs on a thread," Canning warned, "and we know that, with the monstrous power of Russia, Turkey would be overwhelmed, and Greece too, whenever Russia chooses to put her armies in motion. A war with Turkey would be popular in Russia—popular with the army, popular with the people, if popular opinion can be said to exist in a country so governed." Bowring tried to argue that an independent Greece could resist Russia, but Canning was sure that Russia would impose a stooge king in Greece as "a blind instrument of the Holy Alliance."

Canning refused to endorse Greek independence, or privately meet with Greek deputies in London to raise a loan. (He did end up going to a Guildhall banquet thrown for them by the London Greek Committee.) Bowring asked if Canning would offer "your interference to stop the effusion of blood, to prevent the continuance of a struggle which will exhaust both?" But Canning replied: "A mediation of this sort, if rejected, would probably involve the interfering mediator in a war." The most that Canning would do was give "a very hard rap" to British consuls who seemed pro-Ottoman. Bowring reminded Canning of his youthful love of Greece: "in reference to Greece, that your situation is one enviable beyond the conception of envy. . . . The [public] enthusiasm that exists you contributed to create, and what you dreamt of as a boy, you may *do* as the minister of England." Canning did not reply, but bowed his head graciously. He invited Bowring to see him again.[12]

Canning had good reason to fear a Russian attack. Russia had already withdrawn its ambassador from Constantinople, to Britain's shock. As Britain tried to cajole Russia into sending an ambassador back, Aleksandr I asked Britain to join Russia in a mediation that would lead to a Russian-dominated autonomous Greece. This, Liverpool predicted, would soon bring Greek statehood.[13]

Wellington fervently hoped that the Ottoman forces would crush the Greeks. If not, he made a strategic argument for trying to ensure that any new Greek government was "not so far under the influence of Russia as to bring Russian power and resources in fact into the Mediterranean." But he feared that possible Greek independence might cause "a general war, or . . . the extension of the mischiefs of war to the neighbouring powers."[14]

Both the Ottomans and the Greeks rejected the tsar's plan, meaning that outside mediation would have to be imposed by military force. This, Canning thought, would be impossible. Wellington agreed. "You cannot *force* them to be reconciled," Liverpool wrote. "You may propose what you think reasonable terms of accommodation . . . ; but if those terms should be refused, the contest must proceed." The prime minister, not wanting to raise Greek hopes that Britain or Russia would rescue them, had warmed to Canning's policy of neutrality: "I am not prepared to say that either party is *so wrong*—the Turks in enforcing their sovereign rights, and the Greeks in struggling for their independence—as would warrant third parties in interfering by force in the contest." When the Greek provisional government tried to put Canning on the spot by rejecting Russia's plan and begging instead for British help, Canning refused to offer anything more than mediation.[15]

Britain's rebuff drove Aleksandr I into what Canning called "a passion." The tsar sent Canning a note, "the amount of which seems to be that 'he will be d——d if he ever talks Greek to us again.'" Canning boycotted a Russian conference held in St. Petersburg on the Greek crisis. For almost nine months, the Russians refused to talk to the British.[16]

Although more liberal than Castlereagh, Canning had a particular aversion to anything that smacked of religious war. He worried that Russia "in all her papers puts forth the character of '*co-religionnaires*,' . . . which entitles the Greeks to her active interposition." And he publicly warned the more evangelical British philhellenes, over Liverpool's objections, of the horrors of "religious war." Canning wrote, "The saints are running wild, and giving their aid to the political fanatics in behalf of Greece."[17]

CHAPTER TEN

The Holy Alliance

"THE HOLY SCOUNDRELS"

"This is the age of the war of the oppressed against the oppressors," Percy Shelley had written in his preface to "Hellas," "and every one of those ringleaders of the privileged gangs of murderers and swindlers, called Sovereigns, look to each other for aid against the common enemy, and suspend their mutual jealousies in the presence of a mightier fear. Of this holy alliance all the despots of the earth are virtual members." There was almost nothing that the philhellenes hated more than the Holy Alliance—personified above all by Metternich, Austria's reactionary foreign minister.[1]

Metternich, having devoted his life to the defeat of liberal revolts, saw the Greek revolutionaries as a pale imitation of his nemesis, Napoléon Bonaparte. So Metternich unwaveringly sought the crushing of the Greek insurgency. His kindest suggestion was that the Ottoman Empire reform its governance and offer amnesty to the rebels; his second kindest was that Ottoman forces "decrease the number of victims." As Canning accurately noted, "Prince Metternich . . . enters, heart and soul, into the Turkish view of this controversy. He considers the Greeks simply as rebels to their natural Sovereign. . . . [H]e would repress the armed resistance of the Greeks with a strong hand." Austrian ships openly ran Greek blockades to resupply Ottoman garrisons and armies.[2]

Metternich reserved particular contempt for Aleksandr I, who had betrayed the Holy Alliance's antirevolutionary principles. He complained about Russia's "disastrous support for the Greeks" and feared "an immediate war" between Russia and the Ottoman Empire. The tsar should stand firm against "the popular voice in Russia."[3]

Metternich despised the philhellenes. He scorned Hobhouse by name and privately loathed Canning: "This is a fine century for all sorts of people: for imbeciles, who pass for men of spirit; for moral myrmidons, who are always ready to threaten with the remote fist." Canning, he wrote, reflected British public opinion: "Canning is only the personified symptom of this disastrous evil which is found in all the pulsations of its fatherland, of an evil . . . which threatens to deliver its exhausted body to dissolution." Worse, Metternich wrote, "Throughout Europe, the public opinion of all countries is mixed up with this business, which has taken on a general popularity." To fight the rising tide of public opinion, the Austrian foreign minister was reduced to secretly inserting antiphilhellene notices in the press.[4]

The London Greek Committee reciprocated Metternich's opinion in full. Byron had named Metternich "power's foremost parasite." He called Austria's troops "the hounds of hell" and fumed that "the interests of millions are in the hands of about twenty coxcombs." In Cefalonia, Byron had worried that the Greeks were only safe "if the Holy Alliance leave the Greeks to themselves." Bentham had warned the Greeks, "What is the Holy Alliance, but an alliance of all kings, against all those who are not kings." Now, Barker warned Bowring, "I very much fear that the holy Scoundrels are going to put their paw on Greece, 'offering such protection, as vultures give to lambs.' . . . If Great Britain would only declare itself decidedly for Greece, the holy Scoundrels durst not meddle, & the Greeks would be strong enough to laugh at them." If the London Greek Committee had hated Castlereagh for betraying British principles, they hated Metternich for upholding Austrian ones.[5]

Metternich Agonistes

Russia's next gambit was a conference at St. Petersburg. Canning boycotted it, despite Wellington's urgings that Britain should try to have a say in the future of a possible new "maritime power in the Mediterranean." That left it up to Metternich to try to rein Russia in from war against the Ottoman Empire. He invoked sovereignty and international law to support Ottoman repression: "Could the powers base on principles of public law the support that they would lend to the cause of Greek independence? This question is sliced by a single word; all Europe is in relations of peace with the Sultan."[6]

But Metternich was sidelined away from the summit by personal agony: his wife, Princess Eleanor, was terribly ill, in Paris. Metternich dared not go to Paris for fear that Canning would see his departure as some kind of diplomatic maneuver. With Metternich distracted, the Austrian summit delegation agreed to try threatening the Ottoman Empire with possible recognition of an independent Greek state in the Morea. Metternich seemed too far sunk in personal misery to notice: "I am sad until my heart melts, and at the moment I am no good for anything." When his wife died, Metternich stoically wrote: "I have been tested by an irreparable loss; Providence wanted it thus." Still angry at Canning, Metternich gathered his daughters and son, and went to Paris. He impatiently sat the conference out.[7]

On April 7, 1825, the powers at St. Petersburg agreed on the principle of intervention in the Greek struggle, and demanded that the Ottoman Empire agree to it. In July, the Ottoman government rejected that demand. Metternich saw his conception of antirevolutionary intervention being turned on its head: the tsar wanted "a Russian intervention with the solidarity of the allies, like the Austrian intervention in Italy and the French intervention in Spain," except that now Russia would be backing the revolutionaries, instead of the reactionaries. With more than a whiff of panic, Metternich urged Russia to renounce conquest, and the Ottoman Empire to rein in some of its thuggish forces. "The whole business is bad, miserable, compromising to everyone's dignity," he wrote in disgust. "As long as the earth has existed, one never saw a similar attitude to that which unhappily seized the St. Petersburg conference." Russia, still refusing to return its ambassador to Constantinople, infuriated Canning by fishing energetically for new pretexts for belligerence.[8]

Metternich could only hope that the British cabinet would remember "the natural mobility of popular opinions and the danger of the extremes to which they lead so quickly." He dreaded a world in which "the triumph of liberalism" means "that the powers would recognize to the peoples or fractions of States the right to pass according to their good pleasure under other masters or protectors."[9]

A Fading British Neutrality

Canning, thoroughly sick of both Metternich ("That rogue Metternich!") and Aleksandr I ("a very foolish figure"), still clung to the fading fiction of neutrality between Greeks and Ottomans. The policy grew more threadbare daily.[10]

Although Canning was proud that both sides accused British ships of partiality, the Ottoman Empire had a better point: British forces on the Ionian Islands, where Byron had found such hospitality, refused to help

Ottoman troop movements and sheltered Greek fugitives. Worse, there was the glaring fact of private British citizens leading the fight against Ottoman rule. In "neutral" Britain, the London Greek Committee agitated, philhellenes joined the Greek army, and bankers funded the Greek struggle. To the reactionaries in Vienna, this was baffling. As the renegade Lord Cochrane busied himself in creating a Greek navy, as a project of the committee, Metternich simply could not understand why Britain had not brought its activists to heel. Canning admitted that Cochrane's ambitious mission would "bring into suspicion the neutrality of England, and give cause of just complaint to the Turkish Government." But he contrasted British domestic freedom with Austrian despotism: "The prevention of individual enterprise is not so easy in this country as Prince Metternich may suppose." British courts could not stop the fighters without legal evidence, which was particularly hard to dig up "when the popular feeling is strongly on the side of the offence, and when the act which the law erects into a crime is of a political character." It was not just in Britain, but in the United States and France, too, that governments could not keep "popular feeling . . . within due bounds." One can almost hear Austrian teeth grinding at this.[11]

The Greeks pressed their advantage. Canning made the bold new step of agreeing to meet with two Greek deputies in London. They told Canning that the provisional government was prepared to offer its lands up as a British protectorate. This was overreaching. Alarmed, Canning flatly refused. Undeterred, the Greek deputies suggested naming an English royal as the leader of Greece (and, knowing their crowd, let slip that France had suggested a member of the house of Orleans). Canning again turned them down. While still professing "strict and impartial neutrality," the foreign secretary reminded the deputies that Britain had recognized them as legitimate belligerents, thus helping to put a "barbarous system of warfare within the rules of civilisation, and prevent[ing] other Powers"—almost certainly meaning Austria—"from making common cause against the Greeks as insurgents, not entitled to the privileges of legitimate warfare." Britain had gone as far as it could: "Were we to go one step further, and transgress the limits of impartiality in favour of the Greeks, it would be in fact to take part with them in the war."

Canning told his guests that the Concert of Europe strictly forebade one great power aggrandizing itself over the others, a principle that, Canning lectured, surely ruled out a British protectorate or prince in Greece. (That, he rather apocalyptically warned, would spark a general scramble, leading to a war "general throughout Europe.") The Greeks should not be snowed by "their sanguine and enthusiastic friends" in Britain. The philhellenes too easily forgot the treaties and common interests that linked Britain and the Ottoman Empire. The most Britain could do was promote compromise, not Greek independence, because "that was asking *everything,* and could not form the subject of a compromise." But the foreign secretary brazenly added, "If they could conquer it, it was well, and that was their affair."

The Greek deputies firmly rejected any accommodation with the Ottomans: "The Greeks must now either be entirely independent or perish." Canning, unimpressed, warned that "he had stated . . . with perfect frankness all that they had to expect from the British government." Canning frostily informed the Greek deputies that "if those persons in England who distinguished themselves most as friends and advisers of the Greeks were to be at the head of the king's councils to-morrow, they would not have the means, or, when they saw all the difficulties of the question, the disposition to go beyond the line . . . prescribed . . . by the British government." Never mentioning that he had defended Britain's activists to Metternich, Canning said that Britain had been forced to declare again its neutrality because of "the stir which had been made and was now making in this country to engage the king's subjects in the Greek contest—contrary to the law of the land—and to procure succour of every description for Greece (the Greek deputies knew very well to what he alluded)."[12]

On the other side of the Atlantic, it seemed like bad news for Greece that John Quincy Adams was elected president of the United States in 1824. But even he yielded somewhat to public pressure. In August 1825, Adams ordered a secret envoy to Greece, who passed himself off as chargé d'affaires to Sweden. In fact, his mission was to head straight for Greece as a show of U.S. support, and to look into whether Greece was really independent. The agent sailed on a frigate with Lafayette, returning to France after visiting the United States, who, loyal to the Greek cause, said he would give up his own berth to the man. But the envoy took ill and died in France, never reaching Greece.[13]

Back in London, in private, Canning was still lukewarm toward the Greek cause. On the one hand, he did nothing to stop Cochrane, although he did want him to show a lower profile. And in Canning's instructions for a new ambassador in Constantinople, his own cousin, Stratford Canning, the foreign secretary was still convinced of the necessity of British recognition of the Greeks as belligerents, lest the war again sink into "disgusting barbarities" or "mutual extermination." On the other hand, Canning was annoyed at "the public and uncontrollable interference of British subjects in the military operations of the Greeks," which made British neutrality look like a bad joke. Britain had to struggle to restrain Russia, where the tsar could barely prevent public opinion "from crying out for war, a war against their ancient and natural enemy, and in behalf of a nation professing the same religion with themselves." The Ottoman Empire could not win its war: "Every success of the Turkish arms renders the Greeks more and more objects of sympathy and compassion, and every failure contributes to place Turkey in the light of a more tempting and easy prey." So Canning wanted the Ottoman Empire to accept some kind of autonomous Greece—hopefully less than full independence.[14]

Wellington was horrified by the prospect of the "establishment of a new Power in Europe, which must be founded on the principles of modern democracy, and therefore inimical to this country." He worried about the possibility of a great power intervention that was "not, as has been the case in other instances, with a view to restore the power of a legitimate government," but "for objects purely Russian." Although Wellington wanted the great powers to deter Russian aggression, he worried that "the Turkish government is so oppressive and odious to all mankind, that we could scarcely expect to carry the country with us" in helping the Ottoman government. Even Wellington, who wished Britain could openly side with the Ottoman Empire, admitted that British neutrality was eroding fast. Wellington would later say that Canning's pro-Greek tilt should have been stopped right at the outset, before it inevitably dragged Britain to war for Greece.[15]

CHAPTER ELEVEN

A Rumor of Slaughter

"A System Little Short of Extermination"

As the Allies fenced among themselves, the only foreign power to go to war in Greece did so with the least humanitarian of motives. Egypt, an Ottoman vassal loyal to the sultan, dutifully sent Ibrahim Pasha's forces to help their Ottoman overlords crush the Greek insurgency. Ibrahim was the son of Mehmet Ali, Egypt's ruler. As a British officer nastily recorded, Ibrahim was "a man of about 40 years old, not at all good-looking, but with heavy features, very much marked with the small-pox, and as fat as a porpoise." Ibrahim would later go on to become khedive of Egypt, but for now, he was simply a brutally effective commander.[1]

The Egyptian navy gave the Ottomans a new advantage at sea, which led to nightmarish atrocities on land. By the end of 1825, Ibrahim's forces had laid to waste much of the Morea. He intensified the siege of Mesologgi. The Greeks were all but defeated. Mavrokordatos's provisional government, forced to consider giving up on independence, secretly asked Britain to mediate an end to the war.[2]

Metternich watched Ibrahim's assault with considerable satisfaction. He claimed that the "liberal Europeans" fighting for the Greeks were flipping sides. "I see the Eastern Question as void," he declared with relief. "Ibrahim Pasha is the master of the Morea." Ibrahim's well-disciplined forces, some of them trained by French officers, stormed across the Greek heartland. Metternich let the Egyptian fleet use five Austrian commercial ships for transport.[3]

For the British, the mere fact of Ibrahim's offensive was alarming enough. But mounting concern turned to outright panic when the Russian ambassador in London gave Canning a terrifying warning: Russia had "positive information" that the Ottoman government had agreed that once Ibrahim had conquered Greece, he was "to remove the whole Greek population, carrying them off into slavery in Egypt or elsewhere, and repeople the country with Egyptians and others of the Mahometan religion." (Russia was still sulkily refusing to talk to Britain about Greek issues, and the ambassador said he was acting "in entire personal confidence" and without official instructions.) Canning was startled. This was, he wrote, "quite new to me," but clearly required fast action.[4]

Canning and Wellington were, in varying degrees, skeptical of Russia's intelligence. In retrospect, it seems unlikely that Ibrahim had any such plan in mind—a depth of systematic modern cruelty only attained by the Ottoman Empire ninety years later in the Armenian genocide. But British officials had no other reliable intelligence. After the brutality of the war thus far, British officials dared not ignore the rumor, and some of them clearly believed it. The British government also had to worry about the press. From 1825 on, the *Times* covered the war with a philhellene reporter, James Emerson, who had first gone to Greece in 1823 to fight alongside the insurgents. If there were such deportations on such a massive scale, they would likely be reported by Emerson and other journalists. The rumor lodged in British consciousness. It would become an article of faith among subsequent British commentators that Ibrahim was, as a distinguished international law scholar would put it four decades later, waging "a war of extermination" that gave "every European State a right of war against Turkey."[5]

Canning was jerked into action. He immediately passed the chilling news to Liverpool: "I begin to think that the time approaches when something must be done." He still wanted to act in tandem with the other great powers, most problematically, Austria: "I am quite clear that there is no honesty in Metternich; and that we cannot enter into joint counsel with him, without the certainty of being betrayed. It is not only his practice; but in our case it will be his pride and pleasure." A few days later, Canning more warily noted, "Things are not yet ripe for our interference, for we must not (like our good Allies) interfere in vain. If we act we must finish what is to be done."[6]

Canning swiftly began military preparations. He secretly sent a series of detailed tactical questions to the first naval lord of the admiralty, checking what naval forces Britain had in the Mediterranean:

> Supposing a case to occur in which it might be deemed expedient—
>
> (1.) To prevent fresh supplies of men, &c., from reaching Egypt;

> (2.) To prevent the Turkish Fleet from advancing into the Archipelago;
> (3.) To prevent the Greeks from taking undue advantage of the opportunity afforded them, by this restraint put upon their enemies;
>
> In other words, to enforce an armistice between the belligerent parties—is the present amount of force in these seas sufficient to execute this purpose in all its different details; and to do so with such effect as to deter opposition, and consequently to avoid actual hostile collision?

This had the potential makings of a small war to save the Greeks.[7]

Canning did not want to just take the Russian ambassador's word for it. Although the British government had no evidence of an actual expulsion plan, British intelligence largely confirmed the darkest views of Ibrahim's conduct. As Stratford Canning, a trusted source, reported from Corfu, the Egyptian record in the Morea was terrifying. Ibrahim had repeatedly destroyed villages and put the villagers "to the sword." This "cruel policy now adopted by Ibrahim is not likely to diminish the number of Greek recruits, otherwise than as it thins the population in general." Stratford Canning had not "heard of any acts of slaughter committed by him in cold blood; but he seems to spare no one where the slightest show of resistance is made. There is room to apprehend that many of his prisoners have been sent to Egypt as slaves, the children, it is asserted, being even compelled to embrace the Mahometan faith." Ibrahim "now acts on a system little short of extermination." All this lent credibility to, at least, some version of the Russian rumor. The extraordinary brutality of Ibrahim's campaign was enough to drive Britain to the brink of war.[8]

"To Extirpate Systematically a Whole Community"

Canning became more overtly pro-Greek. He warned Wellington that it was unimaginable that "the simple question of balance of power . . . would now reconcile Parliament to an active alliance with Turkey, involving in its consequences hostility not only to Russia, but to the Greeks." He decided to try a fresh round of bold mediation, with new initiatives toward Russia, the Ottoman Empire, and the Greek rebels. Britain would finally mediate the end of the bloody war.[9]

As Canning was preparing for his new diplomacy, there was a thunderbolt from Russia. In Vienna, Metternich got a late-night note with "Very urgent" written on it three times. He opened it to discover that Tsar Aleksandr I had dropped dead, on December 1, most likely of typhus. Canning was already planning to send Wellington to St. Petersburg to reopen talks on Greece. Now King George IV personally asked Wellington, while there, to greet the new tsar, Nikolai I, as well as to figure out what made him tick.[10]

Wellington presumed that Nikolai I would claim the right to go to war because of Ibrahim's "indiscriminate destruction of the population, without distinction of guilty or innocent, or of age or sex; his seizure of the youth for circumcision and conversion to the Mahometan religion; his declared intention of transporting the Greeks to Egypt, and of planting colonies of Arabs and Egyptians in the Morea." Even Wellington conceded that Ibrahim's alleged plan, if true, "would afford to every Christian Power ground for complaint, and even for measures to prevent the execution of the designs." If the Ottoman government refused British mediation and compromise, and Ibrahim really did plan mass deportations, Britain, along with Russia, "would not permit the execution of such a design." Britain would use its navy "to prevent the communication between the ports of Egypt and the Morea." Wellington knew full well "that in doing so we shall, in fact, decide the results of the war; but that must be for the consideration of the ministers of the Porte." Even the conservative Wellington now agreed that Britain had to stop the carnage unless "the Turks will change the character of their war in the Morea, and check the cruelties of Ibrahim Pasha."[11]

Canning admitted that he had initially found Ibrahim's alleged "monstrous and extravagant" plan to be "incredible." But Stratford Canning's report from Corfu showed "a prevalent belief in the existence of some such plan," followed up by some other confirmations. This was still "not sufficient" to positively affirm there was a plan, but it did "preclude the possibility of altogether doubting it." And if it proved true, Canning wrote, such warfare probably could not "be tolerated by Christian nations." If the British public knew about it, Canning doubted that the government could avoid intervening.[12]

Canning seems to have cautiously given some credence to the Russian ambassador's rumor. The expulsion plan was already "perfectly notorious" in Parliament, and it took all of Canning's efforts to prevent a question in the House of Commons. While lacking enough firm evidence, he instructed Stratford Canning to "declare in the most distinct terms to the Porte that Great Britain will not permit the execution of a system of depopulation which exceeds the permitted violences of war, and transgresses the conventional restraints of civilization." Britain alone could block it "by interposing . . . her maritime power between the Morea and Egypt." This, Canning unsubtly said, would "incidentally but no doubt materially affect the operations of the war in Greece." He demanded that the Ottoman Empire disavow any such plans, and immediately order Ibrahim to desist from them.[13]

British diplomacy was backed by a real threat of force. Earl Bathurst, the war secretary, wrote that Britain could not allow Ibrahim's plans "to extirpate systematically a whole community, to seize upon the women and children of the Morea, to transport them to Egypt, and re-people the Morea from Africa or Asia; to change, in fact, that part of Greece from an European State to one resembling in character the States of Barbary." He dispatched a trusted naval officer, Captain Robert Spencer, to demand that Ibrahim "explicitly disavow, or . . . formally renounce" the purported plan, with a blunt warning that the British navy would "prevent" Ibrahim from carrying it out.[14]

Spencer, commanding HMS *Naiad,* sailed into the Gulf of Patras, near Mesologgi, to face down Ibrahim, and got a run-around. At Ibrahim's headquarters, the Egyptian commander denied any involvement in "any cruelties"—something that no senior British official would have believed. Spencer insisted that he was only there to discuss the alleged deportation plot. Then an Ottoman Turkish official, overseeing Ibrahim, told Spencer that this was a matter requiring the presence of a top-level Ottoman government official. Ibrahim deferred to the Ottoman official, saying that as a mere general in the sultan's service, he could give "no answers" to larger questions of war and politics. Another Turkish official politely added that such matters were usually reserved at least for ambassadors, not a mere frigate captain. At wit's end, Spencer gave Ibrahim a written note stipulating that not answering would be taken as "a refusal to comply" with Britain's demands. Spencer hung around the Gulf of Patras for a week hoping in vain for a reply. "This answer led me to suspect the imputation to be true," Canning wrote.[15]

Ibrahim stepped up his attack on Mesologgi, one of the most important prizes in the war. Spencer feared fresh atrocities if Mesologgi was conquered. In April, after a long and brave siege, the town where Byron had died finally fell. This quickly became a cause célèbre in much of Europe. Victor Hugo penned a macabre ode, "The Seraglio's Heads," in which he repeated the common European rumor that Ibrahim had sent back to Constantinople "six thousand severed heads." Eugène Delacroix painted his massive and famous *Greece on the Ruins of Missolonghi* (now in the Musée des Beaux-Arts in Bordeaux), to parallel his one of the Scio massacre. His focus on Mesologgi was partially an homage to the death of his hero, Byron. Ibrahim's vile reputation was immortalized in Delacroix's demonizing figure of a swarthy Egyptian soldier, triumphant in black and crimson, with a gold turban against an ominously black sky, gloating as a classically pallid Greek woman in shimmering white stretches out her hands, ready to be shot by the Ottomans. All around her is rubble. At her feet, a dead man's hand sticks grotesquely out from beneath a massive piece of cut stone. The stone next to the hand is streaked with darkening blood.[16]

The Decembrists

Soon before the final assault of Mesologgi, Wellington arrived in St. Petersburg for what he reckoned "the most important" negotiations since the titanic diplomatic efforts at the end of the Napoleonic Wars in 1815. He hoped to get Russia to reinstate its ambassador at Constantinople. Privately, the conservative military hero had no enthusiasm for the Greeks. He saw no "benefit . . . from the establishment in the Mediterranean of an efficient naval Power which is likewise Continental." He knew that public opinion made it impossible for Britain to support the Ottoman Empire, but he doubted that a fickle "Parliament would support us through one single campaign." Still, even Wellington warned that Britain would not tolerate "any violation of the laws of nations or of the ordinary rules of war," and understood that stopping Ibrahim's rumored expulsions would mean putting "an end to the war in Greece by the Egyptian troops."[17]

The iron duke found Nikolai I sitting precariously on his new throne. The tsar's ascension back in December had been challenged by reform-minded Russian officers who, just after Aleksandr I's death, swore loyalty to Russia's constitution rather than the new monarch. Nikolai I had quickly smashed these so-called Decembrists, by execution or Siberian exile. One young poet went to the gallows carrying a book of Byron's poems.[18]

The youthful tsar, with an icy gaze, turned out to be a firm autocrat, terrified of liberal revolutions. One of Nikolai I's major contributions, if that is the word, to Russian political life was the creation of the secret police: the notorious Third Section of the Imperial Chancellery. It answered directly to Nikolai I, investigating subversives and stray Decembrists. Convinced that the Decembrists were the product of dangerous ideas spread by reformist journals, the young tsar also broke new ground in censorship, ending the relatively indulgent period of Aleksandr I's reign and paving the way for the Soviet freeze. This censorship blotted the immortal words of Aleksandr Pushkin, who, for all his imperialism, was an inspiration to many of the Decembrists. "Metternich himself never held such ultra Imperial language as is *now* the tone here," reported the British ambassador in St. Petersburg.[19]

This was very bad news for the Greeks. Many of the Decembrists were pan-Slavists and philhellenes. So, obsessed with the failed coup, the new tsar saw the Greek rebels as the moral equivalent of the Decembrists: traitors to their monarch. As the British ambassador put it, "The young Emperor Nick does not care one straw for the 'virtuous and suffering Greeks.'" Unlike his father, Nikolai I would see any armed intervention in Greece as "an invitation to his own subjects to rebel." The tsar told Wellington that there was "no feeling here in favour of the Greeks"—if true, then a testament to the efficacy of the secret police and censors. As Bathurst observed, remembering the Decembrists, "He who has just escaped with his life from an insurrection at home is not precisely the person to support one, though it is against the Turks."[20]

Thus in a stunning reversal, the tsar told Wellington that his "quarrel with the Porte was not about the Greeks, but for his own just rights under treaties which the Porte had violated." Although Russia had been expected to declare that it would block Ibrahim's rampage, Wellington was surprised to find that Nikolai I's latest note to the Ottoman Empire "does not contain one word or the most distant allusion to the Greeks." Instead, the tsar unilaterally demanded a total Ottoman withdrawal from the principalities of Wallachia and Moldavia, something that the Ottoman Empire had long agreed to do.[21]

Metternich was delighted. He had given up entirely on Nikolai I's predecessor: "The moral death of Emperor Alexander preceded his material death." Metternich only wished Russia had seen the reactionary light earlier, which "would have saved the world six years of torments, and the Cabinets the most serious compromises to a factious and seductive public opinion, but still inflamed."[22]

Canning was stupefied by the about-face. "Monstrous and incredible," he fumed. The past two years of diplomacy with Russia were now a dead letter. This was the complete opposite of previous Russian policy: "Why, in the name of common sense, have we been plagued for the last three years with memoirs upon Greece, and obligations to *co-religionnaires,* and were so often reproached by Russia for our apathy in behalf of a Christian people?" Why, he asked, had Russia warned Britain of Ibrahim's alleged deportation plans?[23]

Despite British exasperation, on April 4 Britain and Russia managed to sign a protocol. The Greeks would have an autonomous government, but remain "subjects of the Porte *en suzeraineté.*" The Greeks would pay tribute to the Ottoman Empire, which would maintain a role in picking Greece's rulers. Even Nikolai I agreed to join Britain in its policy of fighting to prevent "the attempt to establish a Mahometan State upon the destruction of the Greek population in the Morea." The document stood as the first international recognition of the Greeks, at a time when Greek military strength alone could never have won full independence.[24]

The dire expulsion rumor that had kicked Canning into action faded. In Constantinople, Stratford Canning finally got an audience with the Reis Effendi, the Ottoman equivalent of foreign minister. Their meeting left the British ambassador inclined to believe that "the Porte is no party" to such an "atrocious and extensive" plan. The ambassador tried to confirm this with a formal note, but got no answer. Without any definite Ottoman statement, he was "left to hope that either the imputed plan never existed or that the Sultan will silently take measures to prevent its execution."[25]

In London, George Canning was less than convinced by Stratford Canning's "provisional" information. He worried that Ibrahim had never answered the British captain sent to confront him over the deportation allegations, and still wanted an official Ottoman disavowal of any such plans by Ibrahim. At the same time, Canning notified the prime minister of the "necessity of reinforcing our squadron in the Archipelago"—a military step aimed directly at backing up Britain's threats to Ibrahim. As a British general reported from Corfu, the desperate Greeks would need the help: "There is nothing to oppose the Egyptian army but a mob kept together by the small sums sent by the different [philhellene] committees in foreign countries."[26]

Although Wellington had joined in threatening the Ottoman Empire over Ibrahim's rumored plans, he came to believe there was "no evidence whatever" of them. Canning, wary of handing Russia an easy pretext for attacking the Ottoman Empire, told Russian diplomats, with some exaggeration, that Britain had finally secured a "positive verbal denial," and that the Ottoman government's refusal to put that denial in writing was "not unusual" and not enough to prove that they were lying. Even so, Canning would carry out Britain's military threat "if what is as yet only matter of suspicion should ever become matter of proof." While Wellington thought that Ibrahim had been defamed, Canning seemed to believe that Ibrahim had been deterred.[27]

"An Evil of So Extraordinary a Character"

As he slid closer to war to save the Greeks, Canning remained somewhat aloof from the philhellene activists. When Capo d'Istria resurfaced in Paris, still agitating for war, Canning cursed his "impudences" and shut him out of all diplomacy. He heaped scorn upon Lord Cochrane, the scandal-plagued philhellene who had been kicked out of the British military, exiled, and was now off fighting alongside the Greek insurgents. But Canning and the cabinet would not arrest the renegade lord, and Canning claimed—not very plausibly—that there was little Britain could do to stop Cochrane's private war.[28]

In fact, as a matter of policy, Canning was looking more and more like a Byron in the Foreign Office. Conservative Tories were appalled to see him embrace "a very popular cause among a large description of well-meaning people, as well as with all democrats." Over bitter Ottoman protests, Canning allowed the Greek insurgents to buy British weapons, standing up for both the British military-industrial complex and the Greeks. While still warning Russia not to go to war, except to stop Ibrahim from expelling the Greeks from the Morea, Canning was shaken by the cruelty of the ongoing war. It was "so ferocious in its details, so hopeless of termination" that it became "an evil of so extraordinary a character as to justify extraordinary interposition"—anything short of outright attack. Canning wanted to threaten to recognize Greek statehood if the Ottoman Empire resisted international mediation that would bring Greek autonomy. Wellington was infuriated when he caught Canning trying to sneak references to Greek statehood and independence into the protocol, which only spoke of autonomy.[29]

Now that Britain and Russia had a protocol, they hoped to sign up more allies and then implement it. Of course, Austria refused to have anything to do with it. "The establishment of an independent Greece would be synonymous with the expulsion of the Turks from Europe," Metternich warned. But Metternich was not surprised: "Canning always does the opposite of what I would do." Consumed with irritation, he wrote, "Canning flies; I walk; he rises in a region where men do not live,

I am stuck at the level of human things. The result of this difference will be that Canning will have for him the romantics, while I will be reduced to the simple prose-speakers. His role is brilliant like a flash, but momentary like one; mine does not dazzle, but it preserves what the other consumes!"[30]

Heaping fresh contempt on "the philhellenic shop," Metternich knew he would be accused of having "taken on the turban"—going Ottoman. But, he indignantly wrote, "I am a better Christian than Benjamin Constant, Mr. Hobhouse, Chateaubriand, the abbey of Pradt"—some of the most prominent philhellenes—"and all the subscription shops." The Greeks and Turks were "barbarians both." Above all, "I declaim against that very villainous game which takes religion and humanity for a pretext in order to upset all regular order of things." If the "miserable wretched committees" were to win the day, "I would prefer to abdicate, to descend from the peak of an illusory power, and cede the reins of Government to the philhellenic committees."[31]

With the crisis over Ibrahim fading, Wellington hoped that Russia would lose interest in the Greek insurgency. At a special conference, the Ottoman Empire did its best to mollify Russia. But Nikolai I, with all the capriciousness of a fledgling despot, had gotten over his Decembrist shock and was now leaning toward an outright recognition of Greece. If the Ottoman Empire refused British-Russian joint mediation, Russia now wanted to threaten to break diplomatic relations and instead recognize an independent Greece. Wellington, seeing the slipperiness of the slope he had put Britain on, protested that Russia had "forgotten the principle of the Protocol, which is not to render Greece an independent State." "Russia wants to go too fast," Canning wrote, "and the D[uke]. of W[ellington]. . . . goes too slow." The foreign secretary refused to consider breaking off diplomatic relations with the Ottoman Empire, and urged Russia not to see refusal of mediation as a justification for war.[32]

As Britain and Russia drew closer to war, Metternich frantically tried to stop them. Britain preferred to act with all five great powers in unanimity, but Metternich flatly refused. Greek independence was too much for the Austrian Empire, no stranger to nationalist rebellions itself, to accept. Metternich was horrified even by Greek autonomy: "The manifest violation of principles is the proposal addressed to the Sultan to give up his *sovereignty* and to modify it into a *suzerainty.*" And Greek appeals to humanity darkly reminded him of "certain addresses presented, in a time that nobody likes to recall, . . . *in the name of mankind*"—that is, the gory horrors of the French Revolution.[33]

The Treaty of London

Canning's power only grew. In February 1827, Britain's prime minister, Liverpool, was "seized with apoplexy" that cost him his control of the right side of his body, and mentally hobbled him in a way that forced him out of public life. He would never recover. Bizarrely, Canning, the likely next prime minister, was stricken with violent headaches, although he soon seemed to be recovered enough to get out of bed and return to work.[34]

In March, a debilitated Canning announced a conference of the five great powers in London, with the Greek crisis at the top of the agenda. The plan was to draft a London treaty, following on and expanding the principles of the protocol that Wellington had already brokered with Russia. The diplomats of the great European powers locked horns over the same familiar issues: whether the provisional Greek government would be recognized, and whether enforcement would mean war. The courts in London and St. Petersburg were openly rumbling about severing diplomatic relations with Constantinople. Wellington, resigned to the stretching of his protocol, unhappily admitted, "This Greek State will sooner or later become independent." He wanted to make the best of a mess: "It will be a continental maritime Power; and it will certainly not be advisable to leave it under the influence of France or Russia, or both."[35]

On April 10, King George IV named Canning as prime minister. Britain's conservatives were appalled, particularly over Canning's staunch support for letting Catholics serve in the British government. Bathurst and four other cabinet members resigned rather than be in a government led by "the most powerful advocate of the Roman Catholic claims." Canning was forced to accept Whig help to hold power. Wellington, who had barely been able to stomach Canning as foreign secretary, and had his own ambitions for the top job, promptly resigned both from the cabinet and from his post as commander in chief of the army, alluding faintly to "our difficulties." He was not even named foreign secretary, a plum job that went to a Canning crony, John William Ward, the Earl of Dudley, who, in 1809, had been impressed by a meeting with a young Byron en route to Greece for the first time. The iron duke whinged, "Nobody will consider that I was treated with confidence, respect, or even common civility, by Mr. Canning."[36]

Ibrahim kept up his offensive. In Athens, the Acropolis itself surrendered to the Egyptian forces. The Greek insurgents, divided and out of money, were losing all hope. Their only chance was international support, which they bid to squander when Greek troops opened fire on Ottoman soldiers who had already surrendered at a monastery. Thomas Gordon, the London Greek Committee commander, saw two hundred men who "were cut to pieces." Gordon, who had quit his Greek service after the Tripolitza massacre, once again resigned and left Greece.[37]

Only Austria seemed inclined to resist the new British prime minister. Metternich was horrified at Britain and Russia's plans for "the use of squadrons for the goal of intercepting communications between Ibrahim's army and Egypt"—a fateful step that almost certainly meant war to stop Ibrahim's rampage. Metternich still hoped that Ottoman forces would crush the Greeks. More sweepingly, he wanted an amnesty for the Greek insurgents, a separation of the Christian and Muslim populations, and international guarantees of the settlement. He found it "impossible" to have anything to do with the impending treaty, for all the same reasons that he had scorned the protocol. But Austria was totally isolated, and Canning thought that Metternich could not stand alone against the rest of Europe.[38]

In stark contrast, the Russian foreign minister argued that, with Russian prestige now fully committed, the new treaty needed to have a real threat of "coercive measures" against the Ottoman Empire. The foreign minister argued that past threats had not worked: "Orientals enter into engagements only from absolute necessity." With such "hatred" between Greeks and Ottomans, "the war . . . can only finish by the destruction of one of them, and Europe has unanimously agreed that . . . the destruction of a whole Christian people was not an event admissible by Christianity." Russia, invoking Christianity more than humanity, had more crass motives too: it "cannot be required to allow a people which professes her religion, which was one of the most useful intermediaries of her commerce, which sent 300 vessels to the ports of her southern provinces, to perish entirely by the sword of the Mussulman." If the Ottoman Empire was not cowed by the recall of Allied ambassadors, Russia would join with Britain in dispatching "squadrons of the contracting Powers, with the object of preventing all help of men, arms, or of Egyptian or Turkish vessels, from arriving in Greece or in the Archipelago." Only force would work with the Ottoman Empire: "She has required, so to say, to see the glitter of our arms before deferring to our wishes."[39]

Canning tried to bring France on board as a counterweight to Austria. After the signing of the St. Petersburg protocol, he spent six weeks in Paris assiduously pursuing the French king, Charles X, so successfully that he became the only nonroyal to dine with the royal family in the Tuileries.

France, still on probation just a decade after the end of the Napoleonic Wars, played only a limited role in the Greek crisis. Charles X, a relative liberal, had abolished the censorship of journals, and the opening press encouraged French philhellenism. The king himself was sympathetic to the Greeks. Like Britain, France feared that Russia was seeking expansion in the Mediterranean. Although the British suspected that France had an eye on Egypt, France officially professed the loftiest of motives: "The excesses of the most dreadful tyranny made Greece rise. The Turks believed they could choke virtuous insurrection in the blood of the heroic Hellenes, the bloody ruins of opulent Scio." The Greeks faced massacre and enslavement if France did not listen to "the voice of religion and humanity as well as that of policy."[40]

On July 6, the new prime minister proudly watched the signing of the Treaty of London. Metternich had refused to sign, and reactionary Prussia followed him; but Canning had managed to get France on board with Britain and Russia. Unlike Wellington's protocol, the treaty began with the invocation, "In the name of the most holy and undivided Trinity," a bullying Russian touch. Where Wellington's protocol had claimed to act only in the name of "the principles of religion, justice, and humanity," the new treaty invoked both humanity and "the interest of the repose of Europe." Britain, Russia, and France would offer a mediation and expect a swift armistice from both sides. The final settlement, as in the protocol, would be an autonomous but tribute-paying Greece under Ottoman suzerainty. Most important, in a secret article, the Allies put teeth in their commitment. If the Ottomans did not yield within a month, then the Allies would use "all the means" necessary to impose an armistice. As soon as the secret article was signed, the three united powers sent "instructions . . . to the admirals commanding their squadrons in the seas of the Levant."[41]

The stage was set for war. Capo d'Istria reappeared in London, proclaimed as president of Greece, and cheered the Treaty of London as delivering his people from "the calamities which would have inevitably ended up by annihilating the Hellenes." The Ottoman Empire refused the threatened Allied mediation, and Ibrahim's bloody offensive continued.[42]

Canning's war was now all but inevitable. But the curse that had taken the lives of almost all the main players in the Greek crisis—Castlereagh, Byron, Aleksandr I—had one more name on its list. Canning had been too sick to get out of bed for much of the politicking over his premiership, and he ran the government in a daze of exhaustion and illness. With his inflammation growing, he said, in a lucid moment, "If all the pain which I have suffered throughout my life were collected together, it would not amount to the one-hundredth part of the pain which I have suffered these last three days." In agony, he screamed, "My God! my God!" His doctor replied that he was right to pray, and had him seek redemption through Jesus Christ. The doctor considered asking Canning about his country, but feared agitating the dying man. On August 8, Canning's pulse stopped, and then his breathing. His funeral procession went from Downing Street to Westminster Abbey, with somber crowds thronging around. As a Russian princess in London said, "The people [are] in tears, everybody who is not Metternich is in despair."[43]

Metternich, the one surviving leader who had seen the whole drama through, thought no better of Canning dead than alive: "England is delivered from a great plague." But Canning's diplomacy had taken the future of the Greeks out of the Austrian diplomat's hands, and into the hands of a British navy man sailing a warship off the Greek coast: Sir Edward Codrington, the admiral in the Mediterranean. "I hear the report of the death of Mr. Canning causes the Greeks to despair of English assistance," Codrington reassured Mavrokordatos. "Believe me, unless they disgust England altogether by their piracy and other unjust proceedings, they will still find us their best and most disinterested supporters." This was the quiet before devastating battle.[44]

CHAPTER TWELVE

Navarino

"I Have Never Felt a Wish to See Another War till Now"

In late July, Admiral Codrington sailed past the island of Scio. Codrington was a haughty and bald aristocrat turned into a seasoned combat sailor. He had commanded HMS *Orion* under Admiral Horatio Nelson himself at the legendary naval battle at Trafalgar in 1805, his ship blasted by French cannons. In the Mediterranean, Codrington now commanded from his flagship HMS *Asia,* a hulking two-decker ship of the line with eighty-four guns, and a crew of seven hundred men. The blistering Greek summer heat—wafting from the land and on siroccos—kept the crew from sleep, wrecked the ship's furniture, and cracked the *Asia*'s bulkheads. Although Codrington had been inspired by Byron, he was not firmly pro-Greek, and was particularly sick of local Greek piracy.[1]

But even now, more than five years after the Scio massacre, the admiral could still see the devastated houses of the Greeks "who were annihilated in that horrid massacre, which has disgraced even the name of *Turk,* already so stained in blood." He remembered with horror that it had taken two months for the Ottoman fleet to carry out "this butchery . . . 30,000 were murdered in cold blood, and the houses reduced to ruins!" One of Codrington's officers had told the admiral that "long after the massacre, he could hardly find his way about the town, owing to the destruction and the heaps of putrid bodies, which nauseated him even to vomiting. I assure you I have never contemplated a scene more sickening to the mind than this view of Scio."[2]

Codrington was deeply shaken by what he saw at Scio. He tried to offer a substantial £100 subscription to the London Greek Committee, until being waved off by Dudley, the new British foreign secretary, since it would seem "too warlike." This was precisely the right fear. "I have never felt a wish to see another war till now," privately mused Codrington, the hardened veteran of the Napoleonic Wars. But "I really think it might prove a more humane way of settling affairs here than any other. One strong act of coercion would place the Porte at our mercy."[3]

Codrington sailed from Scio to Smyrna, to await fresh instructions on Britain's new policy, coming by courier from Stratford Canning. Codrington, sweltering in "ovenly" ninety-degree heat, was to be joined by Russian and French squadrons. In addition to the *Asia,* he had two other ships of the line, HMS *Genoa* and HMS *Albion.* Having spent much of his career fighting or planning to fight Frenchmen, Codrington now reluctantly prepared to meet his new ally, Rear Admiral H. de Rigny of France. "You may judge how comfortable it will make me to have to rely upon French and Russians," he wrote. "In truth, I shall place no reliance upon any but ourselves." Codrington was a little calmer about the Russians: "A bear cannot resist this temperature without changing his nature."[4]

To his surprise, Codrington first read his fateful instructions in the *Times,* which had enterprisingly found a leaker. (The official orders, preceded by a copy of the Treaty of London, arrived several weeks later.) If the Ottoman Empire did not agree to an armistice, the Allied squadrons would "prevent any Turkish or Egyptian assistance, as men, weapons, vessels, and war munitions, from arriving in Greece." De Rigny reckoned that "a certain number of guns will produce submission," and Codrington was sure that Ibrahim would "gladly grasp at any excuse for keeping the fleet at Alexandria" and that "the Turks, or rather the Sultan, will at last yield to circumstances—I was going to say with what grace he may, but more probably without any grace at all."[5]

As the admirals boasted, their foreign ministries still insisted on their peaceful intentions. The admirals were baffled by this diplomatic grace note. They were policing an armistice that was not being respected either by Ibrahim or by the Greeks and the philhellenes leading them; Church and Cochrane were planning new military operations; the Ottoman forces would not respond to harsh language alone. De Rigny and Codrington, finding common military ground in berating diplomats, impatiently wrote to Stratford Canning: "Neither of us can make out how we are by force to prevent the Turks, if obstinate, from pursuing any line of combat which we are instructed to oppose, without committing hostility. Surely it must be like a blockade; if an attempt be made to force it, by force only can that be resisted."[6]

While waiting for ambassadorial clarification, despairing at the responsibilities weighing on him, Codrington's mind again turned to "Turkish barbarity." He wrote to his wife about a gruesome incident at Ipsara ("Ipsara—or Ypsara—or Psara,—for we know not how to give the Greek sounds") where Ottoman forces vowed to kill all Greeks. So seven hundred Greeks reportedly blew themselves up rather than face death at Ottoman hands. This was, Codrington thought, proof of "that excessive barbarity which has distinguished the reign of this Sultan even amongst his cruel predecessors." En route to ask the Greek provisional government to accept the Treaty of London, he once again ominously sailed past Scio.[7]

Diplomacy had its last gasp. The Greek provisional government immediately agreed to the Treaty of London. But a large Egyptian fleet had sailed from Alexandria, and the Russian squadron was on its way. On August 31, Stratford Canning wrote that the Reis Effendi had "refused [the Treaty] in the most positive terms." On September 8, Codrington finally received his clarification from the ambassador, in blunt words that could not mean anything other than war: "the prevention of supplies is ultimately to be enforced, if necessary, and when all other means are exhausted, by cannon shot." The admiral immediately sent those dire words out as a general order to his fleet. Codrington was also ordered to intercept any ships resupplying the Ottoman forces.[8]

Codrington now sailed for Hydra, to stop the Ottoman fleet. When the Ottoman forces moved on to Navarino, on the west coast of the Morea, he followed them, without waiting for French or Russian support. On September 11, Codrington finally found his object: the joint Turkish-Egyptian fleet, in Navarino Bay, ready for war. The Egyptian force, upon reconnaissance by HMS *Dartmouth,* a frigate with forty-four guns, included three ships of the line and fifteen sturdy frigates. Codrington knew this fleet was the key to the whole war: "The interception of the expedition from Alexandria would at once put an end to further operations on the part of the Turks in the Morea." The admiral impatiently waited for Ottoman provocation. "I wish the Sultan would declare war, as it would simplify matters at once." Emulating Nelson, Codrington's fleet lurked in harbor, sails furled, waiting for bloodshed.[9]

On September 19, the Ottoman fleet made ready to sail, presumably for fresh combat against the Greeks. Codrington, still without French or Russian backup, warned the Turkish admiral with macabre politeness that the Allies had "taken the humane precaution of sending a very large force" to impose an armistice, and that if "any one shot should be fired at the British flag on this occasion it will be fatal to the Ottoman fleet." If the Ottomans would back down, Codrington offered to protect them from the Greek naval forces led by the renegade Cochrane. Two days later, some of the Turkish ships sailed out of Navarino Bay. As the British fleet chased after them and made ready to open fire, de Rigny's frigates and four French ships of the line suddenly appeared windward of the Turkish fleet. This dramatic arrival stopped the Turkish fleet cold. The Turkish ships outside Navarino were held by the Allies, until being returned to Ibrahim's control later.[10]

To add to the tension, there was a terrifying risk that Britain would be dragged into actually fighting Austria—not just the grouchy diplomatic fencing between Canning and Metternich, but the real thing. Metternich still backed the Ottoman forces, and Codrington heard a rumor that Austrian warships had been involved in an Egyptian expedition. So the British admiral fired off a démarche warning that he would not make "any distinction between the Austrian and Turkish ships." Codrington told the British foreign secretary that "the barefaced way in which the Austrian flag covers Turkish property, will eventually require our interference." Codrington sent the *Dartmouth* to chase an Austrian corvette, which would have caused a major crisis if the Austrian ship had not gotten away. Worse, an Austrian ship, the *Vigilant,* had been in Navarino Bay before the Egyptian fleet got there. An indignant Metternich argued that the "blockade of the port of Navarino by ships of the European powers was not regularly announced," and that none of the three big powers had yet formally declared war on the Ottoman Empire. Only after the Foreign Office decided not to rise to Austrian provocations did the confrontation abate.[11]

Codrington and de Rigny continued to warn Ibrahim. On September 25, they came ashore for a meeting with Ibrahim in his cool and shady tent, just outside the town of Navarino. After their Turkish coffee, sitting on velvet cushions, the officers talked war. When the Allied admirals told Ibrahim of their orders to blockade his fleet, Ibrahim replied that he, too, was under orders—in his case, to attack Hydra. The admirals replied by threatening "the total destruction of his fleet." As the fleets stood eyeball to eyeball, Britain's long alliance with the Ottoman Empire was reduced to, as a British officer in the tent remembered, the admirals' "little humbug about their regret at having to destroy, without reason, so many brave men"—this said while pointing at the Turkish officers. But Ibrahim put his hand on his heart and vowed to suspend his operations, and leave his fleet in Navarino Bay to await fresh instructions from Constantinople and Alexandria. As a parallel gesture, Codrington promised to rein in Cochrane. Ibrahim chillingly claimed that Greek villages under his rule were "very quiet," and joked that he read most English and French newspapers: "Never did he see one in favour of the *Turks;* he saw by them that the *Greeks* were always successful everywhere, and the Turks always massacring, but the Greeks never!"[12]

Codrington marveled at his "unparalleled" situation: "Here we are now, De Rigny and myself, surrounded by above 120 vessels in their own port, whom we are forcing into obedience to the allies, in direct contradiction of the orders of a Sovereign whose slightest disapprobation deprives his subjects of their heads." Ibrahim promised not to do anything for twenty days, so the Allied squadrons temporarily moved out of Navarino to Zante. But then Ibrahim saw a chance to sail out again, this time sending some frigates out toward Patras in stormy weather on October 1. The British squadron doubled back to Navarino. Codrington, fuming at this "breach of parole," threatened to sink the entire fleet. Ibrahim had fifty-four ships against Codrington's three (although the *Asia* was a ship of the line). Still, Codrington fired thirty-two-pound shots across the bow of some Turkish ships that were not yet heaving to. At this, somewhat to Codrington's surprise, Ibrahim backed down. Codrington, deeply distrustful, called him "the *dirty dog.*"[13]

The Russian squadron finally arrived on October 13. Led by a rear admiral, Count Lodewijk Heiden (who was Dutch-born), commanding the *Azov,* the Russians brought four ships of the line, two frigates, and a corvette. Heiden was surprisingly amenable to taking orders from either of the other two admirals. Still, Codrington had "to keep the French and Russians, who evidently bore no good will to each other, as much separated as possible." With ten ships of the line, Codrington slowly warmed to his mission: "I feel somewhat proud of my mixed and most extraordinary command."[14]

"Putting a Stop to the Atrocities"

With the Allied squadrons united at full power, they turned to "forcing Ibrahim to come out and proceed to Turkey." In London, Dudley's Foreign Office was "on the tiptoe" waiting to hear if the Ottoman government would give in.[15]

Instead, some of Ibrahim's army defiantly set off across the plain of

Kalamata on another of his rampages. After two near misses, this new provocation was more than the Allied fleet could swallow. It was, Codrington furiously wrote, a "direct breach" of Ibrahim's promise. Ibrahim's forces were "ravaging the country, destroying the habitations, and burning the olive and other fruit trees." Codrington ordered Captain G. W. Hamilton of HMS *Cambrian* to sail after the Egyptian troops, and defend the Greeks "against these barbarities"—and to "drive back the army of the Pacha within the lines of Navarin." The Allied admirals also sent the *Dartmouth* off to deliver a threat to Ibrahim at Navarino: "Such a strange violation of your engagements place you, Sir, outside the law of nations, and beyond the existing Treaties between our Courts and the Ottoman Porte."[16]

Hamilton, of the *Cambrian,* was horrified to find a massive refugee crisis in Kalamata created by Ibrahim's troops, with starving "women and children dying every moment. . . . It is supposed that if Ibrahim remained in Greece, more than a third of its inhabitants will die of absolute starvation." The *Dartmouth* could not deliver its letter to Ibrahim, since he was not at Navarino and the Ottoman officers said they had no idea where he was. The Allied admirals, at the end of their patience, fired off a final blistering threat to Ibrahim, this time in the formal form of a protocol. The Allies accused the Egyptian commander of breaking his cease-fire pledges: Ibrahim's troops were still "carrying on a species of warfare more destructive and exterminating than before, putting women and children to the sword, burning habitations, . . . in order to complete the devastation of the country." The previous Allied warnings, meant to put "a stop to the atrocities which exceed all that has hitherto taken place," had "been treated as mockeries."[17]

It would be almost impossible to maintain a full blockade through the winter, since a storm would make it possible for Ibrahim to slip out. So the Allied admirals decided to sail smack into Navarino Bay, where Ibrahim could either yield to them or face destruction. The Russians were eager to go. It was, Codrington told a reluctant de Rigny, "our only means of preventing the barbarities of Ibrahim and effecting the objects of the Treaty." The night before the final confrontation, Codrington wrote to his wife, "This Ibrahim, who boasted to us his humanity and complained of being called in the newspapers the 'Sanguinary Ibrahim,' is ravaging the whole country; and Hamilton, whom I sent to drive back his army near Kalamata, tells me that some of the poor houseless wretches in the country which he has desolated are living upon boiled grass!"[18]

"Wreck and Devastation"

On October 20, the Allied squadron gathered outside Navarino Bay for the final confrontation. Eating a last Saturday lunch, the British sailors drank extra, and nervously toasted: "May we all meet again to-morrow!" The *Dartmouth* had scouted out the situation before in the process of delivering the final Allied protocol, and it was a clear trap. The waiting Ottoman forces had formed a horseshoe around the bay (Victor Hugo, reading reports of the battle, would be reminded of a Muslim crescent), with their broadsides facing into the middle. This forced the Allied ships either to anchor as sitting ducks in the middle, or blast their way into a better tactical position by opening fire.[19]

Numerically, the Allies were significantly outgunned and outmanned. There were 1,298 Allied guns against over 2,000 Ottoman guns. Codrington's combined squadron of twenty-four ships would be exposed to potential fire from three Ottoman ships of the line, five double-banked Egyptian frigates, fifteen Ottoman frigates, and eighteen Ottoman and eight Egyptian corvettes, plus other smaller ships, for a total of eighty-nine. But the Allies hoped that a qualitative superiority would carry the day: they had ten ships of the line and several frigates.[20]

Codrington's *Asia* led the Allied squadron as it sailed smack into the horseshoe at about two p.m. on a bright fall afternoon. A gentle breeze nudged the British ships directly beneath the heavy Ottoman batteries at the entrance to the bay, with the *Asia* anchoring when it matched up against a Turkish ship of the line. The Russian and French squadrons followed. A small ship sent by a Turkish admiral, urging the Allies to desist, was rebuffed by the *Asia.* Behind the *Asia* came the two other monstrous British ships of the line, the *Genoa* and the *Albion,* and then the four Russian ships of the line, to finish up the formation. Next, the four Russian frigates squared off against Turkish frigates. The three French ships of the line, led by de Rigny's *Syrène,* were abreast of Egyptian frigates. On tenterhooks, the Ottomans held their fire from the artillery batteries on both sides of the mouth of the bay as the Allied ships sailed in, within easy pistol range. The *Dartmouth,* the big British frigate, had the provocative task of luring the Ottomans' dangerous fire-vessels out of position. With strict orders not to fire unless fired upon, Codrington ended his instructions by quoting Nelson: "No captain can do very wrong who places his ship alongside that of an enemy."[21]

For a precarious moment, the enemy fleets faced each other, with not a shot fired. But when the *Dartmouth* sent out a small boat to intercept one of the Turkish fire-vessels, the Turks fired muskets. According to the captain of the *Dartmouth,* this killed or wounded several crew members. He sent a cutter out to rescue the beleaguered little boat, which ran into more Turks. They opened up more musket fire, killing the British lieutenant commanding the cutter.[22]

Later, the enemies blamed each other for the outbreak of firing. Codrington's version, confirmed by that of a sailor on the *Genoa,* faulted the Ottoman side for firing first. Ibrahim did not dispute this, but blamed the *Dartmouth* for being "the first, and without reason, to try to seize the fire-ships, and that it was the just resistance on this side which caused the first fire."[23]

Those first shots ignited a cataclysm: cannon, musket, smoke, and devastation. The *Dartmouth* fired muskets back, as did de Rigny's *Syrène.* An Egyptian corvette fired at the *Syrène,* which responded in kind. By then, all around the bay, cannon after cannon was firing in open combat. The *Asia* blasted away an Egyptian ship of the line. Other Egyptian ships opened up a raking fire that ripped off the *Asia*'s mizzenmast and killed some of the crew. The bay was filled with smoke and fiery explosions. The smoke was so thick that often crews could not see more than a few yards, and the thunderous detonations were so loud that sailors were deafened for two days after.[24]

The cannon broadsides at close range ripped ships to fiery pieces of iron and wood, setting off explosions so massive that they could shake even a ship of the line. The bombardment left the deck of one British ship "so bestrewed with splinters of wood" that it looked like "a carpenter's shop." The cannon fire did vastly worse to frail human tissue. On the *Genoa,* which destroyed two Turkish ships of the line and a frigate, a sailor wrote that his lieutenant drew his sword and ordered the outgunned men to hold their fire until ordered: "Make every shot tell—that's the way to show them British play!" The lieutenant threw his hat on the deck, and told the sailors to give the Turks three cheers, which the British heartily did. Warning his men to stand clear of the guns, the lieutenant yelled "FIRE!" and the *Genoa* devastatingly pounded the side of the Turkish admiral's ship. The lieutenant called out, "Fire away, boys, as hard as you can!" After the *Genoa* had taken five or six Ottoman rounds, the *Genoa* sailor witnessed his first death. He turned around to see a British marine "at my feet with his head fairly severed from his body, as if it had been done with a knife." The incessant firing was met with loud cheers, audible even over the cannons—but, according to the *Genoa* sailor, "distincter than these could be heard the dismal shrieks of the sufferers, that sounded like death knells in the air, or like the cry of war-fiends over their carnage." The British navy used boys as young as twelve as servants; one of whom, still smiling in the thrill of combat, was killed "by a shot on the back of the head" and delivered to "a watery grave."[25]

The enemy ships were packed so near that a British marine on the *Genoa* could clearly see "a great stout fellow of a Turk, in a red flannel shirt" on a ship of the line, firing a gun with lethal effectiveness. The marine aimed his musket and shot the Turk through the head. He collapsed back, dead, and was soon thrown overboard by the gunner who replaced him. One Turkish frigate was so close to the *Genoa* that the British sailor could see its elaborate decorations, which "glittered brilliantly" when "the sun pierced the dense cloud of smoke": gilded angels at the stern, a broad gold stripe above the portholes, and a figurehead of a red lion holding a shield with three crescents. A gunner captain on the *Genoa* cried, "She's coming! she's coming! d—— me, if I don't spoil her gingerbread work!" He aimed and fired, and then, above the smoke and deafening noise, he yelled, "I told ye! I told ye! I've done more than I bargained for; I've carried her spanker-boom as well as her gingerbread work away." The Turkish frigate "caught fire and blew up. As she was very near us, pieces of the burning wreck made their way through the ports, and nearly suffocated us with the fumes."[26]

At such tight range, this was more like mutual massacre. Men died random and grotesque deaths at every moment. One officer on the *Genoa,* desperately thirsty, had been badly wounded in his right arm, and his left was so bruised that he could not raise a jug of water. He went aft begging for help, and a middle-aged gunner kindly "took the jug, and after skimming back the blood and dirt from the top of the cask, filled it, and offered it to the officer; but just as he was in the act of holding it to the wounded man's mouth, he dropt a mangled corpse, being cut nearly in pieces with grape-shot." The thirsty officer was knocked off his feet, but not hurt. He was then helped

> down to the cockpit, where, illuminated by the dim light of a few purser's dips, the surgeon and assistants were busily employed in amputating, binding up, and attending to the different cases as they were brought to them. The stifled groans, the figures of the surgeon and his mates, their bare arms and faces smeared with blood, the dead and dying all round, some in the last agonies of death, and others screaming under the amputating knife, formed a horrid scene

of misery, and made a hideous contrast to the "pomp, pride, and circumstance of glorious war."[27]

One midshipman climbed up a mast to tend to a sail that had caught fire. As the *Genoa* sailor recorded, the midshipman "was knocked out of the ship altogether with a shot." He plummeted, and it looked like he had fallen overboard. In fact, the *Genoa* sailor soon saw "the body, with the head down, hanging by the entrails to the boat's davits, the most sickening spectacle I had witnessed during the action." Another British sailor "with one blow severed the parts, and the lifeless body immediately found a grave among hundreds of its fellow creatures."[28]

The *Asia* unleashed massive starboard broadsides. Codrington, tall and in an admiral's uniform as he marched the poop deck, was a prime target for Ottoman snipers. One bullet went right through his hat, another through his loose coat sleeve, and yet another ricocheted off his watch fob—but, although wrenched around a few times, he came out with nothing worse than "several splinter scratches and bruises." Two less lucky officers were shot dead while in the middle of talking to their chief, one with his head blown apart.[29]

Codrington's nineteen-year-old son, Henry, a midshipman aboard the *Asia,* recorded that the ship took "8 round shot in her bowsprit, 18 in foremast, 25 mainmast, mizen-mast dowsed, standing and running rigging cut to pieces, lower yards useless, &c., and 125 round shot in the hull, besides quantities of grape, canister, and musket shot, &c." The midshipman, "astonished at the coolness and intrepidity shown by all the men" and the "precision and steadiness" of the *Asia*'s volleys, got away relatively light: a splinter of wood dislocated his collarbone, a musket ball lodged in his right leg, and a piece of iron railing from his father's cabin blasted into the same leg, which nearly had to be amputated. Like the British sailor on the *Genoa,* Henry Codrington descended into the makeshift hospital in the *Asia*'s cockpit: "almost in the dark, and in an atmosphere which was as hot, though not as pure, as many an oven." Some of the worst wounded could not speak; others shrieked in agony. "Some (generally the least hurt) calling out lustily for the doctor. 'Oh! doctor, my dear doctor, do come here, I'm bleeding to death,' &c., and some saying it was their turn, &c." On the *Syrène,* de Rigny remembered, "When I was able to get down at midnight between-decks to see the victims, I found everywhere limbs and shoulders shattered without benefit of amputation."[30]

It was even more nightmarish on the burning and sinking Turkish and Egyptian vessels. The *Genoa* sailor recalled rescuing ten "poor drowning wretches who were drifting about during the storm of fire and thunder, that made the ancient Island of Sphalactria tremble again." The British rescuers were showered with burning wood and torrents of burned rice and olives from the Turkish ships. "[A]s one of our men, called Buckley, was hauling a tall stout young Moslem out of the water, a shot blew the head of the Turk to pieces, upon which Buckley, turning coolly about, said, 'D—— me, did you ever see the like of that?' "[31]

The British sailor on the *Genoa* reckoned the Turks, if anything, even braver than his own compatriots. One Turkish officer was picked up by a French frigate, but he realized that his arm was

> so shattered that it would need to undergo amputation; so he made his way down the cockpit ladder with as much ease as if he had not been hurt, and as much dignity as if he had made a prize of the frigate. He pointed to his shattered arm, and made signs to the surgeon that he wanted it off. The surgeon obliged him so far, and having bound up the stump and bandaged it properly, the Turk made his way to the deck, and plunging into the water, swam to his own vessel.

He was last seen climbing up the side of the Turkish ship with one arm. After a few minutes, that ship exploded, presumably killing him.[32]

The fighting raged on until it began to get dark, with burning Ottoman ships "illuminating the bay with a vivid glare." For all the chaos, the outcome was crushingly decisive. By around six p.m., the Ottoman fleet was mostly destroyed. Codrington wrote that the "bloody & destructive battle" raged "with unabated fury for four hours," resulting in an almost unprecedented "scene of wreck and devastation." As the *Genoa* sailor wrote, "Out of the large and majestic Turkish fleet that had that day been stretched in the form of a crescent round the bay, only 15 small vessels were to be seen close to the shore; the remainder being either sunk, burnt, or mere wrecks." After nightfall, the Ottomans started to scuttle some of their smashed fleet, so explosions and fire lit up the night. In defeat, Ibrahim wrote, "Do the Admirals think they have made a full harvest of glory by thus engaging with forces so superior . . . , [against those] who had not given grounds for it, and who . . . had not made any defensive preparations yet?"[33]

Not a single Allied ship was sunk, but 174 of their men were killed. The British navy would later estimate that its three ships of the line fired 122 tons of shot in those four hours of combat. On the other side, in total,

Codrington estimated that, out of 116 Ottoman ships, "the whole of these men-of-war, with the exception of one double-banked frigate, and a few corvettes and brigs, were either burned, sunk, or driven on shore [and] totally annihilated." Of about 18,575 Ottoman sailors, at least 6,000 were killed. In his general order to the battered Allied squadron, Codrington told his men to console themselves that their fallen colleagues had "died in the service of their country, and in the cause of suffering humanity." Navarino was as decisive a naval victory as almost any in history. But for that *Genoa* sailor, finally collapsing on the deck in exhaustion, it was an enduring nightmare:

> A slumbering drowsiness came over me, but I could not call it sleep. Visions of the conflict flitted before my eyes, and hideous phantasms, full of terrible combats and strifes, conflagrations and uproar, mingled with dismal apparitions of gory bodies, among whom I could see my messmate Morfiet covered with blood, and casting his dying glance at me.[34]

Aftermath

Here, at last, was the bloody humanitarian intervention that the London Greek Committee had so desperately wanted, that Castlereagh had resisted, that Byron had died for, and that Canning had set up. The battle of Navarino spelled Greek independence. Metternich was beside himself at the "catastrophe of Navarin." More happily, in his annual presidential message to Congress, John Quincy Adams praised the great European powers for encouraging "the friends of freedom and of humanity," and hoped that the Greeks' "independence will be secured by those liberal institutions of which their country furnished the earliest examples in the history of mankind." For all the subsequent diplomatic maneuvering and equivocation, and continuing warfare across the Greek mainland until 1829, the blunt military facts could not be hidden—the Ottoman Empire no longer controlled Greece.[35]

Russia did take Navarino as an opportunity to begin a wider war with the Ottoman Empire in April 1828. With the Ottoman fleet decimated, Russian troops stormed into Moldavia and eastern Anatolia. When Britain and France refused to see that adventure as a humanitarian one, the tsar used Black Sea trade as his pretext for a declaration of war. Fearing an attack on Constantinople itself, the Ottoman Empire signed a peace treaty in September 1829.[36]

Britain was horrified at Russia's expansion of the original intent of the Treaty of London, and quickly drew a stark line between that treaty and the Russian military onslaught. Rather than try to wield influence in a new Greece, Britain foreswore any interference in the formation of a Greek government. Britain's motives at Navarino had been far more limited. That battle was not meant to be the beginning of a full-scale land war, still less an occupation. In Codrington's report to the Admiralty, the victorious admiral emphasized his narrowly humanitarian mission: inducing "Ibrahim Pacha to discontinue the brutal war of extermination." Britain would use its navy to keep Ibrahim from deporting the Greeks to Egypt, to discourage massacres, and to run a partial and temporary blockade to help Greek ground troops push Ibrahim's routed forces out of Greece—but not in any broader Russian campaign to undo the Ottoman Empire.[37]

The same basic principle applied to France. In July 1828, Charles X declared that he was so determined that Ibrahim had to be forced to leave Greece that France would send ground troops to the Morea. Although Britain still would not do the same, it allowed France to do so. By the time the French forces arrived at the Bay of Kalamata, Ibrahim had already agreed to return the deported Greek slaves and to give up on Greece. The French mission was strictly limited to mop-up operations in the Morea, nothing more. When the French general decided to take Attica, he was quickly ordered not to by his own government. By June 1829, the bulk of the French troops had returned to Toulon. A small force of about three thousand French soldiers remained for a few more months, prompting loud British protest until they, too, shipped out at the end of the year.[38]

The London Greek Committee had created the nightmare that Castlereagh had feared: emboldening Russia to attack the Ottoman Empire. In his speech from the throne to Parliament after Navarino, a mortified King George IV decorously lamented the "untoward event" of blasting to smithereens the fleet of an ally. Wellington, not believing there had been "a plan for the extermination of the Greek population," complained of "this melancholy affair of Navarino; as usual, the blame is laid upon us, and principally upon me. But I think we are as far from any concern in this transaction as the moon is from being like a cream cheese!"[39]

It was a strategic disaster for Britain, but for the philhellenes, Navarino was pure glory. In Parliament, Lord John Russell baldly expressed the sentiment of his fellows on the London Greek Committee: "It is my decided opinion that that glorious victory was a necessary consequence of the

Treaty of London." Victor Hugo, in an ode on Navarino, cheered the victory by remembering the fallen poet of Mesologgi:

Behold this black sky, more beautiful than a sky serene.
The old Turkish colossus over the Orient collapses,
Greece is free, and in the tomb
Byron applauds Navarin.

Codrington, when he returned to Britain, was greeted by an old acquaintance who had not been paying attention to world events. "How are you, Codrington?" he asked. "I have not met you for some time; have you had any good shooting lately?" Codrington replied with perfect politeness, "Why, yes, I *have* had some rather remarkable shooting," and walked on.[40]

"Keep It Now"

Mesologgi today is an unglamorous little town in the west of Sterea Ellada, with narrow streets stalked by scrofulous stray dogs. Unlike the magnificently craggy Peloponnese, the land here is tediously flat, with the town perched on a stagnant lagoon. The air is marshy, and it takes only seconds on a hot day to appreciate why the boggy climate dropped Europeans like flies. Almost uniquely among Greek towns, Mesologgi has no ancient history to boast of, and is best known for killing off Greece's most famous European friend. The aesthetics alone would have put Byron halfway in the ground.

The fort is still there, with low walls made of simple gray stone. Its cannons bravely face a Discount Super Market. The fort now encloses a serene and leafy memorial garden for those, Greek and philhellene, who fell in the defense of the town. Byron's white marble statue has pretty good placement, just to the right of the main hill monument. He stands out amid the marble Greeks for two reasons: he has no mustache, and his memorial has no cross. (Byron was too heretical to get a memorial in Westminster Abbey until 1969.) The pedestal beneath his statue is instead adorned with a British seal, poetical masks of comedy and tragedy, and a graven owl of Athens—kept company by real ones hooting softly in the heat. Byron is windswept, his neck kerchief swept dramatically to the right, a classical-looking robe thrown over his British suit, with a scroll clutched in his left hand and his right hand pointing purposefully, except that his finger has been broken off. With a placid expression and dead eyes, he has become, finally, a Greek statue.

The Greek government and the London Greek Committee had squabbled bitterly about what to do with Byron's corpse. Stanhope had suggested a typically outsized gesture: "Had I the disposal of his ashes I should have placed them in the Temple of Theseus or in the Parthenon at Athens." Blaquiere, in Greece, was "surprised then mortified to hear, that there is some idea of depositing the body here." In the end, Byron's body was sent back to the London Greek Committee "in a puncheon of rum."[41]

At least, most of it was. The dispute was resolved with a ghoulish compromise. Byron's innocent love poem on his youthful first trip to Greece ("Maid of Athens, ere we part,/ Give, oh give me back my heart!/ Or, since that has left my breast,/ Keep it now, and take the rest!") has been taken with grotesque literalness. "The heart was . . . very large," Blaquiere noted clinically, "but its fibres were extremely relaxed, so that it must have performed its functions very feebly." Although the rest of the poet's corpse is entombed with his ancestors near Newstead, beneath the pedestal in Mesologgi is buried the heart of Lord Byron.[42]

Byron's legacy has been just as much up for grabs as his sundry parts. He is claimed today by romantics and radicals, as well as by Greek nationalists—including many who argued vehemently against NATO's Bosnia and Kosovo wars, the successors of Byron's own struggle. He probably would have found that funny. He continues to inspire people in hopeless struggles. In 1980, in the Lenin Shipyards in Gdansk, among the Polish workers on strike, one Solidarity activist pinned up Byron's famous words: "For Freedom's battle once begun,/ Bequeath'd by [bleeding] sire to son,/ Though baffled oft is ever won." Byron did not live long enough to fully realize his abilities either as an artist or as a political leader, but he died as the poetic hero of the first modern humanitarian intervention. His real monument is the free Greece where his heart, if not body, lies.[43]

PART THREE
Syrians

On August 7, 1860, Napoléon III, self-styled emperor of the French, assembled his troops at the camp of Châlons-sur-Marne. As if in imitation of the iconic portrait image of his world-conquering uncle, Napoléon III had the affectation of putting his hand in his buttoned coat. He ostentatiously wore a general's uniform that he had not earned, as the exiled Victor Hugo once scathingly noted: "He is fond of tufts, trimmings, spangles, top-knots, and embroideries, of grand words and grand titles, of sound and glitter and all the petty glories and glass beads of power." The heavily mustachioed emperor was, Hugo wrote, "a man of middle height, cold, pale, and heavy. He has the look of a person who is not quite awake." Like so many Frenchmen, Hugo knew that the callow Charles-Louis-Napoléon Bonaparte was hardly the real thing: he had "a pallid face whose spare angular lines were brought out with distinctness by the lamp-reflectors, a nose coarse and long, a lock of hair curled over a straight forehead, eyes small and dull, a timid and troubled demeanour, a likeness to the Emperor [Napoléon I] nowhere."[1]

Napoléon III was not one to miss a parade. At Châlons, he gave a grand send-off to two regiments and a squadron of Hussars about to sail for Syria to protect the Syrian Christians from the Druzes after a horrific series of massacres. The emperor handed out crosses and medals to his soldiers. The troops formed a square, with the French colors flying in the center. Napoléon III made a rousing speech, starting with expressions of humanitarianism:

> Soldiers,
>
> You are starting for Syria, and France greets with happiness an expe-

> dition that has but one object, that of effecting the triumph of the rights of justice and humanity.
>
> You are not, indeed, going to make war on any particular Power, but you are going to aid the Sultan to recall to their allegiance subjects blinded by an antiquated fanaticism.

After these high-minded sentiments, the emperor then sounded a harshly discordant note, invoking the Crusades: "In that distant country, rich in grand traditions, you will do your duty, and will show yourselves to be the worthy children of those heroes who bore gloriously in that country the banner of Christ." He ended in a better key: "You are not going in great force, but your courage and your prestige will supply the want, for now everywhere the flag of France is seen to pass, nations know that a great cause precedes it, a great future follows it." The troops marched past Napoléon III, and enthusiastically shouted "*Vive l'Empereur!*" As a contemporary Syrian historian put it, "The courage of heroes was stirred in their heads and they rose with hearts as if they were mountains."[2]

Napoléon III's awkward, blustery mix of themes paralleled France's mix of motives. On the one hand, there was a genuine idealism in French horror at the worst outburst of sectarian massacres in Ottoman Syria's history. That sense of shock, from ordinary Frenchmen to diplomats, put pressure on the government, which functioned with the bizarre arrangement of an emperor whose legitimacy rested on elections. Ideologically, of course, the idea of the rights of man was still potent in the country that had spectacularly brought that concept to the world in 1789, not so long ago. Institutionally, the picture was more dicey. Neither press nor society was fully free, and government was only sporadically responsive. Because the press was not free to report critically, France's knowledge of Syrian affairs was driven by a network of pro-French Maronite clerics in Syria who supplied much of the information that reached the French government. This in turn created a bias in favor of the Maronite Christians, unlike the more evenhanded British view of the civil war between Druzes and Maronites. Still, even with only the flickerings of liberalism, France under the Second Empire nevertheless could be pushed by the handful of brave progressive newspapers and journals that still existed, and by a public opinion that could express itself at the ballot box. Facing the 1860 massacres in Syria, Napoléon III had to be mindful of his domestic political situation.[3]

On the other hand, nobody could overlook France's obvious imperial aspirations in the Middle East. The emperor said he was acting in the interests of humanity, but many in Europe and the Middle East were appropriately suspicious. Unlike Britain's rescue of the Greeks thirty-three years earlier, France was not acting against its own strategic interest. Especially in Britain and the Ottoman Empire, it was hard to cheer on a French intervention without fearing a new Crusade.

And yet the French troops still sailed for Syria. Although the Syrian crisis seemed an unlikely opportunity for international cooperation, the great powers managed to overcome their suspicions and hammer together arrangements that allowed for a closely watched and strictly limited French-led intervention. Britain, pushed along by its own public opinion, sent its navy to help out, and stood ready to land the marines alongside French ground troops if necessary. In another check, the French occupying troops had to operate in uneasy tandem with a special Ottoman mission. As the immediate danger receded, British leaders preferred to trust in the authority of their Ottoman ally, still seen with considerable trust, rather than Napoléon III's ambitious France. France yielded to the will of the great European powers, limiting its own intervention even when French officials were beside themselves with rage at having to do so. Not despite the ambiguities of the French position but because of them, the 1860–61 intervention in Syria stands out as a success in the management of the tangled international politics surrounding a humanitarian military intervention.

CHAPTER THIRTEEN

Napoléon the Little

France Under the Second Empire

Napoléon III held the baffling title of prince-president. France in the Second Empire was a strange hybrid of liberal and monarchic government. Napoléon III had seized power in a coup d'état in 1851, but now stood as an emperor who was elected by plebiscite. The legislature, elected every six years with universal male suffrage, was actually far too weak to withstand the emperor. Only the government's candidates were allowed to campaign, with the opposition frozen out, with predictable electoral results. Still, Napoléon explicitly based his rule not on his bloodline but the will of the French people. He was constitutionally mandated to seek plebiscites for any notable constitutional changes, and he advocated giving the vote to all Frenchmen. As he brashly promised the public, "If I no longer possess your confidence, if your ideas have changed, there is no need to make precious blood flow, it is enough to place a negative vote in the ballot box. I will always respect the people's judgement."[1]

Politics and press were still largely matters for the cities. Literacy was mostly the stuff of the bourgeoisie and upper classes, with newspapers and libraries making only slow inroads into the countryside. In the 1860s, peasants still favored printed images, often religious or patriotic, or cheap single broadsheets whose frequent gory sensationalism and unreliability are captured in today's meaning of their name: *canards.* Many French peasants did not even know who the emperor was. Proper newspapers—the harbingers of a homogeneous modern nation, with common things on everyone's mind—would not reach the peasants until the beginning of the twentieth century.[2]

Despite the enduring image of France as the revolutionary vanguard of liberty, the free press there had long faced an uphill struggle. French newspaper readership in 1780 was at best a third of what it was in Britain. The French Revolution in 1789 left the revolutionary press unfettered, with the urban French suddenly reading their Revolution in uncensored newspapers. Edmund Burke worried that the revolutionary spirit was being spread "chiefly by newspaper circulations, infinitely more efficacious and extensive than ever they were." This heady moment would, however, last only until the Terror, which ended not just the free press but also the lives of many journalists. Napoléon Bonaparte's dictatorship was a fierce enemy of journalistic liberty. Even during the Third Republic, when the press was uncensored, it was corrupt, often taking orders from the government.[3]

Napoléon III, too, did his best to crack down on France's fledgling free press, imposing harsh censorship. As Victor Hugo furiously wrote:

> We have three-fourths of the republican journalists deported or proscribed, the remainder trailed by mixed commissions, scattered, wandering, hiding from every eye. Here and there, . . . in four or five journals still independent, but closely watched, with the club of Maupas wielded above their heads, fifteen or twenty courageous writers, serious and high-minded men of pure and generous soul, still write with a chain around the neck and a ball hanging from the leg.

Government officials would tell the press which articles to write—and which not to. The administration would write up its own pro-government editorials and distribute them to provincial newspapers, which would slavishly reprint them with fake bylines. The imperial sword hung over every aspect of the business: newspapers needed imperial permission to open shop; editors and owners alike had to be to the regime's liking; each issue was taxed. Errant newspapers got three strikes: a warning each time they published something out of line, and a two-month suspension after three warnings, which would usually be enough to drive the paper out of business. More insidiously, the Second Empire used patronage: the subservient were given government notices to publish, and the independent-minded were starved. Worst of all, the press could simply be paid off, even by savvy foreign countries like Prussia and Italy. Bismarck provided 5,000 francs monthly for bribery in 1859, and bought the *Presse Libre*'s content outright for 1,500 francs. The editor of *Le Figaro*—today probably France's most respected conservative newspaper—once bragged, "Here's the best number we've ever had; every line of it is bought and paid for."[4]

Despite all this, France's liberals and democrats were far from extinguished. Napoléon III's censorship was a kind of homage that imperial vice paid to democratic virtue: a recognition of the power of the press and public opinion, important enough that the emperor had to channel them to his political advantage. The Second Empire went to great pains to track French public opinion as it really was, based on secret Justice Ministry and prefect reports, rather than France's lapdog press. These often showed French sentiment running against imperial policy.[5]

There were still plenty of French citizens who dared speak their minds. No French leader, republican or imperial, could fail to understand the importance of keeping on the right side of public opinion. In October 1860, out of 226,000 newspapers in total, there were about 95,000 progressive newspapers being printed, as against about 57,000 official imperial papers. That progressive number was roughly the same as the circulation of the *Times* in Britain at the same time. Even if the progressive editors had to watch their step, they were a potent force. From exile, Victor Hugo wrote, "What the *fellah,* what the proletarian, what the pariah, what the sold negro, what the oppressed white, what all hope: the chains are a network, they hold them all." In the early 1860s, Baudelaire primly noted in his journal, "Every newspaper, from the first line to the last, is nothing but a tissue of horrors. Wars, crimes, thefts, lecheries, tortures, the evil deeds of princes, of nations, of private individuals; an orgy of universal atrocity. And it is with this loathsome appetizer that civilized man daily washes down his morning repast."[6]

On the eve of the Syria crisis, Napoléon III was in mounting trouble at home. Despite all the patronage and menace, he was unpopular with much of the French electorate, now about 9.5 million strong. Hugo, a stout republican, called for abstention as a sign of principled rejection of what he saw as sham ballots of a dictatorship. It took real courage not to vote for the emperor. Mayors and other officials tried (with decreasing effectiveness) to influence the voting; the police often stepped in; the press was supposed to print only moderate criticism from opposition candidates; and the government's ballots were printed on white paper, allowing anyone to see a voter's choice with frightening ease.[7]

Despite that, in the 1857 elections, Napoléon III's government got 86 percent of the votes cast, with only about 14 percent voting against him. But 38 percent of potential voters chose to abstain altogether, which suggests that huge numbers of Frenchmen either opposed Napoléon III outright or lacked confidence in the Second Empire. Things only got worse with time: 665,000 antigovernment votes in 1857, almost 2 million in 1863, and 3.3 million in 1869.[8]

Adding fuel to the fire, in 1859, French Catholics were enraged at Napoléon III for sending troops to help Sardinian revolutionaries, who menaced Vatican-controlled Romagna. Catholic fury forced him to impose new crackdowns on the press. The prince-president urgently needed to find some way to improve his standing at home.[9]

Napoléon III and the Middle East

In 1860, the world's attention was fixed more on crises far from the Middle East—on matters like chaos on Italy and the impending outbreak of civil war in the United States. France, though, had a clear interest in the Middle East. Napoléon III hoped to maintain and strengthen the French empire in North Africa. Napoléon Bonaparte had conquered Egypt in 1798, only to be driven back by British, Ottoman, and Egyptian forces. In 1830, France had invaded Algeria, which was later declared part of France. As far back as King Louis XIV, the eastern Mediterranean had been dominated by France, but new European challengers were making their presence felt. So the Second Empire wanted to restrain Russia and Britain, which had an overwhelming naval superiority in the Mediterranean.[10]

France's claim to a special status as a defender of Middle Eastern Christians dated back at least to 1535. The great Catholic power had a long-standing relationship with the Maronite churches in Syria, whose doctrine hewed close to Catholicism. Since the 1856 Treaty of Paris, which ended the Crimean War, the Concert of Europe had claimed the right to oversee the Ottoman Empire's treatment of its Christian minorities. But repeated European encroachments on the empire had solidified resentment of Christians among many Muslims.[11]

The Ottoman Empire's grip on Syria was increasingly tenuous. It had briefly lost control of the province to Ibrahim Pasha, the brutal Egyptian commander in the Greek war of independence. Britain and France both supported the Ottoman Empire's subsequent war to regain Syria. But this left the Ottoman authorities in Syria weak and compromised. Even the calls for liberalization and reform coming from the Sublime Porte in Constantinople seemed, in the far-flung provinces of the weakened empire, too obviously an European imposition.

The rest of Europe was concerned about France, not Syria. Britain in particular was increasingly alarmed by the resurgence of France under the aggressive and blustery Napoléon III. On the eve of the outbreak of massacres, Syria was far away from European minds.[12]

CHAPTER FOURTEEN

The Massacres

"Blood Ran in Torrents"

In the late 1850s, ethnic and class tensions ran high in Syria. In particular, trouble seemed likely between two large rival groups: the Maronite Christians and the Druzes. The Maronites had the support of French agents, which earned France the resentment of many Druzes. Since European interventions in 1841 and 1845, Mount Lebanon, while still under Ottoman sovereignty, had been under a special administration: a kind of semi-independence for two special Maronite and Druze self-governing districts, ruled by Ottoman-appointed governors (*qaymaqams*). The Maronites, anticipating further turmoil with the Druzes, rallied the other local Christian factions to their side. Many Muslims, still resentful of European interference during the Crimean War, lined up with the Druzes. By 1859, Muhammad Kurshid Pasha, the Ottoman governor-general of Sidon Province, was hard-pressed to prevent open violence. A particularly brutal season of war seemed all too likely.[1]

The chief French official monitoring the impending catastrophe was Stanislas d'Aragon, Comte de Bentivoglio, the consul general in Beirut. Bentivoglio would become the main French witness to the unfolding bloodbath. He had close ties to the Maronite clergy, who provided him with a rich source of information, although they were also some of the chief instigators of the imminent war. His reporting was therefore extremely detailed and extremely slanted, even if the sincerity of his horror at the massacres cannot be questioned. In March 1860, Bentivoglio could feel trouble brewing. The Ottoman authorities, he thought, did not mind seeing "disorders burst in the Lebanon." Bentivoglio warned the Maronite militants that they were risking disaster.[2]

In May 1860, some of those Maronite Christians rashly prepared to start a broader war against the Druzes. Said Bey Junblat (Djumblat), the most influential Druze leader and a relative moderate, tried to avert further unrest, but it was too late. On May 28, Maronite troops made a fatal act of overt aggression: crossing the Dog River, into ethnically mixed territory. The next day, they attacked the Druzes in multiethnic villages—the first shots of the civil war. In furious retaliation, the Druzes burned Maronite villages and sacked monasteries and churches. Although the Maronites had started the war, it was clear from the start that they were militarily no match for the Druzes. At the end of May, Bentivoglio, while too hazy on the facts to ascertain who the aggressor was, reported: "Civil war is declared."[3]

The Maronite militants had made a terrible mistake. "The local Government," Bentivoglio wrote, "perhaps out of powerlessness, perhaps out of ill will, has only weakly acted to stop the misfortunes." In the mixed districts, Christian villages were in flames. Even the main strategic Maronite strongholds, Zahleh and Dayr al-Qamar, were threatened. So far, Beirut itself did not seem to be in danger, but the city was flooded with women, children, and the elderly, fleeing the fighting elsewhere.[4]

Druze resentment against France ran high. Bentivoglio condemned as "absurd" the "false rumor" among Druzes that the French consulate was authorizing and encouraging the Maronite militants. Bentivoglio, not particularly credibly, tried to spread word of France's "complete neutrality." On May 31, he brought his British, Austrian, Prussian, and Russian counterparts to urge the Ottoman governor Kurshid to "make peace and stop the massacre, the fire and the pillage." Kurshid blamed the trouble on militant Maronites in Beirut, many of them under European protection. The united European consuls pledged to Kurshid to use all their influence to restrain the Christians, on the condition that Kurshid did likewise with the Druzes.[5]

Even before the fighting began in earnest, European forces were braced to step in. On May 25, a French war sloop and a small British ship, HMS *Firefly,* cruised near Beirut in anticipation. Weeks before they would receive instructions mailed from their home capitals, the European consuls flexed military muscles. The first instance was the intimidating appearance at Beirut of the fifty-two-cannon Russian frigate *Vladimir,* carrying six hundred troops ready to land, which Bentivoglio noted with satisfaction, "produced a very good effect."[6]

Bentivoglio persuaded the British consul in Beirut, Noel Moore, to send that small British warship, the *Firefly,* to Sidon (Sayda). This, too, was a success, as a British colonel wrote: "The Moslems hourly vowed death to the Christians; but the opportune arrival of Her Majesty's ship Firefly . . . overawed the dark designs." But the *Firefly*'s was only a partial victory. Jezzin and Hasbayya had been pillaged and burned. Outside Sidon, Bentivoglio reported, Christian refugees from the interior "were pitilessly massacred by the Muslims of the town." In the town, the Christians were safe: "They owe their salvation to the presence of the little English vessel that we sent there."[7]

The European consuls blamed the local Ottoman government. Bentivoglio feared that the fighting could spread to Acre, Tripoli, and other mixed communities in the region. He repeatedly visited Sisters of Charity Hospital to see wounded Christians. Fearing that the Christians could not mount an effective defense, the alarmed consuls sent an "urgent *démarche* to Kurshid Pasha that he use all the means in his power to stop the Druses." The consuls claimed they had restrained the Christians for three days from any further aggression against the Druzes, as Kurshid had asked. Bentivoglio began to press for European intervention: "If the Eastern Question is going to be raised again, what has actually happened provides ample material for action for those who do not wish to sit any longer as indifferent spectators to an intolerable situation." As one British colonel would claim, the fighting looked to European onlookers like a war of extermination: "Not a male adult Christian was to be spared. . . . [W]hen the Christian race had been all but extirpated from among them [the Druzes], and the lands which they had usurped through a long series of years had been restored to their ancient owners, their part of the Lebanon would, as of yore, become the 'Mountain of the Druzes.' "[8]

The naval buildup continued. On June 14, the commander of the French station in the eastern Mediterranean, Baron de la Roncière le Noury, arrived in Beirut aboard his flagship, the frigate *Zénobie.* Kurshid's remonstrations seemed to have blunted the Druze offensive, but only momentarily. On June 11, there was a massacre of disarmed Christians in Hasbayya, followed by another massacre in nearby Rashayya. According to one account, some Druzes at Hasbayya called out, "Give him a slash for the French," and "Another for his consul." Six days later, Bentivoglio reported "horrible scenes" from Hasbayya, with fifteen hundred Christians put to the sword. The richest Greek Catholic convent in Lebanon, near Sidon, Bentivoglio wrote, was "pillaged, burned, and demolished." He blamed Said Bey Junblat, the powerful Druze leader. Many European observers came to see Junblat—however unfairly—as the mastermind of the slaughter.[9]

The strategic Maronite city of Zahleh was under siege, with a pitched battle under way. If "the strongest city in the Lebanon" fell, Bentivoglio wrote, it would be a "disaster" with unimaginable consequences. The French and British consuls agreed that Zahleh had to be saved, and got the other European consuls to quickly march to Kurshid's camp to make their demand. The Ottoman governor swiftly "formally promised to send to Zahlé all the troops he had at his disposal," under orders to get the Druzes to stand down. But, while Bentivoglio was satisfied with Kurshid's response, the French consul feared the Ottoman authorities would not be capable of halting the bloodshed.[10]

Worse, there were ominous reports from Damascus itself: "A great upheaval reigns in the city." The city government, "weak and unpopular," had been unable to stop Druze opportunists from descending on Damascus. After a three-hour talk with Kurshid, who promised to stop the Druzes, Bentivoglio wrote, "The Government of the Sultan seems to me menaced by the indigenous Arab element, always ill-disposed against the white race of Turks."[11]

The Maronite leaders had had enough. They begged Kurshid to restrain the triumphant Druze forces, and consulted with Bentivoglio about terms for peace with the Druzes. The Druzes wanted a deal to shield themselves from punishment for the massacres. Bentivoglio, while sympathetic to Christian demands for reparations, told the Maronites that it was "urgent to make peace in order to suspend the bloodshed, and to stop the murders." He suggested that the Ottoman Empire consider "making severe inquiry into the causes of these events, and inflicting punishments on those, Druses or Christians, who were the provocators."[12]

But there were limits to Ottoman imperial control. The European consuls asked Kurshid to personally go to besieged Zahleh, offering to accompany him. Kurshid, without enough troops, did not manage to stop the Druze army from marching on Zahleh. After days of pitched battle, the strategic town bloodily fell on June 14. Then a massacre of Zahleh's Christians began. The Druzes also reportedly killed French missionaries. According to eyewitness reports to Bentivoglio from two monsignors who had been there, one Christian's "head was sliced and broken into small pieces that were distributed to the crowd." The Druzes next attacked the Ottoman seraglio and began "to massacre the Christians; nothing is respected; nothing is spared; neither age nor sex stops them: women, children, elderly, fall with the men. . . . This massacre lasted four hours; blood ran in torrents." The French consul estimated almost a thousand dead.[13]

Next came Dayr al-Qamar, falling, as Bentivoglio had dreaded, to "an implacable hatred." The small Ottoman garrison there was powerless to stop the defiant Druzes. The town's inhabitants surrendered without resistance, but hundreds were reportedly massacred anyway. The British consul had begged Junblat to use his influence to spare the town, but by the time his letter was penned, the killing had already started. Bentivoglio, with blazing fury, wrote: "Said Djomblat . . . could not forgive Der el Kamar for escaping Druse domination and especially for being, like Zahlé, an important, strong and rich city." Without proper evidence, Bentivoglio accused Junblat and the other Druze leaders of openly calling for a massacre of all the town's inhabitants. The French consul's report, estimating over two thousand deaths, was gory:

> Children's throats were cut on the knees of their mothers, women and girls were violated and broken in front of their husbands and their fathers. They carved up the men in the streets with axe blows. Women were burned after being bathed in the blood of their children.

The Druzes, he wrote, finished by sacking and burning the church and convent, and killing all the monks. The consuls had beseeched Kurshid to come to Dayr al-Qamar's rescue too, but again the Ottoman authorities, according to Bentivoglio, had not been strong or willing enough. Kurshid arrived too late, to find the city in ruins, with the roads blocked by corpses and birds feeding on them. Two British warships ferried over twenty-three hundred survivors—half of them women and children—of the Dayr al-Qamar massacre to safety in Beirut. Refugees flooded toward Beirut and Sidon.[14]

The consuls had already heard the grim news from Zahleh by the time they, on June 20, received official instructions from their ambassadors in Constantinople. Now acting on identical orders from the respective embassies, the European consuls in Beirut once again harangued Kurshid. They sent a joint démarche to the Ottoman governor: "The Five Powers . . . deplore and condemn the regrettable conflicts between the Druzes and the Christians," and would be happy to help end them.[15]

By now, the war was at the consuls' doorsteps. Despite the arrival of an Ottoman man-of-war at Beirut, refugees were fleeing. Bentivoglio reported that, in Beirut, Muslims were throwing little wooden crosses into the streets beneath the feet of Christians. Christian refugees were hiding in the European consulates, as well as the homes of moderate Muslims. So, as Bentivoglio was returning from a meeting with an Ottoman official, a local Muslim screamed at him, "Here is the wretch who's keeping the murderer hidden with him. I'm going to kill him." The Muslim swung a sword at the French consul. Although glancingly hit, Bentivoglio did not have his assailant killed, instead saying, "That man is crazy, let him go."[16]

On June 22, also in Beirut, a young Maronite refugee was accused of killing a Muslim boy. The city teetered on the brink of chaos: a Muslim mob called for "severe and prompt justice," and Christians were gripped by fear. But the young Maronite, despite his protestations of innocence, was hastily sentenced to death by an Ottoman judge. And the European consuls, despite bad consciences, supported the execution to keep the peace. The crowds dispersed.[17]

Sidon, too, trembled on the brink. Kurshid dashed to the mixed city, now swollen with refugees. After reports of an imminent attack in Sidon, Bentivoglio sent France's flagship frigate *Zénobie* and a steam sloop, which landed thirty-five men and a field artillery piece in the port. The British consul sent two warships. The Ottoman garrison seemed weak, but the Ottoman authorities sent a ship of the line, carrying four hundred troops. In Sidon, at least, the peace was kept.[18]

Still, the local European officials had given up on the Ottoman government. On June 27, the Austrian, British, Prussian, and Russian consuls met at Bentivoglio's residence, and, taking matters into their own governments' hands, drew up a joint letter to the Druzes formally demanding an end to the war and the massacres of Christians. They warned that the ongoing "pillage, massacres and devastation" met their "highest disapproval." Menacingly invoking precise instructions from their embassies, the consuls reminded the Druze leaders that "our governments cannot watch with indifference the continuation of this state of affairs." At the same time, the consuls also sent a sympathetic note to the Christian leadership, notifying them that the European powers had sent "a very lively and very energetic letter" to the Druze chiefs, while asking the Christian authorities to do everything in their power to avoid any aggressive steps. The consuls also once again urged Kurshid to bring about "the immediate pacification of the country."[19]

Junblat, the most important Druze leader, told the consuls that he was trying to restrain the Druzes but lacked authority. As even Bentivoglio had to admit, Junblat "never ceases writing to his followers to stay quiet," but other Druze leaders at first snubbed the European great powers. On July 1, the major Christian leaders met in Beirut and sued for peace with the Druzes. Their conciliatory formula, dictated by the Druzes, was "*mada ma mada*"—an Arabic expression meaning "what has passed has passed," or, as Bentivoglio disgustedly put it, "one should cover the past with a veil, to speak no more of it." That meant there would be no Christian attempt to seek reparations or vengeance. The Druzes, led by Junblat, cautiously agreed, although insisting on "impunity for the Druses and the troops." (Bentivoglio's reluctance to grant amnesty for war crimes echoes similar sentiments among human rights activists today, who are reluctant to allow thugs to evade justice in the name of stability.)[20]

"For several days, the situation seems to have been improving," Bentivoglio wrote. "We no longer hear of assassinations or pillage in the Lebanon." He continued to send more details about the "incredible atrocities" in Zahleh and Dayr al-Qamar, and about the massacres in Rashayya. But this was new information about old news. The British consul hopefully expressed "profound satisfaction that we have been thus the means of preventing further effusion of blood and the repetition of the nameless atrocities that have been perpetrated elsewhere during this deplorable war." Thanks largely to tough local Ottoman authorities, the violence had not spread to Jerusalem, Nablus, Acre, Latakia, or Hama. All told, perhaps four thousand Christians had been killed. But the storm seemed to have passed.[21]

"Humanity Demands a Prompt Intervention"

Back in Paris, the news was more than the Second Empire could stomach. It took, at best, about two weeks for letters to get from Beirut to Paris or London. (By contrast, from London to Paris, it took a single day.) There was still no telegraph line between Beirut and Damascus. So Bentivoglio's first reports of massacres in Hasbayya and Zahleh did not reach the Foreign Ministry at the Quai d'Orsay until July 5.[22]

Immediately Edouard-Antoine de Thouvenel, the French foreign minister and a former ambassador to the Ottoman Empire, sprang into action. Thouvenel's first step was to send the chilling dispatches from Beirut and Damascus to Lord John Russell, the British foreign secretary. From the start, France was determined above all to act in close concert with its fellow great powers.[23]

Thouvenel had good reason to hope that Russell would help. Russell had been an early and prominent Whig member of the London Greek Committee, helped pen the pathbreaking 1832 Reform Bill, and had risen to be prime minister from 1846 to 1851. Russell had applauded Britain's battle at Navarino Bay as a "glorious victory." Lord John now served uneasily in the Whig cabinet of his elderly and somewhat more conservative rival Viscount Palmerston, who was a foe of the slave trade and supporter of Catholic emancipation. Lord John's liberalism would live on after him: he would personally raise his grandson, who grew up to be the formidable philosopher and Nobel laureate Bertrand Russell.[24]

Thouvenel next sent a telegraph (the Sublime Porte itself had got a telegraph in 1855) to the Marquis de Lavalette, France's ambassador to the Ottoman Empire. The foreign minister wrote that the "scenes of carnage" at Zahleh and Dayr al-Qamar "has greatly moved the government of the Emperor." He warned of "the regrets and sympathies which the victims of these deplorable events will awake throughout Europe," and that "age-old traditions" would require a strong French response: "We do act today neither from political disagreements nor from rivalries of influence; humanity demands a prompt intervention and urgent arrangements." Thouvenel ordered Lavalette to urge the Ottoman Empire to send enough forces to "stop the bloodshed," because "the blood of Muslims ran with that of Christians" and there was no telling where it would stop. Once peace was reestablished, Thouvenel wrote, the guilty must be punished: European "public sentiment will require it."[25]

France immediately sent troops into position. Napoléon III himself met with his naval minister. On July 7, on the emperor's own command, the minister sent Rear Admiral Jehenne and two screw ships of the line, the *Donawerth* and the *Redoutable,* directly to Beirut. Several other warships were on their way. The naval minister told Jehenne to wait for consular instructions "for the mission of humanity."[26]

Thouvenel sent out identical appeals to Britain, Austria, Russia, and Prussia. Once the great powers learned the bitter facts, he predicted "the most furious repercussion in Europe." He hoped for a "unanimous" response; this was "a question of humanity, and does not comprise any difference of opinion between the cabinets." Thouvenel called not just for a cease-fire but for "steps both to put right appalling calamities and to prevent their return." He proposed the creation of an international commission, with representatives of the five great European powers and the Ottoman government. The commission would investigate the outbreak of civil war, bring guilty Syrians and Ottomans to book, pay reparations to the victims, and suggest steps to prevent future catastrophes.[27]

Thouvenel next urgently summoned Earl Cowley, the British ambassador to France. Based closely on Bentivoglio's reports, an emotional Thouvenel gave a gruesome account of "the massacres and horrors" in Zahleh and Hasbayya: "Neither sex nor age had been spared; priests, women, and children, had been indiscriminately slain; the convents had been plundered, and the Sovereign Authority being impotent, or unwilling to act, there was no saying what the next intelligence might bring." British and French warships could protect their own consulates and citizens, but that would not be enough for French public opinion. *Le Siècle,* France's main liberal newspaper, reported that Zahleh had been "entirely burned," with a thousand people killed. When the news of the massacres of Christians became widely known, Thouvenel warned, "There would be but one cry of indignation in France."[28]

France's diplomatic barrage worked. The British ambassador replied that his own government would "deplore" the massacres as much as France, and would be "most ready" to help France protect the Lebanese Christians and improve Syria's governance. But since Britain was not as reliant on Catholic networks in Syria for its intelligence, Cowley could evenhandedly point out that British diplomats thought (correctly) that the Druzes "had received considerable provocation from the Maronites." The ambassador told Russell that France's reports were based "on information given by fugitive Christians alone," and might be exaggerated. "Still," he wrote, "if but a tenth part be true, enough has occurred to excite universal reprobation."[29]

In London, Russell was not eager to be outdone by the French. He urged the Ottoman government to make the "utmost efforts to repress the disturbances in Syria." Britain quickly sent a squadron to the Syrian coast, with orders for the marines to storm ashore if their consul asked. This use of force was meant to "put an end to bloodshed and the destruction of property, and to restore tranquillity and order." By protecting Syrian Christians and British subjects on the coast "from massacre," Russell hoped to free up Ottoman forces to prevent Damascus itself from the bloodbath. Of course, from a strategic point of view, this was a disaster for the British. Having gone against their empire's interests in 1827 by helping Russia intervene in Greece, Britain now hastily bestowed more or less the same favor upon France. But British public opinion was so shocked by the massacres that Palmerston did not dare to openly stop France from coming to the rescue.[30]

France was sure that international law would allow outside intervention. Thouvenel argued that an 1845 treaty "authorized the interference of Europe." He claimed that European impositions should not be a problem for Ottoman sovereignty. In the past, he wrote, "The Porte has never made any difficulty about admitting the good offices of diplomacy" during violence in Lebanon. He thought Ottoman cooperation would be "indispensable," but suggested that his proposals "would in no way constitute an innovation or an act of intervention, the effect of which might be dreaded upon the position or the independence of Turkey." They were just "a logical consequence of an anterior understanding, to which the Porte itself lent a hand."[31]

The other great powers were even easier to persuade. Aleksandr Gorchakov, Russia's foreign minister, a puffy-faced diplomat in the middle of a long and brilliant career, was found at the royal summer palace at Peterhof, near St. Petersburg. He readily agreed to the French and British moves, with Gorchakov only afraid that the European powers "would come too late to be of much use to the unfortunate Christians in Syria." He ordered Russia's one warship off the Syrian coast to cooperate with the British squadron.[32]

A triumphant Thouvenel struck a pan-European note. He told Russell that the massacres had "caused a profound emotion" that "created duties" for "all the Cabinets"; he emphasized the proposed European commission; he praised "the harmony which was spontaneously established in the views of all the [European] Courts at the news of the massacres in the Lebanon." But he could hardly deny that France had a particular stake in the region. As Thouvenel bluntly told Russell, "The interest of France has at all times been shown in the Lebanon." Napoléon III "could not depart from" this "tradition." But he promised that "we are not actuated by any personal motive, nor by the preconceived desire of obtaining, in favour of one of the two populations between whom the conflict has arisen, any exclusive advantage. We propose to ourselves no other object than to co-operate with the Powers, by an equality of right, in the interest of peace in the East, to re-establish tranquillity and order."[33]

"The Extinction of This Evil": Sultan Abdulmecit

The Ottoman Empire saw its danger. When Sultan Abdulmecit read the French account of the massacres, he immediately summoned his foreign minister, Muhammad Fuad Pasha, and his reformist grand vizier, Ali Pasha. In a stinging sign of disgust with his army's ineffectual performance in Syria, Abdulmecit removed from his own cap the insignia of his military authority. He then told Fuad and Ali that he was counting on them to avenge the honor of his army.

The sultan invested Fuad with sweeping emergency powers in Syria. Fuad was a dashing, handsome reformer, with a broad education in medicine and diplomacy, even though he had started out as a would-be poet. Witty and thoughtful, the sultan's envoy was a Western-leaning modernizer whose selection would go down well in London and Paris. Fuad started for Syria on July 12, on the steam frigate *Taïf,* followed by two corvettes carrying soldiers and munitions. As he set off, Fuad's final words were directed at soothing France: "Tell the French ambassador that, at the risk of my life, I will wash away the stain done to the honor of the army, and that the troops will do their duty."[34]

A few days later, with the prospect of French and British intervention weighing on his mind, the sultan, in his magnificent new marble Dolmabahçe Palace—where he ruled from the largest throne room on earth—telegraphed a soothing letter to Napoléon III and Queen Victoria. Abdulmecit expressed his "grief" over the massacres, and promised to use "all means in my power to re-establish order and security here, to punish severely the guilty, whoever they may be, and render justice to all."[35]

Abdulmecit gave Fuad his orders in a special edict (*firman*). The sultan emphasized that the subjects of his vast multiethnic empire "are all equal in my eyes," and that he particularly desired "that one people should not in any mode whatsoever commit an aggressive act on another." He denounced "the cruel and tyrannical acts which have been perpetrated in Mount Lebanon" as "altogether contrary to my wish." Fuad's task was to "cease the confusion and civil war" and find those "instrumental in the odious act of shedding human blood, and immediately punish them according to the prescriptions of my Imperial Code. In a word, you are freely intrusted with the adoption of all the military and civil measures, for the extinction of this evil." Backing those words up, Abdulmecit sent a ship of the line with a thousand troops, commanded by Ismail Pasha—a choice meant to satisfy European concerns. Ismail, also known by his Hungarian name of Kmety, was a Hungarian Christian refugee who had fled to Constantinople after the Austrian Empire crushed the Hungarian revolution of 1848. His first suggestion, happily rejected, was to start bombing Beirut.[36]

"Slaughter plunder fire and alarm"

But the war was not over. On July 9, Muslim mobs gathered in Damascus, with the Ottoman authorities under Ahmet Pasha, the vali of Damascus, too weak or apathetic to stop them. One of the first targets to be burned and pillaged was the Russian consulate, where they killed the consul's dragoman. Then they stormed to the Austrian and U.S. consulates, as well as the churches, patriarchates, and monasteries in the Christian Quarter. The British consulate was spared. The next day, the violence turned to looting, with opportunistic plunderers descending on Damascus and prolonging the chaos. Although some Muslims tried to shelter Christians, the French estimated five hundred dead on the first day. By July 11, when Muslim moderates gained the upper hand and subdued the mobs, at least three thousand more Christians had been killed. In total, the British consul in Damascus figured five thousand people slaughtered.[37]

As one Syrian historian wrote at the time, "These crowds poured into the Christian quarter, killing the men. And they dismembered the little children and carried off all the furniture and possessions, and took the women and girls captive, and burnt down the monasteries and churches and houses." This Syrian writer accused the mobs of killing pregnant women and raping others, and luridly continued: "Some of the men they urged to embrace Islam, and occasionally they spared him who answered right, but then again they killed him immediately after his conversion to Islam, alleging that, if he remained alive, he would return to his error. And they killed the priests and the monks, the lame and the blind, and whichever woman attempted to defend any of her people." The crowds also turned on the Europeans in Damascus: "It was the devil who prompted them [to think] that the fire of Europe had turned to ashes and [the steel of] their swords to wood." For days, it seemed an apocalypse:

> The night was . . . like the day because the conflagration gave them light with its flames of fire. . . . And during those days [things] of this nature occurred in the Christian quarter, pitiful such as the eye had never beheld, nor the ear heard of, and by worse than which had never been moved because one saw the blood flowing like rivulets and the blaze of the fire mounting to the clouds of heaven; and the smoke obscured the face of the earth like a mist; and the uproar was echoed and reëchoed by the valleys and ravines; and the cries for help of the women and children were enough to rend the stoniest

heart. And the women ran barefoot with their bodies uncovered, and the heads [of the men] rolled like balls before the mallet.[38]

"Damascus is in flames," wrote Bentivoglio on July 11. One Syrian observer described a massacre "the like of which has not occurred in preceding ages"; Ali would later say that the slaughter was "without example not only in the history of Europe but also in that of Turkey." A British missionary reported mobs like "fiends from Hell" yelling, "Kill them, butcher them, plunder, burn, leave not one, not a house, not any thing, fear not the [Ottoman] soldiers, fear nothing, the soldiers will not meddle with you."[39]

As the city blazed, James Brant, the British consul in Damascus, urged the Ottomans "to save what remained of Damascus from destruction by fire and to stop rapine and massacre." The next day, he wrote, "we had an awful day of slaughter plunder fire and alarm and not a person in the city but trembled for his life." Although he praised some Muslims for sheltering Christians, he cursed Ahmet Pasha: "He is a craven and an imbecile." Brant, panicked and exhausted to the verge of hysteria, wrote, "If Great Britain will not come to their aid whence are they to look for it? Heaven protect these poor people." Brant went out in the Damascus streets four times to try to get the Ottomans to impose order, and (as a British official later recounted) spent ten days locked up with his wife and children, "daily expecting death, and listening to the shouts and shrieks which proceeded from the Christian quarter as the massacres were going on." He was "shattered" by the experience, and "the nervous system has given way, and he sometimes wanders in his talk."[40]

France had already been poised to act; now it was galvanized again. With the Damascus massacre, what might have been a small naval expedition would grow into a full-fledged occupation. As soon as the European consuls in Beirut heard of the massacres in Damascus, they sent a letter to Kurshid, the Ottoman governor, demanding guarantees of the safety of their consulates in Beirut and all the city's inhabitants. On July 16, Thouvenel in Paris got the first dark word of the massacre, by a telegraph from Beirut via Smyrna. Frustrated that the Ottomans had not done more, Thouvenel wrote, "In the face of these massacres, reproducing from city to city and everywhere where Christians live, it is impossible not to recognize that humanity commands the Powers to interpose their action."

This was important enough that the foreign minister decided to meet with Napoléon III to get fresh orders.[41]

By the next day, Lavalette in Constantinople had confirmed the news. Thouvenel did not know where this "pitiless war waged on the Christians" might stop, and warned that "the cabinets would not answer the just requirements of public opinion if they did not . . . stop the progress of these scenes of carnage." Although Thouvenel was pleased with the sultan's letter to Napoléon III, he thought the weakened Ottoman Empire would need European pressure to kick it into forceful action. Most important, Thouvenel wanted to expand the mandate of the French warships already on their way to Syria. The original orders given to the squadrons "cannot allow them to reach the insurrection in its center, within the Lebanon, nor especially in the cities of the interior." To do that, France would need troops under broad orders to act at liberty to stop the violence.[42]

France had shown few compunctions about sending its navy into international waters. But landing ground troops was a major step. This would require Ottoman consent. Thouvenel wrote that it would also "be essential that it was the result of an obvious agreement of the Five Courts. The intervention would be thus collective in principle," with "the European troops, sent under common views."[43]

Thouvenel went to see Napoléon III himself at his magnificent royal St. Cloud château. Time was crucial. The French foreign minister hoped for British and Ottoman consent to "obtain the satisfaction due to humanity and to contribute to the reestablishment of peace in Syria." After a long conversation, Thouvenel wrote that the emperor thought that "the state of affairs in Syria required a more active intervention on the part of Europe. Public opinion would not brook the continued suppineness of Europe in presence of such disasters. It was clear that the Porte had no authority left, and that the whole country was in a state of anarchy."[44]

After his session with Napoléon III, Thouvenel wanted more radical action: "Foreign troops might be sent and disembarked at different points along the coast of the disturbed districts." Still, France would not act unilaterally. The troops could be British or Austrian as well as French, and "the consent of the Powers should be asked before any occupation of Turkish soil should take place." Even a symbolic presence would be important: "The very fact of disembarking a few troops would strike terror into the aggressors, and restore confidence to the Christian populations."[45]

In Paris, Thouvenel continued to regale the British ambassador with the latest tales of "atrocity" from the dispatches of Bentivoglio and other

French officials. The British were stuck largely taking France's word about what had happened in Damascus; the British government would not get a reliable report, from a bourgeois Muslim source, until almost a month after the massacre. In London, Count Victor Fialin Persigny, the French ambassador, collared Russell and urged him to help. Russell took the matter seriously, and quickly Britain agreed in principle, although insisting on signing a formal convention with the Ottoman Empire and the European great powers on the terms of the mission. But Britain "will not object to the landing of French or Austrian troops in Syria." Britain "would not furnish British troops, but would have a strong force of Marines on the coast." Pleased, Thouvenel agreed to Russell's demand for a convention: "I am committed to establishing well the collective character of the participation of the Powers."[46]

His success with Britain let Thouvenel send telegrams to Constantinople, St. Petersburg, Vienna, and Berlin asking for their approval, too. Thouvenel suggested a force of ten thousand troops, all of whom could be French if necessary. As part of the proposed international convention, the European courts could determine when the European troops should be pulled out.[47]

Austria and Russia promptly agreed to the project. The Austrian foreign minister—less of a reactionary than Metternich, who had been ousted in the 1848 revolution—was eager to help "arrest cruelties so revolting to the feelings of humanity." Austria sent a frigate to Syria. Gorchakov, evidently entirely without irony, declared that, in all the times that the Russian foreign minister had taken steps to protect Christians, Russia had made no distinctions of race or cult. Russia, Gorchakov said, would see without jealousy and with pleasure and confidence the French flag flying above the riggings.[48]

There was no time to lose. The French military began assembling a full brigade of almost seven thousand soldiers, to be sent as soon as the great powers agreed. "We could not . . . arrive too early," wrote Thouvenel. "Floods of blood have already ran. The same disorders threaten to extend themselves throughout all of Syria; each moment lost could cost the life of numerous victims and add new disasters."[49]

Britain Balks

The Damascus massacre gave the Maronites a brutal incentive to end the war at once. So on July 14, Bentivoglio reported that the Christians had signed a peace deal, with amnesty for the Druzes under the rubric of "*mada ma mada.*" The rampage stopped in Beirut, and Kurshid gave formal assurances to the European consuls that order would be maintained. Still, Bentivoglio reported continued unrest: Christian refugees were fleeing, there were killings around Sidon, and "anarchy reigns every day in the immediate environs of Beyrout."[50]

The waters off Beirut were increasingly thick with battleships. On July 16, France's two screw ships of the line, the *Redoutable* and Rear Admiral Jehenne's *Donawerth,* docked at Beirut. Bentivoglio hoped that they would reassure the Christians who still remained in Beirut, although he said that most had fled. And he was encouraged by the Ottomans' replacement of Ahmet Pasha, the vali of Damascus, who had failed to stop the slaughter there.[51]

Fuad was already racing to Syria—"with fire-ships, which travelled by the strength of vapor, faster than birds," as one Syrian writer put it—when the war spread to Damascus. The gruesome news reached him when his ship, the frigate *Taïf,* was refueling, anchored at Cyprus. As a contemporary Syrian historian wrote, "It made him fume with rage and the sweet stream of his forbearance changed into a burning flame, and he accelerated his voyage to Bayrut that he might punish the guilty Muhammadans and Druzes." He arrived surprisingly early in Beirut on July 17—the same day that, near Paris, Napoléon III told Thouvenel that European ground troops would be needed. But in Beirut, Bentivoglio, impressed with Fuad's energy and firmness, was from the first ready to give him a chance: "The arrival of this high character has completely changed the situation." A few days earlier, an Ottoman ship of the line and two other warships had arrived in Beirut, bearing three thousand troops, a thousand of whom marched the next day toward Damascus. Fuad summoned the commander of the Ottoman garrison at Dayr al-Qamar and sent warships to restore order on the coast. He issued a harsh edict demanding that the violence stop immediately.[52]

Russell, in London, was relieved to hear of the peace deal. However one-sided the terms were, the British foreign secretary now thought that sending French troops would be "unnecessary" and could be at least deferred and possibly "entirely abandoned." Palmerston himself told the French ambassador at dinner that "peace between the Druses and the Maronites happily puts an end to the project of the convention," which would have undermined the sultan's prestige and authority. The ambassador replied that the real threat to the Ottoman Empire was the atrocities, which "would be the shame of Europe if they were not repressed."[53]

Thouvenel wrote, "What was this peace? It would turn out to be nothing more than the submission of the Maronites to the Druses, to save themselves from further massacre." He could not accept a peace that did not include punishment for the Druze killers and reparations for the Christians. "Was nothing to be done to prevent the repetition of such horrors?" He hoped that the Ottoman forces under Fuad might enforce a cease-fire, but he thought the Christians would see "no justice" without the presence of European troops. Thouvenel snapped that he heard with "astonishment" that Britain was balking on their agreement. He furiously reminded Russell of the Damascus massacre, which had necessitated "an immediate and energetic action." With no information about the end of violence, Thouvenel still feared the worst: "At this hour, do we know that the [Damascus] carnage . . . has not continued the following day; are we certain that it will not spread further and that Christian blood is not running in Aleppo, in Diarbekir, in Jerusalem, everywhere, in a word, where the populations are exposed to fanaticism, excited at what has come to pass in Damascus as well as in the Lebanon?"[54]

Thouvenel urged Britain to get back on board, as without a collective action there would be no action at all. He stressed France's multilateral commitments even despite the "pillage of our consulate in Damascus and the murder of French missionaries": "We have from the first had but a single thought, that of concerting ourselves with the other powers." Privately, French officials were more suspicious; Bentivoglio reported "intrigues" swirling around the British consulate in Beirut as it tried "to spare the Druzes."[55]

The Ottomans were understandably miserable at the prospect of European occupation. When the French ambassador in Constantinople proposed a convention to Ali Pasha, now serving both as acting grand vizier and foreign minister while his close friend Fuad was off in Syria, Ali showed "considerable emotion." He was convinced that "the landing of a foreign force in Syria would be the signal for other catastrophes." The sheer insult could cause unrest in Constantinople itself. Thouvenel shrugged this off. As the British ambassador in Constantinople wrote, "The Sultan and the Turkish Government are struck down by this blow."[56]

Russell was torn. On the one hand, the British foreign secretary was deeply shocked by "the most frightful" accounts from Syria. He reckoned that some fifty-five hundred people had been massacred, and that twenty thousand refugees, including new widows and orphans, were at risk of famine. (These statistics were particularly shocking since the French estimated there were 150,000 Christians in Lebanon.) Russell fumed that the Ottoman authorities in Syria had been either "inactive spectators" or actual "accomplices in the work of massacre": "At Deir-el-Kamar, Osman Pasha disarmed the Christian inhabitants, and, after eight days of privation, exposed them to be shot and cut to pieces by their ferocious enemies." These, he thought, were "exceptional circumstances" that "justify this expedition."[57]

Even so, he had reservations about a military mission. He would not commit British "land forces in the effort to prevent these massacres." If the news of the next two weeks showed that the massacres had definitively stopped, then there was no need for "the very hazardous attempt of endeavouring to tranquillize the country by foreign troops." On top of that, Russell had a new reservation, about what today would be called the exit strategy. He wanted the international convention to mandate that the French occupation last only six months: "If Syria is not tranquillized in that time, it will be clear that no period, however long, will suffice to reduce it to peace and order." Russell worried that sending foreign troops into Syria could "provoke a fiercer fanaticism among the Mussulmans" and thus further inflame Syria. So he contented himself with exhorting the Sublime Porte to "[guard] against future massacres."[58]

Thouvenel was disgusted by Britain's new reluctance. He told the British ambassador in Paris that "it was not until the attack had been made on Damascus, that he had proposed an armed expedition to Syria"—an outright lie. Thouvenel, still without information about the peace deal in Syria, warned that the massacres could still be going on in Damascus, and spreading to Aleppo and elsewhere.

Although France could have enforced reparation for the sack of its Damascus consulate and of French-protected convents, France "had no wish to act single-handed in any question arising in the East." The British ambassador pointedly asked about French-made rifles found in the hands of Maronite militants. Thouvenel admitted it was "very likely" that the war had been started by some Maronite priests, who should be punished for it. But even so, "the indiscriminate slaughter of men, women, and children, went beyond the pale of legitimate defence." Thouvenel slapped Russell with a springtime dispatch from Bentivoglio warning of a plot for "the entire destruction of the Christians at Zahlé and Deir-el-Kamar," which Thouvenel had, to his regret, written off as "too hideous to be true." Urging Russell to end his dawdling, he sent Russell fresh "disastrous news" about Damascus, where some ten thousand refugees "expected to be hourly attacked and massacred by the Mussulman population, excited by the Turkish Authorities themselves."[59]

In the end, Britain did not outright block the mission. Thouvenel was "much relieved" to be told that Britain agreed to his proposal "with reluctance" and "advised great deliberation and caution in proceeding to so exceptional a measure"—but did not withdraw their consent. The British ambassador in Paris asked Thouvenel not to undertake so dangerous a venture lightly; Thouvenel, out of patience, did not answer. But France seemed happy to meet most of Russell's terms: paying for the troops, "limiting the number of troops to be employed, and fixing the period of occupation." Although the French commander would keep full responsibility over his soldiers, these troops could be called "auxiliaries . . . operating on behalf of Europe in concert with the contingents of the other powers." Thouvenel pointedly called for the great European powers to gather in Paris, rather than in Constantinople, to draw up and sign the formal convention.[60]

On July 25, word was sent to French officials in Syria to begin preparations for the arrival of occupying troops. The Syrian Christians greeted this news, Bentivoglio wrote, with "undisguised joy," while Muslims glowered and the Druze leadership verged on outright panic. In an open letter, Napoléon III piously denounced the "pitiful jealousies and unfounded distrust of those who suggested that any interests except those of humanity had induced him to send troops to Syria."[61]

CHAPTER FIFTEEN

Public Opinion

"The Avant-Garde of the Armies and the Chancelleries": France

So soon after the revolutions of 1789 and 1848, no French government dared ignore its own public. With the Second Empire depending on elections to provide its legitimacy, Napoléon III had to be keenly aware of his unpopularity, although his executive power gave him opportunities to mold public views that were simply unavailable to British politicians like Palmerston and Russell.

As the Syrian crisis broke, the prince-president was already in trouble at home with Catholics, after a series of embarrassing Italian and papal crises. Around the same time, he sent French troops to China in imperial reprisal for the killings of Catholic missionaries, winning the Catholics the right to hold Chinese land—a clear sop to Catholic opinion at home. In 1858, over objections from his foreign ministry, Napoléon III sent a colonial fleet to begin conquering Vietnam, nominally in defense of beleaguered Catholic missionaries there. It is likely that he thought that a pro-Maronite mission to Syria would help to reaffirm his stature at home.[1]

As one observer noted at the time, the horrifying news from Syria provoked "a veritable explosion of public opinion against the Turkish government." Although the French press did not dare get too far out in front of government policy, progressive newspapers took the lead. *Le Constitutionnel,* a prominent government paper, printed four to five times fewer stories about Syria than the major liberal newspaper, *Le Siècle.*[2]

Telegraphs relayed the basic outlines of the Syrian massacres back to France with startling speed. Thus, French newspaper readers would have seen a fragmentary notice of the massacre at Dayr al-Qamar a full week *before* Bentivoglio sent his report on that town to Thouvenel. From late June, French readers of *Le Siècle* knew that Syria was imploding. There was little independent reporting, with French editors relying instead on British legwork. Press coverage usually lagged behind what the government already knew by about a week, but it reliably caught up.[3]

With the Damascus massacre, the press coverage intensified. But the French government, having already decided on intervention by then, now allowed the press to push harder. Thus the first detailed news of the Damascus massacre came from the official *Moniteur,* reprinted the next day in the other newspapers. *Le Moniteur* also carried a report from the naval minister, relying on the French squadron at Beirut for its information. *La Patrie,* another government paper, added more details. The Paris press immediately predicted strong European intervention.[4]

It was only after the government had given the cue that the liberal French press began to editorialize, although *Le Siècle* did so heartily and with an implicit rebuke of the French government for not acting sooner. One obsequious nobleman dared to write to Napoléon III that "the world is indignant." As with the Greeks forty years before, there were public subscriptions from all over France to pay for relief efforts for Syrians. The Paris press continued to rely heavily on the French government press and the navy for its information.[5]

Since progressive newspapers like *Le Siècle* reached far more readers than the official imperial press, the liberal championing of the Syrian cause put serious pressure on the French government. But even the liberal press voiced almost no criticism of Napoléon III's government, although anger at British obstructionism was perfectly acceptable. Still, *Le Siècle* proudly editorialized: "Public opinion . . . engages the battle; it determines the issues on which governments must take action; it takes the initiative, and marches in the avant-garde of the armies and the chancelleries." The paper demanded action in keeping with "the traditional policy of France, the interests of humanity and those of civilization."[6]

The final source of nongovernment writing was the Catholic press, led by *L'Ami de la Religion.* It relied on flame-throwing reports from Syria by François Lenormant, who would quickly pad them into a histrionic book. The contemporary French histories of the massacres were written mostly by Catholic expansionists, basing their writings on Christian victims' accounts. This meant that French information about Syria was mostly drawn either through government or Catholic sources, both heavily reliant on Maronite Christians in Syria. Small wonder the Druzes and Ottomans would feel that France was deaf to their side of the story.[7]

The French government repeatedly invoked public opinion throughout the crisis. Even the Ottoman government believed that European public opinion demanded intervention. Ali told the French ambassador that he had urged the sultan to allow a French military deployment because he understood "the feelings that may exist in Europe." Once Napoléon III had decided to act, this public pressure even became useful to him.[8]

All the same, French public pressure could only run as far as the emperor let it. The emperor did not have to worry about the kind of rancorous domestic dissension and partisanship that gave such headaches to British politicians. Accounting for the relative sizes of the electorate, Napoléon III faced far less media pressure than his British counterparts. If the French public had demanded something truly obnoxious, Napoléon III might have refused. But since a mission to Syria was not too high a price to pay, the prince-president seemed ready to win support at home by a self-declared humanitarian adventure in Syria.

"No Political Objects Can Make Us Forget the Claims of Humanity": Britain

Things looked different in London. Britain's official reluctance ran afoul of its public opinion. As one European observer in Syria noted, "The general irritation against the Turks was such, even in England, that the government did not dare to articulate its veto categorically." Knowing this, Thouvenel continued to flog British officialdom with whatever bad news he could get from Syria.[9]

Britain's own official information was less detailed, less biased, and more equivocal than France's. The reporting of the British ambassador was a mass of conflicting intelligence: predicting that the Druzes would back off, then belatedly realizing that something awful was happening, but not knowing exactly what. He lamely concluded, "There can be little doubt that something of the kind reported has taken place, but the details and the extent of the mischief it has caused have, I think, as yet to be ascertained."[10]

But British newspapers were tougher. The British press, free from the political pressures on their French colleagues, produced less but more independent coverage. In July, *Le Siècle* ran more stories on Syria than the *Times,* although the *Times* narrowly overtook *Le Siècle* the next month. But while *Le Siècle* was carefully marching along with French policy, the *Times* was pushing against British policy. As Russell was deciding whether to help the French troops, the *Times* was running copious coverage of the

Syrian massacres—about the same amount as the newspaper had given to the Scio slaughter back in the feverish month of August 1822. While Russell stalked the slowly decaying old Foreign Office houses on Downing Street and Fludyer Street, outside the literate classes were reading about the massacres in Hasbayya, Dayr al-Qamar, and Zahleh.[11]

In its first editorial, on July 10, the *Times* admitted it had no clue about the cause of the fighting, but warned that if Damascus fell it would be "the signal for a general extermination of the Christians in Syria." The editors wrote, "England will be untrue to her nature if she does not aid in repressing atrocities which surpass anything that has of late years been perpetrated." The editors understood perfectly well that this went diametrically against Britain's strategic interest in backing the Ottoman Empire: "We have been obliged to support the most wretched, in order to save ourselves from the most formidable, of despotisms. The SULTAN rules in the North through our jealousy of Russia, and in the South through our jealousy of France." Still, "no political objects can make us forget the claims of humanity. If the PORTE cannot repress these outrages the Christian Powers must do it. . . . An intervention there must be." Inspired by the editorial, Moses Montefiore, the most prominent Jewish leader in Britain, wrote a letter suggesting the formation of a committee to gather subscriptions, contributing £200 as a start.[12]

By then, the Damascus massacre was starting. The *Times* broke the news, in a Reuters telegram from Vienna based on official sources, on the same day as *Le Siècle* did. Horrified, the *Times* editorialized that "all our worst fears" had been realized, and feared Aleppo or Jerusalem could be next. The editors wrote, "This frightful event must remove the scruples of the most cautious politician," which must have made Russell and Palmerston wince. "Instant action must take place to save the world from crimes which will be a reproach to it for ages." The Constantinople correspondent gave a sickening account: "Upwards of 1,500 living bodies to be hacked to pieces" in Hasbayya, the entire male population of Dayr al-Qamar "put to the sword," an "extensive massacre" of the men in Zahleh.[13]

When word of the peace between the Druzes and Maronites was announced, the *Times* editorialized against impunity for the Druze killers and warned that new massacres could break out at any moment. Although the editors preferred "to occupy the country only under a convention" with the Ottoman Empire, if that was impossible, then "in the name of humanity let us disregard etiquette, and put an end at once to these horrors."[14]

Unlike in France, though, professional British newspaper coverage presented a much more evenhanded view of Syrian politics. The *Times*' Constantinople correspondent blamed the Maronites for starting the war. And the *Times* acquired a special correspondent in Beirut, whose reporting lacked the one-sided bias of the French press. The reporter exonerated Said Junblat of leading the massacres, and reported stories of Maronite aggression and atrocities. All told, the British government came under great public pressure to save Syria, but as time went on, the free and serious British press gave its readers a more nuanced view. This would, in the months ahead, give Russell more flexibility.[15]

The Paris Conference

France planned to send sixty-eight hundred troops to Syria, under the command of General Charles-Marie-Napoléon Brandouin, the Marquis de Beaufort d'Hautpoul. Despite the fancy name, he was a blustering, boorish soldier who "knew every inch of the country." Chillingly, France's chief peacekeeper had previously worked in Syria alongside the Egyptian commander Ibrahim Pasha, demonized in Europe as a major villain of the Greek war.[16]

On July 26, the haughty ambassadors in Paris gathered for their first session. The Ottoman ambassador, Ahmed Vefik Effendi, was French-educated and worldly: he reputedly spoke sixteen languages, was fond of Dickens and Shakespeare, and translated Hugo and Molière into Ottoman Turkish. But he did not hide his disdain for the Greeks and Syrian Christians ("those terrible people"). Vefik had the miserable task of trying to stall and divide. His orders were to protest against having foreign troops in his country, but to agree to it if the five great powers were unanimous.[17]

Thouvenel, needing unanimity, was at his most agreeable. He accepted Russell's proposal for a special protocol, modeled on one signed by Palmerston in 1840, in which France would renounce any political or commercial advantages from its mission. He seemed likely to agree to the six-month time limit that Russell wanted. And Russell was pleased about the international commission of inquiry that the five great powers and the Ottoman Empire were to set up. The commission's main goal was "the future peace of Syria." But Russell thought there could be no peace without justice: "Internal peace cannot be obtained without a speedy, pure, and impartial administration of justice. Those who suffer wrong, and see that wrong committed with impunity, take punishment into their own hands, or rather substitute revenge for due and legal retribution." Pushed by British public opinion, jolted into action by the Damascus massacre, and with France meeting all his key terms, Russell could hardly say no now. "It is to be hoped that the measures now taken may vindicate the rights of humanity, so cruelly outraged in Syria," he wrote.[18]

The Ottoman Empire made one final last-ditch attempt to play Britain off against France. In Constantinople, Ali, while accepting the European troops and expressing a "horror . . . most profound" at the massacres, warned that the occupation of Damascus and other cities might spark Muslim fury. In London, the Ottoman ambassador, Constantine Musurus, told Russell that the Ottoman Empire regretted the recent upheaval more than anyone, but warned that resentful Syrian Muslims might be "unable to appreciate the true intentions of Europe," resulting in more unrest. Would not Fuad's mission, which did not "injure the right of sovereignty" of the sultan, suffice? These were good arguments. But after the Damascus massacre, Russell had no patience for them. He snapped that he knew well the "evils" of an occupation, but "[n]othing but the extreme misconduct of the Turkish Pashas" could have made Britain "consent to the proposal of France; and even the massacres of the Lebanon might have been left to the vigilant justice of Fuad Pasha, had not the disastrous news from Damascus shown that even in one of the principal cities of the Empire the Turkish Authorities were incapable of protecting the lives of the Christians."[19]

So the Ottoman Empire unhappily gave up, with as much grace as possible. Ali, carefully noting European public opinion, urged the sultan to accept French occupation. He told Vefik in Paris, "His Majesty [Abdulmecit] has been more deeply impressed than any one else by the afflicting events of Syria." Ali set out his rather meek terms for a French occupation: that the French troops move in concert with the Ottoman authorities, that the numbers of soldiers be limited, and that there be some deadline for their withdrawal. He agreed to French military intervention: "If it please God, the matter will be soon settled in accordance with the wishes of the sympathising heart of His Majesty, those of all right thinking Mussulmans, and of Europe itself."[20]

Thus on July 31, the ambassadors assembled again in Paris and agreed to a convention with remarkably little fuss.

Thouvenel, gracious in victory, said that this "should not be considered in the light of a French expedition," but that France had been "delegated by Europe to undertake it." At first, only six thousand French soldiers would go, and the Ottoman Empire would have to consent if any more were needed. In that case, Thouvenel hoped "the other Powers" would send troops, too. As to the time limit, he thought "six months would more than suffice for the restoration of tranquillity in Syria, and . . . troops of occupation might well be brought away within that time." If the French mission became bogged down due to illness or bad weather, the European courts could reconvene to discuss an extension.[21]

The only discordant note came not from France, but from Russia, seeing a chance to score points off its hated Ottoman rival. As Fuad would once write, Russian expansion "towards the East is a fatal law of the Muscovite destiny. If I had myself been a Russian Minister, I would have overturned the world to have conquered Constantinople." So now the Russian government demanded that the convention be applied to other parts of the Ottoman Empire where Christians might need protection. What even France saw as a special case, Russia was trying to make general. Austria and Prussia, the other reactionary courts, quickly agreed. But the stunned Ottoman ambassador protested and refused to sign a convention that was about to become "a direct attack upon the independence of his Sovereign." Thouvenel heatedly told the ambassador he could not walk out without instructions from Constantinople. Cowley, the British ambassador, flatly refused the Russian proposal. Retreating, the Russian ambassador suggested leaving the general question open for later discussion. Cowley again refused. Thouvenel, seeing the wheels falling off the wagon, told the Russian to back off.[22]

On August 3, the five European great powers and the Ottoman Empire signed a protocol to send troops to Syria, plus an additional protocol renouncing any self-interested motives. The main protocol grandly began with the sultan "wishing to stop, by prompt and efficacious measures, the effusion of blood in Syria," and the European powers "having offered their active co-operation"—the kind of glossy statement for which the diplomats earned their salaries. A "body of European troops," which could be increased to twelve thousand men, would "be sent to Syria to contribute towards the re-establishment of tranquillity." France would immediately supply half of this body. The European great powers (except for a delinquent Prussia) would also keep substantial naval forces off the Syrian coast to help maintain peace. The "duration of the occupation of the European troops in Syria" would be "six months," enough "to attain the object of pacification." Napoléon III told Beaufort that he would be "much disappointed if the expedition were not back in France within three months."[23]

In the additional protocol, the Allies reminded the sultan of the need to reform his governance of Christians under a 1856 treaty. Most striking of all, to demonstrate "the true character" and "the perfect disinterestedness" of the imminent European occupation, the European courts "declare in the most formal manner that the Contracting Powers do not intend to seek for and will not seek for, in the execution of their engagements, any territorial advantages, any exclusive influence, or any concession with regard to the commerce of their subjects, such as could not be granted to the subjects of all other nations." Even as the ambassadors pledged their best behavior, that recitation of foresworn potential scams and bad dealings made it clear how rare this flash of honor among thieves was.[24]

CHAPTER SIXTEEN

Occupying Syria

"The Triumph of the Rights of Justice and Humanity"

Two European groups started getting ready to ship out for Syria: the French troops and the international commission. As in more recent nation-building exercises in Bosnia, Afghanistan, and, disastrously, Iraq, there were distinct civilian and military authorities. And, as in those cases, the commission and the troops were interlinked. Thouvenel, like the British, hoped that the commission's success would "cover the withdrawal" of the troops.[1]

The main player on the commission was Britain's representative, Lord Dufferin. He was a young Eton- and Oxford-educated aristocrat with heavy eyelids, whose sole qualification for his new job was a quick trip to Beirut and Damascus in 1859, on the way to Jerusalem and Athens. He had had almost no specific foresight of the impending disaster, beyond a "sense of general insecurity" in the entire Ottoman Empire, and his keenest Syrian memories were of ogling the young Jewish women of Damascus (whose shirts "did not cover but met at the waist beneath their bosoms, which were left quite bare"). Briefing Dufferin before he left London, Russell told him, "Seek to gain no political influence in Syria, nor allow any nation to get any."[2]

The basic outlines of the commission's task were clear enough: to investigate the cause of the massacres, to oversee "the execution of severe and impartial justice" for the guilty, to secure reparations for the Christians for their losses, and to suggest political reforms to ensure "the future order and security in Syria." Although the five European commissioners had identical instructions, there was still bickering: the British wanted to uphold Ottoman sovereignty and pointed out that the Maronites had started the fighting in the first place. Russell urgently called for "rescuing" the "Christian women who have been carried away to Turkish harems," as well as suggesting the purge of Kurshid and Ahmet.[3]

The French army was getting ready, too. Thouvenel reminded the French military that they were "intervening in a collective capacity and in the name of Europe." He ordered the war ministry to cooperate with Fuad and the other European great powers, in order to swiftly stop "the effusion of blood." As a sign of good faith, General Beaufort's instructions from the French war minister were to be circulated to the European great powers. The naval minister instructed Beaufort that his expedition was "remedial and temporary," motivated by public sympathy for the massacre victims. The minister made it clear that Beaufort was not on a mission of conquest: "It will be short and the emperor will be very satisfied if it could return in two months having accomplished its work."[4]

Napoléon III personally met with Beaufort, strictly warning the aggressive general not to "provoke public feeling" among the Druzes and Muslims. But on August 7, he gave his speech to departing French soldiers. Ignoring his own advice, he made that jarringly crude reference to the Crusades, in a way that would make the most moderate Ottoman wince.[5]

"We Must Change All Our Institutions"

Of all the Ottoman officials who could have been appalled when they heard about Napoléon III's thuggish allusion to the Crusades, pride of place must have gone to Fuad Pasha. The reformist Ottoman foreign minister, serving as the Ottoman commissioner for Syria, was the third force on the Syrian political scene. Fuad was the son of a poet who had gone on to medical school and European diplomatic postings, as well as serving as grand vizier. He was a proud and sophisticated Ottoman loyalist, dedicated to the Ottoman ideal of multiethnicity and to reforming the empire to preserve it from European predations. He was one of the driving forces behind the modernizing reforms called the Tanzimat ("reorganization"). Dufferin would admiringly call him "one of the most remarkable public men in Europe—middle-aged, tall and handsome, speaking French in perfection, with the most charming manners, and a kind and amiable character."[6]

Fuad was a man of complicated principles. Dedicated to a multiethnic empire, he extolled "the fusion of our various races." To be sure, he had no patience for insurgents; he scorned the Greeks, and, like many vastly less tolerant Ottoman officials, worried particularly about Armenian insurrections. But Fuad's main concern was saving a crumbling empire: "*The Empire of the Osmanli is in danger.* . . . For the last two centuries they [the European states] have all been moving forward, and all have left us far behind. . . . *We must change all our institutions—political and civil.*" To that end, he wanted to adopt European science, which he saw as perfectly compatible with Ottoman and Muslim principles: "Islamism alone . . . renders it our sacred duty to advance with the world, to develop all our intellectual faculties to the utmost, and to seek instruction and the light of science, not in Arabia, not amongst Mussulman nations solely, but abroad, in China, to the farthest confines of the earth. . . . Science is one. One and the same sun suffuses the world of intelligence."

In foreign policy, Fuad despised Russia, but admired Britain's strength and institutions: "*I would rather lose several provinces than see the Sublime Porte abandoned by England.*" As for France, the power that drove Fuad to Syria, he feared the "most deadly blows." France, he thought, was a "chivalrous nation," with "more of sentiment than calculation. She takes a pride in glory and great ideas." He hoped to preserve good relations, but feared that once France gave up on Ottoman governance, France would "end by causing our destruction."[7]

Fuad's mission to Syria was a chance for him to implement in microcosm in one province the kind of scientific reform that he thought would save the empire. The fact that it was being done at European gunpoint only underlined the consequences of failure.

Fuad sprang into action. Once he reached Beirut, he quickly certified it as "perfectly tranquil" after the "truce between the Druses and Maronites," directly questioning the rationale for European intervention. To show the flag, he ordered Kurshid to sail in a corvette up the coast to Latakia, and sent a vice admiral to Acre with money for wounded Maronites. He told the Ottoman chief at Aleppo "to resort to force at once" to stop any further violence, and "to devote himself and his troops to the last man." Fuad issued a proclamation to the Syrian people. In it, evoking a multiethnic Ottoman tradition that was under increasing strain, he pinned no blame on the Maronites for starting the civil war nor on the Druzes for the massacres. He simply denounced "the wicked shedding of blood." The violence had "excited the indignation and the regrets of His Majesty our Sultan, his mercy and justice extending to all his subjects equally and without distinction." He vowed to "punish the perpetrators of these crimes" and help the refugees, thus showing "Imperial justice and compassion." He warned, "Let hostilities cease altogether. . . . [H]enceforth, the Imperial troops under our command will attack any transgressing party that begins hostilities."[8]

In fact, the situation was hardly tranquil. There was sporadic violence, and refugees were still streaming out of Syria. So on July 27, Fuad marched for Damascus, with two battalions and six artillery pieces to underline his deadly seriousness. He stormed into the city two days later, bristling with military might, with the wicks of his soldiers' guns ready to fire. There were some shots fired at night, presumably by resentful Druzes or Muslims, so Fuad doubled the guards—replacing troops who had been at Hasbayya during the massacre there—and spent the night riding around the city. Fuad "showed the strongest emotion" as he visited the Damascus castle where some twelve thousand famished Christian refugees had gathered, winning over the crowd with his show of sympathy. He offered a government escort for refugees who wanted to leave for the coast. He also sent a battalion out to Hasbayya and its environs, where Christians were still thought to be threatened.[9]

Fuad arrested many of the key Ottoman officials in Syria: Ahmet Pasha, the vali of Damascus; Kurshid Pasha, the governor of Beirut; and the chiefs of the garrisons at Dayr al-Qamar, Hasbayya, and Rashayya. He began planning a series of what today might be called war crimes trials. The Ottoman officers at Hasbayya and Zahleh would be court-martialed, and Kurshid and Ahmet would face trial for letting the violence happen. This must have been personally excruciating for Fuad, since Ahmet, while out of favor at court, was a lifelong friend. Ahmet had the background of a modernizing Ottoman official after Fuad's own heart: raised in Vienna, multilingual, a bold general who had fought off the Russian army, an effective functionary. But now, as a Syrian historian recorded, Fuad had to take "from him his sword and the badges of his official dignity." To compound Fuad's distress, the British ambassador objected to this. A British vice admiral warned Fuad that the "Christian world" could not allow Kurshid to go unpunished for not stopping the Dayr al-Qamar massacre. So Fuad had to come aboard a British ship of the line—not exactly subtle symbolism—to pledge that he would prosecute Kurshid.[10]

Fuad's two battalions in Damascus wasted no time: doubling the guards at the European consulates, disarming Damascenes, and making a wave of arrests. The British consul, Brant, wrote with cruel satisfaction that the Muslims were in "the greatest panic," and "no one ventures to threaten death to the Christians in case of the landing of European troops in Syria." Bentivoglio somewhat more guardedly confirmed that Fuad's efforts had restored calm, at least on the surface. Even the wary Bentivoglio was impressed by Fuad's energy.[11]

By August 4, Fuad had arrested five hundred suspects in Damascus and had appointed an "Extraordinary Tribunal" to judge them. A few days later, immediately after France's announcement that it planned to occupy Syria, Fuad made a fresh round of arrests, bringing the total to eight hundred. The tribunal's standards of evidence and due process were merciless. Since Fuad found it hard to find anyone willing to testify to witnessing any murders—let alone the massacre of thousands—he relied on his own emergency powers. The first execution soon followed. A British major warned Fuad that "the eyes of all Europe were upon him," and recommended "summary proceedings; those of a military court, rather than the delays and quibbles of an ordinary law-court." Fuad said he agreed. His swift action already proved it. The Ottoman minister said that "any reasonable evidence was admitted, even as far as that of a single Christian against a Moslem."[12]

The imminent French intervention left Fuad, one European observer noted, in "a powerfully bad mood . . . wounded in his personal self-esteem as well in his national self-esteem." Fuad said "he yet feared some European Government would not be satisfied." To a British major, Fuad said he regretted the approaching arrival of French troops. The major soothingly replied that the French troops would not be allowed to "mix itself up in the internal affairs" of Syria, and that Fuad should deprive France of pretexts by keeping the peace. Fuad said he feared that France would find excuses anyway.[13]

As Fuad began work, the European navies gathered. One European observer in Beirut noted, "The harbor of Beirut was literally covered with French, Russian and English ships." By early August, there were at least twenty-two warships at Beirut, including a massive first-rate British ship of the line; frigates from Russia, Austria, Holland, and Sardinia; and—in a slap to the Ottomans—a Greek corvette and two gunboats. One of the British commanders might have found his mission familiar. Henry Codrington had been a nineteen-year-old midshipman on board his father's command ship HMS *Asia* during the battle of Navarino Bay in 1827, where the young sailor was shot in the leg. Following in the footsteps of his father, that midshipman rose to be a rear admiral, and now found himself commanding HMS *Hibernia* in the waters off Beirut. This gave him the unusual distinction of participating in two major humanitarian interventions.[14]

British men-of-war raced up and down the coast to protect Syrian Christians and to rescue and feed refugees. A British official successfully urged Fuad to bring relief to the Hasbayya refugees. Russell himself remained personally fixated on the fate of Christian women allegedly abducted by Druze forces, ordering Britain's ambassador in Constantinople to "press this matter most urgently on the Porte . . . it admits of no delay. The sufferings of these women must call forth the strongest feelings of sympathy on the part of all Christian nations."[15]

Despite Fuad's efforts, European officials reported that the Christians were still at risk outside the two big cities of Beirut and Damascus. Bentivoglio, impatiently awaiting the arrival of French ground troops, claimed that his consulate was overrun by victims seeking protection. The British consul sent out Cyril Graham, the British missionary who had been Lord Dufferin's guide in 1859, to Rashayya and Hasbayya, where he saw "bodies lying in every attitude on the paved court of the palace, the stones, naturally white, being stained a deep brown." The missionary reported the Druzes were "more bold and insolent" than ever, bragging of the number of Christians they had killed, threatening to "exterminate them altogether" if anyone acted against the Druzes, as well as to "cut to pieces" any military forces. In response, Fuad sent a battalion from Beirut to Hasbayya, as well as one hundred and fifty troops to Rashayya. It was a risky move, but, to Russell's relief, the Ottoman troops arrived in time to keep the peace.[16]

In such turmoil, Russell still held out the possibility of a British land force—as many as six thousand troops, should France need the help. Although Thouvenel assured the British that France had the situation well in hand, Russell declared Britain "quite ready to agree" to sending at least three thousand.[17]

Trying desperately to bring order before French troops landed, the Ottoman authorities continued their sweeps through Damascus's quarters, arresting accused killers and those who whipped up the mobs. Fuad once again expressed his "horror" at the scale of the Damascus massacre, and promised to start executions, no matter how many he had to kill. Sultan Abdulmecit himself thundered, "My heart and that of all Mussulmans, who are acquainted with God's commands, has been afflicted by the fact that a horde of perverse and ignorant persons among the inhabitants of

Damascus have, by reason of the wickedness and sordidness of their reprobate natures, . . . dared, in opposition to the divine law, to shed the blood, violate the honour, and plunder the property of a number of poor creatures, their countrymen." The sultan ordered Fuad that, while the "authors of such wickedness" would face their ultimate punishment "in the next world," it was still "most necessary that they should receive in this world also the punishment awarded both by the divine and temporal law."[18]

The next day, Fuad began to deal out harsh justice. In the bazaars and public squares of Damascus, fifty-six people who had been swiftly convicted of participating in the massacre were hanged. Their corpses remained on display as a terrifying warning. A European observer wrote, "They rushed the condemned to the gallows in a completely primitive way: the hangman hammered a nail above the door of a shop; he attached a bolt of cord which he wrapped around the neck of the victim, placed upright on a chair; then he yanked the chair, and the trick was done; the body thrashed for a moment, not more." A pedestrian strolling through the streets of Damascus was surprised to find his hat gone; looking up, he realized it had been knocked off as he walked beneath the dangling legs of a hanged man. The following day, 111 more, mostly Ottoman irregular troops accused of participating in the riots, were shot by infantry on a plain outside Damascus.[19]

This was just the beginning. Ahmet, Fuad's old friend, was convicted in Damascus, and was set to be executed. Fuad's tribunal sent more than seven hundred people to jail, forced labor, or exile. As many as four hundred prisoners were bound for Constantinople, and three thousand young men from Damascus would be conscripted in handcuffs into the Ottoman army. Fuad coolly reported, "The town is struck with terror, and no movement has been observed in the town during the executions. . . . The hand of justice is complete mistress of the situation."[20]

Fuad, personally handling all the details from examination to execution, hoped that a few more days would "convince Europe" that the French troops were not necessary. Some British officials were indeed convinced. Bentivoglio warily noted, "It is probable that if one had known in Paris and in London about the acts and success of Fuad Pasha, one would very probably have adjourned the expedition."[21]

But Fuad's grim work was not enough. The British consul, who admired Fuad, thought that the "evil . . . so exceeds all that can be imagined, except by eye-witnesses, that I fear it is beyond the means of the Turkish Government to do more than partially alleviate a very small part of so extensive a calamity." He feared Fuad was slacking his pace, and that the public was not "sufficiently intimidated" yet. With Russell's approval, a bullying British major complained to Fuad that only four or five of those executed were upper class, and that the great bulk of the guilty were still at large. Somehow Fuad's reign of terror was not quite terrifying enough for the British.[22]

Nor for the French. Bentivoglio argued that there was much that the French troops could usefully do in the interior. Thouvenel worried that assassinations were common, if not full-scale massacres. He complained that Fuad had punished lower-level killers, not the leaders. Without French pressure, Thouvenel argued, Fuad would not have the spine to decapitate a few of the most prominent officers. The French occupation was beginning.[23]

Leaving for Syria

One of the French ships was *Le Borysthène,* an elegant steamer that left Marseille on August 6, carrying five hundred soldiers from the Vincennes 16th Light Infantry Battalion. A writer aboard recorded that the suffocating heat was "truly atrocious," with cabins like "ovens in which one cannot breathe." The turbulent waves left the seasick soldiers "paying their tribute to the sea." Still, as night fell, five hundred voices belted out a martial song: "Do not fear the cannon. . . . Maybe one day you will say to others in your turn: Conscripts, weapons in arms! March with the beat! Run to victory!" The soldiers could hardly speak of anything but Syria, as they made their way to Beirut via Alexandria and Jaffa. After a stop in Jaffa, the French troops were overwhelmed with emotion when a friendly British ship's musicians played the French national anthem as *Le Borysthène* cruised out of harbor. Since Napoléon III had banned the too-stirring "Marseillaise" eight years prior, the soldiers sailed to the strains of an appropriate anthem: a gentle love song titled "Leaving for Syria."[24]

On August 16, the bulk of the French soldiers disembarked in Beirut: five thousand men strong, two hundred cavalry, with large supplies of ammunition and artillery. Some Muslim boatmen refused to transport their munitions to land. On the shore, a curious crowd gathered, silent and reserved. As one European observer wrote, "The Christians lowered their eyes, so that the Muslims could not read there the expression of their joy." Thirty European warships and three Ottoman warships loomed in the harbor. In recognition of France's leading role, the French rear admiral, Jehenne, was put in charge of all the ships except for the Ottomans'.

As the day wore on, the French soldiers, exhausted from their journey, sweltered beneath "a sun of fire." Ottoman troops helped their arrival, while French steamships carried in infantry, artillery, and horses. After a grueling march with the soldiers' faces streaming with sweat, Beaufort's force camped two miles outside of Beirut, in the magnificent pine forest. Once again, the military bands played the all-too-apt French national anthem as the soldiers made camp.[25]

The French troops were heavily armed and heavily caffeinated. The soldiers, each fearsomely armed with a rifle and a sword, wore neck kerchiefs and long double-breasted coats. This being the French army, each group of ten men also carried between them eight days' rations of coffee, a coffee grinder, and a tin basin suitable either for bathing or frying. Their knapsacks were stuffed with rifle cartridges, as well as canvas trousers, a flannel vest, and a pair of flannel drawers. This kind of heavy kit, awful for Syria in August, was at that moment helping drop other French soldiers from heat and disease in sweltering Vietnam.[26]

A platoon of Ottoman soldiers had the humiliating duty of leading the way to camp. The French and Ottoman martial bands took turns playing. As the sweaty French soldiers marched, a mob of beaming Christians accompanied them. Despite fears that Druzes and Muslims would resist, only a somber handful showed up. Christian men and women poked up their heads from behind the bushes, where they lurked to avoid being noticed by the Ottomans, and made the sign of the cross, eyes overflowing with tears. Bentivoglio cheered, "The arrival of our troops . . . has excited an extraordinary joy in all classes of the Christian Populations." The French troops were greeted with euphoria by Syria's "overjoyed" Christians, as a British official reported: "On the landing of the troops, Christian refugees relieve the men of their muskets, knapsacks, &c., which they carry for them all the way to the camp; others offer the soldiers water, tobacco, lemonade, &c., gratis." The French soldiers were deeply moved by their first encounters with refugees—a thousand miserable women and children from Dayr al-Qamar, telling harrowing stories of the massacre there. As a writer with the troops opined after hearing the refugees' accounts, "This calculation of extermination was to lead to the extinction of the Christian race in Syria." A contemporary Syrian historian wrote that the French soldiers "were in the highest state of self-exaltation and enthusiasm."[27]

Beaufort egged his men on. Like Napoléon III, the general could strike a more or less humanitarian note: "The Emperor has decided that, in the name of civilized Europe, you will go to Syria to help the Sultan's troops avenge humanity disgracefully vilified. It is a beautiful mission." But he could also sound a parochial and Christian-inflected patriotism: "In these famous lands Christianity was born, and Godfrey de Bouillon and the Crusaders, general Bonaparte, and the heroic soldiers of the Republic honored themselves."[28]

So Fuad and the British feared that the French troops might spark more violence than they would prevent. Russell fervently wanted the French soldiers to stay out of Damascus, lest they "cause a fresh outbreak of Mahometan fanaticism." But Bentivoglio confidently predicted that "the arrival of French troops more inspires fear than it excites fanaticism." If anything, he wanted more troops than the Paris convention would allow.[29]

Beaufort was warmly welcomed by the Maronite leadership in Beirut, and the French military cooperated with Jesuits there in distributing rice, flour, and cash to the Maronites. In the blazing summer heat, over twenty thousand Christian refugees were taking shelter with the Jesuits in Beirut. Just over a week after the French troops landed, Bentivoglio notified Thouvenel that his consular agents reported that Syria seemed largely quiet. Thouvenel reassuringly told the British ambassador that the French troops had no intention of going to Damascus. He added that they could "rely on General Beaufort's doing nothing to provoke public feeling."[30]

This was laughable. As one European observer in Syria noted, given the emperor's lineage, "Napoléon III must have personally felt . . . the desire to enrich the military record of France with some victory of Baalbek or of Damascus like that of the Pyramids, and to show to Europe one more time that the French flag flew everywhere there was 'a fair cause to defend.'" There was also an obvious danger of a clash with Beirut's Muslims. Warships kept bringing thousands of fresh French troops, and the Maronites were spoiling for a fight. Although Beaufort's job should properly have to be as much diplomatic as military, the aggressive general was chomping at the bit. All business, he was offended that the Austrian consulate had thrown a gala ball.[31]

Beaufort's troops were galvanized by the harrowing tales of Christian refugees, and their general was anxious to get out of Beirut. Beaufort, having almost immediately ran out of patience, wanted to march to Damascus, or to Mount Lebanon, but Fuad—at almost every step a far better politician than Beaufort—politely refused. Beaufort would never get to Damascus. No matter what, Fuad wanted Beaufort's troops to stay away from the Druzes. And Fuad insisted that the French soldiers operate alongside his Ottoman troops. Still, as an observer with the French troops wrote, "The Christians of Syria demand the liberty accorded to Greece after six years of heroic combat. . . . They do not want Turkey; they want France."[32]

Fuad made the best of it. He menacingly issued a proclamation announcing that French troops were coming due to "the illegal and inhuman" massacres, and that he hoped that the sultan's law would bring calm so there would be no need for the French troops. Fuad made a show of meeting with hundreds of mourning widows from the Damascus massacre, and pledging to support them. He urged his troops to welcome the French and British soldiers as "comrades" and "guests": "Thus, they will see . . . that you do not require to be assisted or encouraged in punishing the authors of the crimes that have been perpetrated against Christians, who are equally our countrymen, nor in exacting vengeance in the name of humanity."[33]

The Druze leaders, startled at Fuad's firmness and at the imminent French deployment, began to panic. Said Junblat plaintively reminded Fuad and the British consul that he had tried "to prevent evil." To dodge the blame, some Druzes hoped to implicate the Ottoman government instead. This was something that Fuad could not tolerate, even though one British naval officer acidly pointed out the "remarkable fact, that the only points at which serious massacres occurred were precisely and exclusively the points at which there were Turkish garrisons."[34]

Many other Syrians resented the occupation. When the French soldiers reached Beirut, Fuad had to ban all firearms in Beirut to prevent unrest, as well as launching "new measures of repression." Even so, one British official reported, "the occupation is viewed with the utmost aversion by the Mahometans; a scowl is visible on their faces as the troops march past; and their general manner is irritable and sullen, breaking out occasionally in sneers and insult to the Christians, and in some cases personal violence upon the slightest occasion or fancied provocation." There were brawls between French soldiers and Muslims.[35]

The ongoing trials, brutal as they were, did not satisfy the Europeans. Russell wanted Kurshid executed as an example. But as Fuad turned to higher-ranked officers, legal proof was maddeningly difficult to find, although hearsay and rumor were plentiful. Fuad knew that "it would hardly be believed in Europe that evidence against individuals of the higher class was so difficult to obtain." He would have formed juries, but feared they would "acquit every Moslem brought before them." So Fuad had to do the investigations himself. Even so, Russell thought that incriminating witnesses were kept away. Still, from the receiving end, Fuad's rough justice was awful to behold. As one European observer in Syria wrote, "Real terror struck the Muslims, who no longer dared to leave their houses; a doleful silence reigned in the streets, in the deserted bazaars."[36]

Throughout the crisis, the French were noticeably more pro-Christian while the British tilted toward the Druzes. As we have seen, France was influenced strongly by information from the French-aligned Maronite clergy, which had played a major role in Bentivoglio's reporting of the massacres. That Maronite influence continued during the occupation, often driving the British to distraction.

French officialdom saw the British as cynically tilting toward the Druzes, even after the 1860 massacres, as a way of offsetting French influence in Syria. At a minimum, the British took a more nuanced view of Syria's convulsions. British officials blamed the war on the Maronites, and saw little to recommend them over the Druzes. Dufferin was exasperated by talk of the Christians as "saintly martyrs." The violence "was a feud between two equally barbarous tribes, in which the victors inflicted on their enemies the fate with which they themselves had been threatened." And the British understood that many Muslims had protected Christians: Russell formally thanked the heroic Emir Abd al-Qadir for "his noble exertions" in saving Christians in Damascus, while the British ambassador in Constantinople praised the Muslim clergy and elites for saving Christian lives.[37]

Still, Britain was not quite as duplicitous as the French supposed. Although the Druze leaders somewhat desperately tried to win British protection from the double menace of the French general and the Ottoman lord, Russell was in no mood for it. The reports of British consuls made Russell think that Fuad was not doing enough. The British missionary who had been sent to see the ruins of Hasbayya had been mysteriously murdered a few weeks afterward. Russell worried that Christian refugees were still homeless, some reportedly dying from exposure to the elements.[38]

Crucially, Russell remained ready to send as many as three thousand troops to reinforce the French expedition. Alongside an equal number of Prussian soldiers, this would double the European military force. Although Russell worried of the dangers of sailing off the Syrian coast, the British ambassador in Paris told Thouvenel that Britain would send troops if needed, to Thouvenel's "great satisfaction." Marshal Randon, the French war minister, did not think reinforcements would be necessary, unless the troops actually had to fight.[39]

A key part of Britain's counterweight to France was the European commission. As one European observer in Syria noted, for Britain, "It was necessary to demonstrate at all costs that there was nothing left to do, not for the commission, above all not for the French army; it was necessary to block the activity of the expeditionary corps, to hold back the marquis de Beaufort, who burned with a natural desire to play an active role in Syrian affairs, in the enchanted pine forest of Beirut."[40]

The first of the international commissioners, Dufferin of Britain, arrived in Beirut on an Ottoman government steamship on September 2. As if for counteremphasis, a French battalion off-loaded in Beirut the same day. In Constantinople, the British commissioner had had an audience with Sultan Abdulmecit himself, where the sultan "expressed in a most energetic manner his horror of what had taken place." The international commission began holding regular meetings.[41]

Dufferin, while "[i]mbued with humanitarian ideas," started out largely ignorant of Syrian realities. Like Bentivoglio, Dufferin at first relied on European missionaries for his understanding of Syrian politics and the massacres. When he got to Damascus, the horrified British commissioner wrote to his beloved mother:

> Imagine upwards of two thousand houses utterly destroyed, and their inhabitants buried beneath the ruins. . . . As far as the eye could reach in every direction, there was nothing to be seen but vistas of ruined walls, burnt rafters, and courtyards choked up with rubbish. The utter silence made the scene all the more terrible, and gangs of dogs that went sniffing and prowling among the piled-up *débris* told all too plainly what lay beneath our feet. Such a monument to human wickedness and sorrow I have never beheld. When I left the town I felt inclined to shake off the dust of my shoes against it.

Dufferin's draft instructions had emphasized the need for "pure, and impartial administration of justice. Those who suffer wrong, and see that wrong committed with impunity, take punishment into their own hands, or rather substitute revenge for due and legal retribution." He estimated that fifteen thousand people had committed murder (three per victim), and thus reckoned that Fuad's fifty-six executions were "inadequate" to "the enormity of their crimes."[42]

Fuad was wary of the commissioners. A lordly foreign minister, he could not be too impressed with lower-ranked functionaries in their respective bureaucracies. Nor did the commissioners make much of a first impression. In his first meeting with Fuad, the Ottoman minister told Dufferin that he was "still undecided" about whether to execute Ahmet, and Fuad seemed "careful to speak almost in a laudatory manner" of the man whom the British commissioner did not seem to realize was his old friend. But after meeting Dufferin, Fuad finally had to act: Ahmet was shot in the barrack square. Three other senior Ottoman officials were executed along with him.[43]

Even after this horror, one observer wrote, the underwhelmed European great powers "saw these executions as an expedient policy, like a bloody retraction, more than the work of impartial and conscientious justice." One British major grumbled that the executions had not been public, and hoped for hundreds more death sentences for murder charges. On the other hand, the British consul, delighted at the death of a top-ranked official, gave Fuad "the highest applause for the firmness which pronounced, and the courage which carried out a sentence vindicating at once the claims of humanity and the honour of his Government"—and, as European officials failed to notice, betraying a dear friend. A *Times* special correspondent wrote that Fuad was in agony, but said he would go ahead with his duty even if it meant shooting his own brother. Fuad had earned a bitter popular nickname: "Father of the Cord."[44]

"The Whole Nation Is Struck with Terror"

There was worse to come. Although Fuad's purge in Damascus and Beirut was winding down, he now turned his attention to the interior. If Fuad had hoped to show more mercy outside the main cities, continued European pressure clearly made that impossible. The British naval forces were considering helping Fuad attack the Druzes. Fuad issued a summons to thirty-seven Druze chiefs and thirty-five Christian chiefs to come to Beirut in five days to try to clear their names, or face sentence by default—before, as Dufferin wrote, "the impending storm bursts upon the Mountain." Some of the Druzes had already fled. Junblat asked the British for a formal guarantee of his safety to obey the summons. The British, still furious that Junblat had not saved Zahleh from falling, refused to even answer his plea.[45]

Twelve Druze chiefs came to Beirut to face arrest, "like birds in a cage." One day, as Dufferin was visiting Fuad in his tent, an aide came in and whispered in Fuad's ear. Fuad turned to Dufferin and told him that Junblat himself was waiting outside the tent. He faced grim prospects. Although the Druze chiefs were supposed to get impartial trials, Dufferin did not think that any Ottoman tribunal could give a fair trial to the surrendered Druzes. He thought that the Druzes were "designated for trial by public opinion" and that their guilty verdicts had an "almost accidental" relation to the crimes. "Europe requires satisfaction," Dufferin wrote in disgust. "[T]he reputation of the Porte must be cleansed in the blood of the guilty." If there was no evidence, Fuad often would not acquit the suspect, but just skip the death penalty. The Druzes who did not surrender were branded guilty for refusing to show up, and would be punished as soon as they were caught.[46]

On September 23, thousands of Ottoman troops stormed into the interior, occupying Dayr al-Qamar and other mixed districts. Fuad cut off the Druzes' possible lines of retreat. Some two hundred fleeing Druzes were quickly killed by Ottoman troops. To stem a flood of Druze refugees, Fuad issued a notice to Druzes "given way to terror" that they would all be treated justly and that those who "served the Government and the cause of humanity, will be duly rewarded." Dufferin smugly wrote, "I hear the whole nation is struck with terror."[47]

The Ottoman forces were followed closely by French troops. The Druzes thus faced the dismal prospect of a combined attack by both, so terrifying that Fuad figured that the advance would become just "a military promenade." Still, there was a real danger that Beaufort's men might confront the Druzes in the eastern interior. "It would have been impossible to have kept General Beaufort here doing nothing," Dufferin wrote. "He is a determined man himself, his troops and officers were getting very discontented, and kept pressing him on. Fuad Pasha is mortally afraid of him, and can only get the better of him by cunning and deception."[48]

Two columns of French troops, each with about two thousand soldiers, marched out of Beirut at 7 a.m. on September 25, with Beaufort in command. They headed toward Dayr al-Qamar, to take up strategic positions in the Lebanon and patrol the area. At the Dog River, with awesome arrogance, the soldiers inscribed the names of Napoléon III, Beaufort, and his officers on ancient tablets also bearing the marks of Egyptian pharaohs, Assyrian kings, and Roman emperors. A French polemicist who arrived in Dayr al-Qamar around the same time was horrified: "The sun had charred the cadavers; their skin was tanned and black; they were nothing more than skeletons." One corpse held two dead children in her arms. Another held the head of an old man, evidently his father.[49]

Three days later after crossing the Dog River, the first French column reached Dayr al-Qamar, but not before disgracing themselves. Some Maronites accompanying the troops took the chance to launch their own atrocities. As Dufferin reported, an eighty-year-old blind Druze man was "savagely murdered"; a young Druze man was shot; and, near the French camp, a Druze woman was stoned and then decapitated. At this news, the French delegate on the international commission asked Beaufort to punish the Maronite killers. But Dufferin soon heard of "the murder of twenty more Druses by the Maronites that accompany the French army." Then Dufferin was told of eight more innocent Druzes "wantonly murdered," as well as "many instances of rape, pillage and wanton destruction of property." A visiting British official found ten more Druzes killed at Dayr al-Qamar. Horrified British officials urged Fuad to stop these killings, and Russell himself expressed "the greatest indignation" and asked that Beaufort arrest the Maronite killers. By the end of January 1861, a British military official would reckon that in total 176 Druzes had been killed by Maronites during the French occupation of Mount Lebanon.[50]

The sullied French troops proceeded on to Zahleh. Fuad told Beaufort he could go no farther, to the French commander's anger. As a French observer with Beaufort's troops noted, "They are only missing one thing: an occasion to fight." When an Ottoman captain was turned back by a French officer, the Ottoman told his restless troops, "We only have to endure them for four months! Patience!" To that, a pipe-smoking French corporal caustically launched into the traditional French song "Bon homme": "You are not the master of your house/ While we are here."[51]

Meanwhile, the Ottoman troops marched from Sidon across the interior to the Beqaa Valley, without encountering any Druze resistance. Many Druze leaders had already fled to the far side of the mountain or to Jebel ash-Shaykh (Mount Hermon). So Beaufort joined Fuad in a fresh expedition to Jebel ash-Shaykh. After about twenty-four days of a largely futile chase, Fuad returned to Damascus, expecting to smoke the Druze chiefs out when the weather turned colder. After a demand from Dufferin for swift justice, Fuad replied, "Thank you for the kind invitation to cut off heads; I would have preferred an invitation to dinner."[52]

One of the major tasks of the military expedition was returning Christian refugees to their homes. On a tour of the countryside, Bentivoglio could not stop himself from bursting into tears at the sight of the ruins of Dayr al-Qamar. He reported misery in Sidon, Jezzin, Hasbayya, and Rashayya. The French consul helped set up local relief committees, assisted by some of Beaufort's officers. The French troops helped the local populations to rebuild houses in places like Dayr al-Qamar, an unconventional role that both Bentivoglio and Beaufort wholeheartedly endorsed. France paid 300,000 francs toward refugee relief and supported care for the wounded and ill in Beirut, including efforts by a private Anglo-American relief committee.[53]

Fuad's own efforts to return Christian refugees to their homes won him some British praise. Ottoman troops in the interior imposed military rule and helped get refugees back into their homes. The international commissioners also oversaw Fuad's rebuilding of "the burnt villages of the Lebanon." In Damascus, some destitute Christian refugees were housed by displacing Muslims. Those houses were marked with ominous chalk crosses, which scared some of the Christians away.[54]

In Constantinople, on October 1, Sultan Abdulmecit told the British ambassador once again of his "horror" at the Syrian massacres, and his desire for punishment of all the guilty. But in Damascus, the British consul fretted that order had quickly slipped while Fuad was off marching against the Druze chiefs, leaving "pretty much the same state of affairs as existed before the outbreak." If Fuad left, he expected "a worse calamity than we have already witnessed."[55]

"Guilty or Not"

Britain belatedly began to show signs of scruples about the palpable unfairness of Fuad's tribunal. The British and French had breezily approved his first round of executions. But now the international commissioners demanded that a reluctant Fuad allow them to oversee the tribunal. Noel Moore, the British consul in Beirut, was sent to watch for even the "minutest" irregularities.[56]

He found plenty. Moore was immediately scandalized. After just a week of watching Said Junblat's trial, he wrote in shocked tones that it was "not conducted in a spirit of impartiality." The testimony of Junblat and sympathetic witnesses was omitted; Junblat was not given enough time to challenge hostile witnesses; and criticism of Ottoman officials "is harshly, though indirectly, repressed." Dufferin was convinced that "guilty or not, the members of the Court are determined on the prisoner's speedy ruin." Although "the Turks were prepared to throw Europe as many heads as she required," Dufferin wrote, all the accused—not just Ottoman officials but Druzes, too—deserved "the securities of impartial justice." Dufferin angrily denounced Fuad's tribunal and asked that Junblat get a defense lawyer, as afforded even to Europeans facing court-martial. The commissioners criticized Fuad for not allowing defendants to hear testimony against themselves.[57]

These European qualms had not managed to manifest themselves until hundreds of people had faced Fuad's wrath. Still, under this British pressure, Fuad adjourned the tribunal and offered to let Junblat complain about his trial. Fuad's next purge was somewhat more restrained: lacking evidence, he exiled a group of notables to Cyprus as a threat to "public tranquillity." The Russian and Prussian commissioners, of all people, professed shock that perpetual detention was being used against reputedly innocent people. Even Fuad admitted that "the prisons were full of persons against whom nobody appeared to substantiate the charges on which they had been arrested." In a show of more profound fair-mindedness, the British ambassador suggested that Fuad's tribunal should prosecute Christians, too.[58]

But the Europeans could also be remarkably high-handed. Beaufort, with the mailed fist of the French army behind him, loudly and repeatedly demanded a brutal crackdown on the Druzes. The French international commissioner, realizing that there were too many responsible Druzes to possibly be prosecuted, called for "exemplary punishment of the principal criminals," done by swift "summary procedure." Dufferin, too, agreed to summary procedure. He also asked Fuad to execute at least a few exemplary Druze chiefs, since so far no one had been punished for the massacres at Hasbayya, Rashayya, and Dayr al-Qamar. Dufferin wrote that "the work of reconciliation and of peace" could not be done "until the appointed measure of chastisement shall have been inflicted. It is a mockery to talk of peace while the perpetrators of such foul deeds as those which deluged the streets of Hasbeya, Rasheya, and Deir-el-Kamar with blood remain unmolested in their homes."[59]

The fate of Damascus's Jews was another sore point. Here, French and British moral concern went beyond Christians—and even against them. The capriciousness of Fuad's tribunal made it an easy instrument for Christian vengeance, expressed in flimsy charges from Christians that the Jews had participated in the massacres.[60]

Russell, disgusted, ordered his subordinates "to preserve the Jewish population of Damascus from becoming the victims of such monstrous calumny," even viewing them with "the same severity as would be wrongs done to Christians." He was under pressure from Sir Moses Montefiore, the most prominent Jewish Briton, an influential financier who had been the first British eminence to call for a subscription on behalf of the suffering Syrians.[61]

The French agreed with Russell. Bentivoglio met with Fuad, complaining about unfair evidence used against the Jews. Fuad replied that two Jews had been condemned, but the rest would be freed. A British consul demanded that Fuad issue "an equal decree of protection to Jew and Christian," and lectured Fuad against anti-Semitism (although not without mentioning how rich and powerful Jews were). Under British pressure, Fuad let the chief rabbi attend any tribunal prosecutions of Jews. After the issue reached the level of the Ottoman grand vizier, Fuad freed another Jew who had not been able to disprove the charges against him. That left only one Jew in jail, on whose behalf Montefiore again wrote to Russell "in the interests of humanity" and of "saving . . . a human life." Russell asked Dufferin, whose interest in the Jewish women of Damascus in 1859 had been all too human, to do whatever he could. British and French diplomacy was mostly but not exclusively on behalf of the Christians.[62]

"Inspiring a Wholesome Terror"

Fuad found himself torn between two competing European demands: harsh punishment and due process. In November, yielding to European calls for punishment, he proceeded to the Lebanon to arrest Druze suspects. The international commission agreed to give amnesty to "the Druse nation" once the "more notorious" killers in Mount Lebanon had been punished.[63]

Dufferin, satisfied in his calls for vengeance, now veered toward due process: he asked that "only those whose hands are deeply dyed in blood should be required to expiate the guilt of the [Druze] nation." Fuad duly made a few hundred final arrests, to fuel a final round of executions. In a moment of splendid hypocrisy, Dufferin now criticized Fuad for, essentially, listening to Dufferin: "Unfortunately Fuad Pasha on his arrival inaugurated a system of retribution calculated rather to satisfy the public opinion of Europe than to convince the sufferers on the spot of the heartiness with which he espoused their cause."[64]

When the tribunal issued its sentences, the international commissioners complained that Ottoman officials were sentenced to jail while Druzes faced death. Kurshid, to take the most prominent example, had faced trial in Beirut in front of a panel of five Ottoman officials, who found the Ottoman governor remiss in not moving fast enough to stop the Druze militants, especially in Dayr al-Qamar. Kurshid pleaded that he did not have enough troops to stop the violence, which convinced the court that he could not be legally executed, and that he should instead face "perpetual imprisonment in a fortress." The British, French, and Russian commissioners wanted to see Kurshid die. Junblat, in contrast, was blamed for wrongly reassuring Christians that they would be safe and for not quelling the Druze onslaught against the Christians. For that the Druze leader was sentenced to death as "the moral organizer and author of the insurrectionary combination."[65]

The international commission permitted execution for committing or encouraging massacre, as well as for burning and plundering. Dufferin, showing some restraint, suggested never using the death penalty unless two eyewitnesses could verify the murder of unarmed men, women, or children. He did not want to prosecute Druzes for fighting in self-defense, particularly because it was becoming "clearer . . . that the Christians had provoked the Druses into a war of extermination."[66]

The Maronite elites showed even less restraint. The leading clergy came up with a list of forty-six hundred people they wanted killed. Dufferin, disgusted, warned against "the blind vindictiveness of the Christian prosecutors" and "the unscrupulous denunciations of the priesthood." Fuad only managed to bargain the Maronite priests down to demanding twelve hundred rolling heads. Dufferin instructed a British officer with Fuad to make sure the Ottoman government did not try to "destroy the Druse aristocracy" under cloak of law. Dufferin insisted that "no considerations of expediency, no desire to get the thing over quickly, no fear of public opinion, ought to induce his Excellency to order any one for execution unless the evidence against him shall amount to a moral certainty of his guilt." Still, his legalistic scruples only went so far: "We have to deal with an occasion and with a state of society in which a nice adherence to the refinements of European legal practice would be out of place; we must, therefore, content ourselves with taking such precautions as the circumstances of the case admit."[67]

In Mukhtara, a Druze stronghold, Fuad weighed the fates of some eight hundred Druze prisoners. The Maronite leaders there refused to single out any of them as the most guilty or to give evidence against individuals, instead arguing that all deserved death. Fuad heatedly told them that the summary execution of hundreds of prisoners "was a course quite inconsistent with justice, and one which would not be permitted by the general sentiment of Europe." In Dayr al-Qamar, Dufferin noted, Fuad "was surrounded by crowds of Christian women crying out for blood; and both here [Beirut] and elsewhere similar demonstrations are being organized." Fuad seemed embarrassed by these shows of vindictiveness. Worse, Dufferin reckoned that "the lists of the accused are composed in a great measure of names designated either by chance or by motives of private animosity."[68]

Fuad could not get the Mukhtara Maronites to relent from the call for twelve hundred executions. Instead, he requested a new list of about two hundred Druze names, ranked from most to least guilty, without committing to put anything like that number to death. The Maronites flatly refused. In Constantinople, the British ambassador went to Ali, and they agreed on the need to avoid "an unjust and indiscriminate persecution of the whole Druse people." Fuad finally sent a list of three hundred names to the international commission, suggesting about twenty executions, which the international commission thought was too little. Fuad pointedly made his number of Lebanon executions less than those before in Damascus—a sign of waning Ottoman appetite for European-sponsored purges. Dufferin warned the commissioners of "the utter want of evidence" and that "names chosen at hap-hazard form a list of persons whose criminality was attested by indications so unsatisfactory as scarcely to justify a presumption of their guilt." The commission decided to execute only those "against whom there was really some tangible proof." If there was no testimony against a Druze, the prisoner should be freed. Dufferin warned again against "summarily" dealing with the Druzes.[69]

The French remained the most outraged, but even they showed some signs of restraint. Beaufort was impatient at the delays and furious at British efforts to go easy on the Druze chiefs, and the French commissioner demanded their execution. When there were cheers for the Druzes on their way to exile, Beaufort was beside himself with indignation. Still, even Thouvenel, no friend of the Druzes, gagged at Fuad's "unnecessary vengeance," instructing the French commissioner that "it is not a holocaust which is wanted, but the execution of one or two of the ringleaders of the Druses with a view of inspiring a wholesome terror among the rest." In London, Russell agreed. The international commission had thought that twenty death sentences for the Druzes at Mukhtara would suffice, but

Thouvenel's intercession got it down to one or two. Thus Fuad ultimately freed most of the Druzes arrested at Mukhtara. Bentivoglio was outraged, writing bitterly that they "seemed to triumph in their impunity." Still, the divergence was clear: the Maronite leadership wanted forty-six hundred executions; their French rescuers wanted one or two.[70]

Britain, in addition to punishing Druzes, also successfully prodded Fuad to punish some Maronites. Dufferin was appalled at the toll of 176 Druzes killed during the French occupation of Mount Lebanon, including twenty-five women and fifteen children. Putting these Christian killers on the same moral level as the Druze killers in the massacres in Damascus and Hasbayya, he saw the Maronite killings of Druzes as a "renewal of those very barbarities we have come to put an end to." Dufferin urged Fuad that "those who have butchered women and infants in cold blood ought to be dealt with by an equally summary process and with the same severity as the Druses." Fuad quickly agreed and sent men out to make arrests.[71]

Faced with the sentencing of the leaders who had surrendered to Fuad, the international commissioners mostly pushed for the death penalty for Ottoman officials like Kurshid. But the British and Austrian commissioners wanted to commute the sentences for some of the Druze leaders, and acquit some of the others. By now, even the French commissioner was urging Fuad to go easy on the Druze prisoners at Mukhtara, leaving Dufferin to point out the double standard of leniency for worse perpetrators at Mukhtara while those who had given themselves up to Fuad faced death. There were twenty-two death-penalty cases where a British military officer, and later the government, approved of Fuad's court-martial verdicts. But six Druzes, despite prosecution, seemed blameless. Thus Russell wrote, "Her Majesty's Government could not give their consent to the execution of the six whom their Commissioner believes to be innocent of the massacres." He added that "the Maronites had intended to be the aggressors, and had planned an attack on the Druses, and Fuad Pasha ought, therefore, to ask the Porte to apply with great discrimination, and in a perfectly impartial spirit, the severe law."[72]

Dufferin, too, blamed the war on the Maronites: "It was the lamb who dirtied the stream, and if the wolf standing lower down took it amiss, it must thank its own folly for the consequences." He warned that the Druzes were becoming Ottoman "scapegoats," and reminded Russell that he had not made himself "the partizan of any particular community, or still less become the apologist of murderers and assassins." Dufferin found his position close to impossible:

> The other Commissioners are merely prosecutors. Provided that those whom their governments are determined to think guilty do not get off, they need have no other care. But I am judge, jury, prosecutor, and counsel for the plaintiff all at once. These unfortunate Druses are in a most pitiable position. They have committed the most horrible crimes, they are being pursued with the extremity of rancour by the Maronites out of revenge, and by the French out of ambition; they are being sacrificed by the Turks out of fear, and in the hope of saving their own people; and yet their only friend [Dufferin] is obliged to a certain extent to place himself in the ranks of their accusers.

Britain, for all the imperfections of its applications of legalism, was in the grip of scruples that Fuad and Beaufort lacked.[73]

CHAPTER SEVENTEEN

Mission Creep

"An Endless, and Indeed a Hopeless Work"

Napoléon III was getting further and further involved in what today could only be called nation-building. The massacres had stopped, but France was now invested in refugee return, war crimes trials, governmental reform, sheltering the homeless, and hunting down potentially threatening leaders. Beaufort had hunkered down into his role of military viceroy, sending detailed reports on political progress and civil order back to the French war minister and foreign minister. The French commander estimated he would need a strong occupation forcc for at lcast two more years. One French observer in Syria wrote, "France is now in the middle of them [the Maronites], weapons in arms, and she will not leave them without having definitively ensured their destiny!" Bentivoglio was deeply worried that the Ottoman authorities were too weak to protect against a new outbreak of violence.[1]

In contrast, Britain had more faith in the Ottoman Empire, and wanted out. As the Ottoman and French troops came inland, Britain began quietly cutting back its presence on the coast in anticipation of the winter. With its mighty ships of the line gone, the British had six warships, including several frigates, still under orders to protect Syrian Christians as well as British interests.[2]

Thouvenel tried to reignite Russell's anger by pointing to the danger posed by the Druze chiefs in Mount Lebanon who had escaped Fuad and Beaufort's dragnet. But Russell's appetite for the Syrian expedition had run out—about four months shy of the great powers' time limit for the French deployment, at the end of February 1861. There were, Russell argued, "insuperable objections to a prolonged occupation of Syria by European troops." He wrote:

> These troops were sent to Syria in consequence of frightful massacres which filled all Europe with horror. They went to support the Sultan's authorities in their task of restoring order, and punishing the principal criminals. By the activity of Fuad Pasha, and the energy of General Beaufort, this work of humanity and justice has been in great part accomplished. To keep the European troops there in order to hunt out other criminals in the caves and recesses of the mountains would be an endless, and indeed a hopeless work.

The phrase *mission creep* had not been coined, but that was what was on Russell's mind. He wrote that stationing troops in Syria any longer would "alter entirely the original purpose" of the great powers:

> What limit, either of numbers or of time, could be placed to such an occupation? It would soon degenerate into a transfer of the local Government of Syria to the Five Powers, and thus, instead of giving a useful example, well fitted to terrify the Mahometan fanatics, the European occupation would be a precedent for other occupations in Bulgaria, in Bosnia, and other Provinces, and thus lead the way to a partition of the Turkish Empire.

Russell preferred renewed Ottoman governance after a French withdrawal, world-wearily shrugging off the possible fate of the Syrians: "No security, it is true, would be thus obtained against a recurrence of the conflicts of Druses and Christians; but so long as the two races exist in the country, no permanent security can be obtained."[3]

The French were less sanguine. Bentivoglio desperately wanted to keep French troops in place. Frightened Christian refugees were streaming out of Damascus. Beaufort, too, argued that the situation on the ground was still dangerously unsettled, and worried about what would happen when his troops left. The French commander groused about "our eternal enemies, the English." Bentivoglio, touring the country, reported, "I heard nothing but a concert of complaints against the Russians and the English."[4]

French officials were hurt by Britain's suspiciousness. Clear in their own minds, at least, about the loftiness of their motives, they were shocked at Britain's willingness to risk chaos in Syria in order to foil France. An official French report would later indignantly blame Britain's "bad will" on "the secret motives which England attributed to the intervention of France." France had offered its official renunciation of any advantages, and all but begged the other European powers to send troops, but none of this could satisfy *perfide Albion,* who saw the French mission as despotic Bonapartist aggression. To Britain, Syria was the key to French control of the region. Thouvenel accepted the terms of the convention governing the French deployment, but hoped that the international commission would put a new reformed government in place in Syria before the European forces left. He lashed back at Russell: "It would be a sorry termination to the intervention of Europe in Syria if the day after the departure of the troops fresh massacres were to occur."[5]

In fact, the international commission had barely begun its consideration of how to remake the government of Syria. France preferred a strong Christian administration. The British plan was put together by Dufferin, and quickly approved by Russell. Dufferin crudely argued that Syria's "ten distinct and uncivilized races" had a "natural instinct" for "submission to superior authority." He thus suggested a firm and knowledgeable governor, more troops, and special "semi-independent" status for Syria, even though this risked "the dismemberment of the Ottoman Empire." Although he would not partition the mixed Druze-Maronite districts, he worried about ethnic balance: "If Druses cannot be suffered to govern Christians, certainly Christians must not govern Druses." In a fair-minded moment, he admitted the perverse consequences of European intervention: "As foreign influences exalted the arrogance and fanaticism of the Christians, their independence became more insufferable to the Turks."[6]

In Paris, Thouvenel wrote that he wanted "an early settlement of a stable Government in the Lebanon, in order that she [France] may bring away her troops," but dreaded the prospect "that their departure should be the signal for a renewal of the atrocities." But even as the foreign minister rankled at Britain's eagerness to end the mission, he remained multilateral. He agreed that "the French troops in Syria represented European troops." When the British ambassador suggested that any "prolong[ation] of the foreign occupation . . . might be effected by a smaller body of mixed troops," Thouvenel gave Napoléon III's personal imprimatur to non-French troops: "The Emperor was most anxious that other troops besides French should undertake this duty."[7]

The Ottoman government saw British reluctance as their best foil against France. Ali thanked Britain, a helpful ally, for "a sure guarantee" against prolonging or expanding the occupation of Syria. That occupation "might be justified" when "Europe saw all Syria in an uproar." But now, Ali suggested, the troubled towns had been pacified "without striking a blow, by the prestige alone of the Sultan's authority, represented by his Excellency Fuad Pasha."[8]

Syria's Christians were equally desperate that the French troops remain permanently. Bentivoglio wrote that as the occupation deadline approached, "the worries that the arrival of our troops had calmed instantly and that their presence had since contained have begun to reappear with a new intensity." Beaufort wrote, "The preoccupation of the Christians on the subject of the prolongation of our intervention is always sharp, and their discouragement grows every day."[9]

The British took a more jaundiced view of Christian fears. The Christians, Dufferin noted, had "come to look upon that army not only as the instrument which was to realize their dreams of domination, but as their sole protection against forces whom they believe to be biding their time when they can with impunity recommence the half-accomplished work of extermination." So long as Fuad and the Ottoman troops were there, Dufferin reckoned, the Christians had not "the slightest reason for alarm." He continued, "there is no longer any necessity for a foreign army in Syria. As the occupation by a foreign force of the territory of an independent Sovereign is, under any circumstances, attended with innumerable evils, its removal, as a matter of course, should take place as soon as the major necessity which occasioned its entry into the country shall have ceased."[10]

Beaufort had other ideas. Dufferin suspected that the French commander would provoke a skirmish in order to create a pretext for indefinitely prolonging the French occupation. Beaufort complained to the French government that Fuad had allowed Druzes to slip away into the mountains—charges that Fuad indignantly denied. Beaufort also provided muscle for another punitive European demand: reparations. France estimated that the Christians were owed £1,250,000, far more than Fuad's suggestion of a 25 million piastre fine, or about £200,000. The Muslim taxpayers of Damascus were hit hardest. The indemnity, of about 16 percent of the annual income of each Damascus taxpayer, was so painful that it had to be collected over eight months, rather than in a week or a month, as had been contemplated. Dufferin was appalled at this "stupid and unscrupulous system of persecution by which the whole nation is being driven to despair." Fuad had to ask Beaufort to use his troops to enforce the collection of money. If France was winding down its Syrian occupation, that point seemed thoroughly lost on the French commander there.[11]

The business of setting up a new government was still deadlocked. Fuad declared that his mission had three goals: "repression, reparation, and reorganization," the latter of which he would get to "by-and-bye"—which left it hard for France to withdraw. The Ottoman Empire would not agree to any loss of sovereignty; Thouvenel wanted to preserve Maronite semi-independence as established back in 1845; and Britain was now worrying about the future of the Druzes. Britain particularly objected to the French idea of putting Mount Lebanon under a Maronite ruler answerable to the great European powers. Dufferin hoped to "insure the future well-being of either tribe." The Druzes, he wrote, were not just "barbarous assassins," and warned Fuad not to oppress them. This kind of wrangling over Syria's future would continue all the way through the ultimate withdrawal of French troops.[12]

The attempt to get occupying troops out on a strict timetable pegged to political reform was going no better than it would in Bosnia after 1995. Much as it would almost a century and a half later, the deadline had been casually set as a reassurance before the troops went in, and came to look increasingly unworkable as it actually drew near. The British ambassador in Constantinople warned Russell that if withdrawal depended on reforming Syria's government, "the term of six months was an illusory one." In Beirut, the French commissioner suggested prolonging the occupation, and the Prussian and Russian commissioners agreed. Dufferin vehemently said that "the French army, useful as its arrival had originally been, was become an embarrassment to the Government. . . . [T]he police duties it was now discharging in the Lebanon were never intended to form part of its mission."[13]

"The Extermination of a Hostile Tribe"

Napoléon III himself notified Russell that the emperor was "quite ready to withdraw his troops from Syria, but if your Government urge this evacuation, remember that they make themselves responsible if massacres and outrages against the Christians are renewed." Russell, somewhat apprehensive for Syria's future, in turn warned the Ottoman government that Britain's "continued friendship and support" depended on firm Ottoman action in Syria. If there was "a new harvest of corruption on the Bosphorus, and new murders in Damascus and the Mountain, the countenance of the British Government must be withheld, and humanity will require the most decided and effectual measures." Russell reminded Ali that Ottoman order must hold: "If the massacres of Syria are renewed, foreign occupation will probably again take place; . . . no jealousies will prevent the Great Powers from taking effectual measures for the security of Christian life and property."[14]

France was preoccupied abroad with other crises in Poland and China, and at home with Napoléon III's cautious expansion of constitutional and parliamentary liberties. This, a French report would later note, "absorbed all the attention of the Imperial Govt. and public opinion," making a withdrawal possible, if not desirable. Without a new Syrian government in place, Thouvenel said, "it would be impossible to recall the troops." Still, withdrawal or extension "was a question for Europe to decide," and Thouvenel would "act by the wishes of the Great Powers."[15]

Britain would have none of it. Its ambassador in Paris told Thouvenel that "occupation could not be prolonged for a day, without the consent of the Porte." Russell told Thouvenel that both Ali and Dufferin thought that "the presence of the French troops encourages the insolence and the violence of the Maronites, and thus keeps up the feeling of hostility between them and the Druses." He reminded Thouvenel of the Christian demand for forty-five hundred executions: "This is the manner in which these Christian bishops in the East preach 'peace on earth and goodwill towards men.'" British and Ottoman consent to the occupation, he said, was based on the six-month deadline. Thouvenel fired back that "in the present state of the Ottoman Empire, a strong Government in the Lebanon would be impossible." He planned to ask "all the great Courts" for "their opinion as to the withdrawal of the troops." France would "express no opinion one way or the other," but rely on the other great powers.[16]

The British ambassador insisted that nothing could override the Paris convention's time limit. Thouvenel replied that he believed "in my soul and conscience" that "the withdrawal of the troops would be followed by a massacre far more extensive than that for which we were now asking redress," and thus "the Imperial Government would not take the responsibility of acting alone." Napoléon III's "greatest desire was to bring away his troops as soon as possible," but needed a government in the Lebanon first. As a halfway step, the British ambassador suggested withdrawing French troops from the interior, since they continued "to excite the Maronites and irritate the Druses."[17]

Britain tried to sway the other great powers. Russell lobbied Austria and Prussia, arguing that, despite the shock of the massacres, the Ottoman Empire's calls for an end to French occupation were "perfectly reasonable" and any French violation of the convention would be "a breach of faith." Like many opponents of humanitarian intervention to this day, Russell argued that the barbarous locals were in the grip of ancient ethnic hatreds, with both sides guilty. He loftily reminded Austria and Prussia: "From time to time, massacres and murders have desolated the district of the Lebanon. Maronites have been as forward in acts of cruel revenge, and in the indulgence of hatred, as the Druses." He blamed the war on the Maronites, and pointed out that Maronites had murdered twenty or thirty Druzes "in cold blood." Indeed, as for the Maronites, "though nominally Christians, they are in reality a fierce and barbarous race. They seek the extermination of a hostile tribe, and Her Majesty's Government cannot think that the idolatry and superstition of that tribe justify the Powers of Europe in promoting or consenting to their extermination."[18]

The British foreign secretary forgot his own outrage in the spring and summer of 1860, and seemed not to notice that he could only point to at most thirty murdered Druzes, as against his own government's toll of five thousand Christians killed in Damascus alone. Dufferin, while increasingly sympathetic to the Druzes, wrote, "It still remains a fact that they slaughtered in cold blood upwards of 5,000 unarmed men and children." As he put it later, "The Christian population of the Lebanon are almost, if not quite, as savage as any of their non-Christian neighbours." Russell was reduced to this convoluted argument for ignoring the fears of the Christians: "It is the nature of foreign occupation to keep alive an apprehension of the dangers which that occupation professes to prevent; and thus, if such apprehensions were to be admitted as reasons for the continuance of foreign occupation, that occupation would, by the effect which it produces, have a tendency to perpetuate itself." That is a foreign minister earning his salary.[19]

The End of the Affair

Russell's round of diplomacy was a complete flop. Austria wanted the French troops out but only if this would not lead to new massacres. Prussia, too, worried about fresh massacres, and only asked that France get formal permission from the great powers for an extension. The Russian commissioner in Beirut thought the French occupation was, "as a matter of principle, philanthropic and charitable rather than military." Gorchakov decided that Russia would not accept any responsibility for what might happen if the French troops got out before a new government was in place.[20]

Russell, too, seemed somewhat uneasy about what he was doing. He nervously instructed his ambassador in Constantinople not to be too vigorous about calling for a withdrawal, lest the Ottomans blame Britain for any disaster after the French troops left.[21]

In Syria, France kept its troops busy. The French commissioner noted that the presence of French detachments in Zahleh and other mixed areas was vital, and had been "blessed by the public." Dufferin was sure that the French troops were trying to dawdle: "They are so evidently *bent* on remaining here beyond the stipulated time, that they threaten to cause commotions, in order to make work for themselves! A young officer said . . . that it would be a disgrace to French arms to leave Syria *sans coup férir* [without firing a shot]. This is their idea of glory, and such is the discretion of troops sent to keep order and prevent bloodshed." Another French soldier had reportedly said, "We are 8,000 [*sic*] men here—we do not need to take anyone into account, we will dictate the law to this country."[22]

Thouvenel invited the other great powers to a conference to consider an extension of France's occupation. "The Powers did not propose to themselves any political object in Syria," he wrote. "They are executing a work of humanity: is this work accomplished?" If the great powers agreed to extend the occupation, Thouvenel wrote, "having accepted the task of furnishing the effective expeditionary body, we [France] certainly would not refuse to continue the sacrifices which we have imposed on ourselves, in order to afford the Sultan the co-operation of our troops." But trying to demonstrate that the mission was European and not just French, he added that if other powers wanted to send troops, "we should be ready to accept their assistance."[23]

Russell, in his reply, agreed that France's motives were pure. Thouvenel "affirmed, with truth, that the interests of humanity, and not any political object, were the motives of that expedition." The troops had been sent "upon a sudden emergency, when all Europe was in a state of horror and indignation at the intelligence of the massacres perpetrated in the Lebanon and at Damascus. The object of the five Powers was to prevent a renewal of those massacres, and to show the fanatical tribes of Syria that such outrages upon humanity could not be committed without punishment and reparation." But the British foreign secretary coolly noted, "It must be recollected that Syria is a province of the Turkish Empire. The Sultan is the Sovereign of that country, and not the five Powers." (The sultan had, of course, accepted the principle of temporary European intervention.) Returning to his theme of ancient ethnic hatreds in Syria, he wrote that Britain was "not prepared to maintain European troops in Syria until means are found of totally preventing for the future those bloody encounters of hostile tribes which have been for ages the scourge of that country. They care not whether those European troops should belong to France or to any other country. Her Majesty's Government will not agree to become responsible for the future administration of a province of the Sultan by the agency of foreign troops."[24]

In Paris, Thouvenel fought a round with the British ambassador, Lord Cowley. Thouvenel solemnly informed him that Napoléon III had no desire to prolong the occupation indefinitely, but Thouvenel feared withdrawing and thus "leaving the people we went to protect in a worse position than before." All France wanted was the installation of a new Syrian government: "We shall then have done all that under the circumstances it was possible to do, and we can defend ourselves before the Catholic world, should fresh atrocities ensue." According to the ambassador's account, Thouvenel crassly added: "There is not a post that arrives from Syria that does not bring petition upon petition to the Emperor for continued protection, and it is difficult to abandon altogether these people who have at all times looked to us, for I will not deny that we place a certain value in the preservation of our influence over the Maronites." What if, Cowley asked, the Ottomans insisted on sticking to the deadline? "Why then," Thouvenel said, "the troops must go; of that there can be no doubt. Without the Porte's assent they cannot remain." The foreign minister soothingly insisted that France would "respect the decision" of the great powers, no matter what.[25]

Russell was greatly relieved. He shifted Britain to a compromise position: while Britain opposed an extension, the choice was the Ottoman Empire's to make. If the French troops were sent packing, the Porte would have to declare that "the Sultan has means to prevent a renewal of massacre." Russell agreed to France's call for the Maronites to retain the semi-independence granted in 1845. He sent Cowley to the upcoming Paris conference, with instructions not to agree to anything that the Ottoman Empire refused. At long last, he ordered Cowley to accept an extension of the French occupation to the end of April if the Ottoman Empire agreed. Russell did so warily: "if Turkish authority is unfit to rule in Syria now, why should it be fit at the end of two months, or of six months?"[26]

Britain shouldered some of the peacekeeping burden. Russell offered to join France in maintaining "a naval force on the coast of Syria for the protection and succour of the Christian inhabitants" through the summer of 1861. Russell gave the admiralty discretion "to land Marines in the case of urgent danger of massacre of British subjects or of the Christian population." Still, unlike the anti-Druze French, Russell also hoped "to save the Druse population from becoming victims to the atrocities which the Maronites are too ready to exercise against them."[27]

Meanwhile in Beirut, at a glacial pace, the commissioners kept working on a new government for Syria and Mount Lebanon. The Ottoman Empire stuck to the 1845 framework, allowing guarantees for the Christians, but not an independent or semi-independent state. The Ottoman government, jealous of its battered sovereignty, opposed any special autonomous status for Syria. At almost the same time as Thouvenel was inviting the ambassadors to meet in Paris, and just three weeks from the original withdrawal deadline, the commissioners in Beirut were still only moving toward the outlines of a Lebanese government. Their plans were sweeping: a non-Syrian and non-Maronite Christian governor; new administrative districts that roughly followed ethnic lines; abolishing feudalism; minority rights; equality before law and an independent judiciary. Dufferin, thoroughly dissatisfied with the proposed Ottoman reforms, predicted a massive flood of Christian refugees from Damascus and Beirut and a "general exodus" of those wealthy enough to flee—something that was already starting.[28]

Three More Months

The Paris conference met at the Foreign Ministry on February 19. In Syria, the inhabitants were on tenterhooks waiting for the result. The conference was raucously contentious from start to finish. Vefik, the Ottoman ambassador, opened by saying that Syria had been pacified "by the sole agency of the Turkish authorities"—a slap at the French troops, whom he wanted out. Thouvenel disagreed completely: "bitter passions" were still raging, held back only by troops; seven thousand Druzes were arming themselves; no government was in place yet.[29]

Cowley fought back. Britain could not countenance "the permanent occupation of Syria." Thouvenel exclaimed that "nothing was further from his thoughts." He only wanted a sturdy government in place. Cowley, relying on Dufferin's more optimistic reports from Syria, backed Vefik's call for a quick French pullout. Thouvenel repeatedly warned that "the departure of the troops would be followed by fresh horrors, which, this time, would not stop at Damascus." Cowley, invoking "many acts of atrocity" by Christians against Druzes, parried that the French troops were now "pernicious." The occupation "tended to raise extravagant expectations on the one side, and to keep up irritation on the other, while the authority of the Sovereign was almost in abeyance." Thouvenel replied that he knew nothing of such atrocities, which if true was a pretty dim reflection on Beaufort and Bentivoglio.[30]

Multilateralism, in practice, meant the Austrian and Prussian ambassadors, presumably wishing they were somewhere else, sitting silently as their Ottoman and British and French colleagues scorched one another. The Russian ambassador piped up only to back Thouvenel, almost certainly as a way of spiting the Ottoman Empire. Prussia had quietly decided in advance to back Thouvenel, too, fearing renewed massacres and instability.[31]

Cowley invited the other maritime powers to join Russell's proposal to maintain naval squadrons off Syria's coast, which could land troops if needed. Thouvenel, having had a bellyful of the British, pointed out "that ships would be of no use in the Mountain." The Russian ambassador agreed. The Austrian ambassador finally asked when spring weather would allow a British squadron to arrive. May 1, Cowley replied. So the Austrian ambassador suggested prolonging the occupation until, say, May 1.[32]

Cowley had talked himself into a corner. The Ottoman ambassador did not object. This meant that Cowley could not object either. With a deal tantalizingly close, Thouvenel tried to make the May 1 deadline not "absolutely binding" if there was no government in place. He said that if a government were installed tomorrow, he "would abandon the Lebanon to its fate the next day." With Cowley and Vefik fearing that a single commissioner—namely, the French or Russian ones—could stop the withdrawal by dragging out the process of creating a new Syrian government, the exhausted ambassadors adjourned in frustration to get new instructions. But the basic result was clear: two more months for the French occupation.[33]

Russell accepted this. Now that a British squadron would indeed be sent, he had set Britain up for grave potential trouble: if there was violence in Syria as the French troops withdrew, it would be British marines who would have to come to the rescue, alongside Ottoman and French soldiers. If Thouvenel was plotting to establish "exclusive Maronite supremacy," Russell thought, that could take a decade. But he urged modesty: a quick execution for the remaining Druze prisoners, and a prompt final report from the international commission, all of which could be done by May.[34]

Thouvenel, defeated, showed even less grace. He huffily reported to Cowley that Napoléon III's cabinet would probably rather withdraw at once than be pinned to a deadline. Cowley, having none of it, said that he "rejoiced" to hear this news. Trying again, Thouvenel wrote a long dispatch to Russell, arguing that France, while seeking "for itself no object of special advantage in Syria," just wanted to prevent fresh massacres. He regretted that France had been left alone to do Europe's work, and thought it "essentially desirable that other troops should be joined with ours in order to give to the occupying force a truly European character." If not, France would bail out of Syria at once.[35]

After that, even Russell found it hard to believe that France was making a land grab: "France is perfectly willing that the foreign occupation of Syria should be European, furnished . . . by a mixed force, and not one exclusively French." But Russell worried that pacifying Syrian rivalries would take forever: "The Maronites and Druses are two fierce tribes who are constantly indulging their implacable hatred against each other. . . . What is a foreign force to do in these circumstances? If the Commander undertakes to try and punish the offenders, he assumes all the duties and responsibilities of the internal administration of the province. If he refrains from interference, the foreign occupation is justly charged with leaving crime and outrage unpunished." Calling France's bluff, Russell would prefer for European troops to leave immediately than stay forever.[36]

Thouvenel made a final offer. He agreed on a fixed deadline, but wanted it to be June 5. This seemed acceptable to the Ottoman Empire, as well as to Austria and Prussia. Russell decided to agree, too, ending the wrangling. France had capitulated: it would withdraw.[37]

All that remained were a few final fits of pique in the best British-French tradition, including French gripes about whether June 5 was carved in stone. (It was.) The Paris ambassadors assembled again on March 15, this time as farce. Thouvenel truculently said that he still thought the occupation should be extended. Cowley suggested three more months, and Thouvenel accepted with limited grace. Everyone agreed to sign the final convention four days later.[38]

As the ambassadors were filing out of the Paris conference, Thouvenel asked Cowley if Britain would agree to "a combined squadron in the Syrian waters." Russell concurred without hesitation. He had already ordered a British squadron to cruise off the coast from May 1 until the end of the summer, "to overawe those who might be inclined to repeat the massacres of last year." Britain's admiralty was instructed that the squadron could land marines to protect British subjects or Christians "from massacre," but to "in no case direct or allow any officer . . . to march into the Interior."[39]

Beaufort had no such compunctions. He was still menacingly going about his occupation. He sent troops up to the Litani Valley and Hasbayya, "to contradict the rumor . . . that, under the demand of Turkey supported by England, the French troops are definitely going to leave Syria," even though that rumor was true. He let his officers and soldiers travel to Jerusalem for Easter, sending them through Nazareth and the Galilee to calm Christian fears there. The French commander and his troops were eager to return to the interior, to relieve the "agony" of the people that France had pledged to protect. The Christians, he wrote, "have no hope except in us." From his windows in Beirut, Beaufort saw every day caravans of Christian refugees arriving from Damascus. The Christians, he wrote, "continue to be menaced and insulted everywhere." The French general was bluntly executing a mandate that he no longer had.[40]

French officials were upset. As Fuad began enforcing order without French military backup, Beaufort was disgusted by "the effrontery of Fuad Pasha to dare to write that *order and tranquillity reigns in all the provinces of the Empire.*" Thouvenel complained that Fuad, now that European pressure was off, was no longer doing enough to satisfy France. He got Ali to send Ottoman reinforcements to Syria quickly in anticipation of the French withdrawal. The French ambassador in Constantinople asked Thouvenel, "without speaking of the formal desire of the Emperor to withdraw his troops, in what kind of cruel embarrassment will we be if nothing is done before June 5?"[41]

The French were reduced to hare-brained schemes. Thouvenel secretly tried (unsuccessfully) to get all the foreign residents of Beirut and the Lebanon to request that the French troops stay on. The French ambassador, knowing that France could do nothing without an Ottoman invitation, suggested to Ali that the empire request maintaining fifteen hundred French troops and five hundred British marines for a few more weeks. He warned that France would hold the Ottomans responsible for new instability. In response, Ali blamed the media: he complained of "the language of the newspapers of Europe and especially of the French newspapers on the subject of Turkey." Ali asked, "Can one reasonably attribute to an entire nation, to all Islamism, the massacres of Syria?"[42]

Britain and France had one final collision over the fate of Said Junblat, the Druze leader. He had been sentenced to death by Fuad's tribunal despite British complaints that the evidence was hopelessly flimsy. Dufferin was appalled that the Russian commissioner would let Junblat die, and that the French and Prussian commissioners took "for granted that the whole Druse nation is guilty." As the French prepared to evacuate Syria, Russell demanded that Fuad spare Junblat from execution.[43]

The Ottoman Empire agreed. But Beaufort still urged Junblat's speedy execution. He was sure that Junblat "well deserved" it, and thought Britain was trying to spare "the most active agent" of British influence. When Ali suggested imprisoning Junblat for life in a fortress, the French ambassador protested energetically that this "impunity" would provoke "a cry of indignation in all of Europe." To French shock, Britain evidently made a stunning escalation: quietly threatening to withdraw its ambassador in Constantinople if Junblat was executed.[44]

With bad grace, Russell backed down from this dire threat. The French, too, sullenly gave up on the issue, allowing Junblat to live. Dufferin went to visit Junblat in jail. He asked the prisoner directly if the massacres had been provoked by the Ottoman government. Junblat answered evasively. A few days later, the Druze leader died in prison—an outcome so convenient to all sides that it is impossible not to be suspicious about it. Bentivoglio conspiratorially noted that Junblat's son, coming to Beirut after his father's death, was "accompanied constantly by an Englishman."[45]

"The Fatal Date"

In Syria, Bentivoglio begged for more time to safeguard the Christians. They were terrified of what would happen after the three-month extension was past. Beaufort, too, warned that Syria would lapse back into chaos when his troops left. Bentivoglio reported, "The news of the imminent departure of the Expeditionary Corps has plunged the Christians of Syria into consternation and they are preparing a general emigration which must be effectuated before the fatal date of June 5."[46]

For their part, the Christian leaders sent a petition to the great European powers with fifteen hundred signatures begging for the continuation of the occupation. They later gathered more signatures in Zahleh, the Beqaa Valley, and the mixed districts. They claimed that they would have been exterminated if the French troops had arrived four weeks later, and that they had not yet been compensated or seen the guilty sufficiently punished: "How, then, when your generosity is well known, can you have decided to allow your troops to abandon Syria before any disposition has been taken?"[47]

Thouvenel received the petition, and Bentivoglio's pleas, but offered no hope. Even though the international commissioners were still working on the long-promised reorganization of the Syrian government, the French troops were preparing to leave. That protocol would not be signed until a few days after the June 5 deadline. Although Thouvenel still felt "the obligations of humanity," the most that France could do now was send a squadron to Syria's coast, to deter further atrocities or land some ground troops in an emergency—although that would require a fresh agreement with the other great powers. Instead, Fuad was to be left in charge, with at least seventeen thousand Ottoman troops.[48]

On May 29, the first part of the French squadron arrived. As Bentivoglio noted, this "imposing" display of France's "magnificent vessels" somewhat intimidated the Muslims and reassured the Christians in Beirut. But two of the more formidable warships were there not as reinforcements, but to carry off the French ground troops. As one French writer put it, "I beg diplomacy's pardon, but to me nothing seems less practical than decisions of this sort. How to admit, in truth, that an army must abandon on a fixed date the populations of which it is the only hope? . . . I do not believe that a French army could cross the seas to protect populations who are being assassinated, and foresake them before their future has been assured!"[49]

Thwarted, all Bentivoglio could do was try to induce guilt. He wrote, "The news, which the English do not fail to spread everywhere, of the departure of our troops produces in these unfortunates an impression of despair and dejection that is difficult to describe." He blew up at Dufferin, telling him off with bitterness and pomposity: "I strongly regret seeing another young diplomat starting his career by following a line of conduct that was maybe imposed on him by the policy of his Governmt. but diametrically opposed to justice and humanity." This was sour enough that Beaufort, who happened to be there for the confrontation, stepped in to shut Bentivoglio up.[50]

It was time for Dufferin to go, too. The British commissioner tried to reassure the Christians, reportedly telling two youngsters: "Your Father is dead, but I will replace him. Do not worry; England will protect you." He wrote that he had arrived in Syria gripped with "natural sentiments of indignation," but later realized "there were two sides to the story. . . . However criminal may have been the excesses into which the Druses were subsequently betrayed, the original provocation came from the Christians, and that they are themselves, in a great measure, responsible for the torrents of blood which have been shed."[51]

Dufferin was horrified by his duties. "If when I left England I had had any notion of the terrible responsibilities I should have to undertake," he wrote to a friend, "I do not think I should have had the heart to come." His "sole consolation" had been reading Shakespeare every morning, while his hair was brushed: "I read a couple of scenes in some pleasant comedy, filling the room with a vision of sunshine, roses, and quaint old-world merriment. It does take one so out of the present." As he was leaving Syria, sent off with tender and just possibly insincere kisses on both cheeks from Beaufort, Dufferin's wife saw the toll his job had taken on "his poor, worn, hatchet face!" He would recover. Dufferin went on to a prosperous career in the service of the empire, as governor-general of Canada, high commissioner for Egypt, and viceroy of India—where thoughts of withdrawal were not on his mind.[52]

The French began the evacuation on June 1. Bentivoglio gloomily reported

> continual cries and tears. The men, women and children throw themselves on our departing soldiers and prevent the detachments from advancing. At night, it was nearly necessary to use force and especially trickery and money to allow the embarkment on the *Colbert* of the company. . . . The house of General de Beaufort has been invaded since the morning by a compact crowd of widows and orphans who demand help, protection and vengeance, their pain is almost a frenzy; at my house, similar scenes of desolation, these poor women surround me and choke me almost when I try to reassure them and cling to me as the only anchor of salvation which will remain to them in the future. Officers and soldiers tell me that the regrets that they felt when leaving France never equalled that which they currently feel while separating from these unfortunates whom they have helped and with whom they formed a single family.

Not everyone was so upset. There were, according to a secondhand account by Bentivoglio, insulting chants throughout the city against Beaufort and the French.

Bentivoglio took final stock: "After a laborious campaign, after nine months of constraint and self-denial, our brave soldiers are returning to France without laurels, true, but with the conscience of having largely fulfilled a task of humanity and charity, faithfully and disinterestedly." He then immediately undermined his own claims of disinterestedness, telling Thouvenel—in a rare explicit French declaration of political interest—that the "deep roots which we leave behind in the esteem and affection of the Christians of Syria will bear their fruit one day or another."[53]

Bentivoglio, whose reports had sparked the French mission, did not linger in Beirut to watch it expire. Instead, he went to Dayr al-Qamar, site of one of the worst massacres in 1860, to try to stem the flow of refugees. With an implicit rebuke to Thouvenel, he wrote that it was impossible to describe "the despair" there. "The women threw themselves at our feet, crying and sobbing; we ourselves were so moved at their pains that we had to hide our tears." The new streets cleared by French soldiers had been named Rue Napoléon, Rue de Beaufort, and Rue Bentivoglio.[54]

Thouvenel could do nothing more than urge Fuad to maintain order. As the French troops were departing, Fuad finally named a new Christian governor for Syria, supported by an assembly made up of two members of the major ethnic groups, including two Druzes, two Maronites, two Greek Orthodox, and two Muslims. Thouvenel thought this was "true progress." In fact, the Règlement Organique of June 9 would prove remarkably durable, lasting until the creation of an independent Lebanon in 1920.[55]

As the French foreign minister turned his mind to other diplomacies, Bentivoglio was left alone to crisscross the countryside, from Beirut to Dayr al-Qamar to smaller towns. Many Druzes, he wrote, regretted the replacement of French troops with Ottomans. In a final valedictory, he wrote, implausibly, "the regrets left behind by the departure of our troops are felt by all the inhabitants of this country, without distinction of race nor religion."[56]

The French consul returned to Beirut to bid Beaufort farewell. Beaufort, in one of his last addresses to his troops, bluntly told them, "I do not need to tell you how much I regret not having had the happy opportunity to lead you in combat." The general had a final excruciating dinner with Fuad, with a full menu of mutual hypocrisy. If Fuad had mostly run political circles around Beaufort throughout the French expedition, Beaufort had at least the sheer firepower to push back. No more. Now Fuad reached new heights of chivalry in making false declarations of sorrow to see Beaufort go. The Ottoman minister, affecting mournful dejection, gallantly told the French general, "Do not lament for those who are leaving, but really for those who are staying!" He then ordered his myriad functionaries to bid farewell to Beaufort, each one dispensing "seasoned compliments of honey and rose water." Eventually Beaufort could take it no longer. "Let's go!" he snapped at his officers. "We will never finish this. Obviously Fuad Pasha does not want to let me leave!"[57]

As smooth as Fuad seemed to Beaufort, he was torn by what he had done in the name of preserving the Ottoman Empire. Less than a year later, he would be struck down with what he thought was a fatal illness. On what he believed was his deathbed, with his "weak and trembling hand" about to give out, the reforming minister wrote what he thought was his final testament to the sultan: "I know that the greater part of our Mussulmans will curse me as a *ghiaour* and an enemy to our religion. I forgive their anger, for they can understand neither my sentiments nor my language." But he said that the "ignorant zealots" who cursed him would "one day come to know that I, a *ghiaour*, an 'impious innovator,' have been much more religious, much more truly a Mussulman" than they. "They will recognize, but unhappily too late, that I have striven more than any other martyr to save the religion and the empire which they would have led to an inevitable ruin."[58]

It was perhaps a final snub to the British that, after all the wrangling about the deadline of June 5, the French managed to miss it. Beaufort sailed, with the last of his troops, on June 17, bound for Alexandria and then Marseille. At seven a.m. that morning, the high clergy of all the different Christian sects, including those under French protections, gathered to send him off. Beaufort arrived with Fuad, followed by an honor guard of Ottoman cavalry. He paused for a few moments to survey the crowd, spoke a few words of farewell, and then walked to the dock in the midst of the throngs. (To French annoyance, the British admiral had chosen that day to steam offshore in a showy exercise, visible from shore.) Beaufort paid his respects to the Russian and Ottoman navies. He was the last to come aboard. They sailed at noon.[59]

After Occupation

As Bentivoglio had predicted, France's mission would one day bear fruit. But much of what it bore was distinctly poisonous. Although the Règlement Organique held until 1920, the 1860 massacres remain to this day a rallying point for Maronite nationalists and extremists in Lebanon. Repeated European interventions in the Middle East would embitter local politics and stoke nationalist furies. In Syria and Lebanon, this would prove to be one of the factors driving them toward further factionalism and civil war. By the time Dwight Eisenhower sent U.S. troops to Lebanon in 1958, local resentments of this kind of thing were already almost exactly a century old.[60]

Still, from the vantage point of 1860, the Syrian occupation was not foreordained to turn so sour. From the first, the idea of a humanitarian military deployment in Syria had actually been a milder proposition than what had happened in Greece in 1827. The European intervention had been approved by the sultan himself. The philhellenes had urged a war not just to protect the Greeks, but to liberate them as a new nation; the Ottoman Empire had refused to tolerate such a violation of its own imperial rule. But there were no serious calls for an independent Syria, and the Ottoman Empire accepted the French occupation. Even France generally hoped that Fuad would be successful in pacifying the province, rather than agitating definitively for a new Maronite Christian state. European troops were supposed to work hand in glove with Ottoman ones, and had in fact cooperated substantially with Fuad's mission.

Facing growing domestic unpopularity, a successful humanitarian mission in Syria must have seemed like a welcome opportunity for Napoléon III. But his decision also suited French imperial interests. A Syrian mission offered a way of enhancing France's international stature, while undermining British influence in the Middle East—a region where the French Empire had clear aspirations. Bentivoglio, while evidently mostly motivated by his genuine shock at the massacres, was not above noting that the French occupation had strategic benefits for the empire. This potential imperialism properly set off alarm bells in Europe and the Middle East.

It thus took an astonishing diplomatic effort to allow the French occupation of Syria. The mission required the consent not just of the bullied Ottoman Empire, but also of the entire Concert of Europe, justifiably suspicious of Napoléon III's professed humane motives. After all, in Vietnam at roughly the same time, French troops seized Saigon and pressed onward in a colonial conquest—ending definitively only when the Vietnamese trounced the French in 1954. But in Syria, France based its mission on recognized treaty obligations; foreswore any imperial or commercial gains from its mission; repeatedly invited European military participation alongside French troops; participated without reservations in the international commission; worked alongside Fuad's own mission; allowed the Concert to dictate the parameters of the expedition; and accepted European restrictions on the size and duration of the French occupation.[61]

In the end, for Syria, those international considerations were trumped.

While Napoléon III wanted to score some points at home, he was not prepared to take on the full weight of European consensus. When British suspicions became too overwhelming, France backed down. Thouvenel was disappointed and Bentivoglio was outright disgusted, but Napoléon III's will was clear. Europe mattered more than Syria. The final achievement of the international management of the Syria mission was France's willingness to abandon it.

PART FOUR

BULGARIANS

In the muggy Balkan summer heat of 1876, a reporter from Ohio rode into a small mountain town in Bulgaria. Januarius Aloysius MacGahan, an Irish-American journalist with almost no discernible self-preservation instincts, had already made his name with a tour of Uzbekistan and Turkmenistan, and a stirring Arctic expedition. In the swashbuckling hack tradition, he had covered the Franco-Prussian War, and had nearly got himself killed reporting on the Paris Commune. Although the *Times* thought him too "sensational" to hire, an upstart liberal British newspaper, the *Daily News,* gambled by sending him to the Balkans to cover uprisings against Ottoman rule there. When the paper got wind of reports of Ottoman massacres, MacGahan was sent into the Bulgarian interior to check them out.[1]

The Ottoman authorities, alarmed that MacGahan refused an official Ottoman escort, had told him there were no horses. But local Bulgarian villagers provided them. The trek up the mountain path took hours. The reporter was joined by local guides with knives and pistols, and a sad procession of some fifty Bulgarian women and children. As MacGahan rode toward remote Batak, on the first day of August, he saw dogs. When they ran off, he saw skulls and a pile of skeletons. From his horse, he counted a hundred skulls, white and clean of flesh. At the church and the town school, there were more piled corpses. Dogs had dug up bodies from narrow graves. The riverbanks were covered with corpses. He had to hold tobacco up to his nose to keep out the overwhelming stench of decaying human beings.

Horrified, he returned to Tatar Bazardjik, about thirty miles away, and wrote up his story. It was an article to turn the stomach:

> On every side were skulls and skeletons charred among the ruins, or lying entire where they fell in their clothing. There were skeletons of girls and women with long brown hair hanging to the skulls. . . . The whole churchyard for three feet deep was festering with dead bodies partly covered—hands, legs, arms, and heads projected in ghastly confusion. I saw many little hands, heads, and feet of children of three years of age, and girls, with heads still covered with beautiful hair. The church was still worse. The floor was covered with rotting bodies quite uncovered. I never imagined anything so fearful. There were three thousand bodies in the churchyard and church. . . . In the school, a fine building, two hundred women and children had been burnt alive. All over the town there were the same scenes.

He filed the story by telegraph, the story ricocheting to London by an underwater cable. Six days later, the *Daily News* ran the article.[2]

Only a handful of MacGahan's shocked readers could have readily found Bulgaria on a map. Bulgaria was at least as obscure to Britons then as it is now. But these distant horrors against an unknown people, made immediate by a modern mass media, transfixed British society and political life for years—as well as sparking a Russian invasion of the Ottoman Empire. A popular protest movement surged across Britain, from Queen Victoria herself on down. William Ewart Gladstone, a thundering moralistic former prime minister, roared out of retirement to denounce the "Bulgarian horrors." Even Benjamin Disraeli, the invincible Tory prime minister who championed Britain's realpolitik alliance with the Ottoman Empire, was forced to secretly propose a British occupation of Bulgaria.

Disraeli would never recover from the accusations of coldness toward Bulgarian suffering, and would, in the next British election, be hounded out of office by Gladstone. Disraeli was undone by a newly powerful press, a vastly larger electorate, a mass public, and the skilled activists known as the atrocitarians. More than ever before, British foreign policy was driven by pressure from below. MacGahan's scoop, echoed throughout British society, became part of Disraeli's downfall.[3]

In Russia, imperial interests had indulged pan-Slavist propaganda over the last few decades, as a useful way of undermining the Ottoman Empire. For Russia, with long-standing expansionist designs on the Balkans, MacGahan's story was a godsend: an awful tale of defenseless Bulgarian Slavs suffering at Ottoman hands. Tsar Aleksandr II disliked the pan-Slavists, but made the near-fatal mistake of indulging them inside and outside his government. Their outcry drove Russia to the brink of war.

Disraeli only managed to keep Britain from launching a humanitarian intervention because Russia overreached: Russia unilaterally invaded the Ottoman Empire. This ringingly reminded Britons of the menace of Russian expansionism, and Gladstone was discredited for long enough for Disraeli to dodge the atrocitarians—although not to survive politically.

Gladstone's moral campaign has left a kind of legacy. In May 1999, during the NATO war for the Kosovars, Tony Blair went to Sofia University in Bulgaria to give a speech invoking Gladstone:

> Today we face the same questions that confronted Gladstone over 120 years ago. Does one nation or people have the right to impose its will on another? Is there ever a justification for a policy based on the supremacy of one ethnic group? Can the outside world simply stand by when a rogue state brutally abuses the basic rights of those it governs? Gladstone's answer in 1876 was clear. And so is mine today.[4]

CHAPTER EIGHTEEN

The Eastern Question

"A Proud Reserve"

Like so many sensitive young Britons growing up while Byron's legend was thick in the air, Benjamin Disraeli modeled himself after the martyred poet. His novels are full of Byronic characters, and he tried to wear Byronic clothes and exude the requisite air of mystery. Disraeli's Byronic affectations went so far as a maudlin Mediterranean tour two years after his hero's death. In Geneva, Disraeli hired the boatman who had once rowed for Byron, who summoned the future prime minister to go for a row in a lightning storm like the one immortalized in *Childe Harold.* Disraeli even hired Tita Falcieri as a servant, because the Venetian had been one of Byron's servants at Mesologgi, and had held Byron's hand as the poet died. Decades later, when Disraeli was prime minister, he would rank Byron alongside Shakespeare and Dante as an "immortal."[1]

Disraeli was a dandyish man, with dark curly hair over a high forehead, and a semitragic look from the enormous bags under his hound-dog eyes. He craved Byron's style, not his politics. Byron would have despised Disraeli's conservatism, especially in foreign policy. On Disraeli's youthful tour through the east, he, like Byron, got involved in local politics, except Disraeli backed the other side. In 1830, soon after Byron's death, the future prime minister went to Albania hoping to help the Ottoman Empire put down a revolt there. Disraeli did lots of drinking and no fighting, and when he met the grand vizier, he breezily bragged of the "delight of being made much of by a man who was daily decapitating half the province."[2]

As prime minister, Byron's fan took a line close to Castlereagh's. Disraeli was a principled conservative, desperately wanting Britain to avoid the scourge of revolution, and by so doing enjoy freedom and prosperity. He had no patience for partisanship or public enthusiasms; he liked stability. Abroad, he was a loyal imperialist, while aiming to maintain a European balance of power: "The policy of England with respect to Europe should be a policy of reserve, but a proud reserve." He secured the way to India by boldly buying out the khedive's shares in the Suez Canal Company ("You have it, Madam," he gloated to Queen Victoria); and he would cajole a reluctant Parliament into declaring Victoria the empress of India.[3]

Disraeli was, with considerable consistency, uninterested in the suffering of minorities in the Ottoman Empire. Revolutionary nationalism, the great destabilizing force of the era, left him cold. On a tour of the Middle East, he was more impressed with the Ottoman Turks than with their Christian subjects, and frankly admitted to detesting the Greeks. He was frustrated by a "superhuman" sluggishness in Constantinople, without which he thought the nationalist uprisings should have been easily quashed.[4]

Disraeli was bolstered by the confidence of the ultimate Victorian authority: Queen Victoria herself. She had despaired after the early death of her beloved husband, Prince Albert, in 1861, and wore mourning black for the rest of her reign. But Disraeli had coaxed her back into public life. She could not stand Gladstone's radicalism and moralism, and preferred Tory to Liberal rule—a preference solidified as Disraeli unctuously buttered her up. (Behind her back, Victoria's favorite prime minister liked to snottily refer to her as "the Faery.") It does not quite do her justice to call her an imperialist; she was an empress, foundationally dedicated to her empire. But unlike her prime minister, Victoria felt some sympathy for the Ottoman Christians, and was initially happy to flex British muscle on their behalf: "All that would seem really necessary is a few ships in different parts to protect the Christians."[5]

Britain versus Russia

That was not so easily done. Victorian diplomats were haunted by the Eastern Question: the fate of the slowly collapsing Ottoman Empire. Britain's core strategic goal was to resist Russia—the biggest and most populous country in Europe, with the only European army capable of threatening British access to India. "They [the Russians] are the great and rising military power," Disraeli wrote. To thwart Russia, Britain was reluctantly stuck supporting the crumbling Ottoman Empire. "Constantinople is the Key of India," Disraeli argued, with considerable, but widely shared, paranoia. Victoria despised Russia, to the point of once bursting out, "Oh, if the Queen were a man she would like to go and give those Russians, whose word one cannot believe, such a beating."[6]

Britain had few other potential friends to confront Russia: Bismarck had cannily aligned his newly unified Germany with his fellow conservative monarchies in Russia and Austria-Hungary; and France, usually a player in the Eastern Question, was still staggered by its humiliating defeat in the Franco-Prussian War. As Disraeli wrote in 1875, "There is no balance, and unless we go out of our way to act with three northern Powers [Germany, Russia, and Austria-Hungary], they can act without us, which is not agreeable for a State like England." In short, Victorian Britain was driven to its Ottoman alliance by much the same logic that sent Richard Nixon to China, to offset a latter-day Russian imperial menace.[7]

The British looked on the Ottoman Empire with a mixture of wistful optimism and simple bigotry. During the Crimean War, when Britain disastrously fought Russia on behalf of the Ottoman Empire, many Britons were sympathetic to the Ottoman Empire. There was a widespread belief that the empire was successfully reforming itself under British tutelage. But by the 1870s, the Ottoman Empire seemed to its critics in many respects just as much anathema to British liberal pretensions as Russia itself. The empire, in the eyes of the more skeptical Britons, was a prison of nationalities, chaotically misgoverned, bankrupt, and prone to revolts from below.[8]

It was those revolts that most plagued European diplomats. Nationalist revolutions—like those that had exploded all across Europe in 1848—were terrifying to the imperial courts, not just in Ottoman Turkey but also Austria-Hungary and Russia. The Victorian British, who had an infinitely more flattering view of their empire than their subjects did, fancied themselves largely insulated against such disorders; they even sympathized with many of the upstart nationalists, so long as they were revolting against somebody else's empire. Still, in the 1870s, the hard logic of realpolitik, championed by Disraeli, offered Britain no choice but backing the Ottoman Empire.[9]

CHAPTER NINETEEN

Pan-Slavism

Russia Under the Tsar Liberator

Russia took a very different view of the Eastern Question, based in its own domestic disarray and the expansionist ideology of pan-Slavism.

Leo Tolstoy was just one among many Russians to recognize how hard the Romanovs worked at controlling Russian public opinion. Tolstoy wrote, "The means of exciting a nation artificially which are at present in the hands of governments and ruling classes, can always evoke any patriotic manifestation they choose, and afterward label it as the outcome of the patriotic sentiments of the people." He laceratingly expressed his disdain for tsarist nation-building:

> From infancy, by every possible means—class-books, church-services, sermons, speeches, books, papers, songs, poetry, monuments—the people is stupefied in one direction; and either by force or by bribe, several thousands of the people are assembled, and when these, joined by the idlers always present at every sight, to the sound of cannon and music, and inflamed by the glitter and brilliance around them, will commence to shout out what others are shouting in front of them, we are told that this is the expression of the sentiment of the entire nation.[1]

But a burst of unusual freedom came in 1855, when Aleksandr II became tsar. He was a tall, handsome blue-eyed man, with bushy mutton-chop whiskers and a huge mustache. Although the son of the reactionary Nikolai I, the new tsar proved to be a progressive modernizer, with bold reforms in education, law, press, city government, and conscription. Above all, he won fame as the Tsar Liberator for emancipating the serfs.

Under the repressive Nikolai I, nobody had dared speak of any ideology that did not match the tsar's line, including pan-Slavism. The *Times* despaired of keeping a full-time correspondent in St. Petersburg, since he was relentlessly tailed by the secret police. But in 1855, Aleksandr II took the fateful step of loosening censorship. There were only 158 books banned between 1867 and 1894 (one of the ones that slipped past was Marx's *Capital*). This loosening allowed the rise of the so-called fat journals: part literary magazine and part commentary on public affairs, the politics carefully coded or muted in order to sneak past the ever-present government censors. They appealed to readers from across the political spectrum, from the radical *Annals of the Fatherland* to the pro-Western and liberal *Messenger of Europe* to the nationalist *Russian Messenger,* which published Tolstoy and Dostoevsky. As the historian Richard Pipes argues, this rare opening in Russian political space allowed the spread of ideas beyond Moscow and St. Petersburg, and even made possible Russia's first political parties. (Lenin would close all the fat journals soon after the Bolshevik Revolution.) Unlike during the Crimean War, Russia went into the 1875–78 Balkan crisis with a newly active political press. Although editors rankled under the risk of censorship, the regime was keenly aware of how useful nationalist domestic opinion could be.

In 1864, Aleksandr II allowed the creation of local governments, known as *zemstva.* This unprecedented loosening of central authority was partially a response to the inability of the central state and its provincial agents to handle problems like education and infrastructure, as well as the need to fill the vacuum left by serf-owners. This was a far cry from the kind of full-throated liberalization and enfranchisement that was taking place in Britain, but it nevertheless brought a sizable group of liberal or social democratic technocrats—who ran the *zemstva*—into Russian politics. Until the end of the nineteenth century, when reactionaries would crush Aleksandr II's reforms, Russians finally had some room to breathe.[2]

"From the Nile to the Neva"

One of the most important movements to take advantage of Aleksandr II's liberalization was pan-Slavism. Pan-Slavism, an updating of Russian nationalism, celebrated the unity of the Orthodox Slav peoples. The Orthodox religion was the key distinction between the mystical, spiritual, and communitarian Slavs of Eastern Europe and the rationalistic, soulless individualists of Western Europe. Pan-Slavists, who denigrated Protestantism and Catholicism, had less impact on the Catholic Slavs in Poland and Austria-Hungary.[3]

The roots of Russian pan-Slavism as a serious political force do not go back much farther than the 1840s, when romantic Russian intellectuals began to find common cause with fellow Slavs outside Russia's borders. Until Aleksandr II took the throne, pan-Slavists faced public indifference and repression by the secret police. Because pan-Slavists glorified the relationship of Russian state and society, they frowned on tsarist dictatorship. But they thrived on Aleksandr II's reforms and even applauded his liberation of the serfs: only a strong Russia could lead the coming fight.[4]

The pan-Slavists looked forward to the disintegration of the Ottoman and Austrian empires. Poets like Feodor Ivanovich Tiutchev, theorists like Nikolai Yakovlevich Danilevsky, and the great novelist Feodor Mikhailovich Dostoevsky all promoted the image of a gigantic and godly Slav empire, led of course by Russia, an Orthodox third Rome, with a messianic mission to bring Orthodoxy to the world. (Other pan-Slavists preferred the image of a more federal Slav union, like a Slav United States of America.) One reactionary general explicitly made pan-Slavism an imperialist doctrine in his *Opinion on the Eastern Question,* aiming at Russian expansion into Ottoman Slav lands. By the Crimean War, pan-Slavists saw Russians as a chosen people in a holy war on behalf of Slavs under Ottoman domination.[5]

Danilevsky took full advantage of Aleksandr II's press reforms, publishing his influential 1869 book *Russia and Europe* over ten issues of the monthly journal *Dawn.* His militant and pseudoscientific tract scorned European civilization, seeing Russia as separate. He had no interest in mankind as a whole, but only in his brother Slavs (as well as sundry Greeks and Magyars, who were thought to be sufficiently Orthodox to make the cut). Danilevsky thought big: envisioning a pan-Slav union incorporating Bohemia, Bosnia-Herzegovina, Bulgaria, Croatia, Dalmatia, Galicia, Greece, Istria, Poland, Montenegro, Moravia, Romania, Serbia, Slovakia, Trieste, and parts of Albania, Bukovina, Macedonia, and Transylvania, with the capital of course in Constantinople. Not to be outdone, Tiutchev ecstatically imagined a new Russian capital in Constantinople, with dominion spreading "from the Nile to the Neva, from the Elbe to China, from the Volga to the Euphrates, from the Ganges to the Danube, Behold the Russian realm." In 1853, Friedrich Engels, usually writing with Karl Marx, wrote, "Sure would the conquest of Turkey by Russia be only the prelude for the annexation of Hungary, Prussia, Galicia, and for the ultimate realization of the Slavonic Empire which certain fanatical Panslavistic philosophers have dreamed of."[6]

An elderly and cranky Dostoevsky was the most famous pan-Slavist. Pale and worn, with a thin reddish beard, he could still deliver speeches of prophetic intensity. His obsessive late-life cause was a pan-Slavist Russian nationalism that would humiliate the arrogant Western Europeans. He became an enthusiastic member of the Slavic Benevolent Society in 1873, joining its governing council in 1880 and penning a jubilee address on its behalf to Aleksandr II. The immortal novelist was beside himself at the publication of Danilevsky's *Russia and Europe,* rushing to the post office to get the new installment in the latest *Dawn.* He incorporated its ideas into *The Devils:* "It will remain for a long time the daily reading of every Russian. . . . It coincides so much with my own opinions and convictions that I am sometimes amazed by the identity of our conclusions." Dostoevsky met his intellectual idol twice in St. Petersburg. Like many pan-Slavists, Dostoevsky justified taking Constantinople as "ancient Tsargrad." This new third Rome would be "something special and unprecedented," not merely an annexation but "a true, new exaltation of the cross of Christ and the ultimate word of Orthodoxy, at whose head Russia has long been standing."[7]

There were some Russians who saw through the militant fantasies of pan-Slavism. Tolstoy dreamed of a peaceful pan-Christian community that rendered Europe's warring states obsolete. During the Crimean War, Aleksandr Ivanovich Herzen, the famed Russian free thinker, bravely declared, "Orthodox Christians, the Tsar adds, are oppressed by the Turks. We have never heard that the Christians in Turkey are more oppressed than our peasants." But Herzen, who also decried Russian cruelty in Poland in 1863, was speaking against a rising chorus of Russian nationalism.[8]

By the 1860s, pan-Slavism had become a mighty force in the small segment of Russian society that counted as public opinion—almost the official ideology of the country. Whatever humanitarianism had been in the doctrine in the 1840s was by now thoroughly expunged, replaced with furious nationalism. At a nakedly political Slavonic Ethnographic Exhibition in Moscow in 1867, participants called on the imperial state to realize their pan-Slavist visions.

Mikhail Nikiforovich Katkov, Russia's most prominent newspaper editor, imagined Russia unifying the Slavs just as Prussia had unified the Germans. (Katkov became so extreme that, as the editor of Ivan Sergeievich Turgenev's *Fathers and Sons,* he tried to water down the classic novel because of its hero's liberalism, and then wrote a vicious anonymous review.) The rector of Moscow University pointed to Piedmont's lead role in Italian unification, hoping ultimately for a mammoth Russian-speaking nation stretching from Prague to the Pacific.[9]

"800,000 Bayonets"

So much for ideology. Pan-Slavism might have had pure beliefs, but its impact on Russian foreign policy depended on the sordid business of politics. In British eyes, pan-Slavism was just a cover for imperial expansion into a contested region.

Until the middle of the nineteenth century, Russian expansionism was not even nominally on behalf of suffering Slavdom. Since 1774, under the Treaty of Kutchuk-Kainardji, Russia had rights to protect Orthodox Christians living under Ottoman rule. As Canning had written during the Greek revolt, "The quarrel of the Emperor of Russia with the Porte was founded upon treaties, which gave to the Emperor a right of interference." But the interpretation of that right varied with imperial calculations.[10]

For instance, during one major Christian revolt—the Serbian uprising that started in 1804—Russia sat idly by. It urged the Serbian rebels to capitulate and accept Ottoman rule. Then, after German unification, the Kremlin found pan-Slavism convenient as a way of containing German influence in Eastern Europe. But this was only sporadically useful, since the Russian foreign ministry preferred to see Germany and Austria-Hungary as fellow conservative monarchies, and therefore make common cause against revolutionary nationalists trying to gain independence, regardless of whether they were Slavs or not.[11]

Most important, pan-Slavism grew into a way of justifying expansion against the Ottoman and Austro-Hungarian empires, which did not lack for Slavs to liberate. Russia, itself a reactionary monarchy, found itself in the hypocritical position of cheering on national revolutions, so long as they were in the Balkans. Of course, imperial Russian sympathy for Slavs suffering under the Ottoman yoke did not mean that Russia had the slightest inclination of applying the same standards to its own imperial subjects. The point was to undermine the Ottoman Empire.[12]

Dostoevsky's grand dreams could only be realized at the cost of a general war against both the Austro-Hungarian and Ottoman empires—something that Russia was nowhere near ready for. The threat of pan-Slavism was widely known in the West. A panicky Karl Marx warned that hundreds of Russian agents were infiltrating the Ottoman Empire and that pan-Slavism "could not realize itself without sweeping from the map Hungary, Turkey, and a large part of Germany. . . . Pan-Slavism is now, from a creed, turned into a political programme, or rather a vast political menace, with 800,000 bayonets to support it."[13]

But the Russian government was more peace-loving than Dostoevsky's crowd. Foreign policy was still made by Aleksandr II himself, who disliked the pan-Slavists and preferred to ignore them. The second most influential official was the elderly Aleksandr Mikhailovich Gorchakov, the long-serving foreign minister, bespectacled and shrewd, who despised the pan-Slavists as a mortal threat to his lifelong attempts to secure a stable place for Russia in the European balance of power. (Gorchakov had approved of the French mission to Syria back in 1860, but put Russian interests above that of saving persecuted Slavs.) Piotr Andreievich Shuvalov, the Russian ambassador in London, was terrified of pan-Slavist agitations that might drag Russia into war; Aleksandr II and Gorchakov were deeply opposed to fomenting revolt in the Balkans.[14]

Pan-Slavism could have a huge impact on Russian peasants, and ideologically it preferred the provinces to the corrupt cities. But in St. Petersburg, and especially in Moscow, the leading pan-Slavists were politically well connected, holding elite posts in the Orthodox church, the military, and the court. In 1858, with Aleksandr II's consent, they set up the Moscow Slavic Benevolent Committee, which later opened branches in Kiev and Odessa.

The most politically important of these elite pan-Slavists was Count Nikolai Pavlovich Ignatiev, a wily, mendacious diplomat who from 1864 onward was Russia's ambassador at Constantinople. He spent thirteen years there, acquiring the sardonic nickname Menteur Pasha (Liar Pasha), and ended his high-flying career as interior minister. In Constantinople, Ignatiev's ultimate goal was to dominate or outright conquer the city itself and the straits for Russia. He lacked the religious commitment of sincere pan-Slavists; for Ignatiev, as for the Winter Palace, pan-Slavism was a policy of opportunism. His objective was not so much that these Slavs be free and happy, but that they be pro-Russian pawns. The tsar hoped to keep out of trouble; Ignatiev tried mightily to get into it.[15]

CHAPTER TWENTY

Bosnia and Serbia

Russians and Bosnians

The immediate precursor to the Bulgarian explosion was an 1875 uprising against Ottoman rule in Bosnia-Herzegovina, eventually given support from Serbia. Palmerston once predicted that Russia would try "fomenting insurrections in Bosnia and elsewhere among the Christian subjects of the Porte." Sure enough, Ignatiev, taking advantage of a long leash from St. Petersburg, went busily to work fomenting and funding two small revolts in Bulgaria in 1867 and 1868. The Moscow Slavic Benevolent Committee began to get state backing for its aid to Bulgaria. There were also state-sponsored cultural exchanges in the name of pan-Slavism. The Russian consulates in Belgrade, Sarajevo, Mostar, Prizren, and other Balkan towns spent much of their time encouraging pan-Slavism.[1]

In July 1875, the Ottoman Empire was rocked by the revolt in Bosnia. While Russian pan-Slavists had probably made some long-term contribution to the revolt, it was more a local effort than a Russian project. Although Ignatiev doubted that Russia's foreign ministry would really stand behind pan-Slavism, he warned the Ottoman grand vizier that the tsar "cannot see the Christians of the Ottoman Empire continually exposed to persecutions, and the Powers will be forced to intervene." Ignatiev bragged, "Wherever there is a Christian, he is ready to bring his complaint to our notice. They are all spies for Russia."[2]

In fact, Aleksandr II's government was rather embarrassed by the uprising. Any turmoil in Bosnia held terrifying risks for Russia, since Austria-Hungary also had its eye on the territory. So Russia sharply cut a deal with the Vienna court to stop the violence before it spread. This left Ignatiev fuming, but despite urgent pleas to Gorchakov and a trip to lobby Aleksandr II himself, the renegade ambassador was unable to convince his own government to break ranks with Austria-Hungary. In December 1875, to the relief of the Russian government, Count Julius Andrássy, Austria-Hungary's foreign minister, sent a note to the Ottoman Empire urging it to reform its administration of its restless Christian areas.[3]

The state-influenced Russian press took no great interest in the Bosnian uprising. Dostoevsky, who would hyperventilate over subsequent revolts in Serbia and Bulgaria, only passingly noted newspaper coverage of "the present turmoil in Herzegovina." Rather than doing their own reporting, the Russian papers recycled information from the Austro-Hungarian press, and stigmatized the Bosnians as illegitimate insurgents. The pan-Slavist societies were slow out of the starting gate and incapable of funding more than a handful of soldiers. The committees were unthreatening enough for Aleksandr II to chip in 10,000 rubles for refugee relief. The relative quiescence of public opinion made it possible for the Russian government to stand firm. In 1914, Russian and Austro-Hungarian rivalry in the Balkans would plunge the world into war, but in 1875, both governments held back.[4]

Britons and Bosnians

Britain, too, barely reacted to the Bosnian revolt. There was no popular outcry sufficient to upset Britain's pro-Ottoman policy. The British press was just beginning to penetrate the Ottoman Empire, despite the best efforts of the Ottomans to stop them. The *Times* had not managed to field a reliable correspondent in Constantinople until 1854; even Reuters would not send a permanent correspondent to Constantinople until 1877.[5]

British journalism about the Bosnian insurrection was hack work: scant original reporting, almost no curiosity, and clichés instead of analysis. The *Times* drowsily contented itself with telegraph reports from its correspondents in Constantinople and Berlin, supplemented by short Reuters telegrams from Vienna and Trieste. Although the Ottomans had telegraph lines in Bosnia (around Trebinje in the south, for instance), Belgrade was as close to the front as Reuters men ever got. Reporters made little effort to interview refugees, as today's professional foreign correspondents would have done. The *Times* admitted it had little idea what was going on in Bosnia. The paper heaped scorn on both the Ottomans ("the Sultan is alike despotic and Mahomedan, the harem a nest of intrigue, and the chief effort of Ministers or Pasha to keep or gain office") and Bosnians ("a half-civilized race").[6]

Given the ferocity of the repression that was about to befall Bulgaria, it seems possible that there were Ottoman atrocities in Bosnia, too; but since *Times* reporters heard only vague rumors about them, there was little in particular to spark the outrage of high-minded Britons. In December 1875, a League in Aid of the Christians in Turkey was created, under the aging John Russell, the former prime minister who had been one of the first to join the London Greek Committee and who, as foreign secretary in 1860, had approved and then ended France's intervention in Syria. A London meeting attracted neither big names nor big numbers. In a faint echo of the London Greek Committee's successes in the 1820s, Russell pledged £50 for the Bosnians, the same amount he had pledged to the Greeks some fifty-two years prior. For this gesture, the *Times* devoted an editorial to flaying Russell for "a benevolence which is no longer chilled by political responsibility."[7]

Disraeli was under precious little pressure to rescue Bosnia. The worldly conservative greeted the Bosnian uprising coolly: "Fancy autonomy for Bosnia with a mixed population; autonomy for Ireland would be less absurd; for there are more Turks in proportion to Christians in Bosnia, than Ulster v. the three other Provinces." Confident that the Bosnian situation had been settled, Disraeli, in a mood for self-congratulation, expansively wrote, "I really believe 'the Eastern Question' that has haunted Europe for a century, and which I thought the Crimean War had adjourned for half another, will fall to my lot to encounter—dare I say—to settle?"[8]

When rioters killed the French and German consuls in Salonika, Russia, Austria-Hungary, and Germany sent an angry complaint to the Ottoman Empire, and asked Britain and France to join it. Disraeli, heartily sick of the alignment of those three conservative great powers, chose instead to snub them. This meant, Disraeli warned the cabinet, that "neither we, nor any other Power, send ships of war to Constantinople on the pretence of protecting the Christians." Instead, Disraeli did dispatch British warships to Besika Bay, just outside the Dardanelles, as a sign of support for the Ottomans. As he privately told Victoria, "Your Majesty's fleet has not been ordered to the Mediterranean to protect Christians or Turks, but to uphold your Majesty's Empire."[9]

Russians and Serbians

Still, the pan-Slavists doggedly kept at their task. Ignatiev concentrated on Serbia, an Ottoman vassal state, as a Russian proxy to dominate the

Balkans. Russia helped Serbia build up its army and enlist Greece and Montenegro in the anti-Ottoman cause.

By now, Aleksandr II and Gorchakov were finding it hard to hold their own civil society back. After desperate pleas from the Serbian Orthodox clergy, the main Slavic Benevolent Committees in St. Petersburg and Moscow raised over 300,000 rubles. When the interior minister reminded city governments that they could not give money to support foreign insurgencies (the Moscow administration had donated 20,000 rubles for Bosnian refugees), public reaction was so strong that Aleksandr II had to undermine his own minister. Instead, the tsar stipulated weakly that fund-raising subscriptions had to go to refugees, not to insurgents. Even so, this kind of fund-raising had never been allowed before in Russia. It netted over 1.5 million rubles (£250,000, although the money was spent in Russia) by November 1876. This was the first ominous sign that the state was losing its grip on its own public opinion.[10]

Even worse, as branches of the Slavic Benevolent Committee sprang up at home, the Russian government did not stop Russian soldiers from volunteering to serve in the Serbian army. The most prominent of them was Mikhail Grigorievich Cherniaev, a hero of the battle of Tashkent who reached the rank of major general before being sacked for trying to play out his militant pan-Slavism by volunteering to lead Serbia in a crusade against Ottoman rule in the Balkans. But the pan-Slavist governor of Moscow gave Cherniaev a visa to go secretly to Belgrade, where he was quickly declared a Serbian citizen and put in charge of much of the Serbian army. Cherniaev also owned his own pan-Slavist newspaper, *Russian World*, to fight a paper war alongside the real one, bragging that by "communicating information to my own newspaper I might be enabled to appreciate correctly the intelligence which is transmitted to Russia chiefly through the Austrian Press which is hostile to all Slavism generally."[11]

It seemed frighteningly likely that Serbia would go to war with the Ottoman Empire. But Aleksandr II personally ordered his Belgrade consul general to tell Serbia not to fight. Gorchakov and much of the cabinet opposed getting dragged into the Balkans. Writing to Victoria, the tsar tried to maintain a united front of the great powers: "I have always seen the concert as the best means for preserving the peace and the interests of humanity." In June 1876, Russia joined Austria-Hungary in urging Serbia not to declare war on the Ottoman Empire. Andrássy bluntly asked Gorchakov, "Do you want Constantinople?" Startled, Gorchakov answered, "Oh, no!" (He did admit that Russia wanted Bessarabia back.) Shuvalov, the Russian ambassador in London, who enjoyed ambassadorial parties and British women about as much as he despised the uncouth pan-Slavists, reassured Disraeli, "We do not care for Servia as much for Montenegro." That was not very much, as Shuvalov pointed out that Montenegro did not need a port, "only a little garden to grow cabbages and potatoes."[12]

But Ignatiev urged Serbia on, with warnings to make its war effort look defensive. The tsar's own war minister suspected that Aleksandr II was playing a double game. So the tsar's peaceful counsel fell on deaf and dismayed ears in Belgrade. In June, Serbia declared outright war on the Ottoman Empire. It did so implicitly trusting that Russia would bail it out after all if the going got rough—that pan-Slavists like Ignatiev, not Gorchakov, really spoke for Russia. As the war started, pan-Slavist feeling in Moscow and St. Petersburg reached a fever pitch, with blue, white, and red flags everywhere. Ignatiev egged on the pan-Slavist committees.[13]

Aleksandr II was enraged at Cherniaev's mission, and would later secretly claim he wanted "to throw cold water" on the volunteers. Still, his government did not dare to shut down a recruiting office that opened in Moscow to send Russian volunteers to fight alongside the Serbians, including the cream of St. Petersburg and Moscow society. Their transit was greased with free train tickets and with visas provided automatically by the same pan-Slavist Moscow governor who had given one to Cherniaev. By one Russian pan-Slavist newspaper's probably exaggerated estimate, there were ten thousand Russian volunteers in Serbia, as well as two thousand Cossacks.[14]

The British government was sure that Aleksandr II had known that the officers joining Cherniaev, who had to resign their commissions, had been informally promised those commissions back when they returned. As one Briton recently back from the Ottoman Empire reported, "The subscriptions of Russia enormous—the connivance at the rush of officers complete—Some Russians much alarmed at the popular manifestations [in favor] of a policy which is known to be in opposition to the personal wishes of the Czar." Even Aleksandr II's own heir was a pan-Slavist who backed Cherniaev. "The Russians have behaved very badly," Disraeli wrote. "In future, they must have not only Ambassadors for their Emperors, but for their adventurous Generals, who have secret orders."[15]

The tsar's plight was empathetically summed up by, of all people, Kaiser Wilhelm I of Germany, who knew well how hard an unruly public was for an emperor to handle. He wrote that his fellow monarch was "placed in the painful alternative of not chilling the enthusiastic feeling of his subjects in favour of their unfortunate co-religionists, and at the same time of declaring his personal and political love of peace." Of course he "winked at the departure of trains of soldiers," in order to avoid revolution.[16]

Aleksandr II had given the press greater freedom. Now one-sided accounts, led by the pan-Slavist editor Katkov, suggested that Serbian victory was at hand and heaped vitriol on Ottomans and Britons. Dostoevsky noted the shift: "Almost all the newspapers have changed to sympathizing with the Serbs and Montenegrins." Tolstoy reflected reality by having a character in *Anna Karenina* say, "It's the newspapers that all say the same thing."[17]

The pan-Slavists were ecstatic. Dostoevsky cheered, "In Moscow the Slavic Committee has launched an energetic appeal to the whole of Russia for aid to our insurrectionary brothers, and all the committee's members, together with an immense crowd of people, went to the church of the Serbian community for a solemn service of prayer for victory of the Serbian and Montenegrin forces." In his rambling *Diary of a Writer,* Dostoevsky was entirely swept away:

> Suddenly this entire Russia awakens, arises, and humbly but firmly expresses its splendid opinion to the whole nation. . . . Russian people take up their staffs and set off in crowds a hundred strong, accompanied by thousands of people, on some sort of new crusade . . . to Serbia, for the sake of some of their brethren, because they have heard that their brethren were being tortured and oppressed. A father—an old soldier— . . . suddenly takes up arms and sets off on foot for thousands of miles, asking directions along the way, to go fight the Turks and support his brethren, and he takes his nine-year-old daughter along with him (this is a fact): "There'll be good Christians to be found who'll look after my daughter while I'm off wandering."[18]

Tolstoy, though impressed, did not abandon his critical faculties. He brilliantly captured the heady mood of the summer of 1876 in *Anna Karenina:* "Nothing else was talked or written about at that time but the Slavic question and the Serbian war. All that an idle crowd usually does to kill time was now done for the benefit of the Slavs. Balls, concerts, dinners, speeches, ladies' dresses, beer, taverns—all bore witness to a sympathy with the Slavs." Tolstoy has a character warily notice that "the newspapers printed a great many useless and exaggerated things," and that "the ones who leaped to the forefront and shouted louder than the rest were all the failures and the aggrieved: commanders-in-chief without armies, ministers without ministries, journalists without journals, party chiefs without partisans." Even so, Tolstoy's protagonist was swept away: "The slaughter of co-religionists and brother Slavs awakened sympathy for the sufferers and indignation against the oppressors. . . . The nation's soul was given expression. . . . [T]his was a cause that would attain vast proportions, that would mark an epoch."

Count Vronsky, suicidal after his beloved Anna Karenina throws herself under the wheels of a train, seeks solace by volunteering to fund and lead a Russian squadron in the fight for Serbia. Dispatching Vronsky to his miserable heroic fate, in another form of suicide by train, Tolstoy gave a pitch-perfect and slightly jaundiced rendition of the real-life bathetic scenes at railway stations—a staple of Russian press coverage that summer. Russians excitedly discussed the latest telegrams from the front, and counted the donations and volunteers. At the platform, there were cries of "God save the tsar" and "*zhivio!*"—the Serbo-Croatian equivalent of *viva!* Tolstoy wrote: "The crowd poured past them. . . . They . . . heard the loud voice of one gentleman who, with a glass in his hand, delivered a speech to the volunteers. 'Serve for the faith, for humanity, for our brothers,' the gentleman spoke, constantly raising his voice. 'Mother Moscow blesses you for a great deed. *Zhivio!*' he concluded loudly and tearfully. Everyone shouted '*Zhivio!*' "

Sending her son off on the train to battle, Vronsky's mother neatly sums up the split between Russian society and tsarist policy: "This is God's help to us, this Serbian war. . . . Of course, as a mother I'm afraid, and above all they say *ce n'est pas très bien vu à Pétersbourg*" (it's not very well regarded in Petersburg). This was the inflamed Russian scene on the eve of the *Daily News* scoop on the Bulgarian horrors.[19]

Britons and Serbians

Disraeli was horrified at the prospect of a Serbian victory. At this point, the prime minister uncharacteristically wobbled, making a tentative case for humanitarian intervention. He told Shuvalov, "We think blood-letting to be necessary and will consult together. If the Christians get the upper hand, we shall only have to register accomplished facts: if Turkey crushes the Christians and the repression becomes tyrannous, it will be the turn of all the Great Powers to interpose in the name of humanity."[20]

Other British officials were nervous about their pro-Ottoman tilt. "We shall have to be on our guard against appearing as the supporters of Turks against Christians in the East," wrote the Earl of Derby, Disraeli's hapless and chubby foreign secretary. "This is the danger, and neither Mr. Disraeli nor I are blind to it." Responding to Russian professions of alleged surprise at British lassitude, Disraeli told Victoria that "the comparative coolness of the English people" was because "the so-called insurgents are not natives of any Turkish province but are simply an invasion of revolutionary bands," backed by Russia.[21]

Disraeli felt he had managed to prevent Russia from helping the Serbians. The great powers, he bragged to Victoria, had been forced "to fall back on the principle of non-interference." He hoped for a decisive Ottoman victory soon, so that "the infamous invasion of the Servians will have been properly punished." With considerable satisfaction, he added, "All the great Powers, Russia included, seem anxious to defer to England and something like the old days of authority appear to have returned." He shrugged off continued reports of trouble in the Balkans: "I do not think . . . matters are as serious as the newspapers make out. Now that Parliament is up they want a sensation subject." Disraeli reckoned he had things well under control when, a few days later, he noted, "as the Emperors have now entirely adopted our policy of non-interference and neutrality, I am in great hope that the Insurrection may be soon subdued and some tolerable settlement brought about."[22]

CHAPTER TWENTY-ONE

Bulgarian Horrors

Massacre

Disraeli was just beginning to relax when, in April 1876, Bulgarian nationalist revolutionaries launched an uprising of their own. It was a pathetic farce in most of Bulgaria (even the timing was off: they had meant to revolt in May, but one town went too soon), but around Plovdiv a number of villages rose up in earnest. For that, in May, they were sacked by Ottoman irregulars, known as *bashibazouks.* In the town of Batak, some five thousand Bulgarians, and possibly many more, were massacred. Most of them were women and children.[1]

A few decades ago, Bulgaria would have lingered in obscurity. But in 1855, the Fiscal Stamp, which had kept the price of newspapers too high to reach a mass market, had been abolished. The result was a rush of rabble-rousing "penny papers," challenging the supremacy of the *Times.* This was now coupled with telegraph technology that got the news home at blazing speed. So the immediate cause of Disraeli's undoing would be a liberal British penny paper, the *Daily News:* cheap enough to attract a wide audience but reputable enough to be taken seriously at the highest levels, and hungry enough to go to the trouble and expense of fielding foreign correspondents.[2]

The prime minister was just about the last man in Britain to believe what he read in a cheap newspaper. Disraeli, like many Victorian conservatives, heartily hated the press's new vigor. Having founded a conservative weekly newspaper in 1853, and dropped £1,500 of his own money trying to prop it up, he saw the British press as slanted against his Tories. He had particular ill will for the *Daily News,* which he saw as an opposition mouthpiece. He also hated the *Times,* which he called "either ignorant or corrupt" on foreign policy, not to mention the "organ" of the Liberals.

Disraeli once grumbled, "To-morrow is the great battle of Armageddon when it will be decided who governs England, I or the newspapers."[3]

Newspapers, Disraeli thought, only encouraged public hysteria. He did not disguise his annoyance when Victoria herself, evidently not immune to newsprint's appeal, once sent him a "harrowing" newspaper clipping about the killing of young seals. Writing to Selina Lady Bradford, a married grandmother fourteen years older than he with whom he was madly in love, he took a sarcastic swipe at the pretensions of the unwelcome new foreign correspondents: "I write quicker to you than 'our own correspondent' at the seat of war, in the midst of a battle."[4]

On June 23, the *Daily News* lit the spark for perhaps the biggest explosion of Disraeli's career. In a huge exclusive from Constantinople, Edwin Pears, the correspondent there, described scores of razed villages and innocent Bulgarians slaughtered by the Ottoman *bashibazouks:* "The dregs of the Turkish and Circassian population, with gipsies and gaol-birds let out for the purpose." He could only guess at the death toll: eighteen thousand was the safest number, while Bulgarians spoke of thirty thousand dead. Despite Ottoman attempts to monitor the mail and censor the local press, Pears demanded that Britain help stop the massacre, out of "the duty to an oppressed people and to humanity." He followed up a few days later with another huge piece from Constantinople, made up mostly of harrowing letters from the Philippopolis district of Bulgaria: "Every Bulgarian feels that his life is in peril, and awaits his death from minute to minute. The Turks are extremely enraged, and the massacres continue."[5]

The *Times* had let itself be scooped; an editor had complacently told one of its reporters that, while "the Public has an insatiable appetite for horrors," the paper was "always under more or less pressure for space." The paper had been tipped off, but had not followed the story. Now, routed by the *Daily News,* a *Times* editor complained that "these Yankees are undoubtedly pushing fellows with a great gift for routing out facts."[6]

Shock waves began to spread across Britain. When Stratford Canning, now Lord Stratford de Redcliffe, read the piece, he reportedly cried, "Good God! I would rather see Russia in Constantinople than the subjugation of the Principalities by such means." On June 28, Disraeli first addressed the massacres in the House of Commons, wanly explaining that the Foreign Office's intelligence did not back up the *Daily News.* There were tougher questions on July 10, by which point stout Liberals, Radicals, nonconformist Christians, and laborers were already holding public meetings and editorializing against Disraeli's forthright support of the Ottoman Empire. Disraeli, not grasping the magnitude of what was about to happen, assured the Commons that Sir Henry Elliot, Britain's Turcophile ambassador in Constantinople, would have interfered if he knew of such massacres. "Wars of insurrection are always atrocious," Disraeli said. He pointed out that Britons looked back with horror at their own subjugation of the Jamaica insurrection, an analogy that put Britain in the shoes of the *bashibazouks*. Doubting that more than ten thousand Bulgarians had been jailed, Disraeli tried a little light atrocity humor: "I doubt whether there is prison accommodation for so many, or that torture has been practised on a great scale among an Oriental people who seldom, I believe, resort to torture, but generally terminate their connection with culprits in a more expeditious manner." Laughter rolled through the House.[7]

As Disraeli scoffed, Pears sent out a special correspondent to Bulgaria: MacGahan. The former *New York Herald* reporter had been on his way to Serbia, but along the way heard rumors of massacres in southern Bulgaria and changed course for Constantinople. There, he met up with a highly placed friend: a rich New Yorker named Eugene Schuyler, who was now U.S. consul general in Constantinople. Schuyler had heard details of the massacres from professors at Robert College, an American missionary school in Constantinople that trained a number of Bulgarian students. Schuyler, too furious to wait for State Department approval, set off with MacGahan—as well as a Bulgarian teacher from Robert College, a German correspondent, and a Russian diplomat—to get the story.[8]

On August 1, MacGahan's party arrived in Batak. This was an innovation in foreign reporting: covering a recent massacre firsthand. MacGahan filed three dispatches, giving a ghoulish immediacy to the horror for British readers. He worked hard to humanize the Bulgarians, arguing that they were not savages like "the American Indians," but as literate as the British or French, and overall "a hardworking, industrious, honest, civilized, and peaceful people," who, in Batak at least, had not even rebelled. In relentless paragraph after paragraph, MacGahan hammered home the gruesome scene in a way that drives even a reader today—inured and desensitized by the litany of industrial slaughter of the twentieth century, with images of Babi Yar and Srebrenica—to the brink of collapse.

MacGahan described the "sickening odour, like that of a dead horse" from "a heap of skulls, intermingled with bones from all parts of the human body, skeletons nearly entirely rotting, clothing, human hair, and putrid flesh lying there in one foul heap." Dogs were eating the decaying corpses. Those left alive made "a low plaintive wail, like the 'keening' of the Irish over their dead." The reporter noticed that the skeletons were small, with women's clothing scattered around: "These, then, were all women and girls." They had been beheaded. One surviving woman sat "on a heap of rubbish, rocking herself to and fro, wailing a kind of monotonous chant, half sung, half sobbed, that was not without a wild discordant melody. . . . 'My home, my home, my poor home, my sweet home; my husband, my husband, my poor husband, my dear husband; my home, my sweet home,' and so on, repeating the words over and over again a thousand times."

Some bodies had been burned, in a failed attempt to cremate them. Many women seemed to have been raped. One mother, moaning piteously, "gazed into her lap, where lay three little skulls with the hair still clinging to them." MacGahan had to stop at the churchyard because the "the odour here became so bad that it was almost impossible to proceed." The yard held "an immense heap of human bodies covered over with a thin layer of stones." He was told there were three thousand dead there:

> There were little curly heads there in that festering mass, crushed down by heavy stones; little feet not as long as your finger on which the flesh was dried hard, by the ardent heat before it had time to decompose; little baby hands stretched out as if for help; babes that had died wondering at the bright gleam of sabres and the red hands of the fierce-eyed men who wielded them; children who had died shrinking with fright and terror; young girls who had died weeping and sobbing and begging for mercy; mothers who died trying to shield their little ones with their own weak bodies, all lying there together, festering in one horrid mass. They are silent enough now.

One can barely imagine the emotions of a Victorian newspaper reader. This was an age before the term *mass grave* was a staple of the news, a time when British readers might have still believed that humans did not do such things.

MacGahan bitterly contrasted the squalid horrors of Batak with lofty European diplomacy, of ambassadors taking their coffee and cigars, obtaining useless promises while the Bulgarians starved and died. He devastatingly concluded his story with a full-bore attack on Disraeli's joke about the Ottomans usually disposing of their victims rather than jailing them: "Mr. Disraeli was right. At the time he made that very witty remark, these young girls had been lying there many days."[9]

This was anything but another minor foreign outrage. No one could treat it as business as usual, just another installment in what the British public thought of as the familiar litany of Balkan barbarism. The Ottoman Empire was now a member of the Concert of Europe, and was supposed to be a part of civilized Europe. Even if one did not quite accept the *Daily News*'s shocking figure of twenty-five thousand killed, the death toll was clearly enormous—probably in the range of twelve thousand, by the eventual admission of Disraeli's government—and the details were stunning. MacGahan and Schuyler rushed out a pamphlet version of their discoveries. The *Times* and the left-wing *Manchester Guardian* raced to match the *Daily News* scoop. By the standards of 1876, the horror was beyond compare.[10]

"Coffee-house Babble"

Almost immediately, town hall meetings were held to condemn the massacres and to urge Britain to act. Newspapers from Manchester (including the *Guardian*), Liverpool, and Leeds editorialized in outrage. The *Daily News* was "overwhelmed with the numbers of letters . . . from all parts of the kingdom," from all classes and political leanings. The League in Aid of the Christians of Turkey met with Derby, asking for an end to British support of the Ottoman Empire—and presented him with a statement from John Russell, who had sent British marines to Ottoman Syria when he had held Derby's job. Independent-minded Anglicans like the Bishop of Manchester, and Liberal politicians, began to lead a surging movement against the atrocities.[11]

Queen Victoria, whose bad habit of reading and believing newspapers had not abated, immediately saw something out of the ordinary. "It is too awful," she told Disraeli. After MacGahan's first Batak story, Victoria, shocked, ordered her prime minister, "I cannot rest quiet without urging the prevention of further atrocities." She repeatedly spoke, telegraphed, and wrote about the massacre, even after Disraeli told her the reports were "not authenticated." Her aide General Henry Ponsonby, speaking for the queen, warned Derby that the atrocities could "obliterate" British public sympathy for the Ottoman government. Victoria "protests most strongly against this aggravation of the horrors of war, and considers it the duty of this country to warn the Porte that these atrocities cannot be tolerated, and that if these Bashi-Bazouks are thus employed by the Turks, without restraint, it will be necessary for us to withdraw our countenance from them altogether."[12]

Disraeli took this royal outrage less seriously than Victoria's alarums about baby seals. "The Faery telegraphs this morning about the continued 'horrors' reported in the *Daily News* of to-day," Disraeli noted. "They appear in that journal alone, which is the real Opposition journal, and I believe are, to a great degree, inventions. But their object is to create a cry against the Government." He warned Victoria that "the Opposition are going to work the 'atrocities' as a party question, and there is to be a great public meeting, with all the most red-hot politicians on the platform." Derby assured her that the *Daily News* story was "one of those fictions by which insurgent leaders try to keep up the spirit of their followers." Even so, there was some significant diplomatic action: Derby, acting "in the interests of Turkey herself, no less than in those of humanity," had to warn "the Porte against the toleration of acts committed by its troops which would arouse the reprobation of the civilized world."[13]

Disraeli's failure of imagination was almost overdetermined. He was skeptical of atrocity reports in general, and of the *Daily News* in particular; and he had realpolitik reasons to support the Ottoman Empire. On top of that, his Foreign Office was asleep at the switch.

No government information had made its way from Bulgaria to Downing Street or Whitehall. Although Disraeli tried to persuade Victoria that her consuls were generally pro-Christian, some British officials in the Ottoman Empire seemed to have gone local, led by the ambassador, Sir Henry Elliot—a classic diplomat with distant eyes, a mop of white hair and sideburns, and a large pointy nose and chin. The faculty of Robert College had first brought their reports of Bulgarian massacres to Elliot, who ignored them. He eventually decided there was too much reliable testimony about the rape of Bulgarian women to be denied; but he also downplayed and suppressed much of his station's reporting. Elliot would later blame the uprising on Ignatiev, accuse the Bulgarians of worse atrocities, and warn against the "imaginary sensational stories of the ingenious manufacturers of horrors." He would also become notorious for telling Derby that it did not matter to British interests whether ten thousand or twenty thousand people had been massacred. There was one consular report that gave credence to the *Daily News* articles, but it did not find its way to Disraeli's desk until mid-July.[14]

Privately, Disraeli soon suspected that he was being made a fool by his own diplomats. Elliot had ignored four Foreign Office telegrams before finally reporting back that both Ottomans and Bulgarians were equally guilty of atrocities. Now Disraeli had, belatedly, found that consular report that backed up the *Daily News.* So he ripped into Derby: "I must again complain of the management of your office, and request your personal attention to it." It was, Disraeli wrote, "impossible" to represent the Foreign Office against parliamentary critics without proper information: "What I receive is neither ample, nor accurate." He bitterly complained of only finding that damning consular report "*[a]fter* I had made the declarations, wh[ich]. I did on y[ou]r. authority, respecting the Bulgarian 'atrocities.'" Faced with an impertinent question "pretty well giving me the lie in the Ho[use]. of Commons," Disraeli had not dared to reply. He now complained, "I have no confidence what[eve]r. in y[ou]r. office, and I was obliged to submit in silence to the indignity." Publicly, Disraeli was stuck doubting the consular report, even when the *Daily News* gleefully reprinted it.[15]

Disraeli went into rhetorical acrobatics that have been unconsciously echoed by today's skeptics about humanitarian intervention. Disraeli told Victoria that "the atrocities seem equally divided," and Derby wrote, "I am afraid in this war there is not much to choose between the two sides." Disraeli also suggested that one should expect no better from savage eastern peoples, calling atrocities "inevitable, when wars are carried on in certain countries, and between certain races." (This would be paralleled some 117 years later when Warren Christopher, Bill Clinton's secretary of state, told Congress of "atrocities on all sides" in Bosnia.)[16]

Still, Disraeli did it with style. On July 31, the prime minister fired off another disastrous witticism in the House of Commons: dismissing the consular report as based on "coffee-house babble brought by an anonymous Bulgarian." The too-pithy phrase almost instantly took on a bit of the same kind of notoriety as Neville Chamberlain's "quarrel in a far-away country between people of whom we know nothing," and opponents would throw it back at him for the rest of his political career.[17]

Behind the scenes, Disraeli was appalled to be so wrongfooted. He again stormed against the "lamentable want of energy and deficiency of information" from Elliot and Derby. Disraeli admitted, "I w[oul]d. never have made those same answers" had he seen the babble-based consular report, and would have demanded that Derby follow up its information. Elliot's conduct, Disraeli told Derby, "has seriously compromised, and damaged, the Government. . . . [A]s a public servant, the nation has utterly condemned him." He hoped that firm action now "will make the excited 'Public' forget, or condone, the Elliotiana."[18]

To seize the initiative, the prime minister dispatched a special envoy,

Walter Baring, to investigate what had actually happened in Bulgaria. Baring's long official report, while denying some of the more lurid accusations about cartloads of heads being paraded in the streets, estimated about twelve thousand people killed. Derby warned the Ottoman government to avoid further massacres, which would "prove more disastrous to the Porte than the loss of a battle. The indignation of Europe would become uncontrollable, and interference in a sense hostile to Turkey would inevitably follow."[19]

The opposition smelled blood in the water. The Marquess of Hartington, the Liberal leader, pushed for an end to Britain's pro-Ottoman tilt; back-benchers were up in arms; and Sir William Harcourt, an influential Liberal, "hoped to God they had at last done with the Turk." Disraeli winced at "a very damaging debate on Bulgarian atrocities." The *Times,* annoyed by his evasions, began to editorialize against his government. On top of it all, Victoria demanded immediate action: "I have been horrified by the details of the massacres in Bulgaria, which Mr. Baring admits already to have amounted to 12,000; and I cannot rest quiet without trying to do something to prevent further atrocities."[20]

As Disraeli made his last appearance in the House of Commons before moving up to the House of Lords as the new Earl of Beaconsfield, he was taking a beating from all sides, royal and common. After Baring's report, Disraeli had to admit that the atrocity was "a horrible event which no one can think of without emotion." But, he said, it was no reason to shift foreign policy. If Britain's treaty obligations to guarantee Ottoman territorial integrity were "to be treated . . . as idle wind and chaff, and if we are to be told that our political duty is by force to expel the Turks to the other side of the Bosphorus, then politics cease to be an art, statesmanship becomes mere mockery." He conceded there was a "high political and moral duty" to prevent incompetent Ottoman rule, but national security trumped it: "Those who suppose that England ever would uphold . . . Turkey from blind superstition, and from a want of sympathy with the highest aspirations of humanity, are deceived. What our duty is at this critical moment is to maintain the Empire of England."[21]

But Disraeli, swamped with diplomatic cipher telegrams as public demonstrations grew, knew that public opinion had swung against him. Queen Victoria, after another long *Daily News* story by MacGahan from Batak, wrote, "More news of the horrors committed by the Turks, which seem to be more and more verified, and are causing dreadful excitement and indignation in England, or indeed in Great Britain." In France, Victor Hugo, who had been a prominent activist for the Greeks, once again brilliantly found his voice, specifically referring to MacGahan's grisly details, like that "dogs gnaw in the streets the skulls of outraged girls." Referring specifically to Batak, he accused the Ottomans of "massacring, burning, pillaging, exterminating, cutting the throats of fathers and mothers, selling the little girls and boys." He wrote:

> A people is being assassinated. Where? In Europe! Has this act witnesses? One witness—the entire world. Do the Governments see it? No. The nations have above them something which is below them—the Governments. . . . What the human race knows Governments are ignorant of. This is because Governments see nothing through that short-sightedness peculiar to them, while the human race looks on with another eye, the conscience. We are about to astonish European Governments by teaching them one thing—viz., that crimes are crimes; that it is no more allowable for a Government than for an individual to be an assassin; that Europe is *solidair;* that all that happens in Europe is done by Europe; that if there exists a wild beast Government it must be treated as a wild beast.

Hugo was particularly tough on evasive European governments who did not share the "universal indignation":

> There are hours when the human conscience speaks and orders Governments to listen. The Governments stammer a reply. . . . To quibble with public indignation, nothing more miserable. The attenuations aggravate. It is subtlety pleading for barbarism. It is Byzantine excusing Stamboul. Let us call things by their name. To kill a man at the corner of a wood called a Forest of Bondy is a crime; to kill a people at the corner of that other wood called Diplomacy is a crime also—a greater one. That is all the difference. Does crime diminish in proportion to its enormity? Alas, that is indeed an old law of history. Kill six men you are Troppmann, kill 600,000 you are Cæsar. To be monstrous is to be acceptable. . . . "But," we are told, "you forget that there are questions!" To murder a man is a crime, to murder a people is a question! Each Government has its question. Russia has Constantinople, England has India, France has Prussia, Prussia has France. We reply, "Humanity also has its question," and that question is this. It is greater than India, England, and Russia. It is the infant in its mother's womb. Let us supersede the political question by the human question.

Hugo's spectacular fulmination, reprinted in the *Times,* was another devastating smack at Disraeli.[22]

Disraeli miserably told Lady Chesterfield, the elder and rather less appealing sister of his beloved Lady Bradford, "Here there is only one business. . . . If we don't get peace it will be owing, in no slight degree, to our enlightened public who, as usual, have fallen into the Russian trap, and denouncing 'Bulgarian atrocities' call for the expulsion of the Turks from Europe, which would lead to another Thirty Years War." A few days later, he complained, "I have not a moment's peace—every day is the same. . . . Everything has gone against us—but nothing so much as the 'Bulgarian atrocities' which have changed the bent of opinion in England as regards Turkey and which are worked not merely by enthusiasts, but of course by the Opposition and by Russia's agents, though the Government have no more to do with the 'atrocities' than the man in the moon." Beset on all sides, Disraeli was losing his grip: "It is the most difficult business I have ever had to touch."[23]

CHAPTER TWENTY-TWO

Gladstone vs. Disraeli

"For Purposes of Humanity Alone"

William Ewart Gladstone had, so far, held his peace. The last Liberal prime minister was still off at his Hawarden estate licking his wounds since his thumping defeat by Disraeli in 1874. The Liberal Party was now headed by Hartington in the House of Commons and Lord Granville in the House of Lords, both vastly milder personalities than Gladstone. Disraeli had once said that Gladstone and his fellow Liberal ministers reminded him of a South American coastal "range of exhausted volcanoes. Not a flame flickers on a single pallid crest. But the situation is still dangerous. There are occasional earthquakes."[1]

It does not quite cover the ground to say that Gladstone—the greatest of the Victorian liberals—was a very weird man. He was glowering and dauntingly intense, slim with a huge head, with a large nose topped by terrifying frowning eyes: Henry James wrote, "His eye that of a man of genius." He read voraciously about classics and religion, and wrote formidable works like *Homeric Synchronism* and *The Impregnable Rock of Holy Scripture.* He was a thunderous orator, whose dense sentences and verbose digressions somehow exhilarated his audiences rather than putting them to sleep; *Punch* nicknamed him the "Colossus of Words." In portraits he wore a glove on his left hand to hide the fact that he had accidentally shot off his forefinger. He relaxed by chopping down enormous trees, in staggering quantities. And he was a religious moralist to the core, guiltily convinced of his own sinful nature, with the habit of trying to redeem prostitutes in the West End and then flogging himself in penance when he yielded to the desires of the flesh.[2]

Gladstone had started out as a conservative, but later in life quit the Tory Party and became a Liberal stalwart. His liberal politics were inextricably bound up with his nationalism and High Church religion. In foreign policy, he was anguished about suffering in a startling array of places. He had been an antislavery prime minister, imposing an antislavery treaty on Zanzibar in 1872–73. He backed the unification of Italy, Germany, and Romania, and sympathized with the French inhabitants of Alsace-Lorraine.[3]

Gladstone's liberalism applied, although not always consistently, to Britain's own empire. His most infamous failure would be taking over Egypt in 1882, a monumental act of hypocrisy that went directly against his own explicit and repeated denunciations of any aggression against Egypt or the expansion of the British Empire into the Middle East. Still, he was often repelled by imperialism. He wanted Britain to flourish through free trade, not through conquest, and did not think empire was any measure of British greatness. He wrote that India was Britain's only so long as the Indians wanted it that way. He preferred to give the maximum possible power of self-government to aboriginal peoples. He denounced Britain's Opium Wars in China (the second of which was instigated in part by John Bowring, the London Greek Committee activist, who, flat broke, had sold out his principles and taken an appointment as governor of Hong Kong). "I am in dread of the judgements of God upon England for our national iniquity towards China," he wrote in his diary. He sympathized with the Greeks, and called Britain's voluntary surrender of the Ionian Islands "one of the very best measures of our time." Touching the most thorny issue in British politics, he—probably influenced in part by his sympathy for the Bulgarians—came to the radical position of supporting Home Rule for Ireland. This was a sensational stance. He loudly objected to Disraeli's acquisition of the Suez Canal, suspecting the start of expansion into the Middle East. Gladstone would despise Disraeli's imperial wars in Afghanistan and South Africa, bitterly denouncing the massacre of thousands of Zulus "for no other offence than their attempt to defend against your artillery with their naked bodies, their hearths and homes, their wives and families."[4]

Perhaps most important, Gladstone had a history of activism against foreign oppression. Even as a Tory, he could be roused to fury by suffering overseas. Back in 1851, while Gladstone was a Tory MP for Oxford, he spent about four months living in Naples, bearing witness to horrors. A dictatorial monarchy was in the process of a brutal crackdown on liberals—arbitrarily detaining tens of thousands of political prisoners, torturing some, condemning some to death, and cramming the rest into filthy and disease-ridden jails. When the prisoners in one jail revolted, soldiers threw hand grenades into the mob.[5]

With growing disgust, Gladstone personally went to see some of the jails. He, as an Italian friend said, "erupted like Vesuvius." When he returned to Britain, he fired off a long letter to an influential Tory friend, who was also Byron's cousin and a strong supporter of the Greeks in the 1820s. Gladstone wrote that the "revolting" practices of the Neapolitan government, unmatched in all of Europe, were "an outrage upon religion, upon civilization, upon humanity, and upon decency." He scrupulously reported the pitiable legal cases of several of the detainees.[6]

Gladstone, in his conservative phase, at first only wanted British diplomatic pressure over "an internal question" for Naples. But three months passed without British action. An official appeal to Austria yielded only a frosty reminder that Austria had not disapproved of British treatment of dissidents in Ireland and Ceylon. Gladstone, almost with a sense of relief, published his letters, appealing to "the bar of general opinion." (He chose pamphleteering over raising the issue in Parliament, for fear of miring "the sacred purposes of humanity" in European diplomacy.) He wrote, "On the Government of Naples I had no claim whatever; but as a man I felt and knew it to be my duty to testify to what I had credibly heard, or personally seen, of the needless and acute sufferings of men."[7]

Gladstone's pamphlet produced a public sensation. Palmerston, then foreign secretary, printed up official copies and formally sent them to every European government, including that of Naples. Britain broke off diplomatic relations with Naples—a potential prelude to war. But the Neapolitan king stood firm.

Stymied, Gladstone tried force. In 1855, as chancellor of the exchequer, he secretly backed a reckless plan to send a fast steamship to Santo Stefano jail to break the prisoners out by cover of darkness. The famous Italian revolutionary Giuseppe Garibaldi was put in charge of the daring rescue. The covert activists quickly raised the massive sum to buy the steamer, bolstered by big donations from Gladstone's wife and friends—and a hefty £500 secured by Gladstone himself from the British secret service fund, with Palmerston's approval. One prisoner in Santo Stefano snuck out a letter written in lemon juice to give the plotters a sketch of the jail.

The spectacular plan failed spectacularly: the steamer sank in a violent storm off the British coast at Yarmouth, drowning three members of the crew. Gladstone set about using the remaining money to help the political prisoners and their relatives. Not long after, the Neapolitan king suddenly caved, offering the political prisoners exile first in Argentina and then, to sweeten the deal, in New York. The liberated prisoners seized the ship and landed in Cork instead, to wild cheering from the British public. As Garibaldi's revolutionaries led Italy to unification, the British government refused to stop him. Gladstone, Russell, and Palmerston all firmly backed Italian liberty, as did much of the public. (Even Henry Elliot supported Italian unification.) Russell, as foreign secretary, told Palmerston he "could not stomach defending Bombino," the nickname for the king of Naples, for the bombardment of rebels.[8]

But that was two decades ago. Gladstone, now a Liberal eminence, had not protested Britain's insistence on a French withdrawal from Syria in 1861. He had said little during the uprisings in Bosnia and Serbia. In a July debate in the House of Commons, he intentionally avoided mentioning the Bulgarian massacres. Despite Gladstone's Christian sentiments, he was initially less fired by the Ottoman massacres (by Muslims) than he had been about Neapolitan oppression (by Christians).[9]

The massive public outcry following the stories in the *Daily News* could not have escaped Gladstone's attention, and he slowly sensed an opportunity, both political and moral. Originally not much of a democrat, he had learned to appreciate the genius of the masses, so long as they agreed with him. When a Hyde Park rally for the Bulgarians asked for donations, Gladstone mildly asked Granville for permission: "I have half a mind to send them a trifle. Do you object?" Hoping that "the pot will be kept boiling," he wrote a letter for use by pro-Bulgarian labor activists. Gladstone thought Disraeli's government "should be challenged . . . on the grounds of the Bulgarian Massacres. . . . Good ends can rarely be attained in politics without passion: and there is now, the first time in a good many years, a virtuous passion." He had, he warned Granville "half, perhaps a little more than half, a mind to write a pamphlet."[10]

Gladstone was now hearing a divine call to arms. Throughout July, he had been reading up on the Eastern Question; now he churned out his famous pamphlet at a ferocious pace. On the side, he read up on Thomas Aquinas and the salvation of the soul. He was fueled by religiosity and self-pity. As he started work, on August 28, he wrote in his diary: "I stupidly brought on again my lumbago by physical exertion." The day after: "Lumbago bad: aggravated by trying to walk and by writing, which (oddly) works the *back*." The next day he rested. After that: "Kept my bed till four & made tolerable play in writing on Bulgarian Horrors: the back is less strained in bed, where I write against the legs." Hot baths helped. The next day, he met with the editor of the *Daily News* to pump him for details about the paper's Bulgarian reporting and to tip him off about the political storm he was about to unleash. Gladstone noted, "Again worked hard in bed: and sent off more than half to the Printer."

Late on September 3, he urgently took an overnight train to London, arriving at Granville's house at the unholy hour of five a.m. and going straight to bed for four hours. The relentless house guest rose and headed for Bloomsbury to work: "In six or seven hours, principally at the B[ritish]. Museum I completed my MS making all the needful searches of Papers and Journals: also worked on proof sheets." Gladstone, toiling in the British Museum's vast gilded and domed reading room, had to read by whatever dim sunlight could pierce the Victorian fog and grime dulling the dome's splendid windows; gaslight might have caught books on fire.

The long-suffering Granville toned down some of Gladstone's more radical phrases. Gladstone had wanted to dedicate the pamphlet to Lord John Russell, who sent British marines to save the Syrians, but after a warning from Granville, chose Stratford Canning instead, a diplomatic hero for pushing Britain toward Navarino and for his long stint as ambassador in Constantinople. Gladstone received the first pamphlets by seven p.m. on September 5, with an initial print run of two thousand. After taking in a play with Granville and Hartington, Gladstone "sent off copies in various directions"—including, gratis, two to Disraeli. These bits of lava were titled *Bulgarian Horrors and the Question of the East.*[11]

"These Are the Bulgarian Horrors"

Gladstone's pamphlet is an unlikely kind of Magna Carta for the human rights movement. It is wild, unhinged stuff: repetitive and histrionic, a heady mix of over-the-top moralizing, bitter sarcasms against British policy, perfervid appeals to public opinion, and raw anti-Turkish bigotry. He methodically went after Disraeli as if the prime minister was a tree that Gladstone was bringing down ax blow by ax blow.

Gladstone was horrified at Britain's "moral complicity with the basest and blackest outrages upon record within the present century, if not within the memory of man." He wrote:

> We now know in detail that there have been perpetrated, under the immediate authority of a Government to which all the time we have been giving the strongest moral, and for part of the time even mate-

rial support, crimes and outrages, so vast in scale as to exceed all modern example, and so unutterably vile as well as fierce in character, that it passes the power of heart to conceive, and of tongue and pen adequately to describe them. These are the Bulgarian horrors; and the question is, What can and should be done, either to punish, or to brand, or to prevent?

He batted away Disraeli's various rebuttals and excuses. Gladstone was sure that British diplomats had known of the massacre: "So silence was obtained, and relief; and the well-oiled machinery of our luxurious, indifferent life worked smoothly on." He flatly denied Disraeli's claims that both sides were equally guilty, or that this was just how people in the Balkans behaved: "For the [British] Government, it was still merely a question of 'civil war.'" But this was either "ignorance, or . . . brutal calumny upon a people whom Turkish authorities have themselves just described as industrious, primitive, and docile."[12]

For Gladstone, as for many Victorians, the root of Ottoman unrest was racial. Showing off his six or seven hours of research in the British Museum, he wrote that the problem was "not a question of Mahometanism simply, but of Mahometanism compounded with the peculiar character of a race." Turks were not like the "mild Mahometans of India, nor the chivalrous Saladins of Syria, nor the cultured Moors of Spain"; they "were, upon the whole, from the black day when they first entered Europe, the one great anti-human specimen of humanity."[13]

Gladstone was not always as appallingly crude. He once wrote, "The question of the East is not a question of Christianity against the Porte and the governing Ottomans." The problem, he then claimed, was Ottoman misgovernment, which also afflicted Muslims and Jews: "I do not, then, recognise any plurality of causes; for me the cause is one only, and I cannot commend either Greeks, who refuse their moral support to the Slavs, or Slavs who refuse it to the Greeks." In *Bulgarian Horrors,* Gladstone sometimes sounded less racist: accusing the Ottoman government of ignoring "the broad and deep interests of humanity," and invoking "the general sentiment of civilized mankind."[14]

Gladstone's hope was in British public opinion. Twenty-five years ago he had personally visited Naples, but this time, MacGahan had been the eyewitness: "a nameless, an irresponsible newspaper correspondent," as Gladstone sarcastically mimicked Disraeli. Gladstone cheered the contributions of "free journalism to humanity, to freedom, and to justice," and singled out "the courage, determination, and ability" of the *Daily News.*

The speed of reporting by telegraph left no excuse for Disraeli's "days of ease purchased by dishonour." Gladstone supported the protests spreading from the working class to the cities, and finally to Parliament: "The nation will have to speak through its Government: but we now see clearly that it must first teach its Government, almost as it would teach a lisping child, what to say."[15]

The solution, Gladstone argued, was military. If Ottoman troops gained the upper hand, it might cause "a new and wide out-break of fanaticism, and a wholesale massacre." But Disraeli was already projecting power, with a fleet at Besika Bay to protect British subjects—and "the Christians in general." Gladstone hoped to transform the British fleet at Besika Bay from a sometime instrument of Disraeli's realpolitik to one of humanitarian intervention. He rejected Disraeli's claim that "our fleet was in the East for the support of British interests. I object to this constant system of appeal to our selfish leanings. It sets up false lights; it hides the true; it disturbs the world." Instead, "through the energetic attitude of the people of England, their Government may be led to declare distinctly, that it is for purposes of humanity alone that we have a fleet in Turkish waters." The fleet should be prepared "to enable its force to be most promptly and efficiently applied, in case of need, on Turkish soil, in concert with the other Powers, for the defence of innocent lives, and to prevent the repetition of those recent scenes, at which hell itself might almost blush."[16]

Gladstone rejected the anti-Russian realpolitik rationale of Disraeli's Ottoman alliance. Although he had helped lead Britain to war supporting the Ottoman Empire against Russia in the Crimean War, and was enduringly suspicious of Russia, he now would not balance against Russia: "The matter has become too painfully real for us to be scared at present by the standing hobgoblin of Russia." Quite the contrary: he hoped to compete with Russia for hearts and minds in the Balkans, lest the Slavs conclude that "Russia is their stay, and England their enemy." Russia, thus far, had actually "played the part which we think specially our own, in resistance to tyranny, in befriending the oppressed, in labouring for the happiness of mankind." Instead, he was committed to cooperative multilateralism, hoping that "the wise and energetic counsels of the Powers, again united" would "afford relief to the overcharged emotion of a shuddering world."[17]

Gladstone had limited patience for international law. Noting the recent Ottoman adoption of the Geneva Convention, Gladstone wrote: "They might just as well adopt the Vatican Council, or the British Constitution." (At a time when the Ottoman Empire had just adopted the Tanzimat reforms, this was distinctly unfair.) Gladstone justified intervention on the grounds that the Ottoman government had reneged on its obligations under the 1856 Treaty of Paris to safeguard its Christian subjects, but he also went further. Most important, he refused to accept absolute Ottoman sovereignty.[18]

This was not because of any imperial designs on Ottoman territory; he dreaded the "wholesale scramble" that would follow the empire's collapse. But "human sympathy refuses to be confined by the rules, necessarily limited and conventional, of international law." British antislavery sentiment, he pointed out, had hardly followed international law. Although Gladstone advocated Bosnian and Bulgarian autonomy under Ottoman rule, he insisted that "humanity" must be the "first and highest" objective, and any new massacres would make the British public "fear lest the integrity of Turkey should mean immunity for her unbounded savagery, her unbridled and bestial lust." Gladstone wrote, "Territorial integrity shuts out the foreign state; the *status quo* shuts out the inhabitants of the country, and keeps (I fear) everything to the Turk, with his airy promises, his disembodied reforms, his ferocious passions, and his daily, gross, and incurable misgovernment."

Having made his case, but evidently feeling he had not fired off quite enough rhetorical ammunition, Gladstone finished his pamphlet with a hysterical crescendo:

> Let the Turks now carry away their abuses in the only possible manner, namely by carrying off themselves. Their Zaptiehs and their Mudirs, their Bimbashis and their Yuzbachis, their Kaimakams and their Pashas, one and all, bag and baggage, shall, I hope, clear out from the province they have desolated and profaned. This thorough riddance, this most blessed deliverance, is the only reparation we can make to the memory of those heaps on heaps of dead; to the violated purity alike of matron, of maiden, and of child; to the civilization which has been affronted and shamed; to the laws of God or, if you like, of Allah; to the moral sense of mankind at large. There is not a criminal in an European gaol, there is not a cannibal in the South Sea Islands, whose indignation would not rise and overboil at the recital of that which has been done.[19]

The Atrocitarian Movement

On September 6, Disraeli got Gladstone's pamphlet (complimentary only in one sense of the word). He had been dreading it: "Gladstone 'who had retired from public life,' can't resist the first opportunity and is going to declaim at Blackheath—having preliminarily given the cue to public opinion in a pamphlet." Disraeli, having just been unfavorably compared to a South Sea cannibal, accepted the pamphlet in the spirit in which it was offered. "Gladstone has had the impudence to send me his pamphlet," he spluttered, "tho' he accuses me of several crimes. The document is passionate and not strong; vindictive and ill-written—that of course. Indeed, in that respect, of all the Bulgarian horrors, perhaps the greatest."[20]

Disraeli reassured Victoria that "when the country goes mad on any subject, . . . for a time, explanation is hopeless." In time, "the public, getting a little wearied at hearing the same thing over and over again, begins to reflect a little more calmly, and opinion often changes just as quickly as it began." Instead, Disraeli found himself embroiled in one of the most vicious public debates ever held in Britain—in the league of Munich and Suez.[21]

After two days, Gladstone's publisher added a print run of twenty-two thousand. Gladstone gloated, "The pamphlet is alive & kicking: four & twenty thousand copies were printed, & they think it is not the end." It was actually selling faster than any pamphlet in British history: a staggering two hundred thousand copies in a month, plus countless more unauthorized copies, as well as reprints in newspapers. Unlike the mostly elite efforts of the philhellenes, this was a truly mass phenomenon.[22]

Disraeli witheringly described the atrocitarian coalition as "the pressure of this Hudibrastic crew of High Ritualists, Dissenting ministers, and 'the great Liberal party.'" The Bulgarian agitation was striking for its spontaneity, unlike previous well-organized movements against slavery or the protectionist Corn Laws. As Gladstone later said, "In August and September 1876 there was an outburst, an involuntary outburst, for the strain could no longer be borne, from the people of this country, in every quarter of the country, denouncing those massacres. But that . . . was not the act of the Liberal party." The atrocitarians organized hundreds of public meetings in the summer and fall, of which Gladstone's Blackheath speech was just one.[23]

The movement attracted some of the most glittering Victorian names. Charles Darwin backed Gladstone enthusiastically and donated £50. (Marx denounced Darwin's support of the "piggish demonstration.") Anthony Trollope read *Bulgarian Horrors* to his family. Oscar Wilde, then an Oxford undergraduate, wrote a surprisingly ham-handed sonnet, urging Jesus to save the Bulgarians:

CHRIST, dost thou live indeed? or are thy bones
Still straitened in their rock-hewn sephulcre? . . .
For here the air is horrid with men's groans,
The priests who call upon thy name are slain,
Dost thou not hear the bitter wail of pain
From those whose children lie upon the stones? . . .
Come down, O Son of Man! and show thy might,
Lest Mahomet be crowned instead of Thee!

Wilde admiringly sent this off to Gladstone, who kindly gave the promising young zealot tips on how to get it published. From her sickbed, Florence Nightingale beseeched the British to take care of the wounded, and donated £10 to the cause: "In the midst of their rose-garden industry their women and children were all at once attacked and butchered with never-to-be-forgotten horrors or worse." Alfred Tennyson, hugely popular for his "Charge of the Light Brigade," was too anti-Russian to join in wholeheartedly (that was who the Light Brigade was charging against), but, after Gladstone extolled the heroism of the Montenegrins, obliged him with a vaguely ludicrous sonnet called "Montenegro":

O smallest among peoples! rough rock-throne
Of Freedom! warriors beating back the swarm
Of Turkish Islam for five hundred years.[24]

These intellectuals were mostly liberals, disgusted by the slaughter. Many of them had earlier called for the prosecution of the British governor of Jamaica in 1865–66 for his harsh crushing of a weak insurrection—including Charles Darwin, his rival biologist Herbert Spencer, the philhellene T. S. Hughes, and Gladstone. (The writers Thomas Carlyle and John Ruskin, later atrocitarians, as well as Tennyson, had hypocritically defended the British Empire.) The more ardent imperialists—like Sir James Fitzjames Stephen—were less likely to support Gladstone's appeals. The Liberal Party, since Richard Cobden, had a reputation as being either anti-imperial or rather passively happy for the British Empire to gradually turn into a voluntary trading association. So now Gladstone was roundly denounced for being anti-imperialist. As one critic put it, Gladstone "regards our Empire in general, and India in particular, as mere accidents of our national greatness—as sources of weakness, not strength—as liabilities to be diminished, rather than as assets to be enlarged and secured."[25]

But the movement's roots went much deeper than intellectuals. Starting in September, Derby received a flood of atrocitarian town resolutions from all across Britain. In a typical example, from Darwin, in the Co-operative Hall there, the locals unanimously passed resolutions expressing their "heartfelt empathy with the sufferers, and . . . intense indignation," and then roasted Disraeli's policies as "disastrous to the interest of humanity and discreditable to the British nation." Similar resolutions flooded in, from Sunderland, Finchley, Rochester, Aberdeen, Bath, Manchester, Stirling, Ludlow, and Woolwich—joined by pamphleteers and individual activists. The activists also sent some 455 petitions, page after page after page of names neatly written on purple paper. They came mostly from southwestern and northern England and Wales, with almost total silence from Ireland (where Irish grievances came first). In the frenzied month of September, Derby was buried under some twelve hundred pages. By the end of 1876, the Foreign Office had received about seventeen hundred pages of protest.[26]

Religious feeling was important. Where the local church was atrocitarian, it became a potent source of organization. Victorian Britain was fertile ground for evangelical revivals. But atrocitarianism was particularly strong among nonconformists (like Baptists, Congregationalists, Methodists, and Quakers) already unhappy with the British social order. There were no protests to Derby from Catholic or Jewish groups. Gladstone blamed the Vatican: "I suppose the Pope has kept Ireland quiet."[27]

The Church of England was, with a few vocal exceptions, mostly unmoved. The Archbishop of Canterbury and his bishops held their tongues. There were almost no Anglican protests sent to Derby, because of a mix of Tory allegiance, conservative temperament, contempt for the Eastern Orthodox, and, for the so-called Dizzy-Derby bishops, simple patronage. The evangelicals, part of the Low Church, were unremittingly hostile to Gladstone's pleas—quite unlike their prominent role in the London Greek Committee. The most prominent High Church atrocitarian was Henry Parry Liddon, who took the rare step of preaching against Disraeli's policies from St. Paul's, caustically suggesting replacing Elliot with "a diplomat of human rather than of Turkish sympathies."[28]

The Tories dominated in high society, where the toffs found common cause not with the rustic Bulgarians, but their imperial rulers. But Gladstone, an aristocrat trying to learn to be a democrat, found unlikely allies in the labor movement, and regularly denounced "the upper ten thousand." Disraeli also did surprisingly well with the press. The *Daily News* carried the flame for the atrocitarians, and the *Times* started strong and faltered. The *Daily Telegraph,* the largest new daily newspaper, was firmly pro-Ottoman. The smaller magazines split, with *The Economist* repelled at the "boiling anger and indignation of our countrymen."[29]

Finally, there was the Liberal Party, which, seeing its political opportunity in this frenetic new movement, belatedly closed ranks behind Gladstone. When Hartington, Granville, and a jolly Gladstone were seen together at the Haymarket Theatre in London, just after Gladstone finished his pamphlet, Disraeli glowered: "3 conspirators."[30]

"Never Again"

As Gladstone's pamphlet hit the streets, Disraeli and Derby met at 10 Downing Street to coordinate their position. "All the world is mad," Disraeli wrote, from the solitude of the prime minister's residence, as rallies sprung up around the country. Disraeli wistfully hoped that it would rain "cats and dogs" on Gladstone at Blackheath in Greenwich, where he was giving a speech. It did, and a huge crowd of ten thousand undaunted soggy atrocitarians wildly cheered Gladstone on from under their umbrellas. Disraeli later claimed he had heard that the speech was "a blank disappointment to the infuriated and merciless humanitarians." Quite the opposite. Gladstone proposed using the British fleet at Besika Bay to blockade Ottoman efforts to supply their troops, and appealed to his audience "on grounds, not of political party, not even of mere English nationality, not of Christian faith, but on the largest and broadest ground of all—the ground of our common humanity." A journalist remembered Gladstone "standing grey-faced and stern, with flashing eyes and hand uplifted in a gesture of indescribable energy and dignity," raging against an imagined Ottoman: "Never again shall the hand of violence be raised by you; never again shall the dire refinements of cruelty be devised by you for the sake of making mankind miserable in Bulgaria."[31]

Victoria was worried about the Tories' loss of popularity. Disraeli wrote, "I hope the general insanity may have subsided in a fortnight; if not, I really can't answer what may be the result of popular passion and the ballot." He worried that "this Bulgarian atrocity" had "weakened Derby's hands" in making peace in the Balkans. Disraeli attacked Gladstone as an anti-Turkish bigot: "I think Gladstone's pamphlet outrageous. Its point was, for ethnological reasons no less, to expel the Turks as a race from Europe." Gladstone had to retreat, claiming he only meant Turkish officials, not the Turkish people. With satisfaction, Disraeli wrote, "He is already beginning to eat his words."[32]

As a matter of principle, Disraeli was against "hysterically 'modifying' our policy, in consequence of the excited state of the public mind," which would make his government "contemptible." But in fact, he was starting to boast of having used the British navy to prevent massacres. He bristled at Gladstone's accusation that Disraeli had "so emboldened the Porte, that these 'atrocities' have taken place!" Quite the contrary: "We sent our fleet to B[esika] B[ay] to defend H.M. subjects and their property, and to prevent Xtian massacres." The result was "tranquillity instead of anxiety . . . and our Ambassador has received the thanks of all the Xtian communities for our having saved them. Nothing can describe the alarm of the Xtian population of Constantinople, and its contiguous territories, at the rumor of our fleet being withdrawn." Although Derby told a group of working-class activists at the Foreign Office that "there are a great many people in England who fancy that Lord Beaconsfield [Disraeli] is the Sultan and that I am the Grand Vizier," he supported protecting the Bulgarians from further atrocities, as well as paying reparations and punishing the killers.[33]

Atrocitarian activists came to Hawarden to ask a surprisingly reticent Gladstone to throw himself into the fray with another of his legendary speeches. He overcame the last of his reluctance, and started a tour of the north. The country was torn between "Turks" and "Russians." Disraeli, his handwriting almost illegible from stress, wrote, "This is the greatest pressure I have ever had during the whole course of my life."[34]

Disraeli was shocked to learn that Sultan Murat V had read all the House of Commons debates over the Bulgarian massacres. He worried that the agitation was hampering "a peace satisfactory to Europe and very honorable to England." At the same time, he was disgusted with Derby ("the great Sec[retar]y.") and particularly Elliot, "a very second-rate man" and "an invalid" with "a torpid liver," who "has managed to nearly pull down a popular and powerful Ministry."[35]

Because Disraeli had just ascended to the House of Lords, his empty old Commons seat, in Bucks County, had to be filled in a by-election. Gladstone was keen to humiliate the prime minister with a defeat there: "I send 250 little ones [pamphlets] . . . as my contribution to the Bucks Election." He added, "Bucks, Bucks, Bucks." At a campaign speech at an agricultural dinner in Aylesbury on September 20, Disraeli's Tory candidate was white with fear. The prime minister, undaunted, rumbled that the "sublime sentiments" of the atrocitarians risked igniting a huge European war, bringing "general havoc and ruin . . . worse than any of those Bulgarian atrocities." Relying on aristocrats, landlords, and prominent farmers, the deeply rattled Tories managed to hold Disraeli's safe former seat by a tiny margin. "The Anti-Russian feeling is very strong," a disappointed Granville noted.[36]

This near miss hardly endeared Disraeli to the atrocitarians: "those rabid cockneys the electors of Greenwich." Fuming at Gladstone's suggestion of expelling the Turks from Europe, Disraeli complained that "England rapturously assembled at Greenwich to hear the statesmanlike development of this wise proposition." When Derby met with a group of bankers who supported Gladstone, Disraeli told the shaken foreign secretary, "You can't be too firm. What the public meetings want is nonsense, not politics." The result of their plans, Disraeli warned, "w[oul]d. be war by England alone against Turkey."[37]

India or Bulgaria?

There was one shocked Briton whom Disraeli dared not ignore: Queen Victoria. To win her back, Disraeli harped on two themes close to her heart: hatreds of partisan politics and of Russia. She wrote that since "Russia *instigated* this insurrection, which *caused* the cruelty of the Turks, it *ought* to be brought home to Russia, and the world *ought* to know that on *their* shoulders and *not* on *ours* rests the *blood* of the murdered Bulgarians!" She understood Disraeli's "motive for *not* expressing 'horror' at the 'Bulgarian atrocities.' She had only suggested a word of *sympathy* if an occasion offered." And she was disgusted by Gladstone's politicking, which was a little too democratic for a queen who was about to be named empress of India, creating "a *party question*" rather than helping Disraeli secure peace and "the great interests of the great Empire."[38]

Victoria's heir—Albert Edward ("Bertie"), the Prince of Wales, who would become King Edward VII—was more forthrightly conservative. He groused that Gladstone had emboldened Russia by stirring up British public opinion, which "makes my blood boil with indignation." Edward Bulwer-Lytton, the British viceroy in India, admitted that the "Bulgarian atrocities are shocking enough," but could not believe that "English interests" would be well served by "uninstructed popular passion." From Shimla, Lytton clinched his case with an ominous warning to the woman who would soon be ostentatiously signing her Christmas cards as "V.R. & I (Regina et Imperatrix)." There had, Lytton wrote, already been peaceful pro-Ottoman demonstrations by Muslims in Bombay and Peshawar, but a British war against the Ottoman Empire could well cause "a

Mohammedan rising in India. . . . We could only put it down by 'blood and iron.' "[39]

For Victoria, Disraeli, and Lytton, imperial interests came before humanitarian ones. India trumped Bulgaria. As Sir Henry Austen Layard, later Britain's ambassador in Constantinople, would put it, "It is the most monstrous piece of folly that we should be ready to sacrifice the most vital interests of our country, India, our position as a first-class Power, the influence that we have hitherto exercised in the cause of human liberty and civilisation . . . *because some Bashibazuks have murdered some worthless and unfortunate Bulgarians!*"[40]

Conversely, many of the atrocitarians struck sharply anti-imperialist notes, refusing to put the British Empire ahead of morality—to put India ahead of Bulgaria. Gladstone rejected the idea of trading off the unhappiness of "twelve or thirteen millions of Christians in Turkey" for the sake of maintaining self-proclaimed benevolent British rule in India. Hartington would not "fight against the forces of nature, and the laws of human progress" to ensure "the security of our Indian Empire." And Edward Augustus Freeman, an intemperate historian and activist, said, "Perish the interests of England, perish our dominion in India, sooner than we should strike one blow or speak one word on behalf of the wrong against the right." Humanity was more important than the empire.[41]

"That Unprincipled Maniac Gladstone"

Touring the north, Gladstone was vaguely put off to find himself a moral celebrity: "I have had the greatest difficulty in maintaining any show of privacy and avoiding strong manifestations. I never saw such keen exhibitions of the popular feeling, appearing so to pervade all ranks and places." He argued that after Bulgaria and Bosnia were granted autonomy, "a temporary military occupation on a small scale might be necessary, for purposes of police, to keep the peace between Mussulman and Christian. It is a pity: but the thing may have to be done." Gladstone presumably envisioned a multilateral peacekeeping mission like the one in Syria in 1860–61.[42]

On the receiving end, Disraeli's thick skin got thicker. He praised Derby, whose "clear, callous, common sense is so shocked by the freaks of the foolish, and so contemptuous of the machinations of the factious, that he quite enjoys discharging a volume of cold water on their unprotected persons." He joked to Derby, "One really wants encouragement right now. I sometimes feel like the juryman who complained of having been sitting along with eleven of the most obstinate men he ever met." The embattled prime minister, contemptuous of atrocitarian "knaves, or fools," professed to "delight in the whole *débâcle,* having never bated an inch, and being quite as 'cynical' and 'heartless,' and everything else, as I was at the beginning."[43]

In fact, Disraeli's policy had already softened considerably. Derby admitted to the City atrocitarians that the massacres had "changed the position . . . of our own Government." Elliot, in Constantinople, was ordered to read Baring's report on the atrocities directly to the sultan, demand that the Ottoman Empire punish the killers and help the victims, as well as propose autonomy in Bosnia and guarantees against further oppressions in Bulgaria. This, Gladstone noted, marked the end of Disraeli's denial of "the crimes of the Turks." As Gladstone joked, "I cannot turn round as often & easily as the Tories; on account of my (late) lumbago."[44]

Some Tories wanted more action. The Marquis of Salisbury, the India secretary—who was a longtime rival of Disraeli and an old friend of the High Church atrocitarian Liddon—wanted to name an official Ottoman "Protector of Christians," with ready access to the sultan, who could only be fired with the approval of the five great powers. Disraeli mildly liked the idea, but responded coolly that "notwithstanding the hullaballoo in which we still live," the government could not afford to look "frightened and perplexed." The Tory base of "all the moneyed and commercial classes" was holding fast, so Disraeli resisted the temptation of "Bulgarian philippics."[45]

Gladstone publicly tried to mask his personal dislike for Disraeli, but could not resist some unveiled anti-Semitic slurs. He opined: "What Dizzy hates is Christian liberty and reconstruction." He cruelly added, "I have a strong suspicion that Dizzy's crypto-Judaism has had to do with his policy. The Jews of the East *bitterly* hate the Christians; who have not always used them well."[46]

Disraeli openly hated Gladstone to the guts. The prime minister labeled Gladstone "the Greenwich Tartuffe"—a religious hypocrite with nefarious motives. He hoped that his rival would end up disgraced, forced into retirement in a French monastery, or a retirement distinctly more permanent: "I can fancy that grim visage digging his own grave." To Derby, Disraeli fulminated: "Posterity will do justice to that unprincipled maniac Gladstone—extraordinary mixture of envy, vindictiveness, hypocrisy, and superstition . . . whether preaching, praying, speechifying, or scribbling—never a gentleman!"[47]

Russians and Bulgarians

MacGahan, who spoke some Russian, had been startled to discover that he could understand much of what the Batak massacre survivors were saying. These rural Bulgarians reminded him keenly of Russian peasants on the Volga. "It is no wonder," he wrote, "the Russians sympathise with these people."[48]

The news of the massacres broke in the Russian press in late June, with a telegram from Bucharest. It was explosive stuff. Ignatiev did everything he could to spread the word, given extra credibility by the British press. The semiofficial Agence Russe was outraged, along with the almost all of the press. The Russian Orthodox Church proved an enormously effective network, with churches serving as the most effective fund-raisers for the pan-Slavist committees. Tsar Aleksandr II's own wife and son were active in supporting the relief efforts. Activists with donation boxes were everywhere, from train stations to steamboats to trams, invoking the empress's name. Others stormed off to join the Serbian army. The Moscow Slavic Benevolent Committee raged that "every description of torment and disaster is now being inflicted on the unarmed Bulgarian population by a fanatically enraged Asiatic horde, which has planted itself on the ruins of an ancient and a great Orthodox Empire." It was "the last terrible bloody struggle between Slavism and Islam," with Britain encouraging Islam.[49]

Above all, the sensationalistic Russian press stoked the fires across all classes. *Voice* editorialized that Russia was under a "moral obligation" to stop the atrocities. *Russian World,* the newspaper edited by Cherniaev before going to help lead Serbia's army, wanted to march a Russian army corps into Bulgaria. Newspapers competed for circulation by trying to outdo each other in pan-Slavist rhetoric.[50]

In his serialized *Writer's Diary,* Dostoevsky gave a wildly exaggerated version of what MacGahan saw: "the terrible massacre by bashibazouks and Circassians of sixty thousand peaceful Bulgarians." This was five times more than sober estimates. He falsely accused Disraeli of claiming that Slavs had actually committed the massacres. And he swore that, despite hateful European suspicions, Russia actually had nothing but the purest of motives, which would have been news to Ignatiev: "It is done as service to the whole of mankind. Indeed, when and how often did Russia act out of a policy of direct benefit to herself?"[51]

Dostoevsky continued the theme in *The Brothers Karamazov.* Ivan Karamazov reports meeting a Bulgarian in Moscow, who tells him of

Ottoman atrocities in Bulgaria: "They burn villages, murder, rape women and children, they nail their prisoners to the fences by ears, leave them so till morning, and in the morning they hang them." This is not simple animal cruelty, he says, but something worse: artistic cruelty. Dostoevsky has his character feverishly imagine a trembling Bulgarian mother cradling her baby, surrounded by Turks who "pet the baby, laugh to make it laugh. They succeed, the baby laughs. At that moment a Turk points a pistol four inches from the baby's face. The baby laughs with glee, holds out its little hands to the pistol, and he pulls the trigger in the baby's face and blows out its brains. Artistic, wasn't it?"[52]

When the Bulgarian massacres hit the headlines, the pan-Slavist campaign in Serbia had actually been going badly. Cherniaev had proven ineffectual in battle, with Serbian soldiers and Russian volunteers bickering. Ignatiev, who knew a lost cause when he saw it, told a Serbian envoy that Russia could do nothing for them. Even with Serbia routed, Dostoevsky still considered Cherniaev a "genius" for raising "the great Slavic question." The Serbians themselves, wary of being annexed by Russia in the name of pan-Slavism, "were dreamers, very like small seven-year-old children who put on toy epaulets and imagine themselves generals." But they would come around: "The great Russian spirit will leave its traces in their souls, and their own Serbian valor will spring up from the Russian blood that was shed for them. Someday, after all, they will satisfy themselves that the Russian help was selfless and that none of the Russians who died for them was thinking of annexation!"[53]

But now the pan-Slavists turned their full attention to the Bulgarians. The British worried that the explosion of pan-Slavism could become a chance for socialist revolutionaries. When Moscow's governor refused to allow permission for a demonstration, the empress herself told him she was "profoundly wounded" by his attitude. That emboldened Moscow's pan-Slavists to go ahead, with some ten thousand pan-Slavists gathering at the train station to see off Red Cross ambulances bound for Serbia. They delivered a banner sewn by the ladies of Moscow, sang Orthodox hymns, and marched to the governor's house to protest the supineness of the government. The British ambassador reported nervously that if there were any more atrocities, "neither the Emperor nor Prince Gorchakow would be able to resist the unanimous appeal of the nation for intervention to protect and save their coreligionists." Gorchakov sent the other great powers a gruesome Russian consular report on the atrocities, and told Britain that the great powers must stop "the effusion of blood which was creating a feeling of horror and exasperation among all classes."[54]

Aleksandr II tried and failed to assert some control over his country. The Third Section secret police attempted to cool off the pan-Slavist committees. Gorchakov complained to the editor of *Voice* about a nastily anti-Britain editorial. The tsar banned newspapers that printed articles too sharply critical of his governance. *Russian World* was banned for two weeks for taking the War Ministry to task. When reopened, the paper celebrated with an article calling for more democratic institutions, which won a new suspension for three months. But repression risked dangerously alienating much of Russia—not least Aleksandr II's wife. He soon relented. His only option was to shift course. Gorchakov saw the pan-Slavist upheaval as a useful tactic, allowing him to plead to foreign diplomats that his hands were tied. So Russia launched a newly belligerent policy against the Ottoman Empire. Disraeli groaned, "Gortchakoff is, of course, in the seventh heaven."[55]

Gladstone's thunderings were a gift to Russian pan-Slavists. Although he was suspicious of Russia, with a deep horror at Russia's bloody crushing of Poles and Hungarians, he believed in "the pulse of humanity which is now throbbing almost ungovernably in her people." *Voice* cheered on Gladstone's call for a European intervention to save the Bulgarians. Gorchakov and the Russian press eagerly followed the rise of the British atrocitarians.[56]

Disraeli himself was a particular pan-Slavist target. One *Voice* editorial blasted his "cynical explanations." Another singled Disraeli out as a profiteering "premier of hebrew extraction," in a conspiracy with bankers who controlled the media. The "clever and astute Jew," *Voice* wrote, was using "the inherent aptitude of his race" to paralyze Europe into allowing "the wholesale slaughter of the Christians."[57]

Gladstone had *Bulgarian Horrors* translated into Russian and priced to move, with an astonishing twenty thousand copies printed and sold. (The proceeds, which were supposed to go to the oppressed in the Balkans, predictably wound up in the pockets of Russian pan-Slavists.) The Agence Russe cheered, "England seems to want to return to the policy of George Canning. We can again see the beautiful days of Navarino!" Disraeli was staggered: "Gladstone has translated his pamphlet into Russian—to assist us!" Ignatiev, riding high, proposed using the basics of Gladstone's polemics—the expulsion of Ottoman troops from Bulgaria and a temporary military occupation—as the basis for a Russian ultimatum to the Ottoman Empire.[58]

Gladstone's efforts had evidently convinced Russian leaders that Britain would have to stand by if Russia went to war. Disraeli nervously reckoned that by the spring, "Russia and Austria will march their armies into the Balkans." But both Disraeli and Derby knew that British public opinion made it all but impossible to stand up to Russia. Derby's meek efforts to broker a Balkan cease-fire looked pathetic as Russia proposed that it occupy Bulgaria. When Serbia rejected that cease-fire, Disraeli blamed the public agitation for encouraging Serbians to imagine that Britain would actually come to their rescue.[59]

In the hothouse atmosphere of the imperial fall palace at Livadia on the Crimean Riviera, Aleksandr II and Gorchakov were surrounded by court pan-Slavists, including Ignatiev. The pressure was intense. Cherniaev asked to visit, but that was too much for Aleksandr II to swallow. As the press in St. Petersburg and Moscow reached new heights of rage, the tsar began military and diplomatic preparations for war if the Ottoman Empire would not grant Bulgarian autonomy. By mid-October, Russia had decided on partial mobilization.[60]

To Disraeli, a massive war seemed inevitable. "I don't see my way," the flummoxed prime minister wrote. He predicted the invasion and destruction of the Ottoman Empire, and the nightmare prospect that Britain might be forced to defend Constantinople itself against a Russian onslaught. Disraeli bitterly wrote, "War seems imminent—and a long one. So much for Mr. Gladstone and his friends who will avenge the 'Bulgarian atrocities' by the butchery of the world."[61]

Disraeli needed to end the Balkan fighting fast, before another atrocity drove him any further. In desperation, he made a wildly dangerous step: demanding that the Ottoman Empire accept an armistice, or have Britain withdraw its support and ambassador. This would silence Russia. "I think Gortchakoff wants war," the prime minister wrote nervously. "The only good thing is the improved feeling in England; but I fear it's too late."[62]

This audacious "last card," Disraeli knew, was necessitated only because of "the conduct of Gladstone and Co." Russia, he wrote, "was feeling her way till Gladstone's move; that decided her." Disraeli complained that his diplomatic efforts had been "immensely aggravated by the treasonable conduct of that wicked maniac Gladstone."[63]

The gamble worked. The Ottoman Empire agreed to a six-month armistice. Disraeli had put his trust in the new young sultan, Abdulhamit II: "Will he be a Soleyman the Great?" Abdulhamit II, in fact, would go on to become notorious across Europe for the massacres of Armenians in the 1890s, in a prelude to the 1915 genocide. But for now, Disraeli could relax: "breathing time." After six months, "the people of England will have quite recovered their senses—and I hope Gladstone will be shut up."[64]

Even though the Ottoman Empire had just accepted a six-month armistice, Ignatiev delivered what Disraeli called an "offensive and hostile ultimatum" demanding a six-week Balkan armistice only. Victoria was appalled at "Emperor Alexander's rash and intemperate act. . . . How can we *ever* trust the Russians?" But the pan-Slavists were thrilled. Dostoevsky wrote that the tsar's "resounding words" were echoed "in the hearts of all Russian people." But he still yearned for war. Dostoevsky argued that the Ottomans would continue to slaughter Bulgarians: "The Slavs need peace, but not that kind of peace. It's not peace at all that's needed now, but simply an end."[65]

Unlike Dostoevsky, Aleksandr II still would rather have avoided war. He personally rejected Ignatiev's proposal of basing Russia's ultimatum on Gladstone's pamphlet. He pledged his honor that he had no desire to own Constantinople, let alone India, although he warned that he might have to temporarily occupy Bulgaria. Aleksandr II reassured the British that he had been forced to send off that ultimatum out of fear that there might be more massacres like Batak after Serbia's defeat. Gorchakov instructed the pathologically unreliable Ignatiev, "His Majesty prefers above all a pacific solution and would rejoice exceedingly if military demonstration is not imposed on us by our dignity." Still, at the last minute, the Ottoman Empire accepted Russia's ultimatum.[66]

"A Kremlin on the Bosphorus"

Disraeli cheered up briefly as Russia overreached. Russia's aggressive drive to occupy Bulgaria "has roused and alarmed John Bull," Disraeli wrote with relief. "England looks upon the proposed occupation of Bulgaria as a real Bulgarian atrocity." Some of the British press, including the *Times,* turned against Gladstone.[67]

Victoria hoped to take away Russia's pretext for expansion, by freeing Bulgaria from Ottoman rule and creating a neutral state. Even with the armistice in hand, Disraeli was gloomily planning for a huge war against Russia. ("The 'Intelligence Dept.' must change its name," he groused. "It is the department of Ignorance.") His war plans were the exact opposite of what the bulk of the British public would have wanted: aiming at checking Russian expansionism, not Ottoman cruelty. Disraeli warned that if

Russia occupied Constantinople before the British navy could come to the rescue, it would be "the most humiliating event, that has occurred to England, since the surrenders of Whitelocke and Burgoyne and Cornwallis, but infinitely in its consequences more important and disastrous." To prevent that, Victoria wrote, "we might have to occupy Constantinople." It would take British troops six weeks to reach Constantinople, racing the Russians there. As Disraeli warned the cabinet, British soldiers would have to seize the Bosphorus and the Dardanelles.[68]

Disraeli scorned Aleksandr II as "that old cox-comb." He could not have been more skeptical of Russia's professed benevolence: "The Emperor of Russia cares as much for the Christians as you do for Spurgeon and he and all his court would doff (don?) the Turban to-morrow if he could only build a Kremlin on the Bosphorus." (Disraeli was somewhat less ambitious, wanting only Malta or Gibraltar, not Egypt or other major territories, if the Ottoman Empire collapsed.)[69]

With a shaky armistice in place, the European powers turned their attention to an international conference at Constantinople. Disraeli chose Salisbury to represent Britain among the assembled "Machiavellian brains." Given Salisbury's calls for protecting the Bulgarians, this showed a significant softening of Disraeli's hard line. Gladstone was delighted.[70]

Britain was worried about what a Russian occupation of Bulgaria would mean. To restrain Russia, Derby formally asked that the conference be based on the same formula used successfully to limit the French occupation of Syria: "the Powers do not seek for territorial advantages, exclusive influence or commercial concessions—as in the protocols . . . of August 3, 1860." Gorchakov agreed, as the British ambassador to Russia noted, to an occupation with "an European character as in the case of Syria, . . . in 1860, and it might be entrusted to Russia and Austria acting in the name of Europe." Citing the Syrian occupation as a precedent, Gorchakov said he would not object to other great powers participating in the occupation.[71]

But Russia never actually signed a protocol. Gorchakov warned that atrocities were still going on in Bulgaria, and that force might be needed. He ordered Ignatiev to insist on Bulgarian autonomy at the conference, and, if Russia was in the minority on that, to quit the talks.[72]

Disraeli lashed back against Russia. Granville knew that Disraeli's strongest card was British public contempt for Russia: "the counter excitement of the Russophobia." Disraeli complained that the *Times* was getting its news dictated directly by the Russian ambassador. In a high-profile speech at the Guildhall banquet in London, the prime minister defiantly attacked the atrocitarians for deluding Serbians into thinking Britain would come to their rescue. He offered one sop to British public opinion, suggesting that Ottoman independence would "vanish" unless its Balkan subjects were treated properly. Disraeli warned Russia that the British Empire would be "inexhaustible" in war.[73]

Two days later, Aleksandr II, unaware of Disraeli's statement, took the sensational step of giving a rare public speech in Moscow—a sign of how much public opinion was pushing the Russian state. He paid warm tribute to "our volunteers, who had paid with their blood for the cause of Slavdom," although he still sought above all to prevent "precious Russian blood being shed." While hoping that the Constantinople conference would bring peace, Aleksandr II warned that he would act independently if the Ottoman Empire did not satisfy "our just demands." He concluded with red meat for the pan-Slavists: "May God help us to fulfil our sacred mission." The Russian interior minister was so stunned by this line—a royal endorsement of pan-Slavist views of an Orthodox holy community—that he had to ask for confirmation before officially publishing the speech.[74]

The war talk startled many other people, including Granville: "Dizzy & the Czar are playing at an unworthy & dangerous game of brag." Gorchakov, while taken aback at Disraeli's London speech, hung tough, telling the British ambassador that they could not allow more atrocities: "It is not a political question; it is one of humanity—which equally regards all Europe."[75]

Despite rumblings of war, Gladstone remained serenely confident, pleased by church sermons and cash donations for the cause. In London, someone dressed up as an Ottoman Turk complete with some little Bulgarians to oppress; he was chased by atrocitarians yelling, "No peace with Turkey!" With no sense of recounting something chilling, Gladstone reported that, in Liverpool, a traditionally Tory town, during a performance of *Othello,* when "the words were reached 'the Turks are drowned' the audience rose in enthusiasm & interrupted the performance for some time with their cheering." Also nastily, Gladstone privately explained that Disraeli was risking his government "for his Judaic feeling, the deepest and truest, now that his wife is gone, in his whole mind."[76]

Disraeli's own government was collapsing both above and beneath him. Above, he had to fend off Victoria's recommendation of an independent Balkan state to prevent further oppression. Below, at least half of Disraeli's cabinet was repelled by Britain's alliance with the Ottoman Empire. Disraeli found one of them, Lord Carnarvon, the colonial secretary (with the unfortunate nickname of "Twitters"), "insufferable" for openly keeping company with atrocitarians. Disraeli repeatedly complained of religious feeling in his own cabinet, getting in the way of a realpolitik resolution "of a purely political question, wh[ich]. referred to the distribution of power." He reserved his ire for the Bulgarians: "If the 'Eastern Xtians' will be tolerably tranquil—sensible on such matters they can never be—I by no means despair of ultimate success."[77]

Disraeli's Bulgaria

While Salisbury prepared for peace talks, the Russian army slowly mobilized for war. By the end of 1876, almost two hundred thousand Russian soldiers were poised to strike. And the Russian press added anti-British outbursts to its steady anti-Ottoman drumbeat.[78]

To block Russia from occupying Bulgaria, Disraeli instead secretly proposed a British occupation of Bulgaria and Bosnia. The model was the French occupation of Syria sixteen years before. He instructed Salisbury that, if Russia proposed an occupation at the peace conference, Britain would only agree "with the full consent, of the Porte—as in the Syrian case." The Ottoman government, Disraeli thought, would accept this, so long as Russia was not doing the occupying. Disraeli thought that a joint British-Russian occupation would be "highly objectionable," and that "the Porte . . . would prefer fighting." Instead, Britain itself had the troops to handle the job: "We have a force of 40,000 men ready, and I cannot doubt that, if 6,000 French were sufficient for Syria, 40,000 English would be ample for European Turkey: say 10, or 15,000 for Bosnia, etc., and 25 or 30,000 for Bulga[ria]." These British troops would be helped by regular Ottoman soldiers placed under British command.

The prime minister, while desperate, was not bluffing. He was confident the cabinet would endorse his occupation plan, and that it would "be cheerfully accepted by Parliament, and be popular outside." He instructed Salisbury that this British occupation plan would be "the last card to be played, and it must be so done, that we must seem almost unwillingly to consent." This secret proposal, Disraeli wrote, should always be on Salisbury's mind: "a polestar to guide you, and a great end always to be working up to."[79]

This was an intervention on a grander scale than either the battle of

Navarino, or even France's occupation of Syria. While Disraeli's own motives were to foil Russia, a great many people—much of the cabinet, Parliament, and public, not to mention the queen—would have cheered the departure of British troops to end the Bulgarian horrors.

Constantinople and Piccadilly

As Salisbury sailed for the Constantinople peace conference, the British atrocitarians held a parallel star-studded conference in St. James's Hall in Piccadilly, which usually hosted concerts. It was, for atrocitarians, a shadow Parliament, while Parliament itself was out of session; the name "conference" summoned up heroic memories of the antislavery struggle. Held on December 8, it was a sensationally popular event, drawing activists from across Britain and sending ripples across the country. The *Times* gave it prominent coverage. The conference included eighty-nine MPs, and luminaries like Darwin, the novelist Anthony Trollope, the biologist Herbert Spencer (eclipsed by Darwin but evidently willing to swallow his pride in the name of Bulgaria), the scholar James Bryce, and the poet Robert Browning.[80]

When Gladstone entered the hall around eleven a.m., pandemonium broke out in the audience, with hats and handkerchiefs waving, as he bowed and smiled. The Duke of Westminster started the proceedings by calling for sending the British navy and army to Constantinople to whip the Ottoman government into line. He won his biggest cheers for declaring that Britain would not go to war on behalf of the Ottoman Empire. Liddon, the High Church priest and friend of Salisbury, demanded a military occupation, using some one hundred thousand British troops. Thomas Carlyle wrote in: "The unspeakable Turk should be immediately struck out of the question, and the country left to honest European guidance." To cheers and laughter, Trollope, sporting gold spectacles and white hair, urbanely compared the Ottoman Empire to a dissolute friend or relative who had to be broken with: "England had now to declare that if the Turk was to live in Europe, it must be under other laws than his own, and he must adopt other customs than those which outraged the feelings of civilized humanity." George Otto Trevelyan warned Disraeli against honoring Britain's alliance with the Ottoman Empire on the battlefield: no matter how his "fingers . . . may finger the hilt of the sword, the nation will take care it never leaves its scabbard." In a hysterical burst, Edward Augustus Freeman, a historian and activist who regularly denounced Disraeli as a Jew, and who wore a bushy beard that was bigger than his head, asked, "Will you fight for the integrity and independence of the Empire of Sodom?" The crowd roared.[81]

Moderate Liberals like Granville and Hartington (who largely agreed with Derby) skipped the conference, but Gladstone was its main speaker. Gladstone, oddly reticent about leading the movement, gave relatively few speeches, but this was a "great, notable, almost historical" occasion. As he took the stage, the hats and handkerchiefs flew again, with round after round of applause. Gladstone talked for an hour and a half, urging an "attack in the name of humanity." Rather than Ottoman dominion or Russian conquest, he called for freedom for the Balkans. He recalled the fight against the slave trade. And he closed to loud cheers by invoking the precedent of Canning's war for the Greeks. Against Tory claims that Britain had a traditional pro-Ottoman policy, Gladstone said, "I know not where that policy was in . . . 1827, when the Battle of Navarino was fought. But . . . there is a higher and broader traditional policy; that traditional policy of England was not complicity with guilty power, but was sympathy with suffering weakness." And then as the crowd went wild, Gladstone, flushed with success, headed off for dinner with a Russian pan-Slavist friend and the Russian ambassador.[82]

This was, at last, too much for the queen. Her fear of Russia and jealousy for India trumped her humanitarian sentiments. Gladstone had "taken leave of his reason!" He had done "irreparable mischief" by convincing Russia that Britain would not fight, which was "not patriotic and has nothing to do with Conservative or Liberal, or the general jealousy and dislike of Lord Beaconsfield [Disraeli]." With blithe royal conviction of the identicality of her preferences and public opinion, Victoria insisted that "*all really* sensible people of *all classes* and all opinions in the country, would never for an instant stand our honour and interests being sacrificed for the sake of Bulgarian atrocities." Disraeli was relieved to find "the Faery most indignant about the St. James's Hall 'Conference.'" She suggested unleashing the attorney general on the activists. "She seems now really to hate Gladstone." As Victoria wrote to Disraeli, "It is *impossible* for the Queen to say what she *feels* at the *conduct* of Mr. Gladstone and others." She called them "unpatriotic" and "disloyal." A few days later, Disraeli wrote, "She really thinks G[ladstone]. mad."[83]

Disraeli thought that the St. James's meeting had, once again, weakened Britain's hand. "The occupation [of Bulgaria]—even by soi-disant 'police'—will be difficult for Othman to digest." In fact, Aleksandr II began to exert pressure on Russia's press from the start of December, which had some impact in dampening pan-Slavist agitation. Disraeli frostily reported to Derby that the Russian ambassador had told him that "Russia did not care a pin for Bulgaria, or Bosnia, or any other land—what it really wanted was 'the Straits.' . . . I said, I knew that."[84]

But Aleksandr II and Shuvalov were not the only Russian voices. As the peace conference convened in Constantinople, Ignatiev was already planning for a Russian occupation of Bulgaria. Disraeli had explained to Salisbury that the conference "will consist of a meeting between you and Ignatieff." Salisbury, finally meeting the notorious Ignatiev at dinner, said, "I am told you are a terrible man, and that you have so many spies and agents all over the East." The suave Ignatiev, who affected an ironically sulfuric charm, calmly admitted as much, but swore that they were not paid agents: "Every one who fights for his country, who fights for his faith, who struggles for freedom in all these lands, is my helper. I have thousands of these—yes, twenty thousand. . . . But you are the support of the savagery and tyranny of the Turks."[85]

Ignatiev wanted international approval for a Russian occupation of a huge new Bulgaria. He pressed Salisbury by asking him "what will they say in England" if Salisbury delivered only half measures "in response to Mr. Gladstone's agitation against atrocities." Salisbury was stunned when, while his back was turned, Ignatiev redrew the proposed boundaries to give Russia several thousand more miles of Bessarabia. Caught red-handed, the Russian count smiled, shrugged, and urbanely said, in French, "*Monsieur le Marquis* is so sharp, one cannot hide anything from him."[86]

Instead of Ignatiev's expansive plans, the great powers proposed European-supervised Bulgarian autonomy within the Ottoman Empire. And rather than have Russian troops provide security, Salisbury suggested that Belgium send gendarmes. Ignatiev complained that the Belgians would not be able to keep the peace and that Russian troops would have to come to their rescue, and Salisbury worried that he might be right: "If massacre [were] afterwards to occur, our positions would be hard to defend and Russian occupation inevitable."[87]

This was still more than the Ottoman government could swallow. On the first day of the conference, a new reformist grand vizier put out a new Ottoman constitution, promising fresh liberties and better governance. That, as far as the Ottomans were concerned, was that. Bizarrely, one of the two Ottoman plenipotentiaries, Edhem Pasha, started life as a Greek child born in Scio, who was found and adopted by an Ottoman officer after the 1822 massacre there. He was raised as a Muslim Turk, and became, as Salisbury wrote, "one of the most fanatical Turks at the Porte. His temper is very violent: and he sometimes relieves the tedium of the sittings by insulting the Plenipotentiaries all round." The Ottoman Empire, furious at pan-Slavist intrigues, would go no further. As Disraeli wrote, "The Porte cannot accept the preposterous proposals."[88]

Disraeli spent a miserable Christmas dinner alone with only the enigmatic consolation of a copy of *Faust* as his present from the queen. He keenly regretted his conciliatory decision to send Salisbury to Constantinople: "He is much duped by Ig[natiev]." He was appalled by his envoy's sympathy for the Bulgarians: "Sal[isbury]. seems most prejudiced, and not to be aware, that his principal object . . . is to keep the Russians out of Turkey, not to create an ideal existence for Turkish Xtians. He is more Russian than Ignatieff: *plus Arabe que l'Arabie!*"[89]

The prime minister, wracked with a wicked case of gout and bronchitis, was sunk in misery: "I wish they were all—Russians and Turks—at the bottom of the Black Sea." Disraeli noted that "the Porte . . . seems resolved to make the Emperor and his princely Minister [Ignatiev] eat the leek—very difficult to digest, if not impossible." The new Queen-Empress Victoria, just as interested in her elevation ceremony as she was with the devastating famine in Bengal, sulked and said, "It is most disappointing and annoying!" Disraeli privately urged the Ottoman Empire to grant more Balkan autonomy, but did not delude himself: "It is hopeless. The Turks will yield nothing. I'm not sure, were I a Turk, I should think them wrong."[90]

The European great powers made a last-ditch offer for autonomy for Bosnia and Bulgaria, without the obnoxious gendarmerie. But despite a threat by all the other powers to withdraw their ambassadors, on January 18, 1877, the sultan and his court rejected this, too. Russia now had a free hand to wage war, since the demands of the great European powers had been snubbed.[91]

With no wider settlement in place, the armistice expired. Salisbury slunk back to London. The hard-line Scio survivor, Edhem, became grand vizier—ready for confrontation. Europe braced for war.[92]

"Constantinople Must Be Ours"

At the beginning of 1877, Gladstone was still riding high, making inroads even in Tory counties. He could barely stay on top of his speaking engagements, some held at railway stations for maximum efficiency. In Glastonbury, for instance, he paraded through with a band and flag-waving crowds stomping happily through the rain and mud. In Parliament, the Tories were lambasted by Gladstone and the Radicals. Gladstone intoned before the House of Commons of the "deep human interests that are involved in every stage of the question."[93]

But privately, Gladstone was worried. He feared that Parliament could turn against him. In the House of Lords, "Turkish or anti-Russian sentiment will have a blinding effect." In the House of Commons, his lead was "remarkably compact, and the Irish Roman Catholics have . . . behaved badly, in deference to the trumpet sounded from Rome."[94]

Above all, the British atrocitarians lost steam as a catastrophic war loomed. The mass following trickled away, leaving the activists and pressure groups, but not a truly national movement anymore. George Eliot was put off by "the bad figure the Opposition makes with its readiness to impeach." Regaining his feet in the House of Lords, Disraeli warned of "wars of no ordinary duration," and argued that Britons felt a "deeper sentiment" than "humanitarian and philanthropic considerations": "the determination to maintain the Empire of England." Disraeli was triumphant: "The Parliamentary collapse of the 'Eastern Question' agitation is almost unprecedented: so rapid and so complete."[95]

Moderate Liberals and Whigs, sensing political disaster for the British left if war broke out with Russia, tried to restrain Gladstone. Granville and Hartington discouraged Gladstone from raising the Bulgarian issue again in Parliament. Over Hartington's objections, Gladstone wrote another pamphlet, *Lessons in Massacre,* which sold only seven thousand copies. He was crestfallen.[96]

Just after Gladstone received the proofs, he went to harangue Charles Darwin himself. Darwin was rendered mute as Gladstone, as soon as seated, inexhaustibly read from the proofs of *Lessons in Massacre* for almost two hours. Somehow, Darwin enjoyed it. As a witness recorded, Gladstone's "great, wise, simple, and truth-loving listener, then, I think, busy on digestive powers of the drosera in his green-house, was intensely delighted." Darwin wrote, "I expected a stern, overwhelming sort of man, but found him as soft & smooth as butter, & very pleasant." As Gladstone strode off, the immortal Darwin said with satisfaction, "What an honour that such a great man should come to visit me."[97]

Aleksandr II was at the end of his rope. In his Moscow speech, he had all too publicly committed his word to rescue the Balkan Slavs. Dostoevsky wrote, "Oh, Europe, whose interests would so suffer should she earnestly forbid the Turks to strip the fathers' skins in the presence of their children!" Aleksandr II showed his limits by denying a Serbian request for two Russian divisions. Serbia, defeated on the battlefield and with no Russian rescue in sight, made peace with the Ottoman Empire.[98]

But the pan-Slavists still demanded that the tsar hold to what he had recklessly called "our sacred mission." Dostoevsky fulminated, "No matter what happens . . . sooner or later, Constantinople must be ours." The British, he wrote, hoped for more Balkan massacres to "completely exterminate the Christian community." Ignatiev urged Aleksandr II not to demobilize the Russian army with Ottoman commitments to reform. The wavering tsar, feeling that his honor was at stake after his ostentatious pan-Slavist pledges, backed Ignatiev, and sent him on a tour of the European courts to whip up anti-Ottoman sentiment.[99]

In mid-March, Ignatiev made his stunning debut in London society. Salisbury had committed the error of casually suggesting to Ignatiev that when the turmoil was over, Ignatiev should visit him at Hatfield, Salisbury's estate in Hertfordshire. A week later, Ignatiev was on his way. Disraeli groaned, "The Ignatieff arrival is a thunderbolt: nothing could be more inopportune and nothing more awkward."[100]

Nothing more awkward, definitely. The Ignatievs, unaccustomed to British hospitality, found the estate damp and freezing. One British lady made the polite mistake of asking Ignatiev how he felt after his long trip, to which the indefatigable count replied, "I always feel well. My conscience is clear because I defend the Christians." Victoria found Ignatiev "a very disagreeable, vulgar-looking man, with a bad countenance." They studiously avoided talking about politics, and instead discussed family events, which later made Derby burst out laughing. Ignatiev briefly met Gladstone, and for once the British orator could not get in a word edgewise.[101]

Disraeli, cringing, could not manage to avoid hosting a dinner party for his hated Russian adversary. There, British high society met the Russians with social dynamics just a notch above kindergarten: the Prince of Wales snubbed Ignatiev; the Russian women skipped water and instead belted back enough sherry to scandalize even the British; and, as Disraeli merrily reported, Britain's finest ladies were determined to show up Countess Ignatiev. Thus "Lady Londonderry staggered under the jewels of the 3 united families of Stewart and Vane and Londonderry, and on her right arm set in diamonds the portrait of the Empress of Russia." Another British duchess "set everything on fire, even the neighboring Thames; . . . her hair *a la Marie Antoinette,* studded with diamonds, which by the by were stuck in every part of her costume." It was a rare British triumph.[102]

. . .

Ignatiev demanded that the Ottoman Empire unilaterally stand down its military forces before Russia would demobilize. Victoria, increasingly obsessed with India, hoped that Disraeli's cabinet would be "very firm." She offered to whip Salisbury and the "somewhat weak and sentimental Lord Carnarvon" into line. She herself had entirely recovered from her bout of humanitarianism: "This mawkish sentimentality for people who hardly deserve the name of real Christians, as if they were more God's creatures and our fellow-creatures than every other nation abroad, and forgetting the great interests of this great country—is really incomprehensible."[103]

Bolstered by the queen, Disraeli convened his nervous cabinet for a climactic meeting. He told his ministers that they had to choose between "the Imperial policy of England, and the policy of crusade." Salisbury, knowing at whom this was aimed, replied that, despite public opinion, he would yield to the majority of the cabinet. Only Carnarvon briefly stood up to Disraeli and Victoria. He coughed, and sharply criticized Disraeli's policy, but then fell into line. The newly united cabinet refused to join Russia's demand for Ottoman demobilization. Disraeli crowed, "Yesterday was the most important meeting of the Cabinet which has yet been holden, and I trust we shall never hear any more . . . Gladstonism, within those walls."[104]

Disraeli suffered a brief attack of optimism: "I think after all we shall have peace, though there are so many slips between Russian cups and Russian lips that I shall never be sure till I hear that the Grand Signor has asked the Russian Ambassador to dinner at his palace on the Bosphorus." The great powers signed a watered-down protocol politely urging the Ottoman Empire to reform its governance and asking both the Ottoman and Russian armies to stand down, so long as there were no more massacres. Disraeli was thrilled: "In fact Russia has surrendered at discretion and England has completely triumphed in her main object: prevented her invasion of Turkey!" In fact, neither the Ottoman nor the Russian government took this new protocol seriously. Ignatiev, having left Britain convinced the British public could not stomach supporting the Ottoman Empire, was hoping for a quick war. But Disraeli, for once underestimating the impact of the atrocitarians, was giddy with relief: "Firmness and tact will, I think, carry us through. . . . It is nearly all up with Gortchakoff. What fun!"[105]

On April 24, less than three weeks later, Russia declared war on the Ottoman Empire.

CHAPTER TWENTY-THREE

The Russo-Turkish War

Gladstone Alone

Russia's pan-Slavist committees and press were in full cry. Huge crowds gathered in Moscow to cheer on the tsar. Dostoevsky was on the Nevsky Prospect in St. Petersburg when he heard the news, and rushed to the Cathedral of Kazan to join continuous prayers marking the glorious event. Riding the train that spring, Dostoevsky bought food and cigarettes for the Russian soldiers on their way to war. In fresh religious ecstasies at this sudden realization of the Orthodox dream, denouncing peace as degrading and Disraeli as Jewish, Dostoevsky welcomed the historic adventure of messianic violence: "It is the people themselves led by the Czar who have risen for war." Russians poured into churches and crossed themselves; peasants donated carts and horses. The war was not just for fellow Slavs, but also "for our own salvation. The war will clear the air which we breathe and in which we have been suffocating, closeted in spiritual narrowness and stricken with impotence of decay."[1]

Self-pityingly, Aleksandr II said he had been reluctantly forced into war by his wife, Gorchakov, Ignatiev, and Gladstone. Russia had laid the groundwork for war by secretly winning Austro-Hungarian neutrality. In exchange, Russia promised Bosnia to Austria-Hungary, as soon as it was carved off from the Ottoman Empire—a monumental betrayal of the pan-Slavist cause. It is striking to see amicable imperial logrolling disposing of the immediate issue that would start World War I.[2]

Disraeli's cabinet frantically evaluated Ottoman military prospects—with the overwhelming fear that Russian troops would threaten to take Constantinople, dragging Britain into the war to save the Ottoman capital. He wanted to hold the Dardanelles to defend Constantinople. Salisbury cautioned that Britain must not be seen to be acting with Ottoman consent, because the British public would not tolerate seeming to be Ottoman allies. Carnarvon did not want to move the fleet at all. But as the Russian menace became more clear, the more pro-Bulgarian Tories in the cabinet yielded to Disraeli.[3]

Russia's aggression was a calamity for Gladstone and the atrocitarians. Just before Russia struck, Victoria demanded that the cabinet show wartime unity: when Britain's "greatest if not vital interests (viz., our Indian Empire) are involved, *all* private feelings should be overruled. . . . It is not the question of upholding Turkey; it is the question of Russian or British supremacy in the world!" She offered to appeal personally to the opposition to stay quiet. The queen, reprimanding a prominent atrocitarian lord, blamed the war on Gladstone's "*utterly* incomprehensible" agitation, which persuaded Russia it had a free hand. In the boozy halls of London, a belligerently anti-Russian song inspired the term *jingoism:*

We don't want to fight,
But by Jingo if we do,
We've got the ships, we've got the men,
We've got the money too.[4]

Gladstone was proud that he had ruptured the alliance with the Ottoman Empire: "All idea of their going to war avowedly for Turkey is out of the question." He stuck to his guns, to the despair of the more moderate Liberals and Whigs led by Hartington and Granville. Feeling that "the Gov[ernmen]t. grow more Turkish every day," he decided to introduce a provocative series of resolutions in Parliament—although presuming they would be voted down. Hartington tried to block this. But Gladstone felt Disraeli needed continuous pressure. Gladstone did not get to speak until the early evening, at which point he unleashed a typically verbose two-and-a-half-hour performance, introducing five resolutions in the House of Commons blasting Disraeli's government for its callous policies. The last three resolutions were the harshest, calling for "practical self-government in the disturbed Provinces of Turkey, by putting an end to the oppression which they now suffer." He invoked Canning's "wise and honourable policy" that brought war on behalf of the Greeks in 1827, asking that Britain now lead the great powers in demanding "such changes in the Government of Turkey as they may deem to be necessary for the purposes of humanity and justice, . . . and for the peace of the world."[5]

Of course, moderate Liberals were not about to go to war alongside Russia. Gladstone could not fathom this, since Russia's cause was just: "If

Russia should fail, her failure would be a disaster to mankind." Hoping only that Russia would be "tolerably prudent," he was openly rooting for Russia's victory:

> When that work shall be accomplished, though it be not in the way and by the means I should have chosen, as an Englishman I shall hide my head, but as a man I shall rejoice. Nevertheless, to my last day I will exclaim—Would God that in this crisis the voice of the nation had been suffered to prevail; would God that in this great, this holy deed, England had not been refused her share!

That was more than enough to make moderates jump ship. One typical prominent Liberal MP would have liked Gladstone's resolution before the war, but could not stomach it now. Gladstone, with Hartington's loyalists turning on him, had to drop the last three resolutions, and content himself with saying that the Ottoman Empire had lost all claims to British support. If anything, Gladstone—speaking off the cuff, having forgotten his glasses—was purpler in humiliation than in ascendancy. "Sir," he said, "there were other days when England was the hope of freedom. . . . The five million of Bulgarians cowed and beaten down to the ground, hardly venturing to look upwards, even to their Father in Heaven, have extended their hands to you; they have sent you their petition; they have prayed for your help and protection." The Bulgarians did not want a Russian alliance, but their suffering was "the greatest that exists on God's earth," and Britain had done nothing for them. Saving them was "a great and noble prize. It is a prize well worth competing for."[6]

Still, Gladstone knew it was not going well. In the House of Commons, he wrote, he was for over two hours "assaulted from every quarter," except the almost silent Liberal benches. "Such a sense of solitary struggle I never remember." He was "nearly in despair . . . but resolved at least not to fail through want of effort." After five days of fierce debate, Gladstone was defeated by 354 to 223, with a healthy pro-government majority of 131—far more than Disraeli's government usually got. Gladstone wrote, "Never did I feel weaker and more wormlike."[7]

Facing Down Russia

Russian troops poured into the Balkans, with Aleksandr II himself visiting the front. Buckling down for the struggle, Disraeli styled himself after his idol, who would have despised his politics: " 'So,' as Byron says, 'here goes.'" Aleksandr II was hoping for a swift victory, before Britain or other European powers could get involved. Russian forces easily crossed the Danube in late June 1877, and the Ottomans appeared on the verge of total rout. With thirty thousand Russian troops in the Balkans, the invaders seemed ready to march on Constantinople itself. Russian officials were planning the creation of a vast Bulgaria under Russia's wing, ripe for annexation, thus spelling, as the British ambassador in Constantinople put it, "the end of the Ottoman Empire in Europe."[8]

On June 30, Disraeli's cabinet once again dispatched the British fleet to Besika Bay, near the Dardanelles, to defend their unpopular Ottoman ally. Victoria was verging on italicized lunacy: "*if* we allow *this, England . . . would no longer exist as a great power,* and . . . the Government itself could *not* exist, which *permitted this*!! The Queen is feeling quite ill with anxiety." When the *Times* reported Russian war crimes against Ottomans, she demanded an official British protest against these "monstrous cruelties." She had "*insisted* on it . . . about the Bulgarians, and *now* she must do the *same* in this much worse instance." Disraeli, nothing if not evenhanded, at first did not want to protest these atrocities either, but agreed to denounce them.[9]

Many of the atrocitarians were predisposed to dismiss these atrocity reports as Ottoman propaganda. Freeman was unconcerned: "I suppose the Cossacks have done some ugly things, as English troops did at St. Sebastian, French in Algeria, and generally everybody everywhere." But Gladstone, to his credit, asked Derby and Shuvalov to look into the "grave" allegations. He recalled how Russia's cruelty to the Poles had undermined Russia's public standing in Britain, and demanded "severe and prompt punishment" for any Russian soldiers who had committed war crimes against Ottoman troops. "My duty is to proceed with a perfect impartiality," Gladstone wrote. "I think we now know that the armed Bulgarians have been doing cruel and horrible acts." He thought that some Russians were guilty, too. "We cannot take all soldiers to be angels. At the same time, cruelty is *worse* in a Christian than in a Turk."[10]

The imminent nightmare prospect of fighting off the Russians at Constantinople was finally too much for the cabinet. Derby, Salisbury, and the rest—except just two—said they would sooner resign. Victoria suddenly remembered a nonimperialist reason for deploying the fleet: "For the protection of the Christians at Constantinople the fleet would seem necessary." At the end of August, Disraeli sent a secret warning directly to Aleksandr II that if the Russians occupied Constantinople, Britain would go to war against Russia.[11]

But Ottoman troops rallied and stoutly fought back the Russians at Plevna. Some three thousand Russian soldiers died in the first attempt to take the fort; another seven thousand died in a second try. Britain warned that a second attempt at taking Constantinople would not be allowed. Russia continued to speak with several voices. Dostoevsky rejected all compromise: "Constantinople must be ours . . . and remain ours for ever." Ignatiev, at Aleksandr II's side as the Russian army laid siege to Plevna, similarly begged the tsar to push on to Constantinople. But Gorchakov tried to restrain the military, prompting the Grand Duke Nikolai, Aleksandr II's uncle and Russia's top wartime commander, to epic denunciation: "Horrible fellow! Horrible fellow! Pigwash! Pigwash!" Although the pan-Slavists remained keen for war, and glad to fight Britain, too, their adventures seemed less and less appealing as the grinding death toll at Plevna mounted. The direst scenario was the prospect of a second military campaign in 1878, which both Karl Marx and the tsar's own Third Section thought would ignite a Russian revolution.[12]

Pan-Slavism's starkest ideological failure came when Russian troops did finally encounter the fabled Bulgarians. The Russians were nonplussed: the Bulgarians actually seemed richer than Russian peasants, rather than on the verge on starvation. The Russian army fed itself off of Bulgarian resources, and then retreated, leaving the Bulgarian villagers to face Ottoman authorities indignant at this collaboration. The soldiers paid scant attention to the well-being of the Bulgarians—the ostensible cause of the invasion.[13]

The war took an appalling toll. Some 80,000 Russians would be estimated dead by the end of the year, and Gladstone would later make the standard estimate that "probably 100,000 or 150,000 Russians bit the dust in the course of that war." Thin and haggard, Aleksandr II stayed at the front, ordering the continued battle for Plevna.[14]

His rival empress, Victoria, blamed Russia for "*one* of the most *bloody wars* ever known." Abandoning any sympathy for the Bulgarians, she fumed:

> Under the cloak of RELIGION and under the pretence of obtaining just treatment for the so-called "Christians" of the principalities, but who are far worse than the Mussulmans, and who moreover had been *excited* to revolt by General Ignatieff, who prevented regular troops being sent out to quell the revolt, leading thereby to the so-called "Bulgarian atrocities" as the irregular troops were sent out, this *war of extermination* (for that it is) has been iniquitously commenced!

In the name of "*humanity*, justice, and of the *British Empire*"—not necessarily the same thing, a point that seemed to elude her—she was "*determined* to put *an end* to so horrible a *slaughter*." Instead of fearing the extermination of Ottoman minorities, she now worried about "*preventing* her [the Ottoman Empire's] *extermination*." She decided that the Russians "are more barbarous and cruel almost than the Turks, though they may *not* kill or murder in the same way, but the slow killing by imprisonment and exile to Siberia, and ill-usage of every kind which *no* one *hears* of, is as bad if not worse."[15]

Despite all this, Gladstone was not shy about rooting for Russia. But more moderate liberals, like Granville, knew they were much undermined by popular anti-Russian wartime emotions. Granville warned Gladstone that "Dizzy has been using the most violent language," blaming "national feeling" for the war, which might force him "to land 300,000 men in Turkey!!!" Even Gladstone conceded that "chauvinism flourishes, and might prevail," but, being Gladstone, kept his chin up: "Admitting as I do that Turkish prevails on the surface, I could detect no flagging at Nottingham in the best audience of 8000 or 10,000 that I ever addressed under cover in my life." He briefly hoped that Disraeli might "disappear in flame and stench."[16]

Despite the horrific death toll from the protracted siege of Plevna, Dostoevsky was resolute: "Constantinople must be *ours*, conquered by *us*, Russians, from the Turks, and remain ours forever." In December, Plevna finally fell to the Russians, putting Constantinople itself in their path. As British involvement in the war loomed, a mob of jingoes smashed the windows of Gladstone's house in London. Russian troops captured Adrianople, the Ottoman Empire's second capital. Then they marched toward Constantinople. Turkish refugees fled in panic, with many dying miserable deaths from the privations of their flight. Dostoevsky's fantasy of a Russian Constantinople was within reach.[17]

But Aleksandr II stopped. The war had been so devastating that, soon before the fall of Plevna, his government had begun making peace overtures. Gorchakov warned that Britain was not bluffing about rescuing Constantinople. Grand Duke Nikolai decided that a war with Britain was more than he could stomach, and, giving up on Constantinople with the city in sight, signed an armistice with the Ottoman Empire. Even after the armistice, the Russians were briefly tempted to push on. To counter this final threat, in February 1878, Disraeli's cabinet ordered the British fleet to sail from Besika Bay to Constantinople itself. Ignatiev got the news in Bucharest, and rushed to confront Nikolai. As Ignatiev screamed at the grand duke in full view of a startled Russian general staff, Nikolai yelled back that he was damned if he was going to war against Britain. At long last, after years of wavering, Russian moderates stood firm against the militant pan-Slavists. It meant an uneasy peace.[18]

In March, Russia imposed the Treaty of San Stefano (signed in a small town near Constantinople) on the vanquished Ottoman Empire. The punitive treaty would have created a gigantic puppet Bulgarian state that sprawled from the Black Sea to the Aegean and almost to the Adriatic. This was Ignatiev's last gasp—a final attempt to expand Russian hegemony in the Balkans. The news from San Stefano was greeted rapturously in Russia, and Aleksandr II made all Ignatiev's male descendants counts.[19]

This was more than Disraeli could swallow, and he began preparing for a ground war against Russia. A depressed Derby, finally breaking with Disraeli, resigned from the cabinet. But in May, Aleksandr II and Gorchakov chose instead to undo the last fifteen years of work by Ignatiev, who was sulking on his estates near Kiev. Ignatiev was sacked as Russian ambassador in Constantinople, and replaced with a conciliatory new diplomat who disdained pan-Slavism. Britain and Russia alike tried to return to traditional great power politics. Russia agreed to cut its Bulgaria into two zones, with an autonomous northern province under a European-appointed prince, and the southern province under a Christian governor loyal to the Ottoman Empire. Russia's presence in Bulgaria was limited; in a typical Austro-Hungarian proposal, any Russian occupation had to be done with fewer than twenty thousand troops and be over in six months. The devastated Ottoman Empire made fresh pledges to reform its rule in the Balkans, with the guarantee falling not just to Russia but to the other major European powers too. Austria-Hungary, having played off Russia and then Britain, was rewarded with Bosnia as a protectorate. Britain picked off Cyprus. At the Berlin conference, in June and July 1878, Disraeli and Salisbury sealed this new eastern order.[20]

In Russia, the disaster of the war discredited pan-Slavism for a while, but also the tsar. The enormous costs of Aleksandr II's adventure would leave his government horribly unpopular at home, and pave the way for a series of assassinations and a return to reactionary rule. Even Dostoevsky, shortly before his death, concluded reluctantly that Constantinople would not be Russia's after all for the foreseeable future.[21]

One of the casualties of the Russo-Turkish War was the man whose newspaper reports had lit its fuse. MacGahan covered all the major campaigns, but caught typhus in Constantinople after the Ottoman surrender. He died there. Still, he had made his mark. If the *Daily News* had not broken the story of the Batak massacre, European history might have taken untold different paths. The Ottoman Empire, dismembered in Europe and disillusioned with Britain, might not have gone searching for new allies and wound up alongside Germany in World War I. Gladstone would not have had a vehicle to return to politics; Aleksandr II would have been under far less pan-Slavist pressure; and Disraeli might have been able to deter Russia from attacking the Ottoman Empire. Among other remote consequences, this would have meant that Austria-Hungary would not have occupied Bosnia in 1878 (as its payoff from Russia for quiet support of Russia's 1877 aggression), nor annexed it in 1908; and thus Austria-Hungary might not have been in possession of Bosnia in 1914, and would have had no reason to dispatch its archduke Franz Ferdinand to Sarajevo that fatal July.[22]

CHAPTER TWENTY-FOUR

The Midlothian Campaign

"The Sanctity of Life in the Hill Villages of Afghanistan"

The emotions over the Bulgarian horrors remained raw. Gladstone was sure that "the Tory party is travelling towards a great smash." In anticipation of a new election, Gladstone swapped his Greenwich constituency for Midlothian, a Scottish county that he knew was a "citadel of Toryism." On the strength of his efforts to save the Bulgarians, Gladstone had far eclipsed rival liberal politicos like Hartington and Granville, and in 1880 he became Liberal leader once again. As Gladstone later recalled, "I made the eastern question the main business of my life. I acted under a strong sense of individual duty without a thought of leadership; nevertheless it made me again leader whether I would or no. The nation nobly responded to the call of justice, and recognised the brotherhood of man."[1]

This peaked, Gladstone wrote, in "the final consummation in 1879–80": in his political campaign in Midlothian. He launched a full-on moral assault on what he called Beaconsfieldism—against the essence of Disraeli. The core of that assault, he once said, was Disraeli's callous attitude toward the Bulgarian horrors. Disraeli was marked by the atrocities; now he stood to pay the price for it at the polls.[2]

Gladstone stormed across frigid Scotland, eviscerating Disraeli for a few minutes at one railway station before moving on to the next. His longer speeches, to crowds of thousands, could run to almost two hours. They were both hyperbolic and packed with rational argument. He recorded that a trip to Edinburgh "was really more like a triumphal procession." There were crowds of thousands in small towns, and in Edinburgh itself, "the scene even to the West end of the City was extraordinary, both from the numbers and the enthusiasm, here and there a solitary groan or howl. We . . . were received with fireworks & torches. I have never gone through a more extraordinary day." A few days later, again in Edinburgh, he recorded "a wonderful meeting of 20000 at the Waverly market. People were continually handed out over the heads who had fainted and were as if dead." In one two-week period, he unleashed about eighty-six thousand words at eighty-six thousand people.[3]

The remote Scottish riding was not used to this kind of spectacle. *Punch* recalled the wild scenes: "two-hour orations in packed halls, the multiplied addresses of honour and congratulation, the waving flags, the laurelled poles and garlanded arches, the crowded house-tops, the flaring bonfires and the torchlight processions, the exuberance of eloquence, the ardour of applause." As a relaxing break back at Hawarden, the hoarse Gladstone chopped down a sycamore.[4]

Scotland had not been particularly pro-Bulgarian back in 1876, and Gladstone made plenty of more parochial appeals for the Scottish electorate. But the Midlothian campaign was not just about Midlothian; it was also a national touchstone. With the 1868 Telegraph Act making it easier for newspapers to take advantage of the new technology, reprinting long speeches the next day, Gladstone was only incidentally speaking to the electors of Midlothian, but to all of Britain.[5]

His full reproach of Beaconsfieldism included shattering the unity of the Concert of Europe, abusively misgoverning India, waging imperial war in Zululand and Afghanistan, and neglecting "the duties of humanity." His clear-eyed denunciation of the Afghan war showed him forthrightly applying his Bulgarian principles even to Britain's own wars. "Do you attach some value to mercy?" Gladstone asked the villagers of Penicuik.

> What measures does this war entail upon your generals and your soldiers? . . . [W]hen . . . they were making war among the mountain-tops of the passes between India and Afghanistan, the tribes who inhabited them, naturally and not wrongfully, issued forth from their villages to resist. And where they had issued forth, the villages were burned to the ground, and the women and children, by natural and necessary consequence, driven forth to wander and to perish in the snow. These things, in my opinion, are horrible to the last degree.

Gladstone did not blame "your military commanders," who "obey the necessity of the case": "The guilt lies with those who imposed upon them that necessity." That guilt "lay . . . with the majority of the House of

Commons who sanctioned the acts of the British Government; it will lie last with you, the people of Penicuik, and the rest of the people of the country—and with every one among you who gives by his vote his sanction to proceedings so dishonourable to the British name." This was a boldly democratic creed.[6]

Gladstone was moving beyond his religious concern for Christians to a broader humanitarianism, although with Christian faith as his intellectual anchor. As he bravely declared, before a crowd of three thousand women, themselves disenfranchised:

> Remember the rights of the savage, as we call him. Remember that the happiness of his humble home, remember that the sanctity of life in the hill villages of Afghanistan among the winter snows, is as inviolable in the eye of Almighty God as can be your own. Remember that He who has united you together as human beings in the same flesh and blood, has bound you by the law of mutual love; that that mutual love is not limited by the shores of this island, is not limited by the boundaries of Christian civilisation; that it passes over the whole surface of the earth, and embraces the meanest along with the greatest in its unmeasured scope.[7]

But it was Bulgaria that made Gladstone's attacks over Afghanistan possible. The atrocities were, he said, "the question out of which almost every other question had grown collaterally." Bulgaria was the theme that he returned to over and over again. Now turned seventy, still regularly chopping down trees, he went back to Scotland for a second round of Midlothian speeches. He was feeling both his own mortality and divinity. "The days of our life are three score and ten," he wrote. "It is hardly possible that I should complete another decade." He yearned for quiet: "Ah what need have I of what I may term spiritual leisure: to be out of the dust and heat and blast and strain, before I pass into the unseen world." But he also had a final mission:

> For the last 3½ years I have been passing through a political experience which is I believe without example in our Parliamentary history. I profess to believe it has been an occasion, when the battle to be fought was a battle of justice humanity freedom law, all in their first elements from the very root, and all on a gigantic scale. The word spoken was a word for millions, and for millions who themselves cannot speak. If I really believe this then I should regard my

> having been morally forced into this work as a great and high election of God. And I certainly cannot but believe that He has given me special gifts of strength, on the late occasion especially in Scotland.[8]

And so to the arena. In the Music Hall in Edinburgh, before a "great & most enthusiastic" crowd, he blasted Disraeli for taking "up arms for maintaining the sovereignty of Turkey against her subject races, or even to prevent the [Russo-Turkish] war," which Gladstone said the tsar had seen as "a great duty to humanity." Although Gladstone had been lambasted for his demand in *Bulgarian Horrors* that the Ottomans should be kicked out of the Balkans, he now felt vindicated: "There is not a Turk at this moment who, as a Turk, holds office under the Sultan . . . in Bulgaria. . . . No, not one! The despised 'bag-and-baggage policy' is at this moment the law of Europe." He jokingly remembered that "the humble individual who stands before you was held up and reviled as a visionary, an enthusiast, or a verbose I forget what, although I believe myself that there was not much verbosity in that particular phrase."[9]

Gladstone traveled beyond the boundaries of Midlothian, sensing a more national opportunity. In Balerno, he brazenly preferred Aleksandr II's foreign policy to Disraeli's. There had been a "great work of liberation" in the Balkans:

> Ten millions of men at least have been set free who were in political servitude of various degrees, and with whom political servitude was not a mere abstraction, but was associated with daily insecurity in all the most essential conditions of human life,—insecurity of life, insecurity of property, insecurity of liberty, insecurity of honour, insecurity in that sense in which it is dearest to all, the honour of the women of the land. This state of things, a state of things painful and horrible to behold, has been put an end to. But it has not been put an end to by your agency. You have done nothing to help it; you—I am not addressing you individually; I am speaking of the Government of the country; I am speaking of the majority who supported that Government—you left it to Russia; you left it to a despotic Power; you broke up the concert of Europe; you would do nothing except use idle words and representations which you knew very well from long experience to be a mockery; you would do nothing to stop the horrible state of things that prevailed in the Turkish provinces; you left that to Russia. The work of emancipation has

> been achieved, and you have been deprived of the honour of it. You have failed to fulfil those traditions of liberty which belong to the history of this country and the character of the people.

This stands as an enduring statement of what the denial of human rights means, and as a classic denunciation of inaction in the face of oppression. Then Gladstone decried how fears of Russia had allowed Britain to abandon the Bulgarians to their fate. Even so, he trusted that the freed Bulgarians would not become Russian tools: "I have faith in freedom, and believe that, as free institutions have been given them, they, knowing the blessings of freedom, will have the good sense and the courage . . . to maintain it for themselves."[10]

Gladstone noted with satisfaction, "Enthusiasm unabated." At Lonehead, he fortified himself with tea, and then, to wild excitement, devoted almost his entire speech to "those horrors which have covered with everlasting infamy the name of the Turks in Bulgaria." Britain had enormous leverage, since so many of the Ottoman Empire's soldiers were based in Asia: "We had only to say no troops, no guns, no munitions of war shall pass by sea between Asia and Europe in order to reduce the Turkish Government to terms." In the end, even Disraeli had left the Ottoman Empire "mangled and mutilated, bleeding, disturbed, invaded on every side, with the Powers of Europe now, under the Treaty of Berlin, all entitled to interfere in the concerns of Turkey between the Sultan and his subjects." His obstinacy had only hurt the Bulgarians: "We left those people to their fate. After the horrors that were enacted in Bulgaria, we allowed the Bulgarians to understand that we were willing to write on their behalf any number of idle remonstrances," but nothing more. Instead, "we left to Russia the place of saviour and deliverer. . . . The name of our free country has become odious in those provinces [Bulgaria and Bosnia]. For them it is associated with the maintenance of tyranny."[11]

In West Calder, Gladstone went a step further: enshrining humanitarianism at the heart of British foreign policy. "We have been busy in alienating the sympathies of free peoples," he said. The "free Slavonic people" had been "painfully taught" to see Britain's own free institutions as only for Britons, but "for them a dream." Under Canning and Palmerston, Gladstone said, "it was well known that England, while regardful of her own just interests, . . . yet was willing to use and willing to find opportunities for giving cordial aid and sympathy to freedom." He wanted liberation to be doctrine: "The sympathies of free people ought to be a dear and precious object of our ambition."[12]

Gladstone, well pleased, explained his crusade with an egregious mixed metaphor: "I have hammered with all my little might at the fabric of the present Tory power." In his final Midlothian speech before election day, Gladstone resoundingly summed it all up: "A great State trial is proceeding. That State trial is the trial of the majority of the last House of Commons at the bar, not merely of public opinion, but at the bar of this nation."[13]

Beaconsfieldism Defeated

This was all a lot less fun from the receiving end of it. Disraeli, aged seventy-five and in ill health, seemed never to manage to gain his footing. He put out a splashy manifesto blasting Gladstone's support of Home Rule for Ireland as part of an attempt to "enfeeble our colonies by their policy of decomposition," now coming home as "the disintegration of the United Kingdom." But Gladstone weathered even that criticism.[14]

As the voters went to the polls, Disraeli was stupefied: "At this awful pause my mind is a blank." The results were crushing: an overwhelming Liberal victory. In Edinburgh, Gladstone rejoiced to the electors of Midlothian, "the party, which termed itself the Constitutional party, the patriotic party, the country party, and the national party, has now seen the NATION rise up and shatter at a stroke the fabric of its power." Privately, he thanked God: "Wonderful, & nothing less, has been the disposing guiding hand of God in all this matter. Finished England under Lord B[eaconsfield]."[15]

Disraeli wrote, "I am alive, notwithstanding this battle of Armageddon where I have to receive and endure blow after blow." He self-pityingly added, "I . . . am now about to pass through the most painful passage in political life, the transition from power to obscurity." He hoped that Hartington would be the next prime minister, but Hartington and Granville refused to serve without Gladstone. So Disraeli had one final pain to face: giving up 10 Downing Street to his nemesis. The agitation over the Bulgarian massacres finally attained its goal.[16]

Byron's Ghost

Throughout their titanic clash, both Disraeli and Gladstone were painfully aware that they were playing out a latter-day version of the debate over the Greeks. Everybody knew it. The *Times* remembered the Scio massacre, and editorialized, "The atrocities in Bulgaria show that such as Turkey was during her fight with the Greeks and during the outbreak of fanaticism in Syria, such she is still."[17]

For Disraeli, the paramount goal was to avoid another Navarino. He once wrote to Victoria, "It is impossible for England to join in coercing the Porte. It would be damaging to our honour; fatal to our interests; Navarino over again." While Disraeli was prepared to occupy Bulgaria and Bosnia temporarily, he refused to let Russia take the Balkans in a carve-up of the Ottoman Empire. He wrote that Russia's ambitions to take Bulgaria "would be most perilous, if not fatal. It would insure another Navarino, and probably was so intended. We must never attempt to occupy Constantinople, but at the instance of the Porte." Preparing for a cabinet meeting, Disraeli kept in mind "Mr. Canning's experience" as the prime example of what not to do.[18]

In equal and opposite reaction, Gladstone had called Disraeli the least decent British minister since Castlereagh. In December 1876, Gladstone wrote a long article on Canning's humanitarian war for the Greeks, complete with showy passages in Greek. (Gladstone had actually met Canning, but he was two years old at the time.) Drawing on the histories of fighting philhellenes like Colonel Thomas Gordon and George Finlay, he argued that Ottoman rule was slavery. Gladstone remembered the Scio massacre as being as bad or worse than Batak: "All, or nearly all, was quenched in blood by a massacre even more sanguinary, though apparently in some respects less fiendish, than the Bulgarian massacres of the present year." His distrust of Russia was still on display: "The religious sympathies of the Emperor Alexander were upon the whole overborne . . . by his horror of democracy." He praised the philhellenes, the obvious forebears of the current atrocitarians: "the noble forms of individual devotion, as from Byron, Church, Gordon, Hastings, and others." Gladstone particularly extolled the "brilliant" Canning. The contrast to the current prime minister was not exactly subtle; but Gladstone, having discovered a new way of getting on Disraeli's nerves, drove it home with an invocation of the hero of Disraeli's youth. "Lord Byron brought to this great cause, and to the dawn of emancipation, for the East then all in grave-clothes, not only the enthusiasm of a poet, or the reckless daring of a rover," Gladstone wrote. "He treated the subject . . . with the strongest practical good sense, and with a profound insight, which has not been shamed by the results." Byron's "lofty part" had encouraged "the bold policy of Canning," and Gladstone hoped that remembering Byron "may yet supply a guiding light to some British statesman." The dig was unsubtle, even by Gladstonian standards.[19]

Although they took the positions of Byron and Castlereagh, Gladstone and Disraeli were actors on a bigger stage. Gladstone, accurate but self-congratulatory, could not help noting, "The Philhellenes of England were but a sect, limited in numbers and in influence"—in implicit contrast to the national campaign he was fronting. Disraeli, facing a more democratic Britain, with a bigger electorate and press, was up against public pressure that went far beyond what the London Greek Committee had ever managed to field.[20]

In the face of that pressure, Disraeli had been totally unable to deter a Russian attack on the Ottoman Empire. His government had largely fallen apart. He had admitted humanitarian intentions in sending the fleet to Besika Bay. Instead of standing behind the Ottoman Empire, as Britain had done in the Crimean War, he largely left it to fend for itself. And he had nearly sent British troops to occupy Bulgaria and Bosnia. If Russia's untimely invasion of the Ottoman Empire had not let him off the hook, there is no telling what Britain would have done—possibly including a second Navarino. The combination of newly far-reaching foreign correspondents, a mass media, and increasingly democratic politics had made it impossible for British realpolitik to function. Byron, over half a century after his death, had bested Disraeli.

PART FIVE

CONCLUSION

CHAPTER TWENTY-FIVE

Armenians

The American Gladstone

Gladstone knew that the next century would be the United States'. He looked forward without qualms to U.S. commercial and political primacy as Britain settled into decline, taking comfort from the knowledge that a liberal country would become the predominant great power: "In this instance, the strongest means the best. She will probably become what we are now, the head servant in the great household of the World."[1]

Woodrow Wilson more than returned the compliment. As a teenager, Tommy Wilson—not yet going by his middle name of Woodrow—had a picture of Gladstone above his desk. "That is Gladstone, one of the greatest men that ever lived," he explained. He added that he wanted to grow up to be a statesman, too. At Princeton, he wrote essays for the literary magazine on his favorite public man, Gladstone. The Victorian prime minister made a splendid exemplar: upright, a genius of rhetoric, a commander of the world. In Sigmund Freud's psychobiography of Wilson (coauthored with a U.S. diplomat who served under Wilson at the Paris peace conference), Freud even argued that the adolescent Wilson needed a godlike father figure to replace his fallible actual father: "He refound the 'incomparable father' of his early childhood in Mr. Gladstone. . . . He felt himself a man like Gladstone." Freudian analysis aside, Wilson's admiration was so strong that, as president, he kept a portrait of Gladstone on his desk in the Oval Office.[2]

Wilson was a shy, lonely undergraduate at Princeton in 1876, while Gladstone struggled against the Bulgarian horrors. But Wilson did not grow up into his hero's heir in the fight against atrocity. He had a sense of higher calling and a potent if abstract devotion to humanity—although badly undermined by his support for racial segregation and racism against

African-Americans, whom he privately called "an ignorant and inferior race." The most famously moralistic modern U.S. president took a very different course from Gladstone when confronted, four decades later, with the Armenian genocide—the start of a new century of industrial massacre. Countless Americans rallied to the Armenian cause, championed by Theodore Roosevelt and Wilson's own ambassador in Constantinople. But rather than taking on the mantle that Gladstone intended for him and his country, Wilson remained stuck in isolation.[3]

"An Obligation to Repress Evil External to Its Borders"

Well before Wilson became president, Americans were already alert to the suffering of the Armenians. In the 1890s, there was a series of atrocities against Armenians that foresaged worse to come. In 1894, an elderly Gladstone recalled the Bulgarian horrors in demanding action for the Armenians: "Do not let me be told that one nation has no authority over another. Every nation, and if need be every human being, has authority on behalf of humanity and of justice."[4]

Much of liberal American society would have agreed with him. One of the most prominent activists was Julia Ward Howe, the abolitionist and author of "The Battle Hymn of the Republic," whose husband, Samuel Gridley Howe, had fought alongside the Greeks in the 1820s. She became president of the Friends of Armenia. In an 1895 article on the Armenians for the *Women's Journal,* she demanded military action: "I am an advocate of peace, and in my younger days I traveled far and wide to advance its sacred claim. But it is not peace to sit still while villages are burning and streets are running with blood."[5]

Some of the most prominent names in Massachusetts—including Frederic Greenhalge, the governor; William Russell, a former governor; Francis Walker, the president of the Massachusetts Institute of Technology; and William Lloyd Garrison Jr., son of the famous abolitionist leader—signed a petition of "righteous condemnation." For decades before the outbreak of the Great War, Americans were inundated with pro-Armenian and anti-Ottoman magazine articles, generating widespread sympathy and rather less comprehension. In American culture and politics, the adversity of the Armenians loomed large.[6]

Although the United States might fear to meddle in Europe, it showed no such restraint in its own hemisphere. Under the Monroe Doctrine, the United States had a free hand in the New World, without fear of how the great European powers might react. From 1895 on, Spanish oppression in Cuba, trumpeted by the sensationalistic newspapers of William Randolph Hearst, infuriated much of American society, with widespread calls for military action. American motives here were hardly pure: although President William McKinley at first resisted going to war, doing so would suit U.S. economic and strategic interests, driving Spain out and allowing U.S. domination.[7]

Many Americans recalled the European tradition of intervention, invoking recent European protests against the Armenian massacres. In 1895, Hearst's *San Francisco Examiner* wrote: "It may not be our duty to interfere in Turkey, but we certainly cannot permit the creation of another Armenia in this hemisphere. . . . Cuba is our Armenia, and it is at our doors." In 1896, as Spain's General Valeriano "Butcher" Weyler crowded Cuban peasants into concentration camps, with tens of thousands of deaths at least, the *New York Journal* (another Hearst paper) editorialized, "The American people will not tolerate in the Western Hemisphere the methods of the Turkish savages in Armenia, no matter what the cost of putting an end to them might be."[8]

The immediate catalyst of the Spanish-American War was the sinking of the USS *Maine,* but Theodore Roosevelt, then assistant secretary of the navy, typically, linked it to Weyler's oppressions: "The blood of the Cubans, the blood of women and children who have perished by the hundred thousand in hideous misery, lies at our door; and the blood of the murdered men of the *Maine* calls not for indemnity but for the full measure of atonement which can only come by driving the Spaniard from the New World."[9]

Even without the hysterical yellow press, more responsible reporting of Weyler's atrocities would likely have prompted the American public to act. McKinley did not dare risk attacks from the Democrats about bloodshed just off the Florida coast. In 1898, he asked Congress for permission to go to war in the "cause of humanity."[10]

This could have looked like the United States' first humanitarian intervention, but it was sullied by imperialism. Under the December 1898 treaty with Spain, the United States did not just drive Spain out of Cuba, but also took for itself Puerto Rico, Guam, and the Philippines. After the war, the Senate debated whether to cash in the U.S. victory for a small empire. One Indiana senator said, "We will not renounce our part in the mission of our race, trustees under God, of the civilization of the world." But other senators warned of the corruptions of imperialism and pointed out that the United States itself had had a revolution to throw off colonial domination. The United States was "trampling on our own great Charter," said George Hoar of Massachusetts. In the end, in February 1899, the Senate approved the treaty by a single vote.

The United States crushed Filipino resistance, in a vicious war that Roosevelt, as president, inherited from McKinley. Roosevelt welcomed both the war and the imperial mandate. Although he initially was wary of grabbing the Philippines, he soon became a firm supporter of annexation. In 1899, he argued that many Filipinos were "utterly unfit for self-government," and steeled his countrymen for their new imperial duties: "I have even scanter patience with those who make a pretense of humanitarianism to hide and cover their timidity, and who cant about 'liberty' and the 'consent of the governed,' in order to excuse themselves for their unwillingness to play the part of men." As president, he backed these words up with a devastating campaign against the Filipinos, taking a horrific toll on civilians.

Still, in 1913, Wilson pledged that the United States would support the independence of the Philippines. He had at first resisted the annexation of the Philippines, and had only a rather tepid flirtation with imperialism before settling on a dedicated opposition to it. He and Congress granted home rule in 1916. Even Roosevelt, appalled by the Russo-Japanese War, began to lose some of his excitement about warfare and its fruits. By 1907, he privately told William Howard Taft, his war secretary, "I gravely question" whether the American people wanted to hold on to the Philippines. The islands, he wrote, were of no immediate value, and were frighteningly vulnerable to Japan. Thus, "I think we shall have to be prepared for giving the islands independence of a more or less complete type," although far sooner than Roosevelt would have wanted. Independence was not fully achieved until 1946.[11]

Unlike Cuba, the suffering of Armenians offered no imperial benefits to the United States. Still, some Americans saw Cuba as a precedent for a humanitarian American role in the world. Wilson pointed to the Cuban mission as a precursor to a wider U.S. defense of liberty in Poland, Bohemia, and Yugoslavia after World War I. In 1900, Alfred Thayer Mahan, an influential American naval thinker with strong expansionist impulses, gave a speech to a Christian conference in Providence, Rhode Island. He told his audience that "in the present imperfect and frequently wicked state of mankind, evil easily may, and often does, reach a point where it must be controlled, perhaps even destroyed, by physical force." Pointing to the brutalized Armenians and Cubans, he said, "Under some circumstances, an obligation to repress evil external to its borders rests upon a nation, as surely as responsibility for the slums rests upon the rich quarters of a city."[12]

"The 'Americans' in Your Telegram Should Have Read 'Armenians'"

The Armenian genocide came in the thick of World War I, in 1915. The U.S. response was driven by the Wilson administration's need to stay out of the war. The United States was officially neutral, with a public still deep in isolationism. Confronting the Ottoman Empire, which was allied with Germany and Austria-Hungary, could have meant a major war.[13]

Wilson was hardly a pacifist. He had intervened to restore an elected Mexican government in 1913, in what was widely seen as a frightening overreaction. In the name of democracy or at least civil order, as well as checking foreign economic intrusions and keeping control of the sea routes to the Panama Canal, he occupied Haiti and the Dominican Republic in 1915–16. The United States became an exponent of the spread of democracy, especially in the Philippines and in Latin America—often with unhappy results. But for a state with a small army (despite an excellent navy), bullying smaller countries in South America was far less dangerous than entering the Great War. When there were reports that Germany was deporting French civilians for forced labor, Wilson would not speak out: "If I were to begin making protests along lines such as this, where would I stop?"[14]

One of the most vociferous voices for war was Theodore Roosevelt's. Although initially not taking sides, he was shocked by German cruelty in Belgium. He soon came to loathe Wilson as a coward for keeping out of the Great War. "Wilson is a physically timid man," Roosevelt wrote. "He is an entirely cold-blooded self-seeking man." The former president told his son Archibald: "The murder of the thousand men, women and children on the *Lusitania* is due, solely, to Wilson's abject cowardice and weakness." He was equally tough on "the screaming and shrieking and bleating of the peace people," as well as on Wilson's supporters: "Every soft creature, every coward and weakling, every man who can't look more than six inches ahead, every man whose god is money, or pleasure, or ease . . . is enthusiastically in favor of Wilson."[15]

In contrast, Roosevelt was enraptured by war. He believed in international organizations to enforce peace, like Wilson, but ones with military force behind them. He wrote, "A sillier falsehood has never been uttered than the falsehood that 'war settles nothing.' War settled the independence of this country; war settled the question of union, and war settled the question of slavery. . . . Many of the greatest advances in humanity have been due to successful wars for righteousness." For him, the current war—"in its essence one between militarism and democracy"—was surely another such instance. He wrote to a British friend wishing that "I and my four boys would now be in an army getting ready to serve with you in Flanders or else to serve against Constantinople." His sons all served and most paid a terrible price honoring their father: Theodore Jr. was gassed and shot, but lived; Archibald was wounded severely (although this did not stop him from reenlisting in World War II at the age of forty-eight, where he was injured again, becoming the only U.S. serviceman retired on full disability in both World Wars); and Quentin, the youngest, became a pilot and was shot down and killed in France.[16]

But despite Wilson's own sympathies for the Armenians, joining the Great War was far more than he was prepared to do. At most, the atrocities could help tilt the United States toward the Allies, but not jolt the country out of neutrality.[17]

The ruling Committee of Union and Progress, better known as the Young Turks, began its extermination and deportation campaign against their Armenian population in April 1915. In Europe, the reaction was not so different from what had happened after previous, lesser Ottoman atrocities.

Throughout British society, there was horror at this new version of the Bulgarian massacres. David Lloyd George, Lord Curzon, and Arthur Balfour were all enraged. Lloyd George later accused the Ottoman Empire of "exterminating and deporting the whole race, whom they regarded as infidels and traitors. In this savage task they had largely succeeded." Echoing Gladstone's worst moments, he added, "The Turk is a blight and a curse wherever he pitches his tent, and . . . he ought in the interests of humanity to be treated as such. When a race which has no title to its lands other than conquest, so mis-manages the territories it holds by violence . . . , the nations have a right—nay, a duty—to intervene in order to restore these devastated areas to civilisation."[18]

That cry was echoed by influential parliamentarians like Viscount James Bryce, who had been at the Piccadilly conference for the Bulgarians in 1876. Along with the eminent writer Arnold Toynbee, he now helped compile a voluminous Foreign Office documentary report on the massacres. Since the 1890s, there had been a number of influential pro-Armenian groups in Britain, including Bryce's Anglo-Armenian Association, the British Armenia Committee, and the Friends of Armenia—the various descendants of the London Greek Committee. Toynbee worked on the British Armenia Committee's propaganda subcommittee. In a popular 1915 pamphlet, in the Gladstonian tradition, he accused the Ottoman Empire of plotting "nothing less than the extermination of the whole Christian population within the Ottoman frontiers."[19]

As in previous instances of mass atrocity, Russia was more overt about winning strategic benefits. It fielded a few Armenian volunteer army units, made up of a tiny fraction of the overall Armenian population, and many of them non-Ottoman Armenians. Russia, the main Ottoman enemy, tried to sponsor Armenian insurrections, even though the Armenians could hardly be claimed as Slavs. Indeed, the Young Turks' choice for extermination was prompted in part by a desperate wartime fear of Russia. As for Britain, it was not above fomenting unrest among Ottoman subjects, like T. E. Lawrence's mission to the Arabs. But the British government thought that the Armenians were militarily useless, and thus repeatedly refused to back any Armenian revolts.[20]

Early in the genocide, a British diplomat remembered the French occupation of Syria back in 1860: "The final result was the establishment of the autonomy of the Lebanon under a Christian Governor-General, and we must provide the parallel to that by defeating the Turks, not by writing to them." Sir Edward Grey, the foreign secretary, even remembered how France had pressured Fuad in Syria: "Fuad Pa[sha]. was forced to inflict punishment." But since Britain, France, and Russia were already at war with the Ottoman Empire, in an era before air power, there was no obvious military way of rescuing the Armenians.[21]

The U.S. ambassador in Constantinople, Henry Morgenthau Sr., became the Wilson administration's most passionate advocate for saving the Armenians. An immigrant from Germany, he grew up to be a New York lawyer and real estate magnate, active in the city's Jewish community. He had been a stout Wilson loyalist since 1911, when the New Jersey governor came to a dinner celebration for a new synagogue Morgenthau had helped found for poor Eastern European Jews. (His grandson, Robert Morgenthau, today the Manhattan district attorney, remembers, "My grandfather always used to say to me, you know, 'I had to wait until I was fifty-five to go into public service. You have no excuse for waiting that long.'") Morgenthau gave $30,000 to fund Wilson's presidential race, a substantial portion of the total campaign war chest. In return, Wilson made Morgenthau chairman of his campaign finance committee. The day after Wilson won the White House, Morgenthau was among the inner circle gathered at the president-elect's home in Princeton. He had hoped to be named Treasury secretary, but was offended to be offered only the traditional "Jewish slot" of the Constantinople ambassadorship, keeping an eye on the Jewish community in Palestine. He turned Wilson down, only to later reconsider—and thus find himself watching a genocide unfold.[22]

The deportations, Morgenthau later wrote, meant "giving the death warrant to a whole race." He was stunned: "I am confident that the whole history of the human race contains no such horrible episode as this." On April 27, Morgenthau cabled to the State Department that over a hundred "Armenians of better class were arrested ostensibly to prevent revolutionary propaganda." This was part of a "concerted movement against all non-Turkish and non-Union-and-Progress elements." He had received "unfavorable reports about Armenians in interior provinces." Without instructions, he began "strong efforts to prevent excesses and stop the movement." Later the same day, he got a telegram from William Jennings Bryan, in his final months as Wilson's secretary of state, telling him to urge the Ottoman government to protect the Armenians from violence.[23]

Morgenthau, joined by the Italian ambassador, made "strong representations to the Sublime Porte." In response, Talaat Pasha, the interior minister and mastermind of the genocide, told him that provincial officials had been ordered to protect the innocent. In his memoirs, Morgenthau recalled that Talaat angrily snapped, "Are *they* Americans?" Later that month, Britain, France, and Russia had Morgenthau deliver a far more public threat on their behalf: those guilty of "these new crimes of Turkey against humanity and civilization" would be held "personally responsible." This was front-page news in the *New York Times*.[24]

The Ottoman Empire cloaked its atrocities under national sovereignty. The German and Austro-Hungarian ambassadors did not want to meddle in the domestic affairs of their Ottoman ally. Unfazed by the Allied threat of war crimes prosecutions, the grand vizier told Morgenthau that he resented the "attempted interference by foreign governments with the sovereign rights of the Turkish Government over their Armenian subjects." At the same time, Morgenthau reported, the persecution of Armenians was getting worse. Hinting broadly that he needed more robust instructions from the State Department, Morgenthau pointed out that his "unofficial efforts, though frequent and persistent, have resulted in occasionally mitigating the hardships but have failed to dissuade them [from] their course which they attempt to justify on the ground of military necessity."[25]

Bryan resigned in protest of Wilson's strongly worded note to Germany protesting the sinking of the *Lusitania.* He was replaced with Robert Lansing, previously the State Department counselor: an unemotional, detail-minded lawyer, who supported neutrality. He took office as Morgenthau was being deluged with shocking reports from far-flung U.S. consuls and missionaries across the Ottoman Empire. The consul in Harput, for instance, wrote, "There seems to be a systematic plan to crush the Armenian race." So one of Lansing's first challenges as secretary was a long, detailed, and gruesome telegram from his man in Constantinople:

> Persecution of Armenians assuming unprecedented proportions. Reports from widely scattered districts indicate systematic attempt to uproot peaceful Armenian populations and through arbitrary arrests, terrible tortures, whole-sale expulsions and deportations from one end of the Empire to the other accompanied by frequent instances of rape, pillage, and murder, turning into massacre, to bring destruction and destitution on them.

Morgenthau wrote that the assaults were "not in response to popular or fanatical demand, but are purely arbitrary and directed from Constantinople in the name of military necessity, often in districts where no military operations are likely to take place." There were some Armenians who had joined the Russian army, he noted, but most of the victims "are innocent and have been loyal to Ottoman Government," many of them old men and women. U.S. officials had tried to help the deportees, but had been blocked by Ottoman authorities.

Morgenthau's pleas to Talaat and Enver, the war minister, had been rebuffed. The Young Turk leaders, Morgenthau reported, "state that it is the Union and Progress committee's nationalistic policy which they refused to modify even when Russia, France, and Great Britain threatened Ottoman Cabinet Ministers with personal responsibility." They would do anything to hold power, he explained, and wanted to take advantage of a moment when the Allies were already at war with them, and they could count on Germany to stand by. "Turkish authorities have definitely informed me that I have no right to interfere with their internal affairs," Morgenthau wrote. "Still I desire to ask whether you have any suggestions."[26]

Lansing barely reacted. He approved of continuing "pleading" with Talaat and Enver to stop persecuting the Armenians, and of getting the German and Austro-Hungarian ambassadors to add pressure. In response to Morgenthau's request for a new policy, perhaps with political or economic consequences for Ottoman intransigence, Lansing ordered up more of the same. His only novel thought was to ask if any American citizens had been injured.[27]

Lansing held a conservative view of sovereignty, with obligations to defend Americans but not Armenians. At the height of the slaughter, James Barton, an American missionary leader in New York state, begged him for help. But Barton made a typographical error: "Advices from different parts of Turkey report inhuman treatment of Americans by Turks. Cannot something be done to alleviate the horrors?" Lansing smugly replied that the State Department had "received no reports of any inhuman treatment of Americans by the Turks, and would be pleased to receive details from you if you have received information to this effect. The Department believes, however, that the 'Americans' in your telegram should have read 'Armenians.'" He then went further, repeating the Ottoman government's assertion that "large bodies of Armenians are in armed rebellion against the Turkish Government, and . . . the Turkish Government claim that such measures as it has taken are only such as necessary for its own protection against the members of this race." This was, in fact, the exact opposite of what Morgenthau and his consuls were reporting.[28]

Morgenthau made another personal appeal to Talaat. As the ambassador later recorded, Talaat asked, "Why are you so interested in the Armenians, anyway? You are a Jew; these people are Christians. The Mohammedans and the Jews always get on harmoniously. We are treating the Jews here all right. . . . Why can't you let us do with these Christians as we please?" Morgenthau, ignoring the fact that Wilson had actually chosen him specifically for his Jewishness, replied: "You don't seem to realize that I am not here as a Jew but as American Ambassador. My country contains something more than 97,000,000 Christians and something less than 3,000,000 Jews. So, at least in my ambassadorial capacity, I am 97 per cent Christian. But after all, that is not the point. I do not appeal to you in the name of any race or religion, but merely as a human being." Talaat, accusing the Armenians of revolting at Van and helping Russia, was undaunted.[29]

After a bloody month, an agonized Morgenthau tried another long telegram to Washington: "Turkish anti-Armenian activities continue unabated." He sent copies of more consular reports. Unless "this atrocious campaign" was somehow stopped, he wrote, "these people also will be forced from their homes and herded like cattle into the arid and hostile wastes of the interior, where the greater number, possibly excepting those who in desperation embrace Mohammedanism, will doubtless perish by murder or slow starvation." Talaat had said that "he realizes no Armenians can remain friendly to Turkish Government after present treatment and hints at drastic measures against all in Constantinople if slightest offense is committed against Government." The only good news was a protest from the German ambassador.

Throwing diplomatic niceties to the wind, Morgenthau continued, "I earnestly beg the Department to give this matter urgent and exhaustive consideration with a view to reaching a conclusion which may possibly have the effect of checking this Government and certainly provide opportunity for efficient relief which now is not permitted." He choked on the need to respect the sovereignty of a government engaged in massacre: "It is difficult for me to restrain myself from doing something to stop this attempt to exterminate a race, but I realize that I am here as Ambassador and must abide by the principles of non-interference with the internal affairs of another country."[30]

Lansing ignored this. He sent back only one brusque sentence: "Has protest by German Ambassador improved conditions?"[31]

"A Wrong on Humanity"

Morgenthau had lost to the policy of neutrality. He continued to pass along the latest grim news from his consuls, like the brutalization of a caravan of deported Armenians in Urfa, but without much hope of action. He was reduced to smaller efforts, saving lives where he could, but unable to stop the overall extermination. He managed to get Talaat to pledge to spare Protestant and Catholic Armenians, while the massacre of the Gregorians—some 90 percent of the population—went on. He asked for mercy for Armenian teachers, students, and nurses in U.S. institutions in the Ottoman Empire. (Lansing later wrote that these small concessions were not fulfilled.)[32]

Abandoned by the White House, the ambassador asked Lansing to suggest that Morgenthau's influential friends back home form a committee to raise money for the surviving Armenians and to help some emigrate. This followed in the tradition of relief committees for Belgians: a symbol of moral purpose, but without contradicting official neutrality. "Destruction of Armenian race in Turkey is progressing rapidly," Morgenthau wrote, as he asked for half measures. In September, as Morgenthau had requested, Cleveland Dodge, a New York philanthropist who was an old

Princeton friend of Wilson, founded the Committee on Armenian Atrocities. Its leadership included Barton and Morgenthau's friend Rabbi Stephen Wise, who led the Jewish Emergency Relief Commission. They quickly ruled out large-scale emigration of Armenians, but began work on relief. The committee raised enormous amounts of money, helped by the new Rockefeller Foundation, under John D. Rockefeller Jr. It also helped feed articles to the press, led by the *New York Times.* By the end of 1915, the efforts for the "starving Armenians" were widespread.[33]

The deportations and massacres were too large to be secret, and Morgenthau was not the only person reporting them. Based on accounts by travelers and missionaries, as well as U.S. and European government officials, the *New York Times* provided copious coverage from April onward—although not as much as the British press had printed over the Bulgaria atrocities. In August, a *New York Times* headline read, "Turks Accused of Plan to Exterminate Whole Population." In September, there was a front-page headline in a story about Morgenthau: "He Protests Against the War of Extermination Now in Progress." When Barton and Charles Crane, a Democratic Party activist from Chicago and a friend of Wilson, visited the State Department to lobby for the Armenians, the paper reported it under a chilling headline: "500,000 Armenians Said to Have Perished." In October, it ran a long story on the findings of a study by the Committee on Armenian Atrocities with a front-page warning of "A Policy of Extermination." *The Nation* complained of "a deliberate policy of persecution." In response, there were widespread protests and donations on behalf of the Armenians.[34]

So by October 1915, the Wilson administration realized that public opinion would not ignore the Armenians. Edward M. House, Wilson's foreign policy confidant, suggested to the president a protest against the Armenian massacres. As Lansing wrote, private letters "published in the newspapers have aroused a general and intense feeling of indignation among the American people." Finally jerked into some action, he ordered Morgenthau to keep trying to rescue Armenians, as well as "informing Turkish Government that this persecution is destroying the feeling of good will which the people of the United States have held towards Turkey." Lansing's message was immediately leaked to the press. Wilson himself seems to have known at least the basics of the atrocities. Pressed by a missionary friend, who sent the president an eyewitness account from Armenia, Wilson wrote, "The situation with regard to the Armenians is indeed nothing less than appalling . . . we have been doing everything that is diplomatically possible to check the terrible business."[35]

. . .

Nobody was more contemptuous of Wilson's sense of what was "diplomatically possible" than Theodore Roosevelt. If John Quincy Adams had articulated the American creed of refusing to intervene to stop massacres abroad, Roosevelt put forward the opposite about a century later: a doctrine of U.S. military intervention in the name of humanity.

Roosevelt disdained Wilsonian ideals of humanitarianism, unless rooted in patriotism. He wrote, "The man who loves other nations as much as he does his own, stands on a par with the man who loves other women as much as he does his own wife. The United States can accomplish little for mankind, save in so far as within its borders it develops an intense spirit of Americanism. A flabby cosmopolitanism, especially if it expresses itself through a flabby pacifism, is not only silly, but degrading. It represents national emasculation." Instead, he stood for "a nationalism of duty, to oneself and to others; and, therefore, for a nationalism which is a means to internationalism."[36]

In practice, Roosevelt supported a militaristic and interventionist kind of foreign policy. He condemned slavery and said that the United States had been properly castigated for supporting it. He nostalgically remembered the "period when Americans were proud of standing for Kossuth and for Garibaldi, when they subscribed for those who had suffered from wrong in Ireland or Poland, when they sympathized with patriots wrongfully oppressed in any land." He believed that the United States had been right when it, in his rosy phrase, "championed orderly freedom in Cuba, the Philippines, and Panama." He even criticized Disraeli's response to the Bulgarian massacres: "In 1878 it was right to champion Russia and Bulgaria against Turkey and England." His causes included the fate of the Congo, and persecuted Jews in Russia and Rumania.[37]

Roosevelt was famous for fighting against Spanish cruelty in Cuba, risking death with his Rough Riders at San Juan. But unlike the United States' imperialists, he wanted to grant Cuba its independence. In May 1902, as president, he had ended the occupation of Cuba, terminated the military government, and taken down the United States flag in Havana. Despite his expansionist rhetoric, he resisted efforts to establish new military bases in China and the Caribbean, and eventually admitted that the annexation of the Philippines had been a bloody mistake.[38]

He was especially annoyed by Wilsonian neutrality: "It is a wicked thing to be neutral between right and wrong. Impartiality does not mean neutrality." Thus he concluded: "No man can support Mr. Wilson without being false to the ideals of national duty and international humanity."[39]

Roosevelt's commitment to the Armenians went back at least to June 1897, after that earlier round of atrocities. Then, in his first public speech as assistant secretary of the navy, at the Naval War College in Newport, Rhode Island, Roosevelt had sounded like a militaristic New York Gladstone. He had specifically endorsed a duty to wage war against oppression: "Thanks . . . to the cold-blooded brutality and calculating timidity of many European rulers and statesmen, the peace of Europe has been preserved, while the Turk has been allowed to butcher the Armenians with hideous and unmentionable barbarity." Just as he would during the Great War, he blamed pacifism: "War has been averted at the cost of blood-shed and infinitely more suffering and degradation to wretched women and children than have occurred in any European struggle since the days of Waterloo. No war of recent years, no matter how wanton, has been so productive of horrible misery as the peace which the powers have maintained during the continuance of the Armenian butcheries." For someone so obsessed with conflict, Roosevelt seemed blind to the dangers and unintended consequences of military action. War, he was convinced, was a glorious instrument of righteousness: "The men who would preach this peace, and indeed the men who have preached universal peace in terms that have prepared the way for such a peace as this, have inflicted a wrong on humanity greater than could be inflicted by the most reckless and war-loving despot. Better a thousand times err on the side of over-readiness to fight, than to err on the side of tame submission to injury, or cold-blooded indifference to the misery of the oppressed."[40]

In November 1915, a Newark judge sent Roosevelt, in Oyster Bay, on Long Island, a description of the massacres. Roosevelt promised to use it immediately. Later that month, Roosevelt made good on that pledge with a letter to the Committee on Armenian Atrocities in New York. When he was president, in his State of the Union address in 1904, Roosevelt had stated the need to "interfere by force of arms" to stop suffering, with Cuba as his example. Now he unreservedly included the Armenians under that principle.[41]

He wrote to the committee, "Even to nerves dulled and jaded by the heaped-up horrors of the past year and a half, the news of the terrible fate that has befallen the Armenians must give a fresh shock of sympathy and indignation." He went on: "The crowning outrage has been committed by the Turks on the Armenians. They have suffered atrocities so hideous that it is difficult to name them, atrocities such as those inflicted upon conquered nations by the followers of Attila and of Genghis Khan." But that public indignation needed to lead to action: "If this people through its government had not shirked its duty . . . in connection with the world war for the last sixteen months, we would now be able to take effective action on behalf of Armenia. Mass meetings on behalf of the Armenians amount to nothing whatever if they are mere methods of giving a sentimental but ineffective and safe outlet to the emotion of those engaging in them."

Roosevelt took direct aim at Wilson: "A nation too timid to protect its own men, women and children from murder and outrage and too timid even to speak on behalf of Belgium, will not carry much weight by 'protest' or 'insistence' on behalf of the suffering Jews and Armenians." It was "evil pacifism" that encouraged "alien militarism." Attacking Wilson's famous phrase, he wrote, "It is dreadful to think that these things can be done and that this nation nevertheless remains 'neutral not only in deed but in thought,' between right and the most hideous wrong, neutral between despairing and hunted people, people whose little children are murdered and their women raped, and the victorious and evil wrongdoers."[42]

In Roosevelt's other writings on the genocide, he cast about for historical parallels: "Unoffending, industrious and law-abiding peoples like the Armenians, have been subjected to wrongs far greater than any that have been committed since the close of the Napoleonic Wars; and many of them are such as recall the days of the Thirty Years' War in Europe, and, indeed, in the case of the Armenians, the wars of Genghis Khan and Tamerlane in Asia." Or, to take another example: "The Armenians have been butchered under circumstances of murder and torture and rape that would have appealed to an old-time Apache Indian."[43]

Roosevelt was reluctant to back a cause that could not realistically be pursued by arms. Despising peace supporters like Andrew Carnegie, he shunned any activists who did not also call for war. As he told that Newark judge, "I very particularly do *not* want to be put in the position of seeming to demand verbal action that will not be backed by deeds, or of taking action about the Armenians that I would not venture to take about the Belgians." He later wrote, "Some of the professional pacifists and praisers of neutrality have ventured to form committees and speak about—not act about—the 'Armenian atrocities.' These individuals did not venture to say anything about the Belgian atrocities. . . . They were afraid of Germany;

they were afraid of the German vote"—that is, German-Americans, a sizeable group. "But there is no Turkish vote, and they are not afraid of Turkey." Even if less hawkish people managed to save lives, he was unimpressed. Roosevelt's humanitarianism was always militarized.[44]

"The Greatest Crime of the War"

After Roosevelt's letter to the Committee on Armenian Atrocities, as public outrage grew, Lansing belatedly passed one of Morgenthau's reports on to Wilson himself. In Constantinople, Morgenthau was too sickened to stay at his post. "My failure to stop the destruction of the Armenians had made Turkey for me a place of horror," he later wrote. He left for home, to help Wilson's reelection campaign and, he hoped, to tell the president personally what he had witnessed.[45]

In February 1916, the Wilson administration began making angrier complaints to the Ottoman Empire. In addition to pressure from Morgenthau, Roosevelt, and the broader public, the policy shift likely reflected a White House and State Department realization that sending aid to the survivors was a less risky proposition than making military threats. Lansing noted that the constant flow of new accounts of Armenian suffering was "increasing the horror and indignation which the people of this country feel." The U.S. government, he wrote, "earnestly appeals to the sense of humanity and justice of the Turkish Government and urges it to take immediate steps towards the amelioration of the conditions at present existing among the Armenians."[46]

Strikingly, Lansing admitted that the State Department had been "withholding from the American people the facts now in its possession"—an official cover-up of genocide. But, he now threatened the Ottoman government, the State Department was considering whether that whitewash was "justified." His department's decision would be "greatly influenced" by whether the Ottoman Empire took up this appeal. Lansing repeated the same threat to the German ambassador in Washington: he was "greatly in doubt as to whether I am longer justified in keeping from the American people the terrible facts in my possession." He implied that he might make a speech to the American public about the Armenian atrocities.[47]

But by now, the bulk of the killing was over. The Ottoman foreign minister assured the U.S. chargé in Constantinople, Hoffman Philip—who hewed closely to Morgenthau's pro-Armenian line—that the deportations were over, although the chargé continued to fear new ones. Philip, hearing of fresh expulsions from Aleppo and elsewhere, next complained forcibly to Talaat. The Ottoman leader replied that the State Department's information was exaggerated, although he admitted that "many innocent Armenians had suffered." As Philip skeptically reported, Talaat claimed that his orders to stop persecutions and dispossessions had been botched or intentionally misunderstood at lower levels, but that his government would try to stop further atrocities. The chargé doubted that the Ottoman government had much inclination to provide properly for the survivors, and certainly lacked the means: "very extensive outside financial assistance is required immediately to enable survivors to exist."[48]

Lansing, on receiving reports of Armenians in Mesopotamia dying of hunger and disease, had his embassy in Constantinople "urge Turkish Government in name of humanity to alleviate condition remnants of this race." Philip delivered this message, which carried no consequences for ignoring it, "without apparently making much impression." The Young Turks, he wrote, were "violently opposed to the open administration of relief by foreigners to subjects under their control."[49]

The State Department was startled by further deportations of Armenians in Aleppo. "It is a complete extermination," wrote one U.S. consul. Since Talaat seemed increasingly unwilling to hear his complaints in person, Philip sent a stern note reminding him of his promises to stop such expulsions. Talaat sent Philip to talk to the foreign minister, who informed the chargé that this was "only a partial deportation." The Ottoman authorities continued to block relief aid, according to Philip. He concluded, "The decimation of the unhappy Armenian people continue[s] apace, even though the more active and violent processes of elimination are now in abeyance."[50]

This time, Philip recommended stronger action. In October, he told Lansing that he had long felt that the most effective policy "would be to flatly threaten to withdraw our diplomatic representative from a country where such barbarous methods are not only tolerated but actually carried out by order of the existing government." It was a risky course. Breaking diplomatic ties would endanger "American interests . . . in Turkey" and make it impossible to help Armenian survivors. And as far as the Ottoman officials were concerned, "the entire question is relegated to class of 'internal measures' with which foreign powers have no right to interfere." Still, without tougher outside pressure, Philip thought, the remaining Armenians would die from deprivation.[51]

The Wilson administration never acted on this. The most Wilson did was declare two official Syrian and Armenian Relief Days in October.

Lansing did tell the German ambassador that the "true facts, if publicly known, would shock the whole civilized world," and he asked him to restrain Germany's Ottoman ally from its "studied intention . . . to annihilate a Christian race." To Wilson, though, the secretary of state showed a more pro-Ottoman view of the slaughter. He privately told the president that the Ottoman authorities had good reasons for the expulsions: "In the case of the Armenians I could see that their well-known disloyalty to the Ottoman Government and the fact that the territory which they inhabited was within the zone of military operations constituted grounds more or less justifiable for compelling them to depart from their homes. It was not to my mind the deportation which was objectionable but the horrible brutality which attended its execution." Despite that, though, Lansing told Wilson that the cruelty of the deportations was "one of the blackest pages of this war," and that "we were fully justified in intervening as we did in behalf of the wretched people, even though they were Turkish subjects"—a reversal of his position just a few months earlier, when he had insisted on only acting to protect Americans, not Armenians.[52]

Roosevelt had no patience for these relief efforts for the remaining Armenians, unless they included military steps, too. Otherwise, he told one activist, aid was the equivalent of "putting a soothing plaster on a broken leg," rather than choosing to "interfere by force of arms in entirely disinterested fashion for the oppressed nationalities that are ground under the Turkish rule." As Roosevelt wrote in 1918, "To allow the Turks to massacre the Armenians and then solicit permission to help the survivors and then to allege the fact that we are helping the survivors as a reason why we should not follow the only policy that will permanently put a stop to such massacres is both foolish and odious." When he donated $1,000 from his Nobel Peace Prize to help destitute Armenians, he was careful to earmark it for an activist who "has never sought to excuse or justify what I regard as our inexcusable dereliction in duty in having failed to declare war on Turkey."[53]

For the rest of World War I, the fate of the Armenians remained one of Roosevelt's signature complaints against Wilson's neutrality and the U.S. wish for peace. He wrote, in 1916: "If this nation had feared God it would have stood up for the Belgians and Armenians." Turning the tables on Wilson's Christian ideals, he added: "If . . . these people, when the concrete case arises, as in Belgium or Armenia, fear concretely to denounce and antagonize the wrongdoer, they become not merely passive, but active agents of the devil."[54]

Roosevelt invoked the Armenians as a prime example of the need for force. The diffuse power of public outrage was not enough: "Public opinion has been absolutely useless as regards Belgium, as regards Armenia, as regards Poland." He added, "One outspoken and straightforward declaration by this government against the dreadful iniquities perpetrated in Belgium, Armenia and Servia would have been worth to humanity a thousand times as much as all that the professional pacifists have done in the past fifty years." The Armenians, he argued (with considerable exaggeration), tragically demonstrated the inadequacy of pacifism in a dangerous world: "At this moment the Armenians, who for some centuries had sedulously avoided militarism and war, and have practically applied advanced pacifist principles, are suffering a fate, if possible, worse than the Belgians; and they are so suffering precisely and exactly because they have been pacifists whereas their neighbors, the Turks, have not been pacifists but militarists."[55]

But Wilson was never prepared to take such a military course against genocide. He finally chose war against Germany in 1917, not for the Belgians or Armenians, but only after U-boat warfare struck at American lives and ships. Wilson, repelled by German militarism, went to war convinced of the benefits for liberty of an Allied victory. But although he declared war on Austria-Hungary as well as Germany, he pointedly did not break off U.S. diplomatic relations with the authoritarian Ottoman Empire. Roosevelt, finding new heights of fury, demanded that Wilson expand the war on behalf of the Armenians. In May 1918, he told off Dodge, who preferred peace with the Ottoman Empire, in typically unequivocal terms:

> We should go to war because not to do so is really to show bad faith towards our allies, and to help Germany; because the Armenian massacre was the greatest crime of the war, and failure to act against Turkey is to condone it; because the failure to deal radically with the Turkish horror means that all talk of guaranteeing the future peace of the world is mischievous nonsense; and because when we now refuse to war with Turkey we show that our announcement that we meant "to make the world safe for democracy" was insincere claptrap.

In the end, though, the Ottoman Empire broke its ties with the United States, not the other way around. Britain urged the Wilson administration to go to war against the Ottoman Empire, but Gallipoli must have shown that as a daunting prospect. When Morgenthau suggested the making of a movie about the Armenian atrocities, Wilson rebuffed him: "There is nothing practical that we can do for the time being in the matter of the Armenian massacres." Roosevelt, seemingly undaunted by the calamities of World War I, later wrote, "The Armenian horror is an accomplished fact. Its occurrence was largely due to the policy of pacifism this nation has followed for the last four years."[56]

"There Is No Pity in the World"

As the war drew to a close, Armenian leaders made the case to Lansing that, after the massacres, they could not be left under Ottoman rule. Roosevelt, soon before his death in January 1919, had no hesitations about redrawing the world's map from Yugoslavia to Siberia. As for the Armenians, he was blunt: "The Turk should be driven from Europe, Armenia made independent under a guarantee of the Allies."[57]

But none of the great European powers was about to use military force to safeguard a new Armenia—and the United States least of all. In part because the Wilson administration came late to helping the Armenians, the United States was left behind in the dust during the Allied deliberations over the future of the Ottomans and Armenians. "Not having declared war upon Turkey," wrote the chief of the Near Eastern division of the U.S. delegation to the Paris peace conference, "we were always, during the period of discussion, outsiders, impotent to affect the actual course of the negotiations or put our stamp upon the decisions taken."[58]

Back while Wilson was keeping out of the war, the Allies had already made detailed secret and not-so-secret predatory plans for carving up the Ottoman Empire among the victors. Under the shadowy Sykes-Picot Agreement of 1916, the Armenian portions of the Ottoman Empire were to be divided between France and Russia. This was the antithesis of Wilson's own ideal of transparent, open diplomacy. He once disgustedly said that Sykes-Picot sounded like the name of a tea. The president pushed back in perhaps his most celebrated act of public statecraft: the Fourteen Points speech before Congress in January 1918. The twelfth of them vaguely promised autonomy, if not independence, to Armenians, as well as perhaps Arabs and Kurds: "The Turkish portions of the present Ottoman Empire should be assured a secure sovereignty, but the other nationalities which are now under Turkish rule should be assured an undoubted security of life and an absolutely unmolested opportunity of autonomous development." Wilson had suggested an explicit reference to Armenia, as well as Mesopotamia and Syria, but Colonel House preferred ambiguity. On July 4, at Mount Vernon, the president put forward his own alternative to the spirit of Sykes-Picot, declaring that all questions should be settled "upon the basis of the free acceptance of that settlement by the people immediately concerned, and not upon the basis of material interest or advantage of any other nation or people which may desire a different settlement for the sake of its own exterior influence or mastery."[59]

The atrocities cemented the Allied wish to partition the Ottoman Empire. "From the moment war was declared," wrote Lloyd George, Britain's prime minister, "there was not a British statesman of any party who did not have it in mind that if we succeeded in defeating this inhuman Empire, one essential condition of the peace we should impose was the redemption of the Armenian valleys for ever from the bloody misrule with which they had been stained by the infamies of the Turk." Balfour, as foreign secretary, told the cabinet, "The Turks had voluntarily sided with Germany; they had treated our prisoners with unexampled barbarity; they had massacred hundreds of thousands of their own subjects. They therefore deserved any fate which was inflicted upon them." Impoverished Armenia was not much of a colonial prize, but it could serve European imperial interests by thwarting Turkish or Muslim expansion.[60]

Wilson sailed for Paris in December 1918. In January 1919—a year after the Fourteen Points—Britain, France, Italy, Japan, and the United States agreed that "particularly because of the historical mis-government by the Turks of subject peoples and the terrible massacres of Armenians and others in recent years, . . . Armenia, Syria, Mesopotamia, Palestine and Arabia must be completely severed from the Turkish Empire." These lands would, along with Germany's colonies, be placed under mandates, for the ostensible benefit of peoples too underdeveloped to stand by themselves: "The tutelage of such peoples should be entrusted to advanced nations." As Lloyd George once unblushingly told Wilson and Georges Clemenceau of France: "We were saying to Turkey 'we cannot leave you to run alone any longer; you have got in a rut; and you will remain in it until some big country comes along and pulls you out.' Gaul and Britain would have remained in such a rut if Rome had not come along and pulled them out."[61]

But if the delegates at Paris were serenely convinced of Ottoman barbarity, they had more difficulty finding a suitable great power to take up the mandate for Armenia, which had declared itself a republic.

Russia—now the Soviet Union—was a pariah. Britain and France had more promising territories in mind. So that left the United States. Some of the country's Christian leaders urged Wilson to take on the task, and Bryce argued that the United States stood uniquely above the imperial aspirations of the other great powers. Still, as a U.S. diplomat in Paris noted, "the independence and protection of Armenia became a thing men talked about, but did not work for."[62]

To study the future of Armenia and the other lands to be cut loose from Ottoman rule, the Wilson administration sent Henry Churchill King, the president of Oberlin College, and Charles Crane, now treasurer of the American Committee for Armenian and Syrian Relief. Crane knew little about the Ottoman Empire outside of its Armenian lands, and King still less; they did not bother to visit Mesopotamia. They decided that partition between Turks and Armenians was "imperative and inevitable," but warned that Turks would resent the creation of a new Armenian state. The commissioners concluded that "the demonstrated unfitness of the Turks to rule over others" and "the adoption of repeated massacres as a deliberate policy of State" justified the creation of "a separate Armenian State." But this would require "a strong Mandatory Power," which the Armenians hoped would be the United States. To safeguard Armenia, King and Crane recommended that the United States also take up "a general Mandate over all of Asia Minor"—something that they somehow believed that Turks might welcome.[63]

Wilson, in an off-the-record talk to the Democratic National Convention in February, reported that the United States had been asked to assume the mandate for Armenia. According to an account by Herbert Hoover, Wilson was cautious but tempted. "I had to say offhand that it [the United States] would not be willing," Wilson said, offering to "go home and stump the country and see if they will do it." But he added, "Personally, and just within the limits of this room, I can say very frankly that I think we ought to. I think there is a very promising beginning in regard to countries like Armenia." House asked Hoover, then overseeing relief efforts in Armenia, to become governor for the mandate. Hoover was reluctant, pointing out the huge refugee population and the military threats of neighboring Turkey and Azerbaijan. As for Lansing, he declared himself "not particularly interested" in the fate of Armenia.[64]

In May, in Paris, Lloyd George brought a map into Wilson's residence there and used it to make his case for a U.S. mandate for Armenia and Constantinople, while France and Italy divided up Anatolia. Wilson argued against splitting Turkey, and said that he had to return home to see "whether the United States would accept a mandate." Later that month, Lloyd George, fearing Muslim unrest, backtracked and said he was reluctant to partition Asia Minor, although he still believed that "the Turks should not rule over alien races like the Greeks, Armenians, and Arabs, whom they had always misgoverned." Clemenceau said that the United States would be the best choice to protect the Greeks and Armenians, since it had a reputation for liberty and fairness, and "America had no past in dealings with Mohammedans." Wilson, this time armed with his own ethnographical map of the Ottoman Empire, told these two imperialists that "America desired nothing in Asia Minor" and would not take a mandate there: "It was difficult for her to take a mandate even for Armenia, where she had permanent interests of long standing, and where a good deal of money had been spent by Americans for the relief of the Armenian people."[65]

While the delegates maneuvered, Armenia was besieged by both Turkish and Bolshevik forces. Hoover warned of widespread starvation: "It is impossible to depict the situation in Armenia, for until the last sixty days the population has been eating the dead." But he added, "I quite realise that the situation is one beyond the strength of the Allied military forces at present." He was right. Fearing further atrocities, Clemenceau offered to send French troops to Armenia, but not to take on responsibilities for the territory. When Britain proposed deploying soldiers to the Ottoman Empire "to prevent the Armenians from being massacred," Wilson dodged, saying he did not want to send U.S. troops to grapple with territorial issues. The proposal got no further than the dispatch of another U.S. fact-finding mission, which was in one town greeted by a hopeful banner: "*Vive l'Art. 12 des Principes de Wilson.*" As a U.S. diplomat in Paris pointed out, having not declared war on the Ottoman Empire, "We could not, in the period of the armistice, send troops into Turkish Armenia when such action might have saved many thousands of people from starvation."[66]

Wilson had good reason to be wary of public opinion back home. The same isolationist currents that doomed U.S. participation in the League of Nations would likely have undone such a massive undertaking as an Armenian mandate. On one of his returns from Paris, he disembarked at Boston and told a crowd, "You poured out your money to help succor Armenians after they suffered. Now set up your strength so that they shall never suffer again." He campaigned to the end of his physical endurance for the League in the western states, storming across Missouri, Iowa, and the Dakotas by train like Gladstone in Scotland. Several times, he used the

Armenians as an example of how the League would shelter small nations. In Sacramento, California, he did so with a flash of his racism, saying the League would safeguard both the advanced Armenians and "the poor, naked fellows in jungles of Africa." The next day, in Salt Lake City, Utah, he remembered "the horrible massacres which have made that country [Armenia] a graveyard." In Kansas City, an uncharacteristically emotional Wilson sounded almost like Roosevelt:

> At this moment, my fellow citizens, it is an open question whether the Armenian people will not, while we sit here and debate, be absolutely destroyed. When I think of words piled on words, of debate following debate, while these unspeakable things that cannot be handled until the debate is over are happening in this pitiful part of the world, I wonder that men do not wake up to the moral responsibility of what they are doing. Great populations are driven out upon a desert where there is no food and can be none and there compelled to die, and the men and women and children thrown into a common grave, so imperfectly covered up that here and there is a pitiful arm stretched out to heaven and there is no pity in the world.

On a train outside of Pueblo, Colorado, Wilson suffered a collapse from his exertions. He had to cancel his tour. The League and the peace treaty went down to defeat by the Republican-controlled Senate.[67]

In 1920, at the San Remo conference, the United States was again asked to consider an Armenian mandate. Wilson, his health failing, beseeched the Senate: "It is to this people and to their government that hopes and earnest expectations of the struggling people of Armenia turn as they emerge from a period of indescribable suffering and peril." Despite significant American activism for a mandate, the Senate, including some Democrats, turned him down flat. Senator Henry Cabot Lodge of Massachusetts, the Republican who had successfully led the fight against U.S. involvement in the League, once a supporter of the Armenians, privately said, "Do not think I do not feel badly about Armenia. I do, but there is a limit to what they have a right to put off on us." The Allies asked the newborn League of Nations to assume responsibility for Armenia's safety. In one of the League's first humiliations, it had to refuse, lacking its own money and army.[68]

This left the Soviet Union free to seize Armenia and turn it into a Soviet socialist republic. "Lenine [*sic*] and Mustapha Kemal have cracked the whip," wrote William Westermann, the head of the Near Eastern division of the U.S. delegation at the Paris conference. He accepted blame: "We, the people of the United States, might have saved the Armenians, had we been willing to accept a mandate. . . . We feared foreign entanglements. That fear was justified. But it *is* fear." As the U.S. high commissioner in Constantinople wrote in 1921, "Since the withdrawal of the United States from the Turkish settlement in the fall of 1919 we have had no voice and have shown no real interest in Near East affairs." He warned against encouraging Armenian hopes for statehood: "No power is justified in encouraging the Armenians in working for independence unless that power is willing to pour blood and treasure into this country. It is clear that we are not willing to do this, nor is any other country."[69]

Superpower

A century after John Quincy Adams's 1821 declaration that the United States "does not go abroad, in search of monsters to destroy," his doctrine came to fruition for the Armenians. Adams's position was unexceptional for a small power wanting primarily to be left alone. The young republic was more afraid of being on the receiving end of an intervention than it was hopeful of doing good across the seas. As Adams said, the United States' "glory is not *dominion,* but *liberty.*" This is admirable in itself, and anyway made sense in a world where much stronger powers were setting the rules of international politics. The United States was in no position to provide an international order.[70]

Not so in the next century. As the United States grew into a superpower, it could shoulder serious responsibilities, like confronting genocide. On his return from Paris, Wilson tried to convince his country of the dangers gathering around the Poles, Czechoslovaks, and Yugoslavs: "We set this Nation up to make men free and we did not confine our conception and purpose to America, and now we will make men free." After the United States withdrew from Europe, the subsequent history of those peoples did not quite vindicate his hopes. In the recriminations as the Versailles settlement began to come undone, Westermann wrote, "A caution justified at the turning of the nineteenth century has become a counsel of cowardice in the twentieth century." He added, "The decision was ours and we took it. American safety first."[71]

Instead of following Gladstone, Wilson had taken his own path—and then been further constrained by an isolationist Senate. During the 1915 slaughter, Wilson never made serious political, economic, or military threats; neither he nor his senior officials made any public speeches. Strangely, it was the idealistic Wilson who began the U.S. trend of ignoring genocide, from the Holocaust to Rwanda. The world order envisioned after World War I did not aim to establish a regular way of stopping mass atrocity. The United States did go abroad, of course, in countless interventions, but not in search of monsters, even when there really were monsters.

Still, the tradition of Byron and Gladstone did find a place in the United States. There was James Madison and Daniel Webster; and then Theodore Roosevelt (for all his excesses) and Henry Morgenthau Sr.; and new generations. When Morgenthau first set out for his post in Constantinople, he brought his son with him to the Ottoman Empire. Henry Jr., who would go on to be Treasury secretary under Franklin Delano Roosevelt, was twenty-two years old when he and his father sailed for Constantinople. The younger Morgenthau absorbed his father's outrage and became the most vocal member of the Roosevelt cabinet trying to stop the Holocaust. "What the Turks did to the Armenians made a terrific impact on me," he recalled. "Later on when the Germans did the same things to the Jews, I remembered the feelings I had had in Turkey during World War I." In a January 1944 meeting, Morgenthau told the president of "the results that his father, Henry Morgenthau Sr., had obtained when he was Ambassador to Turkey in getting Armenians out of Turkey and saving their lives."[72]

CHAPTER TWENTY-SIX

The Uses of History

"Wars to Extermination"

People in Britain were shaken to the core by the Bulgarian massacres. The genuine shock at the Bulgarian horrors rested on a Victorian belief in progress that is heartbreaking today. But back in 1876, the slaughter in Batak was seen as something bizarrely out of time and place, premodern and precivilizational. Henry Sidgwick, a progressive Cambridge philosopher and economist, wrote, "Altogether I have to fight against optimism rather vigorously, or should have to, except for Bulgarian atrocities and the like." Henry Parry Liddon, an Oxford professor and canon of St. Paul's Church, was sure that, a century later, the massacre would stand out as a horrible aberration. One prominent British activist was so shocked that he could not believe he was "really living in the nineteenth century."[1]

After the subsequent century, we have totally lost that innocence. They could believe that Scio, Damascus, and Batak were radical departures from the usual way of things; we just look back and see earlier examples of the kind of massacre that we have come to expect as grisly routine.[2]

In 1823, the London Greek Committee warned of "the absolute annihilation of the Greek people"; in 1860, the *Times* editorialized about the danger of "a general extermination of the Christians in Syria"; in 1895, the *San Francisco Examiner* concluded that Spain was gearing up to "fight a war to extermination" in Cuba; and in 1876, Gladstone fumbled for the words to describe "crimes and outrages, so vast in scale as to exceed all modern example, and so unutterably vile as well as fierce in character, that it passes the power of heart to conceive, and of tongue and pen adequately to describe them." The word they were grasping toward was genocide—and the rough idea was enough to send shock waves through public opinion. Today, that world's shuddering has been captured in new terms that blight the post-Victorian vocabulary: mass graves, *Konzentrationslager,* Gulag, killing fields, *laogai.* Few people today would want to go back to the nineteenth-century world of gaslight and empire. But many of us might want to have back their basic belief in human nature.[3]

But that British activist was wrong. He really was living in the nineteenth century. Because massacres turn out to be the regular way of the world, the world will need a regular response to them. And that is why the nineteenth-century experience is worth remembering, in all its strangeness. This is not to suggest that that experience is a precise parallel to Kosovo or Darfur, but merely that it holds lessons. As outlandish as the debates over saving the Greeks, Syrians, and Bulgarians were, they are rare lights along an otherwise dark road.[4]

The Forgotten Fact of Humanitarian Intervention

This history remains largely unknown. In his classic book on the post-Napoleonic era, *A World Restored,* Henry Kissinger writes an entire chapter on the Greek war of independence without mentioning Britain's philhellenes, the Scio massacre, or the climactic battle at Navarino. Kissinger only hints at how the Greek crisis turned British public opinion against Castlereagh. The diplomatic outcome is a triumph for the balance of power, with Castlereagh and Metternich getting Russia to give up on the Greeks. Kissinger's history ends in 1822 with Castlereagh taking his life as a kind of realpolitik martyr for Europe's peace, not with scorched Ottoman and Egyptian ships sinking to the bottom of Navarino Bay.[5]

This kind of oversight has become more or less conventional. But Castlereagh admitted the keen moral appeal of the Greek cause, and threatened possible war after the Scio massacre. Wellington agreed that any attempted expulsion of the Greeks into slavery in Egypt would justify a war to stop it. Disraeli is lionized by today's realists, particularly for holding out against the atrocitarians, although, in fact, even Disraeli said several times that he had sent the British fleet to Besika Bay to protect Ottoman Christians, and in desperation recommended an outright British occupation of Bulgaria. Edmund Burke, claimed as a hero of American conservatives, exhorted William Pitt's foreign secretary on principled grounds to launch a foreign intervention against the slaughter unleashed by the French Revolution: "A more mischievous idea cannot exist than that any degree of wickedness, violence and oppression may prevail in a Country, that the most abominable, murderous and exterminatory Rebellions may rage in it, or the most atrocious and bloody tyranny may domineer, and that no neighbouring power can take cognizance of either, or afford succour to the miserable Sufferers." On humanitarian intervention, even the grand old men of realist foreign policy could sound surprisingly liberal.[6]

Overlooking the history of humanitarian intervention can make for distorted thinking about European politics in the nineteenth century, and world politics today. Greece, Syria, and Bulgaria are by no means the whole of nineteenth-century international politics. But they are crucial enough (as Kissinger himself says) that an account of the century that misses them cannot be a completely sound basis for thinking about international politics today. Understanding the deep roots of humanitarian intervention makes it possible to see today's human rights movement not as newborn, but as coming of age.[7]

Humanitarianism or Imperialism?

This is not a nostalgic book. There is no need to rewind to the nineteenth century, just to learn something from the period's diplomacy. It is as rash to pine for a lost golden age as it is to dimly imagine one in the hypothetical future. The nineteenth century was not a century of humanitarianism. One cannot ignore the arrogant imperialism. Many of the characters in this book held loathsome racial attitudes that played out in the subjugation of countless people.[8]

The British largely missed the irony of carrying on their debates about Greek suffering while simultaneously discussing how to deal with an Indian mutiny and festering Catholic grievances in Ireland. After Indians massacred Britons in Delhi and Kanpur in the summer of 1857, the British sadistically slaughtered Indians by the hundreds, burning old women and children alive, and smearing Muslims with pig fat before killing them. Carnarvon, Disraeli's colonial secretary, spoke inside the cabinet for the Bulgarians, just a few years before he launched widespread brutal reprisals against the Zulus in 1879. In 1876–79, at the height of British public rage over the Bulgarian horrors, an epic drought took the lives of untold millions of Indians, to the enduring historical shame of the British Empire and Edward Bulwer-Lytton in particular.[9]

Ali, the Ottoman acting grand vizier, had a point when he parried British anger over Syria by noting Britain's own "like disasters in her possessions in India." There was a monstrous disconnect between the growing liberalism in Britain and the brute authoritarianism in the British

Empire. But the Georgians and Victorians were not pure evil either, and our contempt for their imperialistic vices should not stop us from trying to learn something from their humanitarian virtues. In rightly condemning John Stuart Mill and Tocqueville for justifying imperialism, we should not forget the anti-imperialism of Burke, Diderot, and Kant.[10]

Humanitarianism was and is a real force in world politics. It is not the same thing as imperialism, even when it uses military force. There is some overspill: these interventions all took place in an imperial era, when statesmen had few compunctions about imposing changes on foreign countries. The British and the French in this period were convinced that they were heralds of superior culture and enlightened government. In that sense, they did have a kind of imperialistic consciousness that was part of the argument for rescuing Greeks, Syrians, and Bulgarians; the humanitarians were happy to reshape other societies. But these were ventures that, for Britain, went directly against their well-understood imperial interests. While monumental national arrogance is a big part of imperialism, it is not imperialism itself.[11]

The last thing we need today is a new imperialism. Authors like David Rieff are right to warn about the potential dangers of "echoes of 19th-century imperialism." Still, precision counts, because imperialism is, properly, such a loaded term. If an intervention is imperialistic or colonialistic, it is beyond the moral pale: a throwback to an era of domination and oppression. Today, imprecise accusations of Western neoimperialism can cloud the current debate about when the free world should defend human rights abroad.[12]

So, precisely, according to the political scientist Michael Doyle, empire means a dominant "metropole . . . exerts political control over the internal and external policy—the effective sovereignty—of . . . the subordinate periphery." This is not the same as hegemony, where a very powerful state influences others around it, but does not directly control others.[13]

Russia and France clearly had imperial motives in the Balkans and the Middle East respectively, even though France left Syria in 1861. But the other major incidents in this book are not easily tarred as imperial. Britain did not want to exert political control over Greece, Poland, Naples, Bosnia, or Bulgaria.[14]

Britain's realpolitik interest was to contain the rise of the alarmingly blustery Napoléon III, but Britain sent its navy and marines to stand with French troops. As imperialist British leaders like Castlereagh and Disraeli stoutly argued, safeguarding the British Empire meant supporting the Ottoman Empire as a bulwark against Russia, not fighting Britain's

Ottoman ally. Castlereagh and Disraeli's logic was exactly the same as that of Richard Nixon jotting down notes for a meeting with Zhou Enlai ("*Russia:* 1. Maintain balance of power"), or of Churchill explaining Britain's uneasy World War II alliance with the Soviet Union against Nazi Germany ("If Hitler invaded Hell I would make at least a favourable reference to the Devil in the House of Commons"). So one cannot explain Canning's policy toward the Greeks, Russell's toward the Syrians, or Gladstone's toward the Bulgarians as imperialist—or even strategic.[15]

Realists still predict that balance-of-power considerations will trump domestic politics. But the idea of the balance of power seemed hopelessly dated even to some diplomats in the early nineteenth century, like Canning. Metternich himself agreed that "the rise of public opinion" made it impossible for Austria to help crush the Greek revolt.[16]

Of course, many nineteenth-century British colonialists saw their empire as a progressive force, bettering backward societies and racial inferiors. There was some effort to rein in the worst imperial excesses, where British settlers on the frontiers tormented indigenous peoples in southern Africa, Australia, and New Zealand. But even these reforms, for all their flaws and inadequacies, are not the same thing as the proposed interventions in this book; the humanitarian goal was to rescue the Greeks, Syrians, or Bulgarians, not to rule over them. Philhellenes like Bentham and Byron wanted Greek self-rule, with Bentham exhorting them to choose democracy.[17]

The distinction between imperialism and humanitarianism gets sharper the closer one looks at British debates. In fact, some of the most important humanitarian interventionists were also deeply critical of imperialism. Despite Victor Hugo's early weakness for Napoléon Bonaparte's military adventures, he matured into a critic of French bullying. He was horrified at the French sack of the Summer Palace in Beijing. Hugo despised French despotism—in the form of Napoléon III—as much as he did other despotisms around the world, and had a humanism that went beyond borders.[18]

Even William Wilberforce, for all his prejudices against Muslims, struggled against British cruelties in India. Byron and Bentham, the key stalwarts of the Greek cause, were deeply skeptical about British imperialism. Instead, the philosophical star of the London Greek Committee attacked French ("Emancipate Your Colonies!"), Spanish ("Rid Yourselves of Ultramaria"), and British colonialism with characteristic gusto. He condemned Britain's empire in India, Canada, South Africa, and the West

Indies as a "rotten sceptre," bringing "denial of justice, oppression, extortion, corruptive influence, despotism." Instead of expanding British rule into Greece, he denounced Britain's control of the Ionian Islands as tyranny. (Gladstone would agree, hoping to see the Ionian Islands turned over to Greek rule.) Bentham warned the Greeks of the evils of British imperialism: "Under England, six millions and a half of Irishmen groan in irremediable distress, under unrelenting tyranny."[19]

The more imperialist one was, the less likely one was to support Gladstone's calls for saving the Bulgarians. Disraeli, flashily imperialist, dreaded Russia as the only land power that could threaten India. He also sympathized with the Ottomans' difficulties in managing rebellious subjects, like Britain's brutal repression of Jamaicans. Victoria, although initially pro-Bulgarian, chose India when Disraeli pushed her. Fitzjames Stephen, a bitter critic of the atrocitarians, was obsessed with India; the same is true of Prince Albert and Lytton.[20]

But Gladstone, Hartington, and other Victorian-era liberals and atrocitarians often explicitly put the moral demands of the Bulgarians above British imperial interests in India. Stratford Canning said he would rather see Russia conquer Constantinople than let the Ottoman Empire carry out such massacres. The atrocitarians were the heirs of the antislavery movement, and the forerunners of the Congo Reform Association, which would demand an end to rapacious Belgian colonial rule. In the Midlothian campaign, Gladstone attacked Disraeli and Lytton for spending India's desperately needed famine fund on the imperial war in Afghanistan; Florence Nightingale wrote letters to the *Times* against the famine; liberals protested; and even Salisbury, Disraeli's pro-Bulgarian India secretary, tried to stop the famine. Gladstone set himself on the side not just of Bulgarians, but also of Zulus, Afghans, aborigines, Indians, and even Irishmen.[21]

The picture is less clear in the United States in its period of imperial temptation after the Spanish-American War. Theodore Roosevelt and Woodrow Wilson were critics of American imperialism in Cuba. Wilson was too, in varying degrees, in the Philippines. Roosevelt's record was awful there. He had in 1899 invoked British rule of India as a noble precedent for a U.S. colonial project in the Philippines. He later turned against annexation, not so much out of a principled renunciation of imperialism as out of weighty democratic and strategic considerations: the American public did not want the islands, and they were precariously exposed to Japan. At best, Roosevelt, battered by the Filipino insurgency, slowly learned the dangers of empire. Still, Wilson told a Salt Lake City crowd, with some exaggeration, "When we fought the war with Spain there was many a cynical smile on the other side of the water when we said that we were going to win freedom for Cuba and then present it to her." But, he said, "we kept that promise and proved our absolute disinterestedness."[22]

Of course, it would be preferable to have better humanitarian agents in this book than Britain and France. Russia is worse still, but all of them should by rights have concentrated on ending their own oppressions before they turned to those of other empires. But even bad agents sometimes do good things. In *All the King's Men,* the demagogic Willie Stark lectures the pure-minded Adam Stanton on making good: "You got to make it, Doc. If you want it. And you got to make it out of badness. Badness. . . . And you know why? Because there isn't anything else to make it out of."[23]

Humanitarianism or Pan-Christianity?

The nineteenth century's humanitarian interventions were about more than just rescuing fellow Christians. Still, there is no doubt that both Christian sympathies and bigotry against Muslims mattered.

There are plenty of examples of crude European prejudice against Muslims. A British sailor at Navarino was disgusted to hear a fellow sailor explain that the Turks planned to burn the British to death. Wilberforce and T. S. Hughes saw the world mostly in religious terms, with a crude contempt for the Muslims of the Ottoman Empire. In Syria, Dufferin sneered at "the stupidity of Turkish officials, and the unthinking folly of these Orientals." In MacGahan's most gruesome *Daily News* dispatch from Bulgaria, he wrote: "When a Mahometan has killed a certain number of infidels, he is sure of Paradise, no matter what his sins may be. . . . Here in Batak the Bashi-Bazouks, in order to swell the count, ripped open pregnant women, and killed the unborn infants."[24]

Gladstone wrote that "negro slavery . . . was a race of higher capacities ruling over a race of lower capacities," while Ottoman rule over Slavs meant "a race of lower capacities . . . rules over a race of higher capacities." In *Bulgarian Horrors,* he nastily wrote that the Turks "were, upon the whole, from the black day when they first entered Europe, the one great anti-human specimen of humanity. Wherever they went, a broad line of blood marked the track behind them." And Disraeli, after a visit from an Ottoman envoy who was in fact Armenian, wrote, "All Turks look to me exactly alike. Strange, that should be the effect of so simple and unimpressive a headdress as the Fez."[25]

French Catholics were particularly worried about the plight of fellow Catholics in Poland and Maronites in Syria; Russian pan-Slavists sympathized with fellow Orthodox Slavs, not all humanity. Woodrow Wilson, who kept African-Americans out of Princeton and implemented racial segregation in the federal government, often referred to the Armenians as a Christian nation. This certainly shows a disproportionate emphasis on Christian suffering.[26]

But that is not the whole story. It is too easy to write off even Byron as a kind of tool of Britain's imperial stake in India, as Edward Said did. The Ottoman Empire faced European imposition not just because it was Muslim, but also because it was relatively weak. There are three broad categories of reasons to think there was more to the humanitarianism of this period than just solicitude for fellow Christians.[27]

First, Britain, at least, was hardly monolithically anti-Muslim. The British in this period often admired Muslim courage, energy, and industry. Bentham, as he signed onto the London Greek Committee, argued that Muslims in Greece should be "treated with . . . gentleness." They would then become a force for liberty: "Natural and supposed irreconcilable enemies would thus be converted into grateful and steady allies." Bentham urged good government in a Muslim state in Tripoli much as he did elsewhere, with scarcely a mention of Islam.[28]

The Ottoman Empire was widely recognized as part of the "system of civilized states"—a status that imposed obligations of decency, but was couched not in terms of religion but of civilization. In the 1850s, the British public was sympathetic to the Ottomans. The Ottomans were seen as victims, in roughly the same category as Poles or Hungarians. Gladstone, of all people, had been in the cabinet supporting the Ottoman Empire against Russia in the Crimean War, and there was real popular pressure behind the Crimean War alliance with the empire. There was a widespread belief that the Ottoman Empire was successfully reforming.[29]

In Syria, for instance, it was British confidence in Fuad and Ottoman reformers that allowed the Europeans to depart in 1861 with a relatively easy conscience. Many Britons affectionately compared the Druzes to the Scots—hardly a demonic group even in English eyes. Disraeli complained repeatedly of Gladstone's anti-Turkish "ethnological" bigotry. The United States had in 1796 signed a treaty with Tripoli officially declaring that "the Government of the United States is not in any sense founded on the Christian religion" and had "no character of enmity against the laws, religion, or tranquillity of Musselmen." During the Armenian genocide, *The Nation* defended missionaries from accusations of bias: "Their evidence is not prejudiced. American missionaries have no dislike for the Turkish people." So an implacable hostility to all things Muslim cannot be the whole story.[30]

Second, there are many cases when Western Christians showed no interest in helping fellow Christians (as in Serbia in 1804–06 or Bosnia in 1875), or when Western Christians helped non-Christian peoples (as in the fight against the slave trade), or when Western Christians wanted to help the victims of oppression by Christians (as in Belgium, Naples, Poland, and Hungary). Dufferin was not won over by the Maronites in Syria: "The Christian population of the Lebanon are almost, if not quite, as savage as any of their non-Christian neighbours." And John Stuart Mill supported intervention to protect civilians, including in cases, like Portugal and Holland, where the oppressors were Christian.[31]

Twenty-five years before the Bulgarian massacres, many people in Britain and France were horrified by reactionary oppression in the Papal States and in Naples, where the thugs were Christian. The diplomatic reprimands over cruel misgovernment sent to the pope looked much like the ones sent to the sultan. Gladstone wrote that the crackdown in Naples was "an outrage upon religion, upon civilization, upon humanity, and upon decency." If anything, the fact that the oppressors in Naples were Christian made it worse for him. The repression in Naples, while smaller and less bloody than the Bulgarian massacres would be, was enough to make Britain break off diplomatic relations. And Gladstone and Palmerston showed no compunctions about trampling Neapolitan sovereignty with their ill-starred 1855 covert operation, led by Garibaldi, to free the political prisoners there.[32]

Little Naples was easier to bully than Russia or Austria. But even those powerful conservative empires faced fierce liberal European criticism. As Palmerston once wrote, "there are a vast number of Christians under the Governments of Russia, Austria, Rome, and Naples who would be rejoiced to be as well treated, and to enjoy as much security for person and property as the Christian subjects of the Sultan." In 1877, denouncing Russian war crimes, Gladstone wrote, "Cruelty is *worse* in a Christian than in a Turk." Even a pan-Slavist ideologue like Nikolai Danilevsky admitted, "The Slavs prefer the heavy yoke of the Mohammedans to the civilized domination of Austria."[33]

Although coverage is a crude measure, there was substantially more reporting of Russia's crushing of Poland in 1831 than there was of the Scio massacre in 1822. Atrocities by Christians got more press than atrocities by Muslims, and the content was just as vehement. For instance, the *Times* editorialized that Russian "troops have destroyed whole towns or villages, out of mere wantonness or revenge."[34]

Conversely, organized Christianity showed little solidarity with the Greeks or Bulgarians. The establishment Church of England, stacked with Tory loyalists, either ignored or resisted the philhellene agitations in the 1820s, and largely sat out the Bulgarian agitation in 1876. It was only the nonconformists and some of the High Church that rallied behind Gladstone—a small slice of British Christianity, and not its most powerful members. Other factors, like region, class, and ethnicity, were equally as important as religion as drivers of sympathy for Greeks or Bulgarians.

Third, Western European prejudices were a many-splendored thing. Russian pan-Slavists despised Protestants and Catholics; the British scorned Catholics and the French scorned Protestants; and the British and French were united in their disgust at Orthodox Christians. Many Anglicans were repelled at the Eastern Orthodox faith of the Bulgarians—barely Christianity at all in some eyes. Queen Victoria, for one, repudiated the Orthodox Bulgarians as not being "real Christians." Taken together, this all hardly adds up to a picture of monolithic Christian hatred for Muslims.[35]

In more recent years, it is hard to explain U.S. interventions as just a matter of saving Christians from Muslims. The Republican evangelist Pat Robertson supported Charles Taylor, the Liberian president now being tried for war crimes, as "a Christian, Baptist president" facing "Muslim rebels." But many evangelicals were appalled at this, and George W. Bush, a decidedly Christian-influenced president, backed Taylor's indictment and pushed him out of power. Despite pressure from American Christians, the United States did not intervene to protect oppressed Christians in Sudan. Under Republican and Democratic presidents, the United States went to war on behalf of Muslims in Somalia, Bosnia, and Kosovo.[36]

Nor is racism by itself a compelling predictor of U.S. humanitarian interventionism. Of course, John C. Calhoun was racist in supporting slavery for American blacks and freedom for the Greeks. Anti-Semitism was, as some of the best historians have argued, an important cause of the United States' lassitude during the Holocaust. And it is impossible to believe that prejudice against Africans was not a factor in the willingness of Americans to ignore the genocide in Rwanda. But there was substantial public outcry over Somalia, leading to a U.S. military mission.[37]

There were, and are, real universalists. It is not particularly plausible that people like Byron and Bentham were mostly driven by bigotry or imperialism. Benthamite philhellenes were likelier to invoke Plato than Jesus, or civilization rather than pan-Christianity. Greece drew attention more for its pagan ancient past than its Orthodox present. Canning was disgusted at the evangelical philhellenes and dreaded religious war. The progressive French press, generally suspicious of Catholicism, loudly supported intervention in Syria. In 1876, at the St. James's Hall conference, Gladstone said he hoped for "liberty . . . for the subject populations of the East—Christian populations they undoubtedly are in the main—but I look upon them as subject populations, and draw no distinction whatever between Christian and Jew and Mussulman and their claims to our sympathy in proportion to their numbers and the degree of oppression." By the time he got to Midlothian, Gladstone was denouncing the cruelty of Disraeli's imperial wars in Zululand and Afghanistan, and arguing for the rights of humanity "over the whole surface of the earth"—a crucial step toward present-day ideas of universal human rights.[38]

Human rights activists should always be acutely aware of their own governments' cruelties and biases. But human rights talk is not always hypocritical or racist—and assuming that it is lends a ready excuse to the likes of Radovan Karadžić or Omar al-Bashir. If all European and U.S. politicians—humanitarian or selfish, imperialist or republican, interventionist or bystander—are written off without distinction as bigots, then all the politics is blotted out, too.

CHAPTER TWENTY-SEVEN

The International Politics of Humanitarian Intervention

Sovereignty

In 1999, Henry Kissinger complained of the "abrupt abandonment of the concept of national sovereignty" in the Kosovo war. But looking back, national sovereignty was actually far more flexible than is commonly realized today. When Slobodan Milošević insisted that what went on within Serbia's borders was nobody else's business, he was forgetting that over a century ago, Serbs frequently appealed to Europeans for rescue in much the same way that the besieged Kosovars were now appealing to the United States. Rather, as the political scientist Stephen Krasner has argued, the long view shows the malleability of sovereignty.[1]

It was usually weaker powers that invoked sovereignty and nonintervention, while stronger powers insisted on their right to interfere. There was always a nineteenth-century double standard: sovereignty in Europe, imperial bullying in the weak and ostensibly barbarous periphery. On top of that, when the reactionary empires of the Holy Alliance were riding high, those empires were strongly in favor of foreign intervention—to help a fellow king crush a revolution or constitutionalist movement, or to pursue the expansion of their empires outside of Europe. The Holy Alliance, in other words, did accept a kind of intervention: antihumanitarian intervention.[2]

This doctrine was cast in broad terms. Canning wrote that Metternich "considers the alliance of the great Powers of Europe as a tutelary Providence watching over the interests of the world, and authorized by that very character to interfere in the concerns of independent States without the sanction of specific obligation." For example, during the revolutionary upheavals of 1848, the most significant international intervention was not on behalf of the oppressed subject peoples of Europe, but of their oppressors. Soon after Louis Kossuth's Hungarian revolutionaries made a bid to form an independent republic, a Russian army marched off to help Austria crush the Hungarians. John Stuart Mill admitted that "assistance to the government of a country in keeping down the people" was "unhappily by far the most frequent case of foreign intervention." (Henry Kissinger's position really does appear to be a modern-day version of Metternich's: during the Cold War, he supported intervention to quash leftism, as in Chile; but he opposed intervention to stop atrocities, as in Kosovo.)[3]

Liberalism, when it was weak, despised this doctrine of intervention. After the Revolution, France, fearing conservative attack, tried to enshrine nonintervention as a bedrock principle of international law. Liberals defensively invoked sovereignty, as the frantic rallying cry of a small nation that had dared to flirt with constitutional liberty and was thus about to be crushed by Russian or Austrian troops. Liberals were appalled by the use of military force to put down freedom-minded Neapolitans and Spaniards in the early 1820s. Daniel Webster, in Washington, denounced the "asserted right of forcible intervention in the affairs of other nations": "Is the whole world expected to acquiesce in principles which entirely subvert the independence of nations?" The Monroe Doctrine was meant to protect the Americas from the Holy Alliance's interventions.[4]

For much the same reasons, in this period, Britain, the most freedom-minded member of the Concert of Europe, was often anti-interventionist. In 1822, Canning declared that Britain would have nothing to do with any Concert intervention against constitutional liberty in Spain. Palmerston—and even Gladstone in 1850, although not later—preferred nonintervention. In much the same way, Hungarians in 1956 and Czechs in 1968 desperately tried to demand their sovereignty against the invading Soviet army. Latin American states would come to insist on nonintervention, out of fear of U.S. imperialism.[5]

Throughout this period, diplomats demonstrated impressive creativity in rethinking sovereignty. After the Crimean War, in 1856, the Ottoman Empire was recognized as fully sovereign by the rest of Europe—an attempt in part to limit Russian bullying. But Gladstone thought that Ottoman sovereignty could contain multitudes of autonomous arrangements: "Why should we be alarmed at the sound of Suzerainty? It is a phrase of infinite elasticity. Even in the present Turkish Empire, Suzerainty exists in half-a-dozen different forms, such as over Tunis, Egypt, Samos, Roumania, and Servia." By the time of the Midlothian campaign, he said, "Why, Turkey in Europe has neither integrity nor independence."[6]

One of the most important tactics for delineating the limits of sovereignty was the creation of treaties specifying exactly which countries were allowed to intervene in which other countries, and under which circumstances. The most famous one was the Treaty of Kutchuk-Kainardji, which allowed Russia to protect Orthodox Christians under Ottoman rule. Both Castlereagh and Wellington had to admit, however reluctantly, that Russia had the right to send troops on behalf of Ottoman Christians. At the end of the Napoleonic Wars, victorious Britain pressured the restored Bourbon monarchy into signing a treaty abolishing the slave trade in France's empire, which, as a U.S. ambassador noted, gave Britain the "right" to "interfere in a domestic concern."[7]

These treaties defined the scope of intervention. Canning preferred to hold off the Holy Alliance with treaties: "We who deny the general abstract right of interference, but admit the possibility of interfering in cases of specific interest or specific obligation, naturally consider treaty as the most authentic title by which one State can claim to busy itself in the concerns of another." Conversely, he noted, "I have no doubt in my own mind that Mett[ernich]. *does* undervalue treaty, *because* he prefers authoritative intervention"—that is, a sweeping right of intervention that did not require a treaty to hammer out the specifics.[8]

After the Napoleonic Wars, British diplomats at first would only cautiously assert a right of humanitarian intervention. But as freedom grew in Britain and France, and as Britain and France became stronger on the world stage, some of the leading liberal thinkers and leaders came to embrace the idea of intervention for humanitarian purposes.[9]

If the despotic powers could intervene as they saw fit, then why could not the free powers do likewise? Canning certainly did not see sovereignty as an absolute. Edmund Burke, seeking to legitimize British intervention to stop the Terror in France, wrote, "I perceive, that much pains are taken by the Jacobins of England, to propagate a notion that one State has not a right to interfere according to its discretion, in the interior Affairs of another. This strange notion can only be supported by a confusion of ideas." And conversely, revolutionary France, although demanding that no state intervene against it, claimed the legal right to intervene in the name of liberty in other countries. In the United States, in a related domestic context, Abraham Lincoln struggled against what he called "the 'gur-reat pur-rinciple' that 'if one man would enslave another, no third man should object,' fantastically called 'Popular Sovereignty.' "[10]

John Stuart Mill was sympathetic to intervention on behalf of "a people in arms for liberty" resisting foreign domination, or to end "a protracted civil war." Mill argued that the "doctrine of non-intervention" could only work if both "despots" and "free States" alike agreed to it. If not, the doctrine would mean "the wrong side may help the wrong, but the right must not help the right." Using the example of the Hungarian revolt in 1848, Mill suggested that if the despots intervened to crush a free people, the big liberal powers could launch a counterintervention too: "When . . . the Russian despot interposed, and, joining his force to that of Austria, delivered back the Hungarians, bound hand and foot, to their exasperated oppressors, it would have been an honorable and virtuous act on the part of England to have declared that this should not be; and that, if Russia gave assistance to the wrong side, England would aid the right."[11]

Today, it is the free states that are strong, and tempted (often unwisely) to intervene to impose their politics on weaker dictatorial states. With a huge number of newly independent postcolonial countries, the principle of nonintervention has been resurrected—doubly so after the Iraq war. Still, in the 1990s, many people have come to think of intervention as a tool of liberal politics, and sovereignty as a tool of brutality. Sovereignty was the best argument of the butchers in the Rwandan and Serbian governments. In September 1999, just over a decade after the Tiananmen Square massacre, Tang Jiaxuan, the Chinese foreign minister, criticized NATO's Kosovo war and championed national sovereignty: "When the sovereignty of a country is put in jeopardy, its human rights can hardly be protected effectively."[12]

But the strength of the democracies today has made the violation of the sovereignty of weaker dictatorships an opportunity too great to resist. Many contemporary human rights activists would agree with the gist—although certainly not the language or specifics—of what Gladstone wrote in *Bulgarian Horrors:* "Territorial integrity shuts out the foreign state; the *status quo* shuts out the inhabitants of the country, and keeps (I fear) everything to the Turk, with his airy promises, his disembodied reforms, his ferocious passions, and his daily, gross, and incurable misgovernment." This is the proper light in which to understand Milošević's argument for Yugoslavia's sovereign right to murder and dispossess the Kosovars.[13]

The Danger of Escalation

Among the many risks from humanitarian intervention, perhaps the scariest is that two great powers will clash—as U.S. and Russian troops nearly did at Pristina airfield in Kosovo. Grotius quotes a saint warning that "by intruding into each other's Provinces they should quarrel among themselves." It would hardly have been moral for Lyndon Johnson to launch a nuclear war trying to protect innocent Czechs from the Soviet Union during the Prague Spring in 1968. In 1994, when NATO proposed air strikes against the Bosnian Serb military after a Serb shell massacred sixty-eight Bosnians at a Sarajevo market, Andrei Kozyrev, the Russian foreign minister, harshly warned, "Already once, in 1914, a provocation had been staged in Sarajevo when a similar horrible act of terror became the reason for a global tragedy."[14]

But in the nineteenth century, the great powers repeatedly shied away from humanitarian commitments that might cause outright war between the most powerful countries. Because leaders really were prudent and deterrable, the dangers of humanitarian intervention became more manageable. Great powers would frequently refrain from intervening not because they did not *want* to intervene, but because they feared what would happen if they did.

The pattern comes up over and over. James Monroe and John Quincy Adams knew that the United States was too weak to help the Greeks. In 1831, Russia smashed an upstart Polish republic. Pushkin, a violent imperialist, wrote privately, "The war which is about to begin will be a war of extermination—or should be." The British House of Commons was so disgusted that it unanimously voted to censure Russia. Russians were infuriated by almost universal liberal European criticism. Like many Russians, Pushkin feared that Britain and France would do more than talk: "If we besiege Warsaw (which will demand a large number of troops), then Europe will have time to interfere in an affair which is not hers. However, France won't butt in by herself; England has nothing to quarrel with us about, so perhaps we'll scramble through." He celebrated the conquest of Warsaw with a poem aimed at French liberals, "To the Slanderers of Russia":

> *Lay off! This is a quarrel of Slavs among themselves,*
> *An old, domestic quarrel already weighed by Fate,*
> *An issue which won't be solved by you.*
> *. . . Leave us alone. You have not read the bloody reckoning.*

For you, these family antagonisms are strange and meaningless.
Neither the Kremlin, nor Praga, means anything to you.
You are thoughtlessly seduced by the courage of this desperate struggle;
And you hate us!

Even Earl Grey, the great Whig prime minister who would end slavery throughout the British Empire, did not dare to go to war with Russia.[15]

During the 1848 revolutions that swept Europe, Britain was vocally shocked by Austria's fierce repression of Italian and Hungarian revolutionaries. A new revolutionary republic in France was particularly worried over the plight of the Piedmontese. A French parliamentary vote to help Piedmont frightened Austria into accepting Anglo-French mediation, to defuse the issue before France took more extreme measures. And when Austria routed the Hungarian revolutionaries, Palmerston ordered his government to "maintain the dignity and honour of England by expressing *openly* and *decidedly*" the British public's "disgust." He wrote, "The Austrians are really the greatest brutes that ever called themselves by the undeserved name of civilised men. . . . [T]he Austrian Government know no method of administration but . . . flogging, imprisoning, and shooting. 'The *Austrians* know no argument but force.'" To help the Ottoman Empire shelter some of the defeated Hungarians who had fled, Palmerston wanted to send British squadrons to the Dardanelles. Austria backed down.[16]

Still, Britain and France dared not go any further against Austria. When the Hungarian revolutionary Kossuth appealed for direct British help, Palmerston—who declared himself totally in sympathy with the Hungarians—had to choose to maintain the cohesion of the Austrian Empire instead. British diplomats had no stomach for a possible war against both Austria and Russia. The situation was not so different from that in 1956, when Eisenhower would have liked to save the Hungarians, but dared not risk a war against the repressive empire that was crushing them.[17]

With the coming of the Crimean War, many Poles hoped that Britain and France would take the opportunity to come to Poland's rescue, too. Napoléon III's government seemed eager to do so; but Britain and France were afraid that saving the Poles would shock Austria and Prussia out of their neutrality and make the two conservative empires enter the war on Russia's side. Poland was left on its own.[18]

In January 1863, once again, Polish nationalists rose up against Russian rule. In Britain, and especially in Catholic France, public sentiment was once again overwhelmingly sympathetic to the Poles—even more so after Bismarck cast himself as an extra villain by helping Russia crush the Poles. The *Times* was indignant, as were Karl Marx and Giuseppe Garibaldi. Lord John Russell, still serving as British foreign secretary, informally warned the Russian ambassador in London that if there were further atrocities, Britain might consider steps beyond diplomacy. Britain and France protested to Tsar Aleksandr II, in tough enough terms that Gorchakov briefly feared that a war might be imminent. Even this protest was not enough to mollify French public opinion, and the entente between France and Russia came unglued. But fear of war kept the clash from going any further.[19]

As Theodore Roosevelt pointed out, Woodrow Wilson did not mind attacking Haiti: "Mr. Wilson nerved himself to wage [war] with tiny Hayti—for Mr. Wilson was not afraid of Hayti." But during the Armenian genocide, Wilson largely sat by because he did fear the Ottoman Empire, and behind it, Germany.[20]

If Russia and Austria were too strong for the liberal European powers to fight, the Ottoman Empire and Naples were not. In 1822, when British officials complained that the Ottoman Empire was selling refugees from Scio into slavery, an Ottoman minister snapped, "Why do not the Christian Sovereigns interfere to prevent the Emperor of Russia from sending his subjects into Siberia? Because they know very well what answer they would receive! Thus there is one law of humanity for Turkey and another for Russia!" It was Ottoman weakness and Russian strength that made such bullying possible. Russian and Austrian cruelty also outraged British and French consciences, even though Austria—if not Russia—was seen as a higher civilization. Had the Romanov and Habsburg imperiums been militarily weaker, it is possible that there would have been humanitarian interventions in Eastern Europe.[21]

Pushkin's brutal poem would be invoked in 1999 by Russia's foreign minister, Igor Ivanov, as good advice that NATO had failed to follow in Kosovo. But Ivanov's analogy does not work. Russia was a mighty state in Pushkin's day; the humanitarians in Britain and France would have been suicidal to go to war against it. In 1989, this was roughly the same kind of calculation that made Richard Nixon urge George H. W. Bush to see past the Tiananmen Square massacre: "What's happened has been handled badly and is deplorable, but take a look at the long haul." But the dangers of confronting Yugoslavia in 1999 were noticeably less than confronting Russia in 1831. These nineteenth-century uprisings from Greece to Armenia could have escalated, with the rivalry between the free and despotic countries erupting into catastrophic warfare. But what exactly was the risk of a great power war in Rwanda?[22]

Controlling Humanitarian Intervention: Self-restraint

By the time the Bulgarian massacres happened, it was almost assumed that, after a major slaughter, European troops might be sent. As the *Times* noted in 1876, "It is only seventeen years since the Syrian massacres brought on the Ottoman Empire the chastisement of foreign intervention, and those iniquities substantially repeated some of the worst stains on the war with the Greeks." Still, the more one looks at these actual interventions, the more one sees how clouded the judgment of the humanitarians was, and how much danger really did lie in the possible consequences.[23]

The most thoughtful conservatives are not amoral. To the contrary, they saw themselves as upstanding men, doing an important job with obvious moral implications. Disraeli was right to worry about "merciless humanitarians." Castlereagh and Disraeli had quite literally a Machiavellian ethic, but an ethic all the same. Kissinger rightly praises Castlereagh and Metternich for almost a century of peace. These leaders had a morality of prudence. Their ultimate goal was preserving order in an era where the uprisings in Greece, Hungary, Syria, Poland, Bosnia, Bulgaria, and Armenia could have escalated into catastrophic warfare among the great powers. The value of stability is that it saves lives. "Political liberty can exist only when there is peace," said Wilson, campaigning for the League of Nations in Des Moines, Iowa. "Social reform can take place only when there is peace."[24]

Even though this book concentrates on interventions, they should only be contemplated in the worst human rights emergencies. Few people today could share Theodore Roosevelt's blithe confidence in military force. Foreign societies are enormously complex, and reshaping them must always be an awful last resort. Humanitarian war—like any other kind of war—is likely to have terrifying unintended consequences. Too-frequent European interventions in the Ottoman Empire sometimes intensified feelings of difference between Christians and Muslims, and helped promote an Ottoman resentment of the West; this could pave the way for nationalist backlash or fresh atrocities. The Greek and Bulgarian rebels recklessly risked their public's brutal suppression, which drew the world's attention and sparked a war to bail them out—much like the

Kosovo Liberation Army taking on Milošević. This is not exactly a model to admire.[25]

Graham Greene wisely warned of the dangers of an American with lofty intentions in Saigon: "Perhaps only ten days ago he had been walking back across the Common in Boston, his arms full of the books he had been reading in advance on the Far East and the problems of China." Greene's world-weary British journalist goes on: "He didn't even hear what I said; he was absorbed already in the dilemmas of Democracy and the responsibilities of the West; he was determined . . . to do good, not to any individual person but to a country, a continent, a world. Well, he was in his element now with the whole universe to improve." Greene could just as well have been writing about Iraq.[26]

Still, in a desperate case like Rwanda, the moral importance of the innocents facing murder make it worth running some risks. But the world will need to find a routine way of cooperating among the big powers for such emergencies. The nineteenth century shows how the practice of humanitarian intervention can be *managed.* In an age where old-style imperialism still swaggered, the great powers had to convince each other that their purported mercy mission was not just a foil for imperial expansion. So the intervening states had to impose limitations on themselves. There were a number of established techniques of self-restraint: delineating spheres of justifiable intervention for each of the great powers, delegating to regional powers, putting time limits on humanitarian interventions, restricting the size of the military force, foreswearing diplomatic and commercial advantages from a humanitarian mission, and, above all, multilateralism. All of these devices helped make humanitarian intervention safer.[27]

SPHERES OF HUMANITARIAN INTEREST

Even Gladstone did not want his country to become the world's policeman, or, as he put it in high Victorian, "I am far from saying that we have taken out a commission of universal knight-errantry." Since the interventions often rested on specific treaties (France in Syria, Russia in Greece), it was clear which country ought to be sending troops. Just as the great powers had spheres of interest, so, too, might they have spheres of humanitarian concern. Revived today, this concept could have several advantages: it makes it harder for a country to dodge its responsibilities; it defuses accusations of imperialism; and it does not leave every disaster today for a deeply unpopular United States to solve.[28]

Where possible, there is much to be said for working with local authorities, rather than having outside powers do all the work. Local rulers know the ground better and have more domestic and regional legitimacy. Their inclusion can also make the intervention less intrusive; it is cheaper and easier to bully a state into reforming its human rights record than to invade it. If international pressure gets the Sudanese government to restrain the Janjaweed militia from mass murder in Darfur, that would be far better than an invasion.

The hitch, of course, is that the local leaders are often either part of the problem or the cause of it. Leaving the human rights problems to local authorities creates a soft option; Britain preferred to leave a volatile Syria in the hands of Fuad Pasha rather than Napoléon III, even when Russell had scant proof that the Ottoman Empire could really maintain order. Still, if humanitarian intervention was a background threat in a human rights crisis, weak governments would have greater incentives to provide order, and cruel governments would have something to fear. As Gladstone noted, "The Ottoman Porte is no more disposed than other governments, in the homely phrase, to drive its head against a brick wall."[29]

In addition, middleweight powers could take the lead in policing their own regions. Australia led the charge on East Timor; the major European countries should have properly done so for Bosnia; and a revitalized South Africa should be doing so for Zimbabwe. In other words, what the world today may need is not a universal right to wage humanitarian intervention, but, paraphrasing Che Guevera: one, two, three, many Treaties of Kutchuk-Kainardji.

Thus international law played an important role, especially the Concert of Europe and some specific treaties. Both Gladstone and Gorchakov agreed that Russia had a special duty to look out for the well-being of the Christians in the Ottoman Empire, from the 1856 Treaty of Paris. The Ottoman Empire also committed itself as part of the system of European public international law by signing the Treaty of Paris, and agreed to reform its treatment of its Armenians in the Treaty of Berlin in 1878. Indeed, during the Armenian genocide, the Ottoman Empire withdrew from the treaties of Paris and Berlin, evidently in an attempt to deprive other countries of the legal grounds for intervening.[30]

It is striking how much Western legal consensus there was on the legitimacy of humanitarian intervention, going back into the nineteenth century, among a host of U.S., British, French (*l'intervention d'humanité*), German, and other authorities. In 1898, a French consul in Constantinople drew up a 1,232-page report for his foreign minister detailing legal justifications for French intervention in the Ottoman Empire, resting on treaties, protocols, and conventions from the years 881, 1327, 1535, and, more recently, 1826, 1827, 1829, 1830, 1831, 1832, 1840, 1841, 1842, 1845, 1846, 1856, 1857, 1858, 1860, 1866, 1867, 1869, 1876, 1877, 1878, 1880, 1882, 1885, 1886, 1895, and much more. Even by the standards of French legal bureaucracy, this is numbing—and the consul was planning a second volume. This legalization did not stop atrocities, any more than the 1948 Convention on the Prevention and Punishment of the Crime of Genocide meant an end to genocide; but it did usefully delineate spheres of justified intervention.[31]

MULTILATERALISM

Admiral Codrington, who had sailed into Navarino Bay in 1827 vaguely wondering if the French and Russian warships might wind up firing at each other, ended up delighted: "There is no instance of the fleet of any one country showing more complete union of spirit and of action than was exhibited by the squadrons of the three Allied Powers together in this bloody and destructive battle." The most obvious benefit of multilateralism is that it provides more military resources. After all, Codrington's Mediterranean squadron had just three British ships of the line—the same number as the Ottomans. It was only with French and Russian help that the Allies gained a qualitative (although not quantitative) advantage over the combined Ottoman naval forces at Navarino Bay. French officials in 1860 seemed genuinely pleased to have help from the British and Russian navies, and the Beirut international commissioners generally worked well together.[32]

But the advantages of multilateralism go beyond ganging up on an enemy. Dufferin, the British commissioner in Beirut, wrote to a fellow commissioner, "We have convinced each other, I think, that the good of the people of the country, and the well government of the Province, is the principal object that each of us has at heart." This is pretty smug, but has the right spirit: multilateralism was the business of mutual convincing. As James Madison wrote in *The Federalist,*

> An attention to the judgment of other nations is important to every government for two reasons; the one is that independently of the merits of any particular plan or measure, it is desirable . . . that it should appear to other nations as the offspring of a wise and honorable policy; the second is that in some doubtful cases, particularly where the national councils may be warped by some strong passion

or momentary interest, the presumed or known opinion of the impartial world may be the best guide that can be followed.

Multilateralism is a powerful way of overcoming the profound suspicion between rival states.[33]

The Concert of Europe was the chief venue for debates over any number of nineteenth-century crises (over Belgium, Poland, Naples, Saxony, and so on), not least the ones over humanitarian interventions. Although many conservatives today are skeptical about international institutions, these were essentially the brainchild of conservatives—the creation not of Wilson, but of Metternich and Castlereagh, who called the Concert "the great machine of European safety."[34]

Multilateralism was a familiar formula for the Concert. For instance, stuck in an unpopular occupation of Rome, France tried to get cover by calling in Belgian, Spanish, Bavarian, and Portuguese troops. The basic idea has endured; Felix Frankfurter, in 1920 (before joining the Supreme Court), wrote that U.S. interventions in Latin America ought to be voted on by a pan-American authority. Today, a deeper kind of multilateralism is possible, embracing not just European great powers, but also the rest of the world.[35]

But multilateralism can be paralyzing. The Concert of Europe was built to preserve peace among the strong, not to protect the weak. Insisting on UN approval for humanitarian interventions could easily become a recipe for stalemate if the great powers are badly split—as they were during the Cold War, or in the aftermath of the Iraq war, or in any number of possible future constellations. Back in 1827, Britain managed to sign up France and Russia to the Treaty of London, as a prelude to intervention in Greece, but not Austria or Prussia. The squadron in Navarino Bay was not the Concert of Europe's ideal of unanimity, but the participation of three great powers gave the mission more legitimacy than if it had just been a single great power—just as the Kosovo war gained legitimacy as a NATO undertaking, even if Russia would not bless it in the UN Security Council.[36]

Still, as Kissinger noted of Castlereagh's effort to restrain Russia from war for the Greeks, "A doctrine of common intervention can furnish a more useful tool to frustrate action than the doctrine of non-interference." In the real world, UN approval means letting Hu Jintao's China and Vladimir Putin's Russia decide who will get rescued. Tibetans and Chechens need not apply. A rising China has used its Security Council seat to shelter Sudan, a major oil source for China.[37]

Unilateralism can be paralyzing in its own way today. The multipolar nineteenth-century European order has been replaced with U.S. unipolarity. But if the United States is the only country that launches humanitarian interventions, then there are grave dangers: U.S. triumphalism and imperial temptations, coupled with passivity, buck-passing, and deep resentment and fear from the rest of the world.

So the nineteenth-century experience suggests what a more effective formula might look like. With a loose consensus on the acceptability of humanitarian intervention in rare last-ditch cases, the great European powers were open to initiatives for action. But the state that brought that initiative was treated with bracing skepticism. A would-be rescuer government had to accept strict constraints about force structure, timing, political and commercial advantages, and international participation. It was quite the opposite of what George W. Bush did in Iraq: undermining his own claims to humanitarian motives in Iraq by excluding France, Germany, and Russia from postwar reconstruction contracts—giving exclusive commercial advantages to the United States.[38]

Of course, in disastrous cases like Russia's 1877 attack on the Ottoman Empire, multilateralism failed outright. Britain had managed to get Gorchakov to agree to use the model of the Syrian occupation in 1860 as the basis for the Constantinople conference in 1876; but, after Gorchakov initially agreed, the conference fell apart, leaving nothing to restrain Russia from its darker ambitions. Troubling as this is, it is not a reason to dismiss multilateralism outright. Obviously international institutions alone cannot prevent a determined aggressor state from attacking. But the point of these institutions is to differentiate that kind of crude aggression from a humanitarian mission. What is so striking about some of these nineteenth-century debates is that states were often surprisingly respectable. Rather than just vetoing any rival initiative, the European powers sometimes confronted a situation on its own merits. After the battle of Navarino, Britain did not mind supporting a limited French ground deployment in Greece to fend off Ibrahim's Egyptian forces, but would not countenance Russia's land grab war.[39]

As Michael Walzer writes, "In practice, we should probably look for some concurrence of multilateral authorization and unilateral initiative—the first for the sake of moral legitimacy, the second for the sake of political effectiveness—but it's the initiative that counts." Something along those lines used to happen in the better moments of the nineteenth century. In Syria, the big European powers held to the principle of multilateral consensus with astonishing fixity. France only went in with unanimous permission; the great powers had repeated conferences about the French mission, with France never denying the principle that any one of the others could veto France's policy; Britain's efforts to get France to withdraw at the end of February 1861 floundered when the rest of Europe was not as insistent; and ultimately it was multilateralism that got a reluctant France back out of Syria in 1861. This was, by the admittedly dismal standards of international cooperation, remarkably effective.[40]

LIMITING MILITARY MISSIONS

The main limitations imposed by all this multilateral diplomacy are simple: keep the mission short, keep the force size small, and give no advantages to the intervening power. Humanitarian interventions are emergency steps; one should be suspicious of a permanent emergency.[41]

In St. Petersburg in 1826, Wellington insisted that none of the great powers would scheme for "its own aggrandisement or advantage." In 1828, French troops sent to Greece had to have a stringently limited mission to win British approval: to get Ibrahim's Egyptian troops out of the Morea, and then to withdraw themselves. When the French general decided to take Attica, he was quickly ordered not to by his own government, rather than exceed his narrow mandate. In 1860, the Concert of Europe signed a formal protocol in Paris demanding that the European troops leave Syria after six months; that the mission consist of no more than twelve thousand troops, of which six thousand would be French; and that no powers (read: France) seek exclusive territorial or commercial gain. In 1878, Austria-Hungary wanted to limit a Russian occupation of Bulgaria to six months, with no more than twenty thousand men.[42]

While this may be good diplomacy, it could be bad peacekeeping or nation-building. It would be disastrous to send in a force that was too small to stop the killing and restore order. The other great powers are reassured to hear that the humanitarian forces won't be staying long; the local murderers are, too, knowing that they can just wait the mission out. This could stymie efforts at enduring reform and postconflict reconstruction. In Syria, the Druzes were acutely aware of the six-month time limit for French occupation. If NATO troops had pulled out of Bosnia after a year, as Clinton had originally said U.S. troops would, then Serb nationalists could have just laid low for a year and then restarted intrigues.[43]

On top of that, discussions of time limits tend to blur into the hotly contested question of what political settlement will be put in place after a humanitarian intervention. Should the victim group gain statehood, autonomy, or what? There was no one nineteenth-century answer: European military power secured a largely independent Greek state, governed by a king who was not too tightly associated with any of the European houses; European military power reformed Ottoman rule in Syria, but did not carve out a new state; and even Gladstone did not want a fully independent Bulgaria. Often there is no obvious stable political end to be found, and the deployment of foreign troops can tempt the victims to expand their political demands. Advocates for Bosnia in 1992–95 only wanted to maintain it as an independent state, but it has been impossible to keep Kosovo as a mere province of Serbia after NATO's humanitarian intervention. The intervening powers often demand a principle of multiethnicity and accommodation, as when the great European powers in 1861 called for the "principle of fusion" in Syria; the insurgent nationalists are equally insistent on self-determination and separation, and see the arrival of foreign troops as their main chance to win their independence.[44]

The kind of occupation that most reassures the other great powers is the one that least scares the *génocidaires.* The answer could simply be a longer time limit; killers would have a hard time waiting out, say, a ten-year occupation. Or one could lay more emphasis on an 1860-style clause stipulating no advantages to the occupying power, so that the occupation would be clearly a duty rather than a prize. The devastating civil war in Iraq shows the terrible risks of taking over another country, even temporarily. The challenge is finding the right middle ground: a mission big and lengthy enough to be effective, but small and swift enough not to be mistaken for imperialism. Still, the distinction is pretty clear: France went into Vietnam in 1858 and finally got out almost a century later; France went into Syria in 1860 and left in under a year.

CHAPTER TWENTY-EIGHT

The Domestic Politics of Humanitarian Intervention

DESPOTIC STATES

Metternich's attitude toward humanitarian intervention was clear: he was dead set against it. He wanted to help the Ottoman Empire to crush the Greeks, just as he supported Russian and Austrian crackdowns on their own restive populations. Without a free press or free society, there was nothing to interfere with his pursuit of Austrian realpolitik.

But even despotic states sometimes use humanitarian rhetoric, decrying human rights violations abroad that look not too different from what that state commits against its own people. This was true in the nineteenth century; it is doubly true today, when human rights rhetoric is so widespread that North Korea styles itself a democratic republic. Dictators can find it useful to stir up their own public opinion to serve their foreign policy goals. As the Palestinians and the Serbs of the Krajina have learned by bitter experience, what the government creates for convenience can sometimes be scrapped when it becomes inconvenient. After Aleksandr I died, his successor, Nikolai I, renounced the Greek cause with lightning speed, choking off pan-Slavist public sentiment and smoothing over Russia's rocky relations with Britain.

But it is not always that easy. When a repressive state creates public sympathy for oppressed foreigners, that sentiment often takes on a life of its own. Pan-Slavism may have been artificial when the Winter Palace first pushed it, but after long years it has become a force to be reckoned with. Arab public sympathy for the Palestinians runs deeper than a diversionary tactic to distract frustration at the Arab states' poor economic and political performance at home. Men make nationalism, but they do not make it as they please.

Nor can a dictatorship count on its repressive apparatus to turn off public opinion as soon as the din gets too loud. In the 1870s, Aleksandr II's government was shot through with pan-Slavists far more militant than their monarch, led by Nikolai Ignatiev but also including the tsar's wife and son. In the summer of 1876, Aleksandr II let pan-Slavist journalists write relatively freely about Serbia, with frighteningly inflammatory results. By the time the tsar unleashed the Third Section on the pan-Slavists and muffled the pan-Slavist press, it was too late: he found it easier to confront the Ottomans abroad than the pan-Slavists at home. The British ambassador in St. Petersburg perfectly captured the calculation: "The internal movement is . . . more threatening than the external danger."[1]

France under the Second Empire does not count as a liberal state. But it was a far more open place than Russia. France had some free elements in its government, which became an important impetus toward the deployment of troops in Syria. *Le Siècle,* the most important nongovernment newspaper, with progressive politics, reached about as many readers each day as the official imperial papers. While the press's ability to cause trouble was limited by government oversight and censorship, public opinion had to be a cause of concern for the prince-president of a government based on universal male suffrage, in a country where public dissatisfaction ran strong—and was expressed at the ballot box. A short and glorious expedition to Syria was a tempting way for Napoléon III to get a boost at home.

Still, Napoléon III might have been prepared to indulge his own public opinion, but only because going into Syria suited his imperial interests. Had a Syrian intervention been diametrically against Napoléon III's view of realpolitik, the emperor could have, like his counterpart in Russia, silenced his public—as he did, for instance, when the Catholic press became too vocal during a crisis over Sardinia. It is only in free societies that something as radical as Navarino could be expected.

Free States

Castlereagh, Palmerston, and Disraeli, as well as Adams and Wilson, were made miserable by their own free press and civil society. Much as they wanted to, they could not directly mandate their public's empathy to suit imperial or strategic interests. As one British philhellene who had been at Mesologgi with Byron later wrote, the British government "had not, like that of Russia, the power to coerce the sympathies of Britons." Instead, reporters could reach out and send reliable news directly from the massacre scene to the public.[2]

Thus, even when Canning was still proclaiming an official neutrality,

Sultan Mahmut II and Metternich alike were baffled at British society's enduring pro-Greek enthusiasm. "In the year 1823," wrote that British philhellene, "the sympathies of Englishmen, with all those engaged in defending the inalienable rights of citizens, were so strong, that the British government feared to act in strict accordance with the recognised law of nations. The people considered that the duties of humanity were more binding than national treaties." Pushkin, while cheering on Russia's crushing of Poland, was worried that pro-Polish public opinion in the more liberal European states would get out of hand: "It is to the advantage of practically all the governments to keep in this case to the principle of non-intervention, that is, to avoid getting a hangover from another's excesses; but their peoples are straining at the leash and baying. Before you know it, Europe will be at us."[3]

IMAGINED HUMANITY

The first step is getting credible information. It is also in some ways the most crucial one—the sine qua non of any humanitarian intervention. Intelligence services often beat the press, and in some cases their dire reports were enough to induce a government to move, like the secret rumor of Egyptian deportations of Greeks in 1825, or Bentivoglio's dispatches from Beirut in 1860. But in a free country, there is also press coverage of an atrocity. It would have made Castlereagh's job much easier if he could have banned British newspapers from publishing information gleaned from *Le Spectateur Oriental*'s reporting about the Scio massacre.

Occasionally, top government officials will be personally touched by foreign atrocities. The British ambassador in Constantinople at the time of the Scio massacre was particularly stunned by the execution of ten Scio hostages whom he knew personally. Thus public decapitation, although a horror dwarfed by the scale of what would soon happen in Scio, was singled out in the British government's complaint to the Ottoman Empire. During the Rwanda genocide, Bill Clinton, while allowing the slaughter to proceed unimpeded, tried personally to find Monique Mujawamariya, a Rwandan human rights activist whom he had recently met at the White House.[4]

But more often, the mass media creates the drive toward a humanitarian intervention. As Disraeli wrote, "As far as the *Times* is concerned, it is a question of who shall rule the country: the Queen's Minister or Printing House Square." In particular, the precise placement of foreign correspondents has a big impact on the policy of free governments. Distant wars are hard to cover, so the few bits of reliable information that make it back to the home country are enormously influential. Gladstone wrote, about atrocity stories from Naples, that the public should "not . . . bar their minds to the entrance of the light, however painful be the objects it may disclose. I have myself felt that incredulity, and wish I could have felt it still; but it has yielded to conviction step by step, and with fresh pain at every fresh access of evidence."[5]

So the resources of the press play a crucial role in determining which atrocities get public attention. As that British philhellene rather quaintly wrote in 1861, "It is difficult for those who travel from London to Constantinople in a week, to form any idea of the difficulty of obtaining information which existed in the East during the first thirty years of the present century." In 1821, the killings of a small number of Greeks in Constantinople were widely covered in the British press, and sparked considerable outrage, unlike the unreported Ottoman massacre of hundreds of Greeks in distant Kydonies just two months later. The first word of the impending slaughter in Scio came because the Ottomans held some Greek merchants from Scio captive in Constantinople—more accessible than Scio itself.[6]

In 1957, French public opinion fixed on Algiers, where a small amount of France's overall cruelty became noticeable to the press corps in the capital city. In 1989, when the Chinese government opened fire on student demonstrators in Tiananmen Square, live television and newspaper reports from Beijing drew worldwide condemnation. There was far more Western interest in Somalia than in Sudan in the 1990s, and in Bosnia than Abkhazia, largely because that was where the reporters happened to be. Otherwise, these places were equally remote and unfamiliar to Western publics. The small Nairobi-based press corps knew that the massive and inaccessible Sudanese south would devour days of reporting time, whereas Mogadishu was potentially a day trip. As Anthony Lake, Clinton's national security adviser, said, "Public pressure for our humanitarian engagement increasingly may be driven by televised images, which can depend in turn on such considerations as where CNN sends its camera crews."[7]

This pattern is true both across countries and within them. The Dili massacre in 1991 got widespread attention, largely because foreign journalists managed to film Indonesian troops firing on a crowd of East Timorese in the Santa Cruz cemetery. In Rwanda, much more was known in real time about killings in the capital of Kigali than in the hills of Bisesero. In Bosnia, there was far more Western public awareness of atrocities in Sarajevo, where the foreign press corps was concentrated, than of those in

Goražde and Tuzla. Even the Srebrenica massacre, the single worst war crime in Europe since 1945, got less coverage, simply because there were no foreign reporters in the town when it fell to Serb nationalist forces in July 1995.

As awful as it is to say so, major massacres are crucial moments for the activists trying to bring such atrocities to an end. Public opinion can coalesce around grisly events. In Greece, it was the execution of Grigorios, the death of Byron, and the Scio massacre; in Kosovo, it was the Račak slaughter. At the outbreak of the Greek rebellion, Constantinople was easier to access than the Morea, and private letters and correspondent reports gave detailed accounts of atrocities there. Relatively early on, this reporting fixed an image of extreme Ottoman cruelty in European imaginations. British sympathy for the Greeks and Bulgarians was caused in large part by the ability of London newspapers to get vivid reports of massacres in Constantinople and Scio in 1821 and 1822, and in Batak in 1876. This was why the Ottoman Empire tried to censor letters and local newspapers from that part of Bulgaria: the gruesome news was a terrible liability. (For the exact same reason, the Sudanese government is restricting foreign press coverage of Darfur today.) In contrast, British press reporting of the 1875 uprising in Bosnia, and of Bulgaria before the *Daily News* got its big scoop in June 1876, provided nothing much to upset the digestion of the British public.[8]

Just as the press was inconsistent in its reach, it was also skewed in its coverage. The British press in the 1820s was pro-Greek, in large part because of its philhellene sources. Without their own on-scene reporting in many cases, newspapers often parroted what they were told by philhellene sources, who disgracefully played down the Greeks' own atrocities against Turks. Brutally honest philhellenes like Byron were the exception, and even Thomas Gordon, who quit his military post in Greece in horror at the massacre of Turks at Tripolitza, muffled his criticism. Thus, although there was substantial press coverage of Tripolitza, the reporters largely missed the real story.[9]

But this does not mean that newspaper reporting should be dismissed as just the voice of national bias. It would be hard to argue that British newspapers were covering Greece or Bulgaria because of a deep and abiding British interest in those particular areas of the Balkans. There was surely more interest in the plight of Christians than in that of Muslims, but, as discussed above, that is only one facet of the overall picture. Still, the nineteenth-century press's overreliance on missionary, Christian, or activist sources is a cautionary tale to today's reporters.

Above all, the press moved independently of government policy. It could be strategically disastrous for the British government to have to face up to credible information in press reports of trouble in Greece, Poland, Hungary, Syria, and Bulgaria. Today, seeing how much the expanding reach of the press mattered in the nineteenth century, it is dispiriting to hear newspaper editors and television broadcasters explaining that they cannot cover a complex and remote bloodbath like Darfur. "If we don't cover the Michael Jacksons, that will be our demise," said John Yearwood, world editor of the *Miami Herald.* "That is what the public wants. But we ought to make the commitment to also give Darfur or Rwanda attention if we can." This does not offer much hope that the next massacre will be covered by the next MacGahan.[10]

There is one element of today's era of human rights that is in retreat: print capitalism, and thus foreign press coverage. Print and capitalism are not getting along. Although U.S. newspapers now field overseas reporters with a skill and a professionalism unknown to nineteenth-century hacks, Wall Street has decided that it hates newspaper stock. Under heavy pressure from investors, some of the country's best newspapers have decided to go local. Foreign bureaus are being closed by many important papers in many important places. When the front offices decide to shut those bureaus, they fritter away a hard-won achievement of centuries. They are reversing the moral gains of modern empathy.

HUMANITARIAN POLITICS IN A FREE COUNTRY

The next step is a domestic reaction to the gruesome news. The word from the free press can hit home in a free society, which in turn puts pressure on an accountable government. In Victorian Britain, while not yet a full democracy, the government had to build a consensus not just among elites but also the middle and working classes.[11]

The scope of the media helped define the ambit of humanitarianism not just abroad, but also at home. The growth of a domestic mass media and faster transit were vital to both Byron's philhellenes and Gladstone's atrocitarians, with the latter far more influential than the former. While the London Greek Committee remained largely an elite group, Gladstone's latter-day supporters had access to more newspapers, with bigger circulations, and farther reach. The *Times* had under six thousand readers at the time of the Scio massacre in 1822, but as many as seventy thousand by the time of Batak. The abolition of so-called taxes on knowledge created an explosion of readership from 1855 onward, including many new papers. To take just one, the *Telegraph* reached about two hundred thousand people at the time of the Bulgarian massacres; by 1888, the *Telegraph* had three hundred thousand readers—about 1 percent of the British population.[12]

The London Greek Committee really was a London group. It had a hard time reaching beyond the capital, even to Cambridge and Manchester. But by the 1870s, telegraphs and railways made it easier to mount a broader movement. It was no coincidence that Gladstone tended to give his speeches at railway stations. During the frenzied Midlothian campaign, he would deliver a five-minute speech in a train station, and then go off to the next rally. (One Tory lord was scandalized by the spectacle of Gladstone "stumping the Country, like a Yankee Presidential agent.") These were the sinews of a new mass nationalism.[13]

The electorate grew, too. The first Reform Act came in 1832, followed by the second Reform Act in 1867, which by itself doubled the size of the British electorate. The press had to reach almost two million voters. The 1867 franchise reform sent a large number of new voters into the mix, just in time to read the gruesome news from the Balkans. Both in absolute terms and adjusted for the size of the electorate and newspaper circulations, there was far more coverage of the Bulgarian horrors than of the Greek uprising. In other words, Palmerston faced more media pressure over the Syrians than Liverpool over the Greeks, and Disraeli had to deal with even more over the Bulgarians.[14]

This all meant more pressure on the British government to act. Humanitarian intervention, emphasizing a common humanity unbounded by state borders, is more an ideology of the left. In Britain, it was more natural for the Liberals to send battleships to Syria in 1860 than it was for the Tories to dispatch a fleet to Greece in 1827. But under Canning, the Tories did yield to British public sentiment. It was only Disraeli who managed to avoid using force. He was under almost unbearable pressure, not just from the Liberals and the public, but also from centrist Tories in his own cabinet like Salisbury, Carnarvon, and Derby, and from Queen Victoria (before the Russians terrified her). If a more moderate Tory like Salisbury had been prime minister, there could well have been a British intervention. Even Disraeli came surprisingly close to it, moving the fleet and planning a Bulgarian occupation. It was only Russian and Ottoman policies that let him off the hook.[15]

A FINAL REALPOLITIK CALCULATION

Domestic politics can put tremendous pressure on a government, but in the end, the decision to send in the troops relies on weighing the international consequences: how much does my public want to see a foreign expedition, and how much trouble will it cause internationally?

For France and Russia, the demands of public opinion lined up with their imperial interests in the Middle East and the Balkans, respectively. France was not prepared to gamble too much for those mixed interests; Russia was ready to gamble hugely, both because of pan-Slavist societal pressure and state imperialism. But imperial and humanitarian motives were closely aligned.

Not so in Britain. Still, there is a final puzzle. Why did Canning and Palmerston choose humanitarian missions while Disraeli did not? It would be shallow to explain it as Disraeli's mere obstinacy; that obstinacy had roots. The real reason has to do with decisions made outside of Britain: in Russia and the Ottoman Empire.

First, Russia's militaristic rumblings in 1876 and after gave Disraeli a devastating reply to the atrocitarians. Like many agitations, the pro-Bulgarian movement lost some steam as time passed. But what really let Disraeli get himself back into the driver's seat was Russian belligerence, which tapped a deep strain of Russophobia in Britain. (In contrast, back in the 1820s, Russia sporadically pushed Britain to move, but did not get too far out in front of British positions.) Unlike Castlereagh, Disraeli did not scorn the dark arts of democratic politicking; he might not have gotten the same sublime thrill from it as Gladstone did, but he knew he had to meet Gladstone head on in the public arena. And there, nothing took the pressure off Disraeli more than Russia's 1877 declaration of war on the Ottoman Empire. He pounded home his message: Gladstone was delivering the British Empire into the hands of Russia.

Second, the crises themselves mattered. The Bulgarian uprising was feeble and quickly crushed; Disraeli only had to deal with one major publicized massacre, at Batak. In contrast, the Greek revolt dragged on for years. This meant that Greece sporadically produced fresh headline-grabbing enormities for British diplomats to confront: Constantinople in 1821, Scio in 1822, Mesologgi in 1824, and the Morea in 1825. After a Vietcong attack on a U.S. barracks at Pleiku, McGeorge Bundy said, "Pleikus are like streetcars"—if you miss this one, another one will come along soon. During the Greek insurgency, Mesologgis were like streetcars. If there had been another major atrocity after Batak, even Disraeli might have had to fold, or be pushed out of office. The prolonged Greek insurgency also gave time for British society to move toward a consensus on intervention, epitomized by the ascension of Canning to the Foreign Office: a Tory, not a Whig, but interventionist all the same. In other words, Bulgaria was a crisis more like Rwanda in 1994, where the genocide lasted three months, and Greece was a crisis more like Bosnia in 1992–95, where the genocide lasted three and a half years.[16]

Just as free institutions can create domestic pressure on a government to launch a particular war, international events and decisions can take that pressure off. Still, in the end, there is a profound difference between debates about humanitarian intervention in free and unfree countries. The roots of Russian interventionism lay in the Winter Palace; the roots of British interventionism lay in Printing-House Square.

CHAPTER TWENTY-NINE

A New Imperialism?

After September 11

Exactly 125 years before the World Trade Center massacre, on September 11, 1876, Benjamin Disraeli was writing that he had sent the British fleet to protect defenseless Ottoman citizens, and Derby was meeting in the Foreign Office with working-class activists about the Bulgarian horrors. The human rights movement long predates the current U.S. national security crisis, and will be with us for a long time to come.[1]

U.S. inaction in the face of mass atrocity dates back to John Quincy Adams. Wilson's abdication in the face of genocide in 1915 set the stage for a century of democratic U.S. indifference to the need for humanitarian intervention. Franklin Delano Roosevelt's administration did far less than it could have to stop the Holocaust. As Samantha Power shows, in the twentieth century, the United States repeatedly failed to intervene to stop genocide. During the Cold War, the Americans or the Soviets would have vetoed any move by the other side. But in the 1990s, the collapse of the Soviet Union made a new liberal interventionism possible. With U.S. military missions in Somalia and Kosovo, and—horribly belatedly—Bosnia, the nineteenth-century practice of humanitarian intervention seemed like it might be poised to make a comeback.[2]

If anything, Bill Clinton's international arena was more favorable to a new humanitarian interventionism than it had been for Canning and Gladstone. A weakened Russia was in the throes of its own precarious democratic experiment; China, while rising, was still only a regional power; and the big countries in Western Europe were all friendly democracies. But Clinton's version of the realpolitik calculation about the costs of a humanitarian intervention weighed even a handful of U.S. casualties far above the saving of hundreds of thousands of foreign lives.[3]

One of the most striking aspects of nineteenth-century British debates about humanitarian intervention is the lack of discussion of casualties or public reaction to them. British diplomats worried about escalation to a major war, not about losing a small amount of their soldiers, along the lines of eighteen U.S. Rangers killed in Mogadishu in October 1993. Britain relied on its navy in much the same way that the United States relies on its air force—as a largely invulnerable instrument of power projection. But a country in the business of running a global empire could not afford the same squeamishness about losing small numbers of soldiers. Although British diplomats were often distracted by domestic issues, they could not put foreign policy aside altogether. Even critics of imperialism like Gladstone would have been mystified by the suggestion of U.S.-style isolationism.[4]

In today's calculations about humanitarian military missions, the loss of a relatively low number of troops weighs heavily on American and European minds, in something a bit like the way that war among the great powers weighed on British minds in the nineteenth century. Even after the Rwandan genocide, American and European publics did not seem to mind much. Flatteringly, one could call this the result of Adams's proper aversion to warfare; unflatteringly, one could call it the isolationism of people still in the habit of thinking themselves distant from world affairs. After Clinton, instead of a U.S. Midlothian campaign against the choice to leave some eight hundred thousand Rwandans to die in 1994, the 2000 presidential campaign was marked by both Al Gore and George W. Bush saying they would not have gone into Rwanda.

"Follow Canning's Example"

Since the massacres of September 11, there have been many calls for a new benevolent U.S. imperialism. The most enthusiastic and erudite advocate is the historian Niall Ferguson, whose main worry is whether the United States is tough enough and shrewd enough to shoulder Britain's old imperial burdens. Michael Ignatieff, too, sees a new "Empire Lite," while the historian John Lewis Gaddis writes of the stirrings of an "empire of liberty" resisting Islamist terrorism—a concept that, he says, goes back to Jefferson. The journalists Robert Kaplan and William Kristol gladly embrace the label of imperialist. Soon after September 11, a neoconservative author,

Max Boot, who was reminded of the post-Napoleonic world, wrote, "Afghanistan and other troubled lands today cry out for the sort of enlightened foreign administration once provided by self-confident Englishmen in jodhpurs and pith helmets."[5]

Some of the toughest critics of recent U.S. foreign policy are horrified at the prospect of a new U.S. imperialism—especially since the Iraq war. Chalmers Johnson, for instance, warns against U.S. "humanitarian imperialists." Once again, some realists and leftists have converged in their critique of imperialism. The same themes come up in Britain and France.[6]

Niall Ferguson sees the ghosts of Canning and Gladstone striding the globe again. At the start of the Iraq war, he recommended that George W. Bush "follow Canning's example" in finding multilateral ways to work with Russia; as the Iraq insurgency grew stronger, Ferguson wished for "a Gladstonian critique of today's inept imperialism." He argued that Tony Blair's foreign policy was the most overtly altruistic since Gladstone's. Timothy Garton Ash, too, saw Blair as "Tony Gladstone." And during the Kosovo war, in his speech in Bulgaria, Blair himself invoked Gladstone as an example for Kosovo:

> Then, as now, it would have been easy to look the other way; easy to argue that bigger strategic issues were at stake than the fate of a few hundred thousand people in the Balkans. Some people made exactly that argument. Some do today. They were wrong in 1876 over Bulgaria; and they are wrong in 1999 over Kosovo.[7]

What to make of this? Canning and Gladstone do offer valuable lessons, but this book tries to stand apart from both the advocates and enemies of a new U.S. imperialism. The nineteenth-century experience of humanitarian intervention suggests three major lessons for U.S. and European foreign policy.

First, humanitarianism and imperialism should not be casually blurred together. They were not the same thing even in the nineteenth century. True, humanitarian intervention is fundamentally an act of force to reshape a country, even if undertaken only in supreme emergency. That imposition came more easily to European imperialists than to someone like Adams, committed to nonintervention. But the use of force alone does not make an act imperialistic—or all wars, not just humanitarian ones, could be called imperial. It took federal marshals to enforce integration in Arkansas and Mississippi, but that does not make the civil rights movement an act of police brutality.

Imperialism is about domination and superiority, not the empathy of humanitarianism. The project of empire had to erode the public conscience, as when the British were asked to support Edward John Eyre's vicious crushing of Jamaica. This could only create different standards of morality for the imperial periphery—the opposite of what Burke wanted. The philhellenes and atrocitarians hoped to see the Greeks and Bulgarians flourish independently; their freedom was a good in itself, even when it went against British strategic interests. Humanitarians do not want to govern other people, let alone the world; they, at their best, just want to resist atrocity.[8]

Of course, power is corrupting. There is always the potential for any military intervention to shade into something much darker. Nietzsche wrote, "Whoever fights monsters should see to it that in the process he does not become a monster." That is why the practice must be so suspiciously watched. Still, as the political scientist Joseph Nye writes, "It is a mistake to confuse the politics of primacy with the politics of empire." The historians Jack Gallagher and Ronald Robinson note that in the thirty years after 1841, Britain took control of New Zealand, the Gold Coast, Labuan, Natal, the Punjab, Sindh, Hong Kong, Berar, Oudh, Lower Burma, Kowloon, Lagos, Sierra Leone, Basutoland, Griqualand, and the Transvaal. In contrast, NATO never wanted to take over Bosnia, and has gladly relinquished its policing duties. The United States cannot hold on to Iraq, and even the Bush administration says repeatedly that it looks forward to leaving. This is hardly comparable with imperial Britain, ruling over hundreds of millions of Indians. Blair's missions in Kosovo and Sierra Leone were aimed at saving lives, not reviving an empire. U.S. concern for human rights does not mean that the United States should take up what George Orwell called "the dirty work of Empire."[9]

Iraq was not a humanitarian intervention. It could have been back in 1988, during the Anfal extermination campaign against the Kurds, but the United States was then supporting Saddam Hussein. Kenneth Roth of Human Rights Watch argued that Saddam's dictatorship, brutal as it was, was not in 2003 engaged in the kind of extraordinary slaughter that would justify an intervention. Instead, George W. Bush's justification for war was mostly about nonproliferation and a safer Middle East—a strategic rationale, not a humanitarian one. The promotion of human rights was a side benefit, although it weighed more heavily in the minds of some of the war's backers. Some advocates of toppling Saddam did so on principled grounds of human rights, like Václav Havel, Bernard Kouchner, José Ramos-Horta, and Ann Clwyd—although none of them, not even Paul Wolfowitz, played a role in White House decisions comparable to that of Donald Rumsfeld or Condoleezza Rice, let alone Bush himself. When there were no weapons of mass destruction to be found, the White House had to fall back on its remaining rationale: democracy and human rights. Today, with Iraq torn apart by a horrific civil war, the Bush administration's debacle threatens to discredit the entire enterprise of spreading freedom. This book tries to show a longer view, so that the disaster in Iraq, as important and troubling as it is, need not invalidate the whole basic idea of promoting human rights—if it is done with greater wisdom and modesty.[10]

Second, humanitarian intervention is possible even in a world where U.S. and European security is not absolutely assured.

After the World Trade Center was destroyed, many conservatives argued that the humanitarian interventions of the 1990s had been frivolous, and even a distraction from the necessity of defending the American homeland. Condoleezza Rice, then Bush's national security adviser, said, "If you go back just a little while, there was a lot of speculation that the future of the U.S. armed forces actually lay largely in so-called operations other than war, in policing civil and ethnic conflicts and in humanitarian missions. Well, I don't hear anybody saying that any more." Robert Kaplan argued that the "luxury" of deployments in Bosnia and Kosovo was over: "Foreign policy must return to what it traditionally has been: the diplomatic aspect of national security rather than a branch of Holocaust studies."[11]

No doubt, free states with real security problems—like terrorism and nuclear proliferation—are going to concentrate on self-preservation. But total security is precious rare in international politics. Britain was mighty in the nineteenth century, but not so mighty that it did not fear for its own security. Even Gladstone was worried by the menace of Russian ascendancy, to say nothing of the challenge posed by Germany after 1871. Al Qaeda is simultaneously a bigger and a smaller threat than what Georgians and Victorians faced: hoping to kill large numbers of American civilians, possibly with nuclear or biological weapons, but incapable of fielding the industry and manpower of Russia and Germany in their nineteenth-century heydays. Even so, British foreign policy still found room for a substantial humanitarianism.[12]

September 11 did not mean the end of all U.S. foreign policy commitments. Human rights policies should not be the only ones to be thrown overboard; there were many other pre-2001 U.S. policies not aimed directly at defending the homeland, like supporting Japan or keeping troops in Saudi Arabia. It is not clear why the NATO missions in Bosnia and Kosovo were incompatible with more robust homeland defense, nor, conversely, what the world's inaction in Rwanda did to discourage Osama bin Laden. If realists are worried about antagonizing other great powers, then presumably Clinton deserves more blame for sending warships into the Taiwan Straits than for bombing Yugoslavia. It is quite right to worry about the blowback consequences of U.S. belligerence and overextension, but that is an argument that cuts against a long list of optional U.S. wars: not just Somalia and Kosovo, but Grenada and Panama, too, just for a start.

Human rights advocates need not ask governments to devote unlimited amounts of resources to protecting noncitizens. In proper historical context, all liberals are asking is for the United States, Europe, and the other major democracies to shoulder as much responsibility as Britain did as long ago as 1827.

Third, and finally, humanitarian intervention can be part of a wider grand strategy of free republics.

Faced with a genocide in some far-off corner of the globe, today's great powers are inclined to let someone else handle it, even if that means nobody does. But in the nineteenth century, there would sometimes be competitions in humanitarianism. In the Midlothian campaign, Gladstone told British voters, "You left it to Russia alone to befriend them [the Bulgarians]; you impressed upon their minds the conviction that they were to expect nothing from you in relieving them from the yoke of the most cruel and debasing despotism; so that . . . we have cast them into the arms of Russia." Gladstone argued that an unselfish Britain could more easily gain the respect of people in the Balkans than an imperialist Russia.[13]

In the post–September 11 world, U.S. and European national security interests clearly include reaching out to the Arab and Muslim worlds. Much as Gladstone wanted to compete with Russia for hearts and minds in the Balkans, George W. Bush, whether he likes it or not, is competing with radical Islamists for hearts and minds in the Middle East—so far distinctly unsuccessfully.

Humanitarian intervention can be a part of an overall effort by the major democracies to do so. Bloody instability that nurtures radicalism can equally well nurture terrorism in the Balkans, the horn of Africa, and other trouble spots around the globe. Just as important, more human-rights-minded policies in Chechnya and the Balkans might diminish some Muslim resentment. Radical Islamists like Egypt's Omar Abdul Rahman accused the United States and Europe of backing the Serbs "in order to completely exterminate the Muslims" in Bosnia. Muhammad Atta, the September 11 terrorist, believed that the Jews had planned the wars in Bosnia and Kosovo to hurt Islam. After September 11, Condoleezza Rice, who had previously opposed humanitarian missions, hoped "the word can get out to remind people that America has . . . used force to save the lives of Muslims against Serbs in Kosovo, or to save the lives of Muslims in Kuwait or in Bosnia." When NATO did intervene promptly in the Kosovo war, radical Islamists struggled to present themselves as truer friends of Milošević's Muslim victims than NATO—not an easy sell in Kosovo, and in many places beyond. Better and more consistent human rights policies show the benevolent side of the planet's most powerful countries.[14]

Rather than a new imperialism, the goal should be the gradual spread of human rights—not for domination, but for a better kind of self-governance. The prevention of mass atrocity is the responsibility not just of the United States, but also of a formidable coalition of free countries: Europe from west to east, Latin America, much of Africa, Japan, and rising democratic powers like India, Brazil, and South Africa. If Russia is recalcitrant, it would be isolated. The issue of humanitarian intervention has thus far been hotly resisted by China, emerging as the most important new great power. But much of China's foreign policy establishment understands the importance of joining the international community. That means playing by certain basic rules, including not allowing genocide.[15]

All the preconditions for a new era of human rights are there, if we only want it. In the world's liberal democracies, we have a more wide-ranging and well-educated press than ever, if we could stop slashing foreign bureaus; we have a public that is freer to express its political opinions than ever, if it could be bothered to figure them out; and we have military forces that could in many cases protect the victims of genocide, if the order came. The idea of protecting human rights is increasingly commonplace, but today's leading democracies have not yet shouldered the responsibilities that previous great powers did. We are all atrocitarians now—but so far only in words, and not yet in deeds.

NOTES

Key to citations

British National Archives Office, Kew, London
ADM: Admiralty papers
CAB: Cabinet papers
FO: Foreign Office papers
Archives diplomatiques, Ministère des Affaires Étrangères, Quai d'Orsay, Paris
CP/T: Correspondance politique, Turquie
CPC/B: Correspondance politique des consuls, Beyrouth (Turquie)
MD/T: Mémoires et documents, Turquie
PA/T: Papiers d'agents et archives privées, Papiers Thouvenel
United States National Archives II, College Park, Maryland
R.G. (Record Group) 59: State Department papers
FRUS: the State Department's *Foreign Relations of the United States* series
London Greek Committee papers, National Library of Greece, Athens
LGC

Unless otherwise noted, translations from French are my own.

EPIGRAPH

Timothy Garton Ash, *The Polish Revolution: Solidarity* (New Haven, Conn.: Yale University Press, 2002), p. 49. The Solidarity member omitted the word "bleeding."

PART ONE: INTRODUCTION

1. *A Compilation of the Messages and Speeches of Theodore Roosevelt, 1901–1905*, ed. Alfred Henry Lewis (New York: Bureau of National Literature and Art, 1906), supplemental vol. 2, p. 858. Clinton told U.S. troops bound for Kosovo, "If somebody comes after innocent civilians and tries to kill them en masse because of their race, their ethnic background or their religion, and it's within our power to stop it, we will stop it." (White House, Office of the Press Secretary, "Remarks by

the President to the KFOR Troops," Skopje, Macedonia, 22 June 1999, 5:43 p.m. local time.)

2. David Brion Davis, *Slavery and Human Progress* (New York: Oxford University Press, 1984); Adam Hochschild, *King Leopold's Ghost: A Story of Greed, Terror, and Heroism in Colonial Africa* (New York: Houghton Mifflin, 1998).
3. Thucydides, *History of the Peloponnesian War,* trans. Rex Warner (London: Penguin, 1972), book 3, section 84, p. 245. Hugo Grotius, *Of the Rights of War and Peace,* trans. J. Barbeyrac (London: W. Innys and R. Manby, J. and P. Knapton, D. Brown, T. Osborn, and E. Wicksteed, 1738; orig. 1625), book 2, ch. 25, section 8, pp. 504–5. See David Halloran Lumsdaine, *Moral Vision in International Politics: The Foreign Aid Regime, 1949–1989* (Princeton, N.J.: Princeton University Press, 1993), pp. 26–28.
4. Arnold J. Toynbee, *Survey of International Affairs 1935: Volume II: Abyssinia and Italy* (London: Royal Institute of International Affairs, 1936), p. 2.
5. On pan-Christianity, see Martha Finnemore, *The Purpose of Intervention: Changing Beliefs About the Use of Force* (Ithaca, N.Y.: Cornell University Press, 2003), pp. 52–84.
6. Walter Clarke and Jeffrey Herbst, eds., *Learning from Somalia: The Lessons of Armed Humanitarian Intervention* (Boulder, Colo.: Westview, 1997); Jon Western, *Selling Intervention and War: The Presidency, the Media, and the American Public* (Baltimore: Johns Hopkins University Press, 2005), pp. 133–74. Samantha Power, *"A Problem from Hell": America and the Age of Genocide* (New York: Basic Books, 2002), pp. 355–57; Ed Vulliamy, *Seasons in Hell: Understanding Bosnia's War* (New York: Simon and Schuster, 1994), pp. ix–x.
7. Lynn Hunt, *Inventing Human Rights: A History* (New York: W. W. Norton, 2007), pp. 15–26; Susan Maslan, "The Anti-Human," *South Atlantic Quarterly,* vol. 103, no. 2–3 (2004), pp. 357–74.

HUMANITARIANISM OR IMPERIALISM?

1. "Sudan Accuses Jewish Groups of Pushing for UN Troops in Darfur," *Sudan Tribune,* 21 September 2006. Steven Lee Myers, "Bringing Down Europe's Last Ex-Soviet Dictator," *New York Times Magazine,* 26 February 2006, p. 50; Larissa Klyuchnikova, "Lukashenko Says No One Can Give Guarantees Against Intervention," TASS, 3 June 2005. Steven Lee Myers and Andrew E. Kramer, "Putin Harnessing Russia's Energy," *International Herald Tribune,* 13 July 2006, p. 3.
2. Thomas Hobbes, *Leviathan* (London: Penguin, 1988; orig. 1651), ch. 13, pp. 187–88; Jean-Jacques Rousseau, "The State of War" (1756), in *A Lasting Peace,* trans. C. E. Vaughan (London: Constable, 1917), p. 127; Kenneth N. Waltz, *Theory of International Politics* (Reading, Mass.: Addison-Wesley, 1979), p. 111; Robert Gilpin, *War and Change in World Politics* (Cambridge: Cambridge University Press, 1981); Robert Jervis, "Cooperation Under the Security Dilemma," *World Politics,* no. 30 (January 1978), pp. 167–214. G. M. Gilbert, *Nuremberg Diary* (New York: Farrar, Straus and Cudahy, 1947), p. 339.
3. Kissinger-Chatchai memorandum of conversation, 26 November 1975, p. 8, at http://www.gwu.edu/~nsarchiv/NSAEBB/NSAEBB193/HAK-11-26-75.pdf.

Condoleezza Rice, *The Soviet Union and the Czechoslovak Army, 1948–1983: Uncertain Allegiance* (Princeton, N.J.: Princeton University Press, 1984), pp. 218–45. Steven Mufson, "A World View of His Own," *Washington Post,* 11 August 2000, p. A1. George Packer, "Unrealistic," *New Yorker,* 27 November 2006; George Packer, "Wars and Ideas," *New Yorker,* 5 July 2004, pp. 29–32; William Safire, "Realism," *New York Times Magazine,* 24 December 2006, p. 20. Martha Finnemore, *The Purpose of Intervention: Changing Beliefs About the Use of Force* (Ithaca, N.Y.: Cornell University Press, 2003), p. 65; Michael Walzer, *Just and Unjust Wars: A Moral Argument with Historical Illustrations* (New York: Basic Books, 1977), p. 101; David Rieff, "A New Age of Liberal Imperialism?" *World Policy Journal,* vol. 16, no. 2 (summer 1999), pp. 1–5; Paul Farmer, *Pathologies of Power: Health, Human Rights, and the New War on the Poor* (Berkeley: University of California Press, 2004), p. 220. Philip Gourevitch, "Damage Control," *New Yorker,* 26 July 2004, p. 55.

4. Waltz, *Theory of International Politics,* pp. 113–14. Reinhold Niebuhr, *Moral Man and Immoral Society: A Study in Ethics and Politics* (New York: Charles Scribner's Sons, 1960; orig. 1932), p. 91. A. J. P. Taylor, *The Origins of the Second World War* (New York: Atheneum, 1983; orig. 1961), p. xiii. For critiques of Taylor's bizarre view of World War II, see H. R. Trevor-Roper, "A. J. P. Taylor, Hitler and the War," and Allan Bullock, "Hitler and the Origins of the Second World War," in Esmonde M. Robertson, ed., *The Origins of the Second World War* (London: Macmillan, 1971), pp. 83–99, 189–224.
5. Niebuhr, *Moral Man and Immoral Society,* p. 84; Stephen John Stedman, "The New Interventionists," *Foreign Affairs,* America and the World issue, 1992–1993, pp. 1–16. Peter Novick, *The Holocaust in American Life* (New York: Houghton Mifflin, 1999), pp. 47–59.
6. Henry A. Kissinger, "Somalia," *Washington Post,* 13 December 1992, p. C7. Henry A. Kissinger, "The End of NATO as We Know It?" *Washington Post,* 15 August 1999, p. B7. For devastating critiques of this view of Westphalian sovereignty, see Stephen D. Krasner, *Sovereignty: Organized Hypocrisy* (Princeton, N.J.: Princeton University Press, 1999); and Robert O. Keohane, "Political Authority After Intervention," in J. L. Holzgrefe and Robert O. Keohane, eds., *Humanitarian Intervention: Ethical, Legal, and Political Dilemmas* (Cambridge: Cambridge University Press, 2003), pp. 275–98.
7. Charles Krauthammer, "The Short, Unhappy Life of Humanitarian War," *National Interest,* fall 1999, p. 6. Stephen Glover, "Does Blair Want Us Endlessly at War?" *Daily Mail,* 13 April 1999, p. 13. Richard N. Haass, *Intervention: The Use of American Military Force in the Post–Cold War World* (Washington, D.C.: Carnegie Endowment, 1994), pp. 12–13, 111–21; Richard N. Haass, "What to Do with American Primacy?" *Foreign Affairs,* September–October 1999, pp. 40, 47. Haass has since become more sympathetic to humanitarian intervention ("What to Do with American Primacy?" pp. 39–40, 45–48). Nicholas Lemann, "The Next World Order," *New Yorker,* 1 April 2002, p. 45. Michael Mandelbaum, "A Perfect Failure," *Foreign Affairs,* September–October 1999, p. 5; Michael Mandelbaum, "Foreign Policy as Social Work," *Foreign Affairs,* January–February 1996,

p. 17. "China Warns UN of Rising Threat of Cold War Interventionism," Agence France Presse, 22 September 1999. Leslie H. Gelb and Justine A. Rosenthal, "The Rise of Ethics in Foreign Policy," *Foreign Affairs,* May–June 2003, p. 6.

8. George F. Kennan, "Morality and Foreign Policy," in George F. Kennan, *At a Century's Ending: Reflections 1982–1995* (New York: W. W. Norton, 1997), p. 273. See his *American Diplomacy* (Chicago: University of Chicago Press, 1984), pp. 53–54; Michael Lind, *Vietnam: The Necessary War* (New York: Free Press, 1999), pp. xii, xiv–xv, 31–75. George F. Kennan, "Somalia, Through a Glass Darkly," in *At a Century's Ending,* pp. 295–97. See Kennan, *Soviet-American Relations, 1917–1920: The Decision to Intervene* (Princeton, N.J.: Princeton University Press, 1958), vol. 2, p. 8; Walter Isaacson, *The Wise Men: Six Friends and the World They Made: Acheson, Bohlen, Harriman, Kennan, Lovett, McCloy* (New York: Simon and Schuster, 1986), p. 172.

9. Niebuhr, *Moral Man and Immoral Society,* p. 86; Paul W. Schroeder, *Austria, Great Britain, and the Crimean War: The Destruction of the European Concert* (Ithaca, N.Y.: Cornell University Press, 1972), pp. xi–xii, 417–27; Max Weber, "Politics as a Vocation," in *From Max Weber: Essays in Sociology,* trans. and ed. H. H. Gerth and C. Wright Mills (New York: Oxford University Press, 1958), pp. 95, 120–21; Harvey C. Mansfield, *Machiavelli's Virtue* (Chicago: University of Chicago Press, 1996), p. xiii. Edward Vose Gulick, *Europe's Classical Balance of Power* (New York: W. W. Norton, 1967), p. 2; Carl Kaysen, "Is War Obsolete?" *International Security,* vol. 14, no. 4 (spring 1990), p. 27; Henry A. Kissinger, *A World Restored: Metternich, Castlereagh, and the Problems of Peace 1812–22* (Boston: Houghton Mifflin, 1973), pp. 320–21; Edward Hallett Carr, *The Twenty Years' Crisis, 1919–1939* (New York: Harper and Row, 1964; orig. 1939), p. 209.

10. Kenneth N. Waltz, "Structural Realism After the Cold War," in G. John Ikenberry, ed., *America Unrivaled: The Future of the Balance of Power* (Ithaca, N.Y.: Cornell University Press, 2002), pp. 29–67. See Michael Ignatieff, "Is the Human Rights Era Ending?" *New York Times,* 5 February 2002, p. A29. Charles A. Kupchan, *The End of the American Era: U.S. Foreign Policy and the Geopolitics of the Twenty-first Century* (New York: Alfred A. Knopf, 2002); Stephen D. Krasner, *Defending the National Interest: Raw Materials, Investments and U.S. Foreign Policy* (Princeton, N.J.: Princeton University Press, 1978), p. 340; Gilpin, *War and Change,* pp. 22–23. See Joseph S. Nye Jr., *Bound to Lead: The Changing Nature of American Power* (New York: Basic Books, 1990); William C. Wohlforth, "The Stability of a Unipolar World," *International Security,* vol. 29, no. 1 (summer 1999), pp. 5–41. Robert Kagan, "Power and Weakness," *Policy Review,* no. 113 (June–July 2002), p. 9. Colin Powell with Joseph E. Persico, *My American Journey* (New York: Random House, 1995), p. 605.

11. Waltz, *Theory of International Politics,* pp. 113–14; Raymond Aron, *Peace and War: A Theory of International Relations,* trans. Richard Howard and Annette Baker Fox (Garden City, N.Y.: Doubleday, 1966), pp. 590–91; Kennan, *American Diplomacy,* pp. 61–62, 66, 73, 93, 100–101, 176; Hans J. Morgenthau, "To Intervene or Not to Intervene," *Foreign Affairs,* April 1967, p. 426. See Jon Elster, "Majority

Rule and Individual Rights," in Stephen Shute and Susan Hurley, eds., *On Human Rights: The Oxford Amnesty Lectures 1993* (New York: Basic Books, 1993), pp. 182–85. Alexander Hamilton, *Federalist* no. 6, in James Madison, Alexander Hamilton, and John Jay, *The Federalist Papers* (New York: Penguin Classics, 1987; orig. 1788), p. 107. Alexis de Tocqueville, *Democracy in America,* vol. 1, trans. Henry Reeve (New York: Vintage, 1945), p. 244. Kissinger, *World Restored,* p. 139; see pp. 1–2, 180–81, 320.

12. Arthur Schlesinger Jr., "Human Rights and the American Tradition," *Foreign Affairs,* America and the World issue, 1978, pp. 507–8.
13. Carr, *Twenty Years' Crisis,* pp. 63–80, 167. Wilhelm Grewe, *The Epochs of International Law,* trans. and rev. Michael Byers (Berlin: De Gruyter, 2001; orig. 1944), p. 23. For a critique of Grewe as a Nazi apologist, see Martti Koskenniemi's review in *International and Comparative Law Quarterly,* vol. 51, no. 3 (July 2002), pp. 746–51.
14. Tolstoy, *War and Peace,* trans. Constance Garnett (New York: Modern Library, 1994; orig. 1869), book 2, ch. 7, pp. 1367–68. Weber, "Politics as a Vocation," p. 118. Niebuhr, *Moral Man and Immoral Society,* p. 105; Hans J. Morgenthau, *Politics Among Nations: The Struggle for Power and Peace,* 3rd ed. (New York: Alfred A. Knopf, 1964), pp. 6–14, 71, 86–97; Waltz, *Theory of International Politics,* pp. 112–13, 200; Edward N. Luttwak, "No-Score War," *Times Literary Supplement,* 14 July 2000, p. 11. Michael Walzer, *Arguing About War* (New Haven, Conn.: Yale University Press, 2004), p. 69. Aron, *Peace and War,* p. 581; Caroline Elkins, *Imperial Reckoning: The Untold Story of Britain's Gulag in Kenya* (New York: Henry Holt, 2005), pp. 5–7; Robin Blackburn, "Kosovo: The War of NATO Expansion," *New Left Review,* no. 235 (May–June 1999), pp. 107–23.
15. Henry A. Kissinger, "Somalia," *Washington Post,* 13 December 1992, p. C7; Mandelbaum, "Perfect Failure," p. 5. James P. Lucier, "Just What Is a War Criminal?" *Insight on the News,* 2 August 1999, p. 13. Waltz, "Structural Realism after the Cold War," pp. 45–46.
16. Lenin, "The Highest Stage of Capitalism," in Harrison M. Wright, ed., *The "New Imperialism": Analysis of Late-Nineteenth-Century Expansion* (Lexington, Mass.: D. C. Heath, 1976), pp. 44–58; Friedrich Engels, "The Real Issue in Turkey," *New York Daily Tribune,* 12 April 1853, p. 4; Michael Hardt and Antonio Negri, *Empire* (Cambridge, Mass.: Harvard University Press, 2001), pp. 36–38. Edward Said, *Orientalism* (New York: Vintage, 1979), pp. 1–28, and *Covering Islam: How the Media and the Experts Determine How We See the Rest of the World* (New York: Vintage, 1997). Noam Chomsky, *Profit over People: Neoliberalism and Global Order* (New York: Seven Stories Press, 1998); *Hegemony or Survival: America's Quest for Global Dominance* (New York: Metropolitan, 2003); *Necessary Illusions: Thought Control in Democratic Societies* (Boston: South End Press, 1989); and "Humanitarian Intervention," *Boston Review,* December 1993–January 1994.
17. Jean-Paul Sartre, "Preface," in Frantz Fanon, *The Wretched of the Earth,* trans. Constance Farrington, pp. 24–25, 28 (New York: Grove Press, 1961). Said, *Orientalism,* pp. 39–40. Edward Said, "The Treason of the Intellectuals," *Al Ahram*

Weekly, 24–30 June 1999. See Mohamed Sid-Ahmed, "A Leading Question," *Al Ahram Weekly,* 4–10 October 2001; Robert Fisk, "This Is Not a War on Terror," *Independent,* 25 September 2001.

18. Richard Wolin, "Kant at Ground Zero," *New Republic,* 9 February 2004, p. 26. See, more generally, Jean Baudrillard, *The Spirit of Terrorism, and Other Essays,* trans. Chris Turner (London: Verso, 2002), p. 91. Baudrillard wrote of the September 11 massacre: "They *did it,* but we *wished for* it" (p. 5). "China Warns UN of Rising Threat of Cold War Interventionism," Agence France Presse, 22 September 1999. Tariq Ali, ed., *Masters of the Universe?: NATO's Balkan Crusade* (London: Verso, 2000) and *Bush in Babylon: The Recolonisation of Iraq* (London: Verso, 2003); Mahmood Mamdani, "The Politics of Naming: Genocide, Civil War, Insurgency," *London Review of Books,* 8 March 2007.

19. Machiavelli, *The Prince,* trans. Harvey C. Mansfield Jr. (Chicago: University of Chicago Press, 1985), ch. 6, p. 24. Weber, "Politics as a Vocation," pp. 119–20. See Michael Walzer, "Political Action: The Problem of Dirty Hands," *Philosophy and Public Affairs,* vol. 2, no. 1 (winter 1973), pp. 160–80; Machiavelli, *The Discourses,* trans. Luigi Ricci (New York: Random House, 1950), book 1, ch. 9, pp. 138–39.

20. Ian Brownlie, *International Law and the Use of Force by States* (Oxford: Clarendon Press, 1963), p. 341. Krasner, *Sovereignty,* pp. 88–89, 152–53. See John Stuart Mill, "A Few Words on Non-Intervention" (December 1859), in John Stuart Mill, *Dissertations and Discussions: Political, Philosophical, and Historical,* vol. 3 (New York: Henry Holt, 1882), p. 238; James M. Goldgeier and Michael McFaul, "A Tale of Two Worlds," *International Organization,* vol. 46, no. 2 (spring 1992), pp. 467–91.

21. Niebuhr, *Moral Man and Immoral Society,* p. 95. Immanuel Kant, "Toward Perpetual Peace," in *Perpetual Peace and Other Essays,* trans. Ted Humphrey, p. 113 (Indianapolis, Ind.: Hackett, 1983). Byron Farwell, *Queen Victoria's Little Wars* (New York: W. W. Norton, 1985), pp. 37–60, 84–133. Mill, "Non-Intervention," pp. 252–53.

22. Peter Singer, *The Expanding Circle: Ethics and Sociobiology* (New York: Farrar, Straus and Giroux, 1981), p. 157. Antoine Rougier, "La théorie de l'intervention d'humanité," *Revue générale du droit internationale,* vol. 17 (1910), pp. 525–26; Carr, *Twenty Years' Crisis,* p. 168. Kennan, *American Diplomacy,* p. 8. Niebuhr, *Moral Man and Immoral Society,* pp. 87, 105.

23. Michael Ignatieff, *Human Rights as Politics and Idolatry* (Princeton, N.J.: Princeton University Press, 2001), p. 10. Chaim D. Kaufmann and Robert A. Pape, "Explaining Costly International Moral Action: Britain's Sixty-year Campaign Against the Atlantic Slave Trade," *International Organization,* vol. 53, no. 4 (fall 1999), pp. 634–36. Finnemore criticizes the anti-slave-trade activists for not moving directly to outright abolition (*Purpose of Intervention,* pp. 68–69). But as a naval power, Britain's military advantage was in choking off the slave trade first, before moving on to total abolition. Liverpool to Castlereagh, 7 July 1815, Arthur Wellesley, Duke of Wellington, *Supplementary Despatches and Memoranda of Field Marshal Arthur, Duke of Wellington, K.G.,* vol. 10, p. 678 (London: John Murray, 1863). FO 92/22, Castlereagh to Liverpool, 31 July 1815, no. 24. See FO 92/22, Castlereagh to Liverpool, 27 July 1815, no. 20; Protocole de Conférence

(Allied ministers' meeting), 13e séance, 24 July 1815 (enclosed); FO 92/22, Castlereagh to Talleyrand, 27 July 1815; FO 92/22, Castlereagh to Liverpool, 29 July 1815, no. 23; FO 92/22, Talleyrand to Castlereagh, 30 July 1815; Wellington to Canning, 21 September 1822, Arthur Wellesley, Duke of Wellington, *Despatches, Correspondence, and Memoranda of Field Marshal Arthur, Duke of Wellington,* vol. 1, pp. 295–96 (London: John Murray, 1867). Gallatin to Adams, 18 January 1823, in *The Writings of Albert Gallatin,* ed. Henry Adams, vol. 2, p. 64 (Philadelphia: J. B. Lippincott, 1879).

24. David Brion Davis, *Slavery and Human Progress* (New York: Oxford University Press, 1984), pp. 238, 285, 301–2. See David Brion Davis, *The Problem of Slavery in the Age of Revolution, 1770–1823* (Ithaca, N.Y.: Cornell University Press, 1975); P. M. Kielstra, *The Politics of Slave Trade Suppression in Britain and France, 1814–48* (London: Macmillan, 2000); Krasner, *Sovereignty,* pp. 106–9. *Times,* 28 April 1821, p. 2. John Stuart Mill, "The Slave Power" (1862), in Mill, *Dissertations and Discussions,* vol. 3, p. 288.

25. Davis, *Slavery and Human Progress,* pp. 285, 300–3. David Herbert Donald, *Lincoln* (New York: Simon and Schuster, 1995), pp. 362–69, 373–80. See Seymour Drescher, *Capitalism and Antislavery: British Mobilization in Comparative Perspective* (New York: Oxford University Press, 1986).

26. David M. Kennedy, *Freedom from Fear: The American People in Depression and War, 1929–1945* (New York: Oxford University Press, 1999), p. 418. See Eugen Weber, *The Hollow Years: France in the 1930s* (New York: W. W. Norton), p. 175.

27. Niebuhr, *Moral Man and Immoral Society,* p. 85; Carlo Ginzburg, "Killing a Chinese Mandarin: The Moral Implications of Distance," *Critical Inquiry,* vol. 21, no. 1 (fall 1994); David Hume, *A Treatise of Human Nature* (Oxford: Clarendon Press, 1979), book 2, part 3, section 7, p. 429.

28. Adam Smith, *The Theory of Moral Sentiments,* ed. A. L. Macfie and D. D. Raphael (Oxford: Clarendon Press, 1976), 3.4, pp. 136–37. Virginia Woolf, *Mrs. Dalloway* (New York: Harcourt Brace, 1981; orig. 1925), p. 120.

29. Thomas Aquinas, *Summa Theologica* (New York: Benziger Brothers, 1947), vol. 2, parts II–III, q. 40, pp. 1359–60. Niebuhr, *Moral Man and Immoral Society,* pp. 53–54, 81. Aristotle, *The Art of Rhetoric,* trans. H. C. Lawson-Tancred (London: Penguin Classics, 1991), book 2, ch. 8, p. 164. Hume, *Treatise of Human Nature,* book 3, part 2, section 1, p. 481. See Amartya Sen, "Other People," *New Republic,* 18 December 2000, p. 23; David Brooks, "People Like Us," *Atlantic Monthly,* September 2003, pp. 29–32.

30. Leo Tolstoy, "On Patriotism," in *Tolstoy's Writings on Civil Disobedience and Non-Violence,* trans. Aylmer Maude (New York: Bergman, 1967; orig. 1894), pp. 99, 101. Finnemore, *Purpose of Intervention,* pp. 53, 61–65. See Martha Finnemore and Kathryn Sikkink, "International Norm Dynamics and Political Change," *International Organization,* vol. 52, no. 4 (fall 1998), pp. 887–917. I will respectfully take issue with Finnemore's important analysis, arguing that it understates the depth of broader non-Christianized humanitarianism in the nineteenth century. My argument is not against Finnemore's social constructivism; to the contrary, Finnemore, a distinguished scholar, makes a major contribution by focusing on

the definition and redefinition of the community. But even in the nineteenth century, a genuine humanitarian concern for fellow humans—not just fellow Christians—was a potent force in world politics. Herzen, "Western European Arabesques, II," in *My Past and Thoughts: The Memoirs of Alexander Herzen,* trans. Constance Garrett (London: Chatto and Windus, 1974), p. 386.

31. Donald L. Horowitz, *Ethnic Groups in Conflict* (Berkeley: University of California Press, 1985), pp. 57–64.

32. Orwell, "The Lion and the Unicorn," in his *Collected Essays, Journalism and Letters: My Country Right or Left, 1940–1943,* vol. 2, ed. Sonia Orwell and Ian Angus (New York: Harcourt, Brace and World, 1968), p. 56. George Kateb, *Patriotism and Other Mistakes* (New Haven, Conn.: Yale University Press, 2006), pp. 3–20; Niebuhr, *Moral Man and Immoral Society,* pp. 91–93; Waltz, *Theory of International Politics,* pp. 93–97; Barry Buzan, "From International System to International Society," *International Organization,* vol. 47, no. 3 (summer 1993), p. 329; Martha Nussbaum et al., *For Love of Country: Debating the Limits of Patriotism* (Boston: Beacon Press, 1996); Alasdair MacIntyre, *Is Patriotism a Virtue?* (Lawrence: University Press of Kansas, 1984), pp. 3–16; David Miller, "The Ethical Significance of Nationality," *Ethics,* vol. 98 (July 1988), pp. 647–62. Carr, *Twenty Years' Crisis,* p. 16.

33. George Canning, "New Morality," in *Select Speeches of the Right Honourable George Canning,* ed. Robert Walsh (Philadelphia: Key and Biddle, 1835), p. 548. Carr, *Twenty Years' Crisis,* pp. 163–64.

34. Edwin M. Borchard, *The Diplomatic Protection of Citizens Abroad* (New York: Banks Law, 1915); Pasquale Fiore, *International Law Codified,* trans. Edwin M. Borchard (New York: Baker, Voorhis, 1918), pp. 259–63. Michael Akehurst, "Humanitarian Intervention," in Hedley Bull, ed., *Intervention in World Politics* (Oxford: Clarendon Press, 1984), pp. 99–104.

35. Kant, "Toward Perpetual Peace," p. 119. P. J. Marshall, ed., *The Writings and Speeches of Edmund Burke: India: The Launching of the Hastings Impeachment* (Oxford: Clarendon Press, 1991), vol. 6, p. 346. Jonathan Glover, *Humanity: A Moral History of the Twentieth Century* (New Haven, Conn.: Yale University Press, 2000), pp. 22–25, 403–4; Charles Beitz, *Political Theory and International Relations* (Princeton, N.J.: Princeton University Press, 1979), pp. 71–92; William F. Schulz, *In Our Own Best Interest: How Defending Human Rights Benefits Us All* (Boston: Beacon Press, 2001), pp. 17–37; David Luban, "Just War and Human Rights," *Philosophy and Public Affairs,* vol. 9, no. 2 (winter 1980), pp. 173–74; Michael W. Doyle, *Ways of War and Peace: Realism, Liberalism, and Socialism* (New York: W. W. Norton, 1997), pp. 396–402; Thomas Nagel, *The Possibility of Altruism* (Oxford: Clarendon Press, 1970); John Fabian Witt, *Patriots and Cosmopolitans: Hidden Histories of American Law* (Cambridge, Mass.: Harvard University Press, 2007), pp. 179–80, 185.

36. Judith N. Shklar, "The Liberalism of Fear," in her *Political Thought and Political Thinkers,* ed. Stanley Hoffman, p. 17 (Chicago: University of Chicago Press, 1998); Lynn Hunt, *Inventing Human Rights: A History* (New York: W. W. Norton, 2007); Smith, *Theory of Moral Sentiments,* p. 137. Victor Hugo, *Napoleon the Little* (New York: Howard Fertig, 1992), p. 216. John Rawls, *A Theory of Justice*

(Cambridge, Mass.: Belknap Press of Harvard University Press, 1971), pp. 118–92. See John Rawls, *The Law of Peoples* (Cambridge, Mass.: Harvard University Press, 1999), pp. 78–81, 94; Walzer, *Just and Unjust Wars,* pp. 90, 101–8. Paul Gomberg, "Patriotism Is Like Racism," *Ethics,* vol. 101 (October 1990), pp. 146–51; Tolstoy, "On Patriotism," p. 103; Nussbaum, *For Love of Country;* Niebuhr, *Moral Man and Immoral Society,* p. 93; Michael Walzer, "The Politics of Rescue," *Dissent,* winter 1995, pp. 35–41; Louis Henkin, *The Age of Rights* (New York: Columbia University Press, 1990), pp. 143–56.

37. David Wyman, *The Abandonment of the Jews: America and the Holocaust 1941–1945* (New York: Pantheon, 1984), p. 340. Nader Mousavizadeh, ed., *The Black Book of Bosnia: The Consequences of Appeasement* (New York: Basic Books/New Republic, 1996), p. ix. Mandela speech, 25 August 2000, in Elizabeth Sidiropoulous, ed., *A Continent Apart: Kosovo, Africa and Humanitarian Intervention,* p. 4 (Johannesburg: South African Institute of International Affairs, 2001). See Steve Coll, "The Other War," *Washington Post Magazine,* 9 January 2000.

38. Carr, *Twenty Years' Crisis,* pp. 164–65. Anna Quindlen, "Some Struggles Never Seen," *New York Times,* 14 November 2001, anniversary section, p. 24. Don Wycliff, "Getting Kicked Off Page 1," *Chicago Tribune,* 7 February 2002.

39. Percy Shelley, preface, "Hellas: A Lyrical Drama," in *The Complete Poems of Percy Bysshe Shelley* (New York: Modern Library, 1994), p. 501. Jean-Marie Colombani, "Nous sommes tous Américains," *Le Monde,* 13 September 2001, p. 1. The antislavery campaign in Britain used the slogan, "Am I Not a Man and a Brother?" (Adam Hochschild, *Bury the Chains: Prophets and Rebels in the Fight to Free an Empire's Slaves* [Boston: Houghton Mifflin, 2005], p. 128). Thomas W. Laqueur, "The Moral Imagination and Human Rights," in Ignatieff, *Human Rights as Politics and Idolatry,* pp. 131–32. See Martha Finnemore's excellent "Constructing Norms of Humanitarian Intervention," in Peter J. Katzenstein, ed., *The Culture of National Security* (New York: Columbia University Press, 1996), pp. 153–85; Martha Finnemore, *National Interests in International Society* (Ithaca, N.Y.: Cornell University Press, 1996), pp. 11–12. See Richard Rorty and Catharine A. MacKinnon's essays in Shute and Hurley, eds., *On Human Rights.* Peter Singer argues for moral concern for all sentient beings, including animals; Richard Posner responds that "we, like other animals, prefer our own," and that Americans prefer American lives over foreigners' lives ("Animal Rights," *Slate,* 12 June 2001).

40. Mill, "Non-Intervention," pp. 243, 238.

MEDIA AND SOLIDARITY

1. Adam Smith, *Theory of Moral Sentiments,* ed. A. L. Macfie and D. D. Raphael (Oxford: Clarendon Press, 1976), p. 136. See pp. 134–35. David Hume, *A Treatise of Human Nature* (Oxford: Clarendon Press, 1978), book 2, part 2, section 7, p. 370.

2. Samantha Power, *"A Problem from Hell": America and the Age of Genocide* (New York: Basic Books 2002), p. 355. Michael Ignatieff, *The Warrior's Honor: Ethnic War and the Modern Conscience* (New York: Henry Holt, 1997), p. 10. Richard N.

Haass, *Intervention: The Use of American Military Force in the Post–Cold War World* (Washington, D.C.: Carnegie Endowment, 1994), pp. 85–86; Hans J. Morgenthau, *Politics Among Nations: The Struggle for Power and Peace,* 3rd ed. (New York: Alfred A. Knopf, 1964), pp. 380–81. George H. W. Bush and Brent Scowcroft, *A World Transformed* (New York: Random House, 1998), p. 101. George F. Kennan, "Somalia, Through a Glass Darkly," in George F. Kennan, *At a Century's Ending: Reflections 1982–1995*, p. 297 (New York: W. W. Norton, 1997). Kissinger, "The End of NATO as We Know It?" *Washington Post,* 15 August 1999, p. B7. See Ronald Steel, *Temptations of a Superpower: America's Foreign Policy After the Cold War* (Cambridge, Mass.: Harvard University Press, 1995), pp. 103–4, 119–20; David D. Laitin, "Somalia: Civil War and International Intervention," in Barbara F. Walter and Jack Snyder, eds., *Civil Wars, Insecurity, and Intervention* (New York: Columbia University Press, 1999), p. 170.

3. Ernest Gellner, *Nations and Nationalism* (Ithaca, N.Y.: Cornell University Press, 1983), pp. 48–49, 138; Reinhold Niebuhr, *Moral Man and Immoral Society: A Study in Ethics and Politics* (New York: Charles Scribner's Sons, 1960; orig. 1932), pp. 83–84; Eric Hobsbawm, "Inventing Traditions," in Eric Hobsbawm and Terence Ranger, eds., *The Invention of Tradition* (Cambridge: Cambridge University Press, 1984), pp. 1–14; E. J. Hobsbawm, *Nations and Nationalism Since 1780: Programme, Myth, Reality* (Cambridge: Cambridge University Press, 1992), pp. 10, 46. Ignatieff, *Warrior's Honor,* pp. 34–39. Benedict Anderson, *Imagined Communities: Reflections on the Origin and Spread of Nationalism* (London: Verso, 1991), p. 26. See Lynn Hunt, *Inventing Human Rights: A History* (New York: W. W. Norton, 2007), pp. 15–34.

4. Eugen Weber, *Peasants into Frenchmen: The Modernization of Rural France, 1870–1914* (Stanford, Calif.: Stanford University Press, 1976), p. 452; Karl W. Deutsch, *Nationalism and Social Communication: An Inquiry into the Foundations of Nationality* (Cambridge, Mass.: MIT Technology Press, 1953), pp. 70–74; Karl W. Deutsch, "Social Mobilization and Political Development," *American Political Science Review,* vol. 55 (September 1961), pp. 493–514; Max Weber, "Politics as a Vocation," in *From Max Weber: Essays in Sociology,* trans. and ed. H. H. Gerth and C. Wright Mills (New York: Oxford University Press, 1958), pp. 96–97; Hannah Barker, *Newspapers, Politics, and Public Opinion in Late Eighteenth-Century England* (Oxford: Clarendon Press, 1998), p. 36; Jack Snyder, *From Voting to Violence: Democratization and Nationalist Conflict* (New York: W. W. Norton, 2000), pp. 41, 294–95. Anderson, *Imagined Communities,* pp. 37, 44; Lucien Febvre and Henri-Jean Martin, *The Coming of the Book: The Impact of Printing 1450–1800,* trans. David Gerard (London: N.L.B., 1976), pp. 248–49. Hobsbawm, *Nations and Nationalism,* pp. 52–63, 73–74; Anderson, *Imagined Communities,* p. 44; Edward Hallett Carr, *The Twenty Years' Crisis, 1919–1939* (New York: Harper and Row, 1964; orig. 1939), pp. 163–64.

5. Anderson, *Imagined Communities,* pp. 37–46; Gellner, *Nations and Nationalism,* p. 127; Benedict Anderson, "Exodus," *Critical Inquiry,* vol. 20 (winter 1994), pp. 316–17, 320–21. Victor Hugo, *Napoleon the Little* (New York: Howard Fertig, 1992), pp. 216–17. Edmund Burke, "Thoughts on French Affairs," in his *Further*

Reflections on the Revolution in France, ed. Daniel E. Ritchie (Indianapolis, Ind.: Liberty Fund, 1992), p. 215. Deutsch, *Nationalism and Social Communication;* Weber, *Peasants into Frenchmen,* p. 469; Bob Harris, *Politics and the Rise of the Press: Britain and France, 1620–1800* (London: Routledge, 1996), pp. 51, 82; Suzanne Hoeber Rudolph and Lloyd I. Rudolph, "Modern Hate," *New Republic,* 22 March 1993, pp. 24–29; Snyder, *From Voting to Violence,* pp. 45–66.

6. Hobsbawm, *Nations and Nationalism,* p. 65. Clifford Geertz, "The Integrative Revolution: Primordial Sentiments and Civil Politics in the New States," in his *The Interpretation of Cultures: Selected Essays* (New York: Basic Books, 2000), pp. 264–65. See Michael Walzer, *Spheres of Justice: A Defense of Pluralism and Equality* (New York: Basic Books, 1983), pp. 42, 49; Anderson, "Exodus," pp. 324–26.
7. George F. Kennan introduction to *The Other Balkan Wars: A 1913 Carnegie Endowment Inquiry in Retrospect* (Washington, D.C.: Carnegie Endowment, 1993). Weber, *Peasants into Frenchmen,* p. 485. Barker, *Newspapers, Politics, and Public Opinion in Late Eighteenth-Century England,* p. 36. Anderson, "Exodus," pp. 320–22.
8. Isaiah Berlin, *Russian Thinkers* (London: Penguin, 1995), p. 204.
9. Andrew Moravcsik, "A Liberal Theory of International Politics," *International Organization,* vol. 51, no. 4 (fall 1997); Michael W. Doyle, "Liberalism in World Politics," *American Political Science Review,* vol. 80 (December 1986); Robert O. Keohane, "International Institutions," in his *International Institutions and State Power: Essays in International Relations Theory* (Boulder, Colo.: Westview, 1989); Helen V. Milner, *Interests, Institutions, and Information: Domestic Politics and International Relations* (Princeton, N.J.: Princeton University Press, 1997); Beth Simmons, *Who Adjusts?: Domestic Sources of Foreign Economic Policy During the Interwar Years* (Princeton, N.J.: Princeton University Press, 1994); Peter B. Evans, Harold K. Jacobson, and Robert D. Putnam, eds., *Double-Edged Diplomacy: International Bargaining and Domestic Politics* (Berkeley: University of California Press, 1993); Dan Reiter and Allan C. Stam, *Democracies at War* (Princeton, N.J.: Princeton University Press, 2002). Immanuel Kant, "Toward Perpetual Peace," in *Perpetual Peace and other Essays,* trans. Ted Humphrey (Indianapolis, Ind.: Hackett, 1983). Power, "*Problem from Hell,*" p. xviii.
10. My definition of a liberal state follows that of Michael W. Doyle, "Kant, Liberal Legacies, and Foreign Affairs," *Philosophy and Public Affairs,* vol. 12, nos. 3–4 (summer and fall 1983). Hugo, *Napoleon the Little,* p. 146. Jean Drèze and Amartya Sen, *Hunger and Public Action* (Oxford: Clarendon Press, 1989), p. 212. See pp. 122, 126, 211–15, 221–25. They note that this has not been enough to stop endemic undernutrition—just the "big news" of major famine (p. 214). See Jean Drèze and Amartya Sen, *India: Economic Development and Social Opportunity* (Oxford: Oxford University Press, 1995), pp. 57–86, 87–92.
11. Brandice Canes-Wrone, *Who Leads Whom?: Presidents, Policy, and the Public* (Chicago: University of Chicago Press, 2006), pp. 39–40. William Ewart Gladstone, *Bulgarian Horrors and the Question of the East* (London: John Murray, 1876), p. 56. See Snyder, *From Voting to Violence,* p. 36.
12. Drèze and Sen, *Hunger and Public Action,* p. 212. Jasper Becker, *Hungry Ghosts: Mao's Secret Famine* (New York: Henry Holt, 1998), pp. 287, 313–39.

13. Metternich to Apponyi, 2 July 1827, Klemens von Metternich, *Mémoires, documents et écrits divers: L'Ère de paix, 1816–1848* (Paris: Plon, 1881), vol. 4, p. 379. Hugo, *Napoleon the Little,* p. 147.
14. Richard J. Evans, *The Third Reich in Power* (New York: Penguin, 2005), pp. 133–36. Zbigniew K. Brzezinski and Samuel P. Huntington, *Political Power: USA/USSR* (New York: Viking, 1965), pp. 88–89.
15. Snyder, *From Voting to Violence,* pp. 45–59, 63–65. Mark Thompson, *Forging War: The Media in Serbia, Croatia and Bosnia-Hercegovina* (Avon: Bath Press, 1994), pp. 51–129, 130–200; Kemal Kurspahić, *Prime Time Crime: Balkan Media in War and Peace* (Washington, D.C.: United States Institute of Peace, 2003), pp. 27–86; Christopher Bennett, *Yugoslavia's Bloody Collapse: Causes, Course, and Consequences* (London: Hurst, 1995); Bogdan Denitch, *Ethnic Nationalism: The Tragic Death of Yugoslavia* (Minneapolis: University of Minnesota Press, 1994), p. 62; Tim Judah, *The Serbs: History, Myth and the Destruction of Yugoslavia* (New Haven, Conn.: Yale University Press, 2000); Stuart J. Kaufman, *Modern Hatred: The Symbolic Politics of Ethnic War* (Ithaca, N.Y.: Cornell University Press, 2001), pp. 37, 169, 179–84; Rui J. P. de Figueiredo Jr. and Barry R. Weingast, "The Rationality of Fear: Political Opportunism and Ethnic Conflict," in Walter and Snyder, eds., *Civil Wars, Insecurity, and Intervention,* pp. 263–64. Alison Des Forges, *Leave None to Tell the Story: Genocide in Rwanda* (New York: Human Rights Watch, 1999), pp. 67–71, 315–16.
16. Emily Nelson, "Through al-Jazeera's Eyes," *Wall Street Journal,* 10 April 2003, pp. B1, B3; David Hoffman, "The Answer to Hate-America TV," *Washington Post,* 14 August 2002, p. A29; Lawrence Wright, "The Kingdom of Silence," *New Yorker,* 5 January 2004, pp. 48–73; Sharon Waxman, "Arab TV's Strong Signal," *Washington Post,* 4 December 2001, p. C1; Noah Feldman, *After Jihad: America and the Struggle for Islamic Democracy* (New York: Farrar, Straus and Giroux, 2003), pp. 11, 191; Samantha M. Shapiro, "The War Inside the Arab Newsroom," *New York Times Magazine,* 2 January 2005.
17. Leo Tolstoy, "On Patriotism," in *Tolstoy's Writings on Civil Disobedience and Non-Violence,* trans. Aylmer Maude (New York: Bergman, 1967; orig. 1894), pp. 107, 114.
18. Jefferson to Carrington, 16 January 1787, *Writings of Thomas Jefferson,* ed. Paul Leicester Ford (New York: G. P. Putnam's Sons, 1894), vol. 4, p. 378. Ralph Waldo Emerson, *Essays and Lectures* (New York: Library of America, 1983), pp. 912–13.
19. George Orwell, "The Lion and the Unicorn," in his *Collected Essays, Journalism and Letters: My Country Right or Left, 1940–1943,* vol. 2, ed. Sonia Orwell and Ian Angus (New York: Harcourt, Brace and World), p. 67. Alan L. Heil Jr., *Voice of America: A History* (New York: Columbia University Press, 2003); Gary D. Rawnsley, *Radio Diplomacy and Propaganda: The BBC and VOA in International Politics, 1956–64* (London: Macmillan, 1996).
20. Some scholars of nationalism argue that the mere fact of a common press is enough to forge a shared identity automatically (Gellner, *Nations and Nationalism,* p. 127). This book argues that the content of the press matters, too, as well as its mere existence (Robert Darnton, "Writing News and Telling Stories,"

Daedalus, vol. 104, no. 2 [1975], p. 176). The existence of telegraph technology is a necessary but not sufficient condition for European outrage; one also needs responsible foreign correspondents getting the story.

21. Paul Starr, *The Creation of the Media: Political Origins of Mass Communications* (New York: Basic Books, 2004), pp. 33–41, 41–46; Harris, *Politics and the Rise of the Press,* pp. 98–99. Emerson, *Essays and Lectures,* pp. 909–11. Aled Jones, *Powers of the Press: Newspapers, Power and the Public in Nineteenth-Century England* (Cambridge: Scolar Press, 1996), pp. 10–13, 19–23.
22. Emerson, *Essays and Lectures,* p. 911.
23. Christopher Hitchens, "Lightness at Midnight," *Atlantic Monthly,* September 2002. Steven Livingstone and Todd Eachus, "U.S. Policy and Television Coverage," in Howard Adelman and Astri Suhrke, eds., *The Path of a Genocide: The Rwanda Crisis from Uganda to Zaire* (New Brunswick, N.J.: Transaction, 1999), p. 209. Telford Taylor, *Anatomy of the Nuremberg Trials: A Personal Memoir* (New York: Alfred A. Knopf, 1992), p. 169. Scott Anderson, "The Target," *New York Times Magazine,* 29 December 2002, p. 50; Cynthia Scharf, "Putin's Other Chechen Campaign," *Wall Street Journal,* 8 January 2003. Martin Shaw, *Civil Society and Media in Global Crises: Representing Distant Violence* (London: Cassell, 1996), p. 95. "Good News Only, from Now On," *The Economist,* 24 May 2003.
24. Barker, *Newspapers, Politics, and Public Opinion in Late Eighteenth-Century England,* p. 36; Harris, *Politics and the Rise of the Press,* pp. 1–52, 87–88, 102. Hannah Barker, *Newspapers, Politics and English Society, 1695–1855* (Essex: Longman, 2000), p. 190.
25. Graham Storey, *Reuters: The Story of a Century of News-Gathering* (New York: Crown, 1951), pp. 6–15.
26. Tom Standage, *The Victorian Internet* (New York: Walker, 1998), pp. 152–53; Byron Farwell, *Queen Victoria's Little Wars* (New York: W. W. Norton, 1985), p. 218. Barker, *Newspapers, Politics and English Society,* p. 221. Johanna Neumann, *Lights Camera War: Is Media Technology Driving International Politics?* (New York: St. Martin's Press, 1996), pp. 30–33. Menahem Blondheim, *News Over the Wires: The Telegraph and the Flow of Public Information in America, 1844–1897* (Cambridge, Mass.: Harvard University Press, 1994). Storey, *Reuters,* p. 62.
27. Standage, *Victorian Internet,* pp. 158–59. Niall Ferguson, *Empire: The Rise and Demise of the British World Order and the Lessons for Global Power* (New York: Basic Books, 2002), p. 140. Disraeli to Bradfield, 6 September 1875, Marquis of Zetland, ed., *The Letters of Disraeli to Lady Chesterfield and Lady Bradford* (New York: D. Appleton, 1929), vol. 1, p. 364.
28. Storey, *Reuters,* pp. 13–18. Jones, *Powers of the Press,* pp. 23, 40. Alan J. Lee, *The Origins of the Popular Press in England 1855–1914* (London: Croom Helm, 1976), pp. 29–33, 59, 64–66.
29. Storey, *Reuters,* pp. 13–18. *The History of The Times: The Tradition Established, 1841–1884* (London: The Times, 1939), pp. 134–35.
30. *History of The Times,* pp. 136–37, 141–43.
31. Phillip Knightley, *The First Casualty: From the Crimea to Vietnam: The War Corre-*

spondent as Hero, Propagandist, and Myth Maker (New York: Harcourt Brace Jovanovich, 1975), p. 4.

32. Ibid., p. 4.
33. Lytton Strachey, *Eminent Victorians* (London: Penguin, 1986; orig. 1918), p. 117. Knightley, *First Casualty,* pp. 4–17. Barker, *Newspapers, Politics and English Society,* pp. 221–22.
34. Storey, *Reuters,* pp. 56–59. Susan E. Tifft and Alex S. Jones, *The Trust: The Private and Powerful Family Behind The New York Times* (Boston: Little, Brown, 1999). Michael Schudson, *Discovering the News: A Social History of American Newspapers* (New York: Basic Books, 1978), pp. 4–5.
35. Schudson, *Discovering the News,* p. 69. Jones, *Powers of the Press,* pp. 40, 113–39.
36. Lee, *Origins of the Popular Press in England,* pp. 160–62.
37. Gladstone's seventh Midlothian speech, 19 March 1880, in his *Political Speeches in Scotland, March and April 1880,* vol. 2 (Edinburgh: Andrew Elliot, 1880), pp. 95–96. Gladstone's second Midlothian speech, 26 November 1879, in his *Political Speeches in Scotland, November and December 1879,* vol. 1 (Edinburgh: Andrew Elliot, 1880), p. 91. Mike Davis, *Late Victorian Holocausts: El Niño Famines and the Making of the Third World* (London: Verso, 2001), pp. 43–44. Jones, *Powers of the Press,* pp. 25–27. Knightley, *First Casualty,* pp. 53–54.

THE DIPLOMACY OF HUMANITARIAN INTERVENTION

1. Thucydides, *History of the Peloponnesian War,* trans. Rex Warner (London: Penguin, 1972), book 6, section 18, p. 421. Ian Kershaw, *Hitler: 1936–1945: Nemesis* (New York: W. W. Norton, 2000), pp. 96–114; Eugen Weber, *The Hollow Years: France in the 1930s* (New York: W. W. Norton, 1994), pp. 175–78. Henderson to Halifax, 15 March 1939, British Foreign Office, *Documents on British Foreign Policy 1919–1939,* ed. E. L. Woodward and Rohan Butler, 3rd series, vol. 4 (London: His Majesty's Stationery Office, 1951), p. 257.
2. John Stuart Mill, "A Few Words on Non-Intervention" (1859), in *Dissertations and Discussions: Political, Philosophical, and Historical,* vol. 3 (New York: Henry Holt and Co., 1882), p. 239. Hans J. Morgenthau, *Politics Among Nations: The Struggle for Power and Peace,* 3rd ed. (New York: Alfred A. Knopf, 1964), pp. 63–64, 68–71, 86–97; John J. Mearsheimer, *The Tragedy of Great Power Politics* (New York: W. W. Norton, 2001), p. 3. Bhiku Parekh, "Rethinking Humanitarian Intervention," *International Political Science Review,* vol. 18, no. 1 (1997); Michael Walzer, "The Politics of Rescue," *Dissent,* winter 1995, p. 36; Michael Ignatieff, *Human Rights as Politics and Idolatry* (Princeton, N.J.: Princeton University Press, 2001), pp. 39, 42; Jack Goldsmith and Stephen D. Krasner, "The Limits of Idealism," *Daedalus,* vol. 132, no. 1 (winter 2003), pp. 57, 59; Michael W. Doyle, *Ways of War and Peace: Realism, Liberalism, and Socialism* (New York: W. W. Norton, 1997), pp. 401, 411–12; Ian Buruma, "Killing Iraq with Kindness," *New York Times,* 17 March 2004, p. A25.
3. Leo Tolstoy, *Anna Karenina,* trans. Richard Pevear and Larissa Volokhonsky (London: Penguin, 2000), p. 805. Harold Pinter, "The NATO Action in Serbia," in Tariq Ali, ed., *Masters of the Universe?: NATO's Balkan Crusade* (London:

Verso, 2000), pp. 327–36. Essays in the same volume by Noam Chomsky, Edward Said, Tariq Ali, and others agree that NATO's motives were imperialistic.

4. Strobe Talbott, *The Russia Hand: A Memoir of Presidential Diplomacy* (New York: Random House, 2002), p. 300. David M. Lampton, *Same Bed, Different Dreams: Managing U.S.-China Relations, 1989–2000* (Berkeley: University of California Press, 2001), pp. 59–61. Edward Hallett Carr, *The Twenty Years' Crisis, 1919–1939* (New York: Harper and Row, 1964; orig. 1939), pp. 71–75; Kenneth N. Waltz, *Theory of International Politics* (Reading, Mass.: Addison-Wesley, 1979), p. 200. Henry A. Kissinger, "Somalia," *Washington Post,* 13 December 1992, p. C7.
5. Reinhold Niebuhr, *Moral Man and Immoral Society: A Study in Ethics and Politics* (New York: Charles Scribner's Sons, 1960; orig. 1932), p. 110; Ronald Steel, *Temptations of a Superpower: America's Foreign Policy After the Cold War* (Cambridge, Mass.: Harvard University Press, 1995), pp. 107–8; Mearsheimer, *Tragedy of Great Power Politics,* pp. 1–14, 360–402. Walter Lippmann, *The Essential Lippmann: A Political Philosophy for Liberal Democracy,* ed. Clinton Rossiter and James Lare (Cambridge, Mass.: Harvard University Press, 1982), p. 80; Stephen M. Walt, *The Origins of Alliances* (Ithaca, N.Y.: Cornell University Press, 1987), pp. 17–26, 278–79; John M. Owen IV, "Transnational Liberalism and American Primacy," in G. John Ikenberry, ed., *America Unrivaled: The Future of the Balance of Power* (Ithaca, N.Y.: Cornell University Press, 2002), pp. 239–59. See Alexander Wendt, *Social Theory of International Politics* (Cambridge: Cambridge University Press, 1999); Charles L. Glaser, "Realists as Optimists," *International Security,* vol. 19, no. 3 (winter 1994–95), pp. 50–90; Ted Hopf, "The Promise of Constructivism in International Relations Theory," *International Security,* vol. 23, no. 1 (summer 1998), pp. 171–200; Thomas Risse-Kappen, "Collective Identity in a Democratic Community," in Peter J. Katzenstein, ed., *The Culture of National Security* (New York: Columbia University Press, 1996).
6. G. John Ikenberry, *After Victory: Institutions, Strategic Restraint, and the Rebuilding of Order After Major Wars* (Princeton, N.J.: Princeton University Press, 2001), pp. 3–7, 233–56; James Fearon, "Signaling Foreign Policy Interests," *Journal of Conflict Resolution,* vol. 41, no. 1 (February 1997), pp. 68–90; Glaser, "Realists as Optimists." On multilateralism, see John G. Ruggie, ed., *Multilateralism Matters: Theory and Praxis of an Institutional Form* (New York: Columbia University Press, 1993); Lippmann, *Essential Lippmann,* pp. 78–79. Multilateralism is neither a basically trivial outgrowth of the balance of power (Mearsheimer, *Tragedy of Great Power Politics,* p. 364), nor a deeply formative and constitutive endeavor that changes the identity and interest of the states participating in it. Instead, multilateralism is a useful midlevel device that states can use to calm fears in an anarchic, competitive world. Multilateral self-retraint made it easier for powerful states in the nineteenth century to launch humanitarian military interventions while lowering the risk of those interventions causing balancing, rivalry, or escalatory war.
7. Michael Walzer, *Just and Unjust Wars: A Moral Argument with Historical Illustrations* (New York: Basic Books, 1977), pp. 101–8; Nicholas J. Wheeler, *Saving*

Strangers: Humanitarian Intervention in International Society (Oxford: Oxford University Press, 2000), pp. 55–77, 111–36. Mill, "Non-Intervention," p. 257.

8. Taner Akcam, *A Shameful Act: The Armenian Genocide and the Question of Turkish Responsibility* (New York: Metropolitan, 2006), pp. 25, 52–54, 78, 207. Marc Trachtenberg, "Intervention in Historical Perspective," in Laura W. Reed and Carl Kaysen, eds., *Emerging Norms of Humanitarian Intervention,* pp. 24–25 (Cambridge, Mass.: American Academy of Arts and Sciences, 1993). This book looks at five major states with radically different domestic systems: illiberal Russia and Austria, liberal Britain and the United States, and, to better illustrate the causal processes at work, the mixed regime of France under the Second Empire. With a limited number of in-depth case studies, this book focuses on process-tracing and causal mechanisms. It aims to show not just what the actors did, but their own private motivations for those actions.

PART TWO: GREEKS

1. Byron to Moore, 27 December 1823, Leslie A. Marchand, ed., *"For Freedom's Battle": Byron's Letters and Journals,* vol. 11 (London: John Murray, 1981), pp. 84–85.
2. Douglas Dakin, *British and American Philhellenes during the War of Greek Independence, 1821–1833* (Thessaloniki: Institute for Balkan Studies, 1955), p. 4.
3. This section, while mostly relying on primary sources, has been helped greatly by a number of excellent histories: William St. Clair, *That Greece Might Still Be Free: The Philhellenes in the War of Independence* (London: Oxford University Press, 1972); Douglas Dakin, *The Greek Struggle for Independence, 1821–1833* (Berkeley: University of California Press, 1973) and his *British and American Philhellenes;* David Brewer, *The Greek War of Independence* (New York: Overlook, 2001); and especially the works of C. M. Woodhouse and George Finlay.

THE GREEK REVOLUTION

1. Thomas Gordon, *History of the Greek Revolution, and of the Wars and Campaigns Arising from the Struggles of the Greek Patriots in Emancipating Their Country from the Turkish Yoke,* vol. 1 (Edinburgh: William Blackwood, 1844), pp. 279–80. George IV to Liverpool, 27 January 1825, Arthur Wellesley, Duke of Wellington, *Despatches, Correspondence, and Memoranda of Field Marshal Arthur, Duke of Wellington, K.G.,* ed. by his son the Duke of Wellington, vol. 2 (London: John Murray, 1867), p. 401. George IV to Liverpool, 27 January 1825, Wellington, *Despatches,* vol. 2, p. 401.
2. Lynn Hunt, *Inventing Human Rights: A History* (New York: W. W. Norton, 2007), pp. 127–30, 160–79.
3. Byron to Murray, 26 April 1821, Leslie A. Marchand, ed., *"Born for Opposition": Byron's Letters and Journals,* vol. 8 (London: John Murray, 1978), p. 102. Fiona MacCarthy, *Byron: Life and Legend* (New York: Farrar, Straus and Giroux, 2002), p. 63.
4. Byron to Hobhouse, 6 July 1821, *Byron's Letters and Journals,* vol. 8, p. 148. MacCarthy, *Byron,* p. 101. Byron, "Written after Swimming from Sestos to Abydos," in Leslie A. Marchand, ed., *Selected Poetry of Lord Byron* (New York: Modern

Library, 2001), p. 193; Byron to Murray, 21 February 1821, *Byron's Letters and Journals,* vol. 8, pp. 80–82. Byron, "Maid of Athens," *Selected Poetry,* pp. 194–95. MacCarthy, *Byron,* pp. 109–15, 118–19. See Amartya Sen, *Identity and Violence: The Illusion of Destiny* (New York: W. W. Norton, 2006), p. 36.

5. Byron to Matthews, 31 July 1811, *Byron's Letters and Journals,* vol. 11, p. 159; MacCarthy, *Byron,* p. 116. Douglas Dakin, *British and American Philhellenes During the War of Greek Independence, 1821–1833* (Thessaloniki: Institute for Balkan Studies, 1955), pp. 8–11.
6. John Stuart Mill, "Grote's History of Greece" (1853), in *Dissertations and Discussions: Political, Philosophical, and Historical,* vol. 3 (New York: Henry Holt, 1882), pp. 193–237. Byron, *Childe Harold's Pilgrimmage,* canto II, lxxiii–lxxiv, lxxxiii–lxxxiv, in *Selected Poetry,* pp. 63, 66.
7. Dakin, *Philhellenes,* pp. 6–8. Byron to Bowring, 21 May 1823, Leslie A. Marchand, ed., *"A Heart for Every Fate": Byron's Letters and Journals* (London: John Murray, 1980), vol. 10, p. 181. See T. J. Binyon, *Pushkin: A Biography* (New York: Alfred A. Knopf, 2003), p. 170.
8. C. M. Woodhouse, *The Philhellenes* (London: Hodder and Stoughton, 1969), pp. 15, 25–32, 38–39, 56. Maria Todorova, *Imagining the Balkans* (New York: Oxford University Press, 1997), p. 99. Byron, *Childe Harold's Pilgrimage,* canto II, xii, *Selected Poetry,* p. 44.
9. Misha Glenny, *The Balkans: Nationalism, War and the Great Powers, 1804–1999* (New York: Viking, 2000), pp. 1–16. John Locke, *Second Treatise of Government* (Indianapolis, Ind.: Hackett, 1980; orig. 1690), ch. 16, §192, p. 98. Byron, *Childe Harold's Pilgrimage,* canto II, lxxiii–lxxiv, lxxxiii–lxxxiv, *Selected Poetry,* pp. 63, 66.
10. Dakin, *Philhellenes,* p. 11; Woodhouse, *Philhellenes,* pp. 54, 61–62. John T. Kakridis, "The Ancient Greeks of the War of Independence," *Journal of Balkan Studies,* vol. 4, no. 2 (1963), p. 252.
11. Byron, *Childe Harold's Pilgrimage,* canto II, lxxv, *Selected Poetry,* p. 64.
12. John Bowring, *Autobiographical Recollections* (London: Henry S. King, 1877), p. 283. Wellington to Canning, 4 October 1822, Wellington, *Despatches,* vol. 1, pp. 350–52. Binyon, *Pushkin,* pp. 130–31.
13. Douglas Dakin, *The Greek Struggle for Independence, 1821–1833* (Berkeley: University of California Press, 1973), p. 59; George Finlay, *History of the Greek Revolution* (London: William Blackwood and Sons, 1861), vol. 1, pp. 172, 179, 181–82, 184–88, 199–203; Gordon, *History of the Greek Revolution,* vol. 1, pp. 149, 168–69.
14. Gordon, *History of the Greek Revolution,* vol. 1, pp. 190, 229, 238–39. Edward Blaquiere, *The Greek Revolution; Its Origin and Progress: Together with Some Remarks on the Religion, National Character, &c. in Greece* (London: G. and W. B. Whittaker, 1824), p. 80. Charles Kingsley Webster, *The Foreign Policy of Castlereagh, 1815–1822* (London: G. Bell, 1925), vol. 2, pp. 354–55; Dakin, *Greek Struggle,* pp. 59–60.
15. *Times,* 26 April 1821, p. 3. *Times,* 13 April 1821, p. 2; "French Papers," *Times,* 28 April 1821, p. 2; "Hamburgh Mail," *Times,* 1 May 1821, p. 2; *Times,* 6 June 1821, p. 2; *Times,* 16 June 1821, p. 3. (For Greek denials, see "Greece," *Times,* 28 April 1821,

p. 3; *Times,* 8 May 1821, p. 2.) "The Greeks," *Times,* 18 May 1821, p. 3; *Times,* 13 June 1821, p. 2. Dakin, *Greek Struggle,* p. 76.

16. Constantinople letters, *Times,* 18 May 1821, p. 3; 28 May 1821, p. 3; 28 May 1821, p. 3. See *Times,* 30 May 1821, p. 3; *Times,* 30 May 1821, p. 3; *Times,* 26 May 1821, p. 2; *Times,* 1 June 1821, p. 3; *Times,* 6 June 1821, p. 2; *Times,* 13 June 1821, p. 3; *Times,* 14 June 1821, p. 2; *Times,* 25 June 1821, p. 2; Lloyd's shipping news, *Times,* 19 June 1821, p. 3. "Flanders Papers," *Times,* 11 June 1821, p. 2. *Times,* 18 June 1821, p. 2; foreign papers, *Times,* 19 June 1821, p. 3; foreign papers, *Times,* 25 June 1821, p. 2. Foreign papers, *Times,* 19 June 1821, p. 3. Gordon, *History of the Greek Revolution,* vol. 1, pp. 187–88.
17. T. S. Hughes, *Address to the People of England in the Cause of the Greeks* (London: Simpkin and Marshall, 1822), p. 11. Blaquiere, *Report on the Present State of the Greek Confederation, and on its Claims to the Support of the Christian World* (London: G. and W. B. Whittaker, 1823), p. 10.
18. Woodhouse, *Philhellenes,* pp. 66–67, 134. "Flanders Papers," *Times,* 13 June 1821, p. 2. Dakin, *Philhellenes,* pp. 1–2.
19. Percy Shelley, "Choruses from Hellas," in *Shelley: Selected Poetry,* ed. Isabel Quigly (London: Penguin, 1956; orig. 1821), pp. 271–73. French dispatch, *Times,* 8 May 1821, p. 2.
20. Webster, *Foreign Policy of Castlereagh,* vol. 2, pp. 29–33; "Famed Foreign Secretaries," *Time,* 11 February 1952.
21. Metternich to Wellington, 14 June 1824, Wellington, *Despatches,* p. 279; Klemens Wenzel Lother Fürst von Metternich, *Mémoires, documents et écrits divers: L'Ère de paix, 1816–1848* (Paris: Plon, 1881), vol. 3, pp. 489–96, 509–17. Webster, *Foreign Policy of Castlereagh,* vol. 2, p. 32. Harold Nicolson, *The Congress of Vienna: A Study in Allied Unity, 1812–1822* (New York: Harcourt, Brace, 1946), p. 294.
22. Richard T. Shannon, *Gladstone and the Bulgarian Agitation 1876* (Sussex: Harvester, 1975), p. xiv. Anthony Trollope, *Can You Forgive Her?* (New York: Oxford University Press, 1999; orig. 1865), p. 1. Webster, *Foreign Policy of Castlereagh,* vol. 2, p. 23.
23. Webster, *Foreign Policy of Castlereagh,* vol. 2, pp. 20–24, 395. John S. Harford, *Recollections of William Wilberforce* (London: Longman, Green, 1864); Samuel Wilberforce, *The Life of William Wilberforce* (London: John Murray, 1868). See Wilberforce's *A Letter on the Abolition of the Slave Trade, Addressed to the Freeholders of Yorkshire* (London: J. Hatchard, 1807); *A Letter to His Excellency the Prince of Talleyrand-Périgord on the Subject of the Slave Trade* (London: J. Hatchard, 1814); and *An Appeal to the Religion, Justice, and Humanity of the Inhabitants of the British Empire: In Behalf of the Negro Slaves in the West Indies* (London: J. Hatchard, 1823).
24. Aled Jones, *Powers of the Press: Newspapers, Power and the Public in Nineteenth-Century England* (Cambridge: Scolar Press, 1996), p. 142. Webster, *Foreign Policy of Castlereagh,* vol. 2, pp. 24–27.
25. Canning to Wellington, 10 February 1826, Arthur Wellesley, Duke of Wellington, *Despatches, Correspondence, and Memoranda of Field Marshal Arthur, Duke of Wellington, K.G.,* vol. 3 (London: John Murray, 1868), p. 93. René Albrecht-Carrié, *A Diplomatic History of Europe Since the Congress of Vienna* (New York:

Harper and Row, 1958), pp. 41, 109. Woodhouse, *Philhellenes,* pp. 60–61. See Planta to Stratford Canning, 8 August 1821, Webster, *Foreign Policy of Castlereagh,* vol. 2, p. 583. Castlereagh to Aleksandr I, 16 July 1821, Robert Stewart, Viscount Castlereagh, *Correspondence, Despatches, and Other Papers of Viscount Castlereagh, Second Marquess of Londonderry,* ed. Charles William Vane, Marquess of Londonderry, vol. 12 (London: John Murray, 1853), p. 405. See Stephen D. Krasner, *Sovereignty: Organized Hypocrisy* (Princeton, N.J.: Princeton University Press, 1999), p. 158.

26. Byron, *Childe Harold's Pilgrimage,* canto III, lxxvii, *Selected Poetry,* p. 94. Byron, *Don Juan,* canto IX, xxiv, *Selected Poetry,* p. 480.
27. Byron, *Childe Harold's Pilgrimage,* canto III, lxiv and xviii, *Selected Poetry,* pp. 90, 76. Byron, "Don Juan," canto IX, ibid., pp. 476–77.
28. Philip Schofield, ed., *The Collected Works of Jeremy Bentham: Securities Against Misrule and Other Constitutional Writings for Tripoli and Greece* (Oxford: Clarendon Press, 1990), p. 193. Byron to Davies, 26 January 1819, *Byron's Letters and Journals,* vol. 11, p. 171.
29. Byron, "Don Juan," dedication, xi, xiv, *Selected Poetry,* pp. 360–61.
30. Percy Shelley, "The Mask of Anarchy," in *The Complete Poems of Percy Bysshe Shelley* (New York: Modern Library, 1994), pp. 366–67.
31. Castlereagh to Aleksandr I, 16 July 1821, Castlereagh, *Correspondence,* vol. 12, p. 407. Castlereagh to Aleksandr I, 28 October 1821, Webster, *Foreign Policy of Castlereagh,* vol. 2, pp. 376–77. Castlereagh to Frere, 29 January 1816, ibid., p. 350.
32. Aleksandr I to Meshcherskia, 22 October 1820, Patricia Kennedy Grimsted, *Foreign Ministers of Alexander I: Political Attitudes and the Conduct of Russian Diplomacy* (Berkeley: University of California Press, 1969), p. 62.
33. Dakin, *Greek Struggle,* p. 58; Dakin, *Philhellenes,* p. 22; Henry A. Kissinger, *A World Restored: Metternich, Castlereagh, and the Problems of Peace 1812–22* (Boston: Houghton Mifflin, 1973), p. 289. Strangford memo, 25 May 1825, Wellington, *Despatches,* vol. 2, pp. 455. Metternich to Rechberg, 25 March 1821, Metternich, *Mémoires,* vol. 3, p. 492; Metternich to Rechberg, 25 March 1821, ibid., p. 493.
34. Theophilus C. Prousis, *Russian Society and the Greek Revolution* (DeKalb: Northern Illinois University Press, 1994); Stella Ghervas, "Le philhellénisme d'inspiration conservatrice en Europe et en Russie," in Elena Siupiur et al., eds., *Peuples, états et nations dans le sud-est de l'Europe* (Bucharest: Editura Anima, 2004), pp. 101–9. Nicolson, *Congress of Vienna,* pp. 243–44; Woodhouse, *Philhellenes,* pp. 96–97. Dakin, *Greek Struggle,* pp. 63–64. Aleksandr I to Castlereagh, 29 August 1821, Castlereagh, *Correspondence,* vol. 12, p. 429.
35. Castlereagh to Aleksandr I, 16 July 1821, Castlereagh, *Correspondence,* vol. 12, p. 407. Castlereagh to Aleksandr I, 16 July 1821, ibid., pp. 406–7. Castlereagh to Aleksandr I, 16 July 1821, Webster, *Foreign Policy of Castlereagh,* vol. 2, pp. 360–61.
36. Castlereagh to Aleksandr I, 28 October 1821, Webster, *Foreign Policy of Castlereagh,* vol. 2, pp. 376–77.
37. Castlereagh to Bagot, 14 December 1821, Castlereagh, *Correspondence,* vol. 12,

p. 445. Strangford to Canning, 3 September 1825, Wellington, *Despatches,* vol. 2, p. 471. Wellington to Castlereagh, 19 April 1822, ibid., vol. 1, pp. 232–35.

38. Metternich, 13 May 1822, Metternich, *Mémoires,* vol. 3, p. 546. Metternich, 22 March 1822, ibid., p. 538. Metternich to Lebzelten, 28 January 1822, ibid., pp. 565–71. Webster, *Foreign Policy of Castlereagh,* vol. 2, pp. 397–98; Kissinger, *World Restored,* p. 308. Metternich note, 15 May 1822, Metternich, *Mémoires,* vol. 3, p. 546.
39. LGC vol. 1, A4, Lempriere to Bowring 21 April 1823. Blaquiere, *Report,* p. 15.
40. Dakin, *Philhellenes,* p. 28; Finlay, *History of the Greek Revolution,* vol. 1, pp. 262, 175–76.
41. Dakin, *Greek Struggle,* pp. 66–67; Dakin, *Philhellenes,* pp. 28–30; F. Rosen, *Bentham, Byron and Greece: Constitutionalism, Nationalism, and Early Liberal Political Thought* (Oxford: Clarendon Press, 1992), pp. 135–40. LGC vol. 1, E4, K4, Gordon to Bowring, 24 and 29 April 1823.
42. Erskine, "The Greeks," *Times,* 30 August 1822, p. 3. Blaquiere, *Report,* p. 11. Blaquiere, *Greek Revolution,* p. 153.
43. *Byron's Letters and Journals,* vol. 11, p. 39. LGC vol. 1, E4, Gordon to Bowring, 24 and 29 April 1823.
44. Leader, *Morning Chronicle,* 6 April 1822, p. 2. Leader, *Times,* 1 July 1822, p. 3. *Times,* 11 September 1822, p. 2.
45. Gordon, *History of the Greek Revolution,* vol. 1, p. 311.

THE SCIO MASSACRE

1. George Finlay, *History of the Greek Revolution,* vol. 1 (London: William Blackwood and Sons, 1861), p. 306.
2. Strangford to Castlereagh, 10 April 1822, Philip P. Argenti, ed., *The Massacres of Chios Described in Contemporary Diplomatic Reports* (London: Bodley Head, 1932), p. 8. Werry to Liddell, 2 May 1822, ibid., p. 38. See CP/T, vol. 235, no. 45, La Tour-Maubourg to Montmorency, 8 May 1822.
3. Strangford to Castlereagh, 10 May 1822, Argenti, ed., *Massacres at Chios,* p. 13. See "Événements arrivés à Scio," *Spectateur Oriental* no. 46, 5 April 1822, ibid., pp. 228–32. Strangford to Castlereagh, 25 May 1822, ibid., p. 21. Strangford to Castlereagh, 25 May 1822, ibid., pp. 16–17.
4. Strangford to Castlereagh, 25 May 1822, ibid., pp. 17–19.
5. Strangford to Castlereagh, 25 May 1822, ibid., pp. 19–20. *Spectateur Oriental,* no. 54, 3 June 1822, ibid., pp. 240–41. Finlay, *History of the Greek Revolution,* vol. 1, pp. 307–19.
6. "Massacre of the Greeks at Constantinople and Scio," *Times,* 28 June 1822, p. 3.
7. *Times,* 29 June 1822, p. 2. "Hamburgh Papers," *Times,* 29 June 1822, p. 4. "Massacre at Scio," *Times,* 6 July 1822, p. 3. Leader, *Times,* 1 July 1822, p. 3.
8. "Parliamentary Intelligence," *Times,* 16 July 1822, p. 2. Parliamentary record, *Times,* 29 June 1822, p. 2. Adam Hochschild, *Bury the Chains: Prophets and Rebels in the Fight to Free an Empire's Slaves* (Boston: Houghton Mifflin, 2005), pp. 122–26. Robert Isaac Wilberforce and Samuel Wilberforce, *The Life of William Wilberforce,* vol. 5 (London: John Murray, 1838), ch. 33, pp. 2–3. "Parliamentary Intelligence," *Times,* 16 July 1822, p. 2.

9. "Parliamentary Intelligence," *Times,* 16 July 1822, p. 2.
10. Ibid., 18 July 1822, p. 1.
11. Ibid., 29 June 1822, p. 2. Castlereagh to Strangford, 9 July 1822, Argenti, ed., *Massacres at Chios,* pp. 25–26.
12. FO 195/37, Strangford to Castlereagh, 10 July 1822. FO 195/37, Strangford to Castlereagh, 25 July 1822.
13. Strangford to Castlereagh, 26 July 1822, Argenti, ed., *Massacres at Chios,* pp. 28–30.
14. Leader, *Times,* 2 August 1822, p. 2. Leader, *Times,* 11 September 1822, p. 2. Edward Blaquiere, *The Greek Revolution; Its Origin and Progress: Together with Some Remarks on the Religion, National Character, &c. in Greece* (London: G. and W. B. Whittaker, 1824), pp. 192–95; T. S. Hughes, *Address to the People of England in the Cause of the Greeks* (London: Simpkin and Marshall, 1822), p. 43. Finlay, *History of the Greek Revolution,* vol. 1, pp. 319–21. Leader, *Times,* 14 August 1876, p. 9.
15. Edward Blaquiere, *Report on the Present State of the Greek Confederation, and on Its Claims to the Support of the Christian World* (London: G. and W. B. Whittaker, 1823), pp. 10, 12. Douglas Dakin, *The Greek Struggle for Independence, 1821–1833* (Berkeley: University of California Press, 1973), p. 108; C. M. Woodhouse, *The Philhellenes* (London: Hodder and Stoughton, 1969), pp. 73–74; Charles Kingsley Webster, *The Foreign Policy of Castlereagh, 1815–1822,* vol. 2 (London: G. Bell, 1925), pp. 399–400.
16. Leader, *Times,* 11 September 1822, p. 2. Blaquiere, *Greek Revolution,* pp. 197, 198.
17. Thomas Erskine, "The Greeks," *Times,* 30 August 1822, p. 3. Hughes, *Address to the People of England,* pp. 5–6, 9–10, 31–34.
18. Victor Hugo, "L'enfant," *Les Orientales,* vol. 2 (Paris: Librairie Marcel Didier, 1954), XVIII: 1–2, 34–36, pp. 29–32.
19. Gordon to Castlereagh, 3 October 1821, Castlereagh, *Correspondence,* vol. 12, pp. 439–40; Metternich note, 14 June 1822, Klemens Wenzel Lother Fürst von Metternich, *Mémoires, documents et écrits divers: L'Ère de paix, 1816–1848* (Paris: Plon, 1881), vol. 3, p. 549.
20. Castlereagh to Wellington, 14 September 1822 (delivered posthumously), Arthur Wellesley, Duke of Wellington, *Despatches, Correspondence, and Memoranda of Field Marshal Arthur, Duke of Wellington,* vol. 1 (London: John Murray, 1867), pp. 285–86.
21. H. Montgomery Hyde, *The Strange Death of Lord Castlereagh* (London: Heinemann, 1959), pp. 49, 52–53. Webster, *Foreign Policy of Castlereagh,* vol. 2, p. 489.
22. Wellington to Arbuthnot, 9 August 1822, Wellington, *Despatches,* vol. 1, pp. 256–57. Hyde, *Strange Death,* pp. 59–63. See Wellington to George IV, 18 August 1822, Wellington, *Despatches,* vol. 1, pp. 258–59.
23. Somerset to Wellington, 12 August 1822, Wellington, *Despatches,* vol. 1, pp. 253–54; Hyde, *Strange Death,* pp. 4, 19–21; *Times,* 13 August 1822, p. 2.
24. Metternich note, 20 August 1822, *Mémoires,* vol. 3, p. 556. See Planta to Bagot, 3 September 1822, Josceline Bagot, ed., *George Canning and His Friends: Containing Hitherto Unpublished Letters, Jeux d'Esprit, Etc.,* vol. 2 (London: John Murray, 1909), pp. 131–32. *Times,* 13 August 1822, p. 2. Hyde, *Strange Death,* pp. 29–32;

Webster, *Foreign Policy of Castlereagh,* vol. 2, p. 486; Wellington to Londonderry, 21 August 1822, Wellington, *Despatches,* vol. 1, pp. 262–63.

25. *Times,* 15 August 1822, p. 2. Byron to Moore, 27 August 1822, Leslie A. Marchand, ed., *"In the Wind's Eye": Byron's Letters and Journals,* vol. 9 (London: John Murray, 1979), p. 197. Byron to Kinnaird, 18 September 1822 and 3 October 1822, ibid., p. 210. Byron to Hardy, 17 May 1823, ibid., vol. 10, p. 173. *Byron: The Complete Poetical Works,* vol. 4, ed. Jerome J. McGann (Oxford: Clarendon Press, 1986), p. 279. Byron preface to *Don Juan* cantos 6–8, July 1822, in *Complete Poetical Works of Lord Byron,* ed. Paul Elmer More (Boston: Houghton Mifflin, 1905), pp. 851–52.

THE LONDON GREEK COMMITTEE

1. Douglas Dakin, *The Greek Struggle for Independence, 1821–1833* (Berkeley: University of California Press, 1973), p. 108. F. Rosen, *Bentham, Byron and Greece: Constitutionalism, Nationalism, and Early Liberal Political Thought* (Oxford: Clarendon Press, 1992), pp. 223–34. This is a superb account of Bentham's role and ideology.
2. William St. Clair, *That Greece Might Still Be Free: The Philhellenes in the War of Independence* (London: Oxford University Press, 1972), p. 141. Bentham to Canning, 11 October 1822, Catherine Fuller, ed., *The Collected Works of Jeremy Bentham: Correspondence,* vol. 11, pp. 161–63 (Oxford: Clarendon Press, 2000); Leslie A. Marchand, ed., *"For Freedom's Battle": Byron's Letters and Journals,* vol. 11 (London: John Murray, 1981), p. 53; John Bowring, *Details of the Arrest, Imprisonment and Liberation, of an Englishman by the Bourbon Government of France* (1823). *Byron's Letters and Journals,* vol. 10, p. 230; John Bowring, *Autobiographical Recollections* (London: Henry S. King, 1877), pp. 83–87. LGC vol. 1, Bowring appeal, 28 January 1823. See LGC vol. 1, Bowring to Liverpool, 1 March 1823.
3. LGC vol. 1, Williams to Bowring, n.d., March 1823; LGC vol. 1, Lansdowne to Bowring, 14 March 1823; LGC vol. 1, Browne to Bowring, 6 March 1823. Bowring, *Autobiographical Recollections,* p. 66. Bentham to Boyer, 29 December 1822, *Collected Works of Bentham: Correspondence,* vol. 11, p. 179. See Rosen, *Bentham, Byron, and Greece.* Bentham had criticized the concept of natural rights after the French Revolution ("Nonsense Upon Stilts, or Pandora's Box Opened," also known as "Anarchical Fallacies," in Philip Schofield, Catherine Pease-Watkin, and Cyprian Blamires, eds., *The Collected Works of Jeremy Bentham: Rights, Representation, and Reform* [Oxford: Clarendon Press, 2002], pp. 317–75) but sometimes used something close to rights language anyway—protections against secret homicide, religious persecution, and censorship ("Securities Against Misrule," in Philip Schofield, ed., *The Collected Works of Jeremy Bentham: Securities Against Misrule and Other Constitutional Writings for Tripoli and Greece* [Oxford: Clarendon, 1990], pp. 25–73). He clearly saw Ottoman misrule in Greece as an affront to principles of good governance.
4. Byron, "My Boy Hobbie O," in Leslie A. Marchand, ed., *Selected Poetry of Lord Byron* (New York: Modern Library, 2001), pp. 286–87. LGC vol. 1, Hume letter, 8 March 1823.
5. LGC vol. 3, A, minutes, 15 March 1823. LGC vol. 1, F5, n.d. May 1823; LGC vol.

3, B, minutes, 22 March 1823. Byron to Bowring, 12 May 1823, *Byron's Letters and Journals,* vol. 10, p. 168; Byron to Bowring, 21 May 1823, ibid., p. 179. They invited seventy-three to join, of whom at least forty-four did (C. M. Woodhouse, *The Philhellenes* [London: Hodder and Stoughton, 1969], pp. 71–75).

6. Woodhouse, *Philhellenes,* pp. 47, 85–91. Rosen, *Bentham, Byron and Greece,* pp. 175, 239.
7. LGC vol. 1, J5, n.d. May 1823. See Thomas Gordon, *History of the Greek Revolution, and of the Wars and Campaigns Arising from the Struggles of the Greek Patriots in Emancipating Their Country from the Turkish Yoke* (Edinburgh: William Blackwood, 1844), vol. 2, pp. 78–79. LGC vol. 3, L, minutes, Crown and Anchor Tavern meeting, 24 May 1823. George Finlay, *History of the Greek Revolution* (Edinburgh: William Blackwood and Sons, 1861), vol. 2, p. 168.
8. Edward Blaquiere, *Report on the Present State of the Greek Confederation, and on Its Claims to the Support of the Christian World* (London: G. and W. B. Whittaker, 1823), p. 16. Bentham to Mavrokordatos, 6 March 1824, *Collected Works of Bentham: Correspondence,* vol. 11, p. 357. Bentham to Greek legislature, 13–20 August 1824, ibid., p. 350.
9. LGC vol. 2, A, Delancey to Bowring, 8 May 1823; Bowring, *Autobiographical Recollections,* p. 400. Byron to Bowring, 26 December 1823, *Byron's Letters and Journals,* vol. 11, p. 83.
10. T. S. Hughes, *Address to the People of England in the Cause of the Greeks* (London: Simpkin and Marshall, 1822), p. 7. E. B. Elliott, *Appeal from the Greek Committee to the British Public in General, and Especially to the Friends of Religion* (London: Richard Taylor, 1823), pp. 2–3. Blaquiere, *Report,* p. 12. LGC vol. 3, V3, Thompson to Bowring, 17 October 1823.
11. Byron to Stoven, 8 March 1824, *Byron's Letters and Journals,* vol. 11, p. 129. Edward Blaquiere, *The Greek Revolution; Its Origin and Progress: Together with Some Remarks on the Religion, National Character, &c. in Greece* (London: G. and W. B. Whittaker, 1824), pp. 79–80. LGC vol. 3, G1, Millingen to Bowring, 21 August 1823. LGC vol. 1, E5, Address of the Greek Committee, Lord Milton MP, Crown and Anchor Tavern, 3 May 1823.
12. LGC vol. 1, J2, Lempriere to Barker, 26 March 1823. LGC vol. 1, U2, Challadarem to Barker, 30 March 1823.
13. Jennifer Pitts, *A Turn to Empire: The Rise of Imperial Liberalism in Britain and France* (Princeton, N.J.: Princeton University Press, 2005), pp. 103–22. In this survey of Bentham's writings on empire, Pitts convincingly undermines Stokes's condemnation of him as a utilitarian imperialist. Eric Stokes, *The English Utilitarians and India* (Oxford: Clarendon Press, 1959), pp. 51–52, 74–75. Bentham, "Emancipate Your Colonies!: Addressed to the National Convention of France, A° 1793, Shewing the Uselessness and Mischievousness of Distant Dependencies to an European State," in Philip Schofield, Catherine Pease-Watkin, and Cyprian Blamires, eds., *The Collected Works of Jeremy Bentham: Rights, Representation, and Reform* (Oxford: Clarendon Press, 2002), pp. 292, 310–12. Bentham, "Rid Yourselves of Ultramaria: Being the Advice of Jeremy Bentham as Given in a Series of Letters to the Spanish People," in Philip Schofield, ed., *The Collected Works of*

Jeremy Bentham: Colonies, Commerce, and Constitutional Law (Oxford: Clarendon Press, 1995), pp. 3–194. See "Summary of a Work Intituled 'Emancipate Your Colonies' in a Letter from Philo-Hispanus to the Spanish People," ibid., pp. 277–344.

14. *Collected Works of Bentham: Securities Against Misrule,* pp. 181–285. Luriottis to Bentham, 10 May 1823, *Collected Works of Bentham: Correspondence,* vol. 11, pp. 233–34; Mavrokordatos to Bentham, 6 July 1823, ibid., p. 269; Bentham to Stanhope, 21 October 1823, ibid., pp. 309–12; Bentham to Greek legislature, 13–20 February 1824, ibid., pp. 349–51; Bentham to Mavrokordatos, 27 February and 1 March 1824, ibid., pp. 353–56; Greek provisional government to Bentham, 24 August 1824, in Luke O'Sullivan and Catherine Fuller, eds., *The Collected Works of Jeremy Bentham: Correspondence,* vol. 12 (Oxford: Clarendon Press, 2006), pp. 23–25; Bentham to Greek legislature, 21 September 1824, *Collected Works of Bentham: Correspondence,* vol. 12, pp. 48–51; Bentham to Greek Senate, 28–30 January 1825, ibid., pp. 96–100. Bentham to Mavrokordatos, 6 March 1824, *Collected Works of Bentham: Correspondence,* vol. 11, pp. 356–57. Bentham to Rivadavia, 5 April 1824, ibid., p. 433.
15. Woodhouse, *Philhellenes,* pp. 75–76. LGC vol. 1, R4, Stanhope to Bowring, 2 May 1823. LGC vol. 1, H3, Leake to Hume, 4 April 1823.
16. LGC vol. 1, E4, Elliot to Bowring, 23 October 1823; LGC vol. 3, V4, Goodwin to Bowring, 2 November 1823. Elliott, *Appeal from the Greek Committee,* p. 3. LGC vol. 3, S4, Hadfield to Bowring, 1 November 1823.
17. Blaquiere, *Report,* pp. 18–19; Blaquiere, *Greek Revolution,* p. vi. LGC vol. 3, S4, Hadfield to Bowring, 1 November 1823. LGC vol. 1, O4, Barker to Bowring, 30 April 1823.
18. LGC vol. 1, Z3, Lempriere to Bowring, 21 April 1823; LGC vol. 4, R3, Barker to Bowring, 5 December 1823; Thomas Erskine, *Appeal to the People of Great Britain on the Subject of Confederated Greece* (London: Whittaker, 1823), p. 3. LGC vol. 3, V3, Thompson to Bowring, 17 October 1823. LGC vol. 1, L3, Barker to Bowring, 13 April 1823. LGC vol. 4, S2, Elliott to Barker, 25 November 1823. See Barker to Bentham, 29 June 1825, *Collected Works of Bentham: Correspondence,* vol. 12, p. 131. LGC vol. 6, Y3, Barker to Bowring, 23 March 1824; LGC vol. 8, Barker to Bowring, 7 May 1824. LGC vol. 1, X4, Pryme to Bowring, 7 May 1823.
19. Bowring, *Autobiographical Recollections,* p. 345. Shelley, "Fragment: To Byron," in *The Complete Poems of Percy Bysshe Shelley* (New York: Modern Library, 1994), p. 608. Byron to Bowring, 12 May 1823, *Byron's Letters and Journals,* vol. 10, pp. 171.
20. LGC vol. 4, E1, Stanhope to Bowring, 18 October 1823. LGC vol. 1, V3, Barker to Bowring, 17 April 1823.
21. Hughes, *Address to the People of England,* p. 28. LGC vol. 8, Routh to Barker, 24 April 1824; in Barker to Bowring, 7 May 1824.
22. Canning to Castlereagh, 20 September 1809, Josceline Bagot, ed., *George Canning and His Friends: Containing Hitherto Unpublished Letters, Jeux d'Esprit, Etc.,* vol. 1, p. 324 (London: John Murray, 1909); C. K. Webster, H. Temperley, and E. Cooke, "The Duel Between Castlereagh and Canning in 1809," *Cambridge Historical Journal,* vol. 3, no. 1 (1929), pp. 83–95.

23. Wendy Hinde, *George Canning* (London: Collins, 1973), pp. 14, 23, 384. Canning speech, 15 May 1823, *Select Speeches of the Right Honourable George Canning,* ed. Robert Walsh (Philadelphia: Key and Biddle, 1835), pp. 403–5. Dakin, *Greek Struggle,* pp. 149–50. Canning, "The Slavery of Greece," Canning, *Speeches,* pp. 541–42. Canning to Giffard, 9 October 1826, *Some Official Correspondence of George Canning,* ed. Edward J. Stapleton, vol. 2 (London: Longmans, Green, 1887), pp. 227–28. Byron to Hunt, 5 May 1823, *Byron's Letters and Journals,* vol. 10, p. 166. See Byron to Hoppner, 13 January 1823, ibid., p. 83. Byron preface to *Don Juan* cantos 6–8, July 1822, in *Complete Poetical Works of Lord Byron,* ed. Paul Elmer More (Boston: Houghton Mifflin, 1905), p. 852.
24. Canning speech, 11 December 1798, Canning, *Speeches,* p. 23. Canning speech, 15 May 1823, ibid., pp. 400–10. Canning speech, 16 March 1821, ibid., pp. 305–31. Finlay, *History of the Greek Revolution,* vol. 2, p. 163; Hinde, *Canning,* pp. 372–73. Canning speech, 4 March 1819, Canning, *Select Speeches,* pp. 271–72. Canning to Wellington, 16 December 1824, Wellington, *Despatches,* vol. 2, p. 366.
25. LGC vol. 3, F, minutes, 12 April 1823. LGC vol. 1, T4, Canning to Bowring, 3 May 1823. LGC vol. 3, M, minutes, 31 May 1823. Hinde, *Canning,* pp. 385–86. Finlay, *History of the Greek Revolution,* vol. 2, p. 169.
26. Blaquiere, *Report,* p. 12.
27. LGC vol. 1, Gordon to Bowring, 18 March 1823. Shelley, preface, "Hellas," *Complete Poems,* p. 501. Byron to Church, 21 June 1823, *Byron's Letters and Journals,* vol. 10, p. 202. LGC vol. 1, Y3, 19 April 1823. LGC vol. 1, N2, Bowring to Reeves, 26 March 1823. LGC vol. 1, I3, Barker to Bowring, 4 April 1823. Bowring, *Autobiographical Recollections,* p. 283. Byron to Kinnaird, 29 October 1823, *Byron's Letters and Journals,* vol. 11, p. 58.
28. Thomas Erskine, *A Letter to the Earl of Liverpool on the Subject of the Greeks,* 4th ed. (London: John Murray, 1823), p. vii. LGC vol. 3, C, minutes of Greek Committee, 22 March 1823. LGC vol. 1, D5, n.d. May 1823. LGC vol. 3, U1, Barker to Bowring, 18 September 1823. LGC vol. 3, I, minutes, 25 April 1823. Blaquiere, *Greek Revolution,* p. vi.
29. LGC vol. 4, O4, Barker to Bowring, 23 December 1823. LGC vol. 1, Y4, Barker to Bowring, 7 May 1823. LGC vol. 1, L3, Barker to Bowring, 13 April 1823; William Gell, *Narrative of a Journey in the Morea* (London: Longman, Hurst, Rees, Orme, and Brown, 1823). LGC vol. 1, W4, Barker to Bowring, 4 May 1823; LGC vol. 1, L3, Barker to Bowring, 13 April 1823. LGC vol. 1, Z4, attached to Barker to Bowring, 7 May 1823.
30. LGC vol. 1, I3, Barker to Bowring, 4 April 1823. LGC vol. 1, Bowring to Liverpool, 1 March 1823. LGC vol. 1, M3, Chatfield to Bowring, 14 April 1823. LGC vol. 1, L3, Barker to Bowring, 13 April 1823. LGC vol. 1, L3, Barker to Bowring, 13 April 1823; LGC vol. 1, F5, n.d. May 1823.
31. "The Greeks," *Gallant,* 10 May 1823, p. 8. LGC vol. 8, Barker to Bowring, 7 May 1824.
32. LGC vol. 3, N, minutes, 7 June 1823. LGC vol. 1, U2, Challadarem to Barker, 30 March 1823. LGC vol. 4, S5, Barker to Bowring, 13 January 1824. LGC vol. 1, X4, Pryme to Bowring, 7 May 1823.

33. LGC vol. 3, U1, Barker to Bowring, 18 September 1823; LGC vol. 3, T3, Barker to Bowring, 16 October 1823. LGC vol. 3, G3, Hadfield to Bowring, 7 October 1823. LGC vol. 3, S4, Hadfield to Bowring, 1 November 1823. LGC vol. 5, W, Manchester Greek Committee minutes, 26 November 1823.
34. LGC vol. 4, I4, Barker to Bowring, 19 December 1823. LGC vol. 4, S5, Barker to Bowring, 13 January 1824. LGC vol. 4, T2, Brown to Bowring, 25 November 1823. LGC vol. 4, Y1, Brown and King to Bowring, 14 November 1823. LGC vol. 6, I4, Ridley note, 28 February 1824.
35. LGC vol. 3, G3, Hadfield to Bowring, 7 October 1823. LGC vol. 1, U2, Challadarem to Barker, 30 March 1823. St. Clair, *Greece Might Still Be Free,* p. 145.
36. LGC vol. 1, Gordon to Bowring, 18 March 1823; LGC vol. 1, P2, Gordon to Bowring, 24 March 1823. LGC vol. 3, M, minutes, 31 May 1823.
37. Byron to Bowring, 12 May 1823, *Byron's Letters and Journals,* vol. 10, pp. 169–70. LGC vol. 1, A4, Lempriere to Bowring, 21 April 1823. LGC vol. 1, J3, Barker to *Iris,* 28 March 1823. LGC vol. 1, Y4, Barker to Bowring, 7 May 1823. LGC vol. 1, C5, Resolutions for Greek Meeting, n.d. May 1823.
38. LGC vol. 1, L3, Barker to Bowring, 13 April 1823. LGC vol. 1, U2, Challadarem to Barker, 30 March 1823. LGC vol. 3, Y4, Yarmouth pamphlet, October 1823.
39. LGC vol. 2, A, Delancey to Bowring, 8 May 1823. LGC vol. 1, Gordon to Bowring, 18 March 1823. LGC vol. 1, E4, Cairness and Gordon to Bowring, 24 and 29 April 1823. LGC vol. 1, I4, Gordon minute, n.d. April 1823. LGC vol. 3, R, minutes, 11 October 1823; LGC vol. 3, L, minutes, Crown and Anchor Tavern, 24 May 1823.
40. LGC vol. 3, O, minutes, 18 June 1823. LGC vol. 3, T1, McNeil to Bowring, 18 September 1823. LGC vol. 3, S2, Gordon to Bowring, 28 September 1823. LGC vol. 4, B2, Schwitzer to Bowring, 15 November 1823. Woodhouse, *Philhellenes,* pp. 179–81.

AMERICANS AND GREEKS

1. James A. Field Jr., *From Gibraltar to the Middle East: America and the Mediterranean World 1776–1882* (Chicago: Imprint, 1991), p. 121. Garry Wills, *Lincoln at Gettysburg: The Words That Remade America* (New York: Simon and Schuster, 1992), p. 42.
2. Edward Mead Earle, "American Interest in the Greek Cause, 1821–1827," *American Historical Review,* vol. 33, no. 1 (October 1927), pp. 44–45. *North American Review,* vol. 7, no. 4 (October 1823), pp. 415–16.
3. Ernest R. May, *The Making of the Monroe Doctrine* (Cambridge, Mass.: Harvard University Press, 1975), pp. 12–21. Samuel Flagg Bemis, *John Quincy Adams and the Foundations of American Foreign Policy* (New York: Alfred A. Knopf, 1950).
4. 7 November 1823 entry, *Memoirs of John Quincy Adams, Comprising Portions of His Diary from 1795 to 1848,* ed. Charles Francis Adams, vol. 6 (Philadelphia: J. B. Lippincott, 1875), p. 129. 9 March 1821 entry, *Memoirs of John Quincy Adams, Comprising Portions of His Diary from 1795 to 1848,* ed. Charles Francis Adams, vol. 5 (Philadelphia: J. B. Lippincott, 1875), pp. 324–25.

5. Adams address, 4 July 1821, *John Quincy Adams and American Continental Empire: Letters, Speeches and Papers,* ed. Walter LaFeber (Chicago: Quadrangle, 1965), pp. 44–45. See Walter A. McDougall, *Promised Land, Crusader State: The American Encounter with the World Since 1776* (Boston: Houghton Mifflin, 1997), pp. 39–75.
6. Adams address, 4 July 1821, LaFeber, ed., *Adams,* pp. 44–45. Gallatin to Adams, 15 September 1821, *The Writings of Albert Gallatin,* ed. Henry Adams, vol. 2 (Philadelphia: J. B. Lippincott, 1879), p. 198. 29 November 1821 entry, Adams, *Memoirs,* vol. 5, pp. 430–31.
7. Jefferson to Everett, 2 March 1822, *The Writings of Thomas Jefferson,* ed. H. A. Washington, vol. 7 (New York: Riker, Thorne, 1854), pp. 232–33. Wills, *Lincoln at Gettysburg,* pp. 41–62.
8. Douglas Dakin, *British and American Philhellenes During the War of Greek Independence, 1821–1833* (Thessaloniki: Institute for Balkan Studies, 1955), pp. 1–4. Wills, *Lincoln at Gettysburg,* p. 43.
9. *Address of the Committee Appointed at a Public Meeting Held in Boston, December 19, 1823, for the Relief of the Greeks, to Their Fellow Citizens* (Boston: North American Review, 1823), p. 8. William Cullen Bryant, "The Massacre at Scio," *Poetical Works* (London: Routledge and Sons, 1891), pp. 38–39. Daniel Webster, "The Revolution in Greece," 19 January 1824, *The Papers of Daniel Webster: Speeches and Formal Writings,* ed. Charles M. Wiltse, vol. 1 (Hanover, N.H.: University Press of New England, 1986), p. 107.
10. 16 November 1822 entry, Adams, *Memoirs,* vol. 6, p. 102. 27 November 1822 entry, ibid., p. 110.
11. Monroe sixth annual message, 3 December 1822, James D. Richardson, ed., *A Compilation of the Messages and Papers of the Presidents 1789–1907,* vol. 2 (Washington, D.C.: Bureau of National Literature and Art, 1908), pp. 193–94.
12. Jefferson to Gallatin, 2 August 1823, *Writings of Gallatin,* vol. 2, p. 273. Jefferson to Page, 20 August 1785, *The Papers of Thomas Jefferson,* ed. Julian P. Boyd, vol. 8 (Princeton, N.J.: Princeton University Press, 1953), p. 418. Jefferson to Wythe, 16 September 1787, *The Papers of Thomas Jefferson,* ed. Julian P. Boyd, vol. 12 (Princeton, N.J.: Princeton University Press, 1955), p. 128. See Jefferson to Thomson, 20 September 1787, ibid., p. 161.
13. Jefferson to Koraes, 31 October 1823, Library of Congress, manuscript division, at http://www.loc.gov/exhibits/jefferson/images/vc204p1.jpg. Also in *Writings of Jefferson,* vol. 7, pp. 318–24. See Monroe to Jefferson, 17 October 1823, *The Writings of James Monroe,* ed. Stanislaus Murray Hamilton, vol. 6 (New York: G. P. Putnam's Sons, 1902), pp. 324–25.
14. Madison to Monroe, 30 October 1823, *The Writings of James Madison* ed. Gaillard Hunt, vol. 9 (New York: G. P. Putnam's Sons, 1910), p. 159. Madison to Jefferson, 1 November 1823, Madison, *Writings,* vol. 9, p. 157.
15. Edward Everett essay, *North American Review,* vol. 7, no. 4 (October 1823), pp. 399–404, 412–13.
16. 15 August 1823 entry, Adams, *Memoirs,* vol. 6, pp. 172–73. Lafayette to Clay, 5 November 1822, *The Works of Henry Clay, Comprising His Life, Correspondence*

and Speeches, ed. Calvin Colton, vol. 4 (New York: G. P. Putnam's Sons, 1904), pp. 132–33.

17. Jefferson to Gallatin, 29 October 1822, *Writings of Gallatin,* vol. 2, p. 258. Gallatin to Ruggles, 16 May 1824, ibid., p. 288. May, *Monroe Doctrine,* p. 48. 15 August 1823 entry, Adams, *Memoirs,* vol. 6, pp. 172–73.
18. 29 June 1823 entry, Adams, *Memoirs,* vol. 6, pp. 35–36. John C. Calhoun, *Union and Liberty: The Political Philosophy of John C. Calhoun,* ed. Ross M. Lence (Indianapolis, Ind.: Liberty Fund, 1992), p. 469. 15 August 1823 entry, Adams, *Memoirs,* vol. 6, p. 173.
19. 15 November 1823 entry, Adams, *Memoirs,* vol. 6, p. 186. 21 November 1823 entry, ibid., p. 194. See Adams to Rush, 16 August 1823, Monroe, *Writings,* vol. 6, p. 361.
20. May, *Monroe Doctrine,* p. 189. 21 November 1823 entry, Adams, *Memoirs,* vol. 6, pp. 194–95.
21. 22 November 1823 entry, Adams, *Memoirs,* vol. 6, pp. 196–98.
22. 24 November 1823 entry, ibid., pp. 198–99. See 26 November 1823 entry, ibid., p. 204.
23. Monroe address, 2 December 1823, Richardson, ed., *Messages and Papers of the Presidents,* vol. 2, pp. 210, 217–18.
24. Earle, "American Interest," pp. 49–50, 53.
25. *Address of the Committee appointed at a Public Meeting Held in Boston, December 19, 1823, for the Relief of the Greeks, To Their Fellow Citizens* (Boston: North American Review, 1823), pp. 9, 15–18.
26. 4 January 1824 entry, Adams, *Memoirs,* vol. 6, p. 227.
27. 27 January 1824 entry, ibid., p. 240. May, *Monroe Doctrine,* pp. 229–32.
28. 4 January 1824 entry, Adams, *Memoirs,* vol. 6, p. 227. 9 January 1824 entry, ibid., p. 230. 17 January 1824 entry, ibid., p. 233.
29. Webster, "The Revolution in Greece," 19 January 1824, *Papers of Webster,* vol. 1, pp. 100, 89, 96, 98. McDougall, *Promised Land,* pp. 74–75. *The Works of Henry Clay, Comprising His Life, Correspondence and Speeches,* ed. Calvin Colton, vol. 6 (New York: G. P. Putnam's Sons, 1904), pp. 245–53. May, *Monroe Doctrine,* pp. 236–40; McDougall, *Promised Land,* pp. 74–75; Edward Mead Earle, "Early American Policy Concerning Ottoman Minorities," *Political Science Quarterly,* vol. 42, no. 3 (September 1927), pp. 356–61. Ichabod Bartlett was the son of Josiah Bartlett, namesake for television's president on *The West Wing,* who sends troops to stop a genocide in a fictional African country and announces a doctrine of humanitarian intervention.
30. Earle, "Early American Policy," p. 349.
31. Solomon Drown, *An Oration Delivered in the First Baptist Meeting-House in Providence, at the Celebration, February 23, A.D. 1824, in Commemoration of the Birth-Day of Washington and in Aid of the Cause of the Greeks* (Providence, R.I.: Brown and Danforth, 1824).
32. Bryant, "To a Cloud," *Poetical Works,* pp. 69–70. Fitz–Green Halleck, "Marco Bozzaris," in Thomas R. Lounsbury, ed., *Yale Book of American Verse* (New Haven, Conn.: Yale University Press, 1912), pp. 10–12.
33. Earle, "American Interest," p. 51.

34. *Letters and Journals of Samuel Gridley Howe: The Greek Revolution* ed. Laura E. Richards (Boston: Estes, 1909), pp. 26, 57.
35. Clinton speech, 4 January 1825, in State of New York, *Messages from the Governors,* vol. 3 (Albany, N.Y.: J. E. Lyon, 1909), pp. 59, 53.
36. 10 May 1824 entry, Adams, *Memoirs,* vol. 6, pp. 324–25.

LORD BYRON'S WAR

1. Fiona MacCarthy, *Byron: Life and Legend* (New York: Farrar, Straus and Giroux, 2002), pp. 263–80.
2. Byron journal, 30 January 1821, Leslie A. Marchand, ed., *"Born for Opposition": Byron's Letters and Journals,* vol. 8 (London: John Murray, 1978), p. 40. Byron journal, 16 February 1821, ibid., p. 45. Byron journal, 18 February 1821, ibid., p. 47. Byron journal, 9 January 1821, ibid., p. 20. Byron journal, 13 January 1821, ibid., p. 26. Byron to Kinnaird, 9 March 1821, ibid., p. 91; Byron to Moore, 28 April 1821, ibid., p. 104. Byron to Kinnaird, 23 March 1821, ibid., p. 96.
3. Byron to Hobhouse, 26 April 1821, ibid., pp. 99–100. Byron journal, 18 February 1821, ibid., p. 47. Byron to Moore, 28 April 1821, ibid., p. 105. Byron to Teresa Guiccioli, 26 July 1821 and 29 July 1821, ibid., pp. 158–61. Byron to Moore, 28 April 1821, ibid., pp. 104–5.
4. Harold Nicolson, *Byron: The Last Journey* (Boston: Houghton Mifflin, 1924), p. 69. John Bowring, *Autobiographical Recollections* (London: Henry S. King, 1877), pp. 344–45; Fiona MacCarthy, *Byron: Life and Legend* (New York: Farrar, Straus and Giroux, 2002), pp. 452–53.
5. Edward Blaquiere, *Narrative of a Second Visit to Greece, Including, Facts Connected with the Last Days of Lord Byron, Extracts from the Correspondence, Official Documents, &c.* (London: G. B. Whittaker, 1825), pp. 3–4; Thomas Gordon, *History of the Greek Revolution, and of the Wars and Campaigns Arising from the Struggles of the Greek Patriots in Emancipating Their Country from the Turkish Yoke,* vol. 2 (Edinburgh: William Blackwood, 1844), pp. 79–80. Bentham to Orlandos and Luriottis, 12 March 1824, Catherine Fuller, ed., *The Collected Works of Jeremy Bentham: Correspondence,* vol. 11 (Oxford: Clarendon Press, 2000), pp. 370–74; Orlandos and Luriottis to Bentham, 13 March 1824, ibid., pp. 378–79; Bentham to Bowring, 14 March 1824, ibid., pp. 381–83; Bentham to Bowring ("J. Be to J. Bo"), 20 March 1824, ibid., pp. 403–7. Byron to Hobhouse, 7 April 1823, Leslie A. Marchand, ed., *"A Heart for Every Fate": Byron's Letters and Journals,* vol. 10 (London: John Murray, 1980), pp. 142–43; Byron to Hobhouse, 17 April 1823, ibid., p. 151.
6. LGC vol. 3, K, minutes, 10 May 1823. Byron to Trelawny, 15 June 1823, *Byron's Letters and Journals,* vol. 10, p. 199.
7. Byron journal, 28 September 1823, Leslie A. Marchand, ed., *"For Freedom's Battle": Byron's Letters and Journals,* vol. 11 (London: John Murray, 1981), p. 29; Byron to Bowring, 7 July 1823, *Byron's Letters and Journals,* vol. 10, p. 210. Byron to Goethe, 24 July 1823, Thomas Moore, ed., *Letters and Journals of Lord Byron: With Notices of His Life,* vol. 2 (New York: Harper and Brothers, 1855), p. 462. Byron to Bowring, 12 May 1823, *Byron's Letters and Journals,* vol. 10, p. 169. C. M.

Woodhouse, *The Philhellenes* (London: Hodder and Stoughton, 1969), pp. 98–102; MacCarthy, *Byron,* p. 446.

8. Byron journal, 19 June 1823, *Byron's Letters and Journals,* vol. 11, p. 29. Byron to Barry, 10 August 1823, ibid., p. 16; Byron journal, 28 September 1823, ibid., p. 29. Byron to Hobhouse, 11 September 1823, ibid., p. 22. Byron to Napier, 9 September 1823, ibid., p. 20. Byron to Leigh, 12 October 1823, ibid., pp. 43–44.
9. LGC vol. 5, E, Mavrokordatos to Byron, 15 August 1823; LGC vol. 5, D, Luriottis to Byron, 15 August 1823. LGC vol. 4, G3, Hobhouse to Bowring, 30 November 1823. See Byron to Hobhouse, 11 September 1823, *Byron's Letters and Journals,* vol. 11, p. 23; Byron to Hobhouse, 15 September 1823, ibid., p. 26.
10. Douglas Dakin, *The Greek Struggle for Independence, 1821–1833* (Berkeley: University of California Press, 1973), p. 152. LGC vol. 4, G3, Hobhouse to Bowring, 30 November 1823. Byron to Bowring, 10 October 1823, Moore, ed., *Letters and Journals of Byron,* vol. 2, p. 475.
11. Bentham to Bowring, 20 March 1824, Catherine Fuller, ed., *The Collected Works of Jeremy Bentham: Correspondence,* vol. 11 (Oxford: Clarendon Press, 2000), p. 405. Byron journal, 28 September 1823, *Byron's Letters and Journals,* vol. 11, p. 33. Byron to Hobhouse, 11 September 1823, ibid., p. 24. LGC vol. 4, G3, Hobhouse to Bowring, 30 November 1823.
12. Byron to Leigh, 12 October 1823, *Byron's Letters and Journals,* vol. 11, p. 44. Byron to Hobhouse, 11 September 1823, ibid., pp. 22–23. Dakin, *Greek Struggle,* pp. 82–88. *Byron's Letters and Journals,* vol. 11, p. 215. Bentham to Mavrokordatos, 6 March 1824, *Collected Works of Bentham: Correspondence,* vol. 11, p. 356. See Bentham to Stanhope, 19 February 1824, ibid., pp. 387–97. Gordon, *History of the Greek Revolution,* vol. 2, p. 80. LGC vol. 4, E1, Stanhope to Bowring, 18 October 1823. Byron to Hobhouse, 6 October 1823, *Byron's Letters and Journals,* vol. 11, p. 40.
13. Byron to Hobhouse, 27 September 1823, *Byron's Letters and Journals,* vol. 11, p. 27. Byron journal, 28 September 1823, ibid., p. 32. LGC vol. 4, Y, Byron to Mavrokordatos, 7 October 1823.
14. LGC vol. 4, L4, Hobhouse to Bowring, 23 December 1823. See Byron to Barry, 25 October 1823, *Byron's Letters and Journals,* vol. 11, pp. 53–54.
15. Moore, ed., *Letters and Journals of Byron,* vol. 2, p. 480. Byron to Greek government, 30 November 1823, *Byron's Letters and Journals,* vol. 11, pp. 69–70.
16. LGC vol. 4, L4, Hobhouse to Bowring, 23 December 1823. See Byron to Hobhouse, 6 October 1823, *Byron's Letters and Journals,* vol. 11, p. 40.
17. LGC vol. 4, L4, Hobhouse to Bowring, 23 December 1823. LGC vol. 5, A, Byron note on Hastings report, 20 October 1823. Byron to Bowring, 26 October 1823, Moore, ed., *Letters and Journals of Byron,* vol. 2, p. 479. Byron journal, 17 October 1823, *Byron's Letters and Journals,* vol. 11, p. 34.
18. LGC vol. 4, G3, Hobhouse to Bowring, 30 November 1823. Byron to Hobhouse, 27 September 1823, *Byron's Letters and Journals,* vol. 11, p. 28. LGC vol. 4, G3, Hobhouse to Bowring, 30 November 1823. See Byron to Knox, 26 August 1823, *Byron's Letters and Journals,* vol. 11, p. 19; E. J. Trelawny, *Recollections of the Last Days of Shelley and Byron* (London: Edward Moxon, 1858), pp. 211, 202, 219. LGC

vol. 6, B, contract, 13 November 1823. *Byron's Letters and Journals,* vol. 11, pp. 215–16.

19. LGC vol. 5, C, Tricoupis to Byron, 15 August 1823. LGC vol. 5, I, Trelawny to Byron, 14 September 1823. Byron to Bowring, 26 December 1823, *Byron's Letters and Journals,* vol. 11, p. 83.
20. Byron to Kinnaird, 23 December 1823, *Byron's Letters and Journals,* vol. 11, p. 80. Byron to Moore, 27 December 1823, ibid., pp. 84–85. Moore, ed., *Letters and Journals of Byron,* vol. 2, p. 478. Byron to Moore, 27 December 1823, *Byron's Letters and Journals,* vol. 11, pp. 84–85. Byron to Hobhouse, 27 December 1823, ibid., p. 85. Byron to Kinnaird, 27 December 1823, ibid., p. 86.
21. Byron to Kinnaird, 21 February 1824, *Byron's Letters and Journals,* vol. 11, p. 116. Byron to Muir, 2 January 1824, ibid., p. 87. Byron to Osborne, 7 January 1824, ibid., p. 91. MacCarthy, *Byron,* p. 490.
22. Byron to Bowring, 28 January 1824, *Byron's Letters and Journals,* vol. 11, p. 102. Byron to Hancock, 5 February 1824, ibid., p. 107. LGC vol. 8, E1, Gill, and Hodges to Stanhope (?), 25 April 1824.
23. Byron to Yusuf, 23 January 1824, *Byron's Letters and Journals,* vol. 11, pp. 98–99. George Finlay, *History of the Greek Revolution,* vol. 1 (Edinburgh: William Blackwood and Sons, 1861), p. 201. Byron to Mayer, n.d., *Byron's Letters and Journals,* vol. 11, p. 118. Byron to Murray, 25 February 1824, ibid., p. 124.
24. LGC vol. 5, E1, Stanhope to Bowring, 8 December 1823. LGC vol. 3, M2, Barker to Bowring, 25 September 1823. Stanhope to Bentham, 1 December 1823, *Collected Works of Bentham: Correspondence,* vol. 11, p. 327. Byron to Bowring, 26 December 1823, *Byron's Letters and Journals,* vol. 11, p. 83.
25. Bowring, *Autobiographical Recollections,* p. 285. Gordon, *History of the Greek Revolution,* vol. 2, p. 108.
26. Blaquiere, *Narrative,* pp. 50, 113.
27. Byron to Bowring, 28 January 1824, *Byron's Letters and Journals,* vol. 11, p. 102. Byron to Hancock, 10 March 1824, ibid., p. 134. Byron to Barff, 19 March 1824, ibid., p. 139.
28. Byron and Stanhope to Mavrokordatos, 5 February 1824, *Byron's Letters and Journals,* vol. 11, p. 105. Byron to Hancock, 7 February 1824, ibid., p. 108; Byron order, 17 February 1824, ibid., p. 115. Byron to Hancock, 5 February 1824, ibid., p. 107. Byron to Barff, 7 April 1824, ibid., p. 152. Byron to Kinnaird, 23 December 1823, ibid., p. 80. Byron to Hancock, 7 February 1824, ibid., p. 108.
29. Byron, "On This Day I Complete My Thirty-Sixth Year," in Leslie A. Marchand, ed., *Selected Poetry of Lord Byron* (New York: Modern Library, 2001), pp. 237–38. Byron journal, 15 February 1824, *Byron's Letters and Journals,* vol. 11, p. 113. Byron to Murray, 25 February 1824, ibid., p. 123. Byron to Londos, 24 February 1824, ibid., pp. 122–23; Byron to Barff, 22 March 1824, ibid., p. 141; Byron to Kinnaird, 30 March 1824, ibid., p. 145; Blaquiere, *Narrative,* part 2, p. 11. Byron note, 15 February 1824, *Byron's Letters and Journals,* vol. 11, p. 112.
30. Byron, "Last Words on Greece," *Selected Poetry,* p. 236.
31. Byron to Barff, 22 March 1824, *Byron's Letters and Journals,* vol. 11, pp. 140–41.

Byron to Bowring, 19 March 1824, ibid., p. 139. Byron to Barff, 26 March 1824, ibid., pp. 141–42. Byron to Kinnaird, 30 March 1824, ibid., p. 145.

32. Byron to Bowring, 30 March 1824, *Byron's Letters and Journals,* vol. 11, p. 147. Byron to Barff, 9 April 1824, ibid., p. 153.
33. LGC vol. 8, L, Stanhope to Murdoch, 18 April 1824. Blaquiere, *Narrative,* part 2, pp. 18–21. Gamba to Hobhouse, 20 April 1824, Doris Langley Moore, *The Late Lord Byron* (London: John Murray, 1961), pp. 10–11; MacCarthy, *Byron,* pp. 512–18.
34. LGC vol. 8, K, Meyer to Stanhope, n.d. LGC vol. 8, B1, Stanhope to Bowring, 30 April 1824.
35. Finlay, *History of the Greek Revolution,* vol. 2, p. 22; Woodhouse, *Philhellenes,* pp. 117–18; C. M. Woodhouse, *The Battle of Navarino* (London: Hodder and Stoughton, 1965), p. 24. T. J. Binyon, *Pushkin: A Biography* (New York: Alfred A. Knopf, 2003), p. 182. *My Past and Thoughts: The Memoirs of Alexander Herzen,* trans. Constance Garrett (London: Chatto and Windus, 1974), p. 389. Victor Hugo, "Les Têtes du Sérail," *Les Orientales,* vol. 1 (Paris: Librairie Marcel Didier, 1952), IV:129, p. 69. MacCarthy, *Byron,* pp. 530–31, 545. Moore, *Late Lord Byron,* p. 12.

CANNING

1. LGC vol. 8, R, Blaquiere to Stanhope, 26 April 1824. LGC vol. 8, Y, Blaquiere to Bowring and Murdorch, 29 April 1824. LGC vol. 8, Y, Blaquiere to Bowring and Murdorch, 29 April 1824.
2. LGC vol. 8, E1, Gill, and Hodges to Stanhope (?), 25 April 1824.
3. Tricoupis funeral oration, in Edward Blaquiere, *Narrative of a Second Visit to Greece, Including, Facts Connected with the Last Days of Lord Byron, Extracts from the Correspondence, Official Documents, &c.* (London: G. B. Whittaker, 1825), pp. 32–33. Blaquiere, *Narrative,* part 2, pp. 22–23. Douglas Dakin, *The Greek Struggle for Independence, 1821–1833* (Berkeley: University of California Press, 1973), p. 124; Blaquiere, *Narrative,* pp. 31–34. Bentham to Bolívar, 13 August 1825, Catherine Fuller, ed., *The Collected Works of Jeremy Bentham: Correspondence*, vol. 12 (Oxford: Clarendon Press, 2000), p. 143. LGC vol. 8, F1, Trelawny to Stanhope, 28 April 1824.
4. Blaquiere to Bentham, 27 June 1825, *Collected Works of Bentham: Correspondence,* vol. 12, p. 130. Bentham to Bolívar, 13 August 1825, ibid., p. 143. Bentham to Mexican legislature, 21 July–1 August 1826, ibid., pp. 231–35; Bentham to Arce, 9 November 1826, ibid., pp. 257–60.
5. James Emerson, "Greece in 1825," *Morning Chronicle,* 12 December 1825, p. 3. LGC vol. 8, Barker to Bowring, 7 May 1824. Blaquiere, *Narrative,* p. xiv; F. Rosen, *Bentham, Byron and Greece: Constitutionalism, Nationalism, and Early Liberal Political Thought* (Oxford: Clarendon Press, 1992), pp. 103–22; C. M. Woodhouse, *The Philhellenes* (London: Hodder and Stoughton, 1969), pp. 125–26, 133. Leslie A. Marchand, ed., *"For Freedom's Battle": Byron's Letters and Journals,* vol. 11 (London: John Murray, 1981), p. 146. "Misapplication of the Greek Loan," *Morning Chronicle,* 13 December 1825, p. 1. Byron to Hobhouse, 27 September 1823, *Byron's Letters and Journals,* vol. 11, p. 28. Byron to Kinnaird, 29 October 1823, ibid., p. 58. Finlay, *History of the Greek Revolution,* vol. 2, p. 26.

6. Thomas Gordon, *History of the Greek Revolution, and of the Wars and Campaigns Arising from the Struggles of the Greek Patriots in Emancipating Their Country from the Turkish Yoke,* vol. 2 (Edinburgh: William Blackwood, 1844), p. 275.
7. Madison to Lafayette, November 1826, *The Writings of James Madison,* ed. Gaillard Hunt, vol. 9 (New York: G. P. Putnam's Sons, 1910), p. 264. Edward Mead Earle, "American Interest in the Greek Cause, 1821–1827," *American Historical Review,* vol. 33, no. 1 (October 1927), pp. 57–58.
8. Liverpool to Canning, 18 October 1824, Arthur Wellesley, Duke of Wellington, *Despatches, Correspondence, and Memoranda of Field Marshal Arthur, Duke of Wellington,* vol. 2 (London: John Murray, 1867), p. 327. Byron, *Don Juan,* canto IX, in Leslie A. Marchand, ed., *Selected Poetry of Lord Byron* (New York: Modern Library, 2001), pp. 476–77.
9. Canning to Wellington, 27 September 1822, Wellington, *Despatches,* vol. 2, pp. 370–72.
10. FO 881/165, Canning conference with Greek deputies, 29 September 1825. Canning to Stratford Canning, 12 October 1825, Wellington, *Despatches,* vol. 2, pp. 533–34.
11. Blaquiere, *Narrative,* p. 147. LGC vol. 1, Barker, *Political Subscription for the Greeks,* 23 March 1823.
12. Dakin, *Greek Struggle,* pp. 110–11. John Bowring, *Autobiographical Recollections* (London: Henry S. King, 1877), pp. 281–87.
13. *Some Official Correspondence of George Canning* (London: Longmans, Green, 1887), Edward J. Stapleton, ed., vol. 1, pp. 150, 179; Wellington to Nesselrode, 7 March 1826, Wellington, *Despatches,* vol. 3, p. 157. Liverpool to Canning, 2 November 1824, ibid., vol. 2, p. 329.
14. Wellington to Canning, 10 November 1824, Wellington, *Despatches,* vol. 2, p. 338. Wellington to Canning, 16 December 1824, ibid., p. 367.
15. Canning, *Correspondence,* vol. 1, p. 198. Canning to Wellington, 10 February 1824, Wellington, *Despatches,* vol. 2, p. 205. Wellington to Canning, 10 November 1824, ibid., p. 338. Liverpool to Canning, 2 November 1824, ibid., p. 329. Canning to Liverpool, 5 November 1824, ibid., p. 331. See Wendy Hinde, *George Canning* (London: Collins, 1973), pp. 387–89.
16. Canning to Granville, 17 January 1825, Canning, *Correspondence,* vol. 1, p. 234. Wellington to Nesselrode, 7 March 1826, Wellington, *Despatches,* vol. 3, p. 158.
17. Canning to Liverpool, 21 November 1824, Canning, *Correspondence,* vol. 1, p. 203.

THE HOLY ALLIANCE

1. Percy Shelley, preface, "Hellas," in *The Complete Poems of Percy Bysshe Shelley* (New York: Modern Library, 1994), p. 502. See Donald H. Reiman, ed., *The Bodleian Shelley Manuscripts* (New York: Garland, 1986), vol. 16.
2. Metternich notes, 5 and 10 August 1825, Klemens von Metternich, *Mémoires, documents et écrits divers: L'Ère de paix, 1816–1848,* vol. 4 (Paris: Plon, 1881), pp. 192, 193–95; Metternich to Lebzeltern, 28 January 1822, ibid., vol. 3, p. 565.

See Klemens von Metternich, *Memoirs of Prince Metternich,* vol. 3, ed. Prince Richard Metternich, trans. Mrs. Alexander Napier (New York: Charles Scribner's Sons, 1881), pp. 456–76. Metternich to Lebzeltern, 28 January 1822, Klemens von Metternich, *Mémoires, documents et écrits divers: L'Ère de paix, 1816–1848,* vol. 3 (Paris: Plon, 1881), pp. 566, 571; Metternich to Ottenfels, 21 June 1823, ibid., vol. 4, pp. 69–77. Metternich to Aleksandr I, 19 April 1822, ibid., vol. 3, pp. 578–79. Metternich to Lützow, 3 June 1822, ibid., p. 594. Canning to Wellesley, 27 September 1825, Arthur Wellesley, Duke of Wellington, *Despatches, Correspondence, and Memoranda of Field Marshal Arthur, Duke of Wellington,* vol. 2 (London: John Murray, 1867), p. 505. Canning to Wellesley, 27 September 1825, ibid.

3. Metternich to Esterhazy, 17 October 1824, Metternich, *Mémoires,* vol. 4, p. 133. Metternich to Lützow, 3 June 1822, ibid., vol. 3, p. 591. Stella Ghervas, "Le philhellénisme d'inspiration conservatrice en Europe et en Russie," in Elena Siupiur et al., eds., *Peuples, états et nations dans le sud-est de l'Europe* (Bucharest: Editura Anima, 2004), pp. 109–10. Metternich to Lützow, 3 June 1822, ibid., p. 591. Metternich to Esterhazy, 17 October 1824 (second dispatch), ibid., vol. 4, p. 137.
4. Metternich note, 1 May 1823, *Mémoires,* vol. 4, p. 8. Metternich note, 18 July 1823, ibid., p. 11. Metternich to Esterhazy, 17 October 1824, ibid., pp. 132–33. Metternich to Gentz, 9 September 1825, ibid., p. 230.
5. Byron journal, 9 January 1821, Leslie A. Marchand, ed., *"Born for Opposition": Byron's Letters and Journals,* vol. 8 (London: John Murray, 1978), p. 20. Byron journal, 11 January 1821, ibid., p. 21. Byron to Kinnaird, 29 October 1823, Leslie A. Marchand, ed., *"For Freedom's Battle": Byron's Letters and Journals,* vol. 11 (London: John Murray, 1981), p. 58. Bentham to Greeks, 24 November 1823, Catherine Fuller, ed., *The Collected Works of Jeremy Bentham: Correspondence,* vol. 11 (Oxford: Clarendon Press, 2000), p. 322. LGC vol. 5, Q2, Barker to Bowring, 1 February 1824. See Thomas Gordon, *History of the Greek Revolution, and of the Wars and Campaigns Arising from the Struggles of the Greek Patriots in Emancipating Their Country from the Turkish Yoke,* vol. 1 (Edinburgh: William Blackwood, 1844), p. 315; Stanhope to Bentham, 24 September 1823, *Collected Works of Bentham: Correspondence,* vol. 11, p. 299. Byron, "The Age of Bronze," in *Complete Poetical Works of Lord Byron,* ed. Paul Elmer More (Boston: Houghton Mifflin, 1905), p. 307.
6. Metternich to Ottenfels, 6 January 1825, Metternich, *Mémoires,* vol. 4, pp. 206–7. Wellington to Canning, 13 January 1825, Wellington, *Despatches,* vol. 2, p. 397. Canning to Stratford Canning, 12 October 1825, ibid., p. 531. Metternich to Lebzeltern, 15 January 1825, Metternich, *Mémoires,* vol. 4, p. 207.
7. Metternich note, 30 January 1825, Metternich, *Mémoires,* vol. 4, p. 150. Austrian note, 4 March 1825, Canning, *Correspondence,* vol. 1, pp. 254–55. Metternich notes, 14 and 29 March 1825, Metternich, *Mémoires,* vol. 4, p. 151. Metternich note, 2 April 1825, ibid., pp. 154–55. Metternich note, 29 March 1825, ibid., p. 152.
8. Metternich note, 11 April 1825, Metternich, *Mémoires,* vol. 4, p. 157. Metternich, *Mémoires,* vol. 4, p. 184. Metternich note, 13 July 1825, ibid., pp. 185–88. Canning to Wellington, 4 June 1825, Wellington, *Despatches,* vol. 2, p. 459; Strangford memorandum, 25 May 1825, ibid., pp. 455–57; Strangford memorandum, 4 June

1825, ibid., pp. 459–61; Strangford to Canning, 3 September 1825, ibid., p. 482.

9. Metternich to Esterhazy, 7 August 1825, Metternich, *Mémoires,* vol. 4, pp. 224–25. Metternich note, 11 September 1825, ibid., p. 234.
10. Canning to Granville, 13 August 1825, Canning, *Correspondence,* vol. 1, pp. 284–85. Canning to Wellesley, 27 September 1825, Wellington, *Despatches,* vol. 2, p. 504; Canning to Wellesley, 3 October 1825, Wellington, ibid., p. 512.
11. Canning to Wellesley, 27 September 1825, Wellington, *Despatches,* vol. 2, pp. 504–5. C. M. Woodhouse, *The Philhellenes* (London: Hodder and Stoughton, 1969), pp. 132–38. Canning to Wellesley, 27 September 1825, Wellington, *Despatches,* vol. 2, p. 506.
12. FO 881/165, Canning conference with Greek deputies, 29 September 1825. See Wellington, *Despatches,* vol. 2, pp. 507–11; Douglas Dakin, *The Greek Struggle for Independence, 1821–1833* (Berkeley: University of California Press, 1973), pp. 158–59, 168–72.
13. FO 881/165, Canning to Stratford Canning, 12 October 1825. 20 July 1824 entry, *Memoirs of John Quincy Adams, Comprising Portions of His Diary from 1795 to 1848,* ed. Charles Francis Adams, vol. 6 (Philadelphia: J. B. Lippincott, 1875), pp. 400–401; 27 August 1825 entry, *Memoirs of John Quincy Adams, Comprising Portions of His Diary from 1795 to 1848,* ed. Charles Francis Adams, vol. 7 (Philadelphia: J.B. Lippincott & Co., 1875), pp. 48–49; Edward Mead Earle, "Early American Policy Concerning Ottoman Minorities," *Political Science Quarterly,* vol. 42, no. 3 (September 1927), pp. 362–64.
14. Dakin, *Greek Struggle,* pp. 176–77. Canning to Stratford Canning, 12 October 1825, Wellington, *Despatches,* vol. 2, pp. 530–35.
15. Wellington to Canning, 22 November 1825, Wellington, *Despatches,* vol. 2, pp. 570–71. Dakin, *Greek Struggle,* p. 228.

A RUMOR OF SLAUGHTER

1. H. J. Codrington to Jane Codrington, 25 September 1827, *Memoir of the Life of Admiral Sir Edward Codrington,* ed. Jane Codrington, Lady Bourchier, vol. 2 (London: Longmans, Green, 1873), p. 15.
2. Douglas Dakin, *The Greek Struggle for Independence, 1821–1833* (Berkeley: University of California Press, 1973), pp. 121–22; George Finlay, *History of the Greek Revolution,* vol. 2 (Edinburgh: William Blackwood and Sons, 1861), pp. 28–29, 45–53, 81, 158. Stratford Canning to Canning, 16 December 1825, Arthur Wellesley, Duke of Wellington, *Despatches, Correspondence, and Memoranda of Field Marshal Arthur, Duke of Wellington,* vol. 2 (London: John Murray, 1867), pp. 580–83; Dakin, *Greek Struggle,* pp. 134–35. Stratford Canning to Canning, 10 January 1826, enclosure to Canning to Wellington, 17 February 1826, Wellington, *Despatches,* vol. 3, pp. 121–24. See Mavrokordatos to Hamilton, 14 December 1826, ibid., pp. 126–27; Canning to Wellington, 17 February 1826, ibid., p. 125.
3. Metternich note, 16 June 1825, Klemens von Metternich, *Mémoires, documents et écrits divers: L'Ère de paix, 1816–1848,* vol. 4 (Paris: Plon, 1881), p. 177. Metternich note, 5 August 1825, ibid., p. 191. Canning to Stratford Canning, 12 October 1825,

Wellington, *Despatches,* vol. 2, pp. 532–33; Stratford Canning to Canning, 16 December 1825, ibid., p. 581. Metternich to Ottenfels, 19 October 1827, Metternich, *Mémoires,* vol. 4, p. 396.

4. FO 881/165, Canning memorandum on Lieven, 25 October 1825.
5. C. M. Woodhouse, *The Philhellenes* (London: Hodder and Stoughton, 1969), pp. 124–25. Augustus Granville Stapleton, *Intervention and Non-Intervention: Or, The Foreign Policy of Great Britain from 1790 to 1865* (London: John Murray, 1866), p. 32. See Ellery C. Stowell, *Intervention in International Law* (Washington, D.C.: John Byrne, 1921), p. 127.
6. Canning to Liverpool, 25 October 1825, *Some Official Correspondence of George Canning* (London: Longmans, Green, 1887), Edward J. Stapleton, ed., vol. 1, p. 317. Canning to Granville, 31 October 1825, ibid., p. 318.
7. Canning to Cockburn, November 1825, Canning, *Correspondence,* vol. 1, p. 321.
8. FO 881/165, Stratford Canning to Canning, 16 December 1825.
9. Canning to Wellington, 10 February 1826, Wellington, *Despatches,* vol. 3, pp. 85–93.
10. Metternich note, 22 December 1825, Metternich, *Mémoires,* vol. 4, p. 205. George IV to Wellington, 27 December 1825, Wellington, *Despatches,* vol. 3, p. 53; Canning to Wellington, 31 December 1825, ibid., p. 55; George IV to Nikolai I, 6 February 1826, ibid., pp. 83–84.
11. Wellington to Canning, 26 January 1826, Wellington, *Despatches,* vol. 3, p. 75. Wellington memorandum, 29 January 1826, ibid., pp. 78–79. Wellington to Canning, 30 January 1826, ibid., p. 77.
12. Canning to Wellington, 10 February 1826, Wellington, *Despatches,* vol. 3, p. 92.
13. Canning to Wellington, 17 February 1826, ibid., p. 125. Canning to Stratford Canning, 10 February 1826, ibid., pp. 105–6.
14. Bathurst to admiralty, 8 February 1826, Wellington, *Despatches,* vol. 3, p. 83. See Bathurst to Wellington, 17 February 1826, ibid., p. 119.
15. Spencer to Neale, 18 March 1826, Wellington, *Despatches,* vol. 3, pp. 285–88. Canning to Granville, 25 April 1826, Canning, *Correspondence,* vol. 2, p. 34.
16. Spencer to Neale, 19 March 1826, Wellington, *Despatches,* vol. 3, pp. 288–89. Salt to Stratford Canning, 14 November 1825, Wellington, *Despatches,* vol. 3, pp. 124–25. Auguste Fabre, *Histoire du siège de Missolonghi* (Paris: Moutardier, 1827); Finlay, *History of the Greek Revolution,* vol. 2, pp. 83–111. Hugo, "Les Têtes du Sérail," *Occidentales,* II:30, p. 63.
17. Wellington to Canning, 26 January 1826, Wellington, *Despatches,* vol. 3, p. 75. Wellington to Bathurst, 17 February 1826, ibid., pp. 113–15. Wellington to Nesselrode, 7 March 1826, ibid., p. 159. Wellington to Canning, 11 March 1826, ibid., p. 182.
18. Benita Eisler, *Byron: Child of Passion, Fool of Fame* (New York: Alfred A. Knopf, 1999), p. 753.
19. Richard Pipes, *Russia Under the Old Regime* (London: Penguin, 1995), pp. 290–93; James H. Billington, *The Icon and the Axe: An Interpretive History of Russian Culture* (New York: Vintage, 1970), pp. 264–70; Hans Kohn, *Pan-Slavism: Its History and Ideology* (New York: Vintage, 1960), pp. 130–31. Binyon, *Pushkin,*

pp. 130–31, 216–222. Strangford to Bagot, 7 March 1826, Josceline Bagot, ed., *George Canning and His Friends: Containing Hitherto Unpublished Letters, Jeux d'Esprit, Etc.* (London: John Murray, 1909), vol. 2, p. 335.

20. Geoffrey Hosking, *Russia: People and Empire 1552–1917* (Cambridge, Mass.: Harvard University Press, 1997), pp. 144–47. Strangford to Bagot, 7 March 1826, Bagot, ed., *Canning and His Friends,* vol. 2, p. 335. Wellington to Canning, 5 March 1826, Wellington, *Despatches,* vol. 3, p. 149. Bathurst to Wellington, 10 April 1826, ibid., p. 282.
21. Wellington to Canning, 16 March 1826, Wellington, *Despatches,* vol. 3, p. 172. Nesselrode to Wellington, 25 March 1826, ibid., p. 237. Wellington to Canning, 16 March 1826, ibid., p. 191. Russian draft note, March 1826, ibid., pp. 233–36.
22. Metternich to Apponyi, 29 January 1827, Metternich, *Mémoires,* vol. 4, p. 349. Metternich note, 12 May 1826, ibid., pp. 281, 282.
23. Strangford to Bagot, 7 March 1826, Bagot, ed., *Canning and His Friends,* vol. 2, p. 335. Canning to Wellington, 11 April 1826, Wellington, *Despatches,* vol. 3, pp. 291–92. Canning to Granville, 4 April 1826, Canning, *Correspondence,* vol. 2, pp. 27–28. Canning to Wellington, 11 April 1826, Wellington, *Despatches,* vol. 3, p. 293.
24. British-Russian secret memorandum, 14 March 1826, Wellington, *Despatches,* vol. 3, pp. 243–44. Canning to Wellington, 11 April 1826, ibid., p. 290. Wendy Hinde, *George Canning* (London: Collins, 1973), pp. 404–5, 408–9; Dakin, *Greek Struggle,* pp. 178–80.
25. Stratford Canning to Canning, 16 March 1826, Wellington, *Despatches,* vol. 3, p. 198. Stratford Canning to Wellington, 6 April 1826, ibid., p. 274.
26. Canning to Granville, 25 April 1826, Canning, *Correspondence,* vol. 2, p. 34; Canning to Wellington, 11 April 1826, Wellington, *Despatches,* vol. 3, pp. 283–89. Canning to Granville, 4 May 1826, Canning, *Correspondence,* vol. 2, p. 49. Canning to Liverpool, 21 June 1826, ibid., p. 59. Ponsonby to Wellington, 15 June 1826, Wellington, *Despatches,* vol. 3, p. 338.
27. Wellington to Canning (draft reply), 3 August 1826, Wellington, *Despatches,* vol. 3, p. 362. Canning to Lieven, 29 August 1826, ibid., p. 393. Canning to Lieven, 4 September 1826, ibid., pp. 398–99.
28. Canning to Liverpool, 21 June 1826, Canning, *Correspondence,* vol. 2, p. 59. Canning to Wellington, 4 August 1826, Wellington, *Despatches,* vol. 3, p. 363. Canning to Stratford Canning (draft), August 1826, ibid., pp. 357–58.
29. Bathurst to Wellington, 5 September 1826, Wellington, *Despatches,* vol. 3, pp. 402–3. Canning to Wellington, 4 August 1826, ibid., p. 364. Canning to Lieven, 4 September 1826, ibid., pp. 398–400. Wellington to Bathurst, 7 September 1826, ibid., pp. 403–4.
30. Metternich note, 24 May 1826, Metternich, *Mémoires,* vol. 4, p. 283. Metternich to Esterhazy, 8 June 1826, ibid., pp. 314, 315. Metternich note, 24 May 1826, ibid., p. 283. Metternich note, 22 June 1826, ibid., p. 289.
31. Metternich to Neumann, 12 June 1826, Metternich, *Mémoires,* vol. 4, pp. 287–88.
32. Wellington to Bathurst, 7 September 1826, Wellington, *Despatches,* vol. 3, pp. 404–5. Stanford J. Shaw and Ezel Kural Shaw, *History of the Ottoman Empire*

and Modern Turkey, vol. 2 (Cambridge: Cambridge University Press, 1977), p. 29. This book, while informative on Ottoman domestic reform politics, sometimes plays down Ottoman atrocities. Lieven to Canning, 7 November 1826, Wellington, *Despatches,* vol. 3, p. 460. Wellington to Canning, 12 November 1826, ibid., p. 455. Canning to Granville, 14 November 1826, Canning, *Correspondence,* vol. 2, p. 160. Canning to Lieven, 20 November 1826, Wellington, *Despatches,* vol. 3, pp. 461–62.

33. Metternich to Bombelles, 24 December 1826, Metternich, *Mémoires,* vol. 4, p. 335. Metternich to Tatistscheff and Wellesley, 22 December 1826, ibid., p. 333. Metternich to Apponyi, 8 November 1826, ibid., p. 328. Metternich to Bombelles, 24 December 1826, ibid., p. 337.
34. Peel to Wellington, 17 February 1827, Wellington, *Despatches,* vol. 3, p. 596. Stapleton to Liverpool, 8 February 1827, Canning, *Correspondence,* vol. 2, p. 256. Stapleton to Liverpool, 12 February 1827, ibid., p. 265.
35. Canning to Wellington, 19 March 1827, Wellington, *Despatches,* vol. 3, pp. 609–10; Wellington to Canning, 20 March 1827, ibid., p. 610. Wellington to Canning, 26 March 1827, ibid., p. 612.
36. Peel to Canning, 17 April 1827, Wellington, *Despatches,* vol. 3, pp. 644–45. Wellington to Canning, 11 April 1827, ibid., p. 638. See George IV to Wellington, 13 April 1827, ibid., p. 631; Wellington memorandum, 13 April 1827, ibid., pp. 636–42. Fiona MacCarthy, *Byron: Life and Legend* (New York: Farrar, Straus and Giroux, 2002), p. 94. Wellington memorandum, 13 April 1827, Wellington, *Despatches,* vol. 3, p. 639. See Canning to Wellington, 5 May 1827, Arthur Wellesley, Duke of Wellington, *Despatches, Correspondence, and Memoranda of Field Marshal Arthur, Duke of Wellington, K.G.,* ed. by his son, the Duke of Wellington, vol. 4 (London: John Murray, 1871), pp. 16–20.
37. Finlay, *History of the Greek Revolution,* vol. 2, pp. 118–26, 147. Woodford to Wellington, 1 July 1827, Wellington, *Despatches,* vol. 4, p. 56. Thomas Gordon, *History of the Greek Revolution, and of the Wars and Campaigns Arising from the Struggles of the Greek Patriots in Emancipating Their Country from the Turkish Yoke,* vol. 2 (Edinburgh: William Blackwood, 1844), p. 391.
38. Metternich to Esterhazy, 25 March 1827, Metternich, *Mémoires,* vol. 4, pp. 359–62. In the end, in 1829, the Greek war ended with an Ottoman general amnesty (FO 421/3/26, Abstract of the Proceedings in the Greek Question, part V, p. 64). Metternich to Apponyi, 11 June 1827, ibid., pp. 373–77. Canning to Wellington, 19 March 1827, Wellington, *Despatches,* vol. 3, p. 610.
39. Nesselrode to Lieven, 6 April 1827, Wellington, *Despatches,* vol. 3, pp. 649–50. Nesselrode to Canning, 21 June 1827, Wellington, *Despatches,* vol. 4, pp. 44–47.
40. David Brewer, *The Greek War of Independence* (New York: Overlook, 2001), p. 317. Metternich note, 25 October 1824, Metternich, *Mémoires,* vol. 4, pp. 144–45. Jean Dimakis, *La Guerre d'indépendence grecque vue par la presse française* (Thessaloniki: Institute for Balkan Studies, 1968). Wellington to Bathurst, 17 February 1826, Wellington, *Despatches,* vol. 3, p. 114. French memorandum, 15 January 1826, ibid., p. 95.
41. Treaty of London, 6 July 1827, Wellington, *Despatches,* vol. 4, pp. 57–62. See

Dakin, *Greek Struggle,* pp. 182–83, 195; Hinde, *Canning,* pp. 455–57; Wellington to Capo d'Istria, 12 October 1827, Wellington, *Despatches,* vol. 4, pp. 136–38.

42. Capo d'Istria to Wellington, 21 September 1827, Wellington, *Despatches,* vol. 4, p. 127. Dakin, *Greek Struggle,* pp. 185–87, 200–206.
43. Augustus Granville Stapleton, *George Canning and His Times* (London: John W. Parker and Son, 1859), pp. 602–5. Brewer, *Greek War of Independence,* p. 321.
44. Metternich to Esterhazy, 19 August 1827, Metternich, *Mémoires,* vol. 4, p. 380. Codrington to Mavrokordatos, 10 September 1827, *Memoir of the Life of Admiral Sir Edward Codrington,* ed. Jane Codrington, Lady Bourchier, vol. 1 (London: Longmans, Green, 1873), p. 452.

NAVARINO

1. Anonymous ("a British seaman"), *Life on Board a Man-of-War; Including a Full Account of the Battle of Navarino* (Glasgow: Blackie, Fullarton, 1829), p. 133; C. M. Woodhouse, *The Battle of Navarino* (London: Hodder and Stoughton, 1965), pp. 28, 32. Codrington to Clarence, 17 September 1827, *Memoir of the Life of Admiral Sir Edward Codrington,* ed. Jane Codrington, Lady Bourchier, vol. 1 (London: Longmans, Green, 1873), p. 470. C. M. Woodhouse, *The Philhellenes* (London: Hodder and Stoughton, 1969), pp. 134–35. The *Asia* was by any standard a massive battleship, although not as intimidating as a full three-decker ship of the line. Frigates are the next smallest warship, with one or two decks; smaller still are corvettes, with a single deck; and finally small escort ships like sloops and brigs.
2. Codrington to Lady Codrington, 23 July 1827, Codrington, *Memoir,* vol. 1, p. 390.
3. Dudley to Codrington, 16 October 1827, ibid., p. 461. Codrington to Bethell, 28 July 1827, ibid., p. 395.
4. Codrington to Wollaston, 2 August 1827, ibid., p. 400. Codrington to Hamilton, 7 August 1827, ibid., p. 404. Codrington to Adam, 15 September 1827, ibid., p. 464.
5. Smyrna diary, 7 August 1827, Codrington, *Memoir,* vol. 1, p. 401; Codrington to Hamilton, 7 August 1827, Codrington, ibid., pp. 404–5. Codrington to Adam, 7 August 1827, ibid., p. 402. Instructions to the Admirals, 12 July 1827, Arthur Wellesley, Duke of Wellington, *Despatches, Correspondence, and Memoranda of Field Marshal Arthur, Duke of Wellington* (London: John Murray, 1867), vol. 4, p. 205. Italics removed. Codrington to Stratford Canning, 1 August 1827, Codrington, *Memoir,* vol. 1, p. 398. Codrington to Dudley, 10 and 11 August 1827, ibid., p. 411.
6. Codrington to Stratford Canning, 12 August 1827, Codrington, *Memoir,* vol. 1, p. 417.
7. Codrington to Lady Codrington, 25 August 1827, Codrington, *Memoir,* vol. 1, p. 434. Codrington to Lady Codrington, 16 August 1827, ibid., p. 422. Codrington to William Codrington, 24 August 1827, Codrington, *Memoir,* vol. 1, p. 431.
8. Codrington to Dudley, 3 September 1827, Codrington, *Memoir,* vol. 1, p. 440. Codrington to Lady Codrington, 28 August 1827, ibid., p. 439. Stratford Can-

ning to Codrington, 31 August 1827, ibid., p. 448. Stratford Canning to Codrington, 1 September 1827, ibid., p. 450. Codrington general order, 8 September 1827, ibid., p. 452. Wellington memorandum, May 1828, Wellington, *Despatches,* vol. 4, p. 413. The Allied fleet was to "hold out . . . every inducement to the Pacha of Egypt and to his son, to withdraw the Egyptian ships and land forces altogether from Greece."

9. Codrington to Admiralty, 12 September 1827, Codrington, *Memoir,* vol. 1, p. 458. See Codrington to Stratford Canning, 16 September 1827, ibid., pp. 466–67. The British at first saw four Egyptian ships of the line, but three seems to be the consensus number. Codrington to Dudley, 13 September 1827, ibid., p. 459. Codrington to Lady Codrington, 15 September 1827, ibid., p. 462. Codrington to Lady Codrington, 18 September 1827, ibid., p. 471.
10. Codrington to Turkish admiral, 19 September 1827, Codrington, *Memoir,* vol. 1, p. 471. Codrington to Stratford Canning, 16 September 1827, ibid., p. 468. Codrington to Lady Codrington, 21 September 1827, ibid., p. 476. Ibid., 472.
11. Metternich to Ottenfels, 3 October 1827, Klemens von Metternich, *Mémoires, documents et écrits divers: L'Ère de paix, 1816–1848,* vol. 4 (Paris: Plon, 1881), p. 388. Codrington to Austrian commander, 19 September 1827, Codrington, *Memoir,* vol. 1, pp. 472–73. Codrington to Dudley, 3 September 1827, ibid., p. 441. Codrington to Stratford Canning, 16 October 1827, *Memoir of the Life of Admiral Sir Edward Codrington,* ed. Jane Codrington, Lady Bourchier, vol. 2 (London: Longmans, Green, 1873), p. 52. Metternich to Esterhazy, 29 October 1827, Metternich, *Mémoires,* vol. 4, p. 399. Dudley to Codrington, 16 October 1827, Codrington, *Memoir,* vol. 1, p. 461.
12. Codrington to Ibrahim, 21 September 1827, Codrington, *Memoir,* vol. 1, p. 475; Codrington and de Rigny to Ibrahim, 22 September 1827, ibid., vol. 2, pp. 1–2. Navarino memorandum, 25 September 1827, ibid., pp. 5–7; H. J. Codrington to Jane Codrington, 25 September 1827, ibid., pp. 14–18.
13. Codrington to Lady Codrington, 26 September 1827, Codrington, *Memoir,* vol. 2, pp. 22–23. Codrington to Admiralty, 2 October 1827, ibid., pp. 30–32; H. J. Codrington to Lady Codrington, 4 October 1827, ibid., pp. 35–36. Codrington to Lady Codrington, 6 October 1827, ibid., p. 39.
14. H. J. Codrington to Lady Codrington, 18 October 1827, Codrington, *Memoir,* vol. 2, p. 43. Codrington to Stratford Canning, 26 September 1827, ibid., p. 22. Ibid., p. 63. Codrington to Lady Codrington, 15 October 1827, ibid., p. 53. One French ship of the line was damaged and unavailable, leaving three French, four Russian, and three British.
15. Codrington to Stratford Canning, 14 October 1827, Codrington, *Memoir,* vol. 2, p. 48. Dudley to Codrington, 5 November 1827, ibid., p. 53.
16. Codrington order, 16 October 1827, Codrington, *Memoir,* vol. 2, pp. 55–56. Codrington, Heiden, and de Rigny to Ibrahim, 17 October 1827, ibid., p. 56.
17. Hamilton to Codrington, 18 October 1827, Codrington, *Memoir,* vol. 2, p. 60. Cradock to Codrington, 18 October 1827, ibid., p. 57. Allied admirals' protocol, 18 October 1827, ibid., pp. 61–62.

18. Codrington, *Memoir,* vol. 2, p. 66. Codrington to Lady Codrington, 19 October 1827, Ibid., p. 70.
19. *Man-of-War,* pp. 129–31. Victor Hugo, "Navarin," *Les Orientales,* vol. 1 (Paris: Librairie Marcel Didier, 1952), III:82, p. 93. FO 78/162/142, Codrington to Croker, 21 October 1827.
20. Woodhouse, *Navarino,* pp. 111–12. Codrington, *Memoir,* vol. 2, p. 71; Codrington memorial, 9 December 1827, Wellington, *Despatches,* vol. 4, p. 261; Ibrahim account, 29 October 1827, ibid., p. 142.
21. FO 78/162/142, Codrington to Croker, 21 October 1827; ADM 51/3018, HMS *Asia* log, 20 October 1827; *Man-of-War,* p. 131. Codrington, *Memoir,* vol. 2, p. 68; Codrington orders, 19 October 1827, ibid., pp. 68–69. See FO 78/162/142, Codrington to Croker, 21 October 1827.
22. Fellowes to Codrington, 11 December 1827, Codrington, *Memoir,* vol. 2, p. 135. See FO 78/162/142, Codrington to Croker, 21 October 1827; *Man-of-War,* pp. 134–35.
23. *Man-of-War,* pp. 131–35. FO 78/162/142, Codrington to Croker, 21 October 1827; Codrington to Clarence, 26 October 1827, Codrington, *Memoir,* vol. 2, pp. 92–97; Codrington to Admiralty, 9 December 1827, ibid., pp. 128–34. See Fellowes to Codrington, 11 December 1827, ibid., pp. 135–36; Gore report, n.d., ibid., 136–39; and FO 421/3/26, Abstract of the Proceedings in the Greek Question, part V, pp. 9–10. Ibrahim account, 29 October 1827, Wellington, *Despatches,* vol. 4, p. 142.
24. FO 78/162/142, Codrington to Croker, 21 October 1827. David Brewer, *The Greek War of Independence* (New York: Overlook, 2001), pp. 332–33.
25. *Man-of-War,* pp. 136–45.
26. Ibid., pp. 139–41.
27. Ibid., pp. 141–42, 158.
28. Ibid., pp. 153–54.
29. ADM 51/3018, HMS *Asia* log, 20 October 1827. Codrington to Bethell, 23 October 1827, Codrington, *Memoir,* vol. 2, p. 90. Ibid., p. 81.
30. ADM 51/3018, HMS *Asia* log, 20 October 1827. Brewer, *Greek War of Independence,* p. 333. Henry Codrington to William Codrington, November 1827, Codrington, *Memoir,* vol. 2, pp. 87–88. See Henry Codrington, *Selections from the Letters (Private and Professional) of Sir Henry Codrington, Admiral of the Fleet,* ed. Jane Barbara Codrington, Lady Bourchier (London: Spottiswoode, 1880). Woodhouse, *Navarino,* p. 119. See E. V. Bogdanovitch, *La bataille de Navarin (1827), d'après les documents inédits des archives impériales Russes* (Paris: Charpentier, 1887), pp. 105–9.
31. *Man-of-War,* pp. 148–49.
32. Ibid., pp. 149–50.
33. Ibid., p. 155. FO 78/162/142, Codrington to Croker, 21 October 1827. ADM 51/3018, HMS *Asia* log, 20 October 1827; Codrington memorandum, n.d. (fall 1827), Codrington, *Memoir,* vol. 2, pp. 75–76; Gore report, n.d. (fall 1827), ibid., vol. 2, pp. 136–39. *Man-of-War,* pp. 163–64. Ibrahim account, 29 October 1827, Wellington, *Despatches,* vol. 4, p. 142.

34. Woodhouse, *Navarino,* p. 140. Codrington memorial, 9 December 1827, Wellington, *Despatches,* vol. 4, p. 261. Codrington general order, 24 October 1827, Codrington, *Memoir,* vol. 2, p. 91. *Man-of-War,* p. 168.
35. Metternich to Apponyi, 13 November 1827, Metternich, *Mémoires,* vol. 4, p. 403. Adams address, 4 December 1827, James D. Richardson, ed., *A Compilation of the Messages and Papers of the Presidents 1789–1907,* vol. 2 (Washington, D.C.: Bureau of National Literature and Art, 1908), p. 384. FO 421/3/26, Abstract of the Proceedings in the Greek Question, part V.
36. Stanford J. Shaw and Ezel Kural Shaw, *History of the Ottoman Empire and Modern Turkey,* vol. 2 (Cambridge: Cambridge University Press, 1977), pp. 30–31. George Finlay, *History of the Greek Revolution,* vol. 2 (Edinburgh: William Blackwood and Sons, 1861), pp. 189–92.
37. FO 78/162/142, Codrington to Croker, 21 October 1827. FO 421/3/26, Abstract of the Proceedings in the Greek Question, part V, pp. 21–25, 27, 36–37, 39, 46–48, 50–54, 65.
38. FO 421/3/26, Abstract of the Proceedings in the Greek Question, part V, pp. 40–44, 69–72, 81.
39. King's speech, 29 January 1828, in Codrington, *Memoir,* vol. 2, pp. 178–79. Wellington memorandum, n.d., October 1827, Wellington, *Despatches,* vol. 4, p. 143. Wellington to Eldon, 1 December 1827, ibid., p. 164. Still, in 1828, when Ibrahim was reported to have hauled off six hundred Greeks as slaves on his remaining ships, to be sold as slaves in Alexandria, Wellington threatened Ibrahim "in the most forcible terms." (Huskisson to Wellington, 6 April 1828, Wellington, *Despatches,* vol. 4, p. 345; Huskisson memo, n.d., Codrington, *Memoir,* vol. 2, p. 175. See FO 421/3/26, Abstract of the Proceedings in the Greek Question, part V, p. 35.)
40. Russell statement, 29 January 1828, Codrington, *Memoir,* vol. 2, pp. 182–83. Hugo, "Navarin," *Les Orientales,* vol. 1, VII:268–71, p. 103. Codrington, *Memoir,* vol. 2, p. 436.
41. LGC vol. 8, J1, Blaquiere to Bowring, 1 May 1824; LGC vol. 8, B2, Blaquiere to Bowring, 8 May 1824; LGC vol. 8, D2, Blaquiere to Bowring, 11 May 1824. LGC vol. 8, B1, Stanhope to Bowring, 30 April 1824. LGC vol. 8, O1, Blaquiere to Hobhouse, 4 May 1824. John Bowring, *Autobiographical Recollections* (London: Henry S. King, 1877), p. 344.
42. Edward Blaquiere, *Narrative of a Second Visit to Greece, Including, Facts Connected with the Last Days of Lord Byron, Extracts from the Correspondence, Official Documents, &c.* (London: G. B. Whittaker, 1825), part 2, p. 24.
43. Timothy Garton Ash, *The Polish Revolution: Solidarity* (New Haven, Conn.: Yale University Press, 2002), p. 49.

PART THREE: SYRIANS

1. Victor Hugo, *Napoleon the Little* (New York: Howard Fertig, 1992), pp. 2, 18.
2. Cowley to Russell, 8 August 1860, Great Britain, Foreign Office, *Correspondence Relating to the Affairs of Syria 1860–61* (London: Harrison and Sons, 1861), pp. 40–41. *Siècle,* 9 August 1860, p. 1; Cowley to Russell, 8 August 1860, *Syria Corre-*

spondence 1860–61, pp. 40–41. Iskander Ibn Yaq'ub Abkarius, *Book of the Marvels of the Time Concerning the Massacres in the Arab Country,* trans. J. F. Scheltema (New Haven, Conn.: Yale University Press, 1920), p. 213.

3. Leila Tarazi Fawaz, *An Occasion for War: Civil Conflict in Lebanon and Damascus in 1860* (Berkeley: University of California Press, 1994), p. xiii. On the difficulties of using both French and Syrian sources, see p. 4.

NAPOLÉON THE LITTLE

1. A real parliamentary system would not be introduced until 1870. Roger L. Williams, *Gaslight and Shadow: The World of Napoleon III* (New York: Macmillan, 1957), p. viii. Roger Price, *The French Second Empire: An Anatomy of Political Power* (Cambridge: Cambridge University Press, 2001), p. 95.
2. Eugen Weber, *Peasants into Frenchmen: The Modernization of Rural France, 1870–1914* (Stanford, Calif.: Stanford University Press, 1976), pp. 109–10, 453–60, 468–69.
3. Edmund Burke, "Thoughts on French Affairs," in Edmund Burke, *Further Reflections on the Revolution in France,* ed. Daniel E. Ritchie (Indianapolis, Ind.: Liberty Fund, 1992), p. 215. Bob Harris, *Politics and the Rise of the Press: Britain and France, 1620–1800* (London: Routledge, 1996), pp. 53–60, 72, 101. Lynn M. Case, *French Opinion on War and Diplomacy During the Second Empire* (New York: Octagon, 1972), pp. 3–4.
4. Victor Hugo, *Napoleon the Little* (New York: Howard Fertig, 1992), p. 40. This paragraph is based on Case, *French Opinion,* pp. 1–6.
5. Case, *French Opinion,* pp. 6–13. The prefect reports from the fall of 1859 to the fall of 1865 have been lost.
6. Pierre Albert, Gilles Feyel, and Jean-François Picard, *Documents pour l'histoire de la presse nationale aux XIXe et XXe siècles* (Paris: Centre Nationale de la Récherche Scientifique, 1977), pp. 23–26; Claude Bellanger, Jacques Godechot, and Pierre Guiral, eds., *Histoire générale de la presse française, de 1815 à 1871* (Paris: Presses universitaires de France, 1969), pp. 258–60. Nora Wang, Ye Xin, and Wang Lou, *Victor Hugo et le sac du Palais d'Été* (Paris: Indes Savantes, 2003), p. 64. Victor Hugo, *Bug-Jargal* (Plymouth: Broadview, 2004; orig. 1826), trans. Chris Bongie. Susan Sontag, "Looking at War," *New Yorker,* 9 December 2002, p. 97.
7. Hugo, *Napoleon the Little,* pp. 142–61; Price, *French Second Empire,* pp. 97, 106–15, 264, 266, 309, 379; Alain Plessis, *The Rise and Fall of the Second Empire, 1852–1871* (Cambridge: Cambridge University Press, 1979), pp. 156–57.
8. Jean Tulard, ed., *Dictionnaire du Second Empire* (Paris: Fayard, 1995), p. 479; Adrien Dansette, *Du 2 décembre au 4 septembre* (Paris: Hachette, 1972), pp. 441; Plessis, *Rise and Fall,* p. 158; Price, *French Second Empire,* pp. 123, 264–65. The growth of the antigovernment vote tracks with a decline in abstentions, suggesting that abstentions were mostly antigovernment.
9. Williams, *Gaslight and Shadow,* p. 86. See Edward D. Mansfield and Jack Snyder, *Electing to Fight: Why Emerging Democracies Go to War* (Cambridge, Mass.: MIT Press, 2005), pp. 182–88.

10. Caesar E. Farah, "The Problem of the Ottoman Administration in the Lebanon 1840–1861," Ph.D. diss. (Princeton University, 1957), p. 74.
11. J. F. Scheltema, *The Lebanon in Turmoil: Syria and the Powers in 1860* (New Haven, Conn.: Yale University Press, 1920), p. 17.
12. Alfred Comyn Lyall, *The Life of the Marquis of Dufferin and Ava,* vol. 1 (London: John Murray, 1905), p. 111.

THE MASSACRES

1. Leila Tarazi Fawaz, *An Occasion for War: Civil Conflict in Lebanon and Damascus in 1860* (Berkeley: University of California Press, 1994), pp. 27–30. Caesar E. Farah, "The Problem of the Ottoman Administration in the Lebanon 1840–1861," Ph.D. diss. (Princeton University, 1957), pp. 228–34. Moore to Fanshawe, 22 July 1858, Great Britain, Foreign Office, *Despatches from Her Majesty's Consuls in the Levant Respecting Past or Apprehended Disturbances in Syria, 1858 to 1860* (London: Harrison and Sons, 1860), p. 31; Samir Khalaf, *Civil and Uncivil Violence in Lebanon: A History of the Internationalization of Communal Conflict* (New York: Columbia University Press, 2002), pp. 79–102; A. L. Tibawi, *A Modern History of Syria* (London: Macmillan, 1969), pp. 121–25, 133.
2. J. F. Scheltema, *The Lebanon in Turmoil: Syria and the Powers in 1860* (New Haven, Conn.: Yale University Press, 1920), p. 19. CPC/B, vol. 12, no. 10, Bentivoglio to Thouvenel, 28 March 1860.
3. Fawaz, *Occasion for War,* pp. 49–53. It is hard to pin down precise responsibility for the outbreak, but most observers put more blame on the Maronites than the Druzes (Dufferin to Russell, 10 March 1861, Great Britain, Foreign Office, *Correspondence Relating to the Affairs of Syria 1860–61* [London: Harrison and Sons, 1861], pp. 485–86; FO 78/1557/366, Bulwer to Russell, 2 July 1860). For a more pro-Maronite view, see Un témoin oculaire (An eyewitness), *Souvenirs de Syrie: Expédition française de 1860* (Paris: Plon, 1903), p. 28. This eyewitness seems to have been an attaché to the international commission of 1860–61 (Alfred Comyn Lyall, *The Life of the Marquis of Dufferin and Ava,* vol. 1 [London: John Murray, 1905], p. 124). CPC/B, vol. 12, no. 15, Bentivoglio to Thouvenel, 24 May 1860. Farah, "Ottoman Administration," pp. 235–45. Churchill blames the Druzes for the outbreak of the war (Charles Henry Churchill, *The Druzes and the Maronites Under the Turkish Rule from 1840 to 1860* [London: Bernard Quaritch, 1862], pp. 140–43), which is just one sign of his bias; I have used him, and many French reports, with considerable skepticism. CPC/B, vol. 12, no. 16, Bentivoglio to Thouvenel, 31 May 1860.
4. CPC/B, vol. 12, no. 17, Bentivoglio to Thouvenel, 3 June 1860. See Scheltema, *Lebanon in Turmoil,* pp. 25–26; Farah, "Ottoman Administration," pp. 241– 42; Churchill, *Druzes and Maronites,* p. 147; Témoin oculaire, *Souvenirs de Syrie,* pp. 28–29. CPC/B, vol. 12, no. 18, Bentivoglio to Thouvenel, 7 June 1860.
5. CPC/B, vol. 12, no. 17, Bentivoglio to Thouvenel, 3 June 1860.
6. Farah, "Ottoman Administration," p. 239. Cowley to Russell, 5 July 1860, *Syria Correspondence 1860–61,* pp. 1–2. CPC/B, vol. 12, no. 17, Bentivoglio to Thou-

venel, 3 June 1860. See CPC/B, vol. 12, no. 18, Bentivoglio to Thouvenel, 7 June 1860; Témoin oculaire, *Souvenirs de Syrie,* pp. 28–29.

7. CPC/B, vol. 12, no. 17, Bentivoglio to Thouvenel, 3 June 1860; Témoin oculaire, *Souvenirs de Syrie,* pp. 28–29. Churchill, *Druzes and Maronites,* p. 158. CPC/B, vol. 12, no. 18, Bentivoglio to Thouvenel, 7 June 1860. See CPC/B, vol. 12, no. 26, Bentivoglio to Thouvenel, 23 June 1860.
8. CPC/B, vol. 12, no. 18, Bentivoglio to Thouvenel, 7 June 1860. Churchill, *Druzes and Maronites,* pp. 160, 169.
9. FO 78/1557/41, Moore to Bulwer, 26 June 1860. CPC/B, vol. 12, no. 20, Bentivoglio to Thouvenel, 9 June 1860. FO 78/1557, Brant to Bulwer, 30 June 1860; FO 78/1557/20, Brant to Russell, 26 June 1860; Iskander Ibn Yaq'ub Abkarius, *Book of the Marvels of the Time Concerning the Massacres in the Arab Country,* trans. J. F. Scheltema (New Haven, Conn.: Yale University Press, 1920), pp. 57–86; Farah, "Ottoman Administration," pp. 254–56; Fawaz, *Occasion for War,* pp. 58–59, 61–64. CPC/B, vol. 12, no. 22, Bentivoglio to Thouvenel, 17 June 1860. One British official estimated nine hundred dead (FO 78/1557, Brant to Bulwer, 30 June 1860). See CPC/B, vol. 12, no. 27, Bentivoglio to Thouvenel, 26 June 1860; Churchill, *Druzes and Maronites,* pp. 148–73, 180, 192–93.
10. Fawaz, *Occasion for War,* pp. 33–37, 64–68. CPC/B, vol. 12, no. 22, Bentivoglio to Thouvenel, 17 June 1860. CPC/B, vol. 12, no. 24, Bentivoglio to Thouvenel, 21 June 1860; PA/T, vol. 5, Bentivoglio to Thouvenel, 21 June 1860; FO 78/1557/20, Brant to Russell, 26 June 1860.
11. CPC/B, vol. 12, no. 22, Bentivoglio to Thouvenel, 17 June 1860.
12. CPC/B, vol. 12, no. 23, Bentivoglio to Thouvenel, 17 June 1860.
13. CPC/B, vol. 12, no. 24, Bentivoglio to Thouvenel, 21 June 1860; FO 78/1557, Abela to Moore, 20 June 1860, 2 p.m.; Farah, "Ottoman Administration," pp. 252–67; Churchill, *Druzes and Maronites,* pp. 179–88; Abkarius, *Book of Marvels,* pp. 86–103. Baptistin Poujoulat, *La vérité sur la Syrie et l'expédition française* (Paris: Gaume frères et J. Duprey, 1861), pp. 100–101. CPC/B, vol. 12, no. 28, Bentivoglio to Thouvenel, 27 June 1860.
14. CPC/B, vol. 12, no. 29, Bentivoglio to Thouvenel, 28 June 1860. CPC/B, vol. 12, no. 24, Bentivoglio to Thouvenel, 21 June 1860; Farah, "Ottoman Administration," pp. 267–72; Churchill, *Druzes and Maronites,* pp. 188–92, 194–95; Abkarius, *Book of Marvels,* pp. 103–63, 154. A death toll of hundreds is more plausible than Bentivoglio's higher estimate (Fawaz, *Occasion for War,* pp. 72, 246). FO 78/1557, Moore to Junblat, 20 June 1860; FO 78/1557/18, Moore to Russell, 28 June 1860. FO 78/1557/41, Moore to Bulwer, 26 June 1860.
15. CPC/B, vol. 12, enclosure, consuls to Kurshid, 20 June 1860. See Farah, "Ottoman Administration," p. 272.
16. Fawaz, *Occasion for War,* pp. 75–76. PA/T, vol. 5, Bentivoglio to Thouvenel, 21 June 1860. François Lenormant, *Les derniers événements de Syrie: Une persécution du Christianisme en 1860* (Paris: W. Remquet et Cie., 1860), pp. 83–84. FO 78/1557/41, Moore to Bulwer, 26 June 1860.
17. CPC/B, vol. 12, no. 25, Bentivoglio to Thouvenel, 23 June 1860. FO 78/1557/41,

Moore to Bulwer, 26 June 1860; CPC/B, vol. 12, no. 43, Bentivoglio to Thouvenel, 8 August 1860.

18. FO 78/1557/41, Moore to Bulwer, 26 June 1860. CPC/B, vol. 12, no. 31 (enclosure), Frantz to Roncière le Noury, 24 June 1860; CPC/B, vol. 12, no. 21, Bentivoglio to Thouvenel, 16 June 1860. FO 78/1557, Abela to Moore, 22 June 1860, 8:30 p.m.; FO 78/1557, Abela to Moore, 26 June 1860. See Fawaz, *Occasion for War,* p. 60.
19. CPC/B, vol. 12, consuls to Druze leaders, 27 June 1860. CPC/B, vol. 12, consuls to Christian leaders, 27 June 1860. CPC/B, vol. 12, consuls to Kurshid, 25 June 1860. FO 78/1557/42, Moore to Bulwer, 27 June 1860; FO 78/1557/43, Moore to Bulwer, 28 June 1860. Churchill, *Druzes and Maronites,* pp. 200–201.
20. Churchill, *Druzes and Maronites,* pp. 202–3. CPB/B, vol. 12, no. 20, Bentivoglio to Thouvenel, 9 June 1860. CPC/B, vol. 12, no. 31, Bentivoglio to Thouvenel, 1 July 1860. CPC/B, vol. 12, no. 33, Bentivoglio to Thouvenel, 5 July 1860. On amnesty, see Raymond Aron, *Peace and War: A Theory of International Relations,* trans. Richard Howard and Annette Baker Fox (New York: Praeger, 1967), pp. 111–16; Samuel P. Huntington, *The Third Wave: Democratization in the Late Twentieth Century* (Norman: University of Oklahoma Press, 1991), pp. 211–31; Jon Elster, *Closing the Books: Transitional Justice in Historical Perspective* (Cambridge: Cambridge University Press, 2004), pp. 188–98; Bruce Ackerman, *The Future of Liberal Revolution* (New Haven, Conn.: Yale University Press, 1992), pp. 72–80; Guillermo O'Donnell and Philippe C. Schmitter, *Transitions from Authoritarian Rule: Tentative Conclusions about Uncertain Democracies* (Baltimore: Johns Hopkins University Press, 1986), pp. 37–47; Gary J. Bass, *Stay the Hand of Vengeance: The Politics of War Crimes Tribunals* (Princeton, N.J.: Princeton University Press, 2000), pp. 284–310; Tina Rosenberg, "Recovering from Apartheid," *New Yorker,* 18 November 1996, pp. 86–95.
21. CPC/B, vol. 12, no. 34, Bentivoglio to Thouvenel, 7 July 1860. CPC/B, vol. 12, no. 31, Bentivoglio to Thouvenel, 1 July 1860. FO 78/1557/42, Moore to Bulwer, 27 June 1860. CPC/B, vol. 12, no. 32, Bentivoglio to Thouvenel, 4 July 1860. FO 78/1557/46, Moore to Bulwer, 4 July 1860. Fawaz, *Occasion for War,* pp. 76–77. Farah, "Ottoman Administration," p. 280. FO 78/1557, Brant to Bulwer, 30 June 1860; FO 78/1557/45, Moore to Bulwer, 30 June 1860.
22. See CPC/B, vol. 13, no. 116, Bentivoglio to Thouvenel, 27 June 1861.
23. Thouvenel to Châteaurenard, 5 July 1860, France, Ministère des Affaires Étrangères, *Documents diplomatiques 1860,* vol. 1 (Paris: Imprimerie Impériale, 1861), p. 193. Fawaz, *Occasion for War,* p. 109.
24. Russell statement, 29 January 1828, *Memoir of the Life of Admiral Sir Edward Codrington,* ed. Jane Codrington, Lady Bourchier, vol. 2 (London: Longmans, Green, 1873), pp. 182–83. Palmerston and Russell had particular bad blood between them on French politics. Russell, as prime minister, had sacked Palmerston, then foreign secretary, for recognizing Louis Napoléon Bonaparte's government after the notorious coup d'état by the man who would later crown himself Napoléon III.
25. Philip Mansel, *Constantinople: City of the World's Desire, 1453–1924* (New York: St.

Martin's Press, 1998), p. 262. Thouvenel to Lavalette, 6 July 1860, *Documents diplomatiques 1860*, pp. 196–97.

26. Hamelin to Thouvenel, 7 July 1860, *Documents diplomatiques 1860*, p. 197.
27. Thouvenel to Châteaurenard, 5 July 1860, ibid., p. 193. Thouvenel to French ambassadors, 6 July 1860, ibid., pp. 194–95.
28. Cowley to Russell, 5 July 1860, *Syria Correspondence 1860–61,* p. 1. *Siècle,* 5 July 1860, p. 1. Cowley to Russell, 5 July 1860, *Syria Correspondence 1860–61,* p. 1.
29. Cowley to Russell, 5 July 1860, *Syria Correspondence 1860–61,* pp. 1–2. FO 27/1341, Cowley to Russell, 5 July 1860.
30. Russell to Cowley, 6 July 1860, *Syria Correspondence 1860–61,* p. 2; Hamelin to Thouvenel, 7 July 1860, *Documents diplomatiques 1860,* p. 197. Russell to Bulwer, 10 July 1860, *Syria Correspondence 1860–61,* p. 3. Russell to Erskine, 12 July 1860, ibid., p. 3. Farah, "Ottoman Administration," p. 12.
31. Cowley to Russell, 5 July 1860, *Syria Correspondence 1860–61,* p. 1. Thouvenel to Russell, 16 July 1860, ibid., p. 5. British translation.
32. Erskine to Russell, 11 July 1860, *Syria Correspondence 1860–61,* p. 6. Erskine to Russell, 14 July 1860, ibid., p. 7.
33. Cowley to Russell, 9 July 1860, *Syria Correspondence 1860–61,* p. 2. Thouvenel to Russell, 16 July 1860, ibid., p. 5.
34. Fawaz, *Occasion for War,* p. 106; Témoin oculaire, *Souvenirs de Syrie,* pp. 199–201. Thouvenel to Persigny, 17 July 1860, *Documents diplomatiques 1860*, p. 198; *Siècle,* 10 July 1860, p. 1. Cowley to Russell, 9 July 1860, *Syria Correspondence 1860–61,* p. 2. Abdulmecit to Fuad, n.d., in Bulwer to Russell, 25 July 1860, ibid., pp. 32–33; Abdulmecit to Napoléon III, 16 July 1860, ibid., p. 10; Abdulmecit to Victoria, 16 July 1860, ibid., p. 22; Abdulmecit to Fuad, n.d., *Documents diplomatiques 1860*, pp. 202–3; Abkarius, *Book of Marvels,* pp. 195–96, 200–4. Lavalette to Thouvenel, 18 July 1860, *Documents diplomatiques 1860*, p. 201. The original French has "tâche" (task) instead of "tache" (stain).
35. Mansel, *Constantinople,* pp. 272–74. Abdulmecit to Napoléon III, 16 July 1860, *Syria Correspondence 1860–61,* p. 10; Abdulmecit to Victoria, 16 July 1860, ibid., p. 22.
36. Abdulmecit to Fuad, n.d., in Bulwer to Russell, 25 July 1860, *Syria Correspondence 1860–61,* pp. 32–33. Churchill, *Druzes and Maronites,* p. 197; Farah, "Ottoman Administration," pp. 275–76.
37. CPC/B, vol. 12, no. 35, Bentivoglio to Thouvenel, 11 July 1860. Abkarius, *Book of Marvels,* pp. 162–96; Farah, "Ottoman Administration," pp. 283–89; Tibawi, *Modern History of Syria,* pp. 125–29. Bulwer to Russell, 1 August 1860, *Syria Correspondence 1860–61,* pp. 54–55. See Moore to Russell, 1 August 1860, ibid., p. 67.
38. Abkarius, *Book of Marvels,* pp. 174–77.
39. CPC/B, vol. 12, no. 35, Bentivoglio to Thouvenel, 11 July 1860. Abkarius, *Book of Marvels,* p. 162. CP/T, vol. 349, no. 73, Lavalette to Thouvenel, 15 May 1861. FO 78/1557, Robson to Brant, 9 July 1860.
40. FO 78/1557/24, Brant to Bulwer, 11 July 1860. FO 78/1557, Brant to Bulwer, 12 July 1860. Lyall, *Dufferin,* vol. 1, pp. 106–7.
41. FO 78/1557/20, Moore to Russell, 13 July 1860; FO 78/1557, consuls to Kurshid,

13 July 1860. Thouvenel to Persigny, 16 July 1860, *Documents diplomatiques 1860*, p. 198.

42. Thouvenel to Persigny, 17 July 1860, *Documents diplomatiques 1860,* pp. 198–99.
43. CPC/B, vol. 12, no. 43 bis, Bentivoglio to Thouvenel, 4 August 1860. Thouvenel to Persigny, 17 July 1860, *Documents diplomatiques 1860*, pp. 198–99. See *Syria Correspondence 1860–61*, p. 9.
44. Thouvenel to Persigny, 17 July 1860, *Documents diplomatiques 1860*, pp. 198–99. Cowley to Russell, 17 July 1860, *Syria Correspondence 1860–61*, p. 7.
45. Cowley to Russell, 17 July 1860, *Syria Correspondence 1860*–61, p. 7. See Thouvenel to Russell, 17 July 1860, ibid., p. 9. British translation.
46. Cowley to Russell, 19 July 1860, *Syria Correspondence 1860–61*, p. 10. Moore to Russell, 4 August 1860, ibid., pp. 68–71. Cowley to Russell, 19 July 1860, ibid., p. 10. Thouvenel to Persigny, 19 July 1860, *Documents diplomatiques 1860*, pp. 203–4.
47. Cowley to Russell, 19 July 1860, *Syria Correspondence 1860–61*, p. 11. Thouvenel to Persigny, 19 July 1860, *Documents diplomatiques 1860*, pp. 203–4.
48. Thouvenel to Persigny, 21 July 1860, *Documents diplomatiques 1860*, pp. 204–5; Moustier to Thouvenel, 22 July 1860, ibid., pp. 207–8. Loftus to Russell, 19 July 1860, *Syria Correspondence 1860–61*, p. 12. Montebello to Thouvenel, 21 July 1860, *Documents diplomatiques 1860*, pp. 205–6.
49. Lavalette to Thouvenel, 18 July 1860, *Documents diplomatiques 1860*, p. 201. Thouvenel to Persigny, 21 July 1860, ibid., pp. 204–5.
50. FO 78/1557/48, Moore to Bulwer, 11 July 1860. FO 78/1557, peace treaty, July 1860. CPC/B, vol. 12, no. 36, Bentivoglio to Thouvenel, 14 July 1860.
51. FO 78/1557/21, Moore to Russell, 18 July 1860. CPC/B, vol. 12, no. 37, Bentivoglio to Thouvenel, 19 July 1860.
52. Abkarius, *Book of Marvels*, pp. 197–98. CPC/B, vol. 12, no. 37, Bentivoglio to Thouvenel, 19 July 1860. FO 78/1557/48, Moore to Bulwer, 11 July 1860. FO 78/1557/21, Moore to Russell, 18 July 1860. Fawaz, *Occasion for War,* p. 107.
53. Russell to Cowley, 21 July 1860, *Syria Correspondence 1860–61,* p. 11. Persigny to Thouvenel, 22 July 1860, *Documents diplomatiques 1860*, pp. 206–7.
54. Cowley to Russell, 22 July 1860, *Syria Correspondence 1860–61,* p. 13. Thouvenel to Persigny, 23 July 1860, *Documents diplomatiques 1860*, p. 208.
55. Thouvenel to Persigny, 23 July 1860, *Documents diplomatiques 1860,* pp. 208–10. Abkarius, *Book of Marvels,* p. 198; CPC/B, vol. 12, no. 37, Bentivoglio to Thouvenel, 19 July 1860.
56. Cowley to Russell, 22 July 1860, *Syria Correspondence 1860–61,* p. 13. Bulwer to Russell, 17 July 1860, ibid., p. 23.
57. CPC/B, vol. 13, no. 75, Bentivoglio to Thouvenel, 16 December 1860. Russell to Cowley, 23 July 1860, *Syria Correspondence 1860–61,* p. 15. For plans for a possible British ground expedition, see FO 221/149, 5 October 1860, Burnaby memorandum, Beirut.
58. Russell to Cowley, 23 July 1860, *Syria Correspondence 1860–61,* p. 15. Russell to Bulwer, 24 July 1860, ibid., p. 18.
59. Cowley to Russell, 23 July 1860, *Syria Correspondence 1860–61,* pp. 15–18. Cowley to Russell, 25 July 1860, ibid., p. 20.

60. Persigny to Thouvenel, 25 July 1860, *Documents diplomatiques 1860,* p. 210; Thouvenel to Persigny, 26 July 1860, ibid., pp. 210–11. Cowley to Russell, 24 July 1860, *Syria Correspondence 1860–61,* p. 19. See Persigny to Thouvenel, 25 July 1860, *Documents diplomatiques 1860,* p. 210.
61. CPC/B, vol. 12, no. 43 bis, Bentivoglio to Thouvenel, 4 August 1860. Napoléon III to Persigny, 25 July 1860, Lyall, *Dufferin,* vol. 1, p. 122.

PUBLIC OPINION

1. Roger L. Williams, *Gaslight and Shadow: The World of Napoleon III* (New York: Macmillan, 1957), pp. 86–87. Stanley Karnow, *Vietnam: A History* (New York: Penguin, 1984), pp. 70–79. William E. Echard, *Napoleon III and the Concert of Europe* (Baton Rouge: Louisiana State University Press, 1983), p. 130; R. W. Seton-Watson, *Britain in Europe, 1789–1914: A Survey of Foreign Policy* (New York: Macmillan, 1937), p. 421.
2. Un témoin oculaire (An eyewitness), *Souvenirs de Syrie: Expédition française de 1860* (Paris: Plon, 1903), p. 217.
3. *Siècle,* 21 June 1860, p. 1. "Bulletins de l'Extérieur," *Siècle,* 11 July 1860, p. 2.
4. *Siècle,* 17 July 1860, p. 1; 18 July 1860, p. 1; 19 July 1860, p. 1; 21 July 1860. *Moniteur,* 17 July 1860; "France," *Siècle,* 18 July 1860, p. 1.
5. Louis Jourdan, "Les massacres en Orient," *Siècle,* 19 July 1860, p. 1. MD/T vol. 122, no. 19, de Nerrier to Napoléon III, 18 July 1860. These totaled about 650,000 francs. CPC/B, vol. 13, no. 92, Bentivoglio to Thouvenel, 5 May 1861; CPC/B, vol. 13, no. 122, Bentivoglio to Thouvenel, 6 June 1861. Bentivoglio hoped a Christian religious orphanage would both do good and expand "French influence." (CPC/B, vol. 13, no. 76, Bentivoglio to Thouvenel, 29 December 1860. See CPC/B, vol. 13, no. 3, Thouvenel to Bentivoglio, 19 April 1861.) See *Siècle,* 19–28 July 1860.
6. Louis Jourdan, "Question d'Orient," *Siècle,* 21 July 1860, pp. 1–2.
7. "France," *Siècle,* 21 July 1860, p. 1. François Lenormant, *Histoire des massacres de Syrie en 1860* (Paris: Hachette, 1861). Caesar E. Farah, "The Problem of the Ottoman Administration in the Lebanon 1840–1861," Ph.D. diss. (Princeton University, 1957), p. 3. See Baptistin Poujoulat, *La vérité sur la Syrie et l'expédition française* (Paris: Gaume frères et J. Duprey, 1861); Saint-Marc Girardin, *La Syrie en 1861* (Paris: Didier, 1862). CP/T, vol. 349, no. 73, Lavalette to Thouvenel, 15 May 1861.
8. Bulwer to Russell, 1 August 1860, Great Britain, Foreign Office, *Correspondence Relating to the Affairs of Syria 1860–61* (London: Harrison and Sons, 1861), p. 56.
9. Témoin oculaire, *Souvenirs de Syrie,* p. 219.
10. Bulwer to Russell, 17 July 1860, *Syria Correspondence 1860–61,* p. 23.
11. The *Times* ran thirty-eight stories on Syria in July 1860, against fifty-five in *Le Siècle;* in August, the *Times* printed forty-nine stories, roughly matching the forty-two in *Le Siècle.* "Syria," *Times,* 5 July 1860, p. 9; "The Civil War in Syria," *Times,* 6 July 1860, p. 11; Reuters Telegrams, *Times,* 9 July 1860, p. 9.
12. Leader, *Times,* 10 July 1860, p. 8. Montefiore letter, *Times,* 12 July 1860, p. 9.
13. "Massacre of Christians at Damascus," Reuters Telegrams, *Times,* 17 July 1860,

p. 9. Leader, *Times,* 18 July 1860, p. 9. Less appealingly, the editors noted the special significance of "the cradle of Christianity," and worried whether Fuad Pasha's mission could "dam up the current of Asiatic fanaticism." "The Civil War in Syria," *Times,* 21 July 1860, p. 10.

14. Leader, *Times,* 25 July 1860, p. 9.
15. "The Civil War in Syria," *Times,* 21 July 1860, p. 10. "The Massacres in Syria," *Times,* 3 September 1860, p. 8. "The Massacres in Syria," *Times,* 17 September 1860, pp. 7–8.
16. Cowley to Russell, 25 July 1860, *Syria Correspondence 1860–61,* p. 21.
17. Philip Mansel, *Constantinople: City of the World's Desire, 1453–1924* (New York: St. Martin's Press, 1998), pp. 276–77. Cowley to Russell, 26 July 1860, *Syria Correspondence 1860–61,* p. 21. Cowley to Russell, 25 July 1860, ibid., p. 20.
18. Cowley to Russell, 26 July 1860, *Syria Correspondence 1860–61,* p. 22. Russell to Cowley, 28 July 1860, ibid., p. 24. MD/T, vol. 122, no. 17, "Note sur les Causes de l'évacuation de la Syrie par la France, 1860–1861." Russell to Dufferin, 30 July 1860, *Syria Correspondence 1860–61,* p. 26. Russell to Cowley, 28 July 1860, ibid., p. 24.
19. Bulwer to Russell, 25, July 1860, *Syria Correspondence 1860–61,* p. 33. Musurus to Russell, 30 July 1860, ibid., p. 28. Russell to Bulwer, 1 August 1860, ibid., p. 31.
20. Bulwer to Russell, 1 August 1860, *Syria Correspondence 1860–61,* p. 56. Ali to Vefik, 27 July 1860, ibid., p. 57.
21. Cowley to Russell, 31 July 1860, *Syria Correspondence 1860–61,* pp. 29–30.
22. Fuad to Abdulaziz, 3 January 1862, J. Lewis Farley, *Turks and Christians: A Solution of the Eastern Question* (London: Simpkin, Marshall, 1876), p. 239. Russia had floated this idea previously, to muted French acquiescence and heated British opposition (Cowley to Russell, 26 July 1860, *Syria Correspondence 1860–61,* p. 22; Russell to Cowley, 28 July 1860, ibid., p. 24). Cowley to Russell, 31 July 1860, ibid., pp. 30–31.
23. FO 93/110, Protocole d'une Conférence tenue au Ministère des Affaires Étrangères, 3 August 1860; Cowley to Russell, 3 August 1860, *Syria Correspondence 1860–61,* pp. 36–38. Cowley to Russell, 7 August 1860, ibid., p. 39; Protocol, 3 August 1860, *Documents diplomatiques 1860,* p. 214.
24. Cowley to Russell, 3 August 1860, *Syria Correspondence 1860–61*, pp. 38–39. FO 93/110, Convention, 5 September 1860; "Convention pour le rétablissement de l'ordre et de la paix en Syria," 5 September 1860, *Documents diplomatiques 1860*, pp. 215–16. In an act of surprising trust all around, the formal convention governing Beaufort's mission was not signed until September 5—almost three weeks after French troops would actually arrive at Beirut.

OCCUPYING SYRIA

1. Cowley to Russell, 7 August 1860, Great Britain, Foreign Office, *Correspondence Relating to the Affairs of Syria 1860–61* (London: Harrison and Sons, 1861), p. 39.
2. Alfred Comyn Lyall, *The Life of the Marquis of Dufferin and Ava,* vol. 1 (London: John Murray, 1905), pp. 1–78, 95–96, 120. See Charles E. Drummond Black, *The*

Marquis of Dufferin and Ava, K.P., G.C.B., G.C.S.I., G.C.M.G., G.C.I.E., P.C.: Diplomatist, Viceroy, Statesman (London: Hutchinson, 1903), pp. 1–22, 37–60.

3. Russell to Dufferin, 14 August 1860, *Syria Correspondence 1860–61*, pp. 58–59. Thouvenel instructions, 16 August 1860, in France, Ministère des Affaires Étrangères, *Documents diplomatiques 1860*, vol. 1 (Paris: Imprimerie Impériale, 1861), pp. 216–17; MD/T, vol. 122, no. 26, Projet d'instructions pour le Commissaire de Sa Majesté en Syrie. Russell to Cowley, 3 August 1860, *Syria Correspondence 1860–61*, pp. 34–35. Russell to Dufferin, 14 August 1860, ibid., p. 59.
4. Thouvenel to Hamelin, 4 August 1860, *Syria Correspondence 1860–61*, pp. 47–48, and *Documents diplomatiques 1860*, pp. 214–15. Cowley to Russell, 7 August 1860, *Syria Correspondence 1860–61*, p. 39. Leila Tarazi Fawaz, *An Occasion for War: Civil Conflict in Lebanon and Damascus in 1860* (Berkeley: University of California Press, 1994), pp. 114–15.
5. Cowley to Russell, 7 August 1860, *Syria Correspondence 1860–61*, p. 39. Cowley to Russell, 14 August 1860, ibid., pp. 59–60. *Siècle*, 9 August 1860, p. 1; Cowley to Russell, 8 August 1860, *Syria Correspondence 1860–61*, pp. 40–41.
6. Stanford J. Shaw and Ezel Kural Shaw, *History of the Ottoman Empire and Modern Turkey*, vol. 2 (Cambridge: Cambridge University Press, 1977), p. 63; Philip Mansel, *Constantinople: City of the World's Desire, 1453–1924* (New York: St. Martin's Press, 1998), p. 265. Lyall, *Dufferin*, vol. 1, p. 107.
7. Fuad to Abdulaziz, 3 January 1862, J. Lewis Farley, *Turks and Christians: A Solution of the Eastern Question* (London: Simpkin, Marshall, 1876), pp. 236–39, 241–43.
8. O'Reilly to Bulwer, 18 July 1860, *Syria Correspondence 1860–61*, pp. 55–56. Iskander Ibn Yaq'ub Abkarius, *Book of the Marvels of the Time Concerning the Massacres in the Arab Country*, trans. J. F. Scheltema (New Haven, Conn.: Yale University Press, 1920), pp. 204–9. Moore to Bulwer, 21 July 1860, *Syria Correspondence 1860–61*, pp. 42–43.
9. Fraser to Russell, 2 August 1860, *Syria Correspondence 1860–61*, p. 75. Moore to Bulwer, 28 July 1860, ibid., p. 54; O'Reilly to Bulwer, 18 July 1860, ibid., pp. 55–56. Un témoin oculaire (An eyewitness), *Souvenirs de Syrie: Expédition française de 1860* (Paris: Plon, 1903), p. 211. Graham to Moore, 30 July 1860, *Syria Correspondence 1860–61*, p. 68. Moore to Russell, 1 August 1860, ibid., p. 67; Un témoin oculaire, *Souvenirs de Syrie*, p. 212. Fraser to Russell, 8 August 1860, *Syria Correspondence 1860–61*, p. 77; Moore to Russell, 12 August 1860, ibid., p. 78; Hasbayya Christians to Moore, 8 August 1860, ibid., p. 79.
10. Bulwer to Russell, 1 August 1860, *Syria Correspondence 1860–61*, pp. 54–55. Un témoin oculaire, *Souvenirs de Syrie*, pp. 205, 244; Fawaz, *Occasion for War*, p. 148. Abkarius, *Book of Marvels*, pp. 214–15. Martin to Fuad, 25 July 1860, *Syria Correspondence 1860–61*, pp. 61–62. Moore to Russell, 26 July 1860, ibid., pp. 60–61. See Fuad to Martin, 26 July 1860, ibid., p. 62 (British translation); Fraser to Russell, 2 August 1860, ibid., p. 76.
11. Brant to Bulwer, 4 August 1860, *Syria Correspondence 1860–61*, p. 84. CPC/B,

vol. 12, no. 43 bis, Bentivoglio to Thouvenel, 4 August 1860. CPC/B, vol. 12, no. 44, Bentivoglio to Lavalette, 6 August 1860.

12. CPC/B, vol. 12, no. 44, Fuad to Bentivoglio, 4 August 1860; Fuad to Moore, 4 August 1860, *Syria Correspondence 1860–61,* pp. 73–74. CPC/B, vol. 12, no. 44, Bentivoglio to Thouvenel, 9 August 1860. Brant to Bulwer, 9 August 1860, *Syria Correspondence 1860–61,* p. 85. Moore to Russell, 10 August 1860, ibid., p. 78. Fraser to Russell, 16 August 1860, ibid., p. 92.
13. Un témoin oculaire, *Souvenirs de Syrie,* p. 225. Fraser to Russell, 16 August 1860, *Syria Correspondence 1860–61,* pp. 92–93.
14. Un témoin oculaire, *Souvenirs de Syrie,* p. 218. Martin to Fuad, 25 July 1860, *Syria Correspondence 1860–61,* pp. 61–62; Moore to Bulwer, 28 July 1860, ibid., p. 54. Moore to Russell, 8 August 1860, ibid., p. 75. FO 78/1557, Codrington to Admiralty, 21 July 1860; J. F. Scheltema, *The Lebanon in Turmoil: Syria and the Powers in 1860* (New Haven, Conn.: Yale University Press, 1920), p. 144.
15. Moore to Russell, 1 August 1860, *Syria Correspondence 1860–61,* p. 68; Moore to Russell, 10 August 1860, ibid., p. 78; Moore to Russell, 15 August 1860, ibid., p. 89. Moore to Russell, 10 August 1860, ibid., p. 78. Russell to Bulwer, 30 August 1860, ibid., p. 80.
16. CPC/B, vol. 12, no. 47, Bentivoglio to Thouvenel, 13 August 1860. Graham report, 13 August 1860, *Syria Correspondence 1860–61,* pp. 86–87; Graham note, 22 August 1860, ibid., pp. 88–89; Russell to Brant, 10 September 1860, ibid., p. 99.
17. Russell to Cowley, 13 August 1860, *Syria Correspondence 1860–61,* pp. 57–58. Cowley to Russell, 14 August 1860, ibid., pp. 59–60. Russell to Fane, 5 September 1860, ibid., p. 94. Prussia would send another three thousand to make up the full twelve thousand set by the Paris Protocol.
18. Brant to Russell, 11 August 1860, *Syria Correspondence 1860–61,* p. 83; Brant to Bulwer, 4 August 1860, ibid., p. 84. Abdulmecit to Fuad, 18 August 1860, ibid., p. 105.
19. Un témoin oculaire, *Souvenirs de Syrie,* pp. 237–38. Fraser to Russell, 20 August 1860, *Syria Correspondence 1860–61,* p. 81.
20. Fraser to Russell, 20 August 1860, *Syria Correspondence 1860–61,* p. 81. Fraser to Russell, 16 August 1860, ibid., p. 93. Un témoin oculaire, *Souvenirs de Syrie,* p. 238. Fraser to Russell, 23 August 1860, *Syria Correspondence 1860–61,* p. 95. Fuad to Ali, 20 August 1860, ibid., pp. 81–82. See Fuad note, n.d., ibid., pp. 98–99.
21. Fraser to Russell, 23 August 1860, *Syria Correspondence 1860–61,* p. 95. Brant to Russell, 11 August 1860, ibid., p. 83; Brant to Bulwer, 16 August 1860, ibid., p. 101. CPC/B, vol. 12, no. 44, Bentivoglio to Lavalette, 6 August 1860.
22. Brant to Bulwer, 31 July 1860, *Syria Correspondence 1860–61,* p. 84. Brant to Russell, 25 August 1860, ibid., p. 103. Fraser to Russell, 23 August 1860, ibid., p. 95; Hammond to Fraser, 12 September 1860, ibid., p. 100.
23. CPC/B, vol. 12, no. 44, Bentivoglio to Lavalette, 6 August 1860. Cowley to Russell, 1 September 1860, *Syria Correspondence 1860–61,* p. 83.
24. Baptistin Poujoulat, *La vérité sur la Syrie et l'expédition française* (Paris: Gaume frères et J. Duprey, 1861), pp. 1–2, 8. Scheltema, *Lebanon in Turmoil,* p. 165.
25. CPC/B, vol. 12, no. 51, Bentivoglio to Thouvenel, 22 August 1860. Un témoin

oculaire, *Souvenirs de Syrie,* p. 227. CPC/B, vol. 12, no. 48, Bentivoglio to Thouvenel, 16 August 1860; Moore to Russell, 16 August 1860, *Syria Correspondence 1860–61,* p. 92. Poujoulat, *Vérité sur la Syrie,* pp. 13, 17; CPC/B, vol. 12, no. 51, Bentivoglio to Thouvenel, 22 August 1860. Moore to Russell, 22 August 1860, *Syria Correspondence 1860–61,* p. 82; Scheltema, *Lebanon in Turmoil,* p. 165.

26. FO 226/149, Burnaby memorandum on French infantry in Syria, n.d. 1860. Stanley Karnow, *Vietnam: A History* (New York: Penguin, 1984), p. 75.
27. Poujoulat, *Vérité sur la Syrie,* pp. 17–18. CPC/B, vol. 12, no. 51, Bentivoglio to Thouvenel, 22 August 1860. Moore to Russell, 22 August 1860, *Syria Correspondence 1860–61,* p. 82. CPC/B, vol. 12, no. 48, Bentivoglio to Thouvenel, 16 August 1860. Abkarius, *Book of Marvels,* p. 213.
28. Fawaz, *Occasion for War,* p. 119.
29. Russell to Cowley, 13 August 1860, *Syria Correspondence 1860–61,* pp. 57–58. CPC/B, vol. 12, no. 44, Bentivoglio to Lavalette, 6 August 1860. CPC/B, vol. 12, no. 53, Bentivoglio to Thouvenel, 25 August 1860.
30. Poujoulat, *Vérité sur la Syrie,* pp. 20–21, 22–23, 34. CPC/B, vol. 12, no. 53, Bentivoglio to Thouvenel, 25 August 1860. CPC/B, vol. 12, no. 54, Bentivoglio to Thouvenel, 31 August 1860. Cowley to Russell, 14 August 1860, *Syria Correspondence 1860–61,* pp. 59–60.
31. Poujoulat, *Vérité sur la Syrie,* pp. 24–27. Un témoin oculaire, *Souvenirs de Syrie,* pp. 239, 228–29. Fawaz, *Occasion for War,* p. 121.
32. CPC/B, vol. 12, no. 61, Bentivoglio to Thouvenel, 14 September 1860; Un témoin oculaire, *Souvenirs de Syrie,* pp. 245–46. Fraser to Russell, 23 August 1860, *Syria Correspondence 1860–61,* p. 95. Fraser notes, 3 September 1860, ibid., p. 117. Poujoulat, *Vérité sur la Syrie,* p. 92.
33. Ottoman proclamation, n.d., *Syria Correspondence 1860–61,* p. 69. CPC/B, vol. 12, no. 61, Bentivoglio to Thouvenel, 14 September 1860. Poujoulat, *Vérité sur la Syrie,* pp. 109–10. Fuad address, August 1860, *Syria Correspondence 1860–61,* p. 106.
34. Fraser to Russell, 23 August 1860, *Syria Correspondence 1860–61,* p. 95. Fraser to Russell, 8 August 1860, ibid., p. 77.
35. Moore to Russell, 22 August 1860, *Syria Correspondence 1860–61,* p. 82. Poujoulat, *Vérité sur la Syrie,* p. 82.
36. Russell to Bulwer, 25 February 1861, *Syria Correspondence 1860–61,* p. 414. Fuad note, 8 September 1860, ibid., pp. 124–25; Brant to Bulwer, 30 August 1860, ibid., pp. 131–33. Fraser notes, 3 September 1860, ibid., pp. 117–18. Russell to Bulwer, 25 February 1861, ibid., p. 414. Un témoin oculaire, *Souvenirs de Syrie,* pp. 235–36.
37. CPC/B, vol. 13, no. 75, Bentivoglio to Thouvenel, 16 December 1860. PA/T, vol. 4, Beaufort to Thouvenel, 21 December 1860. Dufferin to Russell, 19 December 1860, *Syria Correspondence 1860–61,* p. 286. Russell to Brant, 10 August 1860, ibid., p. 42. Bulwer to Russell, 1 August 1860, ibid., pp. 54–55.
38. Morris to Russell, 15 September 1860, *Syria Correspondence 1860–61,* p. 106; Druze petition, 17 August 1860, ibid., pp. 106–14. Russell to Cowley, 15 September 1860, ibid., p. 114. Dufferin to Bulwer, 8 September 1860, ibid., pp. 126–28. Russell to

Bulwer, 22 September 1860, ibid., p. 129. Moore to Russell, 14 September 1860, ibid., p. 135.

39. Cowley to Russell, 21 September 1860, *Syria Correspondence 1860–61,* pp. 129–30. PA/T, vol. 4, Béclard to Thouvenel, 4 November 1861.
40. Un témoin oculaire, *Souvenirs de Syrie,* pp. 234–35.
41. CPC/B, vol. 12, no. 57, Bentivoglio to Thouvenel, 3 September 1860; Moore to Bulwer, 3 September 1860, *Syria Correspondence 1860–61,* p. 119; Dufferin to Bulwer, 3 September 1860, ibid., p. 121; Un témoin oculaire, *Souvenirs de Syrie,* pp. 232–33. Dufferin to Russell, 24 August 1860, *Syria Correspondence 1860–61,* p. 98. Commissioners to Fuad, 26 September 1860, ibid., pp. 156–57; commission protocols, 5 and 9 October 1860, ibid., pp. 169–175.
42. Un témoin oculaire, *Souvenirs de Syrie,* p. 259. Dufferin to Russell, 23 September 1860, *Syria Correspondence 1860–61,* pp. 141–47; Lyall, *Dufferin,* vol. 1, pp. 94–98, 106. FO 78/1624, Russell to Dufferin, 30 July 1860. Dufferin to Bulwer, 8 September 1860, *Syria Correspondence 1860–61,* pp. 122–23.
43. Un témoin oculaire, *Souvenirs de Syrie,* p. 232. Dufferin to Bulwer, 8 September 1860, *Syria Correspondence 1860–61,* pp. 122–23; Poujoulat, *Vérité sur la Syrie,* p. 93. Brant to Russell, 20 September 1860, *Syria Correspondence 1860–61,* p. 140.
44. Un témoin oculaire, *Souvenirs de Syrie,* p. 241. Fraser to Russell, 21 September 1860, *Syria Correspondence 1860–61,* pp. 152–53. Moore to Russell, 14 September 1860, ibid., p. 134. Scheltema, *Lebanon in Turmoil,* p. 154. Dufferin to Bulwer, 26 October 1860, *Syria Correspondence 1860–61,* p. 195.
45. Fraser to Russell, 21 September 1860, *Syria Correspondence 1860–61,* pp. 152–53. Un témoin oculaire, *Souvenirs de Syrie,* p. 248. Fawaz, *Occasion for War,* p. 120. Fraser notes, 3 September 1860, *Syria Correspondence 1860–61,* p. 117. Moore to Russell, 14 September 1860, ibid., pp. 134–35; Dufferin to Bulwer, 13 September 1860, ibid., p. 136. Dufferin to Bulwer, 21 September 1860, ibid., p. 148.
46. Abkarius, *Book of Marvels,* pp. 222–24. Dufferin to Bulwer, 23 September 1860, *Syria Correspondence 1860–61,* pp. 148–49. Fuad to Fraser, 20 October 1860, ibid., pp. 187–88. Dufferin to Bulwer, 23 September 1860, ibid., pp. 149–50.
47. Un témoin oculaire, *Souvenirs de Syrie,* pp. 248–49; Fraser to Russell, 21 September 1860, *Syria Correspondence 1860–61,* pp. 153–54; Fuad notice, n.d., ibid., pp. 149–50. Dufferin to Bulwer, 24 September 1860, ibid., pp. 151–52; Fuad notification, n.d., ibid., p. 152.
48. Dufferin to Bulwer, 14 September 1860, *Syria Correspondence 1860–61,* p. 136. Un témoin oculaire, *Souvenirs de Syrie,* pp. 248–49. Dufferin to Bulwer, 24 September 1860, *Syria Correspondence 1860–61,* pp. 151–52; Fuad notification, n.d., ibid., p. 152. Lyall, *Dufferin,* vol. 1, p. 116.
49. CPC/B, vol. 12, no. 64, Bentivoglio to Thouvenel, 28 September 1860. Scheltema, *Lebanon in Turmoil,* p. 36. Poujoulat, *Vérité sur la Syrie,* p. 181.
50. Dufferin to Russell, 29 September 1860, *Syria Correspondence 1860–61,* pp. 158–59. Russell to Dufferin, 20 October 1860, ibid., p. 168. Dufferin to Fuad, 29 September 1860, ibid., pp. 159–60; Dufferin to Bulwer, 7 October 1860, ibid., pp. 167–68. Fraser to Dufferin, 23 January 1861, ibid., pp. 379. See Scheltema, *Lebanon in Turmoil,* pp. 164–65; Un témoin oculaire, *Souvenirs de Syrie,* pp. 253–54.

51. Brant to Russell, 5 October 1860, *Syria Correspondence 1860–61,* p. 165. Scheltema, *Lebanon in Turmoil,* pp. 165–66. Poujoulat, *Vérité sur la Syrie,* pp. 199, 202. Dufferin to Bulwer, 5 October 1860, *Syria Correspondence 1860–61,* pp. 166–67.
52. Brant to Bulwer, 11 October 1860, *Syria Correspondence 1860–61,* p. 185; Fraser to Russell, 20 October 1860, ibid., p. 187. Un témoin oculaire, *Souvenirs de Syrie,* p. 274.
53. PA/T, vol. 4, Béclard to Thouvenel, 4 November 1860. CPC/B, vol. 13, no. 67, Bentivoglio to Thouvenel, 26 October 1860; CPC/B, vol. 13, no. 71, Bentivoglio to Thouvenel, 14 December 1860; CPC/B, vol. 13, no. 72, Bentivoglio to Thouvenel, 14 December 1860. CPC/B, vol. 13, Thouvenel to Gaillard de Ferry, 27 October 1860. CPC/B, vol. 13, no. 69, Bentivoglio to Thouvenel, 7 December 1860. CPC/B, vol. 13, no. 70, Bentivoglio to Thouvenel, 7 December 1860.
54. Dufferin to Bulwer, 21 September 1860, *Syria Correspondence 1860–61,* pp. 137–38; Dufferin to Abro, 19 September 1860, ibid., p. 139. Dufferin to Bulwer, 23 September 1860, ibid., p. 138–39; Fuad notice, n.d., ibid., pp. 149–50. Dufferin to Bulwer, 26 October 1860, ibid., p. 194. Brant to Russell, 5 October 1860, ibid., p. 165.
55. Bulwer to Russell, 1 October 1860, *Syria Correspondence 1860–61,* p. 159. Brant to Russell, 5 October 1860, ibid., pp. 164–65.
56. The export of domestic legalism from liberal Britain, in contrast to Fuad's overtly political punishments and France's unrestrained and overriding demands for vengeance, basically matches my argument in my *Stay the Hand of Vengeance: The Politics of War Crimes Tribunals* (Princeton, N.J.: Princeton University Press, 2000), pp. 6–29. Commission meeting, 11 October 1860, *Syria Correspondence 1860–61,* pp. 177–79; Russell to Dufferin, 2 November 1860, ibid., p. 186; Dufferin to Bulwer, 26 October 1860, ibid., pp. 189–90; PA/T, vol. 4, for Béclard's letters to Thouvenel. Dufferin to Moore, 15 October 1860, *Syria Correspondence 1860–61,* p. 190.
57. Moore to Dufferin, 23 October 1860, *Syria Correspondence 1860–61,* pp. 191–92. Un témoin oculaire, *Souvenirs de Syrie,* pp. 268, 277–78. Dufferin to Bulwer, 26 October 1860, *Syria Correspondence 1860–61,* pp. 190–91. Dufferin to Fuad, 25 October 1860, ibid., p. 193. Commission meeting, 26 October 1860, ibid., p. 213.
58. Dufferin to Bulwer, 26 October 1860, *Syria Correspondence 1860–61,* pp. 190–91. Dufferin to Bulwer, 1 November 1860, ibid., p. 204. Commission meeting, 23 October 1860, ibid., pp. 205–6. Brant to Russell, 8 November 1860, ibid., pp. 221–22. Bulwer to Dufferin, 11 December 1860, ibid., p. 266.
59. MD/T, vol. 123, no. 7, Beaufort to Randon, 10 March 1861; MD/T, vol. 123, no. 9, Beaufort to Randon, 15 March 1861; PA/T, vol. 4, Beaufort to Thouvenel, 21 December 1860. Commission meeting, 14 November 1860, *Syria Correspondence 1860–61,* pp. 242–46. Dufferin to Bulwer, 1 November 1860, ibid., p. 203; Lyall, *Dufferin,* vol. 1, p. 98. Dufferin speech, 10 November 1860, *Syria Correspondence 1860–61,* p. 225.
60. Scheltema, *Lebanon in Turmoil,* pp. 38–39; Damascus Jews to Montefiore, 23 September 1860, *Syria Correspondence 1860–61,* pp. 162–63.
61. Russell to Brant, 25 October 1860, *Syria Correspondence 1860–61,* pp. 175–76. Montefiore letter, "The Civil War in Syria," *Times,* 12 July 1860, p. 9. In 1876,

Montefiore was less humanitarian, standing behind the Ottoman Empire (Richard T. Shannon, *Gladstone and the Bulgarian Agitation 1876* [Sussex: Harvester, 1975], p. 199).

62. Brant to Bulwer, 11 October 1860, *Syria Correspondence 1860–61,* p. 185. Brant to Russell, 8 November 1860, ibid., pp. 221–22. Brant to Fuad, 26 November 1860, ibid., pp. 256–57; Fuad to Brant, 27 November 1860, ibid., pp. 257–58. Fuad to grand vizier, 5 December 1860, ibid., p. 325. Montefiore to Russell, 24 January 1861, ibid., p. 354. Russell to Dufferin, 31 January 1861, ibid., p. 354.
63. Fraser to Russell, 15 November 1860, *Syria Correspondence 1860–61,* p. 239; commission meeting, 14 November 1860, ibid., pp. 242–43. Dufferin to Bulwer, 17 November 1860, ibid., pp. 235–36.
64. Dufferin to Fraser, 28 November 1860, *Syria Correspondence 1860–61,* p. 255. Fraser to Russell, 29 December 1860, ibid., pp. 316–17. Dufferin to Bulwer, 4 December 1860, ibid., p. 272.
65. Dufferin to Bulwer, 30 December 1860, *Syria Correspondence 1860–61,* pp. 299–300, 314; commissioners to Fuad, 23 February 1861, ibid., pp. 450; MD/T, vol. 123, no. 7, Beaufort to Randon, 10 March 1861; MD/T, vol. 122, no. 27, Evénements de Damas. Dufferin to Bulwer, 21 September 1860, *Syria Correspondence 1860–61,* p. 137. Dufferin to Bulwer, 30 December 1860, ibid., pp. 300–301. Dufferin to Russell, 1 March 1861, ibid., pp. 460–61. Dufferin to Bulwer, 30 December 1860, Sentence on Said Bek Jumblâd, ibid., pp. 303–4.
66. Fraser to Dufferin, 19 January 1861, *Syria Correspondence 1860–61,* p. 379. Dufferin to commissioners, n.d., ibid., pp. 314–15; Dufferin to Bulwer, 30 December 1860, ibid., p. 314. Dufferin to Fraser, 23 January 1861, ibid., pp. 380–81.
67. Dufferin to Fraser, 23 January 1861, *Syria Correspondence 1860–61,* pp. 380–81. Dufferin to Fraser, 23 January 1861, ibid., pp. 380–81.
68. Fraser to Dufferin, 10 January 1861, *Syria Correspondence 1860–61,* p. 342. Fraser to Dufferin, 14 January 1861, ibid., pp. 357–58. Dufferin to Bulwer, 12 January 1861, ibid., p. 334.
69. Fraser to Dufferin, 17 January 1861, *Syria Correspondence 1860–61,* pp. 378–79. Bulwer to Russell, 30 January 1861, ibid., p. 382. Fraser to Dufferin, 23 January 1861, ibid., pp. 379–80. Dufferin to Bulwer, 1 February 1861, ibid., pp. 389–91. Dufferin to Russell, 4 March 1861, ibid., p. 474.
70. MD/T, vol. 123, no. 7, Beaufort to Randon, 10 March 1861; MD/T, vol. 123, no. 10, Beaufort to Randon, 24 March 1861. Un témoin oculaire, *Souvenirs de Syrie,* p. 273. MD/T, vol. 123, no. 10, Beaufort to Randon, 24 March 1861. Cowley to Russell, 7 February 1861, *Syria Correspondence 1860–61,* p. 382. Russell to Cowley, 8 February 1861, ibid., p. 383; Russell to Bulwer, 8 February 1861, ibid., p. 383; Russell to Dufferin, 11 February 1861, ibid., p. 384. CP/T, vol. 349, Russell to Cowley, 23 April 1861. CPC/B, vol. 13, no. 82, Bentivoglio to Thouvenel, 11 February 1861.
71. Dufferin to Bulwer, 29 January 1861, *Syria Correspondence 1860–61,* p. 387. Dufferin to Fraser, 23 January 1861, ibid., p. 388. Dufferin to Bulwer, 29 January 1861, ibid., p. 387; Fraser to Dufferin, 31 January 1861, ibid., pp. 391–92.
72. Dufferin to Russell. 1 March 1861, *Syria Correspondence 1860–61,* pp. 460–61.

Dufferin to Bulwer, 7 March 1861, ibid., p. 509. Russell to Dufferin, 18 March 1861, ibid., p. 462.

73. Dufferin to Russell, 10 March 1861, *Syria Correspondence 1860–61,* pp. 485–86. Lyall, *Dufferin,* vol. 1, p. 115.

MISSION CREEP

1. MD/T, vol. 123, Beaufort to Randon, various; PA/T, vol. 4, Beaufort to Thouvenel, various. J. F. Scheltema, *The Lebanon in Turmoil: Syria and the Powers in 1860* (New Haven, Conn.: Yale University Press, 1920), p. 166. Baptistin Poujoulat, *La vérité sur la Syrie et l'expédition française* (Paris: Gaume frères et J. Duprey, 1861), p. 487. PA/T, vol. 5, Bentivoglio to Thouvenel, 28 January 1861.
2. Martin to Admiralty, 7 October 1860, Great Britain, Foreign Office, *Correspondence Relating to the Affairs of Syria 1860–61* (London: Harrison and Sons, 1861), pp. 168–69. Martin to Heathcote, 10 October 1860, ibid., pp. 200–201.
3. Russell to Cowley, 7 November 1860, *Syria Correspondence 1860–61,* p. 186. The reluctance to hunt down accused war criminals supports my argument in my *Stay the Hand of Vengeance: The Politics of War Crimes Tribunals* (Princeton, N.J.: Princeton University Press, 2000), pp. 29–30, 277. Russell to Cowley, 7 November 1860, *Syria Correspondence 1860–61,* p. 186. Russell to Bulwer, 10 November 1860, ibid., p. 199. Russell to Cowley, 7 November 1860, ibid., p. 186.
4. CPC/B, vol. 13, no. 82, Bentivoglio to Thouvenel, 11 February 1861. Wrench to Russell, 20 October 1860, *Syria Correspondence 1860–61,* p. 199; Wrench to Bulwer, 5 November 1860, ibid., pp. 220–21. PA/T, vol. 4, Beaufort to Thouvenel, 13 January 1861. PA/T, vol. 4, Beaufort to Thouvenel, 24 March 1861. PA/T, vol. 4, Beaufort to Thouvenel, 27 January 1861. CPC/B, vol. 13, no. 75, Bentivoglio to Thouvenel, 16 December 1860.
5. MD/T, vol. 122, no. 17, "Note sur les Causes de l'évacuation de la Syrie par la France, 1860–1861." Cowley to Russell, 13 November 1860, *Syria Correspondence 1860–61,* pp. 201–2.
6. CPC/B, vol. 13, no. 75, Bentivoglio to Thouvenel, 16 December 1860. Russell to Dufferin, 22 November 1860, *Syria Correspondence 1860–61,* p. 223; Russell to Bulwer, 22 November 1860, ibid., pp. 222–23. Dufferin to Bulwer, 14 November 1860, ibid., pp. 229–30. Dufferin to Bulwer, 3 November 1860, ibid., pp. 208–12.
7. Cowley to Russell, 11 December 1860, *Syria Correspondence 1860–61,* pp. 248–49.
8. Ali to Russell, 28 November 1860, ibid., pp. 249–50.
9. CPC/B, vol. 13, no. 82, Bentivoglio to Thouvenel, 11 February 1861. MD/T, vol. 123, no. 10, Beaufort to Randon, 24 March 1861.
10. Dufferin to Bulwer, 4 December 1860, *Syria Correspondence 1860–61,* pp. 271, 74.
11. Un témoin oculaire (An eyewitness), *Souvenirs de Syrie: Expédition française de 1860* (Paris: Plon, 1903), p. 285. Fuad to Ali, 2 January 1861, *Syria Correspondence 1860–61,* pp. 347–48. Dufferin to Bulwer, 18 November 1860, ibid., p. 236. Brant to Russell, 11 August 1860, ibid., p. 83. Fraser to Russell, 2 December 1860, ibid., p. 260. Dufferin to Bulwer, 27 February 1861, ibid., p. 480. Dufferin to Bulwer,

29 November 1860, ibid., p. 261. Dufferin to Russell, 19 December 1860, ibid., p. 286. Dufferin to Bulwer, 11 December 1860, ibid., p. 281.

12. Fraser to Dufferin, 14 January 1861, *Syria Correspondence 1860–61,* p. 357. Russell to Dufferin, 1 February 1861, ibid., p. 364; CP/T, vol. 349, no. 31, Thouvenel to Lavalette, 12 April 1861; CP/T, vol. 349, no. 32, Thouvenel to Lavalette, 14 April 1861; CP/T, vol. 349, Thouvenel to Lavalette, 11 May 1861. Alfred Comyn Lyall, *The Life of the Marquis of Dufferin and Ava,* vol. 1 (London: John Murray, 1905), pp. 116–17. Dufferin to Fraser, 16 January 1861, *Syria Correspondence 1860–61,* p. 359.
13. Bulwer to Russell, 11 December 1860, *Syria Correspondence 1860–61,* pp. 263–64. Dufferin to Bulwer, 18 December 1860, ibid., p. 289.
14. Russell to Bulwer, 1 January 1861, *Syria Correspondence 1860–61,* p. 283. Russell to Ali, 26 December 1860, ibid., p. 268.
15. MD/T, vol. 122, no. 17, "Note sur les Causes de l'évacuation de la Syrie par la France, 1860–1861." Cowley to Russell, 4 January 1861, *Syria Correspondence 1860–61,* pp. 295–96.
16. Cowley to Russell, 4 January 1861, *Syria Correspondence 1860–61,* pp. 295–96. Russell to Cowley, 9 January 1861, ibid., pp. 296–97. Cowley to Russell, 11 January 1861, ibid., pp. 317–18.
17. Cowley to Russell, 11 January 1861, *Syria Correspondence 1860–61,* pp. 317–18.
18. Dufferin to Bulwer, 12 January 1861, ibid., pp. 333–34. Russell to Fane, 16 January 1861, ibid., pp. 321–23.
19. Dufferin to Bulwer, 1 February 1861, *Syria Correspondence 1860–61,* pp. 390–91. Dufferin to Bulwer, 11 February 1861, ibid., p. 403. Russell to Fane, 16 January 1861, ibid., pp. 321–23.
20. Fane to Russell, 17 January 1861, *Syria Correspondence 1860–61,* p. 328. Lowther to Russell, 19 January 1861, ibid., p. 328. Lowther to Russell, 12 January 1861, ibid., p. 318. Commission meeting, 19 January 1861, ibid., pp. 394–97. Cowley to Russell, 12 February 1861, ibid., p. 386.
21. Russell to Bulwer, 17 January 1861, *Syria Correspondence 1860–61,* p. 324.
22. Commission meeting, 19 January 1861, *Syria Correspondence 1860–61,* pp. 394–97. Lyall, *Dufferin,* vol. 1, p. 119.
23. Thouvenel to Russell, 18 January 1861, *Syria Correspondence 1860–61,* pp. 329–31; Thouvenel to ambassadors, 18 January 1861, France, Ministère des Affaires Étrangères, *Documents diplomatiques 1860,* vol. 1 (Paris: Imprimerie Impériale, 1861), pp. 217–19.
24. Russell to Thouvenel, 24 January 1861, *Syria Correspondence 1860–61,* pp. 331–32. Ali to Russell, 21 January 1861, ibid., pp. 369–70. Russell to Thouvenel, 24 January 1861, ibid., pp. 331–32.
25. Cowley to Russell, 28 January 1861, *Syria Correspondence 1860–61,* pp. 350–51.
26. Bulwer to Ali, 29 January 1861, *Syria Correspondence 1860–61,* pp. 381–82; Russell to Cowley, 9 February 1861, ibid., pp. 383–84; MD/T, vol. 122, no. 17, "Note sur les Causes de l'évacuation de la Syrie par la France, 1860–1861." Russell to Cowley, 30 January 1861, *Syria Correspondence 1860–61,* pp. 352–53. Russell to Dufferin, 1 February 1861, ibid., p. 364. Russell to Cowley, 6 February 1861, ibid., p.

371. Russell to Cowley, 19 February 1861, ibid., pp. 393–94. Russell to Cowley, 9 February 1861, ibid., pp. 383–84.

27. Russell to Cowley, 30 January 1861, *Syria Correspondence 1860–61,* pp. 351–52; Russell to Bulwer, 14 February 1861, ibid., p. 386; Russell to Cowley, 14 February 1861, ibid., p. 386. Russell to Admiralty, 15 February 1861, ibid., p. 386. Russell to Cowley, 19 February 1861, ibid., pp. 393–94.

28. Dufferin to Bulwer, 15 December 1860, *Syria Correspondence 1860–61,* pp. 282–83. Ali to Russell, 9 January 1861, ibid., pp. 320–21; Lyall, *Dufferin,* vol. 1, p. 118. Bulwer to Russell, 18 January 1861, *Syria Correspondence 1860–61,* pp. 349. Dufferin to Russell, 10 February 1861, ibid., pp. 405–7. Dufferin to Bulwer, 12 February 1861, ibid., pp. 433–34. Wrench to Bulwer, 25 February 1861, ibid., pp. 459–60.

29. Thouvenel to Cowley, 13 February 1861, *Syria Correspondence 1860–61,* p. 393. MD/T, vol. 123, no. 10, Beaufort to Randon, 24 March 1861. Cowley to Russell, 19 February 1861, *Syria Correspondence 1860–61,* p. 408.

30. Cowley to Russell, 19 February 1861, *Syria Correspondence 1860–61,* p. 409.

31. Loftus to Russell, 16 February 1861, *Syria Correspondence 1860–61,* p. 411. See Loftus to Russell, 2 March 1861, ibid., p. 423.

32. Cowley to Russell, 19 February 1861, ibid., pp. 409–10.

33. Cowley to Russell, 19 February 1861, ibid., p. 410.

34. Russell to Cowley, 21 February 1861, ibid., p. 410. Bulwer to Russell, 27 February 1861, ibid., p. 427. Russell to Cowley, 21 February 1861, ibid., p. 411.

35. Cowley to Russell, 22 February 1861, ibid., p. 412. Thouvenel to Russell, 25 February 1861, ibid., pp. 415–20.

36. Russell to Cowley, 27 February 1861, ibid., pp. 420–21.

37. Ali to Vefik, 7 March 1861, ibid., p. 425. Russell to Cowley, 7 March 1861, ibid., pp. 424–25.

38. Cowley to Russell, 7 March 1861, ibid., p. 426; Russell to Cowley, 8 March 1861, ibid., p. 426. Cowley to Russell, 15 March 1861, ibid., pp. 456–57. MD/T, vol. 122, no. 17, "Note sur les Causes de l'évacuation de la Syrie par la France, 1860–1861."

39. Cowley to Russell, 15 March 1861, *Syria Correspondence 1860–61,* p. 459. Russell to Cowley, 16 March 1861, ibid., p. 459. CP/T, Russell to Admiralty, April 1861.

40. MD/T, vol. 123, no. 7, Beaufort to Randon, 10 March 1861. MD/T, vol. 123, no. 8, D'Arrican to Beaufort, 11 March 1861. MD/T, vol. 123, no. 9, Beaufort to Randon, 15 March 1861. MD/T, vol. 123, no. 10, Beaufort to Randon, 24 March 1861.

41. PA/T, vol. 4, Beaufort to Thouvenel, 20 April 1861. CP/T, vol. 349, no. 51, Lavalette to Thouvenel, 10 April 1861. PA/T, vol. 12, Lavalette to Thouvenel, 10 April 1861.

42. PA/T, vol. 5, Bentivoglio to Thouvenel, 22 April 1861. CP/T, vol. 349, no. 73, Lavalette to Thouvenel, 15 May 1861.

43. Dufferin to Russell, 24 February 1861, *Syria Correspondence 1860–61,* pp. 439–42. Russell to Dufferin, 2 March 1861, ibid., p. 422. CP/T, vol. 349, Russell to Cowley, 23 April 1861.

44. Bulwer to Russell, 7 March 1861, *Syria Correspondence 1860–61,* p. 473. CP/T, vol. 349, no. 69, Lavalette to Thouvenel, 8 May 1861. PA/T, vol. 12, Lavalette to Thouvenel, 27 March 1861; PA/T, vol. 12, Lavalette to Thouvenel, 3 April 1861. MD/T,

vol. 123, no. 7, Beaufort to Randon, 10 March 1861. PA/T, vol. 4, Beaufort to Thouvenel, 5 May 1861. CP/T, vol. 349, no. 49, Lavalette to Thouvenel, 3 April 1861. CP/T, vol. 349, no. 51, Lavalette to Thouvenel, 10 April 1861. See CP/T, vol. 349, no. 52, Lavalette to Thouvenel, 10 April 1861; CP/T, vol. 349, no. 34, Thouvenel to Lavalette, 19 April 1861; CP/T, vol. 349, Russell to Cowley, 23 April 1861.

45. CP/T, vol. 349, Thouvenel to Lavalette, 24 April 1861. CP/T, vol. 349, no. 69, Lavalette to Thouvenel, 8 May 1861. Lyall, *Dufferin,* vol. 1, p. 114. CP/T, vol. 349, Lavalette to Thouvenel, 16 May 1861. CPC/B, vol. 13, no. 98, Bentivoglio to Thouvenel, 18 May 1861.

46. CPC/B, vol. 13, no. 86, Bentivoglio to Thouvenel, 19 April 1861. PA/T, vol. 4, Béclard to Thouvenel, 10 May 1861. PA/T, vol. 4, Beaufort to Thouvenel, 10 May 1861; PA/T, vol. 4, Beaufort to Thouvenel, 24 May 1861. See MD/T, vol. 123, no. 10, Beaufort to Randon, 24 March 1861. CPC/B, vol. 13, no. 88, Bentivoglio to Thouvenel, 20 April 1861.

47. CPC/B, vol. 13, no. 89, Bentivoglio to Thouvenel, 22 April 1861. CPC/B, vol. 13, no. 95, Bentivoglio to Thouvenel, 10 May 1861. CPC/B, vol. 13, Christians to Powers, 22 April 1861.

48. CPC/B, vol. 13, no. 4, Thouvenel to Bentivoglio, 10 May 1861. CP/T, vol. 349, Thouvenel to Lavalette, 17 May 1861; CP/T, vol. 349, no. 49, Thouvenel to Lavalette, 17 May 1861; PA/T, vol. 4, Beaufort to Thouvenel, 10 May 1861. CP/T, vol. 349, no. 78, Lavalette to Thouvenel, 22 May 1861; CP/T, vol. 349, Thouvenel to Lavalette, 28 May 1861. CP/T, vol. 350, Lavalette to Thouvenel, 10 June 1861; CP/T, vol. 350, no. 85, Lavalette to Thouvenel, 12 June 1861; CP/T, vol. 350, no. 85, "Règlement pour l'administration du Liban." CPC/B, vol. 13, no. 5, Thouvenel to Bentivoglio, 17 May 1861. Un témoin oculaire, *Souvenirs de Syrie,* pp. 296–97.

49. CPC/B, vol. 13, no. 107, Bentivoglio to Thouvenel, 2 June 1861. Poujoulat, *Vérité sur la Syrie,* p. xxiii.

50. CPC/B, vol. 13, no. 98, Bentivoglio to Thouvenel, 18 May 1861. PA/T, vol. 5, Bentivoglio to Thouvenel, 5 May 1861.

51. CPC/B, vol. 13, no. 98, Bentivoglio to Thouvenel, 18 May 1861. Dufferin to Russell, 24 February 1861, *Syria Correspondence 1860–61,* pp. 439–40.

52. Lyall, *Dufferin,* vol. 1, pp. 115, 120.

53. CPC/B, vol. 13, no. 105, Bentivoglio to Thouvenel, 1 June 1861.

54. CPC/B, vol. 13, no. 108, Bentivoglio to Thouvenel, 6 June 1861.

55. CPC/B, vol. 13, no. 9, Thouvenel to Bentivoglio, 14 June 1861. CPC/B, vol. 13, no. 108, Bentivoglio to Thouvenel, 6 June 1861; CPC/B, vol. 13, no. 9, Thouvenel to Bentivoglio, 14 June 1861; CPC/B, vol. 13, Firman Imperial relatif à l'administration du Mont Liban, 23 June 1861. Samir Khalaf, *Civil and Uncivil Violence in Lebanon: A History of the Internationalization of Communal Conflict* (New York: Columbia University Press, 2002), pp. 277–82; Stanford J. Shaw and Ezel Kural Shaw, *History of the Ottoman Empire and Modern Turkey,* vol. 2 (Cambridge: Cambridge University Press, 1977), pp. 143–44.

56. CPC/B, vol. 13, no. 111, Bentivoglio to Thouvenel, 16 June 1861.

57. CPC/B, vol. 13, no. 108, Bentivoglio to Thouvenel, 6 June 1861. Leila Tarazi

Fawaz, *An Occasion for War: Civil Conflict in Lebanon and Damascus in 1860* (Berkeley: University of California Press, 1994), p. 127. Un témoin oculaire, *Souvenirs de Syrie,* pp. 298–99.

58. Fuad to Abdulaziz, 3 January 1862, J. Lewis Farley, *Turks and Christians: A Solution of the Eastern Question* (London: Simpkin, Marshall, 1876), p. 244.
59. CPC/B, vol. 13, no. 113, Bentivoglio to Thouvenel, 20 June 1861.
60. Khalaf, *Violence in Lebanon,* pp. 103–50.
61. Stanley Karnow, *Vietnam: A History* (New York: Penguin, 1984), pp. 76–79.

PART FOUR: BULGARIANS

1. Januarius Aloysius MacGahan, *Campaigning on the Oxus, and the Fall of Khiva* (New York: Harper and Brothers, 1874), and *Under the Northern Lights* (London: Low, Marston, Searle, and Rivington, 1876). *The History of The Times: The Tradition Established, 1841–1884,* vol. 2 (London: The Times, 1939), p. 465. Phillip Knightley, *The First Casualty: From the Crimea to Vietnam: The War Correspondent as Hero, Propagandist, and Myth Maker* (New York: Harcourt Brace Jovanovich, 1975), p. 50; Maria Todorova, *Imagining the Balkans* (New York: Oxford University Press, 1997), p. 106.
2. "The War in the East: The Atrocities in Bulgaria," *Daily News,* 7 August 1876, p. 5. See "Turkish Atrocities in Bulgaria," *Daily News,* 22 August 1876, pp. 5–6.
3. Marc Trachtenberg, "Intervention in Historical Perspective," in Laura W. Reed and Carl Kaysen, eds., *Emerging Norms of Humanitarian Intervention* (Cambridge, Mass.: American Academy of Arts and Sciences, 1993), p. 25; Akaby Nassibian, *Britain and the Armenian Question 1915–1923* (London: Croom Helm, 1984), p. 33.
4. John Rentoul, *Tony Blair: Prime Minister* (London: Warner, 2001), p. 529.

THE EASTERN QUESTION

1. Fiona MacCarthy, *Byron: Life and Legend* (New York: Farrar, Straus and Giroux, 2002), pp. 558–60; Robert Blake, *Disraeli* (New York: St. Martin's Press, 1967), pp. 51–52. Disraeli to Bradford, 4 September 1875, Marquis of Zetland, ed., *The Letters of Disraeli to Lady Chesterfield and Lady Bradford,* vol. 1 (New York: D. Appleton, 1929), p. 362.
2. Blake, *Disraeli,* p. 65; W. F. Monypenny and George Earle Buckle, *The Life of Benjamin Disraeli, Earl of Beaconsfield,* vol. 1 (New York: Macmillan, 1912), p. 164.
3. Benjamin Disraeli, *Speech by the Late Earl of Beaconsfield, K.G., at the Free Trade Hall, Manchester, April 3, 1872* (London: National Union of Conservative and Constitutional Associations, n.d.), p. 28. Blake, *Disraeli,* pp. 581, 584. Disraeli's letters to Bradford, 25–30 November 1875, *Letters of Disraeli to Chesterfield and Bradford,* vol. 1, pp. 400–403. Victoria's journal, March 1876, *The Letters of Queen Victoria: A Selection from Her Majesty's Correspondence and Journal between the Years 1862 and 1878,* ed. George Earle Buckle, 2nd series, vol. 2 (New York: Longmans, Green, 1926), p. 451.
4. Blake, *Disraeli,* pp. 578–59. Disraeli to Bradford, 20 August 1875, *Letters of Disraeli to Chesterfield and Bradford,* vol. 1, pp. 357–58.

5. Disraeli to Bradford, 21 October 1875, *Letters of Disraeli to Chesterfield and Bradford,* vol. 1, p. 387. Victoria to Derby, 27 May 1876, *Letters of Victoria,* vol. 2, p. 455.
6. Disraeli to Victoria, 11 November 1876, *Letters of Victoria,* vol. 2, p. 497. Blake, *Disraeli,* pp. 576–77, 589. B. H. Sumner, *Russia and the Balkans 1870–1880* (Oxford: Oxford University Press, 1937), pp. 39–43; Henry Rawlinson, *England and Russia in the East* (London: John Murray, 1875); Charles Marvin, *Russia's Power of Seizing Herat, and Concentrating an Army There to Threaten India* (London: W. H. Allen, 1884); Ármin Vámbéry, *The Coming Struggle for India: Being an Account of the Encroachments of Russia in Asia, and of the Difficulties Sure to Arise Therefrom to England* (London: Cassell, 1885). Robert Blake, *Gladstone, Disraeli, and Queen Victoria* (Oxford: Clarendon Press, 1993), pp. 19–22.
7. Disraeli to Bradford, 6 September 1875, *Letters of Disraeli to Chesterfield and Bradford,* vol. 1, p. 363.
8. Paul W. Schroeder, *Austria, Great Britain, and the Crimean War: The Destruction of the European Concert* (Ithaca, N.Y.: Cornell University Press, 1972), pp. xii, 387; Richard T. Shannon, *Gladstone and the Bulgarian Agitation 1876* (Sussex: Harvester, 1975), p. 15. Ann Pottinger Saab, *Reluctant Icon: Gladstone, Bulgaria, and the Working Classes 1856–1878* (Cambridge, Mass.: Harvard University Press, 1991), p. 1. Palmerston to Canning, 7 November 1849, Evelyn Ashley, ed., *The Life and Correspondence of Henry John Temple, Viscount Palmerston,* vol. 2 (London: Richard Bentley and Son, 1879), p. 117.
9. Monypenny and Buckle, *Life of Disraeli,* vol. 6, pp. 16–17. Derby to Ponsonby, 20 June 1876, ibid., pp. 33–34.

PAN-SLAVISM

1. Leo Tolstoy, "On Patriotism," in *Tolstoy's Writings on Civil Disobedience and Non-Violence* (New York: Bergman, 1967; orig. 1894), pp. 94–95.
2. Hans Kohn, *Pan-Slavism: Its History and Ideology* (New York: Vintage, 1960), p. 131. Graham Storey, *Reuters: The Story of a Century of News-Gathering* (New York: Crown, 1951), p. 100. Richard Pipes, *Russia Under the Old Regime* (London: Penguin, 1995), pp. 264–65, 292–93. B. H. Sumner, *Russia and the Balkans 1870–1880* (Oxford: Oxford University Press, 1937), pp. 3–7, 9.
3. Kohn, *Pan-Slavism,* p. 149.
4. Isaiah Berlin, *Russian Thinkers* (London: Penguin, 1995), p. 18. Kohn, *Pan-Slavism,* pp. 139–40, 149, 159. Sumner, *Russia and the Balkans,* pp. 58, 68.
5. Pipes, *Russia Under the Old Regime,* pp. 266–67. Geoffrey Hosking, *Russia: People and Empire 1552–1917* (Cambridge, Mass.: Harvard University Press, 1997), pp. 368–69; Hans Kohn, ed., *The Mind of Modern Russia: Historical and Political Thought of Russia's Great Age* (New Brunswick, N.J.: Rutgers University Press, 1955), pp. 106–8; Kohn, *Pan-Slavism,* pp. 150–59. James H. Billington, *The Icon and the Axe: An Interpretive History of Russian Culture* (New York: Vintage, 1970), pp. 380, 396. Kohn, *Pan-Slavism,* p. 163.
6. Kohn, *Pan-Slavism,* pp. 157, 190–97; Billington, *Icon and Axe,* p. 396; Sumner,

Russia and the Balkans, pp. 76–77. Engels, "The Real Issue in Turkey," *New York Daily Tribune,* 12 April 1853, p. 4.

7. Kohn, *Pan-Slavism,* pp. 210–11; Billington, *Icon and Axe,* p. 424. Joseph Frank, *Dostoevsky: The Mantle of the Prophet, 1871–1881* (Princeton, N.J.: Princeton University Press, 2002), pp. 22, 243, 275, 478, 480–82. Kohn, *Pan-Slavism,* pp. 190–91. Dostoevsky, *The Diary of a Writer,* trans. Boris Brasol (New York: Scribner, 1949), November 1877, pp. 903–7. Dostoevsky to Strakhov, 16 February 1872, and Dostoevsky to Maykov, 17 January 1877, Dostoevsky, *Complete Letters,* trans. and ed. David A. Love, vol. 4 (Ann Arbor, Mich.: Ardis, 1991), pp. 21, 347. Dostoevsky, *A Writer's Diary,* trans. Kenneth Lantz, vol. 1 (Evanston, Ill.: Northwestern University Press, 1993), June 1876, p. 529.
8. Tolstoy, "On Patriotism," p. 100. Berlin, *Russian Thinkers,* pp. 186–209; Kohn, *Pan-Slavism,* pp. 164–65, 170–71.
9. Billington, *Icon and Axe,* pp. 395–96. Kohn, *Pan-Slavism,* pp. 161–62, 176–78. Sumner, *Russia and the Balkans,* p. 78. Berlin, *Russian Thinkers,* pp. 281, 284, 286. Hosking, *Russia,* pp. 368–69.
10. Kohn, *Pan-Slavism,* p. xv. Canning to Wellington, 27 September 1822, Arthur Wellesley, Duke of Wellington, *Despatches, Correspondence, and Memoranda of Field Marshal Arthur, Duke of Wellington,* vol. 2 (London: John Murray, 1867), p. 371. René Albrecht-Carrié, *A Diplomatic History of Europe Since the Congress of Vienna* (New York: Harper and Row, 1958), pp. 19, 43, 168.
11. Misha Glenny, *The Balkans: Nationalism, War and the Great Powers, 1804–1999* (New York: Viking, 2000), pp. 14–15. Hosking, *Russia,* pp. 370–71; Paul W. Schroeder, *Austria, Great Britain, and the Crimean War: The Destruction of the European Concert* (Ithaca, N.Y.: Cornell University Press, 1972), p. 398.
12. Sumner, *Russia and the Balkans,* p. 74. Schroeder, *Crimean War,* p. 398.
13. Donald Kagan, *On the Origins of War and the Preservation of Peace* (New York: Doubleday, 1994), pp. 103–4. "The Turkish Question," *New York Daily Tribune,* 19 April 1853, Kohn, *Pan-Slavism,* p. 107. Marx, "Pan-Slavism," *New York Daily Tribune,* 5 May 1855, Kohn, *Pan-Slavism,* pp. 108–9. The *Daily Tribune* attributes these pieces to Engels.
14. Sumner, *Russia and the Balkans,* pp. 19, 29, 274–75. Glenny, *Balkans,* p. 129.
15. Sumner, *Russia and the Balkans,* pp. 61, 74–76, 80. David MacKenzie, *Serbs and Russians* (New York: Columbia University Press, 1996), p. 9. Philip Mansel, *Constantinople: City of the World's Desire, 1453–1924* (New York: St. Martin's Press, 1998), p. 300.

BOSNIA AND SERBIA

1. Bernard Lewis, *The Emergence of Modern Turkey,* 3rd ed. (New York: Oxford University Press, 2002), p. 159. Palmerston to Canning, 7 November 1849, Evelyn Ashley, ed., *The Life and Correspondence of Henry John Temple, Viscount Palmerston,* vol. 2 (London: Richard Bentley and Son, 1879), p. 117. B. H. Sumner, *Russia and the Balkans 1870–1880* (Oxford: Oxford University Press, 1937), pp. 110–13. R. W. Seton-Watson, *Disraeli, Gladstone, and the Eastern Question: A Study in*

Diplomacy and Party Politics (London: Macmillan, 1935), p. 19; Sumner, *Russia and the Balkans,* p. 130.

2. Sumner, *Russia and the Balkans,* pp. 141, 154. R. Grant Barnwell, *The Russo-Turkish War: Comprising an Account of the Servian Insurrection, the Dreadful Massacre of Christians in Bulgaria, and Other Turkish Atrocities* (Toledo, Ohio: I. D. Cartright, 1878), pp. 386–87. Seton-Watson, *Eastern Question,* p. 20.
3. Geoffrey Hosking, *Russia: People and Empire 1552–1917* (Cambridge, Mass.: Harvard University Press, 1997), p. 371. Sumner, *Russia and the Balkans,* pp. 138, 142, 144–49, 152. René Albrecht-Carrié, *A Diplomatic History of Europe Since the Congress of Vienna* (New York: Harper and Row, 1958), p. 169.
4. Dostoevsky, *A Writer's Diary,* trans. Kenneth Lantz, vol. 1 (Evanston, Ill.: Northwestern University Press, 1993), March 1876, p. 400. Sumner, *Russia and the Balkans,* pp. 185, 158.
5. Robert Blake, *Disraeli* (New York: St. Martin's Press, 1967), p. 580; W. F. Monypenny and George Earle Buckle, *The Life of Benjamin Disraeli, Earl of Beaconsfield,* vol. 6 (New York: Macmillan, 1920), p. 19. *The History of The Times: The Tradition Established, 1841–1884,* vol. 2 (London: The Times, 1939), pp. 143–46. Graham Storey, *Reuters: The Story of a Century of News-Gathering* (New York: Crown, 1951), p. 98. The reporter had to send almost all of his telegrams in code into Bulgaria and thence to London in order to avoid even tighter Ottoman censorship imposed after the 1876 Bulgarian massacres.
6. *Times,* 2 October 1875, p. 5. "The Herzegovina Insurrection," *Times,* 28 August 1875, p. 3; "Herzegovina," *Times,* 13 September 1875, p. 8. "The Herzegovina," *Times,* 24 September 1875, p. 10; "The Herzegovina," *Times,* 24 September 1875, p. 10. Leader, *Times,* 30 August 1875, p. 9. "The Herzegovina," *Times,* 21 August 1875, p. 6.
7. "Herzegovina," *Times,* 16 September 1875, p. 3. Leader, *Times,* 17 September 1875, p. 9. Richard T. Shannon, *Gladstone and the Bulgarian Agitation 1876* (Sussex: Harvester, 1975), p. 37. "The Herzegovina Meeting," *Times,* 10 September 1875, p. 7. Leader, *Times,* 30 August 1875, p. 9.
8. Monypenny and Buckle, *Life of Disraeli,* vol. 6, p. 13; Blake, *Disraeli,* p. 579. Disraeli to Chesterfield, 16 October 1875, Marquis of Zetland, ed., *The Letters of Disraeli to Lady Chesterfield and Lady Bradford,* vol. 1 (New York: D. Appleton, 1929), p. 384; Disraeli to Bradford, 3 November 1875, ibid., p. 389.
9. Disraeli to Victoria, 16 May 1876, and Ponsonby to Disraeli, 16 May 1876, *The Letters of Queen Victoria: A Selection from Her Majesty's Correspondence and Journal between the Years 1862 and 1878,* ed. George Earle Buckle, 2nd series, vol. 2 (New York: Longmans, Green, 1926), pp. 458–59. Disraeli cabinet memorandum, 16 May 1876, Monypenny and Buckle, *Life of Disraeli,* vol. 6, pp. 24–25. Disraeli to Bradford, 13 June 1876, *Letters of Disraeli to Chesterfield and Bradford,* vol. 2, pp. 64–65; Disraeli to Chesterfield, 20 June 1876, ibid., p. 65; Disraeli to Manners, 7 June 1876, Monypenny and Buckle, *Life of Disraeli,* vol. 6, p. 31; Disraeli to Victoria, 18 May 1876, *Letters of Victoria,* vol. 2, p. 454. Monypenny and Buckle, *Life of Disraeli,* vol. 6, p. 38. Disraeli to Victoria, 29 May 1876, *Letters of Victoria,* vol. 2, p. 455.

10. Sumner, *Russia and the Balkans,* pp. 154, 124–25, 158–59, 194.
11. Hosking, *Russia,* p. 371. Hans Kohn, *Pan-Slavism: Its History and Ideology* (New York: Vintage, 1960), pp. 214–15. Sumner, *Russia and the Balkans,* p. 185. FO 65/938, Cherniaev to *Russki Mir,* 28 May 1876.
12. Edvard Radzinsky, *Alexander II: The Last Great Tsar,* trans. Antonina W. Bouis (New York: Free Press, 2005), p. 259. Aleksandr II to Victoria, 22 June–4 July 1876, *Letters of Victoria,* vol. 2, p. 468. Sumner, *Russia and the Balkans,* p. 173. Disraeli to Derby, 24 June 1876, Monypenny and Buckle, *Life of Disraeli,* vol. 6, pp. 34–35.
13. Radzinsky, *Alexander II,* p. 261. Blake, *Disraeli,* p. 589. Sumner, *Russia and the Balkans,* pp. 177–79, 186, 189.
14. FO 65/941/513, Loftus to Derby, 2 November 1876. FO 65/940/472, Loftus to Derby, 9 October 1876; FO 65/940/474, Loftus to Derby, 10 October 1876. Sumner puts the total at five thousand (*Russia and the Balkans,* pp. 186, 189).
15. Derby to Victoria, 29 September 1876, Monypenny and Buckle, *Life of Disraeli,* vol. 6, p. 76. Granville to Gladstone, 3 October 1876, Agatha Ramm, ed., *The Political Correspondence of Mr. Gladstone and Lord Granville,* vol. 1 (Oxford: Clarendon, 1962), p. 12. Disraeli to Derby, 30 September 1876, Monypenny and Buckle, *Life of Disraeli,* vol. 6, p. 76.
16. Wilhelm I to Victoria, 8 October 1876, *Letters of Victoria,* vol. 2, p. 485.
17. Sumner, *Russia and the Balkans,* pp. 195–97. Dostoevsky, *Writer's Diary,* vol. 1, June 1876, p. 531. Leo Tolstoy, *Anna Karenina,* trans. Richard Pevear and Larissa Volokhonsky (London: Penguin, 2000), p. 808. See also pp. 777, 781.
18. Dostoevsky, *Writer's Diary,* vol. 1, June and October 1876, pp. 531–32, 673. W. T. Stead, ed., *The M.P. for Russia: Reminiscences and Correspondence of Madame Olga Novikoff* (London: Andrew Melrose, 1909), pp. 229–36.
19. Tolstoy, *Anna Karenina,* pp. 771–73, 775, 779. See, for instance, FO 65/940/410, "Off to Servia," *Riga Journal,* 6 September 1876.
20. Disraeli to Derby, 28 June 1876, Monypenny and Buckle, *Life of Disraeli,* vol. 6, p. 36. Seton-Watson, *Eastern Question,* p. 41; Blake, *Disraeli,* pp. 589–90.
21. Derby to Ponsonby, 20 June 1876, Monypenny and Buckle, *Life of Disraeli,* vol. 6, p. 33. Disraeli to Victoria, 29 June 1876, ibid., p. 35.
22. Disraeli to Victoria, 7 July 1876, *Letters of Victoria,* vol. 2, pp. 468–69. Disraeli to Chesterfield, 9 July 1876, *Letters of Disraeli to Chesterfield and Bradford,* vol. 2, p. 69. Disraeli to Bradford, 20 August 1875, ibid., vol. 1, p. 357. Disraeli to Bradford, 13 July 1876, ibid., vol. 2, pp. 70–71.

BULGARIAN HORRORS

1. R. J. Crampton, *A Concise History of Bulgaria* (Cambridge: Cambridge University Press, 1997), pp. 81–83.
2. Graham Storey, *Reuters: The Story of a Century of News-Gathering* (New York: Crown, 1951), p. 18. Phillip Knightley, *The First Casualty: From the Crimea to Vietnam: The War Correspondent as Hero, Propagandist, and Myth Maker* (New York: Harcourt Brace Jovanovich, 1975), p. 50. Maria Todorova, *Imagining the Balkans* (New York: Oxford University Press, 1997), p. 106.

3. Aled Jones, *Powers of the Press: Newspapers, Power and the Public in Nineteenth-Century England* (Cambridge: Scolar Press, 1996), pp. 162–63. Disraeli to Bradford, 25 May 1875, Marquis of Zetland, ed., *The Letters of Disraeli to Lady Chesterfield and Lady Bradford,* vol. 1 (New York: D. Appleton, 1929), p. 319. Disraeli to Bradford, 2 October 1875, ibid., p. 377. Disraeli to Chesterfield, 5 May 1875, ibid., p. 305. Disraeli to Chesterfield, 2 April 1876, ibid., vol. 2, p. 33.
4. Disraeli to Bradford, 21 May 1875, *Letters of Disraeli to Chesterfield and Bradford,* vol. 1, pp. 315–16. Robert Blake, *Disraeli* (New York: St. Martin's Press, 1967), pp. 531–32. Disraeli to Bradford, 2 September 1876, *Letters of Disraeli to Chesterfield and Bradford,* vol. 2, p. 85.
5. "The Assassinations at Constantinople," *Daily News,* 23 June 1876, pp. 5–6. "The Moslem Atrocities in Bulgaria," *Daily News,* 8 July 1876, pp. 5–6.
6. *The History of The Times: The Tradition Established, 1841–1884,* vol. 2 (London: The Times, 1939), p. 465.
7. Richard T. Shannon, *Gladstone and the Bulgarian Agitation 1876* (Sussex: Harvester, 1975), pp. 42–43. Disraeli in Parliament, 10 July 1876, W. F. Monypenny and George Earle Buckle, *The Life of Benjamin Disraeli, Earl of Beaconsfield,* vol. 6 (New York: Macmillan, 1920), p. 43.
8. Michael B. Petrovich, "Eugene Schuyler and Bulgaria, 1876–1878," *Balkan Historical Review,* vol. 1 (1979), pp. 51–69. Knightley, *First Casualty,* p. 50. Todorova, *Imagining the Balkans,* p. 106.
9. "Turkish Atrocities in Bulgaria," *Daily News,* 22 August 1876, pp. 5–6.
10. H. C. G. Matthew, *Gladstone 1809–1898* (New York: Oxford University Press, 1999), p. 273. Januarius Aloysius MacGahan, *The Turkish Atrocities in Bulgaria* (London: Bradbury, Agnew, 1876). Blake, *Disraeli,* p. 592: "To a generation that has known the cold-blooded extermination of six million Jews in Germany and unnumbered millions of political prisoners in the labour camps of Siberia, this may seem small beer. But in the civilized atmosphere of the nineteenth century the reaction was profound. It ought to have been clear at once that this was not a matter which could be shrugged aside."
11. *Daily News,* 24 August 1876, pp. 2, 4. W. T. Stead, ed., *The M.P. for Russia: Reminiscences and Correspondence of Madame Olga Novikoff,* vol. 1 (London: Andrew Melrose, 1909), pp. 247–48. "England and the Eastern Question," *Daily News,* 14 July 1876, p. 5. Shannon, *Bulgarian Agitation,* pp. 46–48.
12. Shannon, *Bulgarian Agitation,* pp. 44, 54. Ponsonby memo, 8 July 1876, *The Letters of Queen Victoria: A Selection from Her Majesty's Correspondence and Journal between the Years 1862 and 1878,* ed. George Earle Buckle, 2nd series, vol. 2 (New York: Longmans, Green, 1926), p. 470. Ponsonby to Derby, 8 July 1876, ibid., pp. 470–71. See Victoria to Disraeli, 15 July 1877, ibid., p. 548.
13. Disraeli to Bradford, 13 July 1876, *Letters of Disraeli to Chesterfield and Bradford,* vol. 2, p. 70. Disraeli to Victoria, 14 July 1876, morning, *Letters of Victoria,* vol. 2, pp. 471–72. Derby to Ponsonby, 3 July 1876, ibid., p. 467. FO 881/2916, Derby to Elliot, 13 July 1876.
14. Disraeli to Victoria, 29 June 1876, Monypenny and Buckle, *Life of Disraeli,* vol. 6, p. 35. Todorova, *Imagining the Balkans,* p. 106. FO 881/2916, Elliot to Derby, 14

July 1876. Blake, *Disraeli,* pp. 591–92. Henry G. Elliot, *Some Revolutions and Other Diplomatic Experiences* (London: John Murray, 1922), pp. 261, 255–56, 268–71. Shannon, *Bulgarian Agitation,* p. 23. Disraeli to Derby, 14 July 1876, Monypenny and Buckle, *Life of Disraeli,* vol. 6, pp. 44–45.

15. Disraeli to Victoria, 14 July 1876, 5 p.m., *Letters of Victoria,* vol. 2, p. 472. Disraeli to Derby, 14 July 1876, Monypenny and Buckle, *Life of Disraeli,* vol. 6, pp. 44–45. "The Affairs of Turkey," *Daily News,* 22 July 1876, p. 5.
16. Disraeli to Victoria, 14 July 1876, 5 p.m., *Letters of Victoria,* vol. 2, p. 472. Derby to Ponsonby, 10 July 1876, ibid. William Ewart Gladstone, *Bulgarian Horrors and the Question of the East* (London: John Murray, 1876), p. 14. Laura Silber and Allan Little, *Yugoslavia: Death of a Nation* (New York: TV Books, 1995), p. 288; Elizabeth Drew, *On the Edge: The Clinton Presidency* (New York: Simon and Schuster, 1994), pp. 138–63.
17. Monypenny and Buckle, *Life of Disraeli,* vol. 6, p. 45.
18. Disraeli to Derby, 15 August 1876, Monypenny and Buckle, *Life of Disraeli,* vol. 6, p. 49. Disraeli to Northcote, 2 September 1876, ibid., p. 51.
19. FO 881/2936, "Report by Mr. Baring on the Atrocities Committed upon the Christians in Bulgaria," *London Gazette,* 19 September 1876. FO 881/2916, Derby to Elliot, 9 August 1876.
20. Monypenny and Buckle, *Life of Disraeli,* vol. 6, pp. 46–47. Disraeli to Derby, 7 August 1876, ibid., p. 46. Shannon, *Bulgarian Agitation,* pp. 55–56. Victoria to Disraeli, 10 August 1876, *Letters of Victoria,* vol. 2, p. 474.
21. FO 65/939/354, Loftus to Derby, 21 August 1876. Richard Millman, *Britain and the Eastern Question 1875–1878* (Oxford: Clarendon Press, 1979), pp. 148–52. Monypenny and Buckle, *Life of Disraeli,* vol. 6, pp. 47–48.
22. Victoria journal, 23 August 1876, *Letters of Victoria,* vol. 2, p. 475. Hugo letter, *Times,* 29 August 1876, p. 3.
23. Disraeli to Chesterfield, 31 August 1876, *Letters of Disraeli to Chesterfield and Bradford,* vol. 2, p. 83. Disraeli to Bradford, 1 September 1876, ibid., p. 84. Disraeli to Salisbury, 3 September 1876, ibid., vol. 6, p. 52.

GLADSTONE VS. DISRAELI

1. Benjamin Disraeli, *Speech by the Late Earl of Beaconsfield, K.G., at the Free Trade Hall, Manchester, April 3, 1872* (London: National Union of Conservative and Constitutional Associations, n.d.), p. 23.
2. *The Political Life of the Right Hon. W. E. Gladstone: Illustrated from "Punch" with Cartoons and Sketches,* vol. 2 (London: Bradbury, Agnew, 1898–99), p. 74. Roy Jenkins, *Gladstone: A Biography* (New York: Random House, 1997), pp. 190, 104–15. H. C. G. Matthew, *Gladstone 1809–1898* (New York: Oxford University Press, 1999), pp. 255–56, 321–23.
3. Matthew, *Gladstone,* pp. 271–74, 282–83. Andrew Porter, "Trusteeship, Anti-Slavery, and Humanitarianism," in Andrew Porter, ed., *The Oxford History of the British Empire,* vol. 3 (Oxford: Oxford University Press, 1999), p. 215. A. J. P. Taylor, *The Struggle for Mastery in Europe: 1848–1918* (London: Oxford University Press, 1971), p. 213; Paul Knaplund, *Gladstone's Foreign Policy* (New York: Harper

and Brothers, 1935), pp. 14–15. Gladstone, less admirably, supported the self-determination of the Confederacy in the American South, which meant self-determination as a way of imposing slavery.

4. William Ewart Gladstone, "Aggression on Egypt and Freedom in the East," *Gleanings of Past Years 1843–78,* vol. 4 (London: John Murray, 1879), pp. 341–65; Gladstone to Granville, 17 November 1876, Agatha Ramm, ed., *The Political Correspondence of Mr. Gladstone and Lord Granville,* vol. 1 (Oxford: Clarendon Press, 1962), p. 20; Gladstone to Granville, 5 January 1878, ibid., pp. 66–67. Harvard historian Niall Ferguson correctly calls it "one of the great U-turns of Victorian foreign policy" (Niall Ferguson, *Empire: The Rise and Demise of the British World Order and the Lessons for Global Power* [New York: Basic Books, 2002], p. 195). See ibid., pp. 193–99; Michael W. Doyle, *Empires* (Ithaca, N.Y.: Cornell University Press, 1986), pp. 211–29; and Matthew, *Gladstone,* pp. 382–94. Paul Knaplund, *Gladstone and Britain's Imperial Policy* (London: Allen and Unwin, 1927), pp. 86–91. John Bowring, *Autobiographical Recollections* (London: Henry S. King, 1877), pp. 216–27; Augustus G. Stapleton, *The Hostilities at Canton* (London: Hatchard, 1857); Maurice Collis, *Foreign Mud: Being an Account of the Opium Imbroglio at Canton in the 1830's and the Anglo-Chinese War That Followed* (New York: Alfred A. Knopf, 1947), pp. 267–71; Jack Beeching, *The Chinese Opium Wars* (New York: Harcourt Brace Jovanovich, 1975), pp. 206–33. John Cam Hobhouse also disgracefully backed the British position (Brian Inglish, *The Opium War* [London: Hodder and Stoughton, 1976], pp. 160, 173). 14 May 1840, William Ewart Gladstone, *The Gladstone Diaries,* ed. H. C. G. Matthew, vol. 3, (Oxford: Clarendon Press, 1974), p. 29. Gladstone, "Aggression on Egypt," *Gleanings,* vol. 4, pp. 347–49. Richard T. Shannon, *Gladstone and the Bulgarian Agitation 1876* (Sussex: Harvester, 1975), pp. 8, 274–81. Paul Kennedy, *The Realities Behind Diplomacy: Background Influences on British External Policy, 1865–1980* (London: George Allen and Unwin, 1981), p. 45. Matthew, *Gladstone,* pp. 307, 257, 266, 275–76. Jenkins, *Gladstone,* pp. 193, 423–35, 532–35. John Morley, *Life of Gladstone,* vol. 2 (London: Macmillan, 1904), p. 595.

5. Denis V. Reidy, "Panizzi, Gladstone, Garibaldi and the Neapolitan Prisoners," *Electronic British Library Journal,* 2005, p. 5. Gladstone to Aberdeen, 7 April 1851, William Ewart Gladstone, *Two Letters to the Earl of Aberdeen on the State Prosecutions of the Neapolitan Government,* 11th ed. (London: John Murray, 1851), p. 28.

6. Christopher Hibbert, *Garibaldi and His Enemies: The Clash of Arms and Personalities in the Making of Italy* (Boston: Little, Brown, 1966), p. 175. Gladstone to Aberdeen, 7 April 1851, Gladstone, *Neapolitan Government,* pp. 3–4.

7. Hibbert, *Garibaldi,* p. 177. Gladstone to Aberdeen, 14 July 1851, Gladstone, *Neapolitan Government,* pp. 4–5, 29, 32–33.

8. Reidy, "Neapolitan Prisoners," pp. 5–15. George Macaulay Trevelyan, *Garibaldi and the Making of Italy* (New York: Longmans, Green, 1911), pp. 26–28, 105–9. Hibbert, *Garibaldi,* pp. 256–57.

9. Matthew, *Gladstone,* p. 266. Shannon, *Bulgarian Agitation,* pp. 91, 51.

10. Morley, *Life of Gladstone,* vol. 2, p. 549. Shannon, *Bulgarian Agitation,* pp. 4,

10–13, 110–12. Gladstone to Granville, 20 August 1876, Ramm, ed., *Political Correspondence of Gladstone and Granville,* vol. 1, p. 1. Gladstone to Granville, 27 and 29 August 1876, ibid., p. 3.

11. Matthew, *Gladstone,* pp. 284–86. 28–30 August 1876, William Ewart Gladstone, *The Gladstone Diaries: With Cabinet Minutes and Prime-Ministerial Correspondence,* ed. H. C. G. Matthew, vol. 9 (Oxford: Clarendon Press, 1986), pp. 150–51. Marjorie Caygill, *The British Museum Reading Room* (London: British Museum, 2000). It was three years before the room would start using electricity. Granville to Gladstone, 1 September 1876, Ramm, ed., *Political Correspondence of Gladstone and Granville,* vol. 1, p. 4. 29–31 August and 1–5 September 1876, *Gladstone Diaries,* vol. 9, pp. 150–51.
12. Gladstone, *Bulgarian Horrors,* pp. 9–12, 19–20, 27–29, 30–31.
13. Ibid., pp. 12–13. See p. 61: "Mahometan, it must be remembered, does mean the same as Turk."
14. Gladstone to Negropontis, 9 January 1877, Matthew, *Gladstone,* p. 278. Gladstone, *Bulgarian Horrors,* pp. 17, 57–58.
15. Gladstone, *Bulgarian Horrors,* pp. 21, 18–19, 23, 9–10.
16. Ibid., pp. 37, 42–43.
17. Ibid., pp. 44–45, 52, 58, 61–63.
18. Ibid., pp. 45, 17.
19. Ibid., pp. 49, 51, 53–55, 61–63.
20. Disraeli to Bradford, 5 September 1876, Marquis of Zetland, ed., *The Letters of Disraeli to Lady Chesterfield and Lady Bradford,* vol. 2 (New York: D. Appleton, 1929), p. 86. Disraeli to Derby, 8 September 1876, W. F. Monypenny and George Earle Buckle, *The Life of Benjamin Disraeli, Earl of Beaconsfield,* vol. 6 (New York: Macmillan, 1920), p. 60.
21. Disraeli to Victoria, 10 September 1876, *Letters of Victoria,* vol. 2, p. 476. Robert Blake, *Disraeli* (New York: St. Martin's Press, 1967), p. 607.
22. Gladstone to Granville, 7 September 1876, Ramm, ed., *Political Correspondence of Gladstone and Granville,* vol. 1, p. 5. Shannon, *Bulgarian Agitation,* p. 88. Blake, *Disraeli,* p. 598. Matthew, *Gladstone,* p. 283.
23. Disraeli to Derby, 6 September 1876, Monypenny and Buckle, *Life of Disraeli,* vol. 6, p. 53. Shannon, *Bulgarian Agitation,* pp. 13–14, 28–30, 150–52, 155–57. Gladstone's first Midlothian speech, 25 November 1879, William Ewart Gladstone, *Political Speeches in Scotland, March and April 1880,* vol. 1 (Edinburgh: Andrew Elliot, 1880), p. 41. Jenkins, *Gladstone,* p. 407.
24. Adrian Desmond and James Moore, *Darwin* (New York: Penguin, 1991), pp. 625–26. Oscar Wilde, "Sonnet on the Massacre of the Christians in Bulgaria," in *Poems by Oscar Wilde,* ed. Temple Scott (New York: Brentano's, 1909), p. 17. Shannon, *Bulgarian Agitation,* p. 187. Matthew, *Gladstone,* pp. 284, 325. Nightingale letter, *Daily News,* 16 August 1876, p. 2. "The Atrocities in Bulgaria," *Times,* 18 September 1876, p. 6. Alfred Tennyson, "Montenegro," in *The Poems of Tennyson,* ed. Christopher Ricks (London: Longmans, Green, 1969), pp. 1239–40.
25. Carlyle to Ruskin, 27 September 1866, George Allan Cate, ed., *The Correspondence of Thomas Carlyle and John Ruskin* (Stanford, Calif.: Stanford University

Press, 1982), pp. 119–20. Uday Singh Mehta, *Liberalism and Empire: A Study in Nineteenth-Century British Liberal Thought* (Chicago: University of Chicago Press, 1999), pp. 196–97; Eric Stokes, *The English Utilitarians and India* (Oxford: Clarendon Press, 1959), pp. 288–89. Shannon, *Bulgarian Agitation,* pp. 204–9, 211–15, 222. A. J. P. Taylor claims that many of the historians who supported the agitation were imperialist (*The Trouble Makers: Dissent over Foreign Policy 1792–1939* [London: Pimlico, 1993], p. 77), but does not give evidence. George Carslake Thompson, *Public Opinion and Lord Beaconsfield 1875–1880,* vol. 1 (London: Macmillan, 1886), p. 42. Edward Dicey, "Mr. Gladstone and Our Empire," *Nineteenth Century,* September 1877, p. 293.

26. Ann Pottinger Saab, *Reluctant Icon: Gladstone, Bulgaria, and the Working Classes 1856–1878* (Cambridge, Mass.: Harvard University Press, 1991), pp. 80–150; Matthew, *Gladstone,* p. 294. FO 78/2551, Manning to Derby, 1 September 1876. FO 78/2551, Snape to Derby, 12 September 1876. FO 78/2551, Nicholson to Derby, 9 September 1876; FO 78/2552; FO 78/2553, Finchley resolutions, 18 September 1876. Shannon, *Bulgarian Agitation,* pp. 69–81, 147–50, 157–60. FO 78/2551, FO 78/2552, FO 78/2553, FO 78/2554, FO 78/2555, FO 78/2556.
27. Shannon, *Bulgarian Agitation,* pp. 28–30, 61–62, 150–52, 155–57, 189–98, 198–201. Gladstone to Granville, 14 September 1876, Ramm, ed., *Political Correspondence of Gladstone and Granville,* vol. 1, p. 7.
28. Shannon, *Bulgarian Agitation,* pp. 63–65, 82–83, 171–86. John Octavius Johnston, *Life and Letters of Henry Parry Liddon* (London: Longmans, Green, 1904), pp. 205–6; Joseph S. Meisel, *Public Speech and the Culture of Public Life in the Age of Gladstone* (New York: Columbia University Press, 2001), p. 153; Liddon, "Turkish Atrocities," *Times,* 23 October 1876, p. 11. Henry G. Elliot, *Some Revolutions and Other Diplomatic Experiences* (London: John Murray, 1922), p. 271.
29. Matthew, *Gladstone,* p. 287. Shannon, *Bulgarian Agitation,* pp. 154–55, 231–38. Jenkins, *Gladstone,* p. 419. Blake, *Disraeli,* pp. 603–4. "The Turkish Atrocities," *The Economist,* 12 August 1876, p. 943.
30. Disraeli to Bradford, 8 September 1876, Monypenny and Buckle, *Life of Disraeli,* vol. 6, pp. 60–61.
31. Disraeli to Bradford, 9 September 1876, ibid., p. 61. Blake, *Disraeli,* p. 602; Shannon, *Bulgarian Agitation,* p. 114. Disraeli to Northcote, 11 September 1876, Monypenny and Buckle, *Life of Disraeli,* vol. 6, p. 61. Matthew, *Gladstone,* pp. 284, 294. *Punch Political Life of Gladstone,* vol. 2, pp. 7–8. Morley, *Life of Gladstone,* vol. 2, p. 554.
32. Disraeli to Bradford, 11 September 1876, *Letters of Disraeli to Chesterfield and Bradford,* vol. 2, p. 90. Disraeli to Bradford, 9 September 1876, ibid., pp. 88–89.
33. Disraeli to Northcote, 11 September 1876, Monypenny and Buckle, *Life of Disraeli,* vol. 6, p. 61; ibid., pp. 63–64.
34. Gladstone to Granville, 16 September 1876, Ramm, ed., *Political Correspondence of Gladstone and Granville,* vol. 1, p. 9. Shannon, *Bulgarian Agitation,* p. 132. Morley, *Life of Gladstone,* vol. 2, pp. 560–61. Disraeli to Chesterfield, 15 September 1876, *Letters of Disraeli to Chesterfield and Bradford,* vol. 2, p. 92.
35. Disraeli to Bradford, 9 September 1876, Monypenny and Buckle, *Life of Disraeli,*

vol. 6, p. 61. Disraeli to Bradford, 24 September 1876, *Letters of Disraeli to Chesterfield and Bradford,* vol. 2, p. 92.

36. Gladstone to Granville, 7 September 1876, Ramm, ed., *Political Correspondence of Gladstone and Granville,* vol. 1, p. 5. Gladstone to Granville, 14 September 1876, ibid., p. 7. Monypenny and Buckle, *Life of Disraeli,* vol. 6, pp. 65–66. Disraeli to Northcote, 11 September 1876, ibid., p. 61. Disraeli to Bradford, n.d. September 1876, *Letters of Disraeli to Chesterfield and Bradford,* vol. 2, pp. 94–95; Salisbury to Disraeli, 23 September 1876, Monypenny and Buckle, *Life of Disraeli,* vol. 6, p. 70. Granville to Gladstone, 4 October 1876, Ramm, ed., *Political Correspondence of Gladstone and Granville,* vol. 1, p. 12.
37. Disraeli to Bradford, 26 September 1876, *Letters of Disraeli to Chesterfield and Bradford,* vol. 2, pp. 93–94. Disraeli to Northcote, 11 September 1876, Monypenny and Buckle, *Life of Disraeli,* vol. 6, p. 61. Disraeli to Derby, 23 September 1876, ibid., p. 68.
38. Victoria to Disraeli, 28 September 1876, *Letters of Victoria,* vol. 2, pp. 480–81.
39. Edward to Victoria, 2 October 1876, ibid., p. 481. Disraeli to Bradford, 25 December 1876, *Letters of Disraeli to Chesterfield and Bradford,* vol. 2, p. 120. Lytton to Victoria, 4 October 1876, *Letters of Victoria,* vol. 2, pp. 483–84.
40. R. W. Seton-Watson, *Disraeli, Gladstone, and the Eastern Question: A Study in Diplomacy and Party Politics* (London: Macmillan, 1935), p. 244.
41. Gladstone, *Bulgarian Horrors,* pp. 44–45. *Punch Political Life of Gladstone,* vol. 2, p. 25. Monypenny and Buckle, *Life of Disraeli,* vol. 6, p. 107.
42. Gladstone to Granville, 3 October 1876, Ramm, ed., *Political Correspondence of Gladstone and Granville,* vol. 1, p. 10. Gladstone to Granville, 7 October 1876, ibid., p. 13.
43. Disraeli to Derby, 1 October 1876, Monypenny and Buckle, *Life of Disraeli,* vol. 6, p. 76. Disraeli to Bradford, 2 October 1876, ibid., p. 79. Disraeli to Bradford, 27 September 1876, ibid., pp. 68–69.
44. Monypenny and Buckle, *Life of Disraeli,* vol. 6, p. 69. Gladstone to Granville, 15 October 1876, Ramm, ed., *Political Correspondence of Gladstone and Granville,* vol. 1, p. 14; *Punch Political Life of Gladstone,* vol. 2, p. 9. Gladstone to Granville, 18 October 1876, Ramm, ed., *Political Correspondence of Gladstone and Granville,* vol. 1, p. 15.
45. Monypenny and Buckle, *Life of Disraeli,* vol. 6, p. 93. Salisbury to Disraeli, 23 September 1876, ibid., pp. 70–71. Disraeli to Salisbury, 26 September 1876, ibid., pp. 71–72.
46. Matthew, *Gladstone,* p. 286. Monypenny and Buckle, *Life of Disraeli,* vol. 6, p. 58.
47. Disraeli to Bradford, 25 and 26 September 1876, *Letters of Disraeli to Chesterfield and Bradford,* vol. 2, p. 93. Disraeli to Derby, n.d. October 1876, Monypenny and Buckle, *Life of Disraeli,* vol. 6, p. 67.
48. "Turkish Atrocities in Bulgaria," *Daily News,* 22 August 1876, p. 5.
49. FO 65/938/288, Loftus to Derby, 28 June 1876. FO 65/938/302, Loftus to Derby, 5 July 1876. B. H. Sumner, *Russia and the Balkans 1870–1880* (Oxford: Oxford University Press, 1937), pp. 187–89. FO 65/939/366, Loftus to Derby, 16 August 1876; FO 65/939/376, Loftus to Derby, 27 August 1876; FO 65/939/378,

Loftus to Derby, 28 August 1876. FO 65/938, Loftus to Derby, 17 July 1876, enclosures.

50. FO 65/939/366, Loftus to Derby, 16 August 1876; FO 65/939/343, Loftus to Derby, 2 August 1876; FO 65/939/396, Loftus to Derby, 2 September 1876. FO 65/939/346, Loftus to Derby, 2 August 1876. FO 65/939/390, "Intervention between Turkey and Servia," *Russki Mir,* 25 August 1876. FO 65/941/501, Loftus to Derby, 21 October 1876.

51. Feodor Dostoevsky, *A Writer's Diary,* trans. Kenneth Lantz, vol. 1 (Evanston, Ill.: Northwestern University Press, 1993), pp. 523–25. Joseph Frank, *Dostoevsky: The Mantle of the Prophet, 1871–1881* (Princeton, N.J.: Princeton University Press, 2002), p. 275.

52. Feodor Dostoevsky, *The Brothers Karamazov,* trans. Constance Garnett (New York: W. W. Norton, 1976), pp. 219–20.

53. Sumner, *Russia and the Balkans,* pp. 192–93. "The War in Servia," *Times,* 12 July 1876, p. 5. Dostoevsky, *Writer's Diary,* vol. 1, October 1876, pp. 660–62.

54. FO 65/939/357, Loftus to Derby, 15 August 1876. FO 65/939/407, Loftus to Derby, 10 September 1876; FO 65/939/408, Loftus to Derby, 10 September 1876. FO 65/939/366, Loftus to Derby, 16 August 1876. FO 65/939/349, Loftus to Derby, 10 August 1876. FO 65/939/373A, Loftus to Derby, 25 August 1876.

55. FO 65/939/356, Loftus to Derby, 15 August 1876. FO 65/940/421, Loftus to Derby, 13 September 1876; FO 65/940/421, Abstracts from the Russian, 13 September 1876. Sumner, *Russia and the Balkans,* pp. 196–97. Disraeli to Bradford, 1 September 1876, *Letters of Disraeli to Chesterfield and Bradford,* vol. 2, p. 84.

56. Gladstone to Granville, 2 November 1876, Ramm, ed., *Political Correspondence of Gladstone and Granville,* vol. 1, p. 17. Matthew, *Gladstone,* p. 277. *Punch Political Life of Gladstone,* vol. 2, p. 7. FO 65/939/390, "Right of Intervention in Turkish Affairs," *Golos,* 23 August 1876. FO 65/939/354, Loftus to Derby, 15 August 1876; FO 65/940/421, Abstracts from the Russian, 13 September 1876; FO 65/940/472, Loftus to Derby, 9 October 1876; FO 65/940/474, Loftus to Derby, 10 October 1876.

57. FO 65/938/330, Loftus to Derby, 19 July 1876. FO 65/939/356, Loftus to Derby, 15 August 1876. FO 65/941/501, "Speculative Policy of Disraeli," *Golos,* 18 October 1876.

58. Matthew, *Gladstone,* p. 277. FO 65/941/475, Loftus to Derby, 10 October 1876. FO 65/941/475, *Agence Russe,* 10 October 1876. Disraeli to Bradford, 25 October 1876, *Letters of Disraeli to Chesterfield and Bradford,* vol. 2, p. 105. Sumner, *Russia and the Balkans,* p. 213.

59. Disraeli to Derby, 4 September 1876, Monypenny and Buckle, *Life of Disraeli,* vol. 6, p. 52. Derby to Victoria, 29 September 1876, ibid., p. 75; ibid., p. 74.

60. FO 65/941/520, Loftus to Derby, 4 November 1876. FO 65/941/525, Loftus to Derby, 6 November 1876. Sumner, *Russia and the Balkans,* pp. 205–20. FO 65/941/534, Loftus to Derby, 15 November 1876; FO 65/939, Wellesley to Loftus, 14 September 1876.

61. Disraeli to Derby, 30 September 1876, Monypenny and Buckle, *Life of Disraeli,* vol. 6, p. 76. Disraeli to Derby, 29 September 1876, ibid., pp. 74–75. Disraeli to

Bradford, 29 September 1876, *Letters of Disraeli to Chesterfield and Bradford,* vol. 2, p. 95.

62. Disraeli to Bradford, 10 October 1876, *Letters of Disraeli to Chesterfield and Bradford,* vol. 2, p. 97.
63. Disraeli to Bradford, 12 October 1876, ibid., p. 98. Disraeli to Bradford, 14 October 1876, ibid., p. 101. Disraeli to Chesterfield, 13 October 1876, ibid., p. 97.
64. Disraeli to Salisbury, 26 September 1876, Monypenny and Buckle, *Life of Disraeli,* vol. 6, pp. 73. Disraeli to Bradford, 12 October 1876, *Letters of Disraeli to Chesterfield and Bradford,* vol. 2, p. 98.
65. Disraeli to Bradford, 1 November 1876, *Letters of Disraeli to Chesterfield and Bradford,* vol. 2, pp. 106–7. Victoria to Disraeli, 26 October 1876, *Letters of Victoria,* vol. 2, p. 493. Dostoevsky, *Writer's Diary,* vol. 1, October 1876, pp. 657–59.
66. FO 65/941/515, Loftus to Derby, 3 November 1876; Sumner, *Russia and the Balkans,* pp. 213, 225; Edvard Radzinsky, *Alexander II: The Last Great Tsar* (New York: Free Press, 2005), p. 260. Seton-Watson, *Eastern Question,* pp. 126–27. FO 65/941/513, Loftus to Derby, 2 November 1876; Disraeli to Bradford, 2 November 1876, *Letters of Disraeli to Chesterfield and Bradford,* vol. 2, p. 107.
67. Disraeli to Bradford, 5 October 1876, *Letters of Disraeli to Chesterfield and Bradford,* vol. 2, p. 96. Granville to Gladstone, 20 October 1876, Ramm, ed., *Political Correspondence of Gladstone and Granville,* vol. 1, p. 15; *History of The Times,* vol. 2, p. 507; Gladstone to Novikov, 17 October 1876, Morley, *Life of Gladstone,* vol. 2, p. 557; Derby to Disraeli, 1 October 1876, Monypenny and Buckle, *Life of Disraeli,* vol. 6, p. 76.
68. Victoria to Disraeli, 17 October 1876, *Letters of Victoria,* vol. 2, p. 488. Disraeli to Corry, 13 December 1876, Monypenny and Buckle, *Life of Disraeli,* vol. 6, p. 106. Disraeli to Derby, 21 October 1876, ibid., p. 99. Victoria journal, 27 November 1876, *Letters of Victoria,* vol. 2, p. 503. Disraeli cabinet paper, November 1876, Monypenny and Buckle, *Life of Disraeli,* vol. 6, p. 101–2; Disraeli to Salisbury, 29 November 1876, ibid., pp. 103–4.
69. Disraeli to Chesterfield, 9 November 1876, *Letters of Disraeli to Chesterfield and Bradford,* vol. 2, p. 110. Disraeli to Chesterfield, 20 October 1876, ibid., p. 102. Monypenny and Buckle, *Life of Disraeli,* vol. 6, p. 102.
70. Disraeli to Bradford, 4 November 1876, *Letters of Disraeli to Chesterfield and Bradford,* vol. 2, pp. 108–9. Gladstone to Granville, 8 November 1876, Ramm, ed., *Political Correspondence of Gladstone and Granville,* vol. 1, p. 18; Gladstone to Granville, 17 May 1877, ibid., pp. 38–39; Disraeli to Derby, 1 November 1876, Monypenny and Buckle, *Life of Disraeli,* vol. 6, p. 95.
71. FO 65/941/522, Loftus to Derby, 5 November 1876. FO 65/941/524, Loftus to Derby, 6 November 1876.
72. FO 65/941/523, Loftus to Derby, 6 November 1876. FO 65/941/517, Loftus to Derby, 3 November 1876.
73. Granville to Gladstone, 27 November 1876, Ramm, ed., *Political Correspondence of Gladstone and Granville,* vol. 1, p. 24. Disraeli to Bradford, 15 November 1876, *Letters of Disraeli to Chesterfield and Bradford,* vol. 2, p. 112. Dis-

raeli speech, 9 November 1876, Monypenny and Buckle, *Life of Disraeli,* vol. 6, pp. 91–92.

74. Sumner, *Russia and the Balkans,* pp. 227–28.
75. Granville to Gladstone, 18 November 1876, Ramm, ed., *Political Correspondence of Gladstone and Granville,* vol. 1, p. 21. FO 65/941/534, Loftus to Derby, 15 November 1876.
76. Gladstone to Granville, 19 November 1876, Ramm, ed., *Political Correspondence of Gladstone and Granville,* vol. 1, p. 22. Shannon, *Bulgarian Agitation,* p. 256. Gladstone to Granville, 26 November 1876, Ramm, ed., *Political Correspondence of Gladstone and Granville,* vol. 1, p. 24. Gladstone to Granville, 2 January 1877, ibid., p. 28. He used the same slur in Gladstone to Granville, 26 November 1876, ibid., p. 24.
77. Victoria to Disraeli, 6 November 1876, *Letters of Victoria,* vol. 2, p. 495; Disraeli to Victoria, 11 November 1876, ibid., p. 496; Victoria to Disraeli, 13 November 1876, ibid., p. 498. Blake, *Disraeli,* pp. 609, 622. Disraeli to Derby, 1 November 1876, Monypenny and Buckle, *Life of Disraeli,* vol. 6, pp. 94–95. Disraeli to Derby, 19 November 1876, ibid., p. 95. Disraeli to Derby, 20 November 1876, ibid., p. 96. Disraeli to Derby, 9 December 1876, ibid., p. 96.
78. Sumner, *Russia and the Balkans,* p. 229.
79. Disraeli to Salisbury, 1 December 1876, Monypenny and Buckle, *Life of Disraeli,* vol. 6, pp. 104–5.
80. Disraeli to Salisbury, 29 November 1876, Monypenny and Buckle, *Life of Disraeli,* vol. 6, pp. 103–4. "St. James's-Hall Conference," *Times,* 9 December 1876, pp. 7–8. Desmond and Moore, *Darwin,* p. 625. Jenkins, *Gladstone,* p. 407. Shannon, *Bulgarian Agitation,* pp. 245–46, 252, 204.
81. Monypenny and Buckle, *Life of Disraeli,* vol. 6, pp. 106–7. "St. James's-Hall Conference," *Times,* 9 December 1876, p. 7. *Punch Political Life of Gladstone,* vol. 2, pp. 11–12; Shannon, *Bulgarian Agitation,* p. 200. (For Freeman's anti-Semitism, see W. T. Stead, ed., *The M.P. for Russia: Reminiscences and Correspondence of Madame Olga Novikoff,* vol. 1 [London: Andrew Melrose, 1909], pp. 333–37, 340–41, 343–44.) Stead, ed., *M.P. for Russia,* vol. 1, pp. 237, 283–88.
82. *Gladstone Diaries,* vol. 9, 8 December 1876, p. 176. Jenkins, *Gladstone,* p. 407. "St. James's-Hall Conference," *Times,* 9 December 1876, p. 8. Stead, ed., *M.P. for Russia,* vol. 1, pp. 289, 291. Gladstone to Granville, 17 May 1877, Ramm, ed., *Political Correspondence of Gladstone and Granville,* vol. 1, p. 39. Blake, *Disraeli,* p. 614.
83. Victoria to Louise, n.d. November 1876, *Letters of Victoria,* vol. 2, pp. 498–99. Victoria to Salisbury, 18 November 1876, ibid., p. 501. Disraeli to Bradford, 16 December 1876, *Letters of Disraeli to Chesterfield and Bradford,* vol. 2, p. 117. Victoria to Disraeli, 18 December 1876, *Letters of Victoria,* vol. 2, p. 504. Disraeli to Bradford, 20 December 1876, *Letters of Disraeli to Chesterfield and Bradford,* vol. 2, p. 119.
84. Disraeli to Victoria, 30 November 1876, *Letters of Victoria,* vol. 2, p. 504. FO 881/2997, Ignatiev proposal for Bulgaria, 14 December 1876. Sumner, *Russia and the Balkans,* p. 230. Disraeli to Derby, 21 December 1876, *Letters of Disraeli to Chesterfield and Bradford,* vol. 2, p. 109.

85. Sumner, *Russia and the Balkans,* p. 234. Disraeli to Salisbury, 29 November 1876, Monypenny and Buckle, *Life of Disraeli,* vol. 6, pp. 103–4. Stead, ed., *M.P. for Russia,* vol. 1, p. 307.
86. Stead, ed., *M.P. for Russia,* vol. 1, p. 308. Michael Ignatieff, *The Russian Album* (New York: Viking, 1987), p. 47.
87. FO 881/3030, 13 December 1876 meeting; FO 881/3048, 21 December 1876 meeting. FO 881/2996, Salisbury to Derby, 11 December 1876, 9:45 p.m.
88. Monypenny and Buckle, *Life of Disraeli,* vol. 6, p. 109; Stanford J. Shaw and Ezel Kural Shaw, *History of the Ottoman Empire and Modern Turkey,* vol. 2 (Cambridge: Cambridge University Press, 1977), pp. 173–80. Disraeli to Bradford, 20 December 1876, *Letters of Disraeli to Chesterfield and Bradford,* vol. 2, p. 119; Salisbury to Victoria, 23 December 1876, *Letters of Victoria,* vol. 2, p. 506; Victoria journal, 1 January 1877, *Letters of Victoria,* vol. 2, p. 513. Disraeli to Derby, 28 December 1876, Monypenny and Buckle, *Life of Disraeli,* vol. 6, p. 111.
89. Disraeli to Bradford, 25 December 1876, *Letters of Disraeli to Chesterfield and Bradford,* vol. 2, pp. 120–21. Disraeli to Derby, 28 and 30 December 1876, Monypenny and Buckle, *Life of Disraeli,* vol. 6, p. 111. See Gladstone to Granville, 17 May 1877, Ramm, ed., *Political Correspondence of Gladstone and Granville,* vol. 1, pp. 38–39.
90. Disraeli to Chesterfield, 3 January 1877, *Letters of Disraeli to Chesterfield and Bradford,* vol. 2, p. 126. Disraeli to Chesterfield, 7 January 1877, ibid., p. 127. Victoria to Lytton, 12 January 1877, *Letters of Victoria,* vol. 2, pp. 518–19. Victoria journal, 8 January 1877, ibid., p. 516. Disraeli to Derby, 9 February 1877, Monypenny and Buckle, *Life of Disraeli,* vol. 6, p. 126. Disraeli to Chesterfield, 13 January 1877, *Letters of Disraeli to Chesterfield and Bradford,* vol. 2, p. 130.
91. Disraeli to Derby, 15 January 1877, Monypenny and Buckle, *Life of Disraeli,* vol. 6, p. 113; ibid., p. 110; Ponsonby to Victoria, 19 January 1877, *Letters of Victoria,* vol. 2, pp. 519–20. Elliot, *Some Revolutions,* p. 292.
92. Disraeli to Salisbury, 6 February 1877, Monypenny and Buckle, *Life of Disraeli,* vol. 6, p. 114. Blake, *Disraeli,* p. 617.
93. Gladstone to Granville, 28 January 1877, Ramm, ed., *Political Correspondence of Gladstone and Granville,* vol. 1, p. 29. Monypenny and Buckle, *Life of Disraeli,* vol. 6, pp. 118–19; *Punch Political Life of Gladstone,* vol. 2, p. 14. Gladstone speech, 16 February 1877, *Punch Political Life of Gladstone,* vol. 2, pp. 17–18.
94. Gladstone to Novikov, 6 February 1877, Stead, ed., *M.P. for Russia,* vol. 1, p. 329.
95. Gladstone to Granville, 17 May 1877, Ramm, ed., *Political Correspondence of Gladstone and Granville,* vol. 1, pp. 38–39; Stead, ed., *M.P. for Russia,* vol. 1, pp. 325–28; Saab, *Reluctant Icon,* pp. 151–91. Eliot to Pattison, 18 February 1877, Gordon S. Haight, ed., *The George Eliot Letters,* vol. 6 (New Haven, Conn.: Yale University Press, 1955), p. 343. Disraeli speech, 20 February 1877, Monypenny and Buckle, *Life of Disraeli,* vol. 6, pp. 120–22. Disraeli to Victoria, 27 February 1877, ibid., p. 124.
96. Granville to Gladstone, 2 March 1877, Ramm, ed., *Political Correspondence of Gladstone and Granville,* vol. 1, p. 32. William Ewart Gladstone, *Lessons in Massacre; Or, The Conduct of the Turkish Government In and About Bulgaria Since*

May, 1876 (London: John Murray, 1877). Gladstone to Granville, 6 March 1877, Ramm, ed., *Political Correspondence of Gladstone and Granville,* vol. 1, pp. 32–33; Blake, *Disraeli,* p. 618. Gladstone to Novikov, 23 April 1877, Stead, ed., *M.P. for Russia,* vol. 1, p. 345.

97. Desmond and Moore, *Darwin,* p. 626. Morley, *Life of Gladstone,* vol. 2, p. 562. Janet Browne, *Charles Darwin: A Biography,* vol. 2 (London: Jonathan Cape, 2002), pp. 440–41. Morley, *Life of Gladstone,* vol. 2, p. 562.
98. Dostoevsky, *The Diary of a Writer,* trans. Boris Basol (New York: Scribner, 1949), February 1877, p. 601. Sumner, *Russia and the Balkans,* p. 248. *Punch Political Life of Gladstone,* vol. 2, p. 19.
99. Dostoevsky, *Diary of a Writer,* March 1877, pp. 628–37. Sumner, *Russia and the Balkans,* pp. 259–62.
100. Disraeli to Bradford, 16 March 1877, *Letters of Disraeli to Chesterfield and Bradford,* vol. 2, p. 137.
101. Ignatieff, *Russian Album,* p. 48. Victoria journal, 20 March 1877, *Letters of Victoria,* vol. 2, p. 524. Blake, *Disraeli,* p. 619.
102 Disraeli to Bradford, 22 March 1877, *Letters of Disraeli to Chesterfield and Bradford,* vol. 2, pp. 138–39.
103. Victoria to Disraeli, 21 March 1877, Monypenny and Buckle, *Life of Disraeli,* vol. 6, p. 130.
104. Disraeli to Victoria, 23 March 1877, *Letters of Victoria,* vol. 2, pp. 524–26. Disraeli to Bradford, 24 March 1877, *Letters of Disraeli to Chesterfield and Bradford,* vol. 2, pp. 139–40.
105. Disraeli to Chesterfield, 29 March 1877, *Letters of Disraeli to Chesterfield and Bradford,* vol. 2, pp. 140–41. Disraeli to Bradford, 31 March 1877, ibid., p. 141. Sumner, *Russia and the Balkans,* pp. 265–70, 274. Disraeli to Bradford, 3 April 1877, *Letters of Disraeli to Chesterfield and Bradford,* vol. 2, p. 142.

THE RUSSO-TURKISH WAR

1. B. H. Sumner, *Russia and the Balkans 1870–1880* (Oxford: Oxford University Press, 1937), pp. 270–71. Edvard Radzinsky, *Alexander II: The Last Great Tsar* (New York: Free Press, 2005), p. 261. Joseph Frank, *Dostoevsky: The Mantle of the Prophet, 1871–1881* (Princeton, N. J.: Princeton University Press, 2002), pp. 243–44. James H. Billington, *The Icon and the Axe: An Interpretive History of Russian Culture* (New York: Vintage, 1970), p. 395. Feodor Dostoevsky, *The Diary of a Writer,* trans. Boris Basol (New York: Scribner, 1949), pp. 660–61, 664, 669.
2. Victoria journal, 8 August 1877, *The Letters of Queen Victoria: A Selection from Her Majesty's Correspondence and Journal between the Years 1862 and 1878,* ed. George Earle Buckle, 2nd series, vol. 2 (New York: Longmans, Green, 1926), p. 560. W. F. Monypenny and George Earle Buckle, *The Life of Benjamin Disraeli, Earl of Beaconsfield,* vol. 6 (New York: Macmillan, 1920), pp. 115–16.
3. Disraeli to Victoria, 2 May 1877, *Letters of Victoria,* vol. 2, pp. 535–36. Disraeli to Victoria, 23 April 1877, ibid., pp. 529–31. Disraeli to Victoria, 28 April 1877, ibid., pp. 532–34.
4. Victoria to cabinet, 19 April 1877, Monypenny and Buckle, *Life of Disraeli,* vol. 6,

p. 132. Victoria to Disraeli, 28 April 1877, *Letters of Victoria,* vol. 2, p. 532. Victoria to Argyll, 4 June 1877, ibid., pp. 538–39. George Carslake Thompson, *Public Opinion and Lord Beaconsfield 1875–1880* (London: Macmillan, 1886), vol. 1, p. 59.

5. Gladstone to Granville, 17 May 1877, Agatha Ramm, ed., *The Political Correspondence of Mr. Gladstone and Lord Granville,* vol. 1 (Oxford: Clarendon Press, 1962), pp. 38–39. Gladstone resolutions, 7 May 1877, *The Political Life of the Right Hon. W. E. Gladstone: Illustrated from "Punch" with Cartoons and Sketches,* vol. 2 (London: Bradbury, Agnew, 1898–99), pp. 21–22.
6. Marquis of Zetland, ed., *The Letters of Disraeli to Lady Chesterfield and Lady Bradford,* vol. 2 (New York: D. Appleton, 1929), p. 151; Disraeli to Victoria, 28 April 1877, *Letters of Victoria,* vol. 2, pp. 532–34. Forster to Ely, 1 May 1877, ibid., p. 535. Granville to Gladstone, 16 May 1877, Ramm, ed., *Political Correspondence of Gladstone and Granville,* vol. 1, pp. 37–38. *Punch Political Life of Gladstone,* vol. 2, pp. 22–27. John Morley, *Life of Gladstone,* vol. 2 (London: Macmillan, 1904), pp. 566–68.
7. *Letters of Victoria,* vol. 2, p. 511; Robert Blake, *Disraeli* (New York: St. Martin's Press, 1967), p. 621. 7 May 1877, William Ewart Gladstone, *The Gladstone Diaries,* ed. H. C. G. Mathew, vol. 9 (Oxford: Clarendon Press, 1974), p. 217.
8. Radzinsky, *Alexander II,* pp. 261–62; Stanford J. Shaw and Ezel Kural Shaw, *History of the Ottoman Empire and Modern Turkey,* vol. 2 (Cambridge: Cambridge University Press, 1977), pp. 182–91. Disraeli to Bradford, 23 May 1877, *Letters of Disraeli to Chesterfield and Bradford,* vol. 2, p. 153. FO 881/3259, Layard to Derby, 19 July 1877. FO 881/3233, Layard to Derby, 19 June 1877.
9. Sumner, *Russia and the Balkans,* p. 317. Victoria to Disraeli, 15 July 1877, *Letters of Victoria,* vol. 2, p. 548. Disraeli to Victoria, 16 July 1877, Monypenny and Buckle, *Life of Disraeli,* vol. 6, p. 151. Victoria journal, 17 July 1877, *Letters of Victoria,* vol. 2, p. 551.
10. Freeman to Novikov, 21 July 1877, W. T. Stead, ed., *The M.P. for Russia: Reminiscences and Correspondence of Madame Olga Novikoff,* vol. 1 (London: Andrew Melrose, 1909), p. 371. Gladstone to Novikov, 3 August 1877, ibid., p. 374. Gladstone to Novikov, 24 August 1877, ibid., p. 376.
11. Victoria journal, 17 July 1877, *Letters of Victoria,* vol. 2, pp. 550–51; Disraeli to Victoria, 16 July 1877, Monypenny and Buckle, *Life of Disraeli,* vol. 6, pp. 151–52. Victoria to Disraeli, 16 July 1877, ibid., p. 153. Sumner, *Russia and the Balkans,* pp. 323–24.
12. Radzinsky, *Alexander II,* pp. 263–64. Hans Kohn, *Pan-Slavism: Its History and Ideology* (New York: Vintage, 1960), p. 213. Michael Ignatieff, *The Russian Album* (New York: Viking, 1987), p. 50. FO 881/3337, Fife to Layard, 26 September 1877. Sumner, *Russia and the Balkans,* pp. 315, 334–37.
13. Sumner, *Russia and the Balkans,* pp. 337–38.
14. *Punch Political Life of Gladstone,* vol. 2, pp. 35–36. Gladstone's thirteen Midlothian speech, 22 March 1880, William Ewart Gladstone, *Political Speeches in Scotland, March and April 1880,* vol. 2 (Edinburgh: Andrew Elliot, 1880), p. 216. Radzinsky, *Alexander II,* p. 266.
15. Victoria memorandum, 7 September 1877, *Letters of Victoria,* vol. 2, p. 567. Vic-

toria to Disraeli, 5 November 1877, ibid., pp. 569–70. See Gladstone to Granville, 5 January 1878, Ramm, ed., *Political Correspondence of Gladstone and Granville,* vol. 1, p. 66.

16. Gladstone to Granville, 7 August 1877, Ramm, ed., *Political Correspondence of Gladstone and Granville,* vol. 1, p. 49. Granville to Gladstone, 4 September 1877, ibid., p. 51. Granville to Gladstone, 21 November 1877, ibid., p. 59. Gladstone to Granville, 5 September 1877, ibid., p. 52. Gladstone to Granville, 10 October 1877, ibid., p. 54. Gladstone to Granville, 21 December 1877, ibid., p. 64.
17. Dostoevsky, *Diary of a Writer,* November 1877, p. 904. H. C. G. Matthew, *Gladstone 1809–1898* (New York: Oxford University Press, 1999), p. 290. Radzinsky, *Alexander II,* pp. 267–69.
18. Sumner, *Russia and the Balkans,* pp. 372, 344. Radzinsky, *Alexander II,* pp. 268–69. Ignatieff, *Russian Album,* p. 51.
19. Ignatieff, *Russian Album,* p. 52; Sumner, *Russia and the Balkans,* pp. 399–424.
20. Granville to Gladstone, 19 July 1878, Ramm, ed., *Political Correspondence of Gladstone and Granville,* vol. 1, p. 72. Ignatieff, *Russian Album,* p. 52. Sumner, *Russia and the Balkans,* pp. 420–21, 448. Monypenny and Buckle, *Life of Disraeli,* vol. 6, pp. 584–85; Geoffrey Hosking, *Russia: People and Empire 1552–1917* (Cambridge, Mass.: Harvard University Press, 1997), p. 372.
21. Kohn, *Pan-Slavism,* pp. 215, 217.
22. Phillip Knightley, *The First Casualty: From the Crimea to Vietnam: The War Correspondent as Hero, Propagandist, and Myth Maker* (New York: Harcourt Brace Jovanovich, 1975), pp. 51–52.

THE MIDLOTHIAN CAMPAIGN

1. Gladstone to Granville, 2 November 1878, Agatha Ramm, ed., *The Political Correspondence of Mr. Gladstone and Lord Granville,* vol. 1 (Oxford: Clarendon Press, 1962), p. 85. *The Political Life of the Right Hon. W. E. Gladstone: Illustrated from "Punch" with Cartoons and Sketches,* vol. 2 (London: Bradbury, Agnew, 1898–99), p. 73. John Morley, *Life of Gladstone,* vol. 2 (London: Macmillan, 1904), p. 550.
2. Morley, *Life of Gladstone,* vol. 2, p. 550. H. C. G. Matthew, *Gladstone 1809–1898* (New York: Oxford University Press, 1999), p. 293; Richard T. Shannon, *Gladstone and the Bulgarian Agitation 1876* (Sussex: Harvester, 1975), p. 272.
3. 24 November 1879, William Ewart Gladstone, *The Gladstone Diaries,* ed. H. C. G. Matthew, vol. 9 (Oxford: Clarendon Press, 1974), p. 461. 29 November 1879, ibid., p. 463. 11 December 1879, ibid., p. 466. Roy Jenkins, *Gladstone: A Biography* (New York: Random House, 1997), p. 428.
4. *Punch Political Life of Gladstone,* vol. 2, p. 73. 9 December 1879, *Gladstone Diaries,* vol. 9, p. 465.
5. Shannon, *Bulgarian Agitation,* p. 157. Matthew, *Gladstone,* pp. 297–300.
6. Gladstone's second Midlothian speech, 26 November 1879, William Ewart Gladstone, *Political Speeches in Scotland, March and April 1880,* vol. 1 (Edinburgh: Andrew Elliot, 1880), pp. 91–92; Gladstone's seventh Midlothian speech, 19 March 1880, William Ewart Gladstone, *Political Speeches in Scotland, March and April*

1880, vol. 2 (Edinburgh: Andrew Elliot, 1880), pp. 95–96. Gladstone's Glasgow speech, 5 December 1879, ibid., vol. 1, p. 190. Gladstone's sixteenth Midlothian speech, 25 March 1880, ibid., vol. 2, p. 294.

7. 26 November 1879, *Gladstone Diaries,* vol. 9, pp. 461–62; Matthew, *Gladstone,* p. 303. Gladstone's second Midlothian speech, 26 November 1879, Gladstone, *Political Speeches in Scotland,* vol. 1, p. 94.
8. Matthew, *Gladstone,* p. 307. 2–3 January 1880, *Gladstone Diaries,* vol. 9, p. 473. 28 December 1879, ibid., p. 471.
9. 17 March 1880, ibid., pp. 492–93. Gladstone's fourth Midlothian speech, 17 March 1880, Gladstone, *Political Speeches in Scotland,* vol. 2, pp. 35, 38.
10. Gladstone's tenth Midlothian speech, 20 March 1880, Gladstone, *Political Speeches in Scotland,* vol. 2, pp. 148–49.
11. 20 and 22 March 1880, *Gladstone Diaries,* vol. 9, pp. 493–94. Gladstone's thirteenth Midlothian speech, 22 March 1880, Gladstone, *Political Speeches in Scotland,* vol. 2, pp. 210–11, 212–13, 214, 219.
12. Gladstone's eighteenth Midlothian speech, 2 April 1880, Gladstone, *Political Speeches in Scotland,* vol. 2, pp. 343–44.
13. 2 April 1880, *Gladstone Diaries,* vol. 9, p. 497. Gladstone's eighteenth Midlothian speech, 2 April 1880, Gladstone, *Political Speeches in Scotland,* vol. 2, p. 327.
14. Disraeli to Marlborough, 8 March 1880, W. F. Monypenny and George Earle Buckle, *The Life of Benjamin Disraeli, Earl of Beaconsfield,* vol. 6 (New York: Macmillan, 1920), p. 515.
15. Disraeli to Bradford, 31 March 1880, Marquis of Zetland, ed., *The Letters of Disraeli to Lady Chesterfield and Lady Bradford,* vol. 2 (New York: D. Appleton, 1929), p. 348. Gladstone speech, 5 April 1880, Gladstone, *Political Speeches in Scotland,* vol. 2, p. 361. 5 April 1880, *Gladstone Diaries,* vol. 9, p. 498.
16. Disraeli to Chesterfield, 4 April 1880, *Letters of Disraeli to Chesterfield and Bradford,* vol. 2, pp. 350–51. Shannon, *Bulgarian Agitation,* p. 239.
17. *Times,* 14 August 1876, p. 9.
18. Disraeli to Victoria, 30 November 1876, *The Letters of Queen Victoria: A Selection from Her Majesty's Correspondence and Journal between the Years 1862 and 1878,* ed. George Earle Buckle, 2nd series, vol. 2 (New York: Longmans, Green, 1926), pp. 503–4. Disraeli to Salisbury, 1 December 1876, Monypenny and Buckle, *Life of Disraeli,* vol. 6, p. 106. Disraeli notes, 22 December 1876, ibid., p. 109.
19. Robert Blake, *Disraeli* (New York: St. Martin's Press, 1967), p. 607. Matthew, *Gladstone,* p. 8. William Ewart Gladstone, "The Hellenic Factor in the Eastern Problem," in his *Gleanings of Past Years 1843–78,* vol. 4 (London: John Murray, 1879), pp. 269, 272, 274, 277, 302–3.
20. Gladstone, "Hellenic Factor," *Gleanings,* vol. 4, p. 281.

PART FIVE: CONCLUSION
ARMENIANS

1. William Ewart Gladstone, "Kin Beyond Sea," in his *Gleanings of Past Years 1843–78,* vol. 1 (London: John Murray, 1879), p. 204.
2. August Heckscher, *Woodrow Wilson: A Biography* (New York: Scribner, 1991), pp.

23, 50. John Milton Cooper Jr., *The Warrior and the Priest: Woodrow Wilson and Theodore Roosevelt* (Cambridge, Mass.: Belknap Press of Harvard University Press, 1983), p. 22. Sigmund Freud and William C. Bullitt, *Thomas Woodrow Wilson: A Psychological Study* (Boston: Houghton Mifflin, 1967), pp. 83–85. Paul Kennedy, *The Realities Behind Diplomacy: Background Influences on British External Policy, 1865–1980* (London: George Allen and Unwin, 1981), p. 161.

3. Richard Hofstadter, *The American Political Tradition* (New York: Alfred A. Knopf, 1948), p. 240. Kendrick A. Clements, *Woodrow Wilson: World Statesman* (Chicago: Ivan R. Dee, 1999), pp. 6–7.
4. Gladstone speech, 29 December 1894, Frederick Davis Green, *Armenian Massacres, or the Sword of Mohammed* (n.p.: American Oxford, 1896), p. 122.
5. Deborah Pickman Clifford, *Mine Eyes Have Seen the Glory: A Biography of Julia Ward Howe* (Boston: Little, Brown, 1978), pp. 264–67.
6. Green, *Armenian Massacres,* pp. 1–5. James B. Gidney, *A Mandate for Armenia* (Kent, Ohio: Kent State University Press, 1967), p. 42. Peter Balakian, *The Burning Tigris: The Armenian Genocide and America's Response* (New York: HarperCollins, 2003), p. xiii. Balakian's book is an excellent overview of the American reaction to the Armenian genocide.
7. Raymond Aron, "The Island-Continent," in *The Dawn of Universal History,* trans. Barbara Bray (New York: Basic Books, 2002), p. 252. For a tough-minded account that emphasizes economic interests, see Walter LaFeber, *The New Empire: An Interpretation of American Expansion 1860–1898* (Ithaca, N.Y.: Cornell University Press, 1998), pp. 333–406.
8. David Nasaw, *The Chief: The Life of William Randolph Hearst* (Boston: Houghton Mifflin, 2001), pp. 125–26.
9. Edmund Morris, *The Rise of Theodore Roosevelt* (New York: Modern Library, 2001), p. 635.
10. John Offner, *An Unwanted War: The Diplomacy of the United States and Spain over Cuba, 1895–1898* (Chapel Hill: University of North Carolina Press, 1992), pp. 229–30. Nasaw, *Chief,* p. 133. Walter A. McDougall, *Promised Land, Crusader State: The American Encounter with the World Since 1776* (Boston: Houghton Mifflin, 1997), p. 110.
11. Robert A. Caro, *The Years of Lyndon Johnson: Master of the Senate* (New York: Alfred A. Knopf, 2002), pp. 35–36. Morris, *Rise of Roosevelt,* pp. 755–56. Theodore Roosevelt, "The Strenuous Life," 10 April 1899, in Ted Widmer, ed., *American Speeches: Political Oratory from Abraham Lincoln to Bill Clinton* (New York: Library of America, 2006), p. 158. Richard Hofstadter, "Cuba, the Philippines, and Manifest Destiny," in Richard Hofstadter, *The Paranoid Style in American Politics and Other Essays* (New York: Alfred A. Knopf, 1965), p. 165. John B. Judis, *The Folly of Empire: What George W. Bush Could Learn from Theodore Roosevelt and Woodrow Wilson* (New York: Oxford University Press, 2006), pp. 59–93. Edmund Morris, *Theodore Rex* (New York: Random House, 2001), pp. 109–10. Stanley Karnow, *In Our Image: America's Empire in the Philippines* (New York: Ballantine, 1989), pp. 241–47, 323.
12. Wilson talk, 23 September 1919, Woodrow Wilson, *The Public Papers of Woodrow*

Wilson: War and Peace: Presidential Messages, Addresses, and Public Papers (1917–1924), ed. Ray Stannard Baker and William E. Dodd (New York: Harper and Brother, 1927), vol. 2, p. 354. Alfred Thayer Mahan, *Some Neglected Aspects of War* (Boston: Little, Brown, 1907), pp. 99, 100, 106–7.

13. Jay Winter, "Under Cover of War," in Jay Winter, ed., *America and the Armenian Genocide of 1915* (Cambridge: Cambridge University Press, 2003), pp. 37–51.

14. Heckscher, *Wilson,* pp. 297–98, 328–30; Frederick S. Calhoun, *Power and Principle: Armed Intervention in Wilsonian Foreign Policy* (Kent, Ohio: Kent State University Press, 1986); Max Boot, *The Savage Wars of Peace: Small Wars and the Rise of American Power* (New York: Basic Books, 2002), pp. 156–81. Margaret MacMillan, *Paris 1919: Six Months That Changed the World* (New York: Random House, 2001), pp. 9–10. Tony Smith, *America's Mission: The United States and the Worldwide Struggle for Democracy in the Twentieth Century* (Princeton, N.J.: Princeton University Press, 1994), pp. 35–83. John Keegan, *The First World War* (New York: Alfred A. Knopf, 1999), pp. 372–75. Wilson to Johnson, 19 August 1916, Ray Stannard Baker, *Woodrow Wilson: Life and Letters* (Garden City, N.Y.: Doubleday, Page, 1937), p. 339.

15. Theodore Roosevelt, *America and the World War* (New York: Charles Scribner's Sons, 1915); Ernest R. May, *The World War and American Isolation, 1914–1917* (Cambridge, Mass.: Harvard University Press, 1966), p. 171; Cooper, *Warrior and Priest,* pp. 276–87; Thomas J. Knock, *To End All Wars: Woodrow Wilson and the Quest for a New World Order* (Princeton, N. J.: Princeton University Press, 1992), p. 61. Roosevelt to Lee, 2 September 1915, *The Letters of Theodore Roosevelt: The Days of Armaggedon 1914–1919,* ed. Elting E. Morison, vol. 8 (Cambridge, Mass.: Harvard University Press, 1954), p. 967. Roosevelt to Archibald Bulloch Roosevelt, 19 May 1915, ibid., p. 922. Roosevelt to Lee, 17 June 1915, ibid., p. 937. Roosevelt to Archibald Bulloch Roosevelt, 19 May 1915, ibid., p. 922.

16. Cooper, *Warrior and Priest,* pp. 281–83. Theodore Roosevelt, *Fear God and Take Your Own Part* (New York: George H. Doran, 1916), p. 196. Roosevelt to Robins, 3 June 1915, *Letters of Roosevelt,* vol. 8, p. 928. Roosevelt to Lee, 17 June 1915, ibid., p. 937. Roosevelt to George V, 22 July 1918, ibid., p. 1353. Edward J. Renehan Jr., *The Lion's Pride: Theodore Roosevelt and His Family in Peace and War* (New York: Oxford University Press, 1998), pp. 232–33.

17. R.G. 59, M-365, roll 2, 711.67; May, *American Isolation,* p. 338.

18. CAB 23/44 (part 2), 19 May 1918, 3 p.m. meeting. David Lloyd George, *Memoirs of the Peace Conference,* vol. 2 (New Haven, Conn.: Yale University Press, 1939), pp. 650, 876.

19. James Bryce and Arnold Toynbee, *The Treatment of Armenians in the Ottoman Empire, 1915–1916* (London: His Majesty's Stationery Office, 1916). FO 371/2488/108070, 29 July 1915; H. A. L. Fisher, *James Bryce* (New York: Macmillan, 1927); James Bryce, *Transcaucasia and Ararat, Being Notes of a Vacation Tour in the Autumn of 1876* (London: Macmillan, 1896). Akaby Nassibian, *Britain and the Armenian Question 1915–1923* (London: Croom Helm, 1984), pp. 44–50. Arnold Toynbee, *Armenian Atrocities: The Murder of a Nation* (London: Hodder and Stoughton, 1915), pp. 14, 27.

20. Taner Akcam, *A Shameful Act: The Armenian Genocide and the Question of Turkish Responsibility* (New York: Metropolitan, 2006), pp. 12, 46, 52, 123–24, 151, 191–96. FO 371/2484/22083, 25 February 1915; FO 371/2484/25073, 4 March 1915; FO 371/2484/25167, 4 March 1915; FO 371/2484/28172, 10 March 1915; FO 371/2485/41444, 9 April 1915; FO 371/2485/101144, 26 July 1915; FO 371/2485/106769, 4 August 1915; FO 371/2485/115866, Sykes to Maxwell, 3 August 1915; FO 371/2485/126836, 7 September 1915; FO 371/2485/136059, 22 September 1915; FO 371/2485/196024, 21 December 1915.
21. FO 371/2488/51010, 28 April 1915.
22. Henry Morgenthau III, *Mostly Morgenthaus* (New York: Ticknor and Fields, 1991), pp. 93–95, 101–7.
23. Henry Morgenthau Sr., *Ambassador Morgenthau's Story* (Garden City, N.Y.: Doubleday, Page, 1918), pp. 209, 321–22. Morgenthau to Bryan, 27 April 1915, *FRUS: 1915 Supplement: The World War* (Washington, D.C.: U.S. Government Printing Office, 1928), p. 980. Bryan to Morgenthau, 27 April 1915, ibid.
24. Morgenthau to Bryan, 2 May 1915, *FRUS: 1915 Supplement,* p. 981. Morgenthau, *Ambassador Morgenthau's Story,* p. 330. 24 May 1915 Allied declaration, Sharp to Bryan, 28 May 1915, *FRUS: 1915 Supplement,* p. 981. "Allies to Punish Turks Who Murder," *New York Times,* 24 May 1915, p. 1.
25. Morgenthau to Bryan, 2 May 1915, *FRUS: 1915 Supplement,* p. 981. Morgenthau to Lansing, 18 June 1915, ibid., p. 982.
26. Heckscher, *Wilson,* pp. 367–69. Balakian, *Burning Tigris,* pp. 225–75. Morgenthau to Lansing, 10 July 1915, *FRUS: 1915 Supplement,* pp. 982–84.
27. Lansing to Morgenthau, 16 July 1915, *FRUS: 1915 Supplement,* p. 984.
28. Barton to Lansing, received 14 July 1915, ibid. Lansing to Barton, 19 July 1915, ibid.
29. Morgenthau, *Ambassador Morgenthau's Story,* pp. 333–34.
30. Morgenthau to Lansing, 11 August 1915, *FRUS: 1915 Supplement,* pp. 985–86. See Morgenthau to Lansing, 12 August 1915, ibid., p. 985.
31. Lansing to Morgenthau, 18 August 1915, ibid., p. 987. Morgenthau to Lansing, 20 August 1915, ibid.
32. Morgenthau to Lansing, 20 August 1915, ibid., p. 977. Morgenthau to Lansing, 18 August 1915, ibid., p. 987. Akcam, *Shameful Act,* p. 172. Lansing to Philip, 4 February 1919, *FRUS: 1916 Supplement: The World War* (Washington, D.C.: U.S. Government Printing Office, 1929), pp. 846–47.
33. Morgenthau to Lansing, 3 September 1915, *FRUS: 1915 Supplement,* p. 988. "Tales of Armenian Horrors Confirmed," *New York Times,* 27 September 1915, p. 5. Polk to Morgenthau, 22 September 1915, *FRUS: 1915 Supplement,* p. 988. "Already Has $75,000 to Help Armenians," *New York Times,* 7 October 1915, p. 3. Balakian, *Burning Tigris,* pp. 278–81, 286–91.
34. There were twenty-four stories in September 1915, and forty-five in October 1915. The total for 1915 was one hundred and forty-five. "Armenians Are Sent to Perish in Desert," *New York Times,* 18 August 1915, p. 5. "Answer Morgenthau by Hanging Armenians," *New York Times,* 16 September 1915, p. 1. "500,000 Armenians Said to Have Perished," *New York Times,* 24 September 1915, p. 2. "Tell of Horrors

Done in Armenia," *New York Times,* 4 October 1915, p. 1. "For Armenia," *Nation,* 7 October 1915. Balakian, *Burning Tigris,* p. xiii.

35. John Milton Cooper Jr., "A Friend in Power?" in Jay Winter, ed., *America and the Armenian Genocide of 1915* (Cambridge: Cambridge University Press, 2003), p. 104. Lansing to Morgenthau, 4 October 1915, *FRUS: 1915 Supplement,* p. 988. "Government Sends Plea for Armenia," *New York Times,* 5 October 1915, p. 3. Wilson to Chambers, 13 December 1915, Baker, *Wilson: Life and Letters,* vol. 6. p. 338.
36. Roosevelt, *Fear God and Take Your Own Part,* pp. 18, 21.
37. Ibid., pp. 152–53, 45. Balakian, *Burning Tigris,* p. 295; Morris, *Rise of Roosevelt,* p. xviii; Morris, *Theodore Rex,* p. 244.
38. Morris, *Theodore Rex,* pp. 104–6. Aron, "Island-Continent," p. 255. John B. Judis, "History Lesson," *New Republic,* 9 June 2003, p. 20.
39. Roosevelt, *Fear God and Take Your Own Part,* pp. 26, 39.
40. Roosevelt, "Washington's Forgotten Maxim," 2 June 1897, *The Works of Theodore Roosevelt* (New York: Charles Scribner's Sons, 1926), vol. 13, pp. 184–85. Morris, *Rise of Roosevelt,* pp. 593–94.
41. Roosevelt to Osborne, 1 November 1915, *Letters of Roosevelt,* vol. 8, p. 976. Theodore Roosevelt, *A Compilation of the Messages and Speeches of Theodore Roosevelt, 1901–1095,* ed. Alfred Henry Lewis, supplemental vol. 2 (New York: Bureau of National Literature and Art, 1906), p. 858.
42. Roosevelt to Dutton, 24 November 1915, Roosevelt, *Fear God and Take Your Own Part,* pp. 377–79, 381–82.
43. Ibid., pp. 112, 133.
44. Roosevelt to Osborne, 1 November 1915, *Letters of Roosevelt,* vol. 8, p. 976. Roosevelt, *Fear God and Take Your Own Part,* p. 134.
45. R.G. 59, M-353, roll 6, 867.00/798-2, Morgenthau to Lansing, 18 November 1915; R.G. 59, M-353, roll 6, 867.00/798-2, Lansing to Wilson, 13 January 1916. Morgenthau, *Ambassador Morgenthau's Story,* p. 385.
46. Lansing to Philip, 4 February 1916, *FRUS: 1916 Supplement,* pp. 846–47. Lansing to Philip, 12 February 1916, ibid., p. 847.
47. Lansing to Philip, 12 February 1916, ibid. Lansing to Bernstorff, 16 February 1916, ibid., pp. 847–48.
48. Philip to Lansing, 15 February 1916, ibid., pp. 848–49. Philip to Lansing, 28 March 1916, ibid., pp. 849–50.
49. Lansing to Philip, 16 June 1916, ibid., p. 852. Philip to Lansing, 21 July 1916, ibid., p. 853.
50. Philip to Lansing, 1 September 1916, ibid., pp. 853–55.
51. Philip to Lansing, 1 October 1916, ibid., pp. 856–57.
52. Baker, *Wilson: Life and Letters,* vol. 6, p. 341; Gidney, *Mandate,* pp. 44–45. Lansing to Grew, 1 November 1916, *FRUS: 1916 Supplement,* p. 858. Lansing to Wilson, 21 November 1916, *FRUS: The Lansing Papers 1914–1920,* vol. 1 (Washington, D.C.: U.S. Government Printing Office, 1939), p. 42.
53. Roosevelt to Shimmon, 10 July 1918, *Letters of Roosevelt,* vol. 8, p. 1349. Roosevelt to Dodge, 11 May 1918, ibid., pp. 1317–18. Roosevelt to Gallivan, 22 August 1918, ibid., p. 1365.

54. Roosevelt, *Fear God and Take Your Own Part,* pp. 21–23.
55. Ibid., pp. 83, 114, 61.
56. Heckscher, *Wilson,* pp. 433–34. May, *American Isolation,* p. 419. Roosevelt to Dodge, 11 May 1918, *Letters of Roosevelt,* vol. 8, pp. 1317–18. Richard G. Hovannisian, *Armenia on the Road to Independence* (Berkeley: University of California Press, 1967), p. 55. Cooper, "Friend in Power?" pp. 106, 111. Roosevelt to Dodge, 11 May 1918, *Letters of Roosevelt,* vol. 8, p. 1318.
57. Nubar to Lansing, 24 May 1917, *FRUS: 1917 Supplement 2: The World War,* vol. 2 (Washington, D.C.: U.S. Government Printing Office, 1932), p. 792. Roosevelt to Bryce, 7 August 1918, *Letters of Roosevelt,* vol. 8, p. 1359. See Roosevelt to Miller, 16 September 1918, ibid., p. 1372.
58. William Linn Westermann, "The Armenian Problem and the Disruption of Turkey," in Edward Mandell House and Charles Seymour, eds., *What Really Happened at Paris: The Story of the Peace Conference, 1918–1919* (New York: Charles Scribner's Sons, 1921), p. 179. MacMillan, *Paris 1919,* pp. 377–80.
59. Gidney, *Mandate,* p. 62. Harold Nicolson, *Peacemaking 1919* (London: Constable, 1933), p. 141. Ray Stannard Baker, *Woodrow Wilson and World Settlement,* vol. 1 (Garden City, N.Y.: Doubleday, Page, 1922), p. 74. Wilson speech, 8 January 1918, Baker and Dodd, eds., *Public Papers of Woodrow Wilson: War and Peace,* vol. 5, pp. 159–60. MacMillan, *Paris 1919,* p. 376. Cooper, "Friend in Power?" p. 105. Wilson speech, 4 July 1918, *Papers of Wilson,* vol. 5, p. 233.
60. Lloyd George, *Memoirs of the Peace Conference,* vol. 2, pp. 811–12. CAB 23/44 (part 2), 19 May 1918, 3 p.m. meeting. Gidney, *Mandate,* p. 76.
61. Allied resolutions, 30 January 1919, *FRUS: The Paris Peace Conference 1919,* vol. 12 (Washington, D.C.: U.S. Government Printing Office, 1947), pp. 745–46. Allied meeting, 13 May 1919, 4 p.m., *FRUS: The Paris Peace Conference 1919,* vol. 5 (Washington, D.C.: U.S. Government Printing Office, 1946), pp. 581–82.
62. Hovannisian, *Armenia on the Road to Independence,* pp. 157–215. Gidney, *Mandate,* pp. 79–80. Westermann, "Armenian Problem," p. 178.
63. Lansing to Wilson, 2 April 1919, *FRUS: Paris 1919,* vol. 12, pp. 747–48. Gidney, *Mandate,* pp. 146–50. King-Crane commission report, *FRUS: Paris 1919,* vol. 12, pp. 781–82, 790, 802, 811–14, 819–28, 834–36, 843–44.
64. Herbert Hoover, *The Ordeal of Woodrow Wilson* (New York: McGraw-Hill, 1958), pp. 225–29. Commissioners' meeting, 13 March 1919, *FRUS: The Paris Peace Conference 1919,* vol. 11 (Washington, D.C.: U.S. Government Printing Office, 1945), p. 116.
65. Allied meeting, 13 May 1919, 4 p.m., *FRUS: Paris 1919,* vol. 5, p. 583. Allied meeting, 21 May 1919, 11 a.m., ibid., pp. 756–65.
66. Hoover to Paris delegations, 16 July 1919, *FRUS: The Paris Peace Conference 1919,* vol. 10 (Washington, D.C.: U.S. Government Printing Office), pp. 482–83. Lloyd George, *Memoirs of the Peace Conference,* vol. 1, p. 117. Five powers' meeting, 15 September 1919, 10:30 a.m., *FRUS: Paris 1919,* vol. 8, p. 207. Gidney, *Mandate,* p. 178. Westermann, "Armenian Problem," p. 179.
67. Wilson speech, 24 February 1919, Baker and Dodd, eds., *Public Papers of Woodrow Wilson, War and Peace,* vol. 1, p. 439. Balakian, *Burning Tigris,* pp.

302–3. Wilson talk, 22 September 1919, *Public Papers of Wilson: War and Peace,* vol. 2, p. 336. Wilson talk, 23 September 1919, ibid., p. 359. Wilson talk, 6 September 1919, ibid., pp. 7–8.

68. Wilson message to Congress, 24 May 1920, *Public Papers of Wilson: War and Peace,* vol. 2, p. 490. MacMillan, *Paris 1919,* pp. 442–44, 449. Balakian, *Burning Tigris,* pp. 360–62. Gidney, *Mandate,* pp. 214–16.

69. Westermann, "Armenian Problem," pp. 179, 203. R.G. 59, M-365, roll 2, 711.67/24, Bristol to State, 17 December 1921.

70. Adams address, 4 July 1821, *John Quincy Adams and American Continental Empire: Letters, Speeches and Papers,* ed. Walter LaFeber (Chicago: Quadrangle, 1965), p. 46.

71. Wilson speech, 24 February 1919, *Public Papers of Wilson: War and Peace,* vol. 1, p. 438. Westermann, "Armenian Problem," p. 179.

72. John Morton Blum, *Roosevelt and Morgenthau* (Boston: Houghton Mifflin, 1970), p. 8. Henry Morgenthau III epilogue in Morgenthau Sr., *Ambassador Morgenthau's Story* (Detroit: Wayne State University Press, 2003), p. 310.

THE USES OF HISTORY

1. Robert Blake, *Disraeli* (New York: St. Martin's Press, 1967), p. 592. Arthur and Eleanor Mildred Sigdwick, *Henry Sidgwick: A Memoir* (London: Macmillan, 1906), p. 325. Richard T. Shannon, *Gladstone and the Bulgarian Agitation 1876* (Sussex: Harvester, 1975), p. 31. Victor Hugo, *Napoleon the Little* (New York: Howard Fertig, 1992), pp. 212–16.

2. A. J. P. Taylor, *The Trouble Makers: Dissent Over Foreign Policy 1792–1939* (London: Pimlico, 1993), p. 74.

3. LGC vol. 1, E5, Address of the Greek Committee, Lord Milton M.P., Crown and Anchor Tavern, 3 May 1823. Leader, *Times,* 10 July 1860, p. 8. David Nasaw, *The Chief: The Life of William Randolph Hearst* (Boston: Houghton Mifflin, 2001), p. 125. William Ewart Gladstone, *Bulgarian Horrors and the Question of the East* (London: John Murray, 1876), pp. 10–12.

4. See Paul Collier, *The Bottom Billion: Why the Poorest Countries Are Failing and What Can Be Done About It* (New York: Oxford University Press, 2007).

5. For an impressive exception, see Martha Finnemore, *The Purpose of Intervention: Changing Beliefs About the Use of Force* (Ithaca, N.Y.: Cornell University Press, 2003), p. 65. Kissinger makes glancing references to "British domestic structure" as constraining (Henry A. Kissinger, *A World Restored: Metternich, Castlereagh, and the Problems of Peace 1812–22* [Boston: Houghton Mifflin, 1973], p. 306; see pp. 312, 323). In a rare mention of human rights violations, Kissinger sounds neutral: "The Greek rebellion continued with countless atrocities by both sides" (p. 296). Kissinger, *World Restored,* pp. 310, 296, 305, 308. The Scio massacre and the rise of British philhellenism happened before Castlereagh's suicide. Kissinger's book ends in 1822, but he is well aware of subsequent events; he refers to World War I (p. 6), the Treaty of Versailles (p. 1), and the 1830 revolutions (p. 315).

6. Henry A. Kissinger, *Diplomacy* (New York: Simon and Schuster, 1994), pp. 89, 92; Simon Chesterman, *Just War or Just Peace?: Humanitarian Intervention and*

International Law (Oxford: Oxford University Press, 2001), pp. 28–32. Harvey Sicherman, "Disraeli's Secret," *National Interest,* spring 2002, pp. 46–57. Burke to Grenville, 18 August 1792, *Selected Letters of Edmund Burke,* ed. Harvey C. Mansfield Jr. (Chicago: University of Chicago Press, 1984), p. 313.

7. Kissinger, *World Restored,* p. 289. One cannot understand the Russo-Turkish War—which ranks alongside the Crimean War and the Franco-Prussian War as one of the crucial episodes of the nineteenth century—without understanding the British and Russian reactions to the Bulgarian horrors.
8. Christopher Lasch, *The True and Only Heaven: Progress and Its Critics* (New York: W. W. Norton, 1991), p. 113.
9. Wynn to Wellington, 27 October 1825, Arthur Wellesley, Duke of Wellington, *Despatches, Correspondence, and Memoranda of Field Marshal Arthur, Duke of Wellington,* vol. 2 (London: John Murray, 1867), pp. 549–53; Wellington's memorandum on Irish Catholics, December 1825, ibid., pp. 592–607; Paget to Wellington, 7 June 1826, ibid., vol. 3, pp. 324–33. A. N. Wilson, *The Victorians* (New York: W. W. Norton, 2003), pp. 213–14. Mike Davis, *Late Victorian Holocausts: El Niño Famines and the Making of the Third World* (London: Verso, 2001), pp. 7–9, 28–30, 102–3.
10. Ali to Russell, 21 January 1861, Great Britain, Foreign Office, *Correspondence Relating to the Affairs of Syria 1860–61* (London: Harrison and Sons, 1861), pp. 369–70. Eric Stokes, *The English Utilitarians and India* (Oxford: Clarendon Press, 1959); Uday Singh Mehta, *Liberalism and Empire: A Study in Nineteenth-Century British Liberal Thought* (Chicago: University of Chicago Press, 1999); Jennifer Pitts, *A Turn to Empire: The Rise of Imperial Liberalism in Britain and France* (Princeton, N.J.: Princeton University Press, 2005); Sankar Muthu, *Enlightenment Against Empire* (Princeton, N.J.: Princeton University Press, 2003), pp. 259–83.
11. Ussama Makdisi, *The Culture of Sectarianism: Community, History, and Violence in Nineteenth-Century Lebanon* (Berkeley: University of California Press, 2000), p. 9. See Taner Akcam, *A Shameful Act: The Armenian Genocide and the Question of Turkish Responsibility* (New York: Metropolitan, 2006), p. 25.
12. I have been arguing against neoimperialism since 1993 ("Lonely Planet," *New Republic,* 14 June 1993, p. 50). David Rieff, "A Nation of Pre-emptors?" *New York Times Magazine,* 15 January 2006, pp. 12.
13. Michael W. Doyle, *Empires* (Ithaca, N.Y.: Cornell University Press, 1986), p. 12.
14. See Engels, "The Real Issue in Turkey," *New York Daily Tribune,* 12 April 1853, p. 4; Finnemore, *Purpose of Intervention,* p. 59.
15. James Mann, *About Face: A History of America's Curious Relationship with China from Nixon to Clinton* (New York: Alfred A. Knopf, 1999), p. 42. Winston S. Churchill, *The Second World War: The Grand Alliance* (Boston: Houghton Mifflin, 1950), p. 370.
16. Canning to Wellington, 10 February 1826, Wellington, *Despatches,* vol. 3, p. 91. Metternich history, 5 January 1826, Klemens von Metternich, *Mémoires, documents et écrits divers: L'Ère de paix, 1816–1848,* vol. 4 (Paris: Plon, 1881), pp. 297–98.
17. Andrew Porter, "Trusteeship, Anti-Slavery, and Humanitarianism," in Andrew

Porter, ed., *The Oxford History of the British Empire* (Oxford: Oxford University Press, 1999), pp. 198–201, 207–11; Pitts, *Turn to Empire,* p. 21.

18. Hugo to Butler, 18 November 1861, Nora Wang, Ye Xin, and Wang Lou, *Victor Hugo et le sac du Palais d'Été* (Paris: Indes Savantes, 2003), pp. 9–10. Claude Millet, *Le despote Oriental: Victor Hugo et l'Orient* (Paris: Maisonneuve, 2001). Wang et al., *Palais d'Été,* p. 64.
19. Pitts, *Turn to Empire,* pp. 15, 103, 109–11. Jeremy Bentham, "Emancipation Spanish: From Philo-Hispanus to the People of Spain," in Philip Schofield, ed., *The Collected Works of Jeremy Bentham: Colonies, Commerce, and Constitutional Law* (Oxford: Clarendon Press, 1995), p. 153. Jeremy Bentham, "Rid Yourselves of Ultramaria: Being the Advice of Jeremy Bentham as Given in a Series of Letters to the Spanish People," in ibid., p. 137. Bentham to Greeks, 24 November 1823, Catherine Fuller, ed., *The Collected Works of Jeremy Bentham: Correspondence,* vol. 11 (Oxford: Clarendon, 2000), p. 322.
20. R. W. Kostal, *A Jurisprudence of Power: Victorian Empire and the Rule of Law* (Oxford: Oxford University Press, 2006); John Fabian Witt, "Anglo-American Empire and the Crisis of the Legal Frame," *Harvard Law Review,* vol. 120, no. 3 (January 2007), pp. 754–97. Shannon, *Bulgarian Agitation,* pp. 214–15.
21. Adam Hochschild, *Bury the Chains: Prophets and Rebels in the Fight to Free an Empire's Slaves* (Boston: Houghton Mifflin, 2005), p. 322. Porter, "Humanitarianism," pp. 218–19. Davis, *Late Victorian Holocausts,* pp. 32, 43–45, 56–57.
22. John B. Judis, "History Lesson," *New Republic,* 9 June 2003, p. 20. Theodore Roosevelt, "The Strenuous Life," 10 April 1899, Ted Widmer, ed., *American Speeches: Political Oratory from Abraham Lincoln to Bill Clinton* (New York: Library of America, 2006), p. 158. Wilson talk, 23 September 1919, *Public Papers of Wilson: War and Peace,* vol. 2, p. 354.
23. Robert Penn Warren, *All the King's Men* (New York: Harvest, 1996), p. 257.
24. Anonymous ("a British seaman"), *Life on Board a Man-of-War; Including a Full Account of the Battle of Navarino* (Glasgow: Blackie, Fullarton, 1829), p. 166. Dufferin to Bulwer, 26 October 1860, *Syria Correspondence 1860–61,* p. 195. "The Turkish Atrocities in Bulgaria," *Daily News,* 22 August 1876, pp. 5–6.
25. H. C. G. Matthew, *Gladstone 1809–1898* (New York: Oxford University Press, 1999), p. 279. Gladstone, *Bulgarian Horrors,* pp. 12–13. Disraeli to Chesterfield, 10 January 1877, Marquis of Zetland, ed., *The Letters of Disraeli to Lady Chesterfield and Lady Bradford* (New York: D. Appleton, 1929), vol. 2, p. 129.
26. John Milton Cooper Jr., *The Warrior and the Priest: Woodrow Wilson and Theodore Roosevelt* (Cambridge, Mass.: Belknap Press of Harvard University Press, 1983), pp. 210–11; Kathleen L. Wolgemuth, "Woodrow Wilson and Federal Segregation," *Journal of Negro History,* vol. 44, no. 2 (April 1959), pp. 158–73. Wilson talk, 6 September 1919, *Public Papers of Wilson: War and Peace,* vol. 2, pp. 7–8.
27. Edward Said, *Orientalism* (New York: Vintage, 1979), p. 192, 40. Finnemore, while a thoughtful supporter of humanitarian interventions, sees nineteenth-century humanitarianism as a matter of rescuing Christians (Finnemore, *Purpose of Intervention,* pp. 58–63). She does not discuss liberals like Byron or Bentham, nor the nonreligious atrocitarians in 1876.

28. Linda Colley, *Captives: Britain, Empire, and the World, 1600–1850* (New York: Anchor, 2004), p. 361. Bentham to Blaquiere, 2 March 1823, *Collected Works of Bentham: Correspondence,* vol. 11, pp. 215–16. His principle was, "Treat them with as much kindness as the indispensable regard for your own [Greek] safety will permit" ("Observations by an Englishman," in Philip Schofield, ed., *The Collected Works of Jeremy Bentham: Securities Against Misrule and Other Constitutional Writings for Tripoli and Greece* [Oxford: Clarendon Press, 1990], p. 254). This did mean making sure that Muslims did not outvote Christians, but with the hope that by participation in political life "the Mahometans [would be] rendered good Citizens" (ibid., pp. 254–55). Bentham reluctantly thought it was necessary to partially exclude Muslims in Greece from civic life temporarily so long as the war continued, but "not a moment longer." He hoped to turn the Muslims in Greece from "necessary enemies" into "actual friends." ("Constitutional Code: Matter Occasioned by Greece," *Collected Works of Bentham: Securities Against Misrule,* p. 263.) See Pitts, *Turn to Empire,* pp. 119–20. Bentham, "Securities Against Misrule," *Collected Works of Bentham: Securities Against Misrule,* pp. 23–73. See Bentham to Muhammad Ali, 28 April 1828, *Collected Works of Bentham: Correspondence,* vol. 12, pp. 468–75.
29. Nico Krisch, "Imperial International Law," January 2004, Global Law working paper, Hauser Global Law School Program, New York University Law School, p. 19. Shannon, *Bulgarian Agitation,* p. 15. Ann Pottinger Saab, *Reluctant Icon: Gladstone, Bulgaria, and the Working Classes 1856–1878* (Cambridge, Mass.: Harvard University Press, 1991), pp. 1, 31.
30. Disraeli to Bradford, 11 September 1876, *Letters of Disraeli to Chesterfield and Bradford,* vol. 2, p. 90; Disraeli to Northcote, 11 September 1876, W. F. Monypenny and George Earle Buckle, *The Life of Benjamin Disraeli, Earl of Beaconsfield,* vol. 6 (New York: Macmillan, 1920), p. 60. W. M. Malloy, ed., *Treaties, Conventions, International Acts, Protocols, and Agreements between the United States of America and Other Powers* (Washington, D.C.: U.S. Government Printing Office, 1910), p. 1768. "For Armenia," *Nation,* 7 October 1915.
31. Dufferin to Bulwer, 11 February 1861, *Syria Correspondence 1860–61,* p. 403. John Stuart Mill, "A Few Words on Non-Intervention" (December 1859), in *Dissertations and Discussions: Political, Philosophical, and Historical,* vol. 3 (New York: Henry Holt, 1882), p. 257. In other words, pan-Christianity is an explanatory variable that does not vary, but the outcomes do vary.
32. René Albrecht-Carrié, *A Diplomatic History of Europe Since the Congress of Vienna* (New York: Harper and Row, 1958), p. 97. Gladstone to Aberdeen, 7 April 1851, William Ewart Gladstone, *Two Letters to the Earl of Aberdeen on the State Prosecutions of the Neapolitan Government,* 11th ed. (London: John Murray, 1851), p. 4. Gladstone to Aberdeen, 14 July 1851, ibid., p. 36.
33. Palmerston to Aberdeen, 1 November 1853, Evelyn Ashley, ed., *The Life and Correspondence of Henry John Temple, Viscount Palmerston,* vol. 2 (London: Richard Bentley and Son, 1879), p. 287. Gladstone to Novikov, 24 August 1877, W. T. Stead, ed., *The M.P. for Russia: Reminiscences and Correspondence of Madame Olga*

Novikoff, vol. 1 (London: Andrew Melrose, 1909), p. 376. Hans Kohn, *Pan-Slavism: Its History and Ideology* (New York: Vintage, 1960), p. 197.

34. Leader, *Times,* 10 May 1831, p. 4. The *Times* ran about twenty-five stories in May 1821 on the outbreak of the Greek uprising and forty-one stories at the peak of its Scio coverage in August 1822—as against about fifty-five stories on Poland in August 1831. The suffering of the Greeks never surpassed that figure. Only Britain's naval victory at Navarino Bay capped it, with about sixty-two *Times* stories in October 1827—more a reflection of British triumphalism than anything else.

35. Maria Todorova, *Imagining the Balkans* (New York: Oxford University Press, 1997). Victoria to Disraeli, 21 March 1877, Monypenny and Buckle, *Life of Disraeli,* vol. 6, p. 130.

36. Alan Cooperman, "Robertson Defends Liberia's President," *Washington Post,* 10 July 2003, p. A19. Jane Perlez, "Suddenly in Sudan, A Moment to Care," *New York Times,* 17 June 2001; Steven Mufson, "Christians' Plight in Sudan Tests a Bush Stance," *Washington Post,* 24 March 2001.

37. Deborah E. Lipstadt, *Beyond Belief: The American Press and the Coming of the Holocaust, 1933–1945* (New York: Free Press, 1986), pp. 240–78; Laurel Leff, *Buried by The Times: The Holocaust and America's Most Important Newspaper* (New York: Cambridge University Press, 2005).

38. Canning to Liverpool, 21 November 1824, *Some Official Correspondence of George Canning,* vol. 1 (London: Longmans, Green, 1887), p. 203. "St. James's-Hall Conference," *Times,* 9 December 1876, p. 8. Gladstone's second Midlothian speech, 26 November 1879, William Ewart Gladstone, *Political Speeches in Scotland, March and April 1880,* vol. 1 (Edinburgh: Andrew Elliot, 1880), p. 94. Matthew, *Gladstone,* p. 294.

THE INTERNATIONAL POLITICS OF HUMANITARIAN INTERVENTION

1. Henry A. Kissinger, "The End of NATO as We Know It?" *Washington Post,* 15 August 1999, p. B7. "Herzegovina," *Times,* 2 October 1875, p. 5. Stephen D. Krasner, *Sovereignty: Organized Hypocrisy* (Princeton, N.J.: Princeton University Press, 1999), pp. 220, 224. See Hans J. Morgenthau, "To Intervene or Not to Intervene," *Foreign Affairs,* vol. 45, no. 3 (April 1967), p. 425; Niall Ferguson, *Colossus: The Price of America's Empire* (New York: Penguin, 2004), p. 170; Max Boot, *The Savage Wars of Peace: Small Wars and the Rise of American Power* (New York: Basic Books, 2002), p. 338; Zbigniew Brzezinski, *The Choice: Global Domination or Global Leadership* (New York: Basic Books, 2004), p. 7; Pasquale Fiore, *International Law Codified,* trans. Edwin M. Borchard (New York: Baker, Voorhis, 1918), pp. 265–66, 269.

2. Krasner, *Sovereignty,* p. 238. Marc Trachtenberg, "Intervention in Historical Perspective," in Laura W. Reed and Carl Kaysen, eds., *Emerging Norms of Humanitarian Intervention* (Cambridge, Mass.: American Academy of Arts and Sciences, 1993), pp. 21–23; Morgenthau, "To Intervene or Not to Intervene," p. 426;

George Finlay, *History of the Greek Revolution,* vol. 2 (Edinburgh: William Blackwood and Sons, 1861), p. 163.

3. Wellington to Canning, 28 November 1824, Arthur Wellesley, Duke of Wellington, *Despatches, Correspondence, and Memoranda of Field Marshal Arthur, Duke of Wellington,* vol. 2 (London: John Murray, 1867), pp. 352–53; Liverpool to Wellington, 8 December 1824, ibid., p. 366. René Albrecht-Carrié, *A Diplomatic History of Europe Since the Congress of Vienna* (New York: Harper and Row, 1958), p. 73. John Stuart Mill, "A Few Words on Non-Intervention" (December 1859), in *Dissertations and Discussions: Political, Philosophical, and Historical,* vol. 3 (New York: Henry Holt, 1882), pp. 256–57.
4. Nico Krisch, "Imperial International Law," January 2004, Global Law working paper, Hauser Global Law School Program, New York University Law School, p. 19. Webster, "The Revolution in Greece," 19 January 1824, *The Papers of Daniel Webster: Speeches and Formal Writings,* ed. Charles M. Wiltse, vol. 1 (Hanover, N.H.: University Press of New England, 1986), pp. 92, 96. See John Fabian Witt, *Patriots and Cosmopolitans: Hidden Histories of American Law* (Cambridge, Mass.: Harvard University Press, 2007), pp. 178–79.
5. Harold Nicolson, *The Congress of Vienna: A Study in Allied Unity, 1812–1822* (New York: Harcourt, Brace, 1946), p. 272; Finlay, *History of the Greek Revolution,* vol. 2, p. 163. Trachtenberg, "Intervention in Historical Perspective," p. 22. José A. Cabranes, "Human Rights and Non-Intervention in the Inter-American System," *Michigan Law Review,* vol. 65, no. 2 (1967), pp. 1147–82.
6. Krasner, *Sovereignty,* p. 86. William Ewart Gladstone, "The Hellenic Factor in the Eastern Problem," in his *Gleanings of Past Years 1843–78,* vol. 4 (London: John Murray, 1879), p. 301. Gladstone's fourth Midlothian speech, 17 March 1880, William Ewart Gladstone, *Political Speeches in Scotland,* vol. 2, pp. 35.
7. Castlereagh to Aleksandr I, 28 October 1821, Charles Kingsley Webster, *The Foreign Policy of Castlereagh, 1815–1822,* vol. 2 (London: G. Bell, 1925), pp. 378; Wellington to Canning, 10 November 1824, Wellington, *Despatches,* vol. 2, p. 339. Gallatin to Adams, 18 January 1823, *The Writings of Albert Gallatin,* ed. Henry Adams, vol. 2 (Philadelphia: J. B. Lippincott, 1879), p. 264.
8. Wellington to Canning, 28 November 1824, Wellington, *Despatches,* vol. 2, pp. 352–53. Canning to Wellington, 30 November 1824, ibid., p. 359.
9. FO 421/3/26, Abstract of the Proceedings in the Greek Question, part V, p. 48.
10. Canning to Stratford Canning, 12 October 1825, Wellington, *Despatches,* vol. 2, pp. 533–34. Burke to Grenville, 18 August 1792, *Selected Letters of Edmund Burke,* ed. Harvey C. Mansfield Jr. (Chicago: University of Chicago Press, 1984), p. 313. Krisch, "Imperial International Law," p. 19. Abraham Lincoln, Cooper Union speech, 27 February 1860, *Selected Speeches and Writings,* ed. Don E. Fehrenbacher (New York: Library of America, 1992), p. 243.
11. Mill, "Non-Intervention," pp. 256–62.
12. "China Warns UN of Rising Threat of Cold War Interventionism," Agence France Press, 22 September 1999. See Rosemary Foot, *Rights Beyond Borders: The Global Community and the Struggle over Human Rights in China* (Oxford: Oxford University Press, 2000), pp. 261–62.

13. William Ewart Gladstone, *Bulgarian Horrors and the Question of the East* (London: John Murray, 1876), p. 55.
14. Hugo Grotius, *Of the Rights of War and Peace,* trans. J. Barbeyrac (London: W. Innys and R. Manby, J. and P. Knapton, D. Brown, T. Osborn, and E. Wicksteed, 1738; orig. 1625), book 2, ch. 25, section 8, p. 504. Italics removed. Paul Lewis, "Russia a Barrier to NATO Air Strike," *New York Times,* 9 February 1994, p. A12. See Roger Cohen, "Calling History to Arms," *New York Times,* 8 September 1995, p. A1.
15. Norman Davies, *God's Playground: A History of Poland* (New York: Columbia University Press, 1982), vol. 2, pp. 327–29. Hans Kohn, *Pan-Slavism: Its History and Ideology* (New York: Vintage, 1960), p. 129. T. J. Binyon, *Pushkin: A Biography* (New York: Alfred A. Knopf, 2003), pp. 337, 363–67.
16. Albrecht-Carrié, *Diplomatic History of Europe,* pp. 66–67, 71; Arthur Schlesinger Jr., "Human Rights and the American Tradition," *Foreign Affairs,* America and the World issue, 1978, pp. 505–8. Palmerston memorandum, 9 September 1849, Evelyn Ashley, ed., *The Life and Correspondence of Henry John Temple, Viscount Palmerston,* vol. 2 (London: Richard Bentley and Son, 1879), pp. 105–7. Palmerston to Normanby, 29 September 1849, ibid., p. 108. Palmerston to Normanby, 23 October 1849, ibid., p. 115.
17. Albrecht-Carrié, *Diplomatic History of Europe,* pp. 73, 81.
18. Davies, *God's Playground,* vol. 2, p. 347.
19. A. J. P. Taylor, *The Struggle for Mastery in Europe, 1848–1918* (Oxford: Oxford University Press, 1971), pp. 133–41; Davies, *God's Playground,* vol. 2, pp. 357–59; Ellery C. Stowell, *Intervention in International Law* (Washington, D.C.: John Byrne, 1921), pp. 92–94; *Massacres de Varsovie: Lettre à S.M. l'empereur Napoléon III* (Paris: n.p., 1861).
20. Theodore Roosevelt, *Fear God and Take Your Own Part* (New York: George H. Doran, 1916), p. 30.
21. Strangford to Castlereagh, 25 May 1822, Philip P. Argenti, ed., *The Massacres of Chios Described in Contemporary Diplomatic Reports* (London: Bodley Head, 1932), pp. 17–19. Krasner, *Sovereignty,* pp. 89, 152–53. See K. Anthony Appiah, "Grounding Human Rights," in Michael Ignatieff, *Human Rights as Politics and Idolatry* (Princeton, N.J.: Princeton University Press, 2001), p. 103. Leader, *Times,* 27 August 1875, p. 8.
22. Binyon, *Pushkin,* p. xxix; Igor S. Ivanov, *Russia: Farewell to Empire?* (Washington, D.C.: Nixon Center and Brookings Institution Press, 2002). George H. W. Bush and Brent Scowcroft, *A World Transformed* (New York: Random House, 1998), p. 98.
23. Leader, *Times,* 14 August 1876, p. 9.
24. Disraeli to Northcote, 11 September 1876, W. F. Monypenny and George Earle Buckle, *The Life of Benjamin Disraeli, Earl of Beaconsfield,* vol. 6 (New York: Macmillan, 1920), p. 61. Machiavelli, *The Prince,* trans. Harvey C. Mansfield Jr. (Chicago: University of Chicago Press, 1985), ch. 17, p. 65. Henry A. Kissinger, *A World Restored: Metternich, Castlereagh, and the Problems of Peace 1812–22* (Boston: Houghton Mifflin, 1973), pp. 6, 323. Wilson talk, 6 September 1919,

Woodrow Wilson, *The Public Papers of Woodrow Wilson: War and Peace: Presidential Messages, Addresses, and Public Papers (1917–1924)*, eds. Ray Stannard Baker and William E. Dodd, vol. 2 (New York: Harper and Brothers, 1927), p. 16.

25. Taner Akcam, *A Shameful Act: The Armenian Genocide and the Question of Turkish Responsibility* (New York: Metropolitan, 2006). Stacy Sullivan, *Be Not Afraid, For You Have Sons in America: How a Brooklyn Roofer Helped Lure the U.S. into the Kosovo War* (New York: St. Martin's Press, 2004).
26. Graham Greene, *The Quiet American* (London: Penguin, 1974), p. 18.
27. Charles R. Beitz, "Sovereignty and Morality in International Affairs," in David Held, ed., *Political Theory Today* (Stanford, Calif.: Stanford University Press, 1991), p. 249. Burke to Grenville, 18 August 1792, *Selected Letters of Edmund Burke,* p. 313. The core of the problem is providing credible commitments to demonstrate that the intervening state has limited humanitarian goals in mind, rather than broader expansionism or imperialism. John Gerard Ruggie, "Multilateralism: The Anatomy of an Institution," in John Gerard Ruggie, ed., *Multilateralism Matters: The Theory and Praxis of an Institutional Form* (New York: Columbia University Press, 1993), pp. 3–8, 19. See Ryan Goodman, "Humanitarian Intervention and Pretexts for War," *American Journal of International Law,* vol. 100, no. 1 (January 2006), pp. 107–41.
28. "St. James's-Hall Conference," *Times,* 9 December 1876, p. 8.
29. Gladstone, *Bulgarian Horrors,* p. 60.
30. Ibid., p. 17; FO 65/941/535, 15 November 1876. Akcam, *Shameful Act,* pp. 218–19. Finnemore has argued that a crucial "shift occurred in humanitarian intervention" between the nineteenth century and the 1990s: "legal understandings and the rules or norms of international organizations," and "a dense web of international legal obligations to protect human rights (Martha Finnemore, *The Purpose of Intervention: Changing Beliefs About the Use of Force* [Ithaca, N.Y.: Cornell University Press, 2003], p. 21). She also claims that modern states, unlike their nineteenth-century ancestors, "will do so [intervene] now only multilaterally with authorization from an international organization" (ibid., p. 3). While Finnemore is right to point to the vital role of international organizations in legitimizing humanitarian intervention, and correctly notes the role of the Concert of Europe (ibid., p. 22; see Anne-Marie Slaughter, *A New World Order* [Princeton, N.J.: Princeton University Press, 2004]), she seems to underestimate the depth of nineteenth-century legalization and overestimate the commitment of today's governments to human rights.
31. Henry Wheaton, *Elements of International Law,* 6th ed. (Boston: Little, Brown, 1855), p. 101; Johann Kaspar Bluntschli, *Le droit international codifié,* trans. M. Charles Lardy, 5th ed. (Paris: Guillaumin, 1895), pp. 269–70; William Edward Hall, *A Treatise on International Law,* 4th ed. (Oxford: Clarendon Press, 1895), p. 303; Antoine Rougier, "La théorie de l'intervention d'humanité," *Revue générale du droit internationale,* vol. 17 (1910), pp. 468–526; W. E. Lingelbach, "The Doctrine and Practice of Intervention in Europe," *Annals of the American Academy of Political and Social Science,* vol. 16 (July 1900), pp. 30–31, p. 25; Augustus Granville Stapleton, *Intervention and Non-Intervention: Or, The Foreign Policy of Great Britain from 1790 to 1865* (London: John Murray, 1866), p. 32; L. F. L.

Oppenheim, *International Law: A Treatise,* 8th ed., ed. H. Lauterpacht, vol. 1 (New York: Longmans, Green, 1955; orig. 1905–6), pp. 312–13; Edwin M. Borchard, *The Diplomatic Protection of Citizens Abroad* (New York: Banks Law, 1915), p. 14; Ellery C. Stowell, *Intervention in International Law* (Washington, D.C.: John Byrne, 1921), p. 126; Fiore, *International Law Codified,* pp. 266, 268; Ian Brownlie, *International Law and the Use of Force by States* (Oxford: Clarendon Press, 1963), pp. 47, 338. MD/T vol. 107, George Outrey, "Étude pratique sur le protectorat religieux de France en Orient" (Constantinople, 1898).

32. Codrington order, 24 October 1827, *Memoir of the Life of Admiral Sir Edward Codrington,* ed. Jane Codrington, Lady Bourchier, vol. 2 (London: Longmans, Green, 1873), pp. 90–91.
33. Alfred Comyn Lyall, *The Life of the Marquis of Dufferin and Ava,* vol. 1 (London: John Murray, 1905), p. 120. Madison, *Federalist* no. 63, in James Madison, Alexander Hamilton, and John Jay, *The Federalist Papers* (New York: Penguin Classics, 1987; orig. 1788), p. 369.
34. Robert Jervis, "Security Regimes," in Stephen D. Krasner, ed., *International Regimes* (Ithaca, N.Y.: Cornell University Press, 1983), pp. 173–94; Louise Richardson, "The Concert of Europe and Security Management in the Nineteenth Century," in Helga Haftendorn, Robert O. Keohane, and Celeste A. Wallander, eds., *Imperfect Unions: Security Institutions over Time and Space* (Oxford: Oxford University Press, 1999); Paul W. Schroeder, "The 19th Century International System," *World Politics,* vol. 39, no. 1 (1986), pp. 1–26. Nicolson, *Congress of Vienna,* p. 258.
35. Mill, "Non-Intervention," p. 257. Roger L. Williams, *Gaslight and Shadow: The World of Napoleon III* (New York: Macmillan, 1957), p. 87. Felix Frankfurter, "Haiti and Intervention," *New Republic,* 15 December 1920, pp. 71–72.
36. Henry A. Kissinger, *Diplomacy* (New York: Simon and Schuster, 1994), p. 160.
37. Kissinger, *World Restored,* p. 284. Human Rights Watch, *Sudan, Oil and Human Rights* (New York: Human Rights Watch, 2003), pp. 456–69, 533; Peter S. Goodman, "China Invests Heavily in Sudan's Oil Industry," *Washington Post,* 23 December 2004, p. A1; Erica Strecker Downs, *China's Quest for Energy Security* (Santa Monica, Calif.: RAND, 2000); Kenneth Roth, "Don't Quench Thirst for Oil with Blood," *Asian Wall Street Journal,* 21 January 2005.
38. Elisabeth Bumiller, "Bush Defends Barring Nations from Iraq Deals," *New York Times,* 12 December 2003, p. A1.
39. Finnemore argues that the nineteenth century's multilateralism was "strategic," whereas today's is "deeply political and normative" (*Purpose of Intervention,* pp. 80–81). This somewhat understates the extent of strategic multilateral thinking today, as seen in instances like NATO's invitation to Russia to send troops to Bosnia, Russia and China's UN objections to the Kosovo war, and the Security Council clash over the Iraq war. It also understates the extent of normative cooperation in the nineteenth century, as seen in instances like the joint Syrian commission and Codrington's allies at Navarino. (FO 65/941/522, Loftus to Derby, 5 November 1876; FO 65/941/523, Loftus to Derby, 6 November 1876; FO 65/941/524, Loftus to Derby, 6 November 1876.)
40. Michael Walzer, "The Politics of Rescue," in *Arguing About War* (New Haven,

Conn.: Yale University Press, 2004), p. 78. See Michael Walzer, *Just and Unjust Wars: A Moral Argument with Historical Illustrations* (New York: Basic Books, 1977), p. 106.

41. Walzer, "Politics of Rescue," p. 72.
42. Wellington to Canning, 26 January 1826, Wellington, *Despatches,* vol. 3, p. 75. FO 421/3/26, Abstract of the Proceedings in the Greek Question, part V, pp. 40–44.
43. Niall Ferguson, "The Empire Slinks Back," *New York Times Magazine,* 27 April 2003, pp. 52–54, and "True Lies," *New Republic,* 2 June 2003, pp. 16–19.
44. Krasner, *Sovereignty,* pp. 160–61. James D. Fearon, "Separatist Wars, Partition, and World Order," *Security Studies,* vol. 13, no. 4 (summer 2004), pp. 394–415. Dufferin to Bulwer, 15 December 1860, Great Britain, Foreign Office, *Correspondence Relating to the Affairs of Syria 1860–61* (London: Harrison and Sons, 1861), p. 282. See Nicholas Sambanis, "Partition as a Solution to Ethnic War," *World Politics,* vol. 52 (July 2000), pp. 437–83; James D. Fearon and David D. Laitin, "Ethnicity, Insurgency, and Civil War," *American Political Science Review,* vol. 97, no. 1 (February 2003), pp. 75–90.

THE DOMESTIC POLITICS OF HUMANITARIAN INTERVENTION

1. FO 65/941/489A, Loftus to Derby, 17 October 1876.
2. George Finlay, *History of the Greek Revolution,* vol. 2 (Edinburgh: William Blackwood and Sons, 1861), pp. 161–62.
3. Ibid., p. 168. T. J. Binyon, *Pushkin: A Biography* (New York: Alfred A. Knopf, 2003), p. 363.
4. Strangford to Castlereagh, 25 May 1822, Philip P. Argenti, ed., *The Massacres of Chios Described in Contemporary Diplomatic Reports* (London: Bodley Head, 1932), pp. 19–20. Castlereagh to Strangford, 9 July 1822, ibid., pp. 25–26. Samantha Power, *"A Problem from Hell": America and the Age of Genocide* (New York: Basic Books, 2002), pp. 365–66.
5. John R. Zaller, *The Nature and Origins of Mass Opinion* (Cambridge: Cambridge University Press, 1992). Disraeli to Bradford, 3 April 1876, Marquis of Zetland, ed., *The Letters of Disraeli to Lady Chesterfield and Lady Bradford,* vol. 2 (New York: D. Appleton, 1929), p. 34. Gladstone to Aberdeen, 14 July 1851, William Ewart Gladstone, *Two Letters to the Earl of Aberdeen on the State Prosecutions of the Neapolitan Government,* 11th ed. (London: John Murray, 1851), p. 37.
6. George Finlay, *History of the Greek Revolution,* vol. 1 (London: William Blackwood and Sons, 1861), pp. 175–76. Douglas Dakin, *The Greek Struggle for Independence, 1821–1833* (Berkeley: University of California Press, 1973), p. 76. In my account, independent reporting leads to greater press coverage, which leads to public outrage, which leads to pressure on the government to act. But there is a potential endogeneity problem here. (Gary King, Robert O. Keohane, and Sidney Verba, *Designing Social Inquiry: Scientific Inference in Qualitative Research* [Princeton, N.J.: Princeton University Press, 1994], pp. 185–96; Douglass North, "The Path of Institutional Change," in *Institutions, Institutional Change, and*

Economic Performance [Cambridge: Cambridge University Press, 1990]; Kathleen Thelen and Sven Steinmo, "Historical Institutionalism in Comparative Politics," in Kathleen Thelen, Sven Steinmo, and Frank Longstreth, eds., *Structuring Politics: Historical Institutionalism in Comparative Analysis* [Cambridge: Cambridge University Press, 1992]; Paul Pierson, "Increasing Returns, Path Dependence, and the Study of Politics," *American Political Science Review,* vol. 92, no. 2 [June 2000].) It could be that greater press coverage is a function of public outrage, not vice versa. Newspaper editors could sniff the market for news about an atrocity and attempt to feed it.

To be sure about causality, I have constructed a measure of this kind of endogeneity. I measure the number of newspaper stories that ran between the first mention of an overseas atrocity and the first story run about a major public response. All of these stories can be considered to be driven by newsworthiness, rather than an attempt to play to public opinion, since the editors have no reason yet to think that public opinion is particularly eager to read stories about this particular obscure part of the world. These lags are often substantial—the equivalent of over a month's, and sometimes several months', worth of coverage. This is enough for me to feel reasonably confident that my causal story is right. It is the news that is driving the newspaper coverage, not the public demand for stories about a far-flung land.

Moreover, this particular measure of endogeneity also allows me to compare across cases to see where the quickest public reaction came. Not surprisingly, the swiftest public response was for the death of a single Briton, not for thousands of foreigners; only about twelve *Times* stories came between the news of Byron's death and the outpourings of grief in Britain. The slowest was for Bosnia in 1875, where both the *Times* and the *Daily News* ran about forty-eight stories before there was any public response. Even in the most inflammatory example, the *Daily News'* coverage of Bulgaria in 1876, there were about twenty-four stories between the first mention of trouble and the first mention of public response. That is roughly equivalent to the paper's total coverage for the whole month of July 1876. This is a rather rough measure, and one would not want to make generalizations across periods where technology shifted; telegraphs could change the whole picture. But overall, it is a useful supplementary measurement—and one that supports my causal story.

7. Gil Merom, *How Democracies Lose Small Wars: State, Society, and the Failures of France in Algeria, Israel in Lebanon, and the United States in Vietnam* (Cambridge: Cambridge University Press, 2003), p. 113. Rosemary Foot, *Rights Beyond Borders: The Global Community and the Struggle over Human Rights in China* (Oxford: Oxford University Press, 2000), p. 113. Steven Livingston, "Suffering in Silence," in Robert I. Rotberg and Thomas G. Weiss, eds., *From Massacres to Genocide: The Media, Public Policy, and Humanitarian Crises* (Washington, D.C.: Brookings Institution, 1996), pp. 68–89. See Steven Livingston, "Clarifying the CNN Effect," research paper R-18, June 1997, Shorenstein Center, Kennedy School, Harvard University, pp. 1–18. Thomas L. Friedman, "U.S. Vision of Foreign Policy Reversed," *New York Times,* 22 September 1993, p. A13.

8. Paul Slovic, "If I Look at the Mass I Will Never Act," *Judgment and Decision Making,* vol. 2, no. 2 (April 2007), pp. 1–17. Wesley K. Clark, *Waging Modern War: Bosnia, Kosovo, and the Future of Combat* (New York: PublicAffairs, 2001), p. 420. Reuters, 18 May 2006.
9. See Clifford Bob, *The Marketing of Rebellion: Insurgents, Media, and International Activism* (Cambridge: Cambridge University Press, 2005).
10. Joe Strupp, "Newspaper Editors Shoot Back at Kristof's Darfur Complaint," *Editor and Publisher,* 26 July 2005, 3 p.m., at http:// www.editorandpublisher.com/eandp/news/article_display.jsp?vnu_content_id=1000991868. See Nicholas D. Kristof, "All Ears for Tom Cruise, All Eyes on Brad Pitt," *New York Times,* 26 July 2005, p. A19.
11. Ann Pottinger Saab, *Reluctant Icon: Gladstone, Bulgaria, and the Working Classes 1856–1878* (Cambridge, Mass.: Harvard University Press, 1991), p. 3.
12. Richard D. Altick, *The English Common Reader: A Social History of the Mass Reading Public 1800–1900* (Chicago: University of Chicago Press, 1957), p. 391, appendix C. Matthew Engel, *Tickle the Public: One Hundred Years of the Popular Press* (London: Victor Gollancz, 1996), p. 36.
13. Gladstone to Granville, 28 January 1877, Agatha Ramm, ed., *The Political Correspondence of Mr. Gladstone and Lord Granville,* vol. 1 (Oxford: Clarendon Press, 1962), p. 29. *The Political Life of the Right Hon. W. E. Gladstone: Illustrated from "Punch" with Cartoons and Sketches* (London: Bradbury, Agnew, 1898–99), p. 73. Saab, *Reluctant Icon,* p. 103.
14. Andrew W. Robertson, *The Language of Democracy: Political Rhetoric in the United States and Britain, 1790–1900* (Ithaca, N.Y.: Cornell University Press, 1995), p. 129. A rough measure of media pressure is the number of atrocity stories multiplied by the total press circulation and divided by the size of the electorate. There were roughly one hundred and two stories on Bulgarians in the *Daily News* alone in August 1876, compared to forty-one stories on the Scio massacre in the *Times* in the peak month of August 1822.
15. Chaim Kaufmann and Robert Pape, in a powerful argument on British antislavery coalitions, hypothesize that more insecure leaders will be more likely to logroll with moral activists (Chaim D. Kaufmann and Robert A. Pape, "Explaining Costly International Moral Action: Britain's Sixty-year Campaign Against the Atlantic Slave Trade," *International Organization,* vol. 53, no. 4 [fall 1999], p. 663). The logic is compelling. But, while Kaufmann and Pape's work holds well for the British antislavery movement, and arguably for France's Syrian mission in 1860, it does not do as well for British humanitarian intervention in the same time period. Tory governments in both the late 1820s and the late 1870s held roughly the same percentage of seats in the House of Commons—56 percent in the 1826 elections, and 54 percent in the 1874 elections. (Colin Rallings and Michael Thrasher, eds., *British Electoral Facts, 1832–1999,* 6th ed. [Aldershot: Ashgate, 2000], pp. 11–12, 67, 89, 91; F. W. S. Craig, *The Parliaments of England, 1715–1847,* 2nd ed. [Chichester: Political Reference Publications, 1973], p. 11; Gordon Strathearns, *Our Parliament,* 6th ed. [London: Cassel, 1964], pp. 76, 196–97; Anthony Seldon, ed., *How Tory Governments Fall: The Tory Party in Power since*

1783 [London: Fontana, 1996], pp. 80–81.) If anything, they were in a more secure position in 1827 than they were in 1876, with Canning reasonably confident of quiet Whig support. (Austin Mitchell, *The Whigs in Opposition, 1815–1830* [Oxford: Clarendon Press, 1967], pp. 182–93, 194–96.) Kaufmann and Pape argue that a "saintly logroll" is more likely when the moral activists are attractive coalition partners ("Explaining Costly International Moral Action," p. 664). But moderate Tories like Derby were eager to make common cause with moderate Liberals like Hartington—and in doing so would have frozen out the atrocitarian movement and Gladstone. (They also would have frozen out Disraeli.) Kaufmann and Pape also suggest that it was the power of nonconformists that kept the issue of slavery alive in British politics ("Explaining Costly International Moral Action," p. 660). The nonconformists played a crucial role in the atrocitarian agitation of the 1870s, but Disraeli still did not go to war. Kaufmann and Pape are not misreading British domestic politics. Quite the contrary; the antislavery and the humanitarian intervention movements were often the exact same people, like Wilberforce himself. Disraeli was under almost unbearable pressure, not just from the Liberals and the public, but also from his own cabinet, from centrist Tories like Salisbury and Carnarvon, and from Victoria. If a moderate Tory like Derby or Salisbury had been prime minister, there could well have been a humanitarian intervention. The key reason why Disraeli did not go to war was an international one: Russian overreach.

16. David Halberstam, *The Best and the Brightest* (New York: Random House, 1972), p. 646.

A NEW IMPERIALISM?

1. Disraeli to Northcote, 11 September 1876, W. F. Monypenny and George Earle Buckle, *The Life of Benjamin Disraeli, Earl of Beaconsfield,* vol. 6 (New York: Macmillan, 1920), p. 61.
2. David S. Wyman, *The Abandonment of the Jews: America and the Holocaust 1941–1945* (New York: Pantheon, 1984); Martin Gilbert, *Auschwitz and the Allies* (New York: Henry Holt, 1981); Richard Breitman, *Official Secrets: What the Nazis Planned, What the British and Americans Knew* (New York: Hill and Wang, 1998). Samantha Power, *"A Problem from Hell": America and the Age of Genocide* (New York: Basic Books, 2002).
3. Peter Baker and Susan Glasser, *Kremlin Rising: Vladimir Putin's Russia and the End of Revolution* (New York: Scribner, 2005). Thomas J. Christensen, "Posing Challenges Without Catching Up," *International Security,* vol. 25, no. 4 (spring 2001), pp. 5–40.
4. Mark Bowden, *Black Hawk Down: A Story of Modern War* (New York: Atlantic Monthly Press, 1999); Walter Clarke and Jeffrey Herbst, eds., *Learning from Somalia: The Lessons of Armed Humanitarian Intervention* (Boulder, Colo.: Westview, 1997), pp. 118–34, 151–72; George Stephanopoulos, *All Too Human: A Political Education* (New York: Little, Brown, 1999), pp. 213–16. The British division of peacekeeping troops sent to Portugal in 1827 was commanded by one Sir William Clinton. (Wellington to Bathurst, 22 January 1827, Arthur Wellesley,

Duke of Wellington, *Despatches, Correspondence, and Memoranda of Field Marshal Arthur, Duke of Wellington,* vol. 3 [London: John Murray, 1867], pp. 557–58; George IV speech, 12 December 1826, *Select Speeches of the Right Honourable George Canning,* ed. Robert Walsh [Philadelphia: Key and Biddle, 1835], p. 442.)

5. Niall Ferguson, *Empire: The Rise and Demise of the British World Order and the Lessons for Global Power* (New York: Basic Books, 2002), p. 317; "The Empire Slinks Back," *New York Times Magazine,* 27 April 2003; *Colossus: The Price of America's Empire* (New York: Penguin, 2004), pp. 7, 286–302. Michael Ignatieff, "The Burden," *New York Times Magazine,* 5 January 2003, pp. 22–54. John Lewis Gaddis, *Surprise, Security, and the American Experience* (Cambridge, Mass.: Harvard University Press, 2004), pp. 106–13. Robert D. Kaplan interview, "Islam vs. the West," *Rolling Stone,* 7 August 2003, p. 38; James Atlas, "A Classicist's Legacy," *New York Times,* Week in Review, 4 May 2003, p. 1. Max Boot, "The Case for American Empire," *Weekly Standard,* 15 October 2001, pp. 28–29. See, variously, Max Boot, *The Savage Wars of Peace: Small Wars and the Rise of American Power* (New York: Basic Books, 2002), pp. xix–xx, 348–52; Robert D. Kaplan, *Warrior Politics: Why Leadership Demands a Pagan Ethos* (New York: Random House, 2002); Sebastian Mallaby, "The Reluctant Imperialist," *Foreign Affairs,* vol. 81, no. 2 (March–April 2002); James Traub, "The Congo Case," *New York Times Magazine,* 3 July 2005, p. 34–39; Deepak Lal, *In Praise of Empires: Globalization and Order* (New York: Palgrave Macmillan, 2004).

6. Andrew J. Bacevich, *American Empire: The Realities and Consequences of U.S. Diplomacy* (Cambridge, Mass.: Harvard University Press, 2002), p. 244; Rashid Khalidi, *Resurrecting Empire: Western Footprints and America's Perilous Path in the Middle East* (Boston: Beacon Press, 2004), pp. ix–xiv, 152–75; Gore Vidal, *Imperial America: Reflections on the United States of America* (New York: Nation Books, 2004), pp. 41–54. Chalmers Johnson, *The Sorrows of Empire: Militarism, Secrecy, and the End of the Republic* (New York: Henry Holt, 2004), pp. 71–72. Coalition for a Realistic Foreign Policy, "The Perils of Empire," http://www.realisticforeignpolicy.org/static/000027.php; Patrick J. Buchanan, *A Republic, Not an Empire: Reclaiming America's Destiny* (Washington, D.C.: Regnery, 1999). David Harvey, *The New Imperialism* (Oxford: Oxford University Press, 2003), p. 6. Emmanuel Todd, *Après l'empire: Essai sur la décomposition du système américain* (Paris: Gallimard, 2002); Alain Joxe, *L'Empire du chaos: Les Républiques face à la domination américaine dans l'après-guerre froide* (Paris: La Découverte, 2002).

7. Niall Ferguson, "In Praise of Failed Diplomacy," *New York Times,* 23 March 2003, Week in Review, p. 13. Niall Ferguson, "A 19th Century Critique of a 21st Century President," *Los Angeles Times,* 7 March 2006. Ferguson, *Empire,* p. 311. Timothy Garton Ash, "Gambling on America," *Guardian,* 3 October 2002, p. 19. John Rentoul, *Tony Blair: Prime Minister* (London: Warner, 2001), p. 529.

8. Bernard Kouchner, *Le malheur des autres* (Paris: Éditions Odile Jacob, 1991). A. N. Wilson, *The Victorians* (New York: W. W. Norton, 2003), p. 272.

9. Friedrich Nietzsche, *Beyond Good and Evil,* trans. Walter Kaufmann (New York: Vintage, 1989), p. 89. Joseph S. Nye Jr., *Soft Power: The Means to Success in World Politics* (New York: PublicAffairs, 2004), p. 135. William Roger Louis, ed., *Impe-*

rialism: The Robinson and Gallagher Controversy (New York: New Viewpoints, 1976), p. 6. George Orwell, "Shooting an Elephant," in his *A Collection of Essays* (New York: Harcourt, 1981), p. 148.

10. Kenneth Roth, "War in Iraq," *Human Rights Watch World Report 2004* (New York: Human Rights Watch, 2004), pp. 13–36. Bernard Kouchner preface in Chris Kutschera, ed., *Le livre noir de Saddam Hussein* (Paris: Oh, 2005), pp. 11–20; Thomas Cushman, ed., *A Matter of Principle: Humanitarian Arguments for the War in Iraq* (Berkeley: University of California Press, 2005); Thomas Cushman, "Antitotalitarianism as a Vocation," *Dissent,* spring 2003, pp. 28–30. Bernard Kouchner, "L'humanitaire a changé le monde," *Les Temps Modernes,* no. 627 (April–May–June 2004), p. 18; Kouchner preface, *Livre noir de Saddam Hussein,* p. 17.
11. White House, Office of the Press Secretary, 31 January 2002, 11:50 a.m., Remarks by the National Security Advisor Condoleezza Rice to the Conservative Political Action Conference, Marriott Crystal Gateway, Arlington, Virginia. See Bill Keller, "The Monster in the Dock," *New York Times,* 9 February 2002, p. A19. Robert D. Kaplan, "U. S. Foreign Policy, Brought Back Home," *Washington Post,* 23 September 2001, p. B5. For critiques, see Michael Ignatieff, "Is the Human Rights Era Ending?" *New York Times,* 5 February 2002, p. A29, and James Traub, "Never Again, No Longer?" *New York Times Magazine,* 18 July 2004, pp. 17–18.
12. Peter R. Lavoy, Scott D. Sagan, and James J. Wirtz, eds., *Planning the Unthinkable: How New Powers Will Use Nuclear, Biological, and Chemical Weapons* (Ithaca, N.Y.: Cornell University Press, 2000); Graham Allison, *Nuclear Terrorism: The Ultimate Preventable Catastrophe* (New York: Times Books, 2004).
13. Gladstone's tenth Midlothian speech, 20 March 1880, William Ewart Gladstone, *Political Speeches in Scotland, March and April 1880,* vol. 2 (Edinburgh: Andrew Elliot, 1880), p. 149. William Ewart Gladstone, *Bulgarian Horrors and the Question of the East* (London: John Murray, 1876), pp. 52–53.
14. Daniel Benjamin and Steven Simon, *The Age of Sacred Terror: Radical Islam's War Against America* (New York: Random House, 2002), pp. 115–16. See Peter L. Bergen, *Holy War, Inc.: Inside the Secret World of Osama bin Laden* (New York: Free Press, 2001), p. 22. Lawrence Wright, *The Looming Tower: Al-Qaeda and the Road to 9/11* (New York: Alfred A. Knopf, 2006), p. 306. U.S. Newswire transcript, Rice press briefing, White House, 15 October 2001.
15. Alastair Iain Johnston, *Social States: China in International Institutions, 1980–2000* (Princeton, N. J.: Princeton University Press, 2007).

ACKNOWLEDGMENTS

This book would not have been possible without the help of scores of good people. Tina Bennett brilliantly and graciously shepherded the book from proposal to publication, improving it every step of the way. It's a privilege and a joy to work with her. Also at Janklow & Nesbit, Svetlana Katz did superb work. At Knopf, Ash Green is the perfect editor, with an unerring eye and unfailing judgment. His fierce intelligence improved this book in countless ways. Thanks also to Andrew Miller and Sara Sherbill for terrific help.

Some old friends went beyond the call of duty. Mike Grunwald showed what a book should be and helped with conceptualization, advice, and editing. Peter Canellos, editor supreme, shaped this book throughout. Nurith Aizenman gave indispensable advice and friendship. Peter Baker, Susan Glasser, and Rory MacFarquhar provided wonderful help and hospitality in Russia. Amy Davidson did magnificent editing. Samantha Power continued our long mutual schlep toward figuring out human rights politics.

Other great friends deserve thanks for their patience and humor: Mike Dorff, Ariela Dubler, Jon and Rebecca Gross, Jed Kolko, Jack Levy, Dan Libenson, Alison Wakoff Loren, Carolyn McKee, Becky Noonan Murray, Emily Nelson, Jennifer Pitts, Richard Primus, Alex Star, Sanjay Wagle, and Mark Wiedman.

Two heroic and brilliant friends died far too young. Elizabeth Neuffer was a brave war correspondent with a deep understanding of politics and personalities. Rosemary Quigley was a profound medical ethicist with incredible courage and warmth. I miss them always.

I've been lucky to have superb editors. At the *New York Times,* thanks again to Alex Star, and to Susannah Gardiner, Scott Malcolmson, Gerald Marzorati, and Jamie Ryerson at the magazine; Barry Gewen, Jennifer Schuessler, and Sam Tanenhaus at the book review; and James Gibney, Laura Secor, and David Shipley at the op-ed page. At *The Economist,* I'm permanently indebted to Peter David, Bill Emmott, John Micklethwait, Zanny Minton Beddoes, Ann Wroe, and Dominic Ziegler—and especially to Daniel Franklin. Thanks again to Susan Glasser, as well as Carlos Lozada and Steve Mufson, at the *Washington Post;* Peter Beinart, Chloe Schama, and Leon Wieseltier at *The New Republic;* and Gideon Rose at *Foreign Affairs.*

Michael Ignatieff (the much nicer great-grandson of Count Nikolai Ignatiev) and Michael Walzer read a full draft of this manuscript and gave trenchant suggestions. David Rohde provided important caution about the risks of intervention. Rebecca Blumenstein, Fu Jun, Mary Gallagher, Philip Pan, Ted Plafker, Sarah Schafer, and Eric Thun helped me out in China. On Byron, thanks to Sophie Gee. On Syria, thanks to Eva Bellin, Amaney Jamal, Maye Kassem, and Julie Taylor. And particular thanks to Stanley Hoffmann, who keeps on teaching me.

Anne-Marie Slaughter and Shirley Tilghman have built Princeton into a wonderful place to study international politics. I'm especially thankful to Anne-Marie for intellectual guidance and support for so many years. I owe a lifetime debt to Thomas Christensen, who knows this book better than any person should, for a particular committee assignment. Thanks, too, to Nancy Bermeo and Jeffrey Herbst.

I'm grateful to other Princeton friends and colleagues: Chris Achen, Anthony Appiah, Mark Beissinger, Charles Beitz, Karen Bennett, Chris Chyba, Chris Eisgruber, Aaron Friedberg, Martin Gilens, Anthony Grafton, Eric Gregory, Constanze Güthenke, Emilie Hafner-Burton, John Ikenberry, George Kateb, Stan Katz, Robert Keohane, Atul Kohli, Steve Kotkin, Evan Lieberman, Jason Lyall, Steve Macedo, Nolan McCarty, Tali Mendelberg, Helen Milner, Andrew Moravcsik, Sankar Muthu, Charles Myers, Alan Patten, Philip Pettit, Jonas Pontusson, Grigore Pop-Eleches, Michael Rothschild, Kim Lane Scheppele, Peter Singer, Paul Starr, Dmitri Tymoczko, Richard Ullman, Maurizio Viroli, Keith Whittington, Bob Wright, and Deborah Yashar. The late David Bradford, whose loss is painfully felt, showed his characteristic generosity. And I'd be lost without the daily rescues of Rita Alpaugh.

For countless insights, thanks to Yevgenia Albats, Mike Allen, Graham Allison, José Alvarez, Arthur Applbaum, Louise Arbour, Phil Bennett, Adam Berinsky, Sheri Berman, Allen Buchanan, Liz Camp, Steve Coll,

Keith Darden, Barbara Demick, Michael Doyle, Kent Eaton, Juliet Eilperin, Grzegorz Ekiert, Jon Elster, Noah Feldman, Page Fortna, Jason Furman, Jesse Furman, Jack Goldsmith, Richard Goldstone, Ryan Goodman, Abby Goodnough, Anna Grzymala-Busse, Oona Hathaway, Iain Johnston, Elena Kagan, Stathis Kalyvas, Dana Kirchman, Stephen Krasner, Peter Maass, Michael McFaul, Kathleen McNamara, Detlev Mehlis, Adam Michnik, Martha Minow, Vanessa Mobley, Robert Morgenthau, Annie Murphy Paul, Alissa Quart, Kal Raustiala, Max Rodenbeck, Stephen Peter Rosen, Kenneth Roth, Scott Sagan, Nicholas Sambanis, Joshua Wolf Shenk, Jack Snyder, Kathryn Stoner-Weiss, Stacy Sullivan, Sabrina Tavernise, Marc Trachtenberg, Richard Tuck, Joshua Tucker, Stephen Van Evera, Jennifer Welsh, Steven Wilkinson, and John Witt.

At Princeton, the Elias Boudinot bicentennial preceptorship supported a year of work. The university's committee on research in the social sciences and humanities funded archival work in London and Paris, and a Seeger fellowship from the program in Hellenic studies paid for my research in Athens. Miguel Centeno, director of the Princeton Institute for International and Regional Studies, generously paid some of the bills. Michelle Greene, Michael Ignatieff, Samantha Power, and Sarah Sewall made the Carr Center for Human Rights Policy at Harvard a terrific place to hunker down for a year. The staff at Firestone Library, and especially Terry Caton, tracked down musty tomes. Thanks to my student research assistants: Patty Aguilo, Alicia Barker-Aguilar, Melissa Bermudez, Alice Farmer, Clare Hunt, Abby Lackman, Andrew Rachlin, and Bianca Sepulveda.

Love and thanks to my family, especially my father, mother, and brother. I can't thank my parents enough. My love, too, to my grandmother, the indomitable Bess Bobrow. And I'll always carry the loving memory of my good and wise grandparents: Gert and Nate Basserabie, and Chona (Joe) Bobrow.

Finally, nobody helped more than Marcella Bombardieri. This book is for her, with love.

INDEX

Abdulhamit II, Sultan, 285–6, 293
Abdulmecit, Sultan, 189, 216
  occupation of Syria accepted by, 173, 176, 184, 187, 188, 202, 220–1, 231
  Syrian massacres and, 172–3, 192–3, 195–6, 200, 202, 206
Acre, 165, 169, 192
Adams, John, 95
Adams, John Quincy, 42, 88–9, 93–9, 121, 148, 327, 339, 356, 368, 376, 377, 378
  as president of United States, 121
Admiralty, British, 149
Adrianople, 302
Afghanistan, Afghans, 6, 16, 27, 37, 378
  Gladstone's sympathy for, 306–7, 346, 351
  nation-building in, 190
Africa, Africans, 23, 345, 382
  enslaved, 6, 17–19, 93
  see also Britain, anti-slavery campaign in; *specific countries*
Agence Russe, 282, 284
Ahmet Pasha, 174, 175, 178, 191
  arrest and conviction of, 193, 196, 203
Albania, Albanians, 53, 65, 239
Albany Greek Committee, 90
Albert, Prince, 240, 346
Albert Edward, Prince of Wales, 279
Albion, HMS, 138, 143
Albright, Madeleine, 7, 42
Aleksandr I, Tsar of Russia, 62–4, 115–16, 117, 129
  death of, 126, 128, 135, 367
Aleksandr II, Tsar of Russia, 242–5, 251, 252–3, 283–8, 295, 311, 358
  Bosnia revolt and, 248–9
  Moscow speech of, 288, 294
  pan-Slavism and, 236–7, 243–4, 245, 247, 285, 288, 291, 295, 304, 368
  reforms of, 243, 244, 253
  Russo-Turkish War and, 297, 299–304, 308
  son of, 282, 368
  wife of, 282, 284, 297, 368
Aleppo, 179, 180, 185, 192, 331
Alexandria, 138, 139, 141, 197, 230, 424*n*
Algeria, 14, 17, 33, 162
Algiers, 370
Ali Pasha, 173, 179, 184, 210, 215–18, 226, 343
  French withdrawal and, 225
  on occupation, 184, 187
All the King's Men (Warren), 347
Al Qaeda, 376–7, 380, 381–2
altruism, 5, 11, 378
American Committee for Armenian and Syrian Relief, 336
American Revolution, 79, 88, 90, 92, 96
Amin, Idi, 41
Amnesty International, 48, 86

Anderson, Benedict, 26
Andrássy, Count Julius, 249, 251
Anglo-Armenian Association, 320–1
Anna Karenina (Tolstoy), 253–4
Anti-Corn Law League, 76
anti-Semitism, 21, 23, 208, 281, 350
anti-slavery campaign, British, *see* Britain, anti-slavery campaign in
appeasement, 19
Arabia, 192, 335
Arabs, 31, 126, 166, 321, 381
 division of Ottoman Empire and, 334, 337
 see also pan-Arabism
Areopagitica (Milton), 34
Aristotle, 20, 92
Armenians, 20, 124, 191–2, 315–40, 348, 359, 361
 genocide of 1915 and, 43, 124, 319–34, 340, 358, 376
 massacres of, 286, 316, 317, 337
 Morgenthau and, 321–6, 330, 334, 340
 Soviet seizure of, 338–9
 U.S. mandate suggested for, 336–7
 U.S. relief committees for, 325–6, 337
Asia, HMS, 137–8, 141, 143, 144, 146, 194, 421*n*
Athens, 53, 133
atrocitarians, 6–7, 42, 236, 237, 273–80, 288–91, 294, 296, 311, 346, 372, 374, 379, 382, 479*n*
 Disraeli's views on, 274, 288, 342
 Russo-Turkish War and, 298, 300
 St. James's Hall conference of, 290–1
 town resolutions of, 276
Atta, Muhammad, 382
Attica, 149, 365
Auschwitz, 33
Australia, 345, 361
Austria-Hungary, 241, 246, 250, 285
 Armenian genocide and, 322, 323
 Bosnia and, 297, 303, 304
 Catholic Slavs in, 244
 press of, 249, 251
 Russia's relations with, 248–9, 251, 353, 365
 Russo-Turkish War and, 297, 303
 in World War I, 319, 333
Austrian Empire, 4, 6, 14, 17, 100, 174, 349, 358, 365
 Greek struggle and, 62–4, 114, 117–21, 123, 124, 126, 131–2, 134, 135, 136, 140, 345, 363
 in Holy Alliance, 51–2
 Hungarian revolution against (1848), 36, 173, 353, 355, 357
 Paris conference of 1860 and, 188–9
 Paris conference of 1861 and, 223, 224
 Syria policy of, 164, 168–9, 171, 176, 177, 188–9, 194, 199, 211, 218–19, 223, 224
Aylesbury, 278–9
Azerbaijan, 336

Baathists, 33
Babi Yar, 258
Baker, James, 12
Bakunin, Mikhail, 28
balance of power, 4, 12, 13, 15, 60, 72, 125, 342, 345
 Disraeli and, 240, 241
 Russia's place in, 247
Balerno, 308–9
Balfour, Arthur, 320, 335
Balkan crisis (1875–78), press and, 235–6, 243
Balkans, 42, 47, 48, 62, 344, 374, 381
 see also specific countries
Bangladesh, 41
Baring, Walter, 263, 281
Barker, Edmund Henry, 81, 84–5, 86, 114, 118
Bartlett, Ichabod, 97, 410*n*
Bartlett, Josiah, 410*n*
Barton, James, 324, 326
bashibazouks (Ottoman irregulars), 256, 257, 258, 260, 282, 347
Bashir, Omar al-, 11, 351
Batak massacre (1876), 256, 286, 304, 311, 341, 371, 372, 374
 MacGahan's reporting on, 235–6, 258–60, 263–4, 271, 282, 347
Bathurst, Earl, 127, 133
Baudelaire, Charles, 161
Baudrillard, Jean, 16
Bavaria, 363
Beaconsfield, Earl of, *see* Disraeli, Benjamin
Beaconsfieldism, 305–6
Beaufort d'Hautpoul, Charles-Marie-Napoléon Brandouin, Marquis de,

186, 191, 198–9, 202, 204–7, 212, 213, 223, 225–30, 229–30, 432*n*
  in departure from Syria, 230
  Druzes as viewed by, 207, 210
  Fuad criticized by, 216, 225
  occupation duration and, 188–9
  on protection of Christians, 216, 225
  troop removal feared by, 214, 226
Beijing, 345, 370
Beirut, 203–4, 210, 229
  communications with, 169, 175
  Dufferin in, 190, 202, 204, 206–7, 362
  European consuls in, 163, 164, 167–8, 175, 195, 199, 206
  European ships at, 164, 165, 178, 183, 194–5, 197, 227
  French soldiers in, 197–200, 202, 225
  Fuad in, 178, 192–3, 203, 204
  international commissioners in, 219, 222, 362
  Junblat's trial in, 206–7
  Kurshid's trial in, 209
  refugees in, 164, 167, 168, 198, 199, 206, 225
  Times special correspondent in, 186
Belgium, Belgians, 292, 325, 349, 363
  Congo colonialism of, 4, 346
  in World War I, 319, 329, 332, 333
Belgrade, 40, 248, 249, 251
Bengal, Bengalis, 17, 293
Bengal mutiny (1857), 37
Bengal Regulations, 37
Bentham, Jeremy, 48, 60, 345–6, 348, 351, 405*n*, 407
  on Byron, 102
  Greeks warned by, 118
  on imperialism, 79, 345–6
  in London Greek Committee, 76–80, 101, 102, 111, 112, 345, 348
  on Mavrokordatos, 103
Bentivoglio, Stanislas d'Aragon, Comte de, 163–9, 171, 175–82, 194–9, 201, 202, 223, 226–32, 369, 431*n*
  Dayr al-Qamar massacre and, 167, 169, 170, 182, 206
  on French troops, 198, 199, 213, 214, 216
  on French withdrawal, 227, 228–9
  on Fuad, 178, 194, 196
  Mukhtara Druzes and, 211
Beqaa Valley, 205, 226
Berlin, 23, 34, 35, 177, 249
Berlin, Treaty of (1878), 309, 361
Berlin conference (1878), 303
Besika Bay, 250, 272, 277, 278, 303, 312, 342
Bessarabia, 251, 292
bin Laden, Osama, 381
Bismarck, Otto von, 37, 160, 241, 358
Blackheath, Gladstone's speech at, 274, 277
blacks, 18, 23, 348, 350
  see also Africa, Africans; Britain, anti-slavery campaign in
Black Sea trade, 148
Blair, Tony, 12–13, 237, 378, 379
Blaquiere, Edward, 55, 57, 64, 65, 76
  in London Greek Committee, 77, 78, 80, 83–4, 85, 101, 105, 111, 112, 114, 151
  Scio massacre and, 71, 72
Bohemia, 318
Bolívar, Simón, 112
Bolshevik Revolution, 243
Bolsheviks, 337
Bolton, John, 15
Bombay, 34, 279
Bonaparte, Charles-Louis-Napoléon, *see* Napoléon III, Emperor of France
Bonaparte, Napoléon, *see* Napoléon I, Emperor of France
Boot, Max, 378
Bosnia, Bosnians, 6, 17, 28, 43, 151, 217, 262, 280, 309, 344, 356, 361, 366, 370, 375, 379, 475*n*
  Austria-Hungary and, 297, 303, 304
  autonomy sought for, 280, 293
  foreign press corps in, 370–1
  nation-building in, 190
  proposed British occupation of, 289, 311, 312
  Russo-Turkish War and, 297, 303
  U.S. policy toward, 5, 7, 23, 42, 43, 350, 365, 376, 380, 382
Bosnia-Herzegovina, uprising in (1875), 248–51, 269, 349, 359, 477*n*
Bouillon, Godfrey de, 199
Bowring, John, 86, 107, 111, 118
  Byron's correspondence with, 102, 105, 106, 109
  Canning's meeting with, 114–15
  London Greek Committee launched by, 76, 77, 80, 81, 267

Boxer Rebellion, 21–2
Bradford, Selina Lady, 257, 265
Brant, James, 175, 193
Britain, 5, 11, 24, 341–51, 353–81
  anti-slavery campaign in, 4, 17–19, 59, 70, 76–7, 93, 170, 267, 273, 274, 290, 346, 354, 357, 388*n*, 478*n*, 479*n*
  Armenian genocide and, 320–1
  Bosnia and, 249–50, 344
  Bulgarians and, 4, 6, 17, 41, 42, 236, 237, 256–65, 269–95, 299, 309, 311, 312, 326, 341, 342, 344, 345, 346, 350, 371–6, 379, 468*n*
  China's relations with, 267
  Constantinople conference and, 287–90, 292–3
  in Crimean War, 36–7, 241, 272, 312, 357
  Eastern Question and, 240–1
  elections in, 236
  French relations with, 18, 34, 137, 162, 171, 176–7, 187, 195, 201, 214–15, 231, 232, 354, 365
  Greek struggle and, 4, 17, 42, 47–9, 51–87, 90, 92, 100–12, 117–51, 157, 170, 298, 342–5, 350, 363, 364, 365, 368–74, 379; *see also* Navarino
  Holy Alliance and, 52, 59
  imperialism of, 14, 17, 18, 37–40, 70, 79, 82, 102, 113, 240, 241, 267, 275–6, 279–80, 291, 293, 294, 296, 298, 306, 343–6, 348, 379
  Jamaica insurrection and, 258, 275, 346, 379
  liberalism in, 6–7, 8, 31, 32, 48, 51, 59, 77, 78, 82, 84, 90, 170, 235, 241, 256, 266–7, 302, 343–4, 346, 398*n*, 437*n*; *see also* Liberal Party, British Midlothian campaign in, 305–10, 346, 351, 353–4, 373, 381
  neutrality of, 113–16, 119–22, 368–9
  Ottoman alliance with, *see* Ottoman Empire, British alliance with Paris conference of 1860 and, 186–9
  Paris peace conference of 1919 and, 335–7
  patriotism in, 21
  press in, 31–8, 48, 56–7, 59–60, 65–6, 68, 71, 72, 124, 160, 161, 184–6, 235–6, 249, 256–64, 277, 282, 286, 326, 369–75
  public opinion in, 19, 71, 83–4, 113–14, 118, 128, 157, 171, 184–7, 271, 273, 274, 279, 285–8, 291, 296, 342, 348
  Russian relations with, *see* Russia, Imperial, British relations with
  Russo-Turkish War and, 297–302
  Syria policy of, 42, 156, 157, 162, 164–81, 184–91, 193–228, 215–16, 232, 250, 269, 343, 344, 345, 361, 372, 373
  in World War I, 321, 333–4
  in World War II, 21, 32, 345
British Armenia Committee, 321
British Museum, 270, 271
British navy, 18, 287, 290, 344, 376, 377
  at Besika Bay, 250, 272, 277, 278, 303, 312, 342
  in Mediterranean, 114, 124–5, 137, 162, 250, 362
  at Navarino, *see* Navarino
  Syria policy and, 157, 164–5, 171, 177, 194–5, 203, 213, 221–5, 260
Brothers Karamazov, The (Dostoevsky), 282–3
Browning, Robert, 290
Bryan, William Jennings, 322, 323
Bryant, William Cullen, 90, 98
Bryce, Viscount James, 290, 320–1, 336
Buchenwald, 33
Bulgaria, Bulgarians, 5, 233–312, 327, 343, 346, 350, 366
  autonomy sought for, 280, 293
  Blair's speech in (1999), 237, 378
  British interest in, *see* Britain, Bulgarians and
  Hyde Park rally for, 269
  massacres in, *see* massacres, in Bulgaria
  proposal for Russian occupation of, 284–7, 289, 292, 311, 365
  proposed British occupation of, 289, 311, 312, 342
  revolts in, 248, 256, 359
  Russia and, *see* Russia, Imperial, Bulgarians and
  Russo-Turkish War and, 299, 300, 301, 303
Bulgarian Horrors and the Question of the East (Gladstone), 269–74, 284, 308, 347, 355
Bundy, McGeorge, 374
Burdett, Sir Francis, 77
Burke, Edmund, 22, 26–7, 160, 342–3, 344, 354, 379
Bush, George H. W., 7, 25, 40, 358
Bush, George W., 5, 12, 15, 350, 364, 377–81
Byron, George Gordon, Lord, 4, 42, 47–9, 52–61, 65, 72–5, 82, 89, 100–13, 119, 133, 137, 268, 311–12, 340, 345, 348, 351, 368, 371

death of, 47, 49, 61, 105, 108–11, 113, 127, 128, 135, 148, 151, 239, 371, 477*n*
as Disraeli's model, 239, 299–300, 311
Greeks as viewed by, 47, 52–4, 102–3, 112
in Italy, 100, 101
in London Greek Committee, 77–9, 81, 86, 87, 101–10, 118, 345, 372, 373
Mesologgi statue of, 150, 151
poetry of, 52–5, 58, 60–1, 75, 82, 98, 101, 102, 108, 109, 113, 128, 151, 239
as pragmatic statesman, 102–10
radicalism of, 47, 60–1, 75, 79, 81, 100, 101, 107, 345

Calhoun, John C., 93, 96, 97, 99, 350
Cambodia, 11–12, 22
Cambrian, HMS, 68, 142
Cambridge, 76, 81, 84–5, 373
Canada, 345
Canning, George, 42, 113–27, 129–36, 140, 148, 246, 284, 345, 346, 353, 368, 374, 376, 378
Byron's Greek mission and, 102
Castlereagh's duel with, 82
death of, 135–6
Disraeli's views on, 311
Gladstone's views on, 291, 298, 309, 311
Greek deportation rumor and, 124–7, 130–1
London Greek Committee and, 82–3, 114–15
London Treaty and, 133, 135
on Metternich, 352, 354
named prime minister, 133
in Paris, 134
Stanhope information rejected by, 107
universalism mocked by, 21
Canning, Stratford (Lord Stratford de Redcliffe), 121, 125, 126–7, 130, 138, 139
Bulgarian massacres and, 257
Gladstone pamphlet dedicated to, 270
Capital (Marx), 243
Capo d'Istria, Count John, 62–4, 81, 131, 135
Carlyle, Thomas, 275, 290
Carnarvon, Lord, 289, 296, 298, 343, 373, 479*n*
Carnegie, Andrew, 329
Carr, E. H., 14, 21, 23, 40
Carter, Jimmy, 3, 4, 22
Castlereagh, Lord (Robert Stewart), 13, 14, 18, 42, 67–76, 116, 312, 344–5, 354, 359, 363, 368, 369
Byron's hatred of, 60, 61, 73–5
Canning's duel with, 82
Disraeli compared with, 239, 311, 359, 374
Greek policy of, 48, 58–64, 67–73, 148, 149, 342
suicide of, 74–5, 76, 113, 135, 342, 467*n*
Catholics, 170, 171, 183, 221, 348, 350, 351, 357–8, 368
Armenian, 325
in British government, 82, 133
in China, 182
Irish, 276, 294, 343
Napoléon III's problems with, 162, 182
Cefalonia (Kefallonia), 102–5, 118
censorship, 7, 34, 37, 38, 129, 135, 257,371
of Napoléon III, 160, 161, 368
in Russia, 243, 284
Ceylon, 268
Chalandritsanos, Lukas, 105, 109
Châlons-sur-Marne, 155–6
Chamberlain, Neville, 19, 21, 25, 39, 262
"Charge of the Light Brigade" (Tennyson), 275
Charles X, King of France, 134–5, 149
Chechnya, Chechens, 17, 33, 364, 382
Cherniaev, Mikhail Grigorievich, 251, 252, 283, 285
Chesterfield, Lady, 265
Chicago Tribune, 23
Childe Harold's Pilgrimage (Byron), 53–4, 55, 239
Chile, 353
China, 13, 27, 40, 192, 363–4, 376, 382, 475*n*
Boxer Rebellion in, 21–2
Catholics in, 182
famines in, 29–30
French relations with, 182, 218, 345
Nixon in, 241
Opium Wars in, 267
Tiananmen Square massacre in, 25, 30, 40, 355, 358, 370
and Tibet, 17
U.S. relations with, 40, 41, 327, 345
Chomsky, Noam, 15, 40
"Choruses from Hellas" (Shelley), 58, 83, 117

Christians, Christianity, 23, 72, 82, 126, 129–30, 134, 199, 307, 359, 371, 469*n*
evangelicals, 59, 69, 77, 78, 80, 276, 350, 351
Mahan's speech to, 318–19
Orthodox, *see* Orthodox Christians
Ottoman, *see* Ottoman Christians
see also Catholics; pan-Christian solidarity; Protestants
Christopher, Warren, 262
Chronicle, 83
Church, Sir Richard, 57, 138, 311
Churchill, Charles Henry, 426*n*
Churchill, Winston, 38, 345
Church of England, 6, 80, 276, 350
civil rights movement, 23
civil society, free, 28, 29, 368
Civil War, U.S., 18, 34, 162
civil wars, 4, 5, 15, 41–2, 231
Druze-Maronite, *see* Druzes, Maronite Christians vs.
Greek, 103, 111
in Iraq, 12, 366, 380
in Spain, 33, 48
Clay, Henry, 14, 93, 96, 97
Clemenceau, Georges, 335, 337
Clinton, Bill, 3, 4, 5, 16, 262, 365, 369, 376–7, 381
Kosovo and, 42, 383*n*
Clinton, DeWitt, 90, 98
CNN effect, 7, 25–7
see also mass media
Cobden, Richard, 275
Cochrane, Lord, 57, 112, 120, 121, 131, 138, 140, 141
Codrington, Henry, 146, 194–5
Codrington, Sir Edward, 136–44, 146–50, 194, 362, 475*n*
Cold War, 32, 81, 353, 363, 376
Committee on Armenian Atrocities, 326, 328–9, 330
concentration camps, 33, 317
Concert of Europe, 13, 51, 120, 162, 231, 251, 260, 306, 353, 361, 363, 365, 474*n*
Confederacy, 450*n*
Congo, Congolese, 5, 43, 327
Belgian colonialism in, 4, 346
Congo Reform Association, 346
Congress, U.S., 94, 95, 96, 148, 262, 317, 318
Monroe's message to, 90–1
Wilson's Fourteen Points speech to, 334–5
see also House of Representatives, U.S.; Senate, U.S.
Congress of Vienna, 4, 13, 51, 59, 117, 342
Conservative Party, British, *see* Tories
Constantinople, 67–71, 96, 127, 141, 148, 162, 167, 173, 177, 181, 188, 196, 240, 250, 257, 374
British ambassadors in, 67–8, 70–1, 121, 130, 179, 195, 201, 206, 210, 217, 220, 226, 258, 270, 280, 300, 369
Dufferin in, 202
fear of Russian occupation of, 287
foreign correspondents in, 36, 185, 186, 249, 257, 258, 370, 371
French ambassador in, 179, 225
French consul in, 361–2
Greeks killed in, 56, 57, 88
Lavalette in, 170, 176
Morgenthau in, 316, 321–6, 330, 331, 340
pan-Slavism and, 244, 245, 247
plans for British occupation of, 287, 289, 311
Russian ambassador withdrawn from, 115
Russian lack of interest in, 286
Russo-Turkish War and, 285, 297, 300–4
U.S. high commissioner in, 339
Constantinople conference (1876), 287–90, 292–3, 364
Convention on the Prevention and Punishment of Genocide (1948), 362
Corfu, 125, 126, 130
Cork, 269
Corn Laws, 33, 274
Correspondence Garnier, 34
Corsair, The (Byron), 101
Courier, 59, 65–6
Cowley, Lord, 171, 188, 221–4
Crane, Charles, 326, 336
Crawford, William, 93, 97
Crimean War, 163, 241, 243, 244, 250, 272, 348, 353, 357, 468*n*
end of, 162
Ottoman Christians and, 40, 162, 245
press and, 36–7
Croatia, Croats, 26, 31
Crusades, 199
Napoléon III's invoking of, 156, 191
Cuba, 18, 32, 318, 327, 346
Spanish-American War and, 3, 17, 317, 328, 341, 347
Curzon, Lord, 320

Cyprus, 83, 178, 207
Czechoslovakia, 19, 21, 39, 353, 356

Dachau, 33
Daily News, 35, 254, 256–64, 269, 270, 277, 371, 477*n*
MacGahan's reporting in, 235–6, 258–60, 263–4, 271, 347
Daily Telegraph, 33, 35, 277, 372–3
Dallaire, Roméo, 25
Damascus, 166, 169, 171, 174, 205
Christian refugees from, 222, 225
Christian refugees in, 193, 206, 214
Christians saved in, 201
Dufferin in, 190, 208
Fuad's efforts in, 193–6, 203, 210
hangings in, 196
Jews in, 190, 207–8
massacre in, 174–5, 177–80, 183, 185, 187, 195–6, 200, 202, 207, 211, 220, 222, 341
Muslim taxpayers of, 216
occupation of, 187, 199
Danilevsky, Nikolai Yakovlevich, 244, 245, 349
Dardanelles, 250, 297, 300, 357
Darfur, 5, 11, 18, 43, 342, 361
press coverage of, 371, 372
Dartmouth, HMS, 139, 140, 142, 143–4
Darwin, Charles, 274, 275, 276, 290, 294
Davis, David Brion, 18–19
Dawn, 244, 245
Dayr al-Qamar, 164, 178, 180, 193, 210
French troops in, 204–5
massacre at, 167, 169, 170, 180, 182, 185, 193, 198, 205, 206, 207, 209, 229
Ottoman troops in, 204
refugees from, 198, 229
Decembrists, 128–9, 132
De Jure Belli et Pacis (Grotius), 4
Delacroix, Eugène, 72–3, 127–8
Delane, John, 36
democracy, 11, 14, 36, 43, 122, 312, 320, 345, 355, 360
in India, 28–9
U.S. role in spread of, 22, 319, 380
Democracy in America (Tocqueville), 14
Democratic National Convention (1916), 336
Democratic Party, U.S., 12, 317, 338, 350
Demosthenes, 91, 92
Deng Xiaoping, 25
Denmark, 18
Derby, Earl of, 255, 260–3, 276–81, 291, 292, 373, 376, 479*n*
in Balkan cease-fire negotiations, 285
Constantinople conference and, 287
Russo-Turkish War and, 300, 303
de Rigny, H., 138, 140–4
Derrida, Jacques, 16
Devils, The (Dostoevsky), 245
Diary of a Writer (Dostoevsky), 253
Dickens, Charles, 35
Diderot, Denis, 344
Dili massacre, 370
Disraeli, Benjamin, 12, 35, 42, 239–41, 252, 254–63, 284–97, 303, 342, 344–8, 376, 479*n*
Bosnian revolt and, 250
Bulgaria policy and, 41, 236, 237, 256–63, 265, 269–74, 277–82, 289–90, 293, 305, 310, 327, 342, 373, 374
Byron as model for, 239, 299–300, 311
conservatism of, 239–40, 359
downfall of, 236, 256
Gladstone vs., 266, 269–74, 277–81, 285, 288, 302, 305–6, 308–12, 351
Guildhall banquet speech of, 288
made Earl of Beaconsfield, 263, 278
press and, 256–7, 271, 277, 288, 368, 369
Russian war plans and, 286–7
Russo-Turkish War and, 297–300, 302–3, 308–9, 374
Serbia and, 252, 254, 255
Victoria's correspondence with, 255, 257, 260–1, 262, 274, 279, 291, 311
Victoria's relationship with, 240, 250, 260–1, 279, 288–9, 291, 373
Dodge, Cleveland, 325–6, 333
Dog River, 164, 204, 205
Dominican Republic, 22, 319
Donawerth (French ship), 170, 178
Don Juan (Byron), 60–1, 101
Dostoevsky, Feodor Mikhailovich, 4, 243, 253
Bosnia revolt and, 249
pan-Slavism of, 244–7, 294–5
Russo-Turkish War and, 297, 302, 303
sensationalism of, 282–3
Doyle, Michael, 344
Drèze, Jean, 28–9, 393*n*

Druzes, 6, 183, 193, 195, 200, 203–19, 224, 229, 348, 365
British tilt toward, 201, 210, 217
French resented by, 163, 164
French troops and, 181, 198, 199, 200, 204, 229
Fuad's efforts and, 203–14, 216, 217, 226
Maronite Christians vs., 155, 156, 163–71, 173, 177–9, 184–6, 195, 205, 209, 211, 214–19, 222, 223, 224, 227–8, 426*n*
Maronite truce with, 169, 177–80, 192
in Mukhtara, 209–11
Dudley, John William Ward, Earl of, 133, 137, 141
Dufferin, Lady, 228
Dufferin, Lord, 190, 195, 201–12, 215–20, 222, 228, 347, 349, 362
Abdulmecit's audience with, 202
in departure from Syria, 227–8
on Fuad, 191, 208
Fuad's meetings with, 203, 204
Junblat's trial and sentencing and, 206–7, 226
on Maronite killings of Druzes, 211

Eastern Question
British views of, 240–1, 250, 294
Gladstone's view of, 269–74, 305
Russian view of, 242–7
East Timor, 361, 370
Economist, 277
Edhem Pasha, 292–3
Edinburgh, 76, 79, 85, 86
Gladstone in, 305–6, 308, 310
Egypt, 123–35, 138–44, 146, 149, 186, 287, 342, 364
French interest in, 135, 162
Gladstone's takeover of, 267
Greek deportation rumor and, 124–7, 130–1, 149, 342, 369, 424*n*
Eisenhower, Dwight, 231, 357
Elgin, Lord, 55
Eliot, George, 294
Elliot, Sir Henry, 258, 261, 262, 269, 276, 278, 281
"Emancipate Your Colonies!" (Bentham), 79
Emerson, James, 124
Emerson, Ralph Waldo, 31–3, 89
Engels, Friedrich, 244–5
England, the English, 11, 14, 24, 27, 28, 276, 279, 355
see also Britain
English Bards and Scotch Reviewers (Byron), 52
Enlightenment, 22
Entebbe, 22
Enver, Ismail, 323
Erskine, Lord Thomas, 65, 72, 77, 83
Ethics (Aristotle), 92
Ethiopia, famine in, 25
"ethnic cleansing," 12, 13
Everett, Edward, 89–90, 92–6
Eyre, Edward John, 379

Falcieri, Tita, 239
famine, 25, 28–30, 179, 393*n*
in China, 29–30
in India, 28–9, 38, 293, 346
Fanon, Frantz, 15
Fathers and Sons (Turgenev), 245–6
fat journals, 243
Federalist Papers, The, 14, 362–3
Ferguson, Niall, 35, 377, 378
Finlay, George, 311
Finnemore, Martha, 20
Firefly, HMS, 164–5
Fiscal Stamp, 256
Fish, Stanley, 15
Foreign Ministry, French, 169, 222
Foreign Office, British, 34, 58, 131, 140, 141, 185, 257, 261–2, 276, 278, 320, 374, 376
Fourteen Points, 334–5
France, 5, 76, 119, 137, 148, 347–50, 356–8, 360–6, 378
anti-slavery campaign and, 18
British relations with, 18, 34, 137, 162, 171, 176–7, 187, 195, 201, 214–15, 231, 232, 354, 365
Bulgarian massacres and, 263–5, 344
China's relations with, 182, 218, 345
in division of Ottoman Empire, 334, 335
Eastern Question and, 241
elections in, 156, 161, 182, 425*n*
Greek struggle and, 49, 57, 67, 68, 72–3, 76, 90, 133, 134–5, 138–44, 147, 149, 344, 363, 365
imperialism of, 14, 17, 18, 39–40, 79, 156–7, 162, 231, 344, 345, 354

liberalism in, 6–7, 90, 156, 159, 160–1, 183, 356–7, 398*n*
multilateralism and, 362, 363
national identity in, 26, 27
Navarino and, 49, 139–44, 147, 362
Paris conference of 1860 and, 186–9
Paris conference of 1861 and, 220–5
Paris peace conference of 1919 and, 335–7
press in, 26–7, 30, 135, 156, 159–62, 171, 182–6, 225, 351, 368
public opinion in, 156, 161, 162, 171, 182–4, 218, 358, 368, 370, 374
Syria policy of, 4, 42, 155–7, 162–232, 344, 437*n*; *see also* Syria, occupation of
Terror in, 51, 82, 354
U.S. relations with, 94, 96
in Vietnam, 182, 198, 231, 366
in World War I, 319, 320, 321
Franco-Prussian War, 37, 241, 468*n*
Frankfurter, Felix, 363
Franklin, Benjamin, 76
Franz Ferdinand, Archduke of Austria-Hungary, 304
freedom, 6–8, 52
see also press, free
Freeman, Edward Augustus, 280, 290–1, 300
free trade, 76, 77, 267
see also Corn Law
French navy, 168, 170, 171, 176
at Beirut, 178, 183, 194, 227
French Revolution, 8, 21, 26 51, 52, 65, 132, 160, 342, 353
Freud, Sigmund, 315
Friends of Armenia, 316, 321
Fuad Pasha, Muhammad, 173, 178, 179, 191–7, 216–17, 227, 231, 321
arrests, trials, and executions by, 193–4, 196–7, 200–1, 203, 204, 206–10, 226, 437*n*
Beaufort's charges against, 216, 225
Beaufort's farewell dinner with, 229–30
beliefs of, 191–2
British views on, 196–7, 206, 348, 361
Druzes and, 203–14, 216, 217, 226
European commission and, 203
French troops as viewed by, 194, 199, 200
Mukhtara Druze and, 209–11
proclamations issued by, 192–3, 200
public opinion and, 187, 432*n*
Gaddis, John Lewis, 377
Gallagher, Jack, 379
Gallatin, Albert, 89, 93, 94–5
Gallipoli, 334
Garibaldi, Giuseppe, 268, 269, 327, 349, 358
Garrison, William Lloyd, Jr., 316
Garton Ash, Timothy, 378
Gdansk, 151
Geertz, Clifford, 27
Gelb, Leslie, 13
Geneva, 239
Geneva Conventions, 272
Genghis Khan, 329
Genoa, 83, 101
Genoa, HMS, 138, 143–8
genocide, 12, 13, 23, 341–2, 362, 375, 379, 381
Armenian (1915), 43, 124, 319–34, 340, 358, 376
Greek struggle and, 78–9
Rwandan (1994), 31, 33, 350, 369, 375, 377
George IV, King of England, 48, 51, 70, 73–4, 126, 133, 149
Germany, Germans, 28, 250, 364, 380
Armenian genocide and, 322, 323
Nazi, 19, 21, 30, 39, 340, 345
Ottoman alliance with, 304, 322, 332, 335
unification of, 241, 245, 246, 267
in World War I, 319, 323, 333, 335
Gibraltar, 287
Gladstone, Sir John, 80
Gladstone, William Ewart, 6, 29, 42, 80, 266–81, 284–8, 290–5, 304–16, 340, 341, 345–51, 353, 360, 361, 366, 376, 377, 378, 479*n*
Afghan war denounced by, 306–7
as anti-imperialist, 275–6, 346
Armenian genocide and, 316
Blackheath speech of, 274, 277
Bulgarian massacres and, 236, 237, 269–74, 277–81, 305, 306, 309, 316, 345, 346, 350
as chancellor of the exchequer, 268
diary of, 267, 269–70
Disraeli vs., 266, 269–74, 277–81, 285, 288, 302, 305–6, 308–12, 351
Lloyd George compared with, 320
in Midlothian campaign, 305–10, 346, 351, 353–4, 373, 381
Naples and, 267–9, 349, 370
pamphlets of, 269–74, 284, 286, 294, 308, 347, 355

Gladstone, William Ewart (*continued*)
  press and, 37, 286, 372
  racism of, 271, 277–8, 347
  Russia as viewed by, 272, 284, 311, 349, 380
  Russo-Turkish War and, 297–302, 308
  as Tory, 266, 267–8
  Victoria's views on, 240, 291
  Wilson compared with, 315–16, 339
  as Wilson's hero, 315
Glastonbury, 293–4
globalization, 16
Glover, Stephen, 13
Goebbels, Josef, 30
Goethe, Johann Wolfgang von, 101
Gorchakov, Aleksandr Mikhailovich, 172, 177, 219, 247, 248, 251, 252, 283–7, 358, 361, 364
  Russo-Turkish War and, 297, 301, 302
Gordon, Thomas, 64–6, 86–7, 104, 107, 112, 134, 311, 371
Gore, Al, 377
Göring, Hermann, 11
Graham, Cyril, 195
Granville, Lord, 266, 269, 270, 277, 279, 287, 288, 291, 294, 305, 310
  Russo-Turkish War and, 298, 302
Greece, Greeks, 5, 6, 17, 21, 23, 41–2, 45–151, 186, 191, 240, 268, 310–11, 316, 359, 362–75, 379
  British and, *see* Britain, Greek struggle and
  British mediation efforts and, 123, 125, 130–5
  British-Russian protocol and, 130, 132–5
  constitution for, 80, 92
  division of Ottoman Empire and, 334, 337
  Muslims in, 56–7, 64–6, 68–70, 86, 106, 114, 134, 371, 348, 470*n*
  press coverage of, *see* press, Greek struggle and
  deportation rumor about, 124–7, 130–1, 149, 342, 369, 424*n*
  Russia and, *see* Russia, Imperial, Greek struggle and
  Syria compared with, 200, 231
  Tripolitza massacre and, 64–6, 86, 134, 371
  U.S. and, 76, 88–99, 112–13, 121, 356
  see also London Greek Committee; massacres, in Greece; Scio massacre
Greece on the Ruins of Missolonghi (Delacroix), 128
Greek navy, 86, 112–13
Greek Orthodox, 54, 56, 57, 63, 78, 80, 229, 244
Greene, Graham, 360
Greenhalge, Frederic, 316
Grenada, 381
Grewe, Wilhelm, 14–15
Grey, Sir Edward, 321, 357
Grigorios, Patriarch, 49, 56, 57, 62, 88, 371
Grotius, Hugo, 4, 356
Guam, 317
Guatemala, 112
Guevara, Ernesto Che, 361
Guiccioli, Countess Teresa, 100–1

Haass, Richard, 13
Hadfield, George, 80, 85
Haiti, 77, 319, 358
Halleck, Fitz-Green, 98
Hamilton, Alexander, 14
Hamilton, G. W., 142
Harcourt, Sir William, 263
Harrison, William Henry, 95
Hartington, Marquess of, 263, 266, 270, 277, 280, 291, 294, 298, 299, 305, 310, 346, 479*n*
Hasbayya, 193, 206, 225
  massacre at, 165, 169, 171, 185, 193, 195, 201, 207, 211
Hastings, Frank Abney, 57, 311
Havana, 18
Havel, Václav, 380
Hawarden, 278, 306
Hearst, William Randolph, 317
Hebrew Melodies (Byron), 53
Heiden, Count Lodewijk, 141
Hellenica Chronica, 107, 110
Henry V, 65
Henry V (Shakespeare), 21
Herzen, Aleksandr Ivanovich, 20, 110, 245
Hibernia, HMS, 194–5
Hitler, Adolf, 12, 19, 39, 40, 345
Hoar, George, 318
Hobhouse, John Cam, 75, 77, 110, 112
  Byron's correspondence with, 100, 105
  on Byron's Greek mission, 102, 103
  Byron's travels with, 52, 53, 77

Don Juan dedication and, 60–1
Metternich's scorn for, 117–18
Hobson, J. A., 15
Holland, 96, 194, 349
Holocaust, 23, 33, 340, 350, 376
Holy Alliance, 62–4, 115, 117–22
Canning's views on, 82, 352, 354
Castlereagh's relations with, 59
intervention as viewed by, 51–2, 352
U.S. relations with, 89, 93, 94, 97, 353
Homer, 55, 67, 91, 92
Hong Kong, 267
Hoover, Herbert, 336
Hours of Idleness (Byron), 52
House, Edward M., 326, 335, 336
House of Commons, British, 69–70, 126, 266, 345, 356, 478*n*
Afghan war and, 306–7
Disraeli and, 257–8, 262, 263, 278
Gladstone and, 269, 294, 299, 310
Russo-Turkish War and, 298, 299
House of Lords, British, 70, 263, 266, 278, 294
House of Representatives, U.S., 94, 96
Houston, Sam, 97
Howe, Julia Ward, 98, 316
Howe, Samuel Gridley, 98, 316
Hughes, Thomas S., 72, 78, 80, 81, 275, 347
Hugo, Victor, 22, 26, 28, 30, 42, 110, 143, 160, 161, 345
on Bulgarian massacres, 263–5
exile of, 155, 161
poetry of, 73, 127, 150
Hu Jintao, 363–4
humanitarian intervention
danger of escalation of, 356–9
despotic states and, 367–8
diplomacy of, 9, 39–43; *see also specific conferences and treaties*
free states and, 368–9, 371–2
imagined humanity and, 27–8, 369–72
imperialism vs., 5–6, 8, 11–24, 39–40, 42, 343–7, 378–9
international politics of, 352–66, 373–5
limiting military missions in, 365–6
pan-Christian solidarity vs., 6, 8–9, 347–51
patriotism vs., 21–2
spheres of interest in, 360–2
tradition of, 3–6, 342–3
see also specific topics
humanity
crimes against, 24
imagined, 27–8, 369–72
human rights, 3–8, 22–4, 351, 379–80, 474*n*
globalization and, 16
power and, 17
human rights groups, 7, 48
Human Rights Watch, 48, 85–6, 379
Hume, David, 20
Hume, Joseph, 77
Hungary, Hungarians, 14, 43, 284, 348, 349, 353, 372
revolution of 1848 in, 36, 173, 353, 355, 357, 359
revolution of 1956 in, 353, 357
Hussars, 155
Hussein, Saddam, 379–80
Hutu, 31
Hydra, 139, 140

Ibrahim Pasha, 123–35, 138, 140–2, 147, 149, 162, 186, 364, 365, 424*n*
Greek deportation rumor and, 124–7, 130–1
Ignatieff, Michael, 25, 377
Ignatiev, Countess, 295
Ignatiev, Count Nikolai Pavlovich, 247–52, 282–6, 292, 293, 295, 296, 368
in Britain, 295–6
Russo-Turkish War and, 297, 301, 303
imperialism, 5–8, 376–82
humanitarian intervention vs., 5–6, 8, 11–24, 39–40, 42, 343–7, 378–9
see also specific countries
India, 27, 41, 286, 346
British colonialism in, 14, 17, 22, 37–8, 79, 82, 102, 240, 267, 275–6, 279–80, 291, 296, 306, 343, 345, 346, 348
democracy in, 28–9
famines in, 28–9, 38, 293, 346
press in, 29, 34, 37–8
Inquirer, 84
international commission for Syria, 186, 190–1, 202–12, 215, 224, 475*n*
government plans for Syrian, 215, 217, 222, 227
tribunal overseen by, 206–7
Ionian Islands, 60, 119–20, 267, 346
Ipsilantis, Alexandros, 56, 58, 62
Iran, 18, 22

Iraq, 42
civil war in, 12, 366, 380
nation-building in, 190
press in, 33
Iraq war, 22, 355, 363, 364, 378, 379–80, 475*n*
Ireland, 14, 51, 59, 60, 77, 100, 250, 268, 327, 346
Catholics in, 276, 294, 343
Home Rule for, 267, 310
Ismail Pasha (Kmety), 173
Israel, 22, 53
Italy, 100–1, 119, 160, 162, 182, 357
Paris peace conference and, 335, 336
Times correspondent in, 36
unification of, 246, 267, 269
Ivanov, Igor, 358

Jackson, Andrew, 96
Jackson, Robert, 33
Jamaica insurrection, 258, 275, 346, 379
James, Henry, 266
Japan, 318, 335, 381
Jebel ash-Shaykh (Mount Hermon), 205
Jefferson, Thomas, 31, 89, 91–2, 93, 377
Jehenne, Rear Admiral, 170, 178, 197
Jerusalem, 169, 179, 185, 225
Jesuits, 199
Jewish Emergency Relief Commission, 326
Jews, 22, 271, 281, 327, 329, 351, 382
American, 321, 322, 324
British, 21, 185, 276
Damascene, 190, 207–8
in Holocaust, 23, 340, 350, 376, 448*n*
in Ottoman Palestine, 322
Jezzin, 165, 206
jingoism, jingoes, 298, 302
Johnson, Chalmers, 378
Johnson, Lyndon B., 22, 37, 356
journalistic professionalism, 7, 35–7
Junblat, Said Bey (Djumblat), 164, 165, 167–9, 186, 200, 203–4
trial and sentencing of, 206–7, 209, 226
Justice Ministry, French, 161

Kagan, Robert, 14
Kalamata, Bay of, 149
Kalamata appeal, 88, 89
Kalamata plain, 142
Kant, Immanuel, 17, 22, 28, 344
Kaplan, Robert, 377, 380
Karadžić, Radovan, 351
Katkov, Mikhail Nikiforovich, 245–6, 253
Kaufmann, Chaim, 17–18
Kemal, Mustafa (Atatürk) 338–9
Kennan, George, 13, 17, 25
Kennedy, John F., 23
Kerry, John, 12, 95–6
Khmer Rouge, 11–12
Kiev, 247
Kim Jong-il, 30
Kissinger, Henry, 11–15, 25, 40, 41, 48, 343, 352, 353, 359
on Castlereagh, 359, 363
on Greek struggle, 342, 467*n*
Koraes, Adamantios, 89, 92
Kosovo, Kosovars, 3, 7, 16, 17, 23, 39, 42, 43, 81, 151, 237, 342, 350, 355, 366, 371, 378, 379, 380, 475*n*
Kissinger and, 12–13, 25
U.S. policy toward, 7, 39, 40, 42, 43, 350, 352, 353, 356, 376, 383*n*
Kosovo Liberation Army, 360
Kosovo Polje, battle of (1389) , 55
Kossuth, Louis, 327, 353, 357
Kouchner, Bernard, 380
Kozyrev, Andrei, 356
Krajina, 367
Krasner, Stephen, 352
Krauthammer, Charles, 13
Kristol, William, 377
Kurds, 33, 334, 379
Kurshid Pasha, Muhammad, 163–8, 175, 178, 191–3, 200, 209, 211
Kutchuk-Kainardji, Treaty of (1774), 56, 62, 246, 354, 361
Kydonies (Aivali), 57, 370

Lafayette, Marquis de, 93, 113
Lagos, explosion in, 23
Lake, Anthony, 370
Lansing, Robert, 323–6, 330, 331, 332, 336
Latakia, 169, 192
Latin America, 93–4, 319, 353, 363
Lavalette, Marquis de, 170, 176
Lawrence, T. E., 321
Layard, Sir Henry Austen, 280
League in Aid of the Christians in Turkey, 250, 260
League of Nations, 8, 337–8, 359

Lebanon, 179, 229–31, 321, 349
creation of (1920), 229
foreign residents in, 225
French army in, 217
French interests in, 172
Fuad in, 208–11
massacres in, 163–9, 172, 187, 219, 220
U.S. troops in, 231
see also Beirut; Mount Lebanon
Lenin, Vladimir Ilyich, 15, 243, 338–9
Lenin Shipyards, 151
Lenormant, François, 183
Lepanto (Nafpaktos), 108
Lessons in Massacre (Gladstone), 294
Liberal Party, British, 257, 260, 263, 274, 275, 291, 294, 373, 479*n*
Gladstone and, 266, 269, 277, 305–10
press and, 256
Russo-Turkish War and, 298, 299
Victoria's views on, 240
liberals, liberal states, 4, 6–8, 12, 13, 15, 16, 22–4, 41, 353
distinctive institutions of, 28
media and, 28–9, 31, 33–8, 369
philhellenes and, 48, 60, 76, 77, 78, 80, 84, 90
Liberia, Liberians, 43, 350
Liddon, Henry Parry, 276, 281, 290, 341
Lincoln, Abraham, 90, 354–5
Litani Valley, 225
Liverpool, 77, 84, 260, 288
Liverpool, Lord, 59, 69, 70, 72, 77, 84, 124, 133, 260, 288, 373
Lloyd George, David, 320, 335–7
Locke, John, 55, 81
Lodge, Henry Cabot, 338
London, 77, 78, 130, 141, 187, 277, 288
anti-Russian "jingo" song in, 298
Byron's funeral in, 110
Canning's funeral in, 136
communications with, 34, 169, 236, 249
Gladstone's house in, 302
Greek deputies in, 120–1
Greek provisional government's loan search in, 101
Guildhall banquet in, 288
newspapers in, 32, 34–8
Persigny in, 177
Russian ambassador in, 123–4, 247, 251–2, 358
St. James's Hall conference in, 290–1, 351
London, Treaty of (1827), 133–6, 138, 139, 149, 150, 363
London conference (1827), 133
Londonderry, Lady, 295
London Gazette, 34
London Greek Committee, 7, 76–87, 100–12, 120, 250, 267, 312, 321, 341
Byron in, 77–9, 81, 86, 87, 101–10, 118, 345, 372, 373
Byron's death and, 111, 151
Canning's relations with, 82–3, 114–15
evangelicals in, 77, 78, 276
fund-raising of, 77–8, 86, 98, 137
Gordon's resignation and, 134
members of, 76–7, 170
military subcommittee of, 86
Navarino and, 148, 149–50
Tories and, 77, 79–82, 86
Lonehead, 309
Louis XIV, King of France, 162
Louis XVIII, King of France, 18
Lukashenko, Aleksandr, 11
Lusitania, 319, 323
Lytton, Edward Bulwer-, 279–80, 343, 346

MacGahan, Januarius Aloysius, 372
on Bulgarian massacres, 235–6, 258–60, 263–4, 271, 282, 347
death of, 303–4
Machiavelli, Niccolò, 16
Macri, Theresa, 53
Madagascar, 18
Madison, James, 42, 92, 95, 113, 340, 362–3
Magyars, 244
see also, Hungary, Hungarians
Mahan, Alfred Thayer, 318–19
Mahmut II, Sultan, 369
"Maid of Athens, Ere We Part" (Byron), 53
Maine, USS, 317
Malays, 27
Malta, 287
Manchester, 61, 77, 80, 84, 85, 373
reformers shot in (1819), 61
Manchester, Bishop of, 260
Manchester Greek Committee, 85
Manchester Guardian, 35, 260
Mandela, Nelson, 23, 33
Mandelbaum, Michael, 13, 15
Mao Zedong, 29–30

Maronite Christians, 162, 177–80, 182, 183, 192, 209–12, 213, 218, 221, 229, 230, 231, 348, 349
  Druzes vs., *see* Druzes, Maronite Christians vs.
  civil war started by, 163–4, 171, 180, 190, 192, 209, 211, 228, 426*n*
  Fuad's punishment of, 211
  pro-French, 156, 199, 201
  semi-independence of (1845), 217, 221, 222
Marseille, 35, 230
Marx, Karl, 15, 243, 244, 246–7, 274, 301, 358
Marxism, 15
massacres, in Armenia, 43, 124, 286, 316–34, 337, 340, 358, 376
massacres, in Bulgaria, 254, 256–65, 269–96, 305, 306, 327, 344, 349, 350, 359, 448*n*, 468*n*
  atrocitarians and, 236, 237, 273–81
  at Batak, 235–6, 256, 258–60, 263–4, 282, 304, 311, 341, 347, 371, 372, 374
  Gladstone's views on, 269–74, 309, 316
  press and, 235–6, 256–64, 271–2, 277, 310–11, 326, 477*n*
massacres, in Greece, 49, 56–7, 63, 67–73, 76, 78–9, 83, 86, 90, 97, 114, 123–8, 130–1, 135, 137, 141–2, 149, 342, 369, 424*n*
  of Turks, 56–7, 64–6, 68–70, 86, 106, 114, 134, 371
massacres, in Syria, 155, 156, 163–87, 190–3, 215–26, 230, 359
  in Damascus, *see* Damascus, massacre in
  at Dayr al-Qamar, 167, 169, 170, 182, 185, 193, 198, 205, 206, 207, 209, 229
  European public opinion and, 156, 171, 176, 182–7
  at Hasbayya, 165, 169, 171, 185, 193, 195, 201, 207, 211
  in Mount Lebanon, 163–9, 172, 187, 219, 220
  at Rashayya, 165, 169, 195, 207
mass media, 8, 9, 25–38, 312
  CNN effect and, 25–7
  domestic politics and, 28–30
  imagined humanity and, 27–8
  see also newspapers; press; *specific publications*
Mavrokordatos, Alexandros, 103–6, 108, 109, 111, 123, 136
Mayaguez, USS, 22
McKinley, William, 317
Mediterranean, 49, 52, 83, 86, 89, 128
  British in, 114, 124–5, 137, 162, 250, 362
  Disraeli's tour of, 239
  French in, 162, 165
  Russians in, 115, 135
  Times correspondent in, 35–6
  U.S. fleet in, 92, 93
Mehmet Ali, 123
Mesologgi, 47, 53, 56, 102–11, 150, 151, 239, 368, 374
  Egyptian forces at, 123, 127
  fall of, 127–8
Mesopotamia, 331, 335, 336
Metternich, Prince Klemens von, 12, 13, 14, 30, 36, 74, 82, 129, 345, 352, 353, 354, 359, 363
  on Canning, 131–2, 136
  at Congress of Vienna, 51, 59
  Greek struggle and, 62, 64, 73, 114, 117–21, 123, 124, 126, 134, 135, 140, 148, 342, 367, 369
  ousting of, 177
Metternich, Princess Eleanor von, 118–19
Mexico, 82, 112, 319
Meyer, Jean-Jacques, 107
Miami Herald, 372
Middle East, 379, 381
  British interests in, 267
  Disraeli's tour of, 240
  French interests in, 162, 231, 344, 374
  see also specific countries
Midlothian campaign, 305–10, 346, 351, 353–4, 373, 381
Mill, John Stuart, 17, 18, 24, 39, 41–2, 54, 344, 349, 353, 355
Milošević, Slobodan, 16, 31, 40, 81, 352, 355, 360, 382
Miłosz, Czesław, 23
Milton, John, 34, 55
mission creep, 214
  in Syria, 213–32
Mogadishu, 25, 370, 377
Moldavia, 56, 62, 148
Monroe, James, 88–96, 99, 356
Monroe Doctrine, 91, 92, 95, 316–17, 353
Montefiore, Sir Moses, 185, 208
Montenegro, 251, 252, 253, 275
"Montenegro" (Tennyson), 275
Moore, Noel, 164, 206

morality, 5, 12–20, 22–4, 64
guilt and, 20
media and, 33–4, 38
see also human rights
Morea (the Peloponnese), 49, 56, 86, 119, 130, 131, 139, 371, 374
colonization plan for, 126, 127
Egyptian forces in, 123, 125, 149, 365
Morgenthau, Hans, 15
Morgenthau, Henry, Jr., 340
Morgenthau, Henry, Sr., 321–6, 330, 334, 340
Morgenthau, Robert, 321
Morning Chronicle, 60, 65–6
Morning Post, 38
Moscow, 243, 245, 247, 251, 252, 283, 297
Aleksandr II's speech in, 288, 294
press in, 285
Moscow Slavic Benevolent Committee, 247, 248, 251, 253, 282
Mount Lebanon, 163, 173, 199, 205, 208, 211, 213, 217, 222–3
Mrs. Dalloway (Woolf), 20
Mugabe, Robert, 33
Mujawamariya, Monique, 369
Mukhtara, 209–11
multilateralism, 5, 8, 41, 179, 215, 223, 272, 280, 362–5, 397*n*, 474*n*, 475*n*
Munich conference (1938), 39, 274
Murat V, Sultan, 278, 281
Muslims, Islam, 18–19, 33, 53, 56, 72, 126, 134, 143, 197–201, 229, 269, 271, 279, 282, 293, 324, 345, 359, 371, 381, 382
in Beirut, 168, 197, 198, 200, 227
Bentham's views on, 348, 470*n*
Druze alliance with, 163
European science and, 192
Fuad's relations with, 230
in Greece, 56–7, 64–6, 68–70, 86, 106, 114, 134, 348, 371, 420*n*
in India, 343
pan-Christian solidarity and, 347–51
in Syria, 162–5, 168, 174, 175, 177, 181, 187, 193, 206, 216
Mussolini, Benito, 5
Musurus, Constantine, 187

Naiad, HMS, 127
Napier, Charles James, 55, 102, 104
Naples, 6, 17, 36, 43, 267–9, 344, 349, 363, 370
Gladstone in, 267–8, 271
revolt in, 59, 353
Napoléon I, Emperor of France, 18, 51, 59, 60, 62, 113, 117
death of, 34
Egypt conquered by, 162
press and, 30, 34, 160
Napoléon III, Emperor of France, 159–62, 170, 172, 178, 181–4, 198–9, 204, 215, 231–2, 344, 345, 357, 361, 428*n*
Abdulmecit's telegram to, 173, 176
censorship of, 160, 161, 368
Crusades invoked by, 156, 191
"Marseillaise" banned by, 197
nation-building and, 213
public opinion and, 156, 162, 182–4
Syria expedition and, 155–7, 181, 184, 188–9, 368
troop withdrawal and, 217, 218, 221, 224
Napoleonic Wars, 13, 18, 32, 33, 40, 51, 59, 60, 329, 354
Nation, 326, 349
National Guard, 23
nationalism, 20–3, 30–1, 230–1, 394*n*
family ties compared with, 20–1
media and, 25–32, 367–72, 394*n*
revolution and, 240, 241
Russian, 243, 245
nation-building, 22, 190, 213, 242, 365
NATO, 13, 16, 17, 40, 151, 237, 355, 356, 358, 363, 365, 366, 379, 381, 382, 475*n*
Naval War College, 328
Navarino, 64, 102, 139–50, 170, 194, 270, 291, 311, 347, 368, 471*n*, 475*n*
Bulgarian conflict compared with, 284, 290
multilateralism and, 362, 363, 364
Ottoman defeat at, 49, 112, 143–8, 342
Nazareth, 225
Nelson, Horatio, 137, 139, 143
newspapers, 7, 28, 30–8, 182–6
Burke's views on, 26–7
in France, 26–7, 156, 159–61, 171, 182–6, 225, 368
"penny papers," 35, 256
yellow journalism and, 317
New York Greek Committee, 95, 98, 112
New York Journal, 317
New York Post, 32

New York Times, 23, 32, 37, 322, 326
New Zealand, 345
Niebuhr, Reinhold, 13, 15, 17
Nietzsche, Friedrich, 379
Nigerians, 23
Nightingale, Florence, 36, 275, 346
Nikolai, Grand Duke, 301, 302, 303
Nikolai I, Tsar of Russia, 126, 128–30, 132, 242–3, 367
Nixon, Richard, 41, 241, 345, 358
No Man's Land (film), 28
North Africa, French empire in, 162
North American Review, 90, 92, 96
North Korea, 367
  media in, 30, 32, 33
Nuremberg war crimes trials, 24, 33
Nye, Joseph, Jr., 379

Ochs, Adolph, 37
Opium Wars, 267
Orientalism (Said), 16
Orion, HMS, 137
Orthodox Christians, 276, 297, 350
  Greek, 54, 56, 57, 63, 78, 80, 229, 244
  Kutchuk-Kainardji Treaty and, 56, 62, 246, 354
  pan-Slavism and, 243–7, 283, 288, 348
Orwell, George, 21, 32, 33, 48, 379
Osman Pasha, 180
Othello (Shakespeare), 288
Ottoman Christians, 40, 78, 188, 189, 248, 249, 254, 255, 281, 295, 324, 342
  Treaty of Paris and, 162, 189, 273, 361
  Victoria's views on, 240, 296, 350
  see also Greek Orthodox; Maronite Christians; Syrian Christians
Ottoman Empire, 4, 6, 17, 18, 52, 53, 91, 162
  Albanian revolt in, 239
  Armenians in, *see* Armenians
  British alliance with, 157, 213, 214, 236, 241, 249, 250, 254–5, 263, 289, 290, 291, 297–8, 304, 312, 344–5, 348, 357, 361
  Bulgarian massacres and, *see* massacres, in Bulgaria
  in Concert of Europe, 260
  Constantinople conference and, 292–3
  Disraeli's views on, 236, 239, 240, 241, 257, 272, 346
  division of, 334–7
  Germany's alliance with, 304
  Greek struggle in, *see* Greece, Greeks
  London Treaty refused by, 139
  modernizing reforms in, 162, 191, 192, 272
  multiethnicity of, 191, 192
  at Navarino, 49, 112, 139–48, 342
  Paris conference of 1860 and, 186–9
  Paris conference of 1861 and, 220–4
  in peace treaty of 1829, 148
  Russo-Turkish War and, *see* Russo-Turkish War
  Serbia's war against, 252–4
  Serb revolt in, 55
  six-month armistice accepted by, 285–6, 287
  slow collapse of, *see* Eastern Question
  sovereignty of, 4–5, 63, 68–72, 81, 92–4, 97, 118, 132, 163, 190, 217, 222, 273, 322, 325, 353–5, 358
  Syrians in, *see* Syria, Syrians
  in "system of civilized states," 348
  threat of Russian war with, 113, 115–18, 122, 134, 138, 139, 141, 143, 148–9
  Treaty of Berlin and, 309, 361
  U.S. ties severed by, 333–4
  weakness of, 162, 213, 348, 358
  in World War I, 319, 321, 333–5
Oxford, 81–2

Pakistan, 27, 41
Palestine, Palestinians, 22, 31, 322, 335, 367
Palmerston, Viscount, 18, 21, 182, 248, 268, 269, 309, 349, 353, 357, 368, 374
  protocol signed by (1840), 186
  Russell's clashes with, 428*n*
  Syria policy and, 170, 171, 178, 185, 373
pan-Africanism, 27
Panama, 327, 381
Panama Canal, 319
pan-Arabism, 20, 23, 27, 29
pan-Christian solidarity, 6, 8–9, 20, 29, 347–51
pan-Serb solidarity, 31
pan-Slavism, 20, 23, 31, 293
  roots of, 244
  in Russia, 4, 41, 129, 236–7, 242–53, 282–6, 288, 291, 294–5, 297, 301, 303, 348, 349, 350, 367–8, 374
  Russian imperialism and, 244

Papal States, 349
Pape, Robert, 17–18
Paradise Lost (Milton), 55
Paris, 118–19, 131, 134, 176–7, 181
  communications with, 34, 169, 175
  foreign correspondents in, 35, 36, 37
  newspapers in, 26–7, 183
Paris, Treaty of (1856), 162, 189, 273, 361
Paris conference (1860), 186–9, 199, 365
Paris conference (1861), 220–5
Paris peace conference (1919), 334–7
Parliament, British, 18, 59, 82, 125, 128, 149, 240, 255, 268, 272, 290, 294
  Disraeli's occupation plan and, 289
  Russo-Turkish War and, 298
  Scio massacre and, 68–70, 72, 73
  see also House of Commons, British; House of Lords, British
Patras, 141
Patras, Gulf of, 127
patriotism, 15, 21–3
Pears, Edwin, 257, 258
Penicuik, 306–7
"penny papers," 35, 256
Pericles, 90
Persigny, Count Victor Fialin, 177
Peshawar, 279
philhellenism, 54, 76–112, 129–31, 135, 231
  in Britain, 4, 17, 47–9, 53–8, 60–1, 64–6, 90, 92, 117–18, 120–1, 124, 131, 311, 312, 342, 345, 350, 351, 368–73, 379, 467*n*; *see also* London Greek Committee
  in United States, 76, 88–99
Philip, Hoffman, 330–1
Philippines, 317, 318, 319, 327, 346
Philippopolis district, 257
Piedmont, 246, 357
Pipes, Richard, 243
Pitt, William, 342
Pitts, Jennifer, 405*n*
Pleiku, 374
Plevna, 301, 302
Plovdiv, 256
Poland, Poles, 14, 43, 65, 100, 218, 327, 333, 344, 348, 349, 357–9, 363
  Catholics in, 244, 348
  press coverage of, 372, 471*n*
  Russian relations with, 245, 284, 300, 349–50, 356–7, 369
  Solidarity in, 151
  U.S. relations with, 318
politics, 41–3
  domestic, 9, 28–30, 367–75
  international, 352–66
Ponsonby, Henry, 260
Portugal, 76, 349, 363
Posner, Richard, 391*n*
Powell, Colin, 14
Power, Samantha, 28, 376
press, 5, 23, 30–8, 367–75, 476*n*–7*n*
  Armenian genocide and, 317, 326
  Bulgarian massacres and, 235–6, 256–64, 271–2, 277, 310–11, 326, 477*n*
  Disraeli's views on, 256–7, 271, 369
  foreign correspondents of, 35, 36, 185, 186, 243, 249, 257, 258, 369–71
  free, 6–7, 28–37, 48, 59–60, 159–60, 368–72
  Greek struggle and, 56–7, 65–6, 68, 71, 72, 83–4, 124, 135, 349–50, 369, 370, 371, 372, 375, 471*n*
  Syrian massacres and, 156, 171, 182–6, 225, 341
  unfree, 29–31, 37–8, 156, 160, 367–8
  see also censorship; newspapers; *specific publications*
Press Libre, 160
Prizren, 248
Protestants, 54, 243–4, 325, 350
Prussia, 135, 160, 245, 357, 363
  in Holy Alliance, 51–2
  Paris conference of 1860 and, 188–9
  Paris conference of 1861 and, 223, 224
  Syria policy of, 164, 168–9, 171, 188–9, 201, 207, 217, 218–19, 223, 224, 226
public opinion, 5, 8, 14, 19, 28, 29, 59, 122, 341, 369, 476*n*–7*n*
  Greek struggle and, 62, 83–4, 96, 113–14, 118, 128, 345
  Syria policy and, 156, 171, 176, 182–9, 218
Puerto Rico, 317
Punch, 266, 306
Pushkin, Aleksandr, 56, 110, 129, 356–7, 358, 369
Putin, Vladimir, 11, 41, 363–4

Qadir, Emir Abd al-, 201
Quakers, 86, 276

racism, racists, 15, 23, 320, 343, 347, 350
of Gladstone, 271, 277–8, 347
of Wilson, 315–16, 338, 348
radio, 28, 30, 31, 32
Rahman, Omar Abdul, 382
Ramos-Horta, José, 380
Randon, Marshal, 202
Rashayya, 193, 206
massacre at, 165, 169, 195, 207
Ravenna, 100
Rawls, John, 22
Reagan, Ronald, 62
realism, realists, 6, 7, 8, 11–19, 40–1, 48, 63, 113, 236, 342, 344, 345, 373–8
CNN effect and, 25
domestic politics and, 373–5
leftists and, 15–16, 378
patriotism and, 21–2
Redoutable (French ship), 170, 178
Règlement Organique, 229, 230
Reis Effendi, 71, 130, 139
reparations, 190, 216, 217
Republican Party, U.S., 12, 338, 350
responsibility to protect, 81
Reuter, Paul Julius, 34
Reuters, 34, 35, 37, 185, 249
revolutions
of 1848, 177, 241, 352, 357
Burke's concerns about, 26–7
see also French Revolution; *specific countries*
Ricardo, David, 48, 77–8, 112
Rice, Condoleezza, 12, 380, 382
"Rid Yourself of Ultramaria" (Bentham), 79
Rieff, David, 344
rights of man, 8, 52, 156
see also human rights
Robert College, 258, 261
Robertson, Pat, 350
Robinson, Ronald, 379
Rockefeller, John D., Jr., 326
Rockefeller Foundation, 326
Rogers, Samuel, 77
Roman Empire, 15
Romania, 56, 267, 327
Roncière le Noury, Baron de la, 165
Roosevelt, Archibald, 319, 320
Roosevelt, Franklin Delano, 340, 376
Roosevelt, Quentin, 320
Roosevelt, Theodore, Jr., 320
Roosevelt, Theodore, Sr., 3, 42, 316–20, 327–30, 332–3, 334, 340, 346, 359
in Spanish-American War, 3, 317, 327
Wilson as viewed by, 319, 327–9, 358
Wilson compared with, 338
Roth, Kenneth, 379
Routledge, James, 38
Rumsfeld, Donald, 380
Ruskin, John, 275
Russell, Bertrand, 170
Russell, Lord John, 201, 217, 250, 260, 269, 358, 428*n*
in London Greek Committee, 77, 149–50, 250
Syria policy and, 169–72, 177–80, 182, 184–7, 190–1, 195, 197, 199, 200, 201, 205, 208–15, 217–26, 250, 270, 345, 361, 432*n*
Russell, William, 316
Russell, William Howard, 36–7
Russia, 11, 17, 40, 356, 363–4, 376, 382, 475*n*
Russia, Imperial, 4, 6, 7, 14, 17, 36, 68, 240–55, 282–304, 327, 346–9, 354, 375, 381, 398*n*
Armenian genocide and, 321, 323
Bosnian revolt and, 248–9, 251
British relations with, 59, 113, 115–16, 123–4, 128–34, 148, 171, 172, 240–1, 272, 279, 285–8, 294, 297–300, 302–3, 311, 344, 356, 357, 363, 367, 374, 380
Bulgarians and, 42, 236–7, 248, 279, 282–96, 299, 300, 301, 303, 311, 365, 468*n*
Constantinople conference and, 287–9, 292–3, 364
in Crimean War, 36, 241, 243, 244, 245, 272, 348, 353, 357
Decembrists in, 128–9, 132
in division of Ottoman Empire, 334, 335
Eastern Question and, 240–7
emancipation of serfs in, 18, 242, 244
expansionism of, 19, 40, 48, 135, 188, 236, 237, 244, 246, 251, 286–7, 292, 303, 344
French relations with, 162, 356–7, 358
Greek struggle and, 42, 49, 56, 62–4, 73, 81, 89, 123–6, 128–32, 134, 135, 138, 139, 141, 143, 171, 251, 342, 360, 363, 364
in Holy Alliance, 51–2, 62–4
Hungarian revolution and, 353, 355
Navarino and, 49, 141, 143, 148–9, 362

Ottoman Empire invaded by, 236, 237, 312, 364
Ottoman Empire's threat of war with, 113, 115–18, 122, 134, 138, 139, 141, 143, 148–9
pan-Slavism in, 4, 41, 129, 236–7, 242–53, 282–6, 288, 291, 294–5, 297, 301, 303, 304, 348, 349, 350, 367–8, 374
Paris conference of 1860 and, 188–9
Paris conference of 1861 and, 223
Poland's relations with, 245, 284, 300, 349–50, 356–7, 369
press in, 31, 243, 249, 253, 254, 282, 284, 285, 289, 291, 297, 368
public opinion in, 242, 249, 251, 288, 374
revolts in, 241, 301
secret police in, 128–9, 243, 244, 284
Serbia's relations with, 250–4, 282, 283
Syria policy of, 164, 168–9, 171, 172, 177, 188–9, 207, 217, 219, 223, 226, 247
U.S. relations with, 94
Victoria's views on, 240–1, 279, 286, 287, 291, 301–2
in World War I, 319, 320, 321
Russia and Europe (Danilevsky), 244, 245
Russian navy, 194
Russian Orthodox Church, 282
Russian World, 251, 282, 284
Russo-Japanese War, 318
Russo-Turkish War, 236–7, 285, 289, 293, 296–304, 308–9, 312, 364, 374, 468*n*
armistice in, 302
deaths in, 301, 303–4
Rwanda, Rwandans, 3, 5, 23, 25, 28, 43, 355, 358, 360, 370, 372, 381
genocide in (1994), 31, 33, 350, 369, 375, 377

Said, Edward, 15, 16, 348
Saigon, 231
St. James's Hall conference, 290–1, 351
St. Petersburg, 34, 133, 177, 297, 368
communications with, 34
conference in (1825), 116, 118–19
pan-Slavism in, 247, 252
press in, 285
Times correspondent in, 243
Wellington in, 126, 128, 129, 365
St. Petersburg Slavic Benevolent Committee, 251
Salamis, 105
Salisbury, Marquis of, 281, 296, 303, 346, 373, 479*n*
Constantinople conference and, 287, 289, 290, 292–3
Russo-Turkish War and, 297–8, 300
Salonika, 250
San Francisco Examiner, 317, 341
San Remo conference (1920), 338
San Stefano, Treaty of (1877), 303
Santo Stefano jail, 268
Sarajevo, 248, 304, 356, 370
Sardinia, 162, 194, 368
Sartre, Jean-Paul, 15–16
Saudi Arabia, 381
Scenes of the Massacre at Scio (Delacroix), 72–3
Schuyler, Eugene, 258, 260
Scio, 137–9
Scio massacre (1822), 49, 67–76, 78, 80, 86, 90, 114, 135, 137, 341, 342, 467*n*
Batak massacre compared with, 311
Edhem Pasha and, 292–3
press coverage of, 68, 71, 72, 185, 310, 349–50, 369–72, 374, 471*n*
Scotland, Scots, 27, 77, 305–6, 348
Scotsman, 35
Scowcroft, Brent, 12
Second Treatise on Government (Locke), 55
Sen, Amartya, 28–9, 393*n*
Senate, U.S., 14, 318, 338, 339
September 11 terrorist attacks (2001), 23, 27, 376–8, 380, 381
"Seraglio's Heads, The" (Hugo), 127
Serbia, Serbs, 26, 43, 81, 88, 248–52, 288, 333, 356, 365–8, 371, 382
Derby's cease-fire negotiations and, 285
media in, 31
Ottoman peace made with, 295
revolts in, 55, 246, 249, 269, 349
Russians in army of, 251, 252, 253, 282, 283
sovereignty of, 352, 355
Serbian Orthodox Church, 251
Shakespeare, William, 21, 228, 239, 288
Shelley, Mary, 103
Shelley, Percy Bysshe, 23, 58, 61, 74, 81, 83, 103
Shia, 33
Shuvalov, Piotr Andreievich, 247, 251–2, 254, 292
Siberia, 68, 128, 302, 448*n*

Sidgwick, Henry, 341
Sidon (Sayda), 164–5, 167, 168, 178, 205, 206
Siècle, 171, 182–5, 368
Sierra Leone, 379
Sikhs, 17
Singer, Peter, 391*n*
Sisters of Charity Hospital, 165
slavery, 68, 71–2, 73, 124
  in U.S., 93, 327, 350, 450*n*
  see also Britain, anti-slavery campaign in
"Slavery of Greece, The" (Canning), 82
Slavic Benevolent Society, 245
Slavonic Ethnographic Exhibition, 245
Slavs, 40, 62
  see also pan-Slavism
Smith, Adam, 20, 22, 25
Smyrna, 56, 57, 67, 69, 138, 175
Sofia University, 237
Somalia, Somalis, 17, 27, 370
  U.S. policy toward, 7, 12, 13, 14, 39, 40, 43, 350, 351, 376
South Africa, 345, 361
South Korea, 32
sovereignty, 4–5, 11–12, 81, 93–4, 118, 132, 187, 190, 352–5
  Krasner's view of, 352
  Lansing's view of, 324
  of Ottoman Empire, 4–5, 63, 68–72, 81, 92–4, 97, 163, 190, 217, 222, 273, 322, 325, 353, 358
  violation of, 5, 12–13, 18, 24, 40, 42, 132
Soviet Union, 336, 353, 356, 357, 376
  Armenia seized by, 338–9
  collapse of, 14, 18, 376
  press in, 30, 33
  in World War II, 345
Spain, 33, 48, 76, 79, 82, 119, 345, 363
  anti-slavery campaign and, 18
  in Cuba, 3, 17, 317, 341
  revolt in, 59, 353
Spanish-American War, 3, 17, 317, 327, 328, 341, 346, 347
Spanish Civil War, 33, 48
Spectateur Oriental, 67, 68, 369
Spencer, Herbert, 275, 290
Spencer, Robert, 127
Srebrenica massacre (1945), 258, 371
Stanhope, Leicester, 77, 103, 106–10, 151
State Department, U.S., 258
  Armenians and, 322–6, 330–1
Stephen, Sir James Fitzjames, 275, 346
Stokes, Eric, 405*n*
Strachey, Lytton, 36
Strangford, Viscount, 67–8, 70–1
Sudan, 11, 38, 350, 361, 370, 371
  see also Darfur
Sudetenland, 19, 39
Suez Canal, 267, 274
Suez Canal Company, 240
Suliotes, 106, 108
Sulzberger, Arthur Ochs, 23
Switzerland, 76, 82
Sykes-Picot Agreement (1916), 334, 335
Syrène (French ship), 143, 144, 146
Syria, occupation of (1860–61), 34, 155–7, 175–81, 184–232, 247, 250, 321, 344, 348, 360, 366, 368, 478*n*
  aftermath of (1860–61), 230–2
  Beirut troop landing in, 197–8, 432*n*
  British reservations about, 157, 180–1, 184, 232, 269
  Bulgarian conflict compared with, 280, 287, 289, 290
  deadline for, 180, 181, 188–9, 216, 217, 218, 221, 227, 230, 365
  extension of, 214, 216, 217, 218, 220, 221, 223, 224, 226, 230
  mission creep and, 213–32
  multilateralism and, 364, 365
  Muslim resentment and, 187, 197–200
  Napoléon III's send-off speech and, 155–6, 191
  Ottoman fears about, 179
  Paris conference of 1860 and, 186–9, 199, 365
  Paris conference of 1861 and, 220–5
  terms of protocol for, 188–9, 365
Syria, Syrians, 153–232, 311, 343, 344, 359
  British policy toward, *see* Britain, Syria policy of
  division of Ottoman Empire and, 335
  Greece compared with, 200, 231
  international commission for, *see* international commission for Syria
  massacres in, *see* massacres, in Syria
  public opinion and, 156, 171, 176, 182–9, 218
Syrian and Armenian Relief Days, 331
Syrian Christians, 177, 185, 193–4, 213–31
  in Beirut, 167, 168, 169, 190–1, 197–200, 203
  in Damascus, 207–8

French relations with, 4, 42, 155–7, 162–81
French troops and, 181, 214, 216, 221, 225, 226–7
reparations for, 190, 216, 217
return to their homes of, 206
see also Maronite Christians

Taft, William Howard, 318
Taïf (Ottoman frigate), 173, 178
Taiwan Straits, 381
Talaat Pasha, 322–5, 331
Talbott, Strobe, 40
Tang Jiaxuan, 13, 16, 355
Tanović, Danis, 28
Tanzania, 41
Tanzimat reforms, 191, 192, 272
Tatar Bazardjik, 235
Taylor, A. J. P., 12
Taylor, Charles, 350
technology, 7, 25, 26, 28, 34–5, 395*n*
Telegrafo Greco, 107
telegraph, 7, 28, 34–5, 37, 38, 395*n,* 477*n*
Armenian genocide and, 324–5
Bosnian revolt and, 249
Bulgarian massacre and, 236, 256, 273
Syrian massacres and, 169, 170, 175, 182, 185
Telegraph Act (1868), 306
television, 25, 28
Tennyson, Alfred, 275
Thackeray, William Makepeace, 37
Thailand, Malays in, 27
Thirty Years' War, 13, 329
Thouvenel, Edouard-Antoine de, 169–72, 175–80, 182, 184, 199, 213, 229, 232
British troops and, 201–2
Cowley's disagreements with, 221, 222–3
French troops and, 190, 191, 195, 215, 218, 227
on Fuad, 197, 210, 225
Mukhtara Druzes and, 210, 211
Napoléon III's meetings with, 176
Paris conference of 1860 and, 186, 187–8
Paris conference of 1861 and, 220–4
Thucydides, 4
Tiananmen Square massacre (1989), 25, 30, 40, 355, 358, 370
Tibet, 17, 363–4
Times, 34–8, 59–60, 69, 74, 83, 124, 161, 286, 288, 290, 346, 350, 358, 369, 471*n*
Bosnian revolt and, 249, 250, 477*n*
Bulgarian massacre and, 235, 257, 260, 265, 310–11
Codrington's instructions in, 138
foreign correspondents of, 35, 36, 243, 249
"penny paper" challenge to, 35, 256
Russo-Turkish War and, 300
Emerson on, 31–2
Scio massacre and, 68, 71, 72, 185, 372, 471*n*
Syrian crisis and, 184–6, 203, 341, 359
Tiutchev, Feodor Ivanovich, 244
Tocqueville, Alexis de, 14, 344
Tolstoy, Leo, 15, 31, 242, 243, 253–4
pan-Christian sentiments of, 20, 245
Tories, 59, 236, 256, 266–8, 281, 288, 291, 293, 350, 478*n,* 479*n*
in elections, 278–9, 305–6, 310
Greek struggle and, 64, 70, 72, 77, 79–82, 86, 131, 373
Russo-Turkish War and, 298
Victoria's relations with, 240, 277
"To the Slanderers of Russia" (Pushkin), 356–7, 358
Toynbee, Arnold, 5, 320–1
Trafalgar, battle of (1805), 137
Trebinje, 249
Trelawny, Edward John, 101, 105, 111, 112
Trevelyan, George Otto, 290
Trieste, 249
Tripoli, 165, 348–9
Tripolitza, 86, 104–5
Tripolitza massacre (1821), 64–6, 86, 134, 371
Trollope, Anthony, 274, 290
Tudman, Franjo, 31
Turgenev, Ivan Sergeievich, 245–6
Turkey, 336–7
see also Ottoman Empire
Tutsi, 31

Uganda, 22, 41
unilateralism, 5, 40, 364
United Nations (UN), 8, 11, 15, 81, 363, 475*n*
Charter of, 13
General Assembly of, 11
Security Council of, 363, 364, 475*n*
United States, 11–14, 28, 39–43, 315–40, 352–6, 358–64, 376–82

United States (*continued*)
  Armenian genocide and, 43, 321–6, 328–32, 358, 376
  Bosnia policy of, 5, 7, 23, 42, 43, 350, 365, 376, 380, 382
  China's relations with, 40, 41, 327, 345
  Damascus consulate of, 174
  Greek struggle and, 76, 88–99, 112–13, 121, 356
  imperialism of, 317–18, 327, 346–7, 353, 377–82
  Kosovo policy of, 7, 39, 40, 42, 43, 350, 352, 353, 356, 376, 380, 381, 383*n*
  liberalism in, 6–7, 31, 316, 398*n*
  Monroe Doctrine and, 91, 92, 95, 316–17, 353
  neutrality of, 319, 320, 323, 325, 327, 332
  Paris peace conference and, 335–7
  press in, 23, 32, 33, 317, 322, 326, 372
  slavery in, 93, 327, 350, 450*n*
  Somalia policy of, 7, 12, 13, 14, 39, 40, 43, 350, 351, 376, 381
  in Spanish-American War, 3, 17, 317, 327, 328, 341, 346, 347
  as superpower, 339–40
  tradition of humanitarian intervention in, 3, 4, 340
  Tripoli treaty of, 348–9
  in World War I, 333–4
utilitarianism, 76, 107

Vefik Effendi, Ahmed, 186, 187
  at Paris conference of 1861, 222, 223
Victoria, Queen of Britain, 34–5, 173, 240, 277, 286, 350, 479*n*
  Aleksandr II's correspondence with, 251
  Bulgarian massacres and, 236, 260–3, 279, 290, 291
  Disraeli's correspondence with, 255, 257, 260–1, 262, 274, 279, 291, 311
  Disraeli's relationship with, 240, 250, 257, 260–1, 279, 288–9, 291, 373
  imperial interests of, 240, 279, 280, 291, 293, 296, 298, 346
  Russia as viewed by, 240–1, 279, 286, 287, 291, 301–2
  Russo-Turkish War and, 298, 300, 301–2
Vienna, 35, 36, 177, 185, 249
Vienna settlement (1814–15), 4, 13, 51, 59, 117, 342
Vietcong, 374
Vietnam, 30, 42, 182, 198, 231, 366
Voice, 282, 284

Wales, the Welsh, 27, 276
Walker, Francis, 316
Wallachia, 56, 58, 62, 129
Waltz, Kenneth, 15
Walzer, Michael, 364
War Ministry, French, 191
War Office, British, 36–7
Warsaw, 356–7
Waterloo, battle of, 60
Weber, Max, 15, 16
Webster, Daniel, 89, 90, 96–7, 340, 353
Wellington, Duke of, 63, 74, 113, 115, 116, 118, 122, 128–35, 354
  Greek deportation rumor and, 124, 130–1, 149, 342, 424*n*
  protocol of, 130, 132–5
  resignation of, 133
  in St. Petersburg, 126, 128, 129, 365
  as Tory, 48, 60
Werry, Francis, 67
Westermann, William, 339
Western Hemisphere, 95, 317
West Indies, 59, 345–6
Westminster, Duke of, 29
Westminster Abbey, 74–5, 101, 136, 150
Weyler, Valeriano, 317
Whigs, 59, 60, 77, 80–1, 112, 133, 170, 294, 298
  see also Liberal Party, British
Wilberforce, William, 59, 69, 80, 345, 347, 479*n*
Wilde, Oscar, 274–5
Wilhelm I, Kaiser of Germany, 252–3
Wilson, Woodrow, 4, 315–16, 318–40, 346–7, 359, 368
  Armenian genocide and, 316, 319–26, 330–4, 348, 358, 376
  in elections, 321–2, 336, 337–8
  Fourteen Points of, 334–5
  health problems of, 338
  isolationism and, 316, 319
  Paris peace conference and, 334–7
  racism of, 315–16, 338, 348
  T. Roosevelt's views of, 319, 327–9, 358
  World War I and, 319–20
Winthrop, Thomas, 95–6

Wise, Stephen, 326
Wolfowitz, Paul, 380
Woolf, Virginia, 20
World Restored, A (Kissinger), 342, 467*n*
World War I, 40, 297, 319–20, 328, 332–7, 340, 353
  Paris peace conference and, 334–7
World War II, 21, 32, 320, 345
Wretched of the Earth, The (Fanon), 15
Writer's Diary (Dostoevsky), 282
Wyman, David, 23

Yearwood, John, 372
Yeltsin, Boris, 40
Young Turks (Committee of Union and Progress), 320, 321, 323, 331
Yugoslavia, Yugoslavs, 26, 318, 355, 358, 381

Zahleh, 164, 193, 205, 226
  massacre in, 166, 167, 169, 170, 171, 180, 185, 204
Zante, 141
Zanzibar, 267
Zanzibar, sultan of, 18
Zhou Enlai, 345
Zimbabwe, 33, 361
Zululand, 306, 351
Zulu War (1879), 38, 343

ABOUT THE AUTHOR

Gary J. Bass is an associate professor of politics and international affairs at Princeton University. He is the author of *Stay the Hand of Vengeance: The Politics of War Crimes Tribunals.* A former reporter for *The Economist,* he has written often for *The New York Times,* as well as writing for *The New Yorker, The Washington Post,* the *Los Angeles Times, The New Republic,* and *Foreign Affairs.* He lives in Princeton and New York City.

A NOTE ON THE TYPE

This book was set in Adobe Garamond. Designed for the Adobe Corporation by Robert Slimbach, the fonts are based on types first cut by Claude Garamond (c. 1480–1561). Garamond was a pupil of Geoffroy Tory and is believed to have followed the Venetian models, although he introduced a number of important differences, and it is to him that we owe the letter now known as "old style." He gave to his letters a certain elegance and feeling of movement that won their creator an immediate reputation and the patronage of Francis I of France.

Composed by Textech, Brattleboro, Vermont

Printed and bound by Berryville Graphics, Berryville, Virginia

Book design by Robert C. Olsson